ADVANCE

MW00583471

General Editors

C. W. J. GRANGER   G. E. MIZON

Time-Series-Based Econometrics

Unit Roots and Co-Integrations

Michio Hatanaka

OXFORD UNIVERSITY PRESS
1996

Oxford University Press, Walton Street, Oxford OX2 6DP
Oxford New York
Athens Auckland Bangkok Bombay
Calcutta Cape Town Dar es Salaam Delhi
Florence Hong Kong Istanbul Karachi
Kuala Lumpur Madras Madrid Melbourne
Mexico City Nairobi Paris Singapore
Taipei Tokyo Toronto
and associated companies in
Berlin Ibadan

Oxford is a trade mark of Oxford University Press

Published in the United States
by Oxford University Press, Inc., New York

British Library Cataloguing in Publication Data
Data available

Library of Congress Cataloging in Publication Data
Data available
ISBN 0-19-877352-8
ISBN 0-19-877353-6 (Pbk)

Typeset by Pure Tech India Ltd., Pondicherry

Printed in Great Britain
on acid-free paper by
Biddles Ltd., Guildford & King's Lynn

Preface

The most vigorous development in econometrics in recent years had undoubtedly been the unit-root field, including error correction and co-integration. I am most grateful to the editors of Advanced Texts in Econometrics, Professors C. W. J. Granger and G. E. Mizon, for allowing me an opportunity to survey these development. The survey has naturally suggested a number of research topics, and the results of one of them are included in the book. It is assumed that readers are acquainted with (*a*) fundamentals of the algebra of liner vector spaces, (*b*) standard time-series analysis of stationary process including the linear prediction theory, and (*c*) standard asymptotic theory of inference used in econometric theory. However, no other mathematics or statistics are presupposed nor is mathematical rigour sought in the writing. In particular unit-root problems are explained from their most elementary starting-points. Graduate students at an advanced level should be able to understand the book. The statistical procedures are explained in detail, and the results of applications are emphasized. The applications that I have in mind are primarily to macro-economic time series rather than to financial series, the analyses of the two kinds of series often requiring different concepts and tools. My survey does not trace the historical sequence of developments, but rather selects the topics worth noting as at the time of writing (the second half of 1992 to the end of 1993).

The book consists of two parts, Part I deals with the univariate unit root, i.e. to see if a stochastic trend is present when each time series is analysed separately. It is summarized in the last part of Chapter 1. Part II discusses co-integration, i.e. the empirical investigation of long-run relationships among a number of time series.

Critics of unit-root tests deny even their motivation. I disagree. The question that the tests try to answer is whether or not the economy is capable of restoring the trend line of a variable after it is forced by shocks to deviate from the line. If the answer is affirmative (negative) the variable is trend (difference) stationary. What the trend line is, and to what extent we can answer the question, is examined in Part I. As in the case of other problems in econometrics one should be warned against optimism about the precision of results, but I cannot imagine that answers to the question can be irrelevant to macroeconomic modelling.

If unit roots are involved in a set of variables we can investigate the long-run relationships among the variables, which is a new branch of econometrics. Moreover, unit roots influence the appropriate selection of inference methods to be adopted in all econometric studies. The new econometrics differs from the old even at the level of a simple regression model in its theoretical aspects, if not in most computations. This is explained in Part II.

Most of Part II was written before I had access to another book on co-integration by Professors Banerjee, Dolado, Galbraith, and Hendry, *Co-integration, Error-Correction, and the Econometric Analysis of Non-Stationary Data* (Oxford University Press, 1993). It turned out that there is virtually no overlapping, which shows that there are divergent developments in this field. Needless to say that I did later take advantage of their book.

Yasuji Koto has kindly permitted me to incorporate a portion of our joint research in this book. Clive Granger, Koichi Maekawa, Kimio Morimune, and Hiro Toda have kindly read the manuscript, and offered valuable advice to improve my writing. Mototsugu Fukushige has provided me with a large number of references that are difficult to obtain in Japan. Noriko Soyama has helped me a great deal with her efficient typing of the manuscript. I feel much obliged to all of them.

Michio Hatanaka

Machikaneyama, Toyonaka, Osaka
July 1994

Contents

List of Figures

PART I
Unit-Root Tests in Univariate Analysis

1
Stochastic Trend and Overview of Part I

For a long time each economic time series has been decomposed into a deterministic trend and a stationary process. In recent years the idea of stochastic trend has emerged, and enriched the framework of analysis to investigate economic time series. In the present chapter I shall (*a*) explain the meaning of stochastic trend, (*b*) consider whether it can be derived from any economic theories, and (*c*) illustrate the impact that it has given to empirical studies of economic theories.

1.1 Stochastic Trend

To explain stochastic trends let us consider two of the simplest models,

$$x_t = x_{t-1} + \mu \tag{1.1d}$$

and

$$x_t = x_{t-1} + \varepsilon_t, \tag{1.1s}$$

where μ is a non-stochastic constant, while $\{\varepsilon_t\}$ is i.i.d., with $E(\varepsilon_t) = 0$ and $E(\varepsilon_t^2) = \sigma_\varepsilon^2$. (The letters d and s associated with the equation numbers stand for 'deterministic' and 'stochastic' respectively.) When these processes start from $t = 0$, (1.1s) and (1.1d) generate $\{x_t\}$ respectively as

$$x_t = x_0 + \mu t \tag{1.2d}$$

$$x_t = x_0 + \sum\nolimits_{s=1}^{t} \varepsilon_s \equiv x_0 + v_t. \tag{1.2s}$$

$\{\mu t\}$ is a deterministic trend while $v_t \equiv \sum_{s=1}^{t} \varepsilon_s$ is a stochastic trend. $\{v_t\}$ is a non-stationary stochastic process as $E(v_t^2) = t\sigma_\varepsilon^2$, which does depend upon t and diverges as $t \to \infty$. $\{v_t\}$ is called the random-walk process. Incidentally x_0 in (1.2s) may be a random variable or a non-stochastic constant.

We are attempting to reveal the meaning of the newly developed stochastic trend by contrasting it with a traditional time-series model. (1.1d) is too simple for the purpose because the traditional model contains not only a deterministic trend but also a stationary process. Therefore let us add a stationary process, $\{u_t\}$, to the right-hand side of (1.2d). I use an autoregressive process in order 1, AR(1), for illustration.

$$x_t - x_0 - \mu t = u_t = (1 - \alpha L)^{-1}\tilde{\varepsilon}_t = \tilde{\varepsilon}_t + \alpha\tilde{\varepsilon}_{t-1} + \dots, \tag{1.3d}$$

where L is the lag operator, $|\alpha| < 1$, and $\{\tilde{\varepsilon}_t\}$ is i.i.d., with $E(\tilde{\varepsilon}_t) = 0$ and $E(\tilde{\varepsilon}^2) = \tilde{\sigma}_\varepsilon^2$.

The best way to understand the meaning of stochastic trend is to compare (1.2*s*) with (1.2*d*) and/or (1.3*d*) in terms of their time-series properties.

1.1.1 *Prediction error*

Let us consider predicting $x_{t+\tau}$ for each of $\tau = 1, 2, \ldots$, from $(x_t, x_{t-1}, \ldots, x_1)$. In the model (1.2*d*), assuming that μ and x_0 are known, the prediction of $x_{t+\tau}$ is $x_0 + \mu(t+\tau)$, and the prediction error is zero. In describing the prediction in the model (1.3*d*) I assume that readers are acquainted with basic parts of the prediction theory in the linear process through, for example, Sargent (1979), Granger and Newbold (1986), or Hamilton (1994).[1] The best linear prediction of $x_{t+\tau}$ is the projection of $x_{t+\tau}$ upon $(x_t, x_{t-1}, \ldots, x_1, x_0)$, which will be denoted by $P(u_{t+\tau}|x_t, \ldots, x_1, x_0)$. Since $x_0 + \mu(t+\tau)$ is perfectly predictable we consider $P(u_{t+\tau}|x_t, \ldots, x_1, x_0)$. Since $u_s = x_s - x_0 - \mu s$, $s = 1, \ldots, t$, it is seen that $(x_t, \ldots, x_1, x_0)$ corresponds one-to-one to $(u_t, \ldots, u_1, x_0)$, and $P(u_{t+\tau}|x_t, \ldots, x_1, x_0) = P(u_{t+\tau}|u_t, \ldots, u_1, x_0)$. This last projection is found equal to $\alpha^\tau u_t$. Therefore the best linear prediction of $x_{t+\tau}$ is

$$x_0 + \mu(t+\tau) + \alpha^\tau(x_t - x_0 - \mu t).$$

The error of prediction of $x_{t+\tau}$ is the error of prediction of $u_{t+\tau}$, and is given by

$$\tilde{\varepsilon}_{t+\tau} + \ldots + \alpha^{\tau-1}\tilde{\varepsilon}_{t+1}. \tag{1.4d}$$

For each of $\tau = 1, 2, \ldots$ its variance is bounded above by the variance of $u_{t+\tau}$, which is $\tilde{\sigma}_\varepsilon^2(1-\alpha^2)^{-1}$. The bound is due to a well-known theorem in the projection theory.

Let us turn to the model of stochastic trend (1.2*s*). The best linear prediction of $x_{t+\tau}$ from $(x_t, \ldots, x_1, x_0)$ is $P(x_{t+\tau}|x_t, \ldots, x_1, x_0)$. Since there is a one-to-one correspondence between $(x_t, \ldots, x_1, x_0)$ and $(\varepsilon_t, \ldots, \varepsilon_1, x_0)$, we may consider $P(x_{t+\tau}|\varepsilon_t, \ldots \varepsilon_1, x_0)$, which is,

$$x_0 + \sum_{s=1}^{t} \varepsilon_s = x_t.$$

And this is the projection of each of $x_{t+\tau}$, $\tau = 1, 2, \ldots$. The error in the prediction of $x_{t+\tau}$ for $\tau = 1, 2, \ldots$ is

$$\varepsilon_{t+\tau} + \ldots + \varepsilon_{t+1}, \tag{1.4s}$$

which should be compared with (1.4*d*). The variance of (1.4*s*) is $\tau\sigma_\varepsilon^2$, and as $\tau \to \infty$ it diverges to infinity.

[1] $\{x_t\}$ is said to be a linear process if $x_t = \mu + \beta_0\varepsilon_t + \beta_1\varepsilon_{t-1} + \ldots$, where $\sum_0^\infty |b_j| < \infty$ and $\{\varepsilon_t\}$ is i.i.d. with $E(\varepsilon_t) = 0$ and $E(\varepsilon_t^2) = \sigma_\varepsilon^2$ for all t. The ARMA process is a linear process.

The model of a deterministic trend plus a stationary process and the model of stochastic trend have totally different views about how the world evolves in future. *In the former the prediction error is bounded even in the infinite horizon, but in the latter the error becomes unbounded as the horizon extends.*

1.1.2 Impulse-response function

For any linear stochastic process $\{x_t\}$

$$x_t - P(x_t|x_{t-1},\ldots) \tag{1.5}$$

is called the innovation or shock at t. In the model (1.3d) $P(x_t|x_{t-1},\ldots)$ is $x_0 + \mu t + \alpha(x_{t-1} - x_0 - \mu(t-1))$, and the shock at t is $\tilde{\varepsilon}_t$. In the model (1.2s) $P(x_t|x_{t-1},\ldots)$ is x_{t-1}, and the shock at t is ε_t.

Let us compare the stochastic trend and the traditional model in regard to the impact of the shock ε_t or $\tilde{\varepsilon}_t$ upon $x_{t+\tau}$. The series of impacts on $x_{t+\tau}$, with index $\tau = 1, 2, \ldots$, while the time t and ε_t (or $\tilde{\varepsilon}_t$) are fixed, is called the *impulse-response function*. In the model (1.3d) $\tilde{\varepsilon}_t$ enters into $x_{t+\tau}$ through $\alpha^\tau \tilde{\varepsilon}_t$. The impulse-response function is $(\alpha, \alpha^2, \ldots)$. Since $|\alpha| < 1$, the impact dies down to zero as $\tau \to \infty$. In the model (1.2s) each of $x_{t+\tau}$, $\tau = 1, 2, \ldots$ contains ε_t. The impulse-response function is $(1, 1, \ldots)$, which never dies down. *The current shock has only a temporary effect in the model (1.3d), while the current shock has a permanent effect in the model (1.2s).*

1.1.3 Returning to a central line

The difference mentioned in Section 1.1.2 may be expressed in another language. *The model (1.3d) has a central line,* $x_0 + \mu t$, around which $\{x_t\}$ oscillates. Even if shocks let x_t deviate temporarily from the line there takes place a force to bring it back to the line. On the other hand *the model (1.2s) has no such central line.* Indeed it is a random walk. One might wonder about a deterministic trend combined with a random walk. Indeed (1.1s) may be extended to

$$x_t = \mu + x_{t-1} + \varepsilon_t,$$

which generalizes (1.2s) to

$$x_t = x_0 + \mu t + \sum_{s=1}^{t} \varepsilon_s,$$

but here the discrepancy between x_t and the line, $x_0 + \mu t$, becomes unbounded as $t \to \infty$.[2]

Having completed the contrast between the stochastic-trend model and the traditional model, we turn to some generalization of the stochastic trend.

[2] Good references for Sections 1.1.1–1.1.3 are Nelson and Plosser (1982) and Stock and Watson (1988a).

If $\{\varepsilon_t\}$ in (1.2*s*) is replaced by a stationary AR(1), (1.1*s*) becomes

$$(1-L)(1-\alpha L)x_t = \varepsilon_t \tag{1.3s}$$

where $|\alpha| < 1$. Determine $b_0 \equiv 1, b_1, b_2, \ldots$ from

$$1/(1-(1+\alpha)L+\alpha L^2) = 1 + b_1 L + b_2 L^2 + \ldots.$$

We get

$$b_i \equiv 1 + \alpha + \ldots + \alpha^i, \qquad i = 0, 1, 2, \ldots .$$

Then the model of stochastic trend (1.3*s*) implies

$$\begin{aligned} x_t &= \varepsilon_t + b_1\varepsilon_{t-1} + \ldots + b_{t-1}\varepsilon_1 + b_t x_0 \\ &= v_T + \alpha v_{t-1} + \ldots \alpha^{t-1} v_1 + b_t x_0, \end{aligned} \tag{1.3s'}$$

where $v_t = \sum_{s=1}^{t} \varepsilon_s$. The projection of $x_{t+\tau}$, $\tau = 1, 2, \ldots$, each upon $(x_t, x_{t-1}, \ldots, x_1, x_0)$ is

$$b_\tau \varepsilon_t + b_{\tau+1}\varepsilon_{t-1} + \ldots + b_{\tau+t-1}\varepsilon_1 + b_{\tau+t}x_0,$$

and the error of prediction is

$$\begin{aligned} &\varepsilon_{t+\tau} + b_1\varepsilon_{t+\tau-1} + \ldots + b_{\tau-1}\varepsilon_{t+1} \\ &= \sum_{s=1}^{\tau} \varepsilon_{t+s} + \alpha \sum_{s=1}^{\tau-1} \varepsilon_{t+s} + \ldots + \alpha^{\tau-1}\varepsilon_{t+1}. \end{aligned} \tag{1.4s'}$$

As $\tau \to \infty$ the variance of the prediction error diverges to infinity. Since the shock at t is ε_t, the impulse–response function is $(b_1, b_2, \ldots)$. Noting that $b_\tau \to (1-\alpha)^{-1}$ as $\tau \to \infty$, the current shock is seen to have a permanent effect.

1.1.4 Important terminology

Now I introduce the *martingale process* as it is often referred to in relation to the stochastic trend. A stochastic process $\{x_t\}$ is called a martingale process if

$$x_{t-1} = E(x_t | x_{t-1}, x_{t-2}, \ldots). \tag{1.6}$$

In the linear process such as (1.3*d*), (1.2*s*), and (1.3*s*) the conditional expectation and the projection are interchangeable so that (1.6) may also be written

$$x_{t-1} = P(x_t | x_{t-1}, x_{t-2}, \ldots), \tag{1.6'}$$

or comparing it with (1.5),

$$\Delta x_t = x_t - P(x_t | x_{t-1}, x_{t-2}, \ldots) \equiv \text{innovation at } t. \tag{1.6''}$$

The innovation is equal to the difference. In (1.3*d*) the innovation at t is $\tilde{\varepsilon}_t$, while $\Delta x_t = \mu + \tilde{\varepsilon}_t - (1-\alpha)(1-\alpha L)^{-1}\tilde{\varepsilon}_{t-1}$. (1.3*d*) is not a martingale. In (1.2*s*) the innovation is ε_t, and Δx_t is also ε_t. (1.2*s*) is a martingale. Continuing on (1.2*s*), if $\{\varepsilon_t\}$ is independently but not identically distributed (1.2s) is still a martingale. In (1.3s) the innovation is ε_t, while $\Delta x_t = (1 - \alpha L)^{-1}\varepsilon_t$ so that it is not a martingale. However, it will be seen in Chapter 2 that the long-run component of $\{x_t\}$ in (1.3s) is a random walk, which is a martingale, and subsequently it will be seen that only the long-run component matters in the unit-root field. It is in this sense that the stochastic trend is a martingale process.

The random walk as a statistical description of stock price is quite old in the economic literature, but the idea of stochastic trend as a general model originates in the statistical literature (Box and Jenkins (1970, ch. 4)). They have proposed a model of $\{x_t\}$ such that Δx_t is stationary but x_t is not, or $\Delta^2 x_t = x_t - 2x_{t-1} + x_{t-2}$ is stationary but Δx_t is not. The former is denoted by $I(1)$, reading that the order of integration is 1, and the latter is written $I(2)$. The series which is stationary without a differencing is $I(0)$. In (1.2s) and (1.3s) Δx_t is stationary but x_t is not so that x_t is $I(1)$. The first difference of a stationary series is also stationary, but it has a special property as described in Chapter 2.

We shall use the words *difference stationarity* and *trend stationarity*. *Difference stationarity* is appropriate for describing the stochastic trend, because it is the differencing operation(s) that is *indispensable* to transform the stochastic trend into a stationary process. In contrast the traditional model such as (1.3d) is called *trend stationary*. There $\{x_t\}$ is not stationary, but subtraction of μt from x_t makes it stationary. Differencing also makes it stationary, but it is not an indispensable operation to get the stationarity.

The equation (1.1s) is a difference equation with a forcing function $\{\varepsilon_t\}$. The characteristic equation is $\lambda - 1 = 0$, and the root is unity. In (1.3s) the characteristic equation is $\lambda^2 - (1 + \alpha)\lambda + \alpha = 0$, and one of its two roots is unity. Stochastic trends are characterized by a unit root, and the entire field that deals with stochastic trends is called the unit root.

Figure 1.1(a) and (b) shows real outputs in log scale in the USA and Japan on a quarterly basis. There have been considerable debates in recent years regarding the presence of a stochastic trend in these series. Figure 1.2(a) and (b) shows stock prices in log scale in the USA and Japan respectively on a quarterly basis.

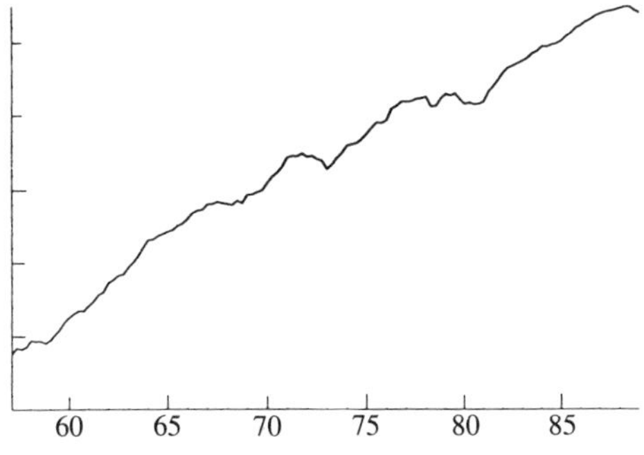

FIG. 1.1(a) *US real GDP*

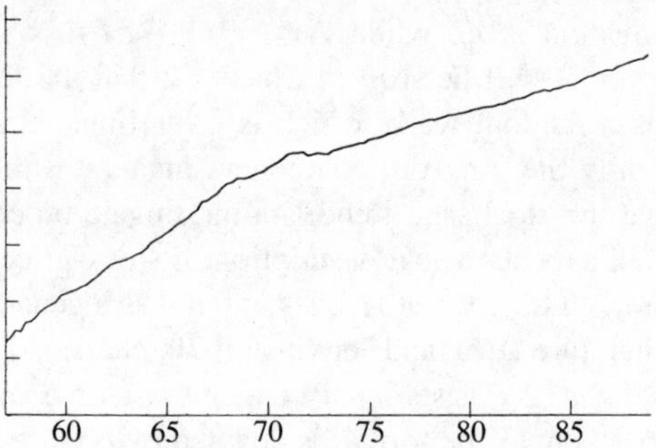

FIG. 1.1(*b*) *Japanese real GNP*

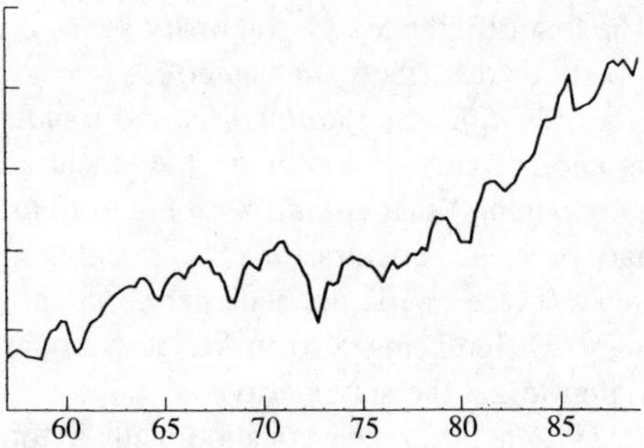

FIG. 1.2(*a*) *US stock price*

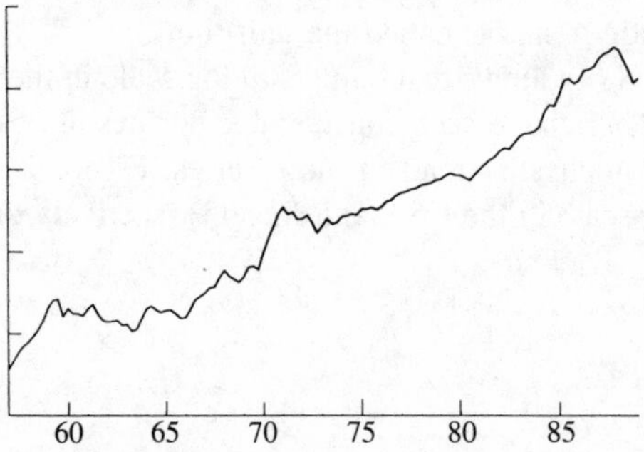

FIG. 1.2(*b*) *Japanese stock price*

For a few decades it has widely been agreed among econometricians that these series contain stochastic trends. Figure 1.3(*a*) is a realization of an i.i.d. process, while 1.3(*b*) is a realization of a random-walk process. The latter is smoother. It is useful for data analysis to keep in mind that the initial value, x_0, in a random walk determines the level of subsequent realizations.

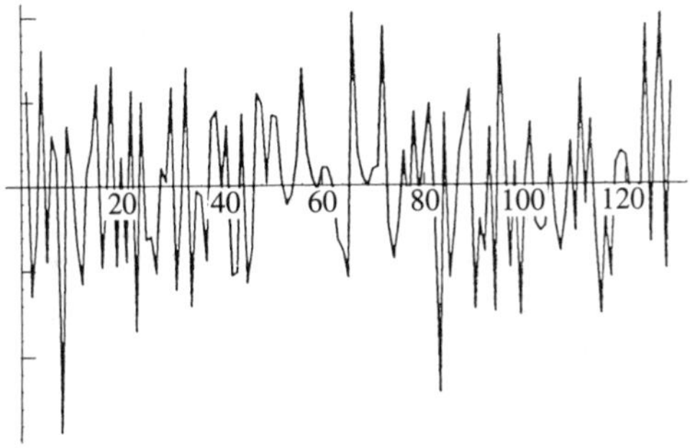

FIG. 1.3(*a*) *White noise*

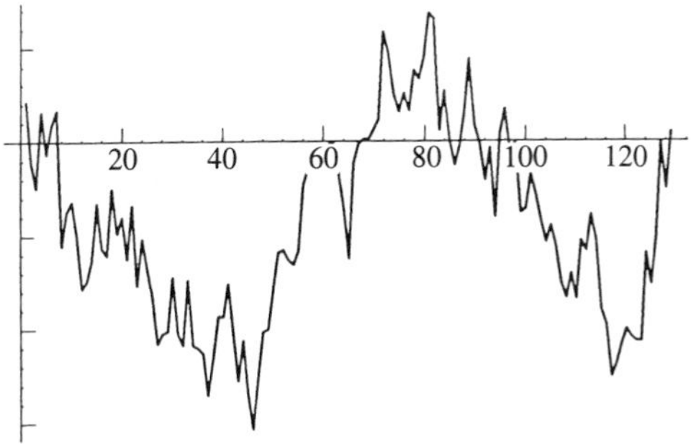

FIG. 1.3(*b*) *Random walk*

Incidentally, visual inspection of time-series charts is indispensable to empirical studies as it suggests what kind of formal tests should be applied.

1.2 Stochastic Trend as a Logical Implication of an Economic Theory?[3]

Let p_t be the price of an asset at time, t, and I_{t-1} be the information set at $t-1$. The rational expectations hypothesis proposes $E(p_t|I_{t-1})$ as the expectation of p_t as of time $t-1$. The efficient market hypothesis suggests that this expectation is realized so that

$$p_{t-1} = E(p_t|I_{t-1}). \tag{1.7}$$

Let us assume that I_{t-1} contains only $(p_{t-1}, p_{t-2}, \ldots)$. Then

$$p_{t-1} = E(p_t|p_{t-1}p_{t-2}, \ldots). \tag{1.7'}$$

[3] Yuichi Fukuta, Hiroshi Osano, and Mototsugu Shintani have kindly commented on an earlier draft of Sections 1.2 and 1.3. Remaining errors are mine.

This is nothing but the definition of $\{p_t\}$ being a martingale process. Note that (1.7′) is equivalent to $E(\Delta p_t | p_{t-1}, p_{t-2}, \ldots) = 0$, i.e. no part of Δp_t is predictable from $(p_{t-1}, p_{t-2}, \ldots)$.

A number of economic theorists have investigated more closely than the above whether or not the martingale property of an asset price can be derived logically from an economic theory of idealized markets of goods and assets. LeRoy (1973) derives the property assuming that investors are risk-neutral or the (relative) risk aversion does not vary over time, but his emphasis is rather on denying the martingale property because investors are risk-averters with a time-varying risk aversion. Lucas (1978) shows that the martingale property of asset price requires more unrealistic assumptions.[4] Finally a random walk is a martingale process, but the martingale process is not restricted to a random walk. The stochastic trend (1.1*s*) is not likely to be derived logically from an economic theory alone.

Incidentally the permanent-income hypothesis has been associated with the random-walk property of consumption in much of the literature. The association is attributed to Hall (1978), but what he obtains from an economic theory is

$$E(u'_{t-1} | I_t) = (1 + r)^{-1}(1 + \delta)u'_t,$$

where u' is the marginal utility and δ and r are respectively the rate of time preference and the real rate of interest. $\{u'_t\}$ is a martingale if $r = \delta$. If $\delta > r$, $\{u'_t\}$ is what is called a sub-martingale process. Since $E(\Delta u'_{t+1} | u'_t) > 0$ a part of $\Delta u'_{t+1}$ is predictable from u'_t, which is fundamentally different from the martingale property.[5]

1.3 Influences upon the Testing of Economic Theories

The stochastic trend has had a profound influence upon empirical studies of economic theories. Logically the influence should follow the empirical plausibility about the stochastic trends in many economic variables. The plausibility was provided by Nelson and Plosser (1982), using a method developed in Dickey and Fuller (1981). However, the research does not necessarily advance in a logical sequence. Earlier Davidson *et al.* (1978) used the error-correction model to relate the stochastic trend to a study of economic relationships. The following review classifies the influences of stochastic trends (i) upon testable implications of economic theories, and (ii) on testing for a kind of theoretical property that has hitherto been taken for granted, i.e. the long-run economic relationship.

[4] Sims (1980*a*) derives the unpredictability of Δp_{t+1} through an approximation that would be justified if the time unit is sufficiently short. Harrison and Kreps (1979) derive the martingale property of option prices from that of stock price.

[5] Hayashi (1982) investigates the permanent-income hypothesis without assuming $\delta = r$.

1.3.1 Influences upon testable implications of economic theories

Many economic theories are expressed as the present-value model,

$$y_t = \sum_{\tau=0}^{\infty} \gamma^\tau E(x_{t+\tau}|I_t) \tag{1.8}$$

where I_t is the information set up to and including t, and the discount factor γ is non-stochastic and $1 > \gamma > 0$. In the permanent-income hypothesis x_t is the labour income, and y_t is that part of consumption that arises from the permanent labour income. Consumption responds to a change in the current income x_t only in so far as the latter alters expectation of future income. Suppose that I_t contains only $(x_t, x_{t-1}, \ldots)$. The new information at t is the innovation, $x_t - E(x_t|I_{t-1})$. Consumers revise the previous expectation $E(\ |I_{t-1})$ into the current $E(\ |I_t)$ by assessing the impact of the innovation upon future labour income as explained in Section 2.2 below. This impact is represented by the impulse-response function, and we have found that the function takes different forms depending upon whether $\{x_t\}$ evolves like a linear trend plus a stationary process or like a stochastic trend. Flavin (1981) assumed the former (trend-stationary case), and found that observed consumptions respond to revisions of the expectation more sensitively than the permanent-income hypothesis (PIH) specifies. Mankiw and Shapiro (1985) and Deaton (1987) examined the latter (difference-stationary case), and concluded that observed responses of consumptions are too insensitive for the PIH.[6]

When y_t in the present-value model (1.8) is stock price, x_t is either the earning or dividend of the stock. Let us write

$$y_t^* = \sum_{r=0}^{\infty} \gamma^\tau x_{t+\tau}.$$

Then it follows that

$$\operatorname{var}(y_t) \leq \operatorname{var}(y_t^*).^7 \tag{1.9}$$

Shiller (1981*a*) intended to test (1.9), which is called the volatility test. The result was definitive rejection of the inequality. However, Kleidon (1986) reveals that the test is invalid if the relevant time series contain stochastic trends.

Note that the var in (1.9) is the variance in the probability distribution of all events that might occur at a fixed time, t. Kleidon calls the distribution 'cross-sectional', and engineers refer to the moments of such a distribution as the ensemble average (or moment). If we are dealing with an ergodic stationary stochastic process, the ensemble moment can be estimated from the sample moments of a single realization, such as $T^{-1}\sum x_t$ and $T^{-1}\sum(x_t - \bar{x})^2$. In fact Shiller (1981*a*) assumes that the stock price in log scale consists of a linear trend and a stationary process, and reformulates (1.9) so that var() can be estimated from the sample moments. However, when $\{y_t\}$ and $\{y_t^*\}$ have a stochastic trend

[6] See Quah (1990) and Campbell and Deaton (1989) for more about this point.

[7] When $\{x_t\}$ is Gaussian the conditional variance never exceeds the unconditional variance. However, it is known that stock price is not Gaussian in terms of a month or shorter time units.

there exists no simple correspondence between var() in (1.9) and the sample moments.[8] Durlauf and Phillips (1988) makes a detailed analysis of this point by the asymptotic theories that will be explained subsequently, and proves that the volatility test may be interpreted as a test of co-integration between $\{y_t\}$ and $\{y^*_\tau\}$ with coefficients 1 and -1.

Given that a stochastic trend is involved in the real output, it has been attributed to supply shocks, especially shocks to the productivity growth, in Nelson and Plosser (1982), Shapiro and Watson (1988), Blanchard and Quah (1989), and King *et al.* (1991). An impact of shock at each time is maintained eternally, and its accumulation produces a stochastic trend. Durlauf (1989) objects to this interpretation on the ground that real outputs of different sectors are in fact co-integrated. (If the stochastic trends are due to productivity shocks, they are sector-specific, and cannot be co-integrated.) However, it can be argued that effects of innovations are interrelated among different sectors. It seems to me that there is no economic interpretation of stochastic trend that is unanimously agreed upon at the present time.

Shapiro and Watson (1988) suggest that the presence or absence of a stochastic trend in the real output decides whether the real business cycle theory or the Keynesian theory should be accepted. DeLong and Summers (1988) deny the validity of such a link, and develop a theory in which the business cycle is unrelated to the stochastic trend. Then the stochastic trend is included in the trend, which is the potential growth of output. Whether or not the central line exists in the real output, real wage, real rate of interest, etc. has a fundamental influence upon macroeconomic theories, but the mode of the influence would perhaps depend upon the models.

1.3.2 Long-run relationships

The concept of stochastic trend has developed a new, important role of econometrics in investigating the empirical validity of long-run economic relationships. This development has been taken in three steps. First, Granger and Newbold (1974, 1986: 207) presented evidence to show that between two independent stochastic trends the regression coefficient estimate does not converge to zero in probability.[9] This confirms an aspect of the well-known nonsense correlations between level variables, but it may also be destructive evidence because an important task of econometrics is to discern the nonsense and the sensible correlations. Incidentally, the statisticians' approach represented by Box and Jenkins (1970) was to eliminate the stochastic trends by differencing. The second step in a study of long-run relationships was taken by Davidson *et al.* (1978) and Hendry and Mizon (1978). They thought that differencing would throw away an important part of the information about the sensible long-run relationships.

[8] To be fair I should say that Shiller (1981*a*) is a quite elaborate study. The only defect is that it ignores the fact that the stock price might very well be difference stationary.

[9] Later Phillips (1986) proved this mathematically.

Instead, they proposed the error-correction model as a device to emphasize the long-run relationships. The model involves current errors in long-run relationships in levels, and describes how the errors set forth adjustments in the next period. The third step was by Granger (1981), Granger and Weiss (1983), and Engle and Granger (1987). They developed the theory of co-integration,[10] and thereby provided a theoretical foundation to discern the nonsense correlations and the sensible long-run relationships.

This new econometrics deserves special emphasis. For some years before its development econometricians had faced a sort of deadlock. Economic theories have very little to suggest on short-run relationships often represented by distributed lags. They are difficult to ascertain, and the relations do not seem to be stable over different periods. On the other hand, economic theories have established a number of hypotheses on long-run relations. Equipped with simultaneous-equations models econometricians had analysed long-run relations by simulations over extended horizons, but they lacked appropriate concepts and tools to cope with the stochastic and the deterministic trends.

1.4 Overview of Part I

Part I examines whether or not a stochastic trend is present in economic time series, treating each series separately. A large part is devoted to the explanation of various methods, but the results of applications of these methods are also our main concern. Chapter 2 sets forth definitions of trend stationarity and difference stationarity in terms of the absence or presence of the long-run component and also in terms of the dominating root of characteristic polynomials. Methods to examine the absence or the presence of the long-run component are introduced in Chapter 3. The difficulty with the non-parametric variance ratio approach is explained by the spectral theory, as it is also found useful to describe difficulties in the Schwert moving average (MA) regarding non-parametric estimations of long-run variance. The absence of the long-run component is equivalent to the presence of an MA unit root in differenced series. The classical hypothesis testing *for trend stationarity against difference stationarity* can be performed by testing for the presence of an MA unit root in differenced series. From Nyblom and Mäkeläinen (1983), Nabeya and Tanaka (1988), Tanaka (1990, 1995*a*), Kwiatkowski *et al.* (1992), and Saikkonen and Luukkonen (1993*a*), who contributed to this development, I follow primarily the last mentioned because they adopt a parametric approach avoiding non-parametric estimations of long-run variance. Chapters 4–7 form the core of Part I in regard to the development of a group of statistical methods. The new asymptotic theories based upon the Wiener process have been emphasized and extended for econometric applications in Phillips (1987), Phillips and Perron (1988), and Ouliaris, Park, and

[10] Earlier Aoki (1968) and Box and Tiao (1977) had ideas close to the co-integration. See Campbell and Shiller (1988) and Aoki (1990) on Aoki (1968).

Phillips (1989). They are introduced without mathematical rigour in Chapter 4 in the case where Δx_t is i.i.d. with zero mean, and in Chapter 6 in the case where the model of $\{\Delta x_t\}$ is more general. The asymptotic distribution of the MA unit-root test statistic is also presented here. The mathematical results in Chapters 4–7 are summarized at the end of Chapter 7. The classical hypothesis testing *for difference stationarity against trend stationarity* has been formulated in terms of the dominating characteristic root. The augmented Dickey–Fuller method is described in fair detail in Chapter 5 for the case where Δx_t is i.i.d., and in Chapter 7 for the case where Δx_t is serially correlated. The method treats difference stationarity as the null hypothesis, but in my judgement this must be combined with an investigation in which trend stationarity is the null hypothesis as mentioned earlier. Moreover, as Perron (1989) emphasized, the discrimination between the difference and the trend stationarity requires appropriate selection of models for deterministic trends. Plausible models are linear trend without a structural change, with structural changes, and polynomial trends. Thus the whole problem should be formulated as model selection regarding both the dominating characteristic root and the modes of deterministic trends. The encompassing principle developed in Mizon (1984) and the general-to-specific principle proposed in Mizon (1977) and Hendry (1979) are found useful in organizing our thinking for model selection along the classical, i.e. non-Bayesian method. Some essence of this thought will be given in Chapter 8. In general the test can discriminate two non-nested models only when they are sufficiently separated, and this will be investigated in Chapter 8 regarding the simplest of difference-stationary and trend-stationary models. The results of the encompassing analysis of macroeconomic time series are shown in Chapter 9. The Bayesian discrimination is introduced at some length in Chapter 10. Various approaches and their results are assessed while emphasizing difficulties due to the point null hypothesis.

Before presenting our conclusions it must be pointed out that with sample size 100 characteristic roots between 0.9 and 1.0 cannot be distinguished from a unit root as will be shown in Chapter 8. With this reservation about the practical meaning of difference and trend stationarity our conclusions are given in the following two statements:

1. *All kinds of macroeconomic variables, real variables, prices, and financial variables, are difference stationary in the post-Second World War quarterly data in the USA*. Since it is mostly the post-war data that are used for studying macroeconomics, the new unit-root econometrics is indispensable to empirical studies of macroeconomics. The price and money stock might even be $I(2)$ rather than $I(1)$.

2. *As for the historical data covering eighty or more years in the USA, it is difficult to offer unequivocal judgement as to whether many real economic variables are difference stationary or trend stationary*. The analysis is hampered by uncertainty about the selection of modes of deterministic trends and also by deviations of possibly appropriate models from the standard time-series model specification. Unemployment rate and real rate of interest are trend stationary,

but real GNP and real wage appear to be near a boundary between the trend and difference stationarity. There is not much that we can propose on the general theory of macrodynamics regarding the self-restoring capability of trend line.

The following topics are left out in Part I though they are undoubtedly related to the outline mentioned above.

(*a*) A large body of literature concerning mathematical analyses of the near unit roots is left out. The analyses contribute to analysing the power of tests for the difference stationarity and also the size of tests for the trend stationarity, but a rough outlook of the power and the size has been obtained by Monte Carlo simulation studies. More important is a possible contribution of the near unit-root analysis to modelling the reality for which the precise unit root has been tried in vain, for example, the time-varying parameter in the regression and AR models, the seasonal fluctuations, etc. Not much investigation has been done to the best of my knowledge.

(*b*) At the time of writing there are appearing a number of tests for difference stationarity other than the augmented Dickey–Fuller test. I have restricted my exposition to the augmented Dickey–Fuller test because it best fits into the framework of the encompassing principle.

(*c*) The fractional differencing model provides bridges between $I(0)$ and $I(1)$ and between $I(1)$ and $I(2)$. It is not introduced in the book because its usefulness in economic time-series analysis seems yet unclear to me.[11]

(*d*) The unit-roots representation of seasonal variations is not introduced because I doubt if seasonal variations are properly modelled by the (complex) unit roots.[12] Deviations of seasonal fluctuations from the deterministic periodicity are bounded in probability *at any time*, and the (complex) unit roots are inappropriate to model the deviations.

(*e*) Beaudry and Koop (1993) find that impulse–response functions of positive and negative shocks are different, negative shocks being less persistent than positive shocks. The finding suggests that some non-linear time-series models should be adopted. The present book does not consider this relatively new field, and readers are referred to Granger and Teräsvirta (1993).

[11] Seeking for the minimum *real number*, d, that makes $(1-L)^d x_t$ a stationary ARMA, x_t is said to have long memory if $0.5 > d > 0$. It is stationary, but the impule–response function goes to zero more slowly than a decaying exponential when the horizon extends to infinity (see Granger and Joyeux (1980) and Hosking (1981)). Diebold, Husted, and Rush (1991) find that a long-memory model fits well the annual data of real exchange-rates under the gold standard system. The long-memory model for Δx_t is a bridge between $I(1)$ and $I(2)$ for x_t. Cheung (1993) finds evidence for it in weekly data of exchange rates and monthly series of ratios of prices among different countries, whereas Lo (1991) finds no evidence in the stock price.

[12] Hylleberg *et al.* (1990) present what seems to be the best analysis of seasonal variation as well as the testing for seasonal unit roots. Using this test Osborn (1990) and Beaulieu and Miron (1993) showed that the seasonal unit roots were not found in the UK and USA data respectively. However, this result has been objected to by Hylleberg (1994). See a nice survey in Ghysels (1994).

2
Trend Stationarity vs. Difference Stationarity

The present chapter introduces difference stationarity and trend stationarity as two non-nested, non-separate hypotheses. After the concepts are defined in Section 2.1, two parameters are introduced to discriminate the two hypotheses. Perhaps less known of the two parameters is a measure of the long-run component, and it will be explained in great length in Section 2.2. It represents the trend stationarity as an MA unit-root in Δx_t and also as a limit of a sequence of the difference-stationary models. The better known is the dominating root of the characteristic polynomial for x_t which will be explained in Section 2.3. It represents the difference stationarity as a limit of a sequence of trend-stationary models. These views in Sections 2.2 and 2.3 are combined in Section 2.4. Finally, the data relevant to the discrimination between the difference and trend stationarity will be explained in Section 2.5.

2.1 Basic Discrimination

One of the hottest debates in recent years has been trend stationarity (TS) vs. difference stationarity (DS) posed in Nelson and Plosser (1982). For a single economic variable, x_t, let d_t, s_t, and c_t be respectively the deterministic trend, stochastic trend, and stationary component in x_t. The TS hypothesis asserts

$$x_t = (d_t +) c_t,$$

whereas the DS hypothesis proposes

$$x_t = (d_t +) s_t + c_t,$$

where placing d_t in parentheses means that the inclusion of d_t is allowed but not required. In fact, deterministic trends are contained in many economic time series, and their existence is seldom an issue. The difference between TS and DS is that s_t is not in TS but is in DS. In other words the question posed is not whether trends are deterministic or stochastic *but* whether the stochastic trend is present or absent in economic time series.

The two hypotheses are differentiated also in regard to what needs to be done in order to achieve the stationarity. In the TS hypothesis it is subtraction of a deterministic function of time. In the DS hypothesis the subtraction is not enough, and differencing is required. Incidentally, the stationarity is a special case of the trend stationarity.

The precise model of deterministic trend is left unspecified here, and insightful readers will anticipate confusions arising in implementing the discrimination between DS and TS. We shall defer the discussion to Chapter 8.

The integration order needs to be redefined with the introduction of deterministic trends. $\{x_t\}$ is $I(1)$ when $\{\Delta x_t\}$ is TS but $\{x_t\}$ is not. $\{x_t\}$ is $I(2)$ if $\{\Delta^2 x_t\}$ is TS but $\{\Delta x_t\}$ is not. A quadratic deterministic trend plus a random walk, for example,

$$x_t = x_{t-1} + \mu t + \varepsilon_t,$$

is $I(1)$, because $\{\Delta x_t\}$ is TS even though it has a linear trend.

There are three purposes for discrimination between DS and TS. First, the discrimination is the purpose by itself for the understanding of economic dynamics. Especially we are concerned with *existence of the central line* which the economy is expected to restore after any temporary deviations from it. The deterministic trend cannot be the central line with this property if the time series also contains a stochastic trend along with a deterministic trend. The second purpose of the discrimination is a sort of pre-tests necessitated by the fact that different results of the discrimination lead to different inference procedures in subsequent, main parts of empirical studies. An example is the determination of integration orders prior to the co-integration analysis. The third purpose is to see which of DS and TS models performs better in outside sample forecasting. To the best of my knowledge this type of discrimination has not been implemented, nor is it attempted in the present book.[1]

Both the first and the second purposes investigate the congruence of DS and TS models with observations. For the first purpose the macroeconomic theory prescribes what data to analyse, and the discrimination is desired to be as sharp as possible. For the second purpose the data are selected in the main parts of the studies, and one would be concerned with the specification error regarding how the subsequent studies are affected by erroneous decisions on the discrimination between DS and TS. Effects of erroneous decisions are investigated in Durlauf and Phillips (1988) and Banerjee *et al.* (1993: 81–93), but a great deal more needs to be done.

There exist two methods to distinguish the DS and TS. One is in terms of the presence or absence of a long-run component, and the other is whether the dominating root of the characteristic polynomial is equal to or less than unity.

2.2 Long-Run Component

Beveridge and Nelson (1981) have presented the concept of a long-run component, which is later found indispensable to all the conceptual and technical developments on the stochastic trend. Given a scalar stochastic process $\{x_t\}$ with

[1] Clive Granger has proposed the discrimination in terms of the forecasting capability.

either $I(1)$ or $I(0)$, suppose that $\{\Delta x_t\}$ is a linear process with zero mean, i.e.

$$\Delta x_t = b_0\varepsilon_t + b_1\varepsilon_{t-1} + \dots, \qquad b_0 \equiv 1, \tag{2.1}$$

where $\{\varepsilon_t\}$ is i.i.d. with $E(\varepsilon_t) = 0$ and $E(\varepsilon_t^2) = \sigma_\varepsilon^2$. Here it is assumed that the process starts at $t = -\infty$. Suppose that we are now at time t. The optimal prediction (i.e. minimum mean-square prediction) of $\Delta x_{t+i} (i > 0)$ from $(x_t, x_{t-1}, \dots)$ is

$$\begin{aligned} E(\Delta x_{t+i}|x_t, x_{t-1}, \dots) &= E(\Delta x_{t+i}|\varepsilon_t, \varepsilon_{t-1}, \dots) \\ &= b_i\varepsilon_t + b_{i+1}\varepsilon_{t-1} + \dots, \end{aligned} \tag{2.2}$$

where the first equality follows from the fact that the projection of Δx_{t+i} upon the space spanned by $x_t, x_{t-1}, \dots$ is identical to that upon the space spanned by $\varepsilon_t, \varepsilon_{t-1}, \dots$. The optimal prediction of $x_{t+k} (k > 0)$ from $(x_t, x_{t-1}, \dots)$ is

$$\begin{aligned} &E(x_{t+k}|x_t, x_{t-1}, \dots) \\ &= E(\Delta x_{t+k} + \Delta x_{t+k-1} + \dots + \Delta x_{t+1} + x_t|\varepsilon_t, \varepsilon_{t-1}, \dots) \\ &= x_t + \left(\sum\nolimits_1^k b_i\right)\varepsilon_t + \left(\sum\nolimits_2^{k+1} b_i\right)\varepsilon_{t-1} + \dots. \end{aligned} \tag{2.3}$$

Let us consider the prediction of the infinitely remote future by taking k to $+\infty$ while fixing t.

$$\hat{x}_t \equiv E(x_\infty|x_t, x_{t-1}, \dots) = x_t + \left(\sum\nolimits_1^\infty b_i\right)\varepsilon_t + \left(\sum\nolimits_2^\infty b_i\right)\varepsilon_{t-1} + \dots \tag{2.4}$$

Do this prediction at each time, t, and form the stochastic process, $\{\hat{x}_t\}$. It is easily seen that

$$\hat{x}_t - \hat{x}_{t-1} = \left(\sum\nolimits_0^\infty b_i\right)\varepsilon_t; \tag{2.5}$$

therefore $\{\hat{x}_t\}$ is a pure random walk unless $\sum_0^\infty b_i = 0$. A more compact derivation will be introduced later with lag operator, and what $\sum_0^\infty b_i = 0$ means will also be explained later.

We shall call $\hat{x}_t$ and $\Delta\hat{x}_t$ the long-run components of x_t and Δx_t respectively. The variance of $\Delta\hat{x}_t$, i.e. $\left(\sum_0^\infty b_i\right)^2\sigma_\varepsilon^2$, is called the long-run variance. (2.5) indicates how the long-run component is revised in the light of the new information given at time, t.

Several remarks will be presented concerning the meaning of $\hat{x}_t$. (i) As seen from (2.2) the impact of ε_t in (2.1) upon $(\Delta x_{t+1}, \Delta x_{t+2}, \dots)$ is $(b_1, b_2, \dots)$. As seen from (2.3) the impact of ε_t upon $(x_{t+1}, x_{t+2}, \dots)$ is $(b_1, b_1 + b_2, \dots)$. $\sum_0^\infty b_i$ is the impact upon $x_{t+\infty}$, i.e. the limit of the impulse–response function as the horizon extends to infinity. (ii) Suppose that $\{x_t\}$ is a stationary linear process so that

$$x_t = c_0\varepsilon_t + c_1\varepsilon_{t-1} + \dots. \tag{2.6}$$

Then

$$\Delta x_t = c_0\varepsilon_t + (c_1 - c_0)\varepsilon_{t-1} + (c_2 - c_1)\varepsilon_{t-2} + \ldots,$$

and in relation to (2.1) $b_0 \equiv c_0, b_1 \equiv c_1 - c_0, \ldots$, from which it follows that $\sum_0^\infty b_i = 0$. The long-run component of Δx_t vanishes. In fact, being a stationary linear process, no part of x_t has a permanent impact upon its future. (iii) Unless $\sum_0^\infty b_i = 0$ $\{\hat{x}_t\}$ and hence $\{x_t\}$ are non-stationary, and include a stochastic trend. In regard to the model (2.1) *the TS is* $\sum b_i = 0$, *and the DS is* $\sum b_i \neq 0$.

I have not bothered to consider convergence conditions on infinite series involved in expressions (2.1)–(2.6). If Δx_t is a stationary ARMA (p, q) (autoregressive moving-average process in order (p, q)),

$$\Delta x_t + \alpha_1\Delta x_{t-1} + \ldots + \alpha_p\Delta x_{t-p} = \varepsilon_t + \beta_1\varepsilon_{t-1} + \ldots + \beta_q\varepsilon_{t-q},$$

and if the AR part is inverted to get

$$\Delta x_t = b_0\varepsilon_t + b_1\varepsilon_{t-1} + \ldots, \qquad b_0 \equiv 1,$$

then $\{b_j\}$ is bounded by a decaying exponential, by which I mean the existence of c such that $1 > c > 0$ and $|b_j| < c^j$, $j = 0, 1, \ldots$. This is because the roots of the equation, $1 + \alpha_1 z + \ldots + \alpha_p z^p = 0$, all have absolute values larger than unity, or, $z^p + \alpha_1 z^{p-1} + \ldots + \alpha_p = 0$ all have absolute values smaller than unity. If $\{b_j\}$ is bounded by a decaying exponential all the infinite series in (2.1)–(2.6) converge. Therefore there should be no worry about the convergence if Δx_t is a stationary ARMA (p, q).

The major points in the above derivation can be reproduced with lag operator, L. The initial values will also be introduced to make the reasoning more useful for the inference based on a finite amount of data. The right-hand side of (2.1) is $b(L)\varepsilon_t$, where $b(L) \equiv b_o + b_1 L + b_2 L^2 + \ldots$. Substituting unity for L, $\sum_0^\infty b_i$ may be written $b(1)$, which is a very common practice in the literature. Thus the long-run component of Δx_t in (2.5) is written $b(1)\varepsilon_t$. From

$$b(L) - b(1) = -(1 - L)[b_1 + b_2(1 + L) + b_3(1 + L + L^2) + \ldots]$$

we get a useful identity

$$b(L) - b(1) = (1 - L)b^*(L), \tag{2.7}$$

where $b^*(L) = b_0^* + b_1^* L + b_2^* L^2 + \ldots$

$$b_0^* = -\sum_{i=1}^{\infty} b_i, \qquad b_1^* = -\sum_{i=2}^{\infty} b_i, \ldots .$$

With this identity (2.1) is

$$\Delta x_t \equiv b(L)\varepsilon_t = b(1)\varepsilon_t + (1 - L)b^*(L)\varepsilon_t.$$

This gives

$$x_t = x_0 + \sum_{s=1}^{t} \Delta x_s = b(1)\sum_{s=1}^{t} \varepsilon_s + b^*(L)\varepsilon_t + x_0 - b^*(L)\varepsilon_0. \tag{2.8}$$

Here the DGP (data-generating process) still starts from $t = -\infty$, but (2.8) has adopted $t = 0$ as an initial time in order to condition our analysis upon $x_0, x_{-1}, \dots$, or $\varepsilon_0, \varepsilon_{-1}, \dots$. In fact the random-walk process cannot be analysed unless so conditioned. We might then alter the previous definition of the long-run component of x_t slightly. The new definition is

$$\hat{x}_t \equiv b(1) \sum_{s=1}^{t} \varepsilon_s.$$

Then (2.8) shows that x_t is decomposed into *the long-run component*, $b(1) \sum_{s=1}^{t} \varepsilon_s$, *the short-run component*, $b^*(L)\varepsilon_t$, and the initial term, $x_0 - b^*(L)\varepsilon_0$. The initial term is independent of the newly defined long-run component. The analysis of the long-run component conditioned upon the initial term is identical to the unconditioned analysis of the long-run component newly defined.

Incidentally, the old expression of long-run component of x_t is (2.4), which is

$$\hat{x}_t = x_t - b^*(L)\varepsilon_t = b(1) \sum_{s=1}^{t} \varepsilon_s + x_0 - b^*(L)\varepsilon_0,$$

so that the old and the new expressions differ in regard to $x_0 - b^*(L)\varepsilon_0$. It still holds for both expressions that

$$(1 - L)\hat{x}_t = b(1)\varepsilon_t.$$

We might set $\hat{x}_0 = 0$ to initiate the random walk $\{\hat{x}_t\}$ in the new definition.

Point (ii) given in connection with (2.6) can be rephrased more compactly. Suppose that $\{x_t\}$ is stationary and that $x_t = c(L)\varepsilon_t$ with $c(L) = c_0 + c_1 L + \dots$. Then $\Delta x_t = (1 - L)c(L)\varepsilon_t$ so that $b(L) = (1 - L)c(L)$. It is immediately seen that $b(1) = 0$ because $b(L)$ has a factor, $(1 - L)$, which vanishes when unity is substituted for L. The TS is $b(1) = 0$, and the DS is $b(1) \neq 0$.

The long-run variance of Δx_t is $\left(\sum_0^\infty b_i\right)^2 \sigma_\varepsilon^2$. This may be represented in a number of expressions.

(i) Recall that the spectral density function of (2.1) is

$$(2\pi)^{-1} \left\| \sum_0^\infty \exp(-ik\lambda) b_k \right\|^2 \sigma_\varepsilon^2, \qquad \pi \geq \lambda \geq -\pi$$

where $i = \sqrt{-1}$ and $\exp(i\lambda) = \cos\lambda + i \sin\lambda$. (Appendix 1 is available for readers who want to brush up their memory about the spectral method.) Setting $\lambda = 0$ we see that the long-run variance of Δx_t is $(2\pi) \times$ (the spectral density at zero frequency).

(ii) The long-run variance of Δx_t is $\lim_{t\to\infty} t^{-1}E(x_t^2)$. To see this suppose that $x_0 = 0$. Then $x_t = \Delta x_t + \Delta x_{t-1} + \dots + \Delta x_1$, and $t^{-1}E(x_t^2) = t^{-1}E\left(\sum_{s'=1}^{t} \sum_{s=1}^{t} \Delta x_s \Delta x_{s'}\right) = \gamma_0 + t^{-1}(t-1)2\gamma_1 + t^{-1}(t-2)2\gamma_2, + \dots + t^{-1}2\gamma_{t-1}$, where $\gamma_j \equiv E(\Delta x_t \Delta x_{t-j})$, i.e. the autocovariance of Δx_t for lag j. Using the Cesaro sum it can be shown that, as $t \to \infty$, $\gamma_0 + t^{-1}(t-1)2\gamma_1 + t^{-1}$ $(t-2)\ 2\gamma_2, + \dots$ converges to $\gamma_0 + 2\gamma_1 + 2\gamma_2, + \dots$, which is $(2\pi) \times$ (the spectral density at zero frequency). Finally, the assumption, $x_0 = 0$, has no effect upon the above result since x_0 is independent of $\varepsilon_t, t > 0$.

(iii) The important relation

$$b(1)^2\sigma_\varepsilon^2 = \gamma_0 + 2\gamma_1 + \dots \tag{2.9}$$

can be directly proved on the model (2.1). First,

$$\gamma_j = \sigma_\varepsilon^2 \sum_{i=0}^{\infty} b_i b_{i+j}. \tag{2.10}$$

Second $b(1)^2 = \left(\sum b_j\right)\left(\sum b_j\right) = \sum b_j^2 + 2\sum b_j b_{j+1} + 2\sum b_j b_{j+2} + \dots$.

Incidentally the long-run variance, i.e. the variance of $\Delta\hat{x}_t$, is equal to the variance of Δx_t if and only if $\sum b_j^2 = \left(\sum b_j\right)^2$. Among a number of processes in which this condition holds, the i.i.d. process is the most important one.

Later in Chapter 3 a special case of (2.6) will play an important role. Suppose that $\{x_t\}$ is a moving-average process in order q, MA(q),

$$x_t = c_0\varepsilon_t + c_1\varepsilon_{t-1} + \dots + c_q\varepsilon_{t-q}, \tag{2.6$'$}$$

which is of course stationary. Then

$$\Delta x_t = b_0\varepsilon_t + b_1\varepsilon_{t-1} + \dots + b_q\varepsilon_{t-q} + b_{q+1}\varepsilon_{t-q-1}, \tag{2.11}$$

where $b_0 = c_0$, $b_i = c_i - c_{i-1}$ for $i = 1, \dots, q$, and $b_{q+1} = -c_q$. The equation

$$b_0 + b_1\lambda + \dots + b_q\lambda^q + b_{q+1}\lambda^{q+1} = 0 \tag{2.12}$$

has a unit root, which is called the MA unit root. Recall that for the general MA($q+1$) model the admissible domain of $(b_0, b_1, \dots, b_q, b_{q+1})$ is restricted to those for which no roots of (2.12) are less than unity in moduli. This is to avoid the lack of identifiability. Also recall that the standard time-series analysis restricts the domain further to those for which all the roots exceed unity in moduli, i.e. what is called the invertibility region. The MA unit root lies on the boundary of the admissible region, which is in fact a point of the non-investibility region. In the model (2.6$'$) the TS is that (2.12) has a real unit root, and the DS is that all roots of (2.12) exceed unity in moduli.

It might be advisable to say that $\{\Delta x_t\}$ is $I(-1)$ in order to emphasize the point that $b(1)$ for Δx_t is zero if $\{x_t\}$ is stationary. This has been suggested in Granger (1986).

One can introduce a simplest type of deterministic trend in $\{x_t\}$ by adding μ to the right-hand side of (2.1),

$$\begin{aligned} \Delta x_t &= \mu + b_0\varepsilon_t + b_1\varepsilon_{t-1} + \dots, \qquad b_0 \equiv 1 \\ &= \mu + b(L)\varepsilon_t = \mu + b(1)\varepsilon_t + (1-L)b^*(L)\varepsilon_t. \end{aligned} \tag{2.1$'$}$$

(2.8) is now replaced by

$$x_t = \mu t + b(1)\sum_{s=1}^{t} \varepsilon_s + b^*(L)\varepsilon_t + x_0 - b^*(L)\varepsilon_0. \tag{2.8$'$}$$

2.3 Dominating Root of Characteristic Polynomial

Another parameter useful for differentiating TS and DS is the dominating root of the characteristic polynomial. I begin with different expressions being used in the economic dynamics and time-series analysis.

In the economic dynamics a homogeneous, linear difference equation

$$x_t - a_1 x_{t-1} - \ldots - a_p x_{t-p} = 0 \tag{2.13}$$

is said to be *stable* if all roots of the corresponding characteristic polynomial

$$z^p - a_1 z^{p-1} \ldots - a_p = 0 \tag{2.14}$$

are less than unity in moduli, and *explosive* if at least one root of (2.14) exceeds unity in moduli. Also the root is said to be stable or explosive. The case where real or complex unity is the root largest in moduli is the borderline between the stability and the explosion.

In time-series analysis an autoregressive process with a possibly infinite order is written as

$$(1 - a_1 L - \ldots)x_t = \varepsilon_t. \tag{2.15}$$

Define $f(z) \equiv 1 - a_1 z - \ldots$, where z is complex-valued. It is often assumed that $f(z) = 0$ never occurs when z is less than unity in moduli. If the order of the autoregressive process is finite, say, p, this assumption means that the equation $f(z) \equiv 1 - a_1 z - \ldots - a_p z^p = 0$ has no roots less than unity in moduli, and it corresponds to absence of explosive roots in the characteristic polynomial (2.14). In the Box–Jenkins modelling of time series $f(z) \equiv 1 - a_1 z - \ldots$ is not zero also when z is complex with unit modulus. In the AR(p) this corresponds to absence of complex unit roots in the characteristic polynomial. In the Box–Jenkins modelling $f(z)$ may be zero at $z =$ real unity. Then with some positive integer r

$$(1 - a_1 L - \ldots) = (1 - L)^r (1 - \tilde{a}_1 L - \ldots),$$

where $\tilde{f}(z) \equiv 1 - \tilde{a}_1 z - \ldots$ cannot vanish when z is less than or equal to unity in moduli. In the AR(p) this corresponds to the presence of real unit root with multiplicity r and stability in regard to all other roots in the characteristic polynomial.

In time-series analysis the *stationary* autoregressive process with a possibly infinite order represented by the condition that $f(z) \equiv 1 - a_1 z - \ldots = 0$ never occurs in so far as z is equal to or less than unity in moduli. Then there exists $g(z) = 1 + g_1 + z - \ldots$ such that $f(z)g(z) = 1$, i.e. $f(z)$ can be inverted.[2] Moreover, $g(z) = 0$ never occurs when z is equal to or less than unity, and $g(z)$ is invertible. In the finite-order autoregressive process $f(z) \equiv 1 - a_1 z \ldots - a_p z^p = 0$ has no roots less than or equal to unity. Then (2.14)

[2] A theorem on the analytic function is behind the statement.

has only stable roots, and $f(z)$ can be inverted, i.e. the difference equation

$$(1 - a_1 L - \ldots - a_p L^p)x_t = \varepsilon_t$$

can be solved to get

$$x_t = \varepsilon_t + b_1\varepsilon_{t-1} + b_2\varepsilon_{t-2} + \ldots.$$

Here $\{b_j\}$ is bounded by a decaying exponential. (This property does not necessarily hold in an infinite order AR.)

In Part I I use the characteristic polynomial (2.13) in order to use the term, dominating root. (I shall switch to the time-series notation in Part II.) The dominating root of the characteristic polynomial is the root that is the largest in moduli. Thus the stationary autoregressive process is characterized by the dominating root of the characteristic polynomial being less than unity in moduli, and the stochastic trend is represented by the dominating root being equal to real unity possibly with some multiplicity. The Box–Jenkins modelling rules out the dominating root being explosive or complex unity.

The explosive root is taken into consideration in Bayesian studies as described in Chapter 10, but it is a priori ruled out in the classical inference explained in Chapters 3, 5, 7, and 8. It should be emphasized that the difference stationarity precludes an explosive root. To see this consider $x_t - \rho x_{t-1} = \varepsilon_t$ with $\rho > 1$. Then $\Delta x_t = \varepsilon_t - (1-\rho)(\varepsilon_{t-1} + \rho\varepsilon_{t-2} + \ldots + \rho^{t-2}\varepsilon_1) + \rho^t x_0$, which is non-stationary. For any positive i the ith difference of x_t is non-stationary, i.e. $\{x_t\}$ is not $I(i)$ for any i.[3]

The multiplicity of unit roots referred to earlier by r is assumed to be 1 in most of the book. In so far as macroeconomic time series are concerned the integration order of the log of price has been an issue in the literature. Hall (1986) judges that the UK price is $I(2)$, but Clements and Mizon (1991) and Johansen and Juselius (1992) think that it is $I(1)$ with structural changes in the deterministic trends or non-stationarity in the variance. I shall present my results on logs of price and money stock in Chapter 9. Charts (of the residuals after the trend fitting) of $I(2)$ variables show even smoother contour than the case of $I(1)$ variables. If one feels from the chart or otherwise a need to check whether or not $r = 2$, one should see if the series of Δx_t has a unit root. $I(2)$ can be tested against $I(1)$ by applying the regression tests given in Chapters 5 and 7 to $\{\Delta x_t\}$ and $I(1)$ can be tested against $I(2)$ by applying the MA unit root test in Chapter 3 to $\{\Delta x_t\}$. The order of integration may not be constant over time in some variables. We cannot be sure of this because the determination of the integration order requires some length of time-span as will be explained in Section 2.5 below.

[3] A simple version of the economic theory of bubbles entails an explosive root. An empirical study of Diba and Grossman (1988) on the historical, annual data of stock price (relative to the general price index) casts doubt on the presence of an explosive root. An extended version of the theory of bubbles given in Froot and Obstfeld (1991) does not necessarily imply an explosive root. It is a non linear model.

The dominating root of the characteristic polynomial is related to $b(1)$ as follows. Suppose that $\{x_t\}$ is $AR(p)$

$$(1 - a_1L - \ldots - a_pL^p)x_t = \varepsilon_t.$$

If the factorization

$$(1 - a_1L - \ldots - a_pL^p) = (1 - L)(1 - \tilde{a}_1L - \ldots - \tilde{a}_{p-1}L^{p-1}) \tag{2.16}$$

is possible, then

$$\Delta x_t = (1 - \tilde{a}_1L - \ldots - \tilde{a}_{p-1}L^{p-1})^{-1}\varepsilon_t,$$

and if $1 - \tilde{a}_1L - \ldots - \tilde{a}_{p-1}L^{p-1}$ is stable,

$$b(1) = (1 - \tilde{a}_1 - \ldots - \tilde{a}_{p-1})^{-1}.$$

If the factorization (2.16) is not possible, $b(1) = 0$.

2.4 Non-Separate Hypotheses

In general two hypotheses, H_1 and H_2, are said to be *non-nested* if neither $H_1 \supseteq H_2$ nor $H_2 \supseteq H_1$ where $A \supseteq B$ means that A is more general than B. The two hypotheses are said to be *separate* if no models in H_1 can be represented as a limit in some sequence of models in H_2 and vice versa. See Cox (1961) for the non-nested and separate hypotheses. The trend stationarity and the difference stationarity are non-nested but not separate. In Figure 2.1 an arbitrary small neighbourhood of $b(1) = 0$ (i.e. TS) contains models of DS. Figure 2.2 is a complex plane for the dominating root of the characteristic polynomial, ρ, and the circle is the unit circle. According to the TS ρ lies *inside* the unit circle, while ρ is real unity according to the DS. In Figure 2.2 an arbitrary small neighbourhood of $\rho = 1$ (i.e. DS) contains models of TS.

It is also worth noting that the parametrization in terms of $b(1)$ represents a TS model as a limit of a sequence of DS models, while the parametrization in terms of ρ represents a DS model as a limit of a sequence of TS models. It will be found later that $b(1)$ is useful to test for TS against DS, whereas the dominating root of the characteristic polynomial is useful to test for DS against TS.

It is not unusual at all that econometricians wish to compare the congruence of two non-nested, non-separate hypotheses with available observations. The statistical inference, either classic or Bayesian, has been useful for the comparison if parameter values of the highest concern are sufficiently separated, and

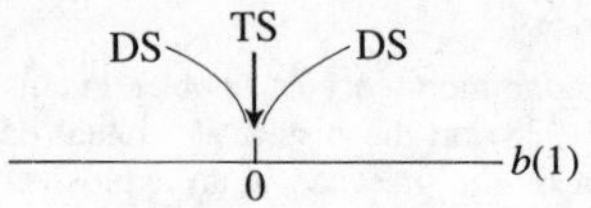

FIG. 2.1 *Long-run component*

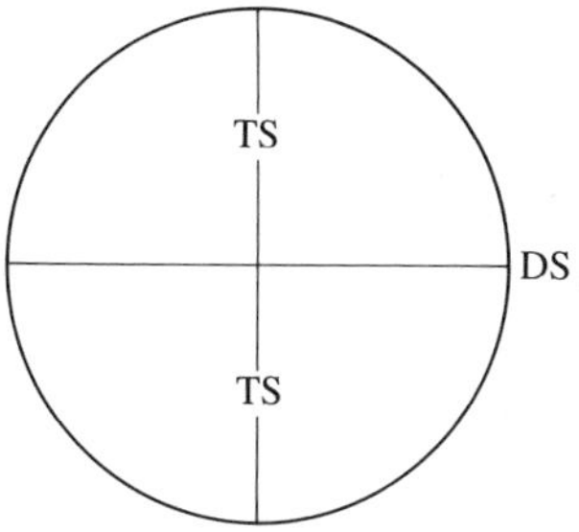

FIG. 2.2 *Dominating roots of characteristic polynomial*

if available data are well behaved. In relation to the discrimination between DS and TS the problem is investigated in Chapter 8. At this point I only warn against overoptimism about precision in discriminating TS and DS.

2.5 Time Aggregation and Other Remarks on the Data

Earlier the purpose of the discrimination between DS and TS was classified into three. Past studies with the first purpose have established a stylized pattern regarding the time-series data to be analysed, and the data are classified into two groups. The first is a set of annual data covering 70–130 years for a number of macroeconomic variables in the USA, and the annual data for at least real output and a few other variables in a number of other countries. As for US data readers are referred to Nelson and Plosser (1982) and Schotman and van Dijk (1991*b*) in which the Nelson–Plosser data have been updated to 1988. Kormendi and Meguire (1990) explore the data in countries other than the USA. The second group is the post-Second World War quarterly or monthly data for a large number of variables in all advanced countries, which must be well known to econometricians. Many studies have been carried out on international comparisons on the real outputs. In the present book the first group will be referred to as the *historical data*, and the second group as the *post-war data*.

In reviewing each empirical study it is advisable to pay attention to which of the two groups is being analysed. Results of analyses are often different between the two groups of data. The post-war era is different from the pre-war with respect to a number of aspects of economic regimes, and this is seen most clearly in the variance of Δx_t being larger in the pre-war period than post-war, where x_t is the real output in log. See also Harvey (1985), DeLong and Summers (1988), and Durlauf (1989). Romer (1986*a*, 1986*b*, 1989) question the comparability of US data between the pre- and post-Second World War periods. Even though she is primarily concerned with the volatility her problem must also be relevant to the stochastic trend.

In spite of these remarks it must be admitted that historical data covering long time-periods are preferred when the presence or absence of stochastic trends is our direct concern as a property of economic dynamics. This is because the persistence of responses to a current impulse even in the infinitely remote future can be verified only with time series covering very long periods.

The post-war data are available on a quarterly basis, which of course can be aggregated into annual data if so desired. On the other hand the historical data are available on an annual basis only. Let us consider the discrimination between DS and TS in relation to different units of time. In terms of the dominating root of the characteristic polynomial the unit root remains unchanged after time aggregation, but the stable root varies its value with time aggregation. Suppose that $x_1 = \rho x_{t-1} + \varepsilon_t$, $1 > |\rho| > 0$, on a quarterly basis, where $\{\varepsilon_t\}$ is i.i.d. with zero mean. Let $y_t = \sum_{i=0}^{3} x_{t-i}$ and $e_t = \sum_{i=0}^{3} \varepsilon_{t-i}$.
Then

$$y_t = \rho^4 y_{t-4} + \sum_{i=0}^{3} \rho^i e_{t-i}.$$

Picking y_t at every fourth time produces the annual data. Even though it is not AR(1) but ARMA(1,1), the root of the characteristic polynomial for the AR part is ρ^4. A DS model with $\rho = 1$ and a TS model with, say, $\rho = 0.95$ on a quarterly basis are separated apart more distinctly as $\rho = 1$ vs. $\rho = 0.95^4$ on an annual basis. Turning to the size of the long-run component let us suppose that Δx_t is MA(q). Construct $\Delta y_t = \sum_{i=0}^{3} \Delta x_{t-i}$ and pick up every fourth observation of Δy_t, which produces the annual data of the differenced series. It is MA $(1 + [(q-1)/4])$. Now suppose that $\{x_t\}$ is TS on the original, quarterly basis so that $b(1) = 0$ in $\{\Delta x_t\}$. Then $b(1) = 0$ in $\{\Delta y_t\}$ but generally $b(1)$ is not zero in the series of every fourth term of Δy_t, because zero frequency and the frequency that corresponds to the annual cycle cannot be distinguished in the annual data.[4] Thus what is TS in the quarterly data is turned into DS in the annual data.[5] Seasonal adjustments do reduce, but do not eliminate the problem. In fact after the seasonal adjustments it is conjectured that the spectral density would resemble that of the Schwert MA to be explained in Section 7.2 below. Incidentally, what is DS in the quarterly data remains as DS in the annual data in terms of the size of long-run component.

In later sections the testing for DS against TS is performed in terms of the dominating root of the characteristic polynomial, and the testing for TS against DS in terms of the size of the long-run component. If the DGP is TS in the quarterly data, the time aggregation separates more clearly the dominating root of the characteristic polynomial from unity, but at the same time it reduces

[4] Let $f(\lambda)$, $\pi \geq \lambda \geq -\pi$, be the spectral density function of Δx_t so that $f(0) = 0$. Let $g(\lambda) = \|1+\exp(i\lambda)+\exp(2i\lambda)+\exp(3i\lambda)\|^2$. Then the spectral density function of Δy_t is $h(\lambda) = f(\lambda)g(\lambda)$. Note that $h(0) = 0$. The spectral density function of the series picking every fourth term of Δy_t is

$$h(\lambda) + h\left(\frac{\pi}{2} - \lambda\right) + h\left(\frac{\pi}{2} + \lambda\right) + h(\pi - \lambda), \qquad \frac{\pi}{4} \geq \lambda \geq -\frac{\pi}{4}.$$

See, e.g. Fuller (1976: 119). Generally the density at $\lambda = 0$ is not zero because $h(\pi/2)$ is not zero. $\pi/2$ is the frequency that corresponds to the annual cycle.

[5] If 4 were an odd number, there would be a simple method to make $h(\pi/2)$ zero and thereby $b(1) = 0$ in the annual data.

the sample size. Perron (1989*b*, 1991*a*) think that the power of discrimination between DS and TS depends upon the absolute length, say in years, of the period covered by the time-series data but not upon the units of time in the data. Continuing on the same assumption, the time aggregation introduces a model misspecification in terms of the size of the long-run component, and distorts the testing for TS against DS. Weighing these factors it may be concluded that we should use the quarterly data without time aggregation when both the annual and quarterly data are available.

In Chapter 9 we shall analyse both the historical annual data and the post-war quarterly data. The former may involve a model misspecification in terms of $|b(1)|$ but it is outweighed by the advantage due to the longer time-spans that they cover. The historical data seem to be useful for any suggestions on the *general* theories of macrodynamics. On the other hand the post-war data are used more frequently for econometric studies in general than the historical data. The discrimination between DS and TS in the post-war data is important from the standpoint of the second purpose of the discrimination, i.e. the analyses of inference procedures.

Macroeconomic time-series data used for DS vs. TS discrimination are logarithms of the variables except in the case of interest rates and unemployment rates. Most of the original variables appear to be explosive. Repeated differencing operations do not transform them into the seemingly stationary series, but the logarithmic transformation possibly does with differencing. See Banerjee *et al.* (1993: 192–9).

In both the historical and the post-war data a typical sample size is 100, and $T = 100$ has been adopted in most of simulation studies regarding finite sample distributions of various statistics. In the post-war data T is close to or more than 150, but the discrepancy between the asymptotic and finite sample distributions is not much affected by increasing T from 100 to 150.

3
Discrimination in Terms of the Long-Run Component: A Test for Trend Stationarity

The present chapter deals with a measure of long-run component, $b(1)$. Section 3.1 describes the non-parametric variance ratio that has been widely used to measure the importance of long-run components in economic time series. While admitting its usefulness as a descriptive statistic, I shall argue in Section 3.2 that it cannot be used to discriminate the difference and the trend stationarity. My argument uses the spectral theory, and the theory will be used again in Chapter 7 to explain the Schwert ARMA. Therefore Appendix 1 provides an elementary description of the spectral theory. Section 3.3 offers a brief comment on the time-series decomposition. Section 3.4 explains the MA unit-root test that has been derived as the locally best test on the basis of the invariance principle. Since this general inference theory is relatively new to econometricians, elementary explanations are given in Section 3.4. It turns out that the MA unit-root test for Δx_t is useful to test for the trend stationarity of x_t against difference stationarity. I shall follow the latest version on this line, Saikkonen and Luukkonen (1993*a*), and also present a particular implementation of the method that will be used in Chapter 8 for an experiment and in Chapter 9 for my analysis of economic time-series data. The deterministic trend is just a constant in the present section, but will be extended in Chapter 6.

3.1 Non-parametric Variance Ratios and Mean-Reverting

A virtually identical type of analysis was made about the same time by Huizinga (1987) on monthly real exchange rates, by Cochrane (1988) on annual US real GNP, and by Poterba and Summers (1988) on stock price and related variables in various time units.[1] All these studies attempt to get information about $b(1)$ in a non-parametric framework though they are not necessarily directed to the discrimination between DS and TS.

I use the notations in Chapter 2 and the model (2.1′). For a given $k > 0$

$$x_{t+k} - x_t = \sum\nolimits_{s=1}^{k} \Delta x_{t+s} = k\mu + b(1) \sum\nolimits_{s=1}^{k} \varepsilon_{t+s} + b^*(L)(\varepsilon_{t+k} - \varepsilon_t)$$

[1] Campbell and Mankiw (1987), Fama and French (1988), and Lo and MacKinley (1989) are also related to this research.

and

$$E(x_{t+k} - x_t - k\mu)^2 = kb(1)^2\sigma_\varepsilon^2 + \sigma_\varepsilon^2 \left(\sum_0^{k-1} b_j^{*2} + 2b(1) \sum_0^{k-1} b_j^* \right.$$
$$\left. + \sum_0^{\infty} (b_{j+k}^* - b_j^*)^2 \right).$$

Define

$$v_k = (E(x_{t+k} - x_t - k\mu)^2)/k. \tag{3.1}$$

Since $\left(\sum_0^{k-1} b_j^{*2} + 2b(1)\sum_0^{k-1} b_j^* + \sum_0^{\infty}(b_{j+k}^* - b_j^*)^2\right)$ remains bounded as $k \to \infty$, $\lim_{k\to\infty} v_k = b(1)^2\sigma_\varepsilon^2$.

Consider $r_k \equiv v_k/v_1$, $k = 2, 3, \ldots$ to turn v_k into a unitless number like a correlation coefficient. Since $E(\Delta x_{t+1} - \mu)^2 = \sigma_\varepsilon^2 \sum_{j=0}^{\infty} b_j^2$,

$$r \equiv \lim_{k\to\infty} r_k = \left(\sum_0^{\infty} b_j\right)^2 \left(\sum_0^{\infty} b_j^2\right)^{-1}. \tag{3.2}$$

If $\{x_t\}$ is TS, $b(1) = 0$, and $r = 0$. If $\{x_t\}$ is DS, $r > 0$.

An alternative view of v_k is

$$\begin{aligned} v_k &= k^{-1}E((\Delta x_{t+1} - \mu) + \ldots + (\Delta x_{t+k} - \mu))^2 \\ &= \gamma_0 + 2\sum_{j=1}^{k-1} k^{-1}(k - j)\gamma_j, \end{aligned} \tag{3.3}$$

where γ_j is the autocovariance of $\{\Delta x_t\}$ for lag j. It is said that in many economic time-series γ_j is positive for small j but negative for large j, even though absolute values of γ_j are small except for j = 1 or 2. In such series r_k is larger than unity for small k because $v_1 = \gamma_0$, but, as k increases, r_k gradually declines because negative γ_js begin to be included in v_k. The case, $r < 1$, is called mean-reverting or trend-reverting, and $r \geq 1$ is called mean (trend)-averting. The trend stationarity is the extreme case of mean-reverting.

Finite amounts of data provide no evidence on the limit of r_k as $k \to \infty$. We should be content with a hint given by $r_1, \ldots, r_{k*}$, where k_* is a cut-off point chosen to maintain the reliability of inference from a given length of available data, T. Since no parametric models are adopted here, I shall call $(r_2, \ldots, r_{k*})$ the non-parametric variance ratios.

The v_ks are estimated by sample analogues of (3.1) except for degrees of freedom adjustment, for which readers are referred to Cochrane (1988). The estimates of $(r_2, \ldots, r_{k*})$ have been plotted against k in a two-dimensional graph, and confidence bands are set by various methods. A standard simulation method is used in Campbell and Mankiw (1987, 1989), Cochrane (1988), Lo and MacKinlay (1989), Christiano and Eichenbaum (1990), and Kormendi and Mequire (1990), and a χ^2 (instead of normal) approximation to spectral estimates is used in Cogley (1990). Confidence bands are not easy to construct because a negative bias and skewness are found.

The studies analysing the non-parametric variance ratios are primarily concerned with discriminating the mean-reverting and mean-averting. Though not entirely irrelevant to our goal of discriminating the TS and DS, my survey of the results will be brief. As for the stock price Poterba and Summers (1988) and Fama and French (1988) conclude that the mean-reverting is supported by monthly and annual data in a number of countries, but Kim, Nelson, and Startz (1991) conclude that the mean-averting is observed in monthly data of the New York Stock Exchange since the Second World War. As for the historical data of real output Cochrane (1988) gets evidence in favour of the mean-reverting for the USA, but the international comparisons in Campbell and Mankiw (1989) on the post-war quarterly data and in Cogley (1990) and Kormendi and Meguire (1990) on the historical data find that the USA is an exception among a number of countries examined.

A linear trend has been taken into consideration in (3.1), but any structural changes in deterministic trends have not been. Banerjee, Lumsdaine, and Stock (1992) observe that the countries for which the real output is found mean-averting are also those for which the structural changes are significant. Demery and Duck (1992) also makes a similar observation. The role that the structural changes play in discrimination between the TS and DS will be discussed in Chapter 8.

3.2 Difficulty of Discrimination through the Non-Parametric Variance Ratios[2]

One might think that the non-parametric variance ratios may be useful also for discriminating TS and DS. If the confidence band does not reach the zero line in the two-dimensional graph of $(r_2, \ldots, r_{k*})$ plotted against k, we should accept the difference stationarity while admitting the limitation of evidence to those ks less than k_*. In fact there have been such attempts.

I shall argue that, when the sequence of v_k is truncated at $k = k_*$, v_{k*} can take any values whatsoever within the models of TS so that the above confidence judgement lacks a theoretical ground. This argument provides a theoretical support to the scepticism that some earlier simulation studies have had about the confidence judgement.

The starting-point of my argument is (3.3). I shall write k for k_* below to simplify the notations. Define

$$w_{j,k} = \begin{cases} k^{-1}(k - |j|), & |j| \leq k \\ 0 & |j| > k. \end{cases} \tag{3.4}$$

Then (3.3) is

$$v_k = \sum_{j=-k+1}^{k-1} w_{j,k}\gamma_j, \tag{3.3$'$}$$

[2] I have benefited from comments by Kimio Morimune on an earlier draft of Section 3.2.

where $\{\gamma_j\}$ is the autocovariance sequence of Δx_t. Keeping k fixed, the Fourier transform of $w_{j,k}\gamma_j$, $j = -k+1, \ldots, 0, \ldots, k-1$, is

$$f_\Delta(\lambda, k) \equiv (2\pi)^{-1} \sum_{j=-k}^{k} w_{j,k}\gamma_j \exp(-i\lambda j), \; -\pi \leq \lambda \leq \pi. \tag{3.5}$$

Then (3.3′) is $2\pi f_\Delta(0, k)$, and this is what we are here concerned with. We shall re-express $2\pi f_\Delta(0, k)$. The Fourier transform of (3.4) is

$$h_B(\lambda, k) \equiv (2\pi)^{-1} \sum_{j=-k}^{k} w_{j,k}\exp(-i\lambda j) \tag{3.6}$$

$$= (2\pi k)^{-1} \left(\sin^2 \tfrac{1}{2}\lambda k\right) \left(\sin^2 \tfrac{1}{2}\lambda\right)^{-1}, \; -\pi \leq \lambda \leq \pi,$$

as shown, for example, in Anderson (1971: 508–9). Let $f_\Delta(\lambda)$ be the spectral density function of $\{\Delta x_t\}$. Then $f_\Delta(\lambda, k)$ is related to $f_\Delta(\lambda)$ through

$$f_\Delta(\lambda, k) = \int_{-\pi}^{\pi} h_B(\lambda - \zeta, k) f_\Delta(\zeta) d\zeta. \tag{3.5′}$$

which is proved in Appendix 1. The right-hand side of (3.5′) is an average of $f_\Delta(\zeta)$ over different values of ζ with weighting function $h_B(\lambda - \zeta, k)$ (as a function of ζ). As seen in Figure 3.1 $h_B(\lambda - \zeta, k)$ is highest at $\lambda - \zeta = 0$. Therefore the weights are highest at $\zeta = \lambda$. In particular, when $\lambda = 0$

$$v_k = 2\pi f_\Delta(0, k) = 2\pi \int_{-\pi}^{\pi} h_B(\zeta, k) f_\Delta(\zeta) d\zeta. \tag{3.7}$$

In this averaging of $f_\Delta(\zeta)$ the heaviest weight is placed at $\zeta = 0$. We are concerned with (3.7).

In general the Fourier transform of weighted autocovariances (such as $w_{j,k}\gamma_j$, $j = -k+1, \ldots, 0, \ldots, k-1$) is called the spectral density 'looked through a window' because it is a weighted average of original spectral densities as shown in (3.5′). The weighting function on the time domain such as (3.4) is called the lag window, and the weighting function on the frequency domain

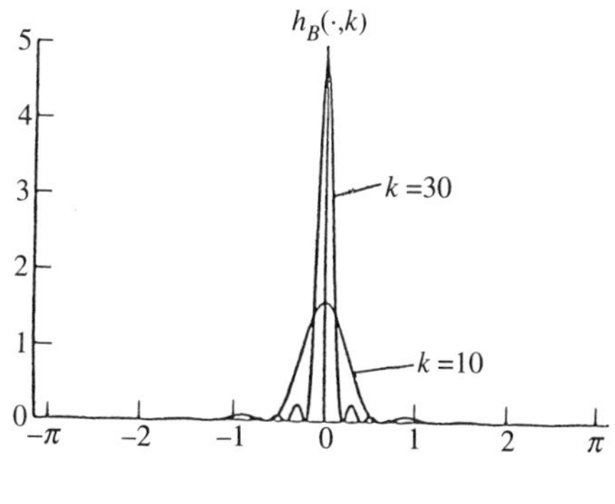

FIG. 3.1 *Bartlett spectral window function*

such as (3.6) is called the spectral window. Specifically, when the weights on autocovariances are (3.4), the expressions (3.4) and (3.6) are called respectively the Bartlett lag window and Bartlett spectral window. The v_k in (3.7) is (2π) times (the spectral density at zero frequency looked through the Bartlett window). So much has been pointed out in Cochrane (1988), Campbell and Mankiw (1989), and Cogley (1990).

Given the spectral density of $\{\Delta x_t\}$, the v_k can be calculated theoretically from (3.7). Figure 3.1 plots $h_B(\lambda, k)$ in (3.6) against λ with k fixed. The base of the central 'hill' narrows as k increases. Now I suppose that $\{x_t\}$ is trend stationary, and after subtracting its deterministic trend the spectral density function is $g(\lambda)$. Then $\{\Delta x_t\}$ has the spectral density function, $2(1-\cos\lambda)g(\lambda) \equiv f_\Delta(\lambda)$, as shown in Appendix 1. Note that $f_\Delta(0) = 0$ no matter what $g(\cdot)$ is, which reconfirms the implication of $b(1) = 0$ given earlier in Section 2.2. The expression (3.7) becomes

$$v_k = 4\pi \int_{-\pi}^{\pi} h_B(\zeta, k)(1 - \cos\zeta)g(\zeta)d\zeta. \tag{3.8}$$

For illustration suppose that $\{x_t\}$ is generated by

$$x_t = \rho x_{t-1} + \varepsilon_t, \qquad |\rho| < 1 \tag{3.9}$$

where $\{\varepsilon_t\}$ is i.i.d. with $E(\varepsilon_t) = 0$ and $E(\varepsilon_t^2) = 1$. Thus

$$g(\zeta) = (1 - 2\rho\cos\zeta + \rho^2)^{-1}, v_1 = E(\Delta x_t^2) = 2/(1+\rho).$$

The graph of $f_\Delta(\lambda)$ with this $g(\cdot)$ is shown in Figure 3.2. The integrand in (3.8) is the product of two functions, h_B in Figure 3.1 and f_Δ in Figure 3.2. For a given $k = k_*$, we can choose ρ sufficiently close to unity so that the valley centred at $\lambda = 0$ in Figure 3.2 has sufficiently steep sides. This in turn makes the product of two functions sufficiently larger than zero over some domain of λ as shown in Figure 3.3. Therefore the integral in (3.8) is positive rather than zero. The TS model (3.9) looks like a DS model.

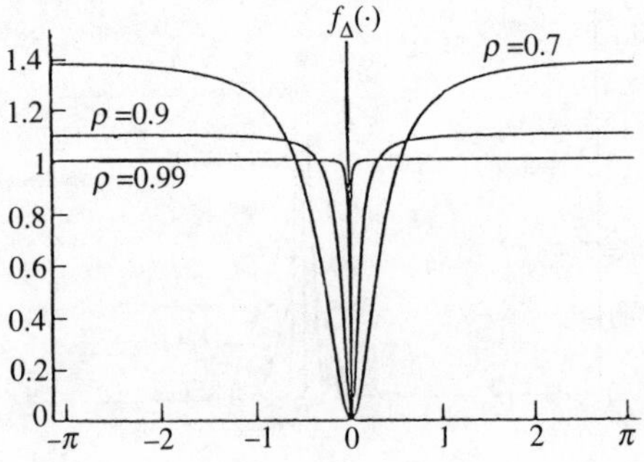

FIG. 3.2 *Spectral density function of* Δx_t

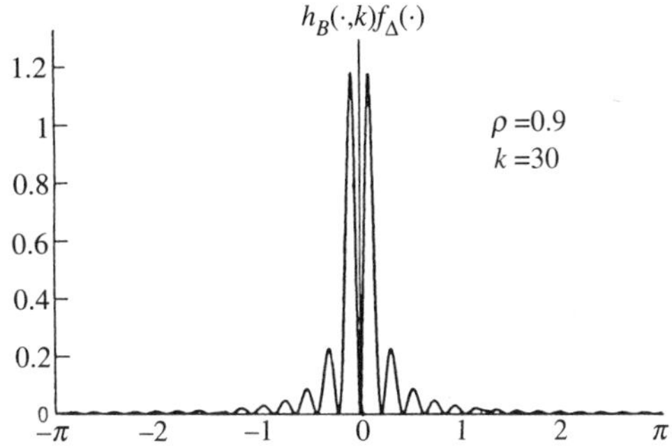

FIG. 3.3 *Product of window and spectral density*

If we have infinite amount of data so that k_* can be made ∞, then $h_B(\lambda, \infty)$ is the Dirac delta function concentrating on $\lambda = 0$. This makes v_∞ zero in the case of the trend stationarity. This is consistent with the condition for TS in (3.2), i.e. $r = 0$.

It is admitted that, no matter what methods are used, the power to discriminate DS and TS with $T = 100$ is limited, but in my view the non-parametric variance ratios are not useful unless one has a priori belief in the difference stationarity. To be able to perform a reliable statistical inference on $b(1)$ one has to assume in addition that $f_\Delta(\lambda)$ for Δx_t is smooth about $\lambda = 0$. The above point is closely related to the long-run variance in the Schwert ARMA, which will be discussed in Sections 7.2 and 7.3.3.

3.3 Time-Series Decomposition

A given time series can be decomposed into unobservable components each representing a specific time-series property with a parametric model. The most comprehensive literature is Harvey (1989). In relation to the discrimination between the trend and the difference stationarity relevant components are (i) the long-run or permanent component and (ii) business cycles or transitory component. Clark (1987) and Watson (1986) demonstrate that there is a number of different decompositions with different correlations between the two components. In response Cochrane (1988) observes that the variance of the long-run component does not depend upon how the decomposition is made. This is because, no matter how a given time series is decomposed, the transitory component does not contribute at all to the spectral density of Δx_t at zero frequency. This theoretical observation notwithstanding, statistical estimates of variances of long-run components diverge among different decompositions. The decomposition in Clark (1989) produces a result in favour of TS contrary to Campbell and Mankiw (1989) concerning the real GNP in different countries.[3]

[3] Lippi and Reichlin (1992) present an interesting inequality concerning the decomposition into unobservable components.

3.4 Parametric MA Unit-Root Test: A Test for Trend Stationarity against Difference Stationarity

Through a simulation study Rudebusch (1992) demonstrates an enormous discrepancy between the impulse–response functions of DS and TS models even when these models can hardly be discriminated in terms of the standard model fitting to the available data. It seems that $(b_0, b_1, \ldots)$ in Chapter 2 is a good indicator for the discrimination between TS and DS. However, non-parametric approaches to $b(1)$ are difficult with $T = 100$ in the available macroeconomic time-series data as shown in Section 3.2. We are thus led to trying a model with a finite number of parameters, i.e. a parametric approach. As indicated in equation (2.11), if $\{x_t\}$ is a stationary MA(q) devoid of a long-run component, i.e. $b(1) = 0$, then $\{\Delta x_t\}$ is an MA $(q+1)$ with an MA unit root. We are thus led to testing for the presence of an MA unit root.

This testing problem is non-standard in so far as the maximum-likelihood approach is adopted, because the null hypothesis specifies a point on the boundary of the admissible region of MA parameters. The maximum-likelihood approach should not be recommended (unless the boundary is properly dealt with).

3.4.1 BLI test

An inference theory called the invariance principle has seldom been used in econometrics, but it is this theory that has made the MA unit-root test possible. A general explanation of the invariance principle now follows. The observation, x, is produced by a member of a parametric family of models with a probability distribution represented by a value of a parameter, θ. Consider a group of transformations, G, on the observation and an associated group of transformations, $\tilde{G}$, on the parameter, such that the distribution of Gx with θ is identical to that of x with $\tilde{G}\theta$. (For example, $x \sim N(\mu, 1)$, G transforms x to $x + c$ with some non-stochastic c, and $\tilde{G}$ transforms μ to $\mu + c$.) We are confronted with an inference problem, testing for H_0 against H_1, and suppose that the differentiation between H_0 and H_1 remains unaltered through the transformations in $\tilde{G}$, symbolically $\tilde{G}(H_0) = H_0$, $\tilde{G}(H_1) = H_1$. Then the invariance principle asserts that the test for H_0 against H_1 should be based upon what is called the maximal-invariant statistic. A statistic, $T(x)$, is maximal-invariant for a given inference problem if the following two conditions are met with G, which is the maximal-invariant group of transformations for the given inference problem: (i) $T(x) = T(g(x))$ for all x and all $g \in G$, and (ii) if there is no $g \in G$ such that $x' = g(x)$, then $T(x) \neq T(x')$. See Cox and Hinkley (1972: 41–4, 157–61, 165) and Ferguson (1967: 143–52, 242–5).

Another inference theory that has been introduced in the MA unit-root test is the locally best (LB) test. Suppose that H_0 states that $\theta = \theta^0$ and H_1 states that

$\theta > \theta^0$. From among all possible ways to construct critical regions, each having given test size α, the theory of the locally best test proposes to choose the one such that the slope of the power function from θ^0 to $\theta^0 + \varepsilon$ (ε being positive and infinitesimal) is the steepest. Suppose that $f(x, \theta)$ is the p.d.f. of x. Then it is seen by a reasoning analogous to the Neyman–Pearson lemma that the steepest slope is attained when the critical region consists of those x such that

$$\frac{\partial}{\partial \theta} \log f(x, \theta^0) > k. \tag{3.10}$$

The left-hand side of (3.10) denotes the partial derivative with respect to θ that is evaluated at $\theta = \theta^0$, and k is chosen to obtain the given test size. See Ferguson (1967: 235–6). If the left-hand side of (3.10) is independent of θ^0, the idea is extended to the curvature (instead of the slope) of the power function, giving the locally best unbiased (LBU) test. It introduces the second-order derivative of $\log f(\cdot)$ in the criterion to construct the critical region (see Ferguson (1967: 237–8)). These tests may be interpreted as an extended version of the score test with explicit recognition of the boundary condition (see Tanaka (1995*a*)).

The invariance principle and the locally best test (or the locally best unbiased test) can be combined into the locally best invariance (LBI) test (or the locally best invariance unbiased (LBIU) test) (see Ferguson (1967: 246)). It has been implemented on the regression model with a disturbance covariance matrix, $\sigma^2 \boldsymbol{\Omega}(\theta)$, where $\boldsymbol{\Omega}(0) = \boldsymbol{I}_T$. The inference problem is to test $H_0 : \theta = 0$ against $H_1 : \theta \neq 0$, or $\theta > 0$. The relevant literature is Durbin and Watson (1971), Kariya (1980), King (1980), and King and Hillier (1985). The LBI test has also been implemented on the regression model with a time-varying parameter. The inference problem is to test H_0: (no variation in the parameter) against H_1: (a random walk is involved in the parameter). The literature is LaMotte and McWhoter (1978), Nyblom and Mäkeläinen (1983), and Nabeya and Tanaka (1988).

3.4.2 MA unit-root test

Nyblom (1986) and Kwiatkowski *et al.* (1992) recognize that the testing for the stationarity of $\{x_t\}$ against the non-stationarity is a special case of the testing mentioned above in relation to the regression with a time-varying parameter. The testing is found invariant through linear transformations of observations (location and scale changes). It is in this background that the MA unit-root test has been developed in Tanaka (1990, 1995*a*), Kwiatkowski *et al.* (1992), and Saikkonen and Luukkonen (1993*a*). The testing methods that they propose are equivalent to each other in so far as $\{\Delta x_t\}$ is MA(1), i.e. $q = 0$ in (2.11).[4] All of them extend

[4] The equivalence between Kwiatkowski *et al.* (1992) and Saikkonen and Luukkonen (1993*a*) is apparent. The equivalence between Tanaka (1990) and Saikkonen and Luukkonen (1993*a*) is indicated in Saikkonen and Luukkonen (1993*b*). I am also indebted to Katsuto Tanaka on this point.

their methods to the more general case, and the extension in Saikkonen and Luukkonen (1993*a*) differs from that in Tanaka (1990) and Kwiatkowski *et al.* (1992). The latter involves non-parametric estimations of long-run variances, the difficulties of which are explained in Section 7.3.3 below. On the other hand Saikkonen and Luukkonen (1993*a*) adopt an ARMA representation of $\{\Delta x_t\}$ avoiding non-parametric estimations of long-run variances.

I am now ready to introduce the MA unit-root test by Saikkonen and Luukkonen (1993*a*). Let $\{\varepsilon_t\}$ be Gaussian i.i.d. with $E(\varepsilon_t) = 0$ and $E(\varepsilon_t^2) = \sigma_\varepsilon^2$, and let $\{\Delta x_t\}$ be an MA(1),

$$\Delta x_t = \varepsilon_t - \delta\varepsilon_{t-1}. \qquad t = 2, \ldots, T \tag{3.11a}$$

For the initial value it is assumed that

$$x_1 = \theta_0 + \varepsilon_1. \tag{3.11b}$$

It follows that

$$x_t = \theta_0 + (1 - \delta)\sum\nolimits_{s=1}^{t-1} \varepsilon_s + \varepsilon_t.$$

If $\delta = 1$, $x_t = \theta_0 + \varepsilon_t$. If $|\delta| < 1$, $\{x_t\}$ is difference stationary. Let $\boldsymbol{x}' = (x_1, \ldots, x_T)$, $\boldsymbol{e}' = (1, \ldots, 1)$, and $\boldsymbol{L}^*$ be the $T \times T$ matrix with unities on the diagonal immediately below the main diagonal and zeros elsewhere. Also let $\boldsymbol{D} = \boldsymbol{L}^* + \boldsymbol{L}^{*2} + \ldots + \boldsymbol{L}^{*T-1}$, and $\hat{\boldsymbol{v}} = \boldsymbol{x} - \bar{x}\boldsymbol{e}$, where $\bar{x} = T^{-1}\boldsymbol{e}'\boldsymbol{x}$. Then the LBIU test for $\delta = 1$ against $\delta < 1$ is based upon

$$S = (\hat{\boldsymbol{v}}'\hat{\boldsymbol{v}})^{-1}\hat{\boldsymbol{v}}'\boldsymbol{D}\boldsymbol{D}'\hat{\boldsymbol{v}}. \tag{3.12}$$

The critical region is set on those S that are larger than a certain value, which is to be decided by the asymptotic distribution of $T^{-1}S$ so as to secure a given test size.

Since $\boldsymbol{e}'\hat{\boldsymbol{v}} = 0$ and $\boldsymbol{I} + \boldsymbol{D} = \boldsymbol{e}\boldsymbol{e}' - \boldsymbol{D}'$ (3.12) is equivalent to

$$S = (\hat{\boldsymbol{v}}'\hat{\boldsymbol{v}})^{-1}\hat{\boldsymbol{v}}'(\boldsymbol{I} + \boldsymbol{D})'(\boldsymbol{I} + \boldsymbol{D})\hat{\boldsymbol{v}}. \tag{3.12'}$$

$(I + D)\hat{v}$ is a vector of partial sums of $\hat{v}_t$ (accumulating from $t = 1$), and the intuitive meaning of the test statistic is clearer in (3.12′) than in (3.12). The limiting distribution of $T^{-1}S$ will be given in Section 6.3.

Let us generalize (3.11*a*) and (3.11*b*) to

$$\Delta x_t = u_t - \delta u_{t-1} \tag{3.13a}$$

$$x_1 = \theta_0 + u_1 \tag{3.13b}$$

$$(1 - a_1 L - \ldots - a_p L^p)u_t = (1 - b_1 L - \ldots - b_q L^q)\varepsilon_t, \tag{3.13c}$$

where L is the lag operator. If $\delta = 1$, $x_t = \theta_0 + u_t$, which is stationary. Let $\boldsymbol{u}' = (u_1, \ldots, u_T)$ and $E(\boldsymbol{u}\boldsymbol{u}') = \sigma_\varepsilon^2\boldsymbol{\Sigma}$, where $\boldsymbol{\Sigma}$ is a function of $\boldsymbol{\gamma} = (a_1, \ldots, a_p, b_1, \ldots, b_q)$ so that we write $\boldsymbol{\Sigma}(\boldsymbol{\gamma})$. When $\delta = 1$ and $\boldsymbol{\gamma}$ is known, $\left(\boldsymbol{e}'\boldsymbol{\Sigma}(\boldsymbol{\gamma})^{-1}\boldsymbol{e}\right)^{-1}\boldsymbol{e}'\boldsymbol{\Sigma}(\boldsymbol{\gamma})^{-1}\boldsymbol{x}$ is the GLS estimator of θ_0, which we write $\tilde{\theta}_0(1, \boldsymbol{\gamma})$.

Let $\tilde{\mathbf{v}}(\gamma) = \boldsymbol{x} - \tilde{\theta}_0(1, \gamma)\boldsymbol{e}$. If γ is known, the LBIU test for $\delta = 1$ against $\delta < 1$ is based on

$$S(\gamma) = (\tilde{\boldsymbol{v}}(\gamma)'\boldsymbol{\Sigma}(\gamma)^{-1}\tilde{\boldsymbol{v}}(\gamma))^{-1}(\tilde{\boldsymbol{v}}(\gamma)'\boldsymbol{\Sigma}(\gamma)^{-1}\boldsymbol{D}\boldsymbol{\Sigma}(\gamma)\boldsymbol{D}' \boldsymbol{\Sigma}(\gamma)^{-1}\tilde{\boldsymbol{v}}(\gamma)). \quad (3.14)$$

Since $\boldsymbol{e}'\boldsymbol{\Sigma}(\gamma)^{-1}\tilde{\boldsymbol{v}}(\gamma) = 0$, (3.14) is equivalent to

$$S(\gamma) = (\tilde{\boldsymbol{v}}(\gamma)'\boldsymbol{\Sigma}(\gamma)^{-1}\tilde{\boldsymbol{v}}(\gamma))^{-1}(\tilde{\boldsymbol{v}}(\gamma)'\boldsymbol{\Sigma}(\gamma)^{-1}(\boldsymbol{I} + \boldsymbol{D})'\boldsymbol{\Sigma}(\gamma) (\boldsymbol{I} + \boldsymbol{D})\boldsymbol{\Sigma}(\gamma)^{-1}\tilde{\boldsymbol{v}}(\gamma)). \quad (3.14')$$

When γ is not known Saikkonen and Luukkonen (1993*a*) suggests to estimate it by fitting

$$(1 - a_1L - \ldots - a_pL^p)\Delta x_t = (1 - \delta L)(1 - b_1L - \ldots b_qL^q)\varepsilon_t \quad (3.15)$$

to $\{x_t\}$. The domain of parameters is that (i) both $1 - a_1L - \ldots - a_pL^p$ and $1 - b_1L - \ldots - b_qL^q$ are invertible and (ii) $-1 < \delta \leq 1$. Note that a possibly non-invertible MA is introduced through $(1-\delta L)$. The $\hat{\gamma}$ that results is consistent under both the null and the alternative hypotheses, which in turn assures the consistency of the test based on (3.14′). The $\hat{\gamma}$ replaces γ in (3.14′).

I introduce one simplification. It is known that if $\{x_t\}$ is TS the asymptotic distributions of GLS and OLS of the mean (or more generally, coefficients in a polynomial trend) are identical.[5] Therefore without altering the asymptotic null distribution the GLS, $\tilde{\theta}_0(1, \gamma)$, may be replaced by the OLS, $T^{-1}\boldsymbol{e}'\boldsymbol{x}$.

When the deterministic trend is generalized from a constant, θ_0, to a polynomial trend, all we have to do is to form $\hat{\boldsymbol{v}}(\gamma)$ by subtracting the OLS estimate of the trend. However, the asymptotic distribution of $T^{-1}S(\hat{\gamma})$ has to be adjusted for the trend subtraction, which will be shown in Section 6.3.

The US historical data have been analysed in Kwiatkowski *et al.* (1992) by a method analogous to but different from (3.14′).[6] The method by (3.14′) will be applied in Chapter 9 to the US historical and post-war data after some investigation about modes of deterministic trends.

I would like to present here some experiences obtained in Hatanaka and Koto (1994) on the estimation of $(a_1, \ldots, a_p, b_1, \ldots, b_q, \delta)$ in (3.15). Saikkonen and Luukkonen (1993*a*) suggests (*a*) to maximize the likelihood function for the ARMA $(p, q+1)$ model for Δx_t and (*b*) to let $\hat{\delta}$ be the largest dominating root of the MA $(q+1)$ on the right-hand side. The (*b*) assumes that the dominating root is real.[7] The (*a*) is not necessarily convenient because the domain of δ is

[5] This is due to a theorem in Grenander and Rosenblatt (1957), for which a good exposition is found in Anderson (1971, ch. 10).

[6] See also Leybourne and McCabe (1994).

[7] The dominating root is real in TS. It may also be justified in the DS models that are close to TS.

$(-1, 1]$ [8] of which the right boundary is important. In Hatanaka and Koto (1994) (3.15) is approximated by

$$(1 - a_1L - \ldots - a_rL^r)\Delta x_t = (1 - \delta L)\varepsilon_t \tag{3.15'}$$

with a sufficiently large r. Our principle for selection of r is that risk of underfitting is unbearable but overfitting may be accepted. The equation, $\lambda^r - a_1\lambda^{r-1} - \ldots - a_r = 0$, has all roots less than unity in moduli. For a given δ in $(-1, 1)$ $(a_1, \ldots, a_r)$ is estimated by OLS on $(1 - \delta L)^{-1}\Delta x_t \equiv \Delta x_t + \delta\Delta x_{t-1} + \ldots + \delta^{t-2}\Delta x_2$. For $\delta = 1$ $(a_1, \ldots, a_r)$ is estimated by OLS on x_t if the resulting equation, $\lambda^r - \hat{a}_1\lambda^{r-1} - \ldots - \hat{a}_r = 0$, has its dominating root less than $1 - \varepsilon(\varepsilon > 0)$. [9] If the dominating root exceeds $1 - \varepsilon$, AR$(r - 1)$ is fitted to $x_t - (1 - \varepsilon)x_{t-1}$. (This idea has been taken from Fukushige, Hatanaka, and Koto (1994).) The sum of squared residuals are calculated for each δ in $(-1, 1]$. The δ at which the sum is minimized is our estimate of δ, and the associated $(a_1, \ldots, a_r)$ is our estimate of AR coefficients. In regard to the asymptotic theory ε is $O(T^{-1})$, but in practice ε is determined by simulation experiments for a given T.

The above procedure can be justified as follows.

(*a*) If $\{x_t\}$ is a stationary AR(r_0) with $r_0 \leq r$ and if the dominating root of the characteristic polynomial does not exceed $1 - \varepsilon$, then $\text{plim}\hat{\delta} = 1$ and $\text{plim}(\hat{a}_1, \ldots, \hat{a}_r) = (a_1, \ldots, a_{r0}, 0, \ldots, 0)$. Overfitting the lag order has no ill effects.[10] If $r_0 < r$ then δ may be made redundant over $(-1, 1 - \varepsilon)$ by letting $(1 - \delta L)$ be a factor of $(1 - a_1L - \ldots - a_rL^r)$, but the minimum of squared residual sums over δ does not occur in the interval $(-1, 1 - \varepsilon)$. (*b*) If $\{x_t\}$ is a non-stationary AR$(r_0 + 1)$ with $r_0 \leq r$ and a single unit root, then the probability that $\hat{\delta}$ converges to unity is asymptotically zero. But $\hat{\delta}$ does not have a probability limit if $r_0 < r$, because $1 - a_1L - \ldots - a_rL^r$ can have a factor $1 - \delta L$, with δ in $(-1, 1 - \varepsilon)$, leading to unidentifiability of δ. As a result $(\hat{a}_1, \ldots, \hat{a}_r)$ is entirely unrelated to $(a_1, \ldots, a_{r0})$. However, this tends to make the test more powerful than in the case where the right lag order is chosen.

With the pure AR(r) model the Yule–Walker equations can be used to form $\mathbf{\Sigma}(\gamma)$, which may now be written $\mathbf{\Sigma}(\boldsymbol{a})$ with $\boldsymbol{a} \equiv (a_1, \ldots, a_r)'$.[11] The inversion

[8] In denoting intervals between a and b both a and b are included in $[a, b]$; b is, but a is not $[a, b]$; and neither a nor b is included in (a, b).

[9] It is after my work was completed that Choi (1993) became available. Choi (1993) proposes a method to set a confidence interval on $(1 - a_1 - \ldots - a_r)$.

[10] Overfitting has been excluded from the consideration in the existing MA unit-root literature, but its consideration is necessitated by the practice of selection of lag orders stated in the text here and in Section 6.2.3, i.e. to avoid underfitting as much as possible while accepting risk of overfitting.

[11] For an illustration consider $a_0x_t + a_1x_{t-1} + a_2x_{t-2} = \varepsilon_t$ with $a_0 \equiv 1$, $E(x_tx_{t-j}) = \gamma_j$, $E(\varepsilon_t^2) = \sigma_\varepsilon^2$. Let $\gamma' = (\gamma_0, \gamma_1, \ldots, \gamma_{T-1})$, $e_1' = (1, 0, \ldots, 0)$, and

(Contd)

of $\boldsymbol{\Sigma}(\boldsymbol{a})$, which is $T \times T$, involves only an inversion of an $r \times r$ matrix, because

$$\boldsymbol{\Sigma}(\boldsymbol{a})^{-1} = \sigma_{\varepsilon}^{-2} \boldsymbol{S}(\boldsymbol{a})' \begin{bmatrix} \boldsymbol{C}^{-1} & 0 \\ 0 & \boldsymbol{I}_{T-r} \end{bmatrix} \boldsymbol{S}(\boldsymbol{a}),$$

where $\boldsymbol{S}(\boldsymbol{a})$ is a banded lower triangular matrix, $\boldsymbol{I} - a_1\boldsymbol{L}^* - \ldots - a_r\boldsymbol{L}^{*r}$, and one can easily determine how $\boldsymbol{C}$ depends on $\boldsymbol{a}$.[12] ($\boldsymbol{L}^*$ was defined earlier above (3.12).)

$$\boldsymbol{A}_1 = \begin{bmatrix} a_0 & a_1 & a_2 & 0 & \ldots & 0 \\ a_1 & a_2 & \iddots & & \iddots & \vdots \\ a_2 & \iddots & & \iddots & & \vdots \\ 0 & & \iddots & & & \vdots \\ \vdots & \iddots & & & & \vdots \\ 0 & \ldots & \ldots & \ldots & \ldots & 0 \end{bmatrix}, \quad \boldsymbol{A}_2 = \begin{bmatrix} 0 & 0 & \ldots & \ldots & \ldots & \ldots & 0 \\ 0 & a_0 & \ddots & & & & \vdots \\ 0 & a_1 & \ddots & \ddots & & & \vdots \\ 0 & a_2 & \ddots & \ddots & \ddots & & \vdots \\ 0 & 0 & \ddots & \ddots & \ddots & \ddots & \vdots \\ \vdots & \vdots & \ddots & \ddots & \ddots & \ddots & 0 \\ 0 & 0 & \ldots & 0 & a_2 & a_1 & a_0 \end{bmatrix}$$

Then $(\boldsymbol{A}_1 + \boldsymbol{A}_2)\boldsymbol{\gamma} = \sigma_{\varepsilon}^2 e_1$, from which $\boldsymbol{\gamma}$ can be obtained. Then $\boldsymbol{\Sigma}(\boldsymbol{a})$ is $\gamma_0 \boldsymbol{I}_T + \gamma_1(\boldsymbol{L}^* + \boldsymbol{L}^{*'}) + \ldots + \gamma_{T-1}(\boldsymbol{L}^{*T-1} + \boldsymbol{L}^{*T-1})$.

[12] In the above illustration

$$\boldsymbol{C} = \begin{bmatrix} a_0 & 0 \\ a_1 & a_0 \end{bmatrix} \begin{bmatrix} \gamma_0 & \gamma_1 \\ \gamma_1 & \gamma_0 \end{bmatrix} \begin{bmatrix} a_0 & a_1 \\ 0 & a_0 \end{bmatrix}$$

4
Unit-Root Asymptotic Theories (I)

In the previous chapter we have learned how to test for TS against DS. In the sequel of developments in the unit-root field, however, it was preceded by the testing for DS against TS. This in turn was made possible by the development of new asymptotic statistical theories on the unit root in Fuller (1976), Dickey and Fuller (1979), Phillips (1987), and Phillips and Perron (1988) among others. These theories are explained in two steps. The first step is given in the present chapter. It deals with the elementary but fundamental case where Δx_t is i.i.d. The second step is given in Chapter 6. It explains more advanced aspects including the case where Δx_t is an ARMA.

Let us recall basic elements of the standard asymptotic theory, for example, Judge *et al.* (1985, ch. 5) or Spanos (1986, chs. 9, 10). If $\{\varepsilon_t\}$ is i.i.d. with $E(\varepsilon_t) = 0$ and $E(\varepsilon_t^2) = \sigma_\varepsilon^2$, then $T^{-1/2} \sum_1^T \varepsilon_t$ converges in distribution as $T \to \infty$ to $N(0, \sigma_\varepsilon^2)$, which is a simplest form of the central limit theorem. Moreover, $T^{-1} \sum_1^T \varepsilon_t^2$ converges in probability to σ_ε^2, which is a version of the law of large numbers. The convergence in probability will be denoted by $\xrightarrow{P}$, and the convergence in distribution by $\xrightarrow{D}$.

The terms such as $T^{-1/2}$ and T^{-1} may be looked upon as normalizers to get a well-defined probability distribution or a constant in the limit. Normalizers for the first and the second-order sample moments are respectively $T^{-1/2}$ and T^{-1}, and the limiting distribution is a normal distribution. Statements in the previous paragraph hold true on a wide class of models more complicated than the i.i.d.

More generally, a stochastic process $\{x_T\}$ with T as index is said to be in the order of $T^{-\alpha}$, abbreviated as $O_p(T^{-\alpha})$ when the following condition holds. For any ε such that $1 > \varepsilon > 0$ there exists A_ε such that $P[|T^\alpha x_T| \leq A_\varepsilon] \geq 1 - \varepsilon$ for all sufficiently large T, i.e. $T^\alpha x_T$ remains bounded in probability while $T \to \infty$. A lemma most frequently used to determine O_p deals with the mean square as follows.

LEMMA. If there exists $c(> 0)$ such that $E(T^{2\alpha} x_T^2) < c$ for all T, then x_T is $O_p(T^{-\alpha})$.[1]

For the i.i.d. $\{\varepsilon_t\}$ with zero mean, $\sum_1^T \varepsilon_t$ is $O_p(T^{1/2})$, and $\sum_1^T \varepsilon_t^2$ is $O_p(T)$.

4.1 Pure Random Walk without a Drift

The situation changes radically when a random walk is involved. Suppose that $\{x_t\}$ is generated from an i.i.d. process $\{\varepsilon_t\}$ by

[1] A proof is found e.g. in Fuller (1976: 185).

$$x_t = x_{t-1} + \varepsilon_t = x_0 + \sum\nolimits_1^t \varepsilon_s. \tag{4.1}$$

Assuming that $E(x_0) = 0$ and $\varepsilon_t, t \geq 1$, is independent of x_0, it is seen that $E(x_t) = 0$ and $\text{var}(x_t) = t\sigma_\varepsilon^2 + E(x_0^2)$. The appropriate normalizer of $\sum_1^T x_t$ is not $T^{-1/2}$. In fact, in considering its mean square,

$$E\left(\sum\nolimits_1^T x_t\right)^2 = E\left(\sum\nolimits_{t=1}^T \sum\nolimits_{s=1}^t \varepsilon_s\right)^2 + TE(x_0^2)$$
$$= \sigma_\varepsilon^2(T^2 + (T-1)^2 + \ldots + 1^2) + TE(x_0^2),$$

it diverges to ∞ as fast as T^3, because $1^2 + 2^2 + \ldots + T^2 = T(T+1)(2T+1)/6$. The appropriate normalizer is $T^{-3/2}$ as $E(T^{-3/2}\sum x_t)^2$ remains bounded as $T \to \infty$. As for $\sum_1^T x_t^2$ it can be shown that it is $O_p(T^2)$, and the appropriate normalizer is T^{-2}.

The mathematics of the stochastic process has long had a continuous-time stochastic process called the Wiener process or the Brownian motion process. The importance of this process in unit-root asymptotic theories was recognized in White (1958), and was emphasized in Phillips (1987). The Wiener process is explained in Appendix 2. Let $w(r)$, $1 \geq r \geq 0$, be the scalar standard Wiener process. It is a continuous-time version of the random walk with $\sigma_\varepsilon^2 = 1$, and for a given value of r $w(r)$ is distributed in $N(0, r)$. Then

$$T^{-3/2}\sum\nolimits_{t=1}^T x_t \xrightarrow{D} \sigma_\varepsilon \int_0^1 w(r)dr, \tag{4.2}$$

as explained in Appendix 2, the equation (A2.2). Here $\xrightarrow{D} X$ means convergence in distribution to the distribution of the random variable, X. Since $T^{-3/2}x_0 \xrightarrow{P} 0$, x_0 has no effect upon the limiting distribution. The right-hand side of (4.2) is Gaussian, in fact $N(0, \sigma_\varepsilon^2/3)$, because it is linear in $w(\cdot)$. See Banerjee *et al.* (1993: 27) for more about this point.

As for $T^{-2}\sum_{t=1}^T x_t^2$ it converges in distribution to a random variable composed by the following functional of the standard Wiener process,

$$T^{-2}\sum\nolimits_1^T x_t^2 \xrightarrow{D} \sigma_\varepsilon^2 \int_0^1 w(r)^2 dr. \tag{4.3}$$

See Phillips (1987: 296) for a proof. The right-hand side of (4.3) is not distributed in a normal distribution. Notice that in (4.2) and (4.3) $\sum_{t=1}^T$ on the left-hand side corresponds to $\int_0^1$ on the right-hand side, and $x_t^i (i = 1, 2)$ on the left-hand side corresponds to w^i on the right-hand side. This kind of correspondence is carried through more complicated expressions.

Consider a model

$$x_t = \rho x_{t-1} + \varepsilon_t, \tag{4.4}$$

where $\{\varepsilon_t\}$ is i.i.d. with zero mean and variance σ_ε^2. The OLS of ρ is

$$\hat{\rho} = \left(\sum_2^T x_{t-1}^2\right)^{-1}\left(\sum_2^T x_t x_{t-1}\right). \tag{4.5}$$

Let ρ^0 be the true value of ρ and consider the case $\rho^0 = 1$. Then the data generating process of $\{x_t\}$ is (4.1), and we have

$$T(\hat{\rho} - 1) = \left(T^{-2}\sum_2^T x_{t-1}^2\right)^{-1}\left(T^{-1}\sum_2^T \varepsilon_t x_{t-1}\right). \tag{4.6}$$

The limiting distribution of the denominator of (4.6) has been given in (4.3). (Note that $T^{-2}x_T^2$ converges in probability to zero so that it can be ignored.) As for the nominator

$$T^{-1}\sum \varepsilon_t x_{t-1} \xrightarrow{D} \sigma_\varepsilon^2 \int_0^1 w(r)dw(r). \tag{4.7}$$

Therefore combining (4.3) and (4.7) we obtain

$$T(\hat{\rho} - 1) \xrightarrow{D} \left(\int_0^1 w(r)^2 dr\right)^{-1}\left(\int_0^1 w(r)dw(r)\right). \tag{4.8}$$

This will be a basis of many developments in the unit-root field.[2] Needless to say that $w(\cdot)$ in the denominator and in the nominator are the same one. The limiting distribution is tabulated by Dickey in Fuller (1976: 371, table 8.5.1, the part for $\hat{\rho}$, the line for $n = \infty$).[3] Sometimes it is called the Dickey–Fuller distribution. Its location is shifted to the left of origin, the distribution is skewed to the left, and $P(\hat{\rho} - 1 < 0)$ is larger than 0.5. See Fuller (1976: 370). Tables in Fuller (1976) also show finite sample distributions of $T(\hat{\rho} - 1)$ for $T = 25$, 50, 100, 250, and 500. That for $T = 100$ is quite close to the limiting distribution. See also part (*a*) of Figure 4.1 and Figure 4.2, which have been compiled by Yasuji Koto.[4]

[2] The representation of limit distribution of $\hat{\rho}$ by the Wiener process originates in White (1958), but the particular expressions in (4.7) and (4.8) are as recent as Chan and Wei (1988). Expressions alternative to (4.7) and (4.8) are also found in the literature. From the identity

$$\left(T^{-1/2}\sum_1^T \varepsilon_t\right)^2 - T^{-1}\sum_1^T \varepsilon_t^2 = T^{-1}\sum_{t \neq s}\sum \varepsilon_t\varepsilon_s = 2T^{-1}\sum_{s<t}\sum \varepsilon_s\varepsilon_t$$

(note that $\varepsilon_t\varepsilon_s \equiv \varepsilon_s\varepsilon_t$) it follows that

$$w(1)^2 - 1 = 2\int w(r)dw(r),$$

i.e. $\int w(r)dw(r) = \frac{1}{2}(w(1)^2 - 1)$.

[3] Nowadays the tables are produced by simulations on the functional of the Wiener process as explained in Section 7.3.1, but Dickey relied upon a simulation on a different expression that is applicable to both the finite sample and limiting distributions.

[4] Figure 4.2 has been obtained from a histogram of simulation results. See the part, $c = 0$, in Nabeya and Tanaka (1990: fig. 1) for a more accurate figure of the p.d.f.

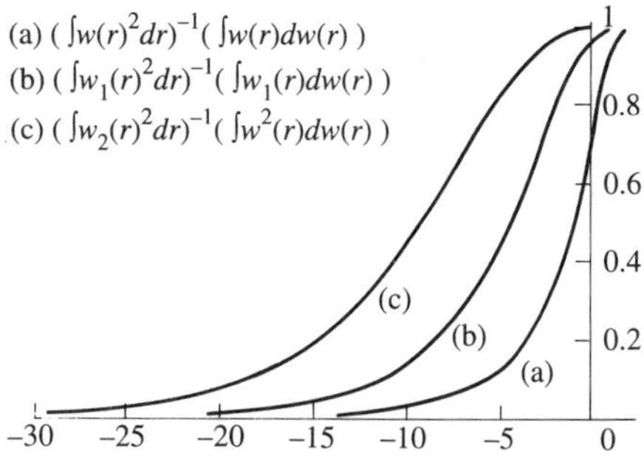

FIG. 4.1 *Cumulative distributions of functionals of Wiener process*

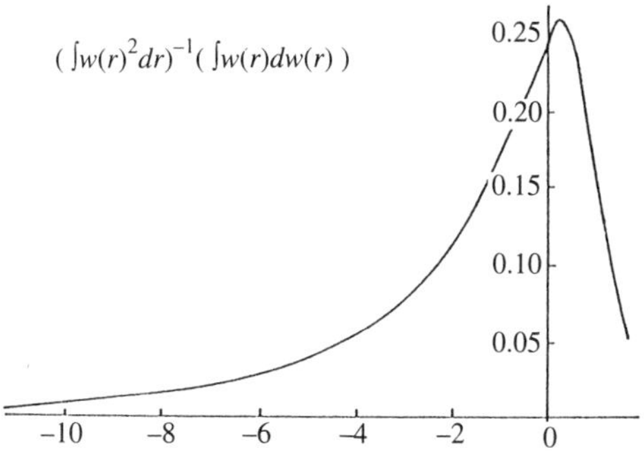

FIG. 4.2 *A rough sketch of probability density function*

In standard models (i) $\sqrt{T}$ times the error of estimation converges in distribution to a random variable, and (ii) the random variable is distributed in normal distributions with zero mean. In the random-walk model the expression (4.8) reveals (i) that T (instead of $\sqrt{T}$) times the error of estimation converges in distribution to a random variable, and (ii) that the random variable has a non-normal distribution. Comparing the above statement (i) for standard models and the statement (i) for the random-walk model, estimators in standard models are $\sqrt{T}$-consistent, but the estimator in the random-walk model is nearly T-consistent,[5] sometimes called 'super-consistent'. Comparing the statements (ii), estimators in standard models have no biases in $O(T^{-1/2})$, and the estimator in the random-walk model has a negative bias in $O(T^{-1})$. Even in standard models there are usually biases in $O(T^{-1})$.

Note that (4.8) is free from σ_ε^2, and there is no need to consider the t-statistic. However I introduce it here for a later reference. The t-statistic to test the

[5] It should not be said to be T-consistent because the expectation of the right-hand side of (4.8) is not zero.

hypothesis $\rho = 1$ is

$$\hat{t} = s^{-1}(\hat{\rho} - 1)\left(\sum_2^T x_{t-1}^2\right)^{1/2} = s^{-1}T(\hat{\rho} - 1)\left(T^{-2}\sum x_{t-1}^2\right)^{1/2} \tag{4.9}$$

$$s^2 = (T-1)^{-1}\sum_2^T (x_t - \hat{\rho}x_{t-1})^2.$$

We have

$$\hat{t} \xrightarrow{D} \left(\int_0^1 w(r)^2 dr\right)^{-1/2} \left(\int_0^1 w(r)dw(r)\right). \tag{4.10}$$

because of (4.3), (4.8), and plim $s^2 = \sigma_\varepsilon^2$. The distribution in (4.10) is tabulated by Dickey in Fuller (1976: 373, table 8.5.2, the part for $\hat{t}$, the line for $n = \infty$). The distribution is shifted to the left of the origin.

4.2 Pure Random Walk possibly with a Drift

Consider an extension of (4.4),

$$x_t = \mu + \rho x_{t-1} + \varepsilon_t. \tag{4.11}$$

Let μ^0 and ρ^0 be the true values of μ and ρ respectively, and assume that $\rho^0 = 1$. The data-generating process of $\{x_t\}$ is

$$x_t = \mu^0 + x_{t-1} + \varepsilon_t = x_0 + \mu^0 t + \sum_{s=1}^t \varepsilon_s. \tag{4.12}$$

If $\mu^0 \neq 0$, $\{x_t\}$ has a linear deterministic trend, and μ^0 is called a drift.

The OLS of ρ in (4.11) is

$$\hat{\rho} = \left(\sum (x_{t-1} - \bar{x}_{-1})^2\right)^{-1} \left(\sum (x_{t-1} - \bar{x}_{-1})(x_t - \bar{x})\right), \tag{4.13}$$

where $\bar{x}_{-1} = (T-1)^{-1}\sum_1^{T-1} x_t$, $\quad \bar{x} = (T-1)^{-1}\sum_2^T x_t$.

We must examine the cases, $\mu^0 = 0$ and $\neq 0$ separately.

4.2.1 *True μ is zero*

Suppose that $\mu^0 = 0$ and $\rho^0 = 1$. Then the data-generating process is (4.1), and appropriate normalizers are identical to the previous ones. However, expressions involved in (4.13) are different from the previous ones, and here we have

$$T^{-2}\sum (x_{t-1} - \bar{x}_{-1})^2 \xrightarrow{D} \sigma_\varepsilon^2 \int_0^1 \left(w(r) - \int_0^1 w(s)ds\right)^2 dr \tag{4.14}$$

$$T^{-1}\sum \varepsilon_t(x_{t-1} - \bar{x}_{-1}) \xrightarrow{D} \sigma_\varepsilon^2 \int_0^1 \left(w(r) - \int_0^1 w(s)ds\right) dw(r). \tag{4.15}$$

The former is obtained from

$$(T-1)^{-2}\sum(x_{t-1}-\overline{x}_{-1})^2 = (T-1)^{-2}\sum x_{t-1}^2 - \left((T-1)^{-3/2}\sum x_{t-1}\right)^2$$

$$\xrightarrow{D} \int_0^1 w(r)^2 dr - \left(\int_0^1 w(r)dr\right)^2 = \int_0^1 \left(w(r) - \int_0^1 w(s)ds\right)^2 dr.$$

Since

$$T(\hat{\rho}-1) = \left(T^{-2}\sum(x_{t-1}-\overline{x}_{-1})^2\right)^{-1}\left(T^{-1}\sum\varepsilon_t(x_{t-1}-\overline{x}_{-1})\right),$$

$$T(\hat{\rho}-1) \xrightarrow{D} \left(\int_0^1 w_1(r)^2 dr\right)^{-1}\left(\int_0^1 w_1(r)dw(r)\right), \tag{4.16}$$

$$w_1(r) \equiv w(r) - \int_0^1 w(s)ds. \tag{4.16$'$}$$

This is due to Phillips and Perron (1988). The distribution in (4.16) has been tabulated by Dickey in Fuller (1976: 371, table 8.5.1, the part for $\hat{\rho}_\mu$, $n=\infty$). It is seen that the leftward location shift is even larger than in (4.8), where the sample means are not subtracted. Compare Figure 4.1(a) and (b).

4.2.2 *True μ is not zero*

Suppose that $\mu^0 \neq 0$ and $\rho^0 = 1$. The data-generating process is now (4.12). In investigating the denominator of (4.13), the term, $(x_{t-1}-\overline{x}_{-1})$, consists of the deterministic part, $d_{t-1} \equiv \mu_0(t-1-T/2)$, and the stochastic part, $v_{t-1}-\overline{v}_{-1}$, where $v_t \equiv \sum_{s=1}^t \varepsilon_s$. For the deterministic part we see $\sum_2^T d_{t-1}^2 = O(T^3)$. For the stochastic part the v_t here is x_t in (4.1) (with $x_0 = 0$), and in view of (4.14) $\sum(v_{t-1}-\overline{v}_{-1})^2$ is $O_p(T^2)$. Thus within $\sum(x_{t-1}-\overline{x}_{-1})^2$ the deterministic part dominates the stochastic part, and $\sum(x_{t-1}-\overline{x}_{-1})^2$ should be normalized by T^{-3}. Moreover

$$T^{-3}\sum(x_{t-1}-\overline{x}_{-1})^2 \xrightarrow{P} \frac{1}{12}\mu^{0^2}. \tag{4.17}$$

Similarly it can be seen that $\sum\varepsilon_t(x_{t-1}-\overline{x}_{-1})$ should be normalized by $T^{-3/2}$, and

$$T^{-3/2}\sum\varepsilon_t(x_{t-1}-\overline{x}_{-1}) = T^{-3/2}\sum\varepsilon_t d_{t-1} + o_p(1),$$

where $o_p(1)$ means a term that converges to zero in probability. It can be shown that

$$T^{-3/2}\sum\varepsilon_t d_{t-1} \xrightarrow{D} N\left(0, \sigma_\varepsilon^2 \lim_{T\to\infty} T^{-3}\sum d_{t-1}^2\right) = N\left(0, \tfrac{1}{12}\mu^{0^2}\sigma_\varepsilon^2\right). \tag{4.18}$$

Therefore, combining (4.17) and (4.18)

$$T^{3/2}(\hat{\rho}-1) = \left(T^{-3}\sum(x_{t-1}-\overline{x}_{-1})^2\right)^{-1}\left(T^{-3/2}\sum\varepsilon_t(x_{t-1}-\overline{x}_{-1})\right)$$

$$\xrightarrow{D} N(0, 12\mu^{0^{-2}}\sigma_\varepsilon^2).$$

This has been pointed out in Dickey and Fuller (1979) and emphasized in West (1988). See Appendix 3, Sections A3.1 and A3.2 for a more accurate derivation of (4.17), (4.18), and (4.19). Keep in mind that $\hat{\rho}$ is $T^{3/2}$ consistent in the present context.

The conclusion derived from Sections 4.2.1–2 is that the asymptotic distribution of $\hat{\rho}$ differs radically, depending on whether $\mu^0 =$ or $\neq 0$. The distribution is Gaussian when $\mu^0 \neq 0$, but given by a functional of Wiener process when $\mu^0 = 0$.

Hamilton (1994: 486–97) is a nice reference that explains the same material as Chapter 4 in a different representation. The contents of the present Chapter 4 are summarized at the end of Chapter 7.

5
Regression Approach to the Test for Difference Stationarity (I)

Let us consider how to test difference stationarity as the null hypothesis against trend stationarity, assuming that $\{x_t\}$ may possibly contain a linear deterministic trend.

5.1 A Method that Does not Work

Suppose that we run the regression

$$x_t = \mu + \rho x_{t-1} + \text{residual}, \qquad t = 2\ldots, T \tag{5.1}$$

and construct the t-statistic to test $\rho = 1$,

$$\hat{t} = s^{-1}(\hat{\rho} - 1)\left(\sum (x_{t-1} - \bar{x}_{-1})^2\right)^{1/2},$$

where s^2 is the sum of squared residuals divided by $(T - 1)$. It turns out that this $\hat{t}$ is useless to test DS against TS.

(i) Let us analyse $\hat{t}$ under the null hypothesis. When $\{x_t\}$ is DS and generated by (4.11) with $\rho^0 = 1$, the distribution of $\hat{t}$ depends upon whether $\mu^0 = 0$ or $\neq 0$. Since μ^0 is unknown we do not know which distribution to use to set the critical values. In the terminology of the testing theory the test based on $\hat{t}$ is not similar. Just to continue on to the next point let us suppose that we choose an arbitrary negative value, c, so that the rejection region is $\hat{t} < c$, because the test would be left one-sided as $\rho > 1$ is a priori ruled out.

(ii) Let us then analyse $\hat{t}$ under the alternative hypothesis. $\{x_t\}$ is TS and generated by a linear trend plus a stationary process. Let $\hat{\rho}$ be the OLS estimate of ρ in (5.1). Then in so far as the coefficient of time variable is not zero in the linear trend, both x_t and x_{t-1} in (5.1) contain the time variable, which leads to plim $\hat{\rho} = 1$. Perron (1988) shows that $(\hat{\rho} - 1)$ is $O_p(T^{-2})$ and that $\left(\sum (x_{t-1} - \bar{x}_{-1})^2\right)^{1/2}$ is $O_p(T^{3/2})$. Thus $\hat{t}$ is $O_p(T^{-1/2})$. Note that $\hat{t} \xrightarrow{P} 0$, while zero is not in the rejection region chosen above. As $T \to \infty$ the test never rejects the DS when the true data-generating process is TS. The test is inconsistent.

Both troubles mentioned in (i) and (ii) above would vanish if the presence of a linear trend is a priori ruled out. See the later Section 5.3.

5.2 Dickey–Fuller Test

We turn to a regression approach that does work, i.e. the widely applied Dickey–Fuller test. In the present chapter it is assumed for simplicity that a deterministic part of $\{x_t\}$ is $\theta_0+\theta_1 t$ and the stochastic part is AR(1). The model is

$$(1-\rho L)(x_t-\theta_0-\theta_1 t)=\varepsilon_t, \tag{5.2}$$

where $\{\varepsilon_t\}$ is i.i.d. with $E(\varepsilon_t)=0$ and $E(\varepsilon_t^2)=\sigma_\varepsilon^2$.

Suppose that $|\rho|<1$ so that (5.2) represents a TS model. Define μ and β by

$$(1-\rho L)(\theta_0+\theta_1 t)\equiv\mu+\beta t. \tag{5.3}$$

When written concretely, $\mu=\theta_0(1-\rho)+\rho\theta_1$ and $\beta=\theta_1(1-\rho)$. Then (5.2) is

$$x_t=\mu+\beta t+\rho x_{t-1}+\varepsilon_t. \tag{5.4}$$

The transformation, $(\theta_0,\theta_1,\rho)\leftrightarrow(\mu,\beta,\rho)$ is one-to-one. The term, βt, distinguishes (5.4) from (5.1), which is the regression equation in the method that has failed.

An important point here is that we do not consider (5.4) by itself separately from (5.2). The β and ρ in (5.4) are not variation-free because of the relation (5.3). If they were variation-free, (5.4) would produce a quadratic deterministic trend in $\{x_t\}$ by setting $\rho=1$.

To consider the DS, set $\rho=1$. Then (5.3) induces $\mu=\theta_1$ and $\beta=0$ in (5.4), and we get

$$x_t=\theta_1+x_{t-1}+\varepsilon_t, \tag{5.5}$$

whether (5.2) or (5.4) is used. (5.5) is nothing but (4.11) with $\rho=1$, a random walk possibly with a drift. (5.5) is also what one would obtain if the constraint $(\beta,\rho)=(0,1)$ is introduced in (5.4). The seminal Nelson and Plosser (1982) use the OLS on (5.4) (and its extension (7.2) below) to test for DS against TS. Indeed we can demonstrate that the F-statistic to test for $(\beta,\rho)=(0,1)$ in (5.4) provides a similar and consistent test for DS against TS.

(i) Let us analyse the F-statistic under the null hypothesis. $\{x_t\}$ is DS and generated by (5.5). The unconstrained OLS, $(\hat{\beta},\hat{\rho})$, in (5.4) converges in probability to $(0,1)$. The F-statistic compares the sum of squares of the constrained OLS residuals with the sum of squares of the unconstrained OLS residuals, where the constraint is $(\beta,\rho)=(0,1)$. Both of these residuals are free from μ in (5.4), and, if $\{x_t\}$ is generated with $\rho^0=1$, it is only in μ that the true value of θ_1, θ_1^0, is contained. It is thus seen that θ_1^0 is not involved in either the constrained or the unconstrained OLS residuals. (This is seen in Appendix 3.3.1(ii) more concretely.) Therefore unlike (4.13′) in the method that has failed, the present F-statistic is free from θ_1^0, i.e. invariant to whether $\theta_1^0=$ or $\neq 0$. The F-test is similar. (ii) Let us then analyse the F-statistic under the alternative hypothesis, $|\rho^0|<1$. The unconstrained OLS estimate of (β,ρ) in (5.4) converges in probability to $(\theta_1^0(1-\rho^0),\rho^0)$ and this is separated away from $(0,1)$ specified by the constraint. The F-statistic diverges as $T\to\infty$, and the test is consistent.

One can recognize another difference from the method that failed. No matter whether $\theta_1^0 = $ or $\neq 0$, the limiting distribution of $T(\hat{\rho} - 1)$ in (5.4) is not normal but a functional of the Wiener process if $\{x_t\}$ is DS. Recall that it is the time variable contained in x_{t-1} that has made $\hat{\rho}$ distributed in a normal distribution in Section 4.2.2. Here in (5.4) the part of x_{t-1} which is linearly related to another regressor, t, is eliminated from x_{t-1} by the well-known logic of the least squares.[1]

Explanations in the present and previous paragraphs have been somewhat intuitive. They will be supplemented by mathematical explanation in Section 6.1.

Dickey and Fuller (1981, table VI) present the finite sample and asymptotic distributions of the F-statistic. The mathematical expression for the limiting distribution will be given in (6.8*c*) below.

The t-statistic to test for $\rho = 1$ in (5.4) also provides a consistent test for the DS against the TS. It is free from θ_1^0, and it diverges to minus infinity if $\{x_t\}$ is generated by a TS model. The finite sample and asymptotic distributions of the t-statistic are tabulated by Dickey in Fuller (1976: 373, table 8.5.2, the part for $\hat{\tau}_r$). The test should be one-sided, setting the critical region on the values smaller than $\rho = 1$.

The t-test has been used most widely in the past empirical unit-root studies ever since Nelson and Plosser (1982), but my opinion is that the F-statistic should be recommended on the ground that it tests a larger number of constraints implied by $\rho = 1$. Readers might wonder if the F- and t-tests are asymptotically equivalent in view of the multicollinearity between two regressors of (5.4), t and x_{t-1}. The conjecture is incorrect. The multicollinearity arises only when $\theta_1^0 \neq 0$. On the other hand Appendix 3.3 shows that the F- and t-tests deal with the terms invariant to $\theta_1^0 = $ or $\neq 0$, as seen from the nominator of the F-statistic shown in equation (A3.12). The limiting distributions of the F- and t-statistics are given in (6.8*c*) and (6.8*b*) below, and they are not identical.[2]

A number of new testing methods are appearing at the time of writing, for example, Choi (1992), Elliot, Rothenberg, and Stock (1992), Schmidt and Phillips (1992), and Ahn (1993). Schmidt and Phillips (1992) and Ahn (1993) develop a Lagrange multiplier test in the parametrization in which all parameters are variation-free (in contrast to (β, ρ) in (5.41)). Levin and Lin (1992) and Quah (1993) consider panel data, and Toda and McKenzie (1994) investigate missing observations. All these will not be surveyed in the present book.

[1] Readers may be perplexed by absence of θ_0 in the above explanation. When $\rho^0 = 1$, θ_0 is not asymptotically identified. When $|\rho^0| < 1$ it is identified.

[2] The t-test is one-sided because $\rho > 1$ is a priori excluded from our consideration. On the other hand the F-test is bound to be two-sided in this sense, and it might make the F-test inefficient. I do not imagine that the loss of efficiency is large. Comparing initially the t and t^2 statistics, it is seen that most of the probability for $(\rho - 1)^2 > \alpha^2$ comes from that for $\rho < 1 - \alpha$ because the distribution of t is left-shifted and left-skewed. Comparing next the t^2 and the F-statistic for $(\beta, \rho) = (0, 1)$, the limit distribution of the latter consists of two terms as seen in (6.8*c*), and the second term is that of the t^2 while the first term is concerned with $\beta = 0$ and irrelevant to the present comparison. None the less it is worth making a simulation study.

5.3 The Case where the Deterministic Trend is Confined to a Constant

So far we have considered how to test for DS against TS in the possible presence of a deterministic linear trend. The test is valid no matter whether the linear trend does or does not exist. Occasionally we wish to perform the test under the constraint that the deterministic trend is just a constant under both the DS and TS hypotheses, i.e. $\theta_1 = 0$ in (5.2). For example, we might be fairly sure of the constraint as a result of the model selection analysis in regard to the form of deterministic trends. Then the equation (5.1) can be reintroduced with $\mu = \theta_0(1 - \rho)$. When $\{x_t\}$ is generated with $\rho^0 = 1$, the constraint forces μ^0 to zero. Run OLS on

$$x_t = \mu + \rho x_{t-1} + \text{ residual}, \qquad t = 2, \ldots, T. \tag{5.6}$$

The F-statistic to test for $(\mu, \rho) = (0, 1)$ in (5.6) can be used to test for DS against TS. The finite sample and asymptotic distributions of the statistic when $\{x_t\}$ is generated with $\rho^0 = 1$ are found in Dickey and Fuller (1981, table IV). The inconsistency mentioned earlier in Section 5.1 does not arise in the present TS hypothesis, i.e. $\{x_t\}$ is a stationary AR with a constant mean.

The t-statistic to test for $\rho = 1$ can also be used. The distributions under the DS hypothesis are found in Fuller (1976: 373, table 8.5.2, the part for $\hat{\tau}_\mu$), but the F-statistic is more desirable.

6
Unit-Root Asymptotic Theories (II)

The present Chapter assembles three unrelated topics of asymptotic theories. Looking back to Chapter 5, Section 6.1 presents the mathematical analysis of the tests on the case where $\{\Delta x_t\}$ is i.i.d possibly with a non-zero mean. Looking forward to Chapter 7, Section 6.2 explains the mathematics used for the case where $\{\Delta x_t\}$ is serially correlated. Section 6.3 gives the asymptotic theory of the MA unit-root test explained in Section 3.4.2.

6.1 Deterministic Trends

I shall present a mathematical explanation of Section 5.2. It should be read in conjunction with Appendix 3.3.

We begin with a basic asymptotic relation. If $v_t = \sum_1^t \varepsilon_s$ and $\{\varepsilon_t\}$ is i.i.d with $E(\varepsilon_t) = 0$ and $E(\varepsilon_t^2) = \sigma_\varepsilon^2$, then

$$T^{-5/2} \sum_{t=1}^{T} t v_t \xrightarrow{D} \sigma_\varepsilon \int_0^1 r w(r) dr, \tag{6.1}$$

which is seen by writing $T^{-5/2} t v_t = (t/T) \cdot T^{-3/2} v_t$. (6.1) is due to Phillips and Perron (1988). The right-hand side of (6.1) is actually Gaussian, $N(0, (2/15)\sigma_\varepsilon^2)$.

The unconstrained OLS estimator, $(\hat{\mu}, \hat{\beta}, \hat{\rho})$, in (5.3) is analysed in Appendix 3.3. OLS residuals unconstrained and constrained by $(\beta, \rho) = (0, 1)$ are also shown there. On the basis of the formulae derived there I shall here show the limit distribution of $T(\hat{\rho} - 1)$, the t-statistic, and the F-statistic on (5.3). It is convenient, though not necessary,[1] to orthogonalize deterministic regressors as we can then proceed along regressions with orthogonal regressors. Let $\tilde{t} = t - (T + 2)/2$ so that $\tilde{t}$ sums to zero over $t = 2, \ldots, T$. Then

[1] All results of the following derivation can be obtained without the orthogonalization. Regress x_{t-1} upon $(1, t)$, and let $\tilde{x}_{t-1}$ be the residual. Then $\hat{\rho}$ is obtained by regressing x_t upon $\tilde{x}_{t-1}$. A normalized $\tilde{x}_{t-1}$ corresponds to a Wiener process

$$w(r) - \left(\int_0^1 w(s)\boldsymbol{\tau}(s)' ds \right) \left(\int_0^1 \boldsymbol{\tau}(s)\boldsymbol{\tau}(s)' ds \right)^{-1} \boldsymbol{\tau}(r), \tag{$*$}$$

where $\boldsymbol{\tau}(r)' = (1, r)$. It is seen that the above Wiener process is identical to $w_2(r)$ defined in (6.5), and that the right-hand side of (6.8a) corresponds to the coefficient in regressing ε_t upon $\tilde{x}_{t-1}$. However, it is likely to use (6.5) rather than ($*$) in tabulating the distributions by simulations as explained in Section 7.3.3.

$\lim_{T\to\infty} T^{-3}\sum \tilde{t}^2 = 1/12$, and, using (4.2) and (6.1), we see that

$$T^{-1}\left(\sum \tilde{t}^2\right)^{-1/2}\sum \tilde{t}v_t \approx \sqrt{12}\left(T^{-5/2}\sum tv_t - \tfrac{1}{2}T^{-3/2}\sum v_t\right)$$

$$\xrightarrow{D} \sqrt{12}\sigma_\varepsilon \int_0^1 \left(r-\tfrac{1}{2}\right) w(r)dr, \tag{6.2}$$

which is actually Gaussian. Upper and the lower limits of all integrals below are 1 and 0 respectively. We are concerned with (A3.10a) and (A3.10b). Using (4.2), (4.3), and (6.2) we see

$$\sigma_\varepsilon^{-2}T^{-2}\left[\sum v_t^2 - T^{-1}\left(\sum v_t\right)^2 - \left(\sum \tilde{t}^2\right)^{-1}\left(\sum \tilde{t}v_t\right)^2\right]$$

$$\xrightarrow{D} \int w(r)^2 dr - \left(\int w(r)dr\right)^2 - 12\left(\int \left(r-\tfrac{1}{2}\right) w(r)dr\right)^2. \tag{6.3}$$

The left-hand side of (6.3) is identical to

$$\sigma_\varepsilon^{-2}T^{-2}\sum\left(v_t - T^{-1}\left(\sum v_t\right) - \left(\sum \tilde{t}^2\right)^{-1}\left(\sum \tilde{t}v_t\right)\tilde{t}\right)^2. \tag{6.4}$$

Using $w_1(r)$ in (4.16′) and writing

$$w_2(r) \equiv w_1(r) - 12\left(r-\tfrac{1}{2}\right)\int \left(s-\tfrac{1}{2}\right) w(s)ds, \tag{6.5}$$

we see that

$$\text{the expression in (6.4)} \xrightarrow{D} \int w_2(r)^2 dr. \tag{6.6}$$

Readers are advised to confirm that the right-hand sides of (6.3) and (6.6) are indeed identical, and also that

$$\int w(s)ds + 12\left(s-\tfrac{1}{2}\right)\int \left(s-\tfrac{1}{2}\right) w(s)ds$$

is the projection of $w(r)$ onto the linear subspace spanned by $\left(1, r-\tfrac{1}{2}\right)$.[2]

If the true data-generating process is (5.2) with $\rho^0 = 1$, it is shown in Appendix 3.3 that $T(\hat{\rho}-1) \approx \Delta^{-1}\Delta_1$, where Δ and Δ_1 are defined in (A3.10a) and (A3.10b). From the above explanations we see

$$\Delta \xrightarrow{D} \sigma_\varepsilon^2 \int w_2(r)^2 dr.$$

Moreover

$$T^{-3/2}\sum \tilde{t}\Delta v_t \approx T^{-3/2}\sum t\Delta v_t - \tfrac{1}{2}T^{-1/2}\sum \Delta v_t \xrightarrow{D} \int \left(r-\tfrac{1}{2}\right) dw(r).$$

[2] For two functions, $f(r)$ and $g(r)$, defined over $1 \geq r \geq 0$ the inner product of f and g is $\int_0^1 f(r)g(r)dr$, the squared length of g is $\int_0^1 g(r)^2 dr$, so that the projection of f on g is $\left(\int g(r)^2 dr\right)^{-1}\left(\int f(r)g(r)dr\right) g(r)$.

Using this it can be shown that

$$\Delta_1 \xrightarrow{D} \sigma_\varepsilon^2 \int w_2(r)dw(r). \tag{6.7}$$

Thus

$$T(\hat{\rho} - 1) \xrightarrow{D} \left(\int w_2(r)^2 dr\right)^{-1} \int w_2(r)dw(r). \tag{6.8a}$$

$$\text{the } t\text{-statistic to test } \rho = 1 \xrightarrow{D} \left(\int w_2(r)^2 dr\right)^{-1/2} \int w_2(r)dw(r). \tag{6.8b}$$

The distribution (6.8*a*) has an even stronger leftward shift of location than (4.16). See Fuller (1976: 371, table 8.5.1, the part for $\hat{\rho}_\tau, n = \infty$) and Figure 4.1(*c*) above. The essential part of the F-test statistic is derived in (A3.12), and we get

$$\text{the } F\text{-statistic to test } (\beta, \rho) = (0, 1) \xrightarrow{D} \tfrac{1}{2}\left[12\left(\int \left(r - \tfrac{1}{2}\right) dw(r)\right)^2 + \left(\int w_2(r)^2 dr\right)^{-1} \left(\int w_2(r)dw(r)\right)^2\right]. \tag{6.8c}$$

(6.8*a*) through (6.8*c*) are due to Ouliaris, Park, and Phillips (1989).

There is an alternative expression for $\int \left(r - \frac{1}{2}\right) dw(r)$. Since

$$\sigma_\varepsilon^{-1} T^{-3/2} \sum t\varepsilon_t = \sigma_\varepsilon^{-1} \left(T^{-3/2} T \sum_{t=1}^T \varepsilon_t - T^{-3/2} \sum_{t=1}^T \sum_{s=1}^t \varepsilon_s + T^{-3/2} \sum_{t=1}^T \varepsilon_t\right) \xrightarrow{D} w(1) - \int w(r)dr,$$

$$\sigma_\varepsilon^{-1} T^{-3/2} \sum \tilde{t}\varepsilon_t \xrightarrow{D} \tfrac{1}{2} w(1) - \int w(r)dr,$$

which is due to Schmidt and Phillips (1992). We thus have

$$\int \left(r - \tfrac{1}{2}\right) dw(r) = \tfrac{1}{2} w(1) - \int w(r)dr. \tag{6.9}$$

In Section 5.3 we considered the case where the deterministic trend is confined to a constant. On the OLS along (5.6) it can be shown that

$$\text{the } F\text{-statistic to test } (\mu, \rho) = (0, 1) \xrightarrow{D} \tfrac{1}{2}\left[\left(\int dw(r)\right)^2 + \left(\int w_1(r)^2 dr\right)^{-1} \left(\int w_1(r)dw(r)\right)^2\right] \tag{6.10}$$

where $w_1(r)$ was defined in (4.16′).

6.2 Serial Correlations in Δx_t

6.2.1 *Asymptotic theories*

Let us consider the case where the process of Δx_t is stationary with the covariance sequence, $\ldots, \gamma_{-1}, \gamma_0, \gamma_1, \ldots (\gamma_{-j} = \gamma_j)$. For simplicity I assume initially that $E(u_t) = 0$. $\{x_t\}$ is generated by

$$x_t = x_{t-1} + u_t = x_0 + \sum\nolimits_1^t u_s. \tag{6.11}$$

Phillips (1987, 1988*a*) shows that

$$T^{-3/2} \sum\nolimits_1^T x_t \xrightarrow{D} \sigma \int_0^1 w(r)dr \tag{6.12}$$

$$T^{-2} \sum\nolimits_1^T x_t^2 \xrightarrow{D} \sigma^2 \int_0^1 w(r)^2 dr \tag{6.13}$$

$$T^{-1} \sum\nolimits_1^T x_{t-1} u_t \xrightarrow{D} \sigma^2 \int_0^1 w(r)dw(r) + \delta \tag{6.14}$$

$$T^{-5/2} \sum\nolimits_1^T t x_t \xrightarrow{D} \sigma \int_0^1 r w(r)dr \tag{6.15}$$

$$T^{-3/2} \sum\nolimits_1^T t u_t \xrightarrow{D} \sigma \int_0^1 r dw(r), \tag{6.16}$$

where $\sigma^2 = \sum_{-\infty}^{\infty} \gamma_j$, i.e. the long-run variance of $\{u_t\}$, and $\delta \equiv \sum_1^{\infty} \gamma_j$. Expressions (6.12), (6.13), (6.14), and (6.15) are generalizations of (4.2), (4.3), (4.7), and (6.1) respectively. Note the role that the long-run variance plays in place of σ_ε^2 and also the presence of δ in (6.14).

The role of long-run variance can be explained by the expression (2.8) because $\Delta x_t = b(L)\varepsilon_t$ there may be equated to u_t here. Then in regard to (6.12)

$$T^{-3/2} \sum\nolimits_1^T x_t = b(1) T^{-3/2} \sum\nolimits_{t=1}^T \sum\nolimits_{s=1}^t \varepsilon_s + T^{-3/2} \sum\nolimits_{t=1}^T b^*(L)\varepsilon_t$$
$$+ T^{-1/2}(x_0 - b^*(L)\varepsilon_0).$$

The last two terms on the right-hand side converge to zero in probability as $T \to \infty$, and the first term converges in distribution to the right-hand side of (6.12), where $\sigma^2 = b(1)^2 \sigma_\varepsilon^2$. As for (6.14), writing $\Delta x_t = b(1)\varepsilon_t + b^*(L)(\varepsilon_t - \varepsilon_{t-1})$ because of (2.7), and assuming $x_0 = 0$, we see that

$$T^{-1} \sum\nolimits_2^T x_{t-1} \Delta x_t$$
$$= T^{-1} \sum\nolimits_t \left(\sum\nolimits_{s=1}^{t-1} b(L)\varepsilon_s \right) (b(1)\varepsilon_t + b^*(L)(\varepsilon_t - \varepsilon_{t-1}))$$

$$= T^{-1}\sum\nolimits_t \left(\sum\nolimits_{s=1}^{t-1} b(L)\varepsilon_s\right) b(1)\varepsilon_t$$

$$+ T^{-1}\sum\nolimits_t \left(\sum\nolimits_{s=1}^{t-1} b(L)\varepsilon_s\right) b^*(L)(\varepsilon_t - \varepsilon_{t-1}). \tag{6.17a}$$

The first term of the last expression is

$$T^{-1}\sum\nolimits_t \left[b(1)\left(\sum\nolimits_{s=1}^{t-1} \varepsilon_s\right) + b^*(L)(\varepsilon_{t-1} - \varepsilon_0)\right] b(1)\varepsilon_t$$

$$\xrightarrow{D} \sigma_\varepsilon^2 b(1)^2 \int w(r)dw(r) + 0. \tag{6.17b}$$

The second term is

$$T^{-1}\sum\nolimits_{s=1}^{T-1} b(L)\varepsilon_s b^*(L)(\varepsilon_T - \varepsilon_s)$$

$$= -T^{-1}\sum\nolimits_{s=1}^{T-1} b(L)\varepsilon_s b^*(L)\varepsilon_s$$

$$+T^{-1}\sum\nolimits_{s=1}^{T-1}\sum\nolimits_j b_j\varepsilon_{s-j}\sum\nolimits_h b_h^*\varepsilon_{T-h}, \tag{6.17c}$$

of which the first term converges in probability to $-\sigma_\varepsilon^2\sum_{j=0}^{\infty} b_j b_j^* = \sigma_\varepsilon^2\sum b_j(b_{j+1} + b_{j+2} + \ldots) = \delta$ because of (2.9) and (2.10), and it can be shown that the second term converges to zero in probability.

6.2.2 OLS and fully modified OLS

Consider the model, $x_t = \rho x_{t-1} + u_t$, in which no deterministic trends are involved. If $\rho^0 = 1$ and $\hat\rho$ is (4.5),

$$T(\hat\rho - 1) \xrightarrow{D} \left(\int_0^1 w(r)^2 dr\right)^{-1}\left(\int_0^1 w(r)dw(r) + \frac{\delta}{\sigma^2}\right), \tag{6.18}$$

which is due to Phillips and Perron (1988). The estimation of δ and σ^2 poses a problem as explained in Section 7.3.3 below.

Applying the fully modified least squares (given in Appendix 6) to a univariate autoregressive process, Phillips (1993) obtains an estimator which is $T^{3/2}$ rather than T-consistent. It is called the hyperconsistency. The new method differs from OLS in adopting $x_t - \Delta x_{t-1}$ for the dependent variable, while x_{t-1} remains to be the independent variable. The crucial point that leads to the $T^{3/2}$ consistency is that $u_t - \Delta x_{t-1} \equiv u_t - u_{t-1}$ has zero long-run variance. At the time of writing we are yet to see the impact of this discovery upon the whole inference problems in the unit-root field. (I comment on the application to co-integrated VAR in Appendix 6.)

6.2.3 *Fuller transformation in the AR*

When the model of $\{\Delta x_t\}$ is parametrically specified one would look for an estimater of ρ better than the above OLS. Fuller (1976: 373–7) considers the case where $\{\Delta x_t\}$ is a stationary AR $(p-1)$,

$$\Delta x_t = a_1 \Delta x_{t-1} + \ldots + a_{p-1} \Delta x_{t-p+1} + \varepsilon_t, \tag{6.19}$$

where $\{\varepsilon_t\}$ is i.i.d. with $E(\varepsilon_t) = 0$ and $E(\varepsilon_t^2) = \sigma_\varepsilon^2$. A model for $\{x_t\}$ that includes (6.19) as well as stationary AR(p) is

$$x_t = \rho x_{t-1} + u_t, \tag{6.20}$$

$$u_t = a_1 u_{t-1} + \ldots + a_{p-1} u_{t-p+1} + \varepsilon_t, \tag{6.20$'$}$$

where (6.20′) is assumed to be a stationary AR$(p-1)$. If $|\rho| < 1$, $\{x_t\}$ is a stationary AR(p). If $\rho = 1$ $\{x_t\}$ is DS, and Δx_t is AR$(p-1)$ as indicated in (6.19). In Fuller (1976: 373) new parameters $(\alpha_1, \ldots, \alpha_p)$ are defined through

$$(1-\rho L)(1 - a_1 L - \ldots - a_{p-1} L^{p-1}) = (1 - \alpha_1 L)$$
$$-(1-L)(\alpha_2 L + \ldots + \alpha_p L^{p-1}). \tag{6.21}$$

The transformation, $(\rho, a_1, \ldots, a_{p-1}) \leftrightarrow (\alpha_1, \alpha_2, \ldots, \alpha_p)$ is one-to-one. In particular it is seen by setting $L = 1$ that

$$1 - \alpha_1 = (1-\rho)(1 - a_1 - \ldots - a_{p-1}). \tag{6.22}$$

Let $f(\lambda) = \lambda^{p-1} - a_1 \lambda^{p-2} - \ldots - a_{p-1}$. The characteristic equation of (6.20′) is $f(\lambda) = 0$. Since it is assumed to have stable roots only, and since $f(+\infty) = +\infty$, $f(1) = 1 - a_1 - \ldots - a_{p-1}$ must be positive. From (6.22) it is seen that $\alpha_1 = 1 \Leftrightarrow \rho = 1$ and that $\alpha_1 < 1 \Leftrightarrow \rho < 1$. Note also that when $\rho = 1$, $\alpha_{i+1} = a_i$, $i = 1, \ldots, p-1$.

The Fuller reparametrization through (6.21) represents the model, (6.20) and (6.20′), as

$$x_t = \alpha_1 x_{t-1} + \alpha_2 \Delta x_{t-1} + \ldots + \alpha_p \Delta x_{t-p+1} + \varepsilon_t. \tag{6.23}$$

or, subtracting x_{t-1} from both sides

$$\Delta x_t = (\alpha_1 - 1) x_{t-1} + \alpha_2 \Delta x_{t-1} + \ldots + \alpha_p \Delta x_{t-p+1} + \varepsilon_t. \tag{6.23$'$}$$

This expression has the advantage that when $\rho = 1$ the stationary and the non-stationary variables are separated, i.e. x_{t-1} is non-stationary but $\Delta x_{t-1}, \ldots, \Delta x_{t-p+1}$ are stationary. Correspondingly $\hat{\alpha}_1$ is T-consistent whereas $(\hat{\alpha}_2, \ldots, \hat{\alpha}_p)$ is $\sqrt{T}$-consistent as shown in Appendix 4. Another advantage is that a non-linear least-squares calculation is required to estimate $(\rho, a_1, \ldots, a_{p-1})$ in (6.20) and (6.20′) while an OLS is sufficient to estimate $(\alpha_1, \ldots, \alpha_p)$ in (6.23).

For a later reference I briefly point out another parametrization of (6.20) and (6.20′). They are combined into

$$x_t = c_1 x_{t-1} + \ldots + c_p x_{t-p} + \varepsilon_t. \tag{6.24}$$

(6.23) and (6.24) are related through

$$\alpha_1 = \sum\nolimits_{j=1}^{p} c_j,\ \alpha_i = -\sum\nolimits_{j=i}^{p} c_j, \qquad i = 2, \ldots, p \tag{6.25a}$$

$$c_1 = \alpha_1 + \alpha_2;\ c_i = \alpha_{i+1} - \alpha_i, i = 2, \ldots, p-1;\ c_p = -\alpha_p. \tag{6.25b}$$

Let us return to the parametrization (6.23′). Let the true value of α_1 be α_1^0 and assume $\alpha_1^0 = 1$. Run OLS along (6.23′). The distribution of the estimator of $\alpha_1 - 1$ depends on the long-run variance σ^2, which in turn depends upon the as and σ_ε^2. In fact

$$\sigma^2 = (1 - a_1 - \ldots - a_{p-1})^{-2}\sigma_\varepsilon^2. \tag{6.26}$$

However, the testing for DS does not require an estimate of σ^2. Construct the t-statistic to test $\alpha_1 - 1 = 0$, and let $\hat{t}$ be the statistic. In Appendix 4 readers find a proof for the statement that if $\alpha_1^0 = 1$

$$\hat{t} \xrightarrow{D} \left(\int_0^1 w(r)^2 dr\right)^{-1/2} \left(\int_0^1 w(r)dw(r)\right). \tag{6.27}$$

A remarkable point here is that unlike (6.18) this limiting distribution is free from all nuisance parameters, $a_1, \ldots, a_{p-1}$, and σ_ε^2. It has been tabulated as mentioned in Section 5.2. On the other hand if $|\alpha_1^0| < 1$, $\hat{\alpha}_1$ converges in probability to $\alpha_1^0 (\neq 1)$, and $\hat{t}$ diverges to $-\infty$. The $\hat{t}$ provides a consistent test for the difference stationarity against stationarity. This method is called the augmented Dickey–Fuller test.

In practice the order of AR, $p-1$, is unknown. To select p one should follow the general-to-specific principle in Hendry (1979). A sufficiently high order, $p_{\max}$, is chosen, and initially one tests for $p_{\max} - 1$ against $p_{\max}$ by one (or all) of the following tests: (i) the t-test to see the significance of the coefficient of Δx_{t-p+1} in (6.23),[3] (ii) the portmanteau test that investigates serial correlations of residual series $\{\hat{e}_t\}$, on which readers are referred to Box and Jenkins (1976, ch. 8), and (iii) the orthogonality test to investigate correlations between $\{\hat{e}_t\}$ and $\{\Delta x_{t-p-\tau}\}$, $\tau > 1$, which has been proposed in Hendry and Richard (1982). If $p_{\max} - 1$ is not rejected, one tests for $p_{\max} - 2$ against $p_{\max} - 1$. The sequential tests are terminated when $p_{\max} - j$ is rejected against $p_{\max} - j + 1$. The asymptotic distributions of these test statistics are identical to those in the stationary AR models, because the limit distribution of $(\hat{\alpha}_2, \ldots, \hat{\alpha}_p)$ is, no matter whether $\alpha_1^0 =$ or $\neq 1$ (see Appendix 4.2)). With each one of the three testing methods different levels of significance imply different selections of lag orders.

Our concern is not symmetric between the choice of p larger than its true value and that of p smaller. The former leads to some loss of efficiency, while the latter may seriously distort the test.

To the best of my knowledge a comprehensive simulation study has not been done on the significance levels. I think we had better focus our concern not

[3] See Anderson (1971: 42) for a theoretical analysis of levels of significance.

on the frequency of a correct selection of lag orders but on the effect that the frequency of incorrect selection has upon the performance of the augmented Dickey–Fuller test. Ignoring α_p that is nearly zero would have no effect upon the performance of the test. On the other hand, ignoring a large value of α_p would have a devastating effect. I wonder if one can design a two-step simulation study as follows. In the first step one determines the c such that the test would be seriously affected if one ignores α_p such that $|\alpha_p| > c$. This defines the underfitting and overfitting of lag orders in terms of the effect upon the test performance. In the second step we determine the level of significance such that the probability of underfitting is very small though the probability of overfitting may be sizeable.

For the case where $p - 1 \geq 1$ in (6.20′) and $\rho^0 = 1$ Choi (1993) proves that the direct OLS of $c = (c_1, \ldots, c_p)$ in (6.24) is $\sqrt{T}$-consistent (rather than T-consistent), and that $\sqrt{T}(\hat{c} - c)$ is asymptotically Gaussian with a rank deficient covariance matrix. (The deficiency is 1.) There are perhaps a number of applications of this interesting discovery. Choi (1993) applies it to a confidence interval for $(1 - c_1 - \ldots - c_p)$ using $\hat{c}$ of an AR with an overfitted lag order. The interval would give some idea regarding how large the dominating root of the characteristic polynomial could be.

In Hatanala and Koto (1994) lag orders in Dickey–Fuller equations such as (6.23′) are chosen with the 5% significance of t-values of the highest lag order coefficient, α_p in (6.23′). With lag orders so determined the dominating roots of characteristic polynomials with coefficients estimated by OLS are found complex-valued in a number of variables, for example, in the historical real GNP and nominal GNP data for the USA. The problem requires a careful examination.[4]

6.2.4 *MA case*

Hall (1989, 1992) considers the case where $\{\Delta x_t\}$ is MA(q),

$$\Delta x_t \equiv u_t = \varepsilon_t + b_1\varepsilon_{t-1} + \ldots + b_q\varepsilon_{t-q}, \tag{6.28}$$

where $\{\varepsilon_t\}$ is i.i.d. with $E(\varepsilon_t) = 0$ and $E(\varepsilon_t^2) = \sigma_\varepsilon^2$. Consider the instrumental variable estimation of ρ in $x_t = \rho x_{t-1} + u_t$ with $\rho^0 = 1$. In so far as $k > q$, x_{t-k} is uncorrelated with Δx_t. Since x_{t-k} is correlated with x_{t-1}, x_{t-k} is a valid instrument for x_{t-1}. The instrumental variable estimator of ρ is

$$\hat{\rho}_I = \left(\sum x_{t-k}x_{t-1}\right)^{-1} \sum x_{t-k}x_t.$$

[4] Chan and Wei (1988) investigate the OLS in the autoregressive process which contains a complex unit root. Fukushige, Hatanaka, and Koto (1994) develop a method to test for stationarity against non-stationarity in the situation in which the dominating roots may possibly be complex-valued.

Let us analyse

$$T(\hat{\rho}_I - 1) = \left(T^{-2}\sum x_{t-k}x_{t-1}\right)^{-1} T^{-1}\sum x_{t-k}\Delta x_t, \tag{6.29}$$

assuming that $\{\Delta x_t\}$ is generated by (6.28). First,

$$T^{-2}\sum x_{t-k}^2 \xrightarrow{D} \sigma^2 \int w(r)^2 dr$$

$$T^{-2}\sum x_{t-k}(x_{t-1} - x_{t-k}) \xrightarrow{P} 0,$$

where σ^2 is the long-run variance of Δx_t. Second, since Δx_t is uncorrelated with x_{t-k}

$$T^{-1}\sum x_{t-k}\Delta x_t \xrightarrow{D} \sigma^2 \int w(r) dw(r).$$

Note that δ in (6.14) and (6.18) does not appear here.[5] Thus

$$T(\hat{p}_I - 1) \xrightarrow{D} \left(\int w(r)^2 dr\right)^{-1} \left(\int w(r) dw(r)\right),$$

which is free from all nuisance parameters. The analogues of the t- and the F-tests are also presented in Hall (1989, 1992).

ARMA models will be dealt with in Chapter 7.

Hamilton (1994: 497–512) is a good reference that gives the same material as Sections 6.1 and 6.2 in a different representation.

6.3 MA Unit-Root Test

I am now ready to explain the asymptotic distribution of the MA unit-root test statistic given earlier in Section 3.4.2.

6.3.1 Constant trend

Suppose that the model is given by (3.11a) and (3.11b) and that H_0 is $\delta = 1$ whereas H_1 is $\delta < 1$. The test statistic is (3.12′) which will be written S_0. Under $H_0 \hat{v} = \boldsymbol{\varepsilon} - T^{-1}(\boldsymbol{e}'\boldsymbol{\varepsilon})\boldsymbol{e}$, where $\boldsymbol{\varepsilon}' = (\varepsilon_1, \ldots, \varepsilon_T)$. The t-th element of $(\boldsymbol{I} + \boldsymbol{D})\hat{\boldsymbol{v}}$ is

$$s_t = \sum_{i=1}^{t} \varepsilon_i - T^{-1} t \sum_{i=1}^{T} \varepsilon_i.$$

[5] That δ in (6.14) does not appear in the present case can be seen as follows. Develop $T^{-1}\sum x_{t-k}\Delta x_t$ along (6.17a) and observe that the second term of the last expression of (6.17a) is here

$$T^{-1}\sum_t \left[\sum_{s=1}^{t-k} b(L)\varepsilon_s\right] [b^*(L)(\varepsilon_t - \varepsilon_{t-1})],$$

where the terms in two [ ] are uncorrelated in the present case where $b_j = 0$ if $j > q$. What corresponds to (6.17c) is $O_p(T^{-1/2})$ here.

Thus $$T^{-1/2}s_t = T^{-1/2}\sum_{i=1}^{t}\varepsilon_i - (t/T)T^{-1/2}\sum_{i=1}^{T}\varepsilon_i$$
$$\xrightarrow{D} \sigma_\varepsilon(w(r) - rw(1)),$$

where $r = (t/T)$. Regarding the nominator of (3.12′)

$$T^{-2}\sum_{t=1}^{T} s_t^2 = T^{-1}\sum (T^{-1/2}s_t)^2 \xrightarrow{D} \sigma_\varepsilon^2 \int_0^1 v_0(r)^2 dr \tag{6.30}$$

$$v_0(r) \equiv w(r) - rw(1). \tag{6.31}$$

Clearly $T^{-1}\times$ the denominator of (3.12′) converges to σ_ε^2, and

$$T^{-1}S_0 \xrightarrow{D} \int_0^1 v_0(r)^2 dr. \tag{6.32}$$

This expression as well as its tabulation is found in Kwiatkowski *et al.* (1992).

6.3.2 *Linear trend*

To introduce a linear deterministic trend modify the model into

$$\Delta x_t = \theta_1 + \varepsilon_t - \delta\varepsilon_{t-1} \tag{6.33a}$$

$$x_1 = \theta_0 + \varepsilon_1. \tag{6.33b}$$

H_0 and H_1 are the same as before. The test statistic is identical to (3.12′) except that what is subtracted is a linear trend instead of mean. Thus $\hat{v}' = (\hat{v}_1, \ldots, \hat{v}_T)$, $\hat{v}_i = x_i - \hat{\theta}_0 - \hat{\theta}_1 i$, where $(\hat{\theta}_0, \hat{\theta}_1)$ is the OLS estimate of $(\hat{\theta}_0, \hat{\theta}_1)$. We denote the new S by S_1. Orthogonalize the regressor $(1, t)$ into $(1, t-(T+1)/2)$. Under H_0

$$\hat{v}_i \approx \varepsilon_i - T^{-1}\sum_{s=1}^{T}\varepsilon_i - \left(\sum_{s=1}^{T}\left(s - \frac{T}{2}\right)^2\right)^{-1}$$
$$\times \left(\sum_{s=1}^{T}\left(s - \frac{T}{2}\right)\varepsilon_s\right)\left(i - \frac{T}{2}\right).$$

The t-th element of $(\boldsymbol{I} + \boldsymbol{D})\hat{\boldsymbol{v}}$ is

$$s_t \approx \sum_{i=1}^{t}\varepsilon_i - T^{-1}t\sum_{i=1}^{T}\varepsilon_i - \left(\sum\left(s - \frac{T}{2}\right)^2\right)^{-1}$$
$$\times \left(\sum\left(s - \frac{T}{2}\right)\varepsilon_s\right)\left(\sum_{i=1}^{t}\left(i - \frac{T}{2}\right)\right).$$

Since $\sum_{i=1}^{t}\left(i - \frac{T}{2}\right) \approx \frac{1}{2}(t^2 - Tt)$,

$$T^{-1/2}s_t \approx T^{-1/2}\sum_{i=1}^{t}\varepsilon_i - (t/T)T^{-1/2}\sum_{i=1}^{T}\varepsilon_i$$

$$-6[t^2/T^2) - (t/T)]T^{-3/2}\sum_{s=1}^{T}\left(s-\frac{T}{2}\right)\varepsilon_s.$$

Using (6.9) we see that this converges to

$$\sigma_\varepsilon\left[w(r) - rw(1) - 6(r^2-r)\left(\tfrac{1}{2}w(1) - \int w(s)ds\right)\right].$$

The result is

$$T^{-1}S_1 \xrightarrow{D} \int_0^1 v_1(r)^2 dr \tag{6.34}$$

$$v_1(r) = v_0(r) - 3(r^2-r)w(1) + 6(r^2-r)\int_0^1 w(s)ds. \tag{6.35}$$

The right-hand side of (6.33) is tabulated in Kwiatkowski *et al.* (1992).

MacNeill (1978) gives a general formula for the partial sum of residuals in the fitting of polynomial trend, and (6.31) and (6.34) are special cases of the formula therein.

6.3.3 ARMA case

Let us revert to a constant trend, θ_0, but generalize the i.i.d. ε_t to u_t in (3.13*c*). The test statistic is (3.14′) with $\boldsymbol{\gamma}$ replaced by $\hat{\boldsymbol{\gamma}}$. I shall give only a sequence of hints to derive the asymptotic distribution. Initially assume that $b_1 = \ldots = b_q = 0$ so that $\{u_t\}$ is AR(p). Let $\boldsymbol{\Pi} = \boldsymbol{I} - a_1\boldsymbol{L}^* - \ldots - a_p\boldsymbol{L}^{*p}$, where $\boldsymbol{L}^*$ is defined in connection with (3.12′). $\sigma_\varepsilon^{-2}\boldsymbol{\Pi}E(\boldsymbol{uu}')\boldsymbol{\Pi}' \approx \boldsymbol{I}$ so that $\boldsymbol{\Sigma}^{-1} \approx \boldsymbol{\Pi}'\boldsymbol{\Pi}$. I replace the GLS estimate of θ_0 by the OLS so that $\tilde{\boldsymbol{v}}(\gamma) = (\boldsymbol{I} - \boldsymbol{e}(\boldsymbol{e}'\boldsymbol{e})^{-1}\boldsymbol{e}')\boldsymbol{u}$. Since $\boldsymbol{\Pi}$ and $\boldsymbol{e}(\boldsymbol{e}'\boldsymbol{e})^{-1}\boldsymbol{e}'$ nearly commute, $\boldsymbol{\Pi}\tilde{\boldsymbol{v}}(\gamma) \approx (\boldsymbol{I} - \boldsymbol{e}(\boldsymbol{e}'\boldsymbol{e})^{-1}\boldsymbol{e}')\boldsymbol{\varepsilon} \equiv \boldsymbol{z}$. Therefore

$$\begin{aligned}&T^{-2}\tilde{\boldsymbol{v}}(\gamma)'\widetilde{\boldsymbol{\Sigma}}(\gamma)^{-1}(\boldsymbol{I}+\boldsymbol{D})'\widetilde{\boldsymbol{\Sigma}}(\gamma)(\boldsymbol{I}+\boldsymbol{D})\widetilde{\boldsymbol{\Sigma}}(\gamma)^{-1}\tilde{\boldsymbol{v}}(\gamma)\\ &\approx T^{-2}\boldsymbol{z}'\boldsymbol{\Pi}(\boldsymbol{I}+\boldsymbol{D})'\boldsymbol{\Pi}^{-1}\boldsymbol{\Pi}^{-1'}(\boldsymbol{I}+\boldsymbol{D})\boldsymbol{\Pi}'\boldsymbol{z}.\end{aligned} \tag{6.36}$$

Since $\boldsymbol{\Pi}$ and $\boldsymbol{D}'$ nearly commute, $\boldsymbol{\Pi}\boldsymbol{D}'\boldsymbol{\Pi}^{-1} - \boldsymbol{D}' = (\boldsymbol{\Pi}\boldsymbol{D}' - \boldsymbol{D}'\boldsymbol{\Pi})\boldsymbol{\Pi}^{-1} \approx \boldsymbol{0}$.

Likewise $\boldsymbol{\Pi}^{-1'}\boldsymbol{D}\boldsymbol{\Pi}' - \boldsymbol{D} \approx \boldsymbol{0}$, and $\boldsymbol{\Pi}\boldsymbol{D}'\boldsymbol{\Pi}^{-1}\boldsymbol{\Pi}^{-1'}\boldsymbol{D}\boldsymbol{\Pi}' \approx \boldsymbol{D}'\boldsymbol{D}$. Thus (6.36) is approximately

$$T^{-2}\boldsymbol{z}'(\boldsymbol{I}+\boldsymbol{D})'(\boldsymbol{I}+\boldsymbol{D})\boldsymbol{z}.$$

The result is that

$$T^{-1}S(\gamma) \xrightarrow{D} \int_0^1 v_0(r)^2 dr,$$

which is the same as (6.32). Replacing $\boldsymbol{\gamma}$ by $\hat{\boldsymbol{\gamma}}$ has no effect upon the asymptotic distribution.

When an MA is added as in (3.13*c*), represent u_t by an AR with its order extending possibly to infinity. Now $\boldsymbol{\Pi} = \boldsymbol{I} - a_1\boldsymbol{L}^2 - \ldots a_{T-1}\boldsymbol{L}^{*T-1}$. Since $\{a_\tau\}$

is bounded by a decaying exponential, the above reasoning goes through. I have followed Saikkonen and Luukkonen (1993*a*) in a part of the above reasoning.

6.3.4 Polynomial trend

The above method can be extended to the case of a polynomial trend in a straightforward manner. See Hatanaka and Koto (1994).

Salient points in Chapter 6 are summarized at the end of Chapter 7.

7
Regression Approach to the Test for Difference Stationarity (II)

In Chapter 5 we have considered how to test for DS against TS in the case where Δx_t is i.i.d. and $\{x_t\}$ may possibly have a linear deterministic trend. In Section 6.2 a mathematical analysis is given on the case where $\{\Delta x_t\}$ is serially correlated with zero mean. Here we reintroduce a non-zero mean, and test for DS against TS with serially correlated Δx_t and possible presence of a linear trend in x_t.

7.1 The Case where $\boldsymbol{\Delta x_t}$ is an AR

Let us consider the case where $\{\Delta x_t\}$ is AR(p) possibly with a non-zero mean under the DS hypothesis. An AR model that includes both the DS and TS is

$$(1 - \rho L)(1 - a_1 L - \ldots - a_{p-1} L^{p-1})(x_t - \theta_0 - \theta_1 t) = \varepsilon_t, \tag{7.1}$$

where $\{\varepsilon_t\}$ is i.i.d. with $E(\varepsilon_t) = 0$ and $E(\varepsilon_t^2) = \sigma_\varepsilon^2$. The Fuller reparametrization (6.21) transforms (7.1) into

$$\Delta x_t = \mu + \beta t + (\alpha_1 - 1)x_{t-1} + \alpha_2 \Delta x_{t-1} + \ldots + \alpha_p \Delta x_{t-p+1} + \varepsilon_t, \tag{7.2}$$

where $\mu + \beta t = (1 - \rho L)(1 - a_1 L - \ldots - a_{p-1} L^{p-1})(\theta_0 + \theta_1 t)$ In particular, $\beta = \theta_1(1 - \rho)(1 - a_1 - \ldots - a_{p-1})$ so that $\beta = 0$ if either $\rho = 1$ or $\theta_1 = 0$. Moreover $\rho = 1 \Leftrightarrow \alpha_1 = 1$, and the constraint on parameters of (7.2) induced by $\rho = 1$ is $(\beta, \alpha_1) = (0, 1)$. The θ_0 vanishes from (7.2) if $\rho = 1$.

When $\{x_t\}$ is generated by $\rho^0 = 1$, the F-statistic to test for $(\beta, \alpha_1) = (0, 1)$ in (7.2) is asymptotically distributed as indicated on the right-hand side of (6.8*c*) free from all nuisance parameters, $(\theta_0, \theta_1, a_1, \ldots, a_{p-1}, \sigma_\varepsilon^2)$. This asymptotic distribution is tabulated in Dickey and Fuller (1981, table VI, $n = \infty$). The t-statistic to test for $\alpha_1 = 1$ can also be used. Its asymptotic distribution is the right-hand side of (6.8*b*) and tabulated in Fuller (1976: 373, table 8.5.2, the part for $\hat{\tau}_\tau$, $n = \infty$), but I recommend the F-statistic because it tests a larger number of constraints implied by $\rho = 1$.

The finite sample distributions in these tables are not applicable to the finite sample distributions in the present case of serially correlated Δx_t. DeJong *et al.* (1992*a*) perform a detailed simulation study, and conclude that the empirical size is close to the nominal size when T is 100. (The empirical size is the size of the test obtained from the simulated, finite sample distribution, and the nominal size is what would be expected if the finite sample distribution is perfectly approximated by the limiting distribution.)

If the deterministic trend is confined to a constant in both the DS and TS hypotheses, we may run the regression

$$\Delta x_t = \mu + (\alpha_1 - 1)x_{t-1} + \alpha_2 \Delta x_{t-1} + \ldots + \alpha_p \Delta x_{t-p+1} + \text{ residual},$$

and apply the F-test for $(\mu, \alpha_1) = (0, 1)$ or the t-test for $\alpha_1 = 1$. The limiting distributions under the DS are free from nuisance parameters $(a_1, \ldots, a_{p-1}, \sigma_\varepsilon^2)$. Moreover, they are identical to those for the case where Δx_t is i.i.d. The limiting distribution of the t-statistic is in Fuller (1976: 373, table 8.5.2, $\hat{\tau}_\mu$, $n = \infty$), and that of the F-statistic in Dickey and Fuller (1981, table IV, $n = \infty$).

Important points in the present Section 7.1 are reproduced at the end of the present chapter.

7.2 ARMA in General and the Schwert ARMA

7.2.1 ARMA in general

As for the case where Δx_t is an MA or an ARMA there exist three lines of thoughts.

(i) Suppose that $\{\Delta x_t\}$ is MA(q) and $k > q$. Then x_{t-k} is uncorrelated with Δx_t, and it leads to the instrumental variable estimator as suggested in (6.29). This idea due to Hall (1989) is extended to an ARMA(p, q) model in Pantula and Hall (1991) and Hall (1992*a*, *b*). Hall (1992*b*) contains determination of lag orders by the general-to-specific principle with the significance of the highest order coefficient.

(ii) An invertible MA can be inverted into a stationary AR, though a nearly non invertible MA requires a large lag order of AR to maintain an adequate degree of approximation. Said and Dickey (1984) provides a mathematical analysis to justify the augmented Dickey–Fuller test performed on the AR approximation of the MA that represents $\{u_t\}$.

(iii) The ARMA model has been dealt with by some forms of the non-linear least squares without inverting the MA part into an AR (see Box and Jenkins (1976: 273), Ansley (1979), and Granger and Newbold (1986: 92)). In this framework Solo (1984) tests the DS by the Lagrange multiplier method.

The approach (i) will be explained in greater details. Admittedly q is not known, but it can be estimated from residuals of the regression of x_t upon $(1, t)$. The k should be chosen to exceed the estimate of q with a sufficient margin. To test the DS set up the equation,

$$x_t = \mu + \beta t + \rho x_{t-1} + u_t. \tag{7.3}$$

Run the instrumental variable calculation with the instrument $(1, t, x_{t-k})$ for the regressor $(1, t, x_{t-1})$. If $\{\Delta x_1\}$ is MA(q) possibly with a non-zero mean, Hall

(1989) shows that

$$T(\hat{\rho}_I - 1) \to \left(\int w_2(r)^2 dr\right)^{-1} \left(\int w_2(r) dw(r)\right),$$

where $\hat{\rho}_I$ is the instrumental variable estimator of ρ and $w_2(r)$ has been defined in (6.5).

If $\{\Delta x_t\}$ is ARMA(p, q), run the instrumental variable calculation in (7.2) with instruments $(1, t, x_{t-k}, \Delta x_{t-k}, \ldots, \Delta x_{t-k-p+1})$ for regressors $(1, t, x_{t-1}, \Delta x_{t-1}, \ldots, \Delta x_{t-p})$, where $k > q$. The asymptotic distribution of the estimator of α_1 as well as the t-statistic here involves the long-run variance of the MA part of Δx_t, which has to be estimated (see Pantula and Hall (1991)).

A computationally simpler method for the case of ARMA is to proceed along Said and Dickey (1984) and apply the augmented Dickey–Fuller test on (6.23′) or (7.2) with a lag order sufficiently large to accommodate a good AR approximation to an MA. This is the method that I have used to get the results presented in Chapter 9. The most serious problem here is how to choose the AR lag order, p. The asymptotic theory in Said and Dickey (1984) suggests that p should go to ∞ as $T \to \infty$ and moreover that $T^{-1/3}p \to 0$. But this hardly provides a useful guide in practical cases where T is small. I have adopted the general to specific principle explained in Section 6.2.3 for the pure AR. The $p_{\max}$ is 12 for the annual data with T ranging between 80 and 120, and 24 for the seasonally adjusted quarterly data with T ranging from 130 to 170. I now wonder if the $p_{\max}$ should have been larger in the quarterly data. The t-value for the highest order coefficient is examined with 5% significance level, which is higher than what seems to be commonly used. Some simulation studies are indicated in Section 8.3, but I have had no time for an adequate simulation experiment.

7.2.2 *Schwert ARMA*

Phillips and Perron (1988), Schwert (1989), and Campbell and Perron (1991) note a case of MA that requires a special caution. Consider the simplest case, $u_t = \varepsilon_t - b_1\varepsilon_{t-1}$, $\beta = \mu = 0$ in (7.3) so that

$$x_t - \rho x_{t-1} = \varepsilon_t - b_1\varepsilon_{t-1}. \tag{7.4}$$

Suppose that $\rho = 1$ so that x_t is DS and that b_1 is close to but less than unity. If b_1 is indeed equal to unity (7.4) contains redundant factors $(1-L)$ on both sides, and after cancelling them (7.4) is reduced to $x_t = \varepsilon_t$; x_t is stationary and Δx_t has an MA unit root. More generally, if the MA representation of $\{u_t\}$ in (7.3) has a root close to but less than unity, there is (i) near-redundancy and also (ii) near-stationarity as well as (iii) near-non-invertibility. The redundancy is a type of non-identification, and the near-redundancy is associated with the likelihood functions which are like a tableland in particular directions.[1] In (7.4) with $\rho = 1$

[1] See Clark (1988) for more about the near-redundancy. The redundancy or, in general, the lack of identification cannot be tested on the basis of data.

it is seen that $b(1)$ defined in Section 2.2 is $1 - b_1$. Thus the near-stationarity here is characterized by $b(1)$ being close to zero, i.e. an MA near unit root. The spectral density of $\{u_t\}$ is lowest at zero frequency in its neighbourhood, because $f(\lambda) \equiv \sigma_\varepsilon^2 \|1 - b_1 \exp(i\lambda)\|^2 = \sigma_\varepsilon^2(1 - 2b_1 \cos\lambda + b_1^2)$, $f(0) = \sigma_\varepsilon^2(1 - b_1)^2$, $f'(0) = 0$, and $f''(0) > 0$. I shall call the situation (where $\rho = 1$ and b_1 is close to unity) the *Schwert MA*, because it is his simulation study that has revealed a devasting effect that it may entail on the inference.

Intensive simulation studies have been made by Schwert (1989), DeJong *et al.* (1992*a*), and Agiakloglou and Newbold (1992) on the augmented Dickey–Fuller t-statistic to test $\alpha_1 = 1$ in (6.23′) for the case where $T = 100$ and (6.20′) is an AR approximation to the MA, $u_t = \varepsilon_t - b_1\varepsilon_{t-1}$. When $b_1 = 0.8$ they find the empirical size appreciably exceeding the nominal size unless the lag order, $p-1$, in (6.20′) is taken much larger than Akaike (1973) suggests. The situation seems hopeless if $b_1 = 0.9$ while $T = 100$. How frequently do we observe the Schwert MA in economic time series? Perron (1988) claims that there are none in the fourteen time series which Nelson and Plosser (1982) analysed. DeJong *et al.* (1992*a*) also make an optimistic conjecture. On the other hand, Schwert (1987) finds the Schwert MA in his fitting of ARMA models to a number of economic time series. The discrepancy among their judgements might be explained in part by difficulties in selecting AR and/or MA orders, about which readers are referred to Christiano and Eichenbaum (1990).

It has been stated that the Schwert MA is a case of DS models which are close to TS. Conversely, if $\{x_t\}$ is DS but close to TS, Δx_t has little spectral density at the origin of the frequency domain. Attempting to generalize the Schwert MA let us consider ARMA representations of Δx_t that could have such spectral density functions.

$$(1 - \rho L)\Delta x_t = (1 - \delta L)\varepsilon_t, \qquad |\delta| < 1, |\rho| < 1. \tag{7.5}$$

Set $\sigma_\varepsilon^2 = 1$. The spectral density function of Δx_t is

$$f_\Delta(\lambda) = (1 - 2\rho\cos\lambda + \rho^2)^{-1}(1 - 2\delta\cos\lambda + \delta^2).$$

It is seen that

$$f_\Delta(0) = (1-\rho)^{-2}(1-\delta)^2, \;\; f'_\Delta(0) = 0,$$
$$f''_\Delta(0) = 2(1-\rho)^{-4}(\delta - \rho)(1 - \rho\delta).$$

Since $(1 - \rho)$ and $(1 - \rho\delta)$ are both positive, $f''_\Delta(0) > 0$ if $\delta > \rho$. Thus if $1 > \delta > \rho > -1$, the spectral density is lowest at the origin over some domain that surrounds it.

The ARMA models of which the spectral density is lowest at the origin over some domain about it will be called the *Schwert ARMA*. They represent a class of DS models that are close to TS. Examples are shown in Figures 7.1(*a*) and (*b*). In Figure 7.1(*a*) $\rho = 0.928$, $\delta = 0.95$, and the valley centred at zero frequency is narrow and shallow. In Figure 7.1(*b*) $\rho = 0$, $\delta = 0.8$, and the valley is wide and

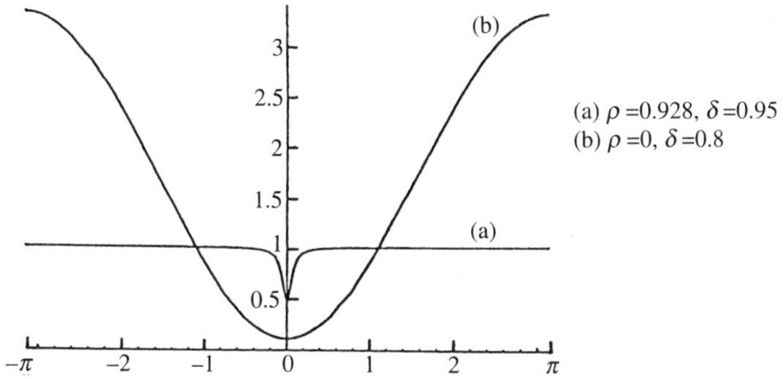

(*a*) $\rho = 0.928$, $\delta = 0.95$ (*b*) $\rho = 0$, $\delta = 0.8$

FIG. 7.1 *Spectral density functions of Schwert ARMAs*

deep. One might say that 7.1(*b*) is closer to TS than 7.1(*a*). Some realizations of Schwert ARMA look as though its integration order is varying over time between $I(1)$ and $I(0)$.

The near-boundary cases between DS and TS consist of (i) the DS that is close to TS and (ii) the TS that is close to DS. There is no way of knowing which of the two is more frequent in economic time series, but we shall see in Section 9.2 how frequent the near-boundary cases are.

7.3 Miscellaneous Remarks

7.3.1 (i) Tabulating limiting distributions

Many researchers including Perron (1989) and Johansen and Juselius (1990) have suggested that the distributions of functionals of the Wiener process can be tabulated by straightforward simulations. For example, to tabulate the limit distribution in (4.8), they would generate Tn pseudo-random numbers distributed in $N(0, 1)$, $\varepsilon_{ti}, t = 1, \ldots, T, i = 1, \ldots, n$, for example, with $T = 1,000$ and $n = 10{,}000$; calculate

$$\left((T-1)^{-2}\sum\nolimits_{t=2}^{T}\left(\sum\nolimits_{s=1}^{t-1}\varepsilon_{si}\right)^{2}\right)^{-1}\left((T-1)^{-1}\sum\nolimits_{t=2}^{T}\left(\sum\nolimits_{s=1}^{t-1}\varepsilon_{si}\right)\varepsilon_{ti}\right)$$

for each i, and compile the results in an empirical probability distribution. The integrals in (4.8) are evaluated by summing relevant functionals over T infinitesimally narrow intervals in which $[0, 1]$ is subdivided. The distributions of far more complex functionals of the Wiener process are derived this way. However, one should carefully investigate properties of expressions to be simulated in each case. Koto and Hatanaka (1994) find that expressions for the statistics concerning structural changes require a larger T (say, 5,000) to deal with the discontinuity involved. In any cases computation costs are little.

As for the bootstrapping method see Basawa *et al.* (1991*a*, 1991*b*) to avoid a pitfall.[2]

7.3.2 *Power*

Powers of the Dickey–Fuller one-sided t-test in (5.3) and of the one-sided t-test and the F-test in (7.2) are investigated in the simulation study of DeJong *et al.* (1992*a*, 1992*b*). Assuming the lag order $p-1=1$ in (6.20′) the powers of the t- and F-tests are very low against $\rho = 0.9$ with $T = 100$. I cannot mention a single number for the power as it depends upon a_1 in (6.20′) and the initial values as well as ρ and T, but I would say it is about 0.15 or 0.20. See also Agiakloglou and Newbold (1992) and Schmidt and Phillips (1992).

7.3.3 *Estimation of the long-run variance*

None of the test statistics that I gave above (except for the method in Pantula and Hall (1991)) estimates the long-run variance, and their limiting distributions do not contain the long-run variance either. However, in some other methods that I have not given above limiting distributions are made free from the long-run variance by an explicit estimator of this parameter. Explanations and cautions are required regarding this estimation. The σ^2 in (6.12) to (6.16) is (2π) times (the spectral density of $\{\Delta x_t\}$ at the zero frequency). The *non-parametric* estimate of σ^2 (the estimate without fitting a model of a finite number of parameters such as ARMA) is equivalent to the estimate of the spectral density at zero frequency.

(*a*) In general the estimate has a downward bias when $\{x_t\}$ and hence $\{\Delta x_t\}$ are demeaned or detrended and T is small, say less than 100. See Granger and Newbold (1986: 64) and Neave (1972).

(*b*) Earlier in (3.4) to (3.5′) the spectral density function was looked through the Bartlett window. Here I reproduce that explanation in a more general context. In estimating the spectral density function some weights such as (3.4) have to be placed on estimates of the autocovariance sequence. The weights are called lag window. The Fourier transform of such weights is called the spectral window (function),[3] and the Parzen window and the Tukey–Hanning window are widely used. See Fuller (1976: 296–9). The k in (3.4) also appears in weights other than that for the Bartlett window, and is called the truncation point in general. It has to be less than $T-1$ by construction, and in fact substantially less than T according to the spectral estimation theory. As a result it is as though we estimate the spectral density function looked through a window rather than the original

[2] I owe this point to Mototsugu Fukushige.
[3] The window is also called the 'kernel'.

spectral density function. This brings about a bias in the spectral estimate unless the original spectral density $f(\lambda)$ is constant over the entire frequency domain $[-\pi, \pi]$. To achieve the consistency, the spectral theory suggests we increase the truncation point k as $T \to \infty$ so that the spectral window (function), which is (3.6) in the case of the Bartlett window, becomes zero at $\lambda \neq 0$ and unity at $\lambda = 0$ as T expands to ∞. But a bias is inevitable in finite samples unless $f(\lambda) =$ a constant.

In relation to the long-run variance we are concerned with the bias of spectral estimate at $\lambda = 0$. If the original density is highest (lowest) at $\lambda = 0$ in its neighbourhood as illustrated by a solid curve in Figure 7.2(*a*) and (*b*), the windowed spectral density, the dotted curve, is lower (higher) than the original density at $\lambda = 0$. Especially in Schwert ARMA one can hardly expect a reasonable estimate of the spectral density at zero frequency in the case where T is about 100. In fact the difficulty in Schwert ARMA is analogous to the one in Section 3.2. We should avoid the non-parametric estimation of the long-run variance in analysing macroeconomic data in so far as we cannot rule out a Schwert ARMA.[4]

The parametric estimation of the long-run variance is simple, at least conceptually. The expression (6.26) may be used in the case of an AR.

The augmented Dickey–Fuller test in its original version or in the version of Said and Dickey (1984) does not use any estimate of the long-run variance. The problem there is instead how to determine lag orders as described in Sections 6.2.3 and 7.2.1.

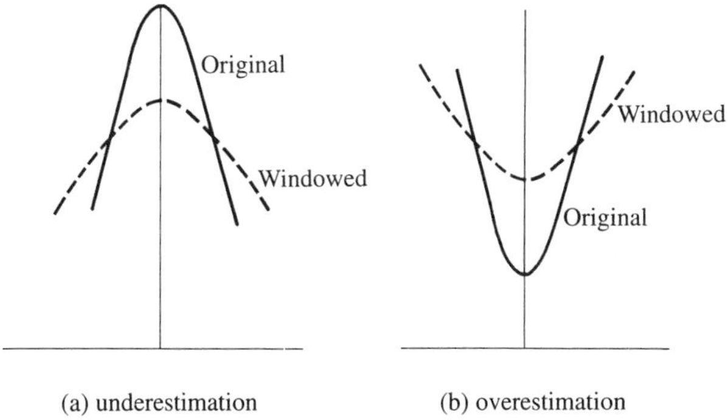

FIG. 7.2 *Original and windowed spectral density functions: (a) underestimation, (b) over-estimation*

[4] There have been attempts to modify the test statistics based upon the OLS using some estimates of δ and σ^2 in (6.12)–(6.16) so that, when applied to the serially correlated Δx, the limiting distribution of the modified statistics are identical to those given in Chapters 4 and 5 for the case where Δx_t is i.i.d. The estimates of δ and σ^2 are non-parametric. The simulation studies, Schwert (1989) and DeJong *et al.* (1992*a*) among others, reveal that the tests are inappropriate in regard to the size not only in the Schwert MA but in all other cases.

As for the selection of lag orders there are some guiding rules of thumb available for the finite sample situation, but there is no rule for the selection of truncation points in spectral estimates useful for the finite sample situation.

7.3.4 *Seasonal adjustment*

The historical data are annual, but the post-war data are quarterly. A problem with the latter is which of the seasonally unadjusted and adjusted data should be used. The most detailed investigation on this problem has been made in Ghysels and Perron (1993). The limiting *null* distribution of the t- and F-test statistics in Section 7.1 may be regarded virtually identical before and after seasonal adjustments by $X - 11$ method. A surprising finding is that when applied to the TS model the seasonal adjustment brings about an upward bias in the OLS estimator of α_1. This renders the tests in Section 7.1 less powerful when applied to the seasonally adjusted data. However, the bias is not large if the lag order, $p - 1$, in (7.1) is as large as 4 in the case of quarterly data (see also Diebold (1993)).

7.3.5 *Applications*

The method given in Section 7.1 has been applied in a large number of empirical studies. The best known is Nelson and Plosser (1982), which has initiated an outburst in the unit-root field. It investigates fourteen historical data in the USA: real GNP, nominal GNP, real per capita GNP, industrial production, employment, unemployment rate, GNP deflator, CPI, wage, real wage, money stock, velocity, bond yield, and stock prices. The t-test rather than the F-test is used, and the DS is not rejected on all but one of the fourteen series. The exception is unemployment rate. A large number of post-war data in a number of countries is investigated in Stultz and Wasserfallen (1985) and Wasserfallen (1986). Readers are also referred to Schwert (1987), and DeJong *et al.* (1992*a*) for studies of a large number of US time series. As for some specific variables Hakkio (1986) analyses exchange rates, and Rose (1988) investigates real rates of interest in many countries. Diebold (1988) investigates exchange rates in the framework of the autoregressive conditionally heteroskedastic (ARCH) model with a unit root. Baillie and Bollerslev (1989) analyse daily data of the spot and the forward foreign-exchange rates.

All the studies mentioned in the previous paragraph had appeared before we began to pay close attention to deterministic trends.

Highlights of Chapters 4–7

The logical aspects of Chapters 4–7 are undoubtedly complicated. Therefore the following reproduction of some of the more important points may help readers.

(1) Let $\{\varepsilon_t\}$ be i.i.d. with $E(\varepsilon_t) = 0$ and $E(\varepsilon_t^2) = \sigma_\varepsilon^2$, and let $v_t = \sum_{s=1}^{t} \varepsilon_s$. When $w(r)$, $1 \geq r \geq 0$, is the standard Wiener process,

$$T^{-3/2} \sum_1^T v_t \xrightarrow{D} \sigma_\varepsilon \int_0^1 w(r) dr, \tag{7.6}$$

$$T^{-2} \sum v_t^2 \xrightarrow{D} \sigma_\varepsilon^2 \int w(r)^2 dr, \tag{7.7}$$

$$T^{-1} \sum \varepsilon_t v_{t-1} \xrightarrow{D} \sigma_\varepsilon^2 \int w(r) dw(r). \tag{7.8}$$

(2) Demeaning and detrending have important effects upon the limiting distributions of relevant statistics. The following points provide a basis on which the effects can be assessed. Let $\hat{\boldsymbol{e}} \equiv (\hat{e}_1, \ldots, \hat{e}_T)'$ be the residual in regressing $v = (v_1, \ldots, v_T)'$ upon $\iota = (1, \ldots, 1)'$. Then

$$T^{-2} \sum \hat{e}_t^2 \xrightarrow{D} \sigma_\varepsilon^2 \int w_1(r)^2 dr,$$

where $w_1(r) \equiv w(r) - \int w(r) dr$.
See (4.14). Let $\tilde{\boldsymbol{e}} \equiv (\tilde{e}_1, \ldots, \tilde{e}_T)'$ be the residual in regressing $\boldsymbol{v} = (v_1, \ldots, v_T)'$ upon $(\iota, \boldsymbol{t})$, where $\boldsymbol{t} = (1, \ldots, T)'$. Then

$$T^{-2} \sum \tilde{e}_t^2 \xrightarrow{D} \sigma_\varepsilon^2 \int w_2(r)^2 dr,$$

where $w_2(r) \equiv w_1(r) - 12 \left(r - \frac{1}{2}\right) \int \left(s - \frac{1}{2}\right) w(s) ds$.
See (6.3) to (6.6) and (A3.10a).

(3) In Chapters 4–7 we have obtained asymptotically normal distributions in some cases, and non-standard distributions expressed as functionals of the Wiener process in others. Let $\{\varepsilon_t\}$ be i.i.d. with zero mean, and consider a model

$$x_t = \rho x_{t-1} + \varepsilon_t, \tag{7.9}$$

and OLS, $\hat{\rho}$. If $\rho^0 = 1$,

$$T(\hat{\rho} - 1) \xrightarrow{D} \left(\int w(r)^2 dr \right)^{-1} \left(\int w(r) dw(r) \right)$$

$$t\text{-statistic to test } \rho = 1 \xrightarrow{D} \left(\int w(r)^2 dr \right)^{-1/2} \left(\int w(r) dw(r) \right).$$

See (4.8) and (4.10). Consider a model

$$x_t = \mu + \rho x_{t-1} + \varepsilon_t, \tag{7.10}$$

and OLS, $(\hat{\mu}, \hat{\rho})$. If $\mu^0 \neq 0$ and $\rho^0 = 1$, $\{x_t\}$ contains a linear trend. $T^{3/2}(\hat{\rho} - 1)$ is asymptotically Gaussian, and the t-statistic to test $\rho = 1$ converges to $N(0, 1)$ (see Section 4.2.2). (However $(\hat{\rho} - 1)$ in the present OLS cannot be used for testing DS against TS in the presence of a deterministic linear trend. The test is inconsistent under the TS model, $x_t = \mu + \beta t + \rho x_{t-1} + \varepsilon_t$, $|\rho| < 1$, as demonstrated in Section 5.1) If $(\mu^0, \rho^0) = (0, 1)$, $\{x_t\}$ contains at most a constant trend, and

$$T(\hat{\rho} - 1) \xrightarrow{D} \left(\int w_1(r)^2 dr\right)^{-1} \left(\int w_1(r) dw(r)\right)$$

$$F\text{-statistic to test } (\mu, \rho) = (0, 1) \xrightarrow{D} \tfrac{1}{2}\left[\left(\int dw(r)\right)^2 + \left(\int w_1(r)^2 dr\right)^{-1} \left(\int w_1(r) dw(r)\right)^2\right].$$

See (4.16) for the former, and (6.10) for the latter. These statistics can be used for testing DS against TS when the deterministic trend is a priori confined to a constant. Finally consider a model

$$x_t = \mu + \beta t + \rho x_{t-1} + \varepsilon_t, \tag{7.11}$$

and OLS, $(\hat{\mu}, \hat{\beta}, \hat{\rho})$. If $\beta^0 \neq 0$ and $\rho^0 = 1$, $\{x_t\}$ contains a quadratic trend, and the situation is analogous to the case where $\mu^0 \neq 0$ and $\rho^0 = 1$ in (7.10). However, as stated in Section 5.2, the Dickey–Fuller test does not admit $\beta^0 \neq 0$ and $\rho^0 = 1$. If $(\beta^0, \rho^0) = (0, 1)$

$$T(\hat{\rho} - 1) \xrightarrow{D} \left(\int w_2(r)^2 dr\right)^{-1} \left(\int w_2(r) dw(r)\right)$$

$$F\text{-statistic to test } (\beta, \rho) = (0, 1) \xrightarrow{D} \tfrac{1}{2}\left[12\left(\int \left(r - \tfrac{1}{2}\right) dw(r)\right)^2 + \left(\int w_2(r)^2 dr\right)^{-1} \left(\int w_2(r) dw(r)\right)^2\right].$$

See (6.8*a*) for the former, and (6.8*c*) for the latter. These statistics can be used for testing DS against TS in possible presence of a deterministic trend.

(4) Suppose that $\{u_t\}$ is a stationary process with zero mean and long-run variance $\sigma^2 = \sum_{-\infty}^{\infty} \gamma_j$ with $\gamma_j = E(u_t u_{t+j})$. Let $v_t \equiv \sum_{s=1}^{t} u_s$. Then (7.6) and (7.7) hold after σ_ε^2 is replaced by σ^2, but (7.8) becomes

$$T^{-1} \sum u_t v_{t-1} \xrightarrow{D} \sigma^2 \int w(r) dw(r) + \sum_1^{\infty} \gamma_j.$$

See (6.14).

(5) Consider the case where $\{u_t\}$ is a stationary AR $(p-1)$. Then all the results on the *test statistics* in (3) above can be carried over with proper modifications through the Fuller reparametrization. Consider

$$\Delta x_t = (\alpha_1 - 1)x_{t-1} + \alpha_2 \Delta x_{t-1} + \ldots + \alpha_p \Delta x_{t-p+1} + \varepsilon_t,$$

and OLS, $(\hat{\alpha}_1, \hat{\alpha}_2, \ldots, \hat{\alpha}_p)$. If $\alpha_1^0 = 1$

$$t\text{-statistic to test } \alpha_1 = 1 \xrightarrow{D} \left(\int w(r)^2 dr\right)^{-1/2} \left(\int w(r)dw(r)\right),$$

which is free from nuisance parameters that comprise those for the AR $(p-1)$. $(\hat{\alpha}_2, \ldots, \hat{\alpha}_p)$ is asymptotically Gaussian (see Appendix (4.2)). Consider

$$\Delta x_t = \mu + (\alpha_1 - 1)x_{t-1} + \alpha_2 \Delta x_{t-1} + \ldots + \alpha_p \Delta x_{t-p+1} + \varepsilon_t,$$

and OLS, $(\hat{\mu}, \hat{\alpha}_1, \ldots, \hat{\alpha}_p)$. If $(\mu^0, \alpha_1^0) = (0, 1)$

$$F\text{-statistic to test } (\mu, \alpha_1) = (0, 1) \xrightarrow{D} \tfrac{1}{2}\left[\left(\int dw(r)\right)^2 + \left(\int w_1(r)^2 dr\right)^{-1}\left(\int w_1(r)dw(r)\right)^2\right].$$

Consider

$$\Delta x_t = \mu + \beta t + (\alpha_1 - 1)x_{t-1} + \alpha_2 \Delta x_{t-1} + \ldots + \alpha_p \Delta x_{t-p+1} + \varepsilon_t.$$

If $(\beta^0, \alpha_1^0) = (0, 1)$ then

$$F\text{-statistic to test } (\beta, \alpha_1) = (0, 1) \xrightarrow{D} \tfrac{1}{2}\left[12\left(\int \left(r - \tfrac{1}{2}\right) dw(r)\right)^2 + \left(\int w_2(r)^2 dr\right)^{-1}\left(\int w_2(r)dw(r)\right)^2\right].$$

However, the limiting distributions of *estimator* $T(\hat{\alpha}_1 - 1)$ contains nuisance parameters in every one of three models introduced above. See Appendix 4.1.

(6) Let us return to the i.i.d. $\{\varepsilon_t\}$, but unlike (2) above consider here regressing $\varepsilon = (\varepsilon_1, \ldots, \varepsilon_T)'$ upon ι. Let $\hat{\boldsymbol{e}} \equiv (\hat{e}_1, \ldots, \hat{e}_T)'$ be the residual, and denote $\hat{s}_t \equiv \sum_{i=1}^t \hat{e}_i$. Then

$$T^{-2} \sum \hat{s}_t^2 \xrightarrow{D} \sigma_\varepsilon^2 \int v_0(r)^2 dr,$$

where $v_0(r) \equiv w(r) - rw(1)$ (see (6.30)).
Then let $\tilde{\boldsymbol{e}} \equiv (\tilde{e}_1, \ldots, \tilde{e}_T)$ be the residual in regressing $\boldsymbol{\varepsilon}$ upon $(\iota, \mathbf{t})$. Then

$$T^{-2} \sum \tilde{s}_t^2 \xrightarrow{D} \sigma_\varepsilon^2 \int v_1(r)^2 dr,$$

where $v_1(r) = v_0(r) - 3(r^2 - r)w(1) + 6(r^2 - r)\int w(s)ds$.
The results in (5) and (6) are extended to different modes of deterministic trends in Hatanaka and Koto (1994).

8
Viewing the Discrimination as a Model Selection Problem including Deterministic Trends

In Chapters 5 and 7 a number of tests are derived under the specification that deterministic trends are linear, $\theta_0 + \theta_1 t$. Even though the tests are invariant to $\theta_1 =$ or $\neq 0$ they would be invalid if deterministic trends are other than a linear function of time. The successful discrimination between TS and DS depends on the valid selection of models for deterministic trends. In the present chapter polynomial trends and linear trends with intercept and slope changes are introduced. The judgement about DS vs. TS has to be made in conjunction with selection of modes of deterministic trends. This suggests a large array of models, and the encompassing theory in Mizon (1984) and Mizon and Richard (1986) will help us to organize our thinking regarding how to select the best one from this array of models in terms of their congruence with observations. The encompassing theory will be extended into a comparison of P-values for the testing for DS against TS and for the testing for TS against DS. Simulation results will be presented to investigate the separability of DS and TS models and the fairness of the comparison.

8.1 Various Modes of Deterministic Trends

A given stochastic process is decomposed into a deterministic part and a stochastic part. The deterministic part is not influenced by the stochastic part so that the former is exogenous to the latter. The deterministic trend is a (non-stochastic) function of time representing a slow and smooth movement. In terms of a polynomial function of time any orders higher than, say, a cubic are unlikely. This smoothness is attributed to that in exogenous variables of the economy such as resources, technology, etc. However, macroeconomic theories provide nothing useful for the model specification of deterministic trends. Especially with respect to the productivity growth the interpretations are divided between a version of the real business cycle theory and its criticism. At any rate sudden discrete changes are allowed in structures of deterministic trends only when they are thought to be caused by exogenous events such as wars, institutional changes, and possibly some decisions of governments and international organizations such as OPEC.

It is important to note that the deterministic trend in the TS model is the central line mentioned in Section 1.1.3. On the other hand the DS model has no central line. There the deterministic trend arises from $E(\Delta x_t)$ being non-zero, but there is no force operating to drive x_t to the deterministic trend. *Roles of deterministic trends are different between the DS and the TS models.*

Especially on the historical data but on the post-war data as well it is obvious from the time-series charts (and in fact borne out by statistical tests) that the linear trend is not adequate to represent deterministic trends in many economic time series. Perron (1989*a*, 1990) introduced structural changes in deterministic trends. His deterministic trend is

$$\theta_0 + \theta_1 I_{TB+1}(t) + \theta_2 t + \theta_3 \max\,(t - T_B, 0), \tag{8.1}$$

where $I_{TB+1}(t) = \begin{cases} 0 & \text{if } t < T_B \\ 1 & \text{if } t \geq T_B + 1. \end{cases}$,

representing changes in the slope and intercept at $t = T_B$. The analyses in Chapter 7 can be easily adapted to this deterministic trend. (7.1) is replaced by

$$\begin{aligned}(1-\rho L)(1 - a_1 L - \ldots - a_{p-1}L^{p-1})(x_t - \theta_0 - \theta_1 I_{TB+1}(t) - \theta_2 t \\ - \theta_3 \max\,(t - T_B, 0)) = \varepsilon_t.\end{aligned} \tag{8.2}$$

It follows from (6.21) that

$$\begin{aligned}&(1-\rho L)(1 - a_1 L - \ldots - a_{p-1}L^{p-1}) I_{TB+1}(t) \\ &\quad = (1-\alpha_1) I_{TB+1} + (\alpha_1 - \alpha_2 L - \ldots - \alpha_p L^{p-1}) U_{TB+1}(t),\end{aligned}$$

and $(1-\rho L)(1 - a_1 L - \ldots - a_{p-1}L^{p-1}) \max\,(t - T_B, 0)$

$$= (1-\alpha_1) \max\,(t - T_B, 0) + (\alpha_1 - \alpha_2 L - \ldots - \alpha_p L^{p-1}) I_{TB+1}(t),$$

where

$$U_{TB+1}(t) = \begin{cases} 1 & \text{if } t = T_{B+1} \\ 0 & \text{otherwise.} \end{cases} \tag{8.3}$$

Thus (8.2) is transformed into

$$\begin{aligned}x_t = \mu_0 + \mu_1 I_{TB+1}(t) + \beta_0 t + \beta_1 \max\,(t - T_B, 0) + \alpha_1 x_{t-1} \\ + \alpha_2 \Delta x_{t-1} + \ldots + \alpha_p \Delta x_{t-p+1} + \varepsilon_t + \xi_t,\end{aligned} \tag{8.4}$$

where ξ_t involves $U_{TB+j}(t)$, $j = 1, \ldots, p$ and $I_{TB+j}(t)$, $j = 2, \ldots, p$. In particular, $\mu_1 = (1-\alpha_1)\theta_1 + \alpha_1\theta_3$ and $\beta_1 = (1-\alpha_1)\theta_3$. The DS, $\rho = 1$, forces $(\beta_0, \beta_1, \alpha_1) = (0, 0, 1)$. $I_{TB+j}(t)$, $j = 2, \ldots, p$ are not distinguishable from $I_{TB+1}(t)$ asymptotically, and dropping $U_{TB+j}(t)$, $j = 1, \ldots, p$ has no effects upon asymptotic distributions of OLS-based test statistics. We can ignore ξ_t and proceed to the F-test for $(\beta_0, \beta_1, \alpha_1) = (0, 0, 1)$. The limiting distributions are given in Hatanaka and Koto (1994).

The intercept shift, $\theta_1 I_{TB+1}(t)$, in (8.1) requires a caution, which does not seem to be noticed in the literature on structural changes in the unit-root field.

The point is that θ_1 is *not asymptotically identified* if $\rho = 1$. (It is if $|\rho| < 1$.) This is seen from the Fisher information matrix of (8.2), assuming that $\{\varepsilon_t\}$ is Gaussian. It is analogous to the asymptotic unidentfiability of θ_0 in the model (7.1) in the case where $\rho = 1$, which has been pointed out in Schotman and van Dijk (1991*a, b*).

The trend function (8.1) contains four subclasses, (i) $\theta_1 = \theta_3 = 0$, i.e. a linear trend, (ii) $\theta_1 \neq 0$ and $\theta_3 = 0$, a shift in the intercept, (iii) $\theta_1 = 0$ and $\theta_3 \neq 0$, a slope change, and (iv) $\theta_1 \neq 0$ and $\theta_3 \neq 0$. Two kinds of model selection are involved. The first is to select one of the four subclasses, and the second is to select the breakpoint, T_B in the subclasses, (ii)–(iv). In Perron (1989*a*, 1990) and Perron and Vogelsang (1992*b*) both kinds of the model selection are made intuitively. Later Zivot and Andrews (1992), Banerjee, Lumsdaine, and Stock (1992), and Perron and Vogelsang (1992*a*) all proposed formal methods to select the most likely, *single* breakpoint, given one of the subclasses, (ii)–(iv).[1] They show that the procedure to select a breakpoint must be explicit in order to derive valid distributions of test statistics for DS against TS. Moreover, this consideration does make a difference in the results of tests on the historical and post-war time-series data. While the DS is rejected in most of the US time series in Perron (1989),[2] the DS is not rejected in many of them once the selection of a breakpoint is taken into consideration in the inference theory. The diametrically opposed emphases in the results of Banerjee, Lumsdaine, and Stock (1992) and Zivot and Andrews (1992) are, as I see them, associated with the difference regarding which of the historical and the post-war time series are emphasized. Raj (1992) confirms the result of Zivot and Andrews (1992) on the international scale.

As for the other kind of model selection, i.e. selection of one of the subclasses, it does not seem to have been examined seriously in the literature. Admittedly the presence of a particular mode of structural change is tested together with selection of a breakpoint, but alternative modes of deterministic trends are not compared to select one from them. For example, a quadratic trend could be an alternative to a linear trend with a slope change and, moreover, a breakpoint need not be selected in the quadratic trend.[3]

A number of specification analyses have borne out the importance of selecting appropriate models of deterministic trends. Rappoport and Reichlin (1989), Perron (1989, 1990), and Hendry and Neale (1991) all find that when the true generating process is trend stationary with a linear trend containing a change in its slope, the test for DS with a simple linear trend fails to reject the DS too often. In short, disregard of a complicated deterministic trend, which is real, unduly favours the DS. On the other hand, I would think that some guard is required against a risk of an unreal, complicated deterministic trend to favour the TS.

[1] Perron (1991*b*) further generalizes the method to allow for possibly multiple breakpoints for a given polynomial trend.

[2] The finding in Mills (1992) on the UK is contrary to Perron (1989).

[3] See Granger (1988*a*) for various forms of the trend function.

Those who have experiences with an extrapolation of economic time series would have recognized that parameters of trend functions vary a little by little as the sample period is altered, indicating necessity to introduce continuous but very slow time variations in parameters. I shall not discuss this problem, but it is advisable to keep in mind this somewhat shaky ground on which the discrimination between DS and TS is based.

A visual inspection of time-series charts for macroeconomic variables suggests plausibility of the following two kinds of non-stationarity in the variance. One is that big shocks enter into the system once in a while apart from small shocks that are continuously operating. See Balke and Fomby (1991). The other is that shocks in a part of the sample period have a larger variance than shocks in the other part. The former may well be a useful model for some macroeconomic variables such as interest rates in the USA in the last twenty years, but I have no experiences with the model. As for the latter kind of variance non-stationarity, it appears typically in historical data, in which the pre-war variance is larger than the post-war. Koto and Hatanaka (1994) show that disregarding the variance non-stationarity deteriorates only slightly the performance of our discrimination procedure to be presented below.

8.2 Encompassing and 'General-to-Specific' Principles on the Model Selection

The above discussions lead us to viewing the whole issue of DS vs. TS as a problem of model selection. The deterministic trends mentioned above are denoted as follows:

M^{1s}: possible change(s) in the slope of a linear trend,
M^{1c}: possible change(s) in the constant term of a linear trend, and
M^{1cs}: possible change(s) in the constant and slope of a linear trend.

Also let M^0, M^1, M^2, and M^3 be respectively a constant, a linear trend, a quadratic trend, and a cubic trend. The DS is denoted by subscript, 0, attached to these Ms and the TS by subscript, 1. Then the entire models under consideration are arrayed as in Figure 8.1.

The lines in Figure 8.1(a) indicate logical implication. Each of M_i^{1s}, M_i^{1c}, and M_i^{1cs}, $i = 0, 1$, is not a single model but a class of models that have different

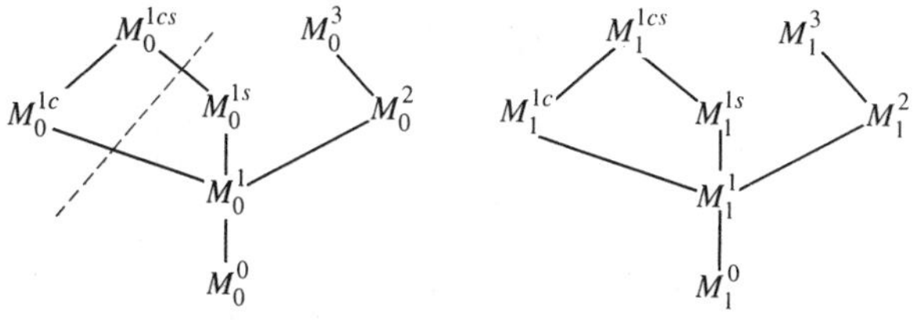

FIG. 8.1(a) *Array of models*

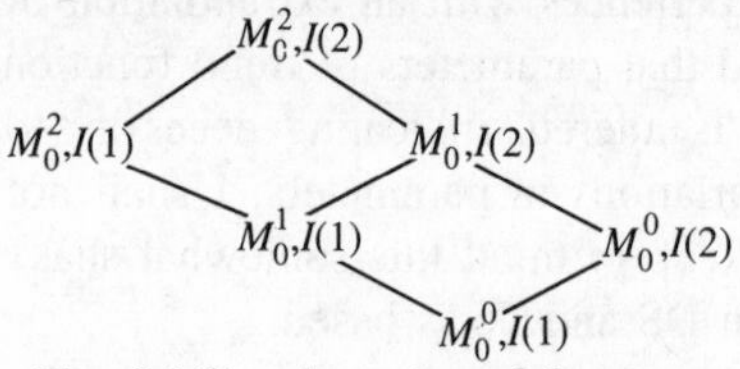

FIG. 8.1(*b*) *A portion of the array*

breakpoints at one or more time points. The broken line at the top left corner of Figure 8.1(*a*) is to remind readers that the intercept shift is not identified asymptotically in the DS model.

Each of DS models with different deterministic trends may consist of $I(2)$ and $I(1)$. Thus the portion of the tree that contains M_0^2, M_0^1, and M_0^0 is as shown in Figure 8.1(*b*).

Our task is to select the best model from this array.

8.2.1 'General-to-Specific' Principle

The theoretically precise inference for the model selection is feasible only for the case where the whole array consists of a single trunk line, for which readers are referred to Anderson (1971: 34–43). However, an important guideline is available for a general case. It is the general-to-specific principle, which has been proposed by Mizon (1977) and Hendry (1979), opposing to what had been done widely before then in practical studies of model selection. The proposal is to start the investigation from the most general model, going down to a more specific model only when it is justified by testing for the latter against the former. In the above array the DS models contain three trunk lines, $M_0^{1cs} \to M_0^{1c} \to M_0^1 \to M_0^0$, $M_0^{1cs} \to M_0^{1s} \to M_0^1 \to M_0^0$, and $M_0^3 \to M_0^2 \to M_0^1 \to M_0^0$. So do the TS models.

It is easy to test for a specific model against a general model in each of these trunk lines. Suppose that we wish to test for M_1^1 against M_1^{1cs} with a single *known* breakpoint.[4] The relevant model is (8.2), and we run the regression

$$x_t = \mu_0 + \mu_1 I_{TB+1}(t) + \beta_0 t + \beta_1 \max\,(t - T_B, 0) + \alpha_1 x_{t-1} \\ + \alpha_2 \Delta x_{t-1} + \ldots + \alpha_p \Delta x_{t-p+1} + \varepsilon_t, \qquad (8.5)$$

which is (8.4) except that ξ_t is dropped. If $|\rho| < 1$ and $\theta_1 = \theta_3 = 0$ so that the true values of β_1 and μ_1 are zero, the t-values of β_1 and μ_1 converge to

[4] On $M_i^{1s}, M_i^{1c}, M_i^{1cs}$, $i = 0, 1$ the selection of breakpoint is inseparable from the testing for M_i^1 against M_i^{1s} (or M_i^{1c} or M_i^{1cs}), and admittedly it is desirable to select the breakpoint by a formal inference procedure as Zivot and Andrews (1992), Banerjee, Lumsdaine, and Stock (1992), and Perron and Vogelsang (1992*a*, *b*) did for testing M_0^1 against M_1^{1s} (or M_1^{1c} or M_1^{1cs}). I point out, however, that the precise inference is not feasible for the model selection from the whole array of Figure 8.1(*a*) aside from the breakpoint, because six trunk lines are involved. In my opinion there is not much gain in adhering to the precise inference on the breakpoint only.

$N(0, 1)$ asymptotically. Next consider testing for M_0^1 against M_0^{1s} within the DS hypothesis, assuming $I(1)$. Since $(\beta_0, \beta_1, \alpha_1) = (0, 0, 1)$ in (8.4) is now a maintained hypothesis, we run the regression

$$\Delta x_t = \mu_0 + \mu_1 I_{TB+1}(t) + \alpha_2 \Delta x_{t-1} + \ldots + \alpha_p \Delta x_{t-p+1} + \varepsilon_t. \tag{8.6}$$

If the true value of $\mu_1 = \theta_3$ is zero, the t-value of μ_1 converges to $N(0, 1)$ asymptotically. Similar procedures can be designed for testing M_i^{j-1} against M_i^j, $i = 0, 1$, $j = 1, 2, 3$.

However, M_0^{1c} requires a caution. Because of the asymptotic unidentifiability mentioned above there is no formal asymptotic testing for the intercept shift in the DS model. My proposal is to look for an outlier in the series of $\Delta x_t = \mu_0 + \mu_1 U_{TB+1}(t) + u_t$, where $\{u_t\}$ is stationary with zero mean and $U_{TB+1}(t)$ is defined in (8.3). See Tsay (1988) for a survey of methods to identify outliers.

8.2.2 Encompassing principle

The traditional hypothesis testing is useful only for a comparison between two models that are in a nested relation. In Figure 8.1(a) any two models in different trunk lines are mutually non-nested. As for the comparison between two mutually non-nested general models, say M_0 and M_1, not necessarily those in Figure 8.1(a), Mizon (1984) and Mizon and Richard (1986) proposed the encompassing principle. To investigate how well M_0 encompasses M_1, to be abbreviated as $M_0 \xrightarrow{E} M_1$, we investigate a statistic of M_1, say $\hat{\beta}_1$. Derive the probability limit of $\hat{\beta}_1$ under the assumption that M_0 is the data-generating process (DGP). The probability limit often depends upon unknown parameters of M_0, and, if it does, any consistent estimators of the parameters are substituted for them, where the consistency is judged under the assumption that M_0 is the DGP. Let an estimator of the probability limit be denoted by $\hat{\beta}_{1(0)}$. The encompassing test statistic to see how well $M_0 \xrightarrow{E} M_1$ is $\hat{\phi}_{01} \equiv \hat{\beta}_1 - \hat{\beta}_{1(0)}$. Suppose further that with a statistic q, which serves as a normalizer of $\hat{\phi}_{01}$,

$$S_{01} \equiv T^{\alpha}\hat{\phi}_{01}/q$$

has a limiting distribution under M_0, where T is the sample size and α is a real number. S_{01} can be used for the analysis of $M_0 \xrightarrow{E} M_1$.

The following example is a special case of an encompassing analysis in Mizon (1984). Two alternative explanatory variables, x and z, are available for the explanation of y. Two alternative models are

$$M_0\colon\ \boldsymbol{y} = \boldsymbol{x}\gamma + \boldsymbol{u}$$

$$M_1\colon\ \boldsymbol{y} = \boldsymbol{z}\beta + \boldsymbol{v},$$

where $\boldsymbol{x}$ and $\boldsymbol{z}$ are each $T \times 1$ and non-stochastic, $\boldsymbol{x} \neq c\boldsymbol{z}$ with any scalar c, β, and γ are each scalar parameters, and $\boldsymbol{u}$ and $\boldsymbol{v}$ are distributed respectively in

$N(\mathbf{0}, \sigma_u^2 \boldsymbol{I}_T)$ and $N(\mathbf{0}, \sigma_v^2 \boldsymbol{I}_T)$. We are concerned with $M_0 \overset{E}{\to} M_1$. A statistic of M_1 is

$$\hat{\beta}_1 = (\boldsymbol{z}'\boldsymbol{z})^{-1}\boldsymbol{z}'\boldsymbol{y},$$

and we shall evaluate $\hat{\beta}_1$ under M_0. All mathematical expectations below are calculated assuming that $\boldsymbol{y}$ is in fact generated by M_0. Then

$$\beta_{1(0)} \equiv E(\hat{\beta}_1) = (\boldsymbol{z}'\boldsymbol{z})^{-1}\boldsymbol{z}'\boldsymbol{x}\gamma,$$

which involves a unknown parameter, γ, of M_0. The γ is estimated by OLS in M_0, and $\beta_{1(0)}$ is estimated by

$$\hat{\beta}_{1(0)} = (\boldsymbol{z}'\boldsymbol{z})^{-1}\boldsymbol{z}'\boldsymbol{x}(\boldsymbol{x}'\boldsymbol{x})^{-1}\boldsymbol{x}'\boldsymbol{y}.$$

The encompassing test statistic is

$$\hat{\phi}_{01} = \hat{\beta}_1 - \hat{\beta}_{1(0)} = (\boldsymbol{z}'\boldsymbol{z})^{-1}\boldsymbol{z}'\boldsymbol{M}_x\boldsymbol{y} = (\boldsymbol{z}'\boldsymbol{z})^{-1}\boldsymbol{z}'\boldsymbol{M}_x\boldsymbol{u}, \tag{8.7}$$

where $\boldsymbol{M}_x = \boldsymbol{I}_T - \boldsymbol{x}(\boldsymbol{x}'\boldsymbol{x})^{-1}\boldsymbol{x}'$. Then $E(\hat{\phi}_{01}) = 0$, and

$$\text{var}\,(\hat{\phi}_{01}) = \sigma_u^2(\boldsymbol{z}'\boldsymbol{z})^{-1}\boldsymbol{z}'\boldsymbol{M}_x\boldsymbol{z}(\boldsymbol{z}'\boldsymbol{z})^{-1}.$$

Let

$$\begin{aligned} S^2 &= \boldsymbol{y}'\boldsymbol{M}_x(\boldsymbol{I}_T - \boldsymbol{M}_x\boldsymbol{z}(\boldsymbol{z}'\boldsymbol{M}_x\boldsymbol{z})^{-1}\boldsymbol{z}'\boldsymbol{M}_x)\boldsymbol{M}_x\boldsymbol{y} \\ &= \boldsymbol{u}'(\boldsymbol{M}_x - \boldsymbol{M}_x\boldsymbol{z}(\boldsymbol{z}'\boldsymbol{M}_x\boldsymbol{z})^{-1}\boldsymbol{z}'\boldsymbol{M}_x)\boldsymbol{u}. \end{aligned} \tag{8.8}$$

Since $\boldsymbol{M}_x - \boldsymbol{M}_x\boldsymbol{z}(\boldsymbol{z}'\boldsymbol{M}_x\boldsymbol{z})^{-1}\boldsymbol{z}'\boldsymbol{M}_x$ is idempotent with rank $(T-2)$, (8.8) is $\sigma_u^2\chi^2(T-2)$. Since $(\boldsymbol{M}_x - \boldsymbol{M}_x\boldsymbol{z}(\boldsymbol{z}'\boldsymbol{M}_x\boldsymbol{Z})^{-1}\boldsymbol{z}'\boldsymbol{M}_x)(\boldsymbol{M}_x\boldsymbol{z}(\boldsymbol{z}'\boldsymbol{z})^{-1}) = 0$, (8.7) and (8.8) are independent. Writing

$$q = S((\boldsymbol{z}'\boldsymbol{z})^{-1}\boldsymbol{z}'\boldsymbol{M}_x\boldsymbol{z}(\boldsymbol{z}'\boldsymbol{z})^{-1})^{1/2}$$

it is seen that

$$S_{01} = \sqrt{(T-2)}(\hat{\phi}_{01}/q)$$

is distributed in the t-distribution with $(T-2)$ degrees of freedom.

For the standard DGP not involving either a stochastic or a deterministic trend Mizon (1984) and Mizon and Richard (1986) demonstrate that the above procedure for $M_0 \overset{E}{\to} M_1$ would be identical to the well-known likelihood ratio test for M_0 against M_1 if it were applied to the case where M_0 is nested in M_1 and if the statistic of M_1 is the Wald test statistic. If $M_1 \overset{E}{\to} M_0$ is investigated in the same situation with the maximum-likelihood estimator of M_0, $\sqrt{T}(\hat{\phi}_{10}/q) = o_p(1)$, i.e., M_1 encompasses M_0 with probability 1.

8.2.3 Comparison of P*-values*

Mizon (1984) has explained the encompassing in terms of the rejection and non-rejection dichotomy, but I shall consider it in terms of the P-value. Indeed if the limiting distribution contains no unknown parameters of M_0, we can determine the asymptotic P-value of an observed value of S_{01}. Provided that the finite sample distribution of S_{01} is well approximated by the limiting distribution, the P-value is an indicator to show the likelihood of an observed value of the statistic of M_1 if the DGP were M_0, or the degree in which behaviours of a statistic of M_1 can be interpreted by M_0.

So far we have investigated how well $M_0 \overset{E}{\rightarrow} M_1$. In comparing mutually non-nested and separate M_0 and M_1 we must also examine how well $M_1 \overset{E}{\rightarrow} M_0$ and form our judgement on the basis of both examinations. The encompassing, $M_1 \overset{E}{\rightarrow} M_0$, is analysed through a statistic, S_{10}, and the asymptotic P-value of S_{10} is P_{10} if the DGP is M_1.

In general the P-values are random variables because they are functions of observations. The joint p.d.f. of the bivariate random variable (P_{01}, P_{10}) is sketched in Figure 8.2. The DGP is a member of M_0 in Figure 8.2(a). If the asymptotic theory provides a good approximation, (P_{01}, P_{10}) is distributed close to the P_{01}-axis, and the marginal densities of P_{01} are uniform over [0, 1]. It can be roughly said that the higher the testing power of S_{10} is, the faster the marginal p.d.f. of P_{10} declines as we move away from the origin. The DGP is a member of M_1 in Figure 8.2(b). (P_{01}, P_{10}) is distributed close to the P_{10} axis, and the marginal densities of P_{10} are uniform.

If the observation at hand reveals large P_{01} and small P_{10}, it may be reasonable to judge that M_0 fits the data better than M_1. It is possible in small probabilities that both P_{01} and P_{10} are small, no matter which of M_0 and M_1 may contain the DGP. If that happens we would be unable to make a comparison between M_0 and M_1. If both P_{01} and P_{10} are large, it would mean that neither M_0 nor M_1 is the DGP.

I propose that the congruence of M_0 and M_1 to the observations be compared through P_{01} and P_{10}. M_0 is judged superior to M_1 if and only if $P_{01} > P_{10}$, and

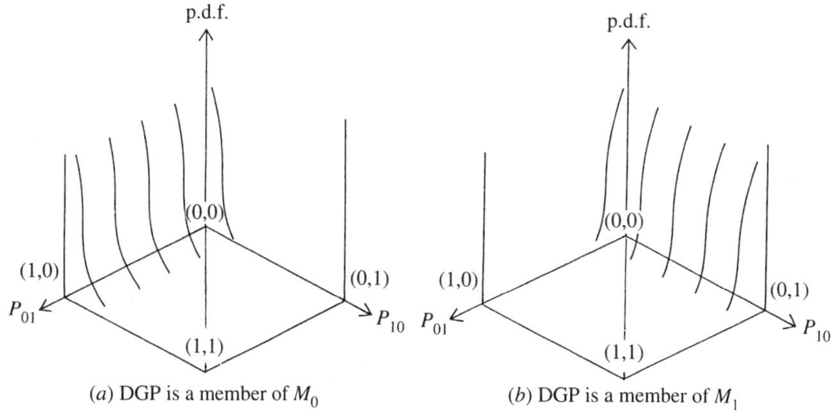

FIG. 8.2 *Illustrations of joint distributions of* P-*values: (a) DGP is a member of* M_0, *(b) DGP is a member of* M_1

vice versa. P_{01} and P_{10} are determined by the limiting null distributions of S_{01} and S_{10} respectively.

This criterion is fair if the joint distributions in Figures 8.2(*a*) and (*b*) are symmetric about the 45-degrees line connecting (0, 0) and (1,1) on the (P_{01}, P_{10}) plane. Or, summarizing the joint distributions compactly, the criterion is thought fair if the probability that $P_{01} < P_{10}$ in Figure 8.2(*a*) and the probability that $P_{01} > P_{10}$ in Figure 8.2(*b*) are equal. Here the fairness is judged on the basis of losses due to two kinds of wrong judgement. The former probability is that of deciding M_1 superior to M_0 when the DGP in fact belongs to M_0. The latter probability is that of deciding M_0 superior to M_1 when the DGP belongs to M_1. If the probability that $P_{01} < P_{10}$ exceeds the probability that $P_{01} > P_{10}$, our criterion has a bias in favour of M_1.

When the DGP belongs to M_0 the probability of correct judgement is that of $P_{01} > P_{10}$ in the joint distribution of (P_{01}, P_{10}) in Figure 8.2(*a*), and the performance of our model comparison under M_0 can be measured by this probability. The minimum requirement on the performance is that the probability of $P_{01} > P_{10}$ exceeds 0.5, because 0.5 can be achieved by tossing a coin without ever analysing relevant data.

Usually M_0 and M_1 are each parametric families of models. The asymptotic (marginal) distribution of P_{01} is, but the finite sample distribution is not invariant throughout different members of M_0 when the DGP belongs to M_0. As for P_{10} even the asymptotic (marginal) distribution is not invariant throughout different members of M_0, one of which is supposed to be the DGP. Therefore the finite sample joint distribution of (P_{01}, P_{10}) depends not just on which of M_0 and M_1 contains the DGP, but also on the particular parameter value of M_0 and/or M_1 that represents the DGP.

8.2.4 *Various encompassing tests*

We have two kinds of comparison between a non-nested pair of models in Figure 8.1(*a*). The first is comparisons within DS models, for example, between M_0^{1s} and M_0^2, and also within TS models, for example, between M_1^{1s} and M_1^2. The second kind of comparison is between a member of DS models and a member of TS models. The ultimate aim of our study, i.e. the discrimination between the DS and TS, is the second kind.

The F-test explained in Section 7.1 is an encompassing test for $M_0^1 \overset{E}{\to} M_1^1$. (7.1) is an AR version of M_1^1, and the OLS estimator of (β, α_1) in (7.2) is a statistic of M_1^1. Under M_0^1 we know that $(\hat{\beta}, \hat{\alpha}_1)$ converges in probability to (0, 1). Therefore $\hat{\phi}' = (\hat{\beta}, \hat{\alpha}_1 - 1)$ is an encompassing statistic for $M_0^1 \overset{E}{\to} M_1^1$. Being a vector statistic its normalization is made through taking a quadratic form of $(\hat{\beta}, \hat{\alpha}_1 - 1)$ with the inverse of a covariance matrix, and the result is what is known as the F-statistic to test for $(\beta, \alpha_1) = (0, 1)$.

As for the analysis of $M_0^0 \overset{E}{\to} M_1^0$ we can use the F-test given in Section 7.1 for the case where the deterministic trend is confined to a constant. However, the modes of deterministic trends need not be identical between M_0 and M_1. For $M_0^0 \xrightarrow{E} M_1^1$ the encompassing may be examined by the F-test for $(\mu, \beta, \alpha_1) = (0, 0, 1)$ in (7.2) because $\rho = 1$ forces μ to zero. Similar F-tests can be used for $M_0^1 \xrightarrow{E} M_1^{1s}$, $M_0^1 \xrightarrow{E} M_1^{1c}$, $M_0^1 \xrightarrow{E} M_1^{1cs}$, $M_0^{1s} \xrightarrow{E} M_1^{1s}$, $M_0^2 \xrightarrow{E} M_1^2$, $M_0^3 \xrightarrow{E} M_1^3$ etc. The test statistics and their limiting distributions are shown in Hatanaka and Koto (1994) and Koto and Hatanaka (1994).

Interpretation of the MA unit-root test as an encompassing test is more complicated. Consider the model and notations in Section 3.4, especially the simplest case, (3.11a) and (3.11b), where Δx_t is MA(1). The entire models may be indexed by δ. The stationary M_1^0 is represented by $\delta = 1$. A class of non-stationary models having a common value of δ and arbitrary values of θ_0 may be represented by that value of δ. Let $\sigma_\varepsilon^2 \boldsymbol{\Omega}(\delta)$ be the covariance matrix of $\boldsymbol{x}$ for a given δ. Then $\boldsymbol{\Omega}(1) = \boldsymbol{I}$. Let $\hat{\theta}_0(\delta)$ be the GLS estimator of θ_0 for a given δ, and $\hat{\boldsymbol{v}}(\delta) = \boldsymbol{x} - \hat{\theta}_0(\delta)\boldsymbol{e}$. Then $\hat{\boldsymbol{v}}(1)$ equals $\hat{\boldsymbol{v}}$ in Section 3.4. $\hat{\boldsymbol{v}}(\delta)'\boldsymbol{\Omega}(\delta)^{-1}\hat{\boldsymbol{v}}(\delta)$ is a statistic of the class of models indexed by δ. According to Saikkonen and Luukkonen (1993a) $\hat{\boldsymbol{v}}'\boldsymbol{DD}'\hat{\boldsymbol{v}}$ is the second-order derivative of $\hat{\boldsymbol{v}}(\delta)'\boldsymbol{\Omega}(\delta)^{-1}\hat{\boldsymbol{v}}(\delta)$ with respect to δ evaluated at $\delta = 1$. The above general definition of encompassing has dealt with a distance between a statistic $\hat{\beta}_1$ and its evaluation $\hat{\beta}_{1(0)}$, but we may extend the idea to the curvature.[5]

Extending the above reasoning to the case where Δx_t is an ARMA, (3.14′) with $\boldsymbol{\gamma}$ replaced by $\hat{\boldsymbol{\gamma}}$ can be used for the study of $M_1^0 \xrightarrow{E} M_0^0$. Moreover, by subtracting a linear trend from the original series as explained in Section 6.3 the MA unit-root test can be used for $M_1^1 \xrightarrow{E} M_0^1$. Hatanaka and Koto (1994) shows the limiting distributions to be used for $M_1^{1s} \xrightarrow{E} M_0^{1s}$, $M_1^{1c} \xrightarrow{E} M_0^{1c}$, $M_1^2 \xrightarrow{E} M_0^2$, $M_1^3 \xrightarrow{E} M_0^3$ etc.

The Saikkonen–Luukkonen test is useful to investigate how well a TS model encompasses a DS model when the two share an identical mode of deterministic trends, for example, $M_1^1 \xrightarrow{E} M_0^1$ and $M_1^{1s} \xrightarrow{E} M_0^{1s}$. But the test cannot be used when the two models have different modes of deterministic trends. I shall present a method that can be used for the encompassing from a TS model to a DS model in so far as the mode of deterministic trend in the TS model is more inclusive than or identical to that in the DS model. I shall illustrate the method by $M_1^1 \xrightarrow{E} M_0^0$. The DGP is

$$x_t = \theta_0 + \theta_1 t + v_t, \tag{8.9}$$

where $\{v_t\}$ is stationary with $E(v_t) = 0$ and $E(v_t^2) = \sigma_v^2$. The sample mean of Δx_t, $\hat{\mu}$, is a statistic of M_0^0. Evaluated under M_1^1 we see that plim $\hat{\mu} = \theta_1$, and θ_1 may be estimated by OLS along (8.9), which is denoted by $\hat{\theta}_1$. Let $\hat{\phi} \equiv \hat{\mu} - \hat{\theta}_1$. Then we have an identity

$$(T-1)(\hat{\mu} - \hat{\theta}_1) = (x_T - \hat{\theta}_0 - T\hat{\theta}_1) - (x_1 - \hat{\theta}_0 - \hat{\theta}_1) = e_T - e_1, \tag{8.10}$$

[5] The point optimal MA unit-root test in Saikkonen and Luukkonen (1993b) can be interpreted as an encompassing test in a simpler manner, but my work was nearly completed when it became available to me.

where $(e_1, \ldots, e_T)$ is the vector of residuals in the OLS. Under M_1^1

$$(T-1)(\hat{\mu}-\hat{\theta}_1) = x_T - x_1 - (T-1)\theta_1 - (T-1)\sum \tilde{t}v_t / \sum \tilde{t}^2,$$

where $\tilde{t} = t - (T+1)/2$. Since the last term is $O_p(T^{-1/2})$,

$$(T-1)(\hat{\mu}-\hat{\theta}_1) \approx v_T - v_1. \tag{8.11}$$

If $\{v_t\}$ is Gaussian, the right-hand side of (8.11) is $N(0, 2\sigma_v^2)$. If M_0^0 were the DGP, $(T-1)\hat{\phi}$ diverges at the speed of $\sqrt{T}$.

To use (8.10) for $M_1^1 \overset{E}{\rightarrow} M_0^0$ it is necessary to design an estimator of σ_v^2, which is consistent under M_1^1 and remains bounded in probability under M_0^0. This is because the test statistic is not $(T-1)(\hat{\mu}-\hat{\theta}_1)$, but

$$\frac{(T-1)(\hat{\mu}-\hat{\theta}_1)}{\sqrt{(2\hat{\sigma}_v^2)}}, \tag{8.12}$$

and if $\hat{\sigma}_v^2$ diverges at the speed of T the test would lack the consistency. One way to construct such $\hat{\sigma}_v^2$ is as follows. I shall write below as though $\{v_t\}$ is observable. In so far as the mode of deterministic trend in M_1 includes that in M_0, $(v_1, \ldots, v_T)$ can be estimated by $(e_1, \ldots, e_T)$. Fit an AR model to $\{v_t\}$, calculate the dominating root, $\hat{\rho}$, of the characteristic polynomial, and choose a sufficiently large n such that $|\hat{\rho}|^n$ can be regarded zero, assuming that $|\hat{\rho}| < 1$. Let $\boldsymbol{\gamma}' \equiv (\gamma_0, \gamma_1, \ldots, \gamma_{n+1})$ be the vector of autocovariances of $\{v_t\}$ for lags $0, 1, \ldots, n+1$. The first element, γ_0, is σ_v^2. Let $\boldsymbol{\gamma}'_\Delta \equiv (\gamma_{\Delta_0}, \gamma_{\Delta_1}, \ldots, \gamma_{\Delta_n})$ be the vector of autocovariances of $\{\Delta v_t\}$ for lags $0, 1, \ldots, n$, and note that $\boldsymbol{\gamma}_\Delta$ can be estimated consistently from $\{\Delta v_t\}$, no matter whether the DGP is M_1^1 or M_0^0. The two vectors $\boldsymbol{\gamma}$ and $\boldsymbol{\gamma}_\Delta$ are related through a known matrix. Let e_i be the ith unit vector of $(n+1)$ elements, $\boldsymbol{F}_1$ be $(n+1)\times(n+1)$ and equal to $2\boldsymbol{I}_{n+1} - \boldsymbol{L}^* - \boldsymbol{L}^{*'} - \boldsymbol{e}_1\boldsymbol{e}'_2$, where $\boldsymbol{L}^*$ has unity one line below the main diagonal and zeros elsewhere, and $\boldsymbol{F} = (\boldsymbol{F}_1, -\boldsymbol{e}_{n+1})$. Then $\boldsymbol{F}\boldsymbol{\gamma} = \boldsymbol{\gamma}_\Delta$. Assuming $\gamma_{n+1} = 0$ and thus writing $\boldsymbol{\gamma}' = (\boldsymbol{\gamma}'_*, 0)$, we obtain $\boldsymbol{F}_1\boldsymbol{\gamma}_* = \boldsymbol{\gamma}_\Delta$, which can be solved for the first element of $\boldsymbol{\gamma}_*$, i.e. σ_v^2. The solution is bounded even under M_0^0 because the estimate of $\boldsymbol{\gamma}_\Delta$ is, even though the assumption that $\gamma_{n+1} = 0$ is invalid under M_0^0.

This kind of test can be performed for $M_1^{1s} \overset{E}{\rightarrow} M_0^1$, $M_1^{1c} \rightarrow M_0^1$, and moreover extended to $M_1^{i+1} \overset{E}{\rightarrow} M_0^i$, $i = 1, 2$ by modifying $\hat{\mu}$ as the sample mean of $\Delta^i x_t$. Relations analogous to (8.10) always hold. I shall call this kind of test the $\hat{\mu}$ test.

8.3 Simulation Studies on the Comparison of P-values

There are at least three reasons why simulation studies are needed on the comparison of P-values proposed in Section 8.2.3 above.

1. All the encompassing tests given in Section 8.2.4 are based upon asymptotic theories, whereas tests will be applied to the time-series data with T ranging from 80 to 180. The only feasible determination of P-values is to assume that the exact, finite sample distributions of test statistics are identical to the limiting distributions under the null hypotheses. Discrepancies between the finite sample and the limiting distributions are revealed as deviations of the marginal distributions of P_{01} and/or P_{10} from the uniform distributions, and the deviations in turn might result in asymmetry of the joint p.d.f.s about the 45-degrees line between Figures 8.2(a) and (b).

2. Related to (1) above is a possible difference between the powers of the test for DS against TS and the test for TS against DS, which would result in asymmetry of the joint p.d.f.s between Figures 8.2(a) and (b).

3. Earlier in Section 2.4 I said that the DS and TS hypotheses are not separate. A serious problem is how far apart the values of discriminating parameters should be in order to differentiate the DS and TS hypotheses with $T = 80$ to 180. The near-boundary cases between the DS and TS consist of the TS models that are close to DS and DS models that are close to the TS. The former can be represented by the dominating root of characteristic polynomials of AR for x_t being close to unity. The latter can be represented by the spectral density of Δx_t in the Schwert ARMA declining as one moves on the frequency domain towards its origin.

In the model

$$(1 - \rho L)\Delta x_t = (1 - \delta L)\varepsilon_t, \tag{8.13}$$

where $\{\varepsilon_t\}$ is i.i.d. with $E(\varepsilon_t) = 0$ and $E(\varepsilon_t^2) = 1$, (1) if $\delta = \rho$ (8.13) is a random-walk model for $\{x_t\}$; (2) if $\delta = 1$ and $|\rho| < 1$, (8.13) is a stationary AR(1) with root, ρ; and (3) if $1 > \delta > \rho > -1$, (8.13) is a Schwert ARMA for Δx_t defined in Section 7.2.2, generating $\{x_t\}$ that is DS but close to TS.

Time-series data with $T = 100$ are generated using each of the above three types of DGP. The augmented Dickey–Fuller test for $M_0^0 \overset{E}{\rightarrow} M_1^0$ and the Saikkonen–Luukkonen test for $M_1^0 \overset{E}{\rightarrow} M_0^0$ are run for each one of the time series. The superscripts 0 on these Ms mean that the data are treated as though they might contain unknown constants. The Saikkonen–Luukkonen test is implemented as described in Section 3.4.2, especially after (3.15′). Lag orders in the AR fitting are determined by the general-to-specific principle as described in Section 7.2.1 with 5% significance level.[6] The $p_{\max}$ in types (1) and (2) is 10, and that in (3) is 20.[7] The AR representation of (8.13) in the form of (6.21) is given by

$$\alpha_1 = 1, a_i = \alpha_{i+1} = (\rho - \delta)\delta^{i-1}, \qquad i = 1, 2, \dots .$$

[6] In fact we choose the lag order one higher than the one determined by the general-to-specific principle.

[7] Since we are not supposed to know the DGP we should adopt the same $p_{\max}$ in the three types of DGP. We intended to save the computing time as it increases with $p_{\max}$.

How large lag orders are required in AR approximations depends upon $|\rho - \delta|$ as well as δ.

Compiling 5,000 replications of simulation results, Figures 8.3–8.7 show the joint distributions of P-values of the Dickey–Fuller statistic and the Saikkonen–Luukkonen statistic. These P-values will be written P_{DF} and P_{SL} respectively. The DGP in Figure 8.3 is a random walk, the case where $\delta = \rho$ in (8.13). The joint distribution in this figure is found just as we should expect from the asymptotic theory. Most of the probability is concentrated in the region in which P_{SL} is low, indicating that the Saikkonen–Luukkonen test is powerful against the random walk even when the lag order is determined from data. P_{DF} is distributed roughly uniformly, which means that the finite sample distribution of the Dickey–Fuller statistic with $T = 100$ is well approximated by its limiting distribution even when the lag order is determined from data. The probability that $P_{DF} > P_{SL}$ is 0.85. Our criterion provides in high probability the correct judgement in discriminating DS and TS.

The DGP in Figure 8.4 is a case of Schwert ARMA, $\delta = 0.95$, $\rho = 0.928$ in (8.13), of which the spectral density function is graphed in Figure 7.1(*a*). It is a DS model that is close to TS. The joint distribution in Figure 8.4 reveals fairly good performance of our encompassing procedure. The probability of correct judgement, i.e. $P_{DF} > P_{SL}$, is 0.77, which is only slightly worse than in the previous random walk. The Dickey–Fuller test in the mode of Said and Dickey (1984) has its finite sample null distribution close to the asymptotic distribution when the AR lag orders are chosen as prescribed above. The Saikkonen–Luukkonen test has adequate power.

The DGP in Figure 8.5 is another case of Schwert ARMA, $\delta = 0.8$, $\rho = 0$ in (8.13), of which the spectral density function is shown in Figure 7.1(*b*). This is a model investigated in Schwert (1989), and may be thought closer to TS than the previous one is. Here the probability that $P_{DF} > P_{SL}$ is 0.70, indicating performance worse than in the previous Schwert ARMA. While the Saikkonen–Luukkonen test retains adequate power, the Dickey–Fuller test in the

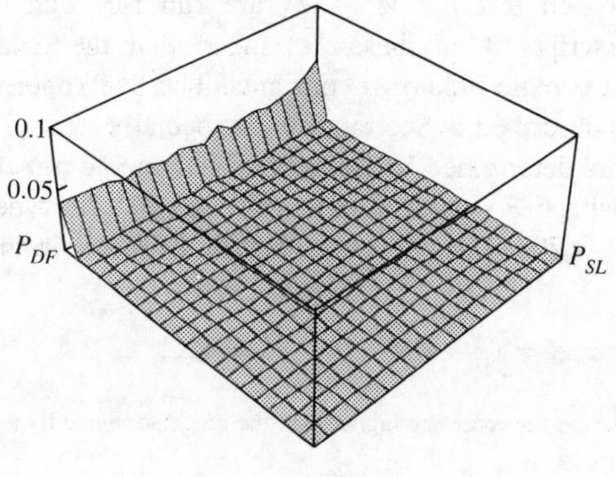

FIG. 8.3 *Joint distributions of* P-*values (random walk)*

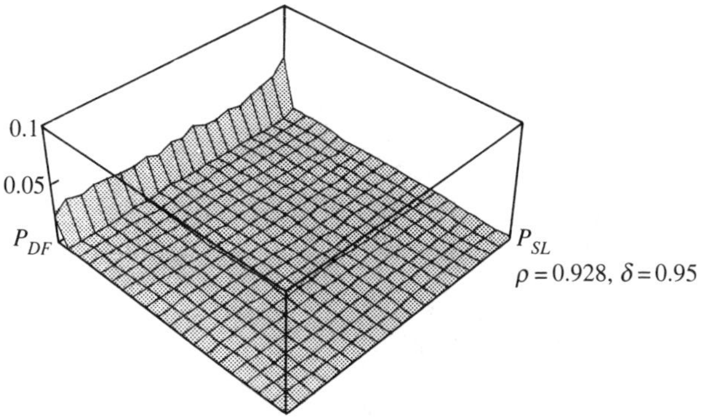

FIG. 8.4 *Joint distributions of* P-*values (Schwert ARMA, I)*

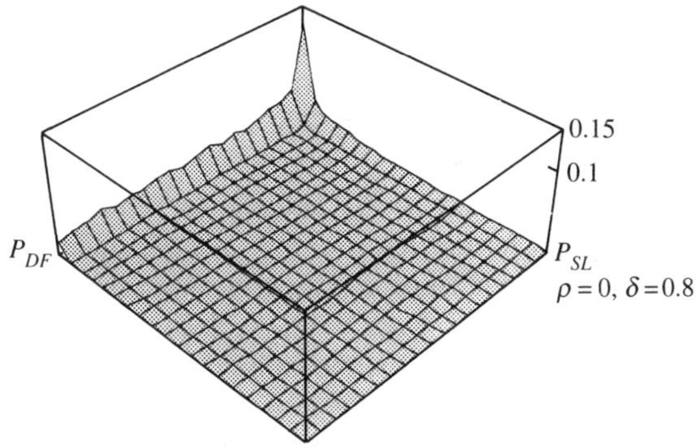

FIG. 8.5 *Joint distributions of* P-*values (Schwert ARMA, II)*

mode of Said and Dickey (1984) has a large-size distortion indicating that the probability of $0 \leq P_{DF} < 0.05$ is as large as 0.30, and causing a sharp peak of joint probabilities of (P_{DF}, P_{SL}) at the origin. Nevertheless one would perhaps be relieved by the probability of correct judgement being 0.70, because the result in Schwert (1989) was miserable. In part this is due to our encompassing analysis performed in both $DS \overset{E}{\rightarrow} TS$ and $TS \overset{E}{\rightarrow} DS$ whereas Schwert (1989) had $DS \overset{E}{\rightarrow} TS$ only.

The DGP in Figure 8.6 is a stationary AR(1) with $\rho = 0.8$, which is taken as a value somewhat displaced from $\rho = 1$. Most of the probability is assembled in the region in which P_{DF} is small, indicating that the Dickey–Fuller test is powerful against $\rho = 0.8$. But the power seems to be less than that of the Saikkonen–Luukkonen statistic against $\rho = 1$ revealed in Figure 8.3. The marginal distribution of P_{SL} is somewhat distorted from being uniform over [0, 1]. There is some size distortion when the Saikkonen–Luukkonen test is

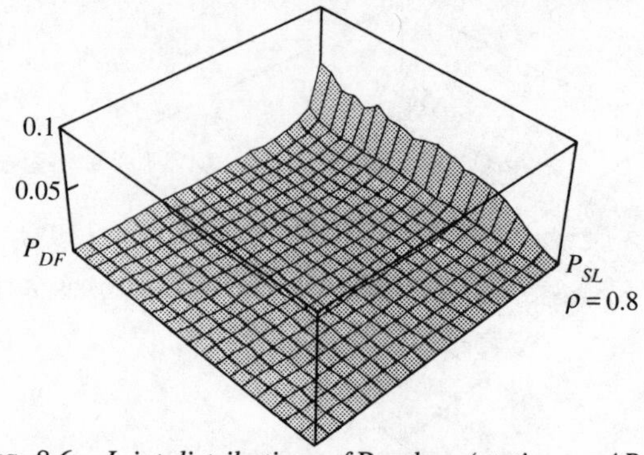

FIG. 8.6 *Joint distributions of* P-*values (stationary AR, I)*

implemented as in Section 3.4.2 with a lag order determined from data. Nevertheless the probability that $P_{SL} > P_{DF}$ is 0.85, and there is a high probability that our criterion provides the correct discrimination between DS and TS.

The DGP in Figure 8.7 is a stationary AR(1) with $\rho = 0.9$, which is closer to the random walk than the DGP in Figure 8.6. A considerable probability is located in the region in which both P_{SL} and P_{DF} are low. The Dickey–Fuller statistic does not have power against $\rho = 0.9$, and the Saikkonen–Luukkonen statistic has a significant size distortion. The probability that $P_{SL} > P_{DF}$ is only 0.60, and it must be admitted that our criterion does not work. With $T = 100$ $\rho = 0.9$ presents a TS model that is sufficiently close to DS.

Common to all five figures is the finding that the region in which both P_{DF} and P_{SL} are larger than, say, 0.3 has virtually zero probability. If both P-values are found larger than 0.3 in our empirical studies, we should suspect model misspecification. The misspecification must be on some parts of the model other than the lag order, because the lag order has been determined from the data in all of the four figures.

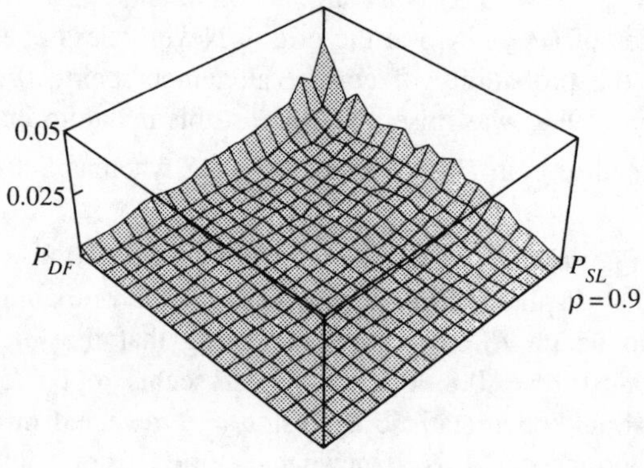

FIG. 8.7 *Joint distributions of* P-*values (stationary AR, II)*

On the other hand it is seen that both P-values are low far more frequently in the DGPs (such as Figures 8.5 and 8.7) near the boundary between DS and TS than in the other DGPs that are definitely TS or definitely DS. Both P-values being low might be taken as indication of boundary cases.

Our criterion is fair in comparing the random walk, which is DS, and the stationary AR(1) with $\rho = 0.8$, which is TS. Two probabilities of wrong decisions, i.e. the probability that $P_{SL} < P_{DF}$ in the former model and the probability that $P_{SL} < P_{DF}$ in the latter, are both 0.15. However, our criterion is not fair when a model near the boundary between DS and TS is one part in comparison. When the random-walk model, which is DS, is compared with the AR(1) with $\rho = 0.9$, which is TS, the probability that $P_{SL} > P_{DF}$ in the former model is 0.15, while the probability that $P_{SL} < P_{DF}$ in the latter is 0.40. The probability of mistaking a TS model for DS exceeds the probability of mistaking the DS model for the TS. The bias is in favour of DS. Likewise there is a bias in favour of TS between a Schwert ARMA and AR(1) with $\rho = 0.8$. In short our criterion is fair in comparing separable models but unfair in comparing inseparable models, admittedly a rather obvious result.

More simulation results are found in Koto and Hatanaka (1994). It includes results on stationary ARs such as $(1 - 0.9L)(1 - 0.8L)x_t = \varepsilon_t$ and $(1 - 0.95L)x_t = \varepsilon_t$ for DGP. The probability of correct discrimination is less than 0.5, that is, worse than tossing a coin. *Characteristic roots between 0.9 and 1.0 are not distinguishable from a unit root with* $T = 100$,[8] and this statement does not assume a particular unit of time.

[8] Fukushige, Hatanaka, and Koto (1994) reached the same conclusion using a discrimination method different from the one adopted here.

9
Results of the Model Selection Approach

Based upon the Bayesian analysis to be reviewed in Chapter 10, Schotman and van Dijk (1991*b*) and Koop (1992) explicitly and Phillips (1991*b*) implicitly present a tentative conclusion that real economic variables are trend stationary *in so far as the US historical data are concerned*. The difference stationarity is also questioned in Rudebuch (1992) using the resampling method, and in Dejong *et al*. (1992*b*) and Kwiatkowski *et al*. (1992),[1] using what may be interpreted as a prototype encompassing method. As for the *post-war* annual data of real outputs a Bayesian analysis in Schotman and van Dijk (1993) reveals that those in eight out of sixteen OECD countries are DS, those in two countries are TS, and the rest undecided.

We shall investigate *both the historical data and post-war quarterly data* in the USA. As for the historical data we analyse real GNP, real wage, real rate of interest, and unemployment rate as the real economic variables, to which are added nominal GNP, CPI, stock price, nominal rate of interest, and nominal money stock. The basic parts of the data set are the Nelson–Plosser (1982) data updated by Schotman and van Dijk (1991*b*) to 1988.[2] All variables other than unemployment rate and interest rate are in logarithmic scales.[3] As for the post-war data of the USA we analyse real GDP, real consumption, real wage, real rate of interest, and unemployment rate, to which are added nominal GNP, CPI, stock price, and nominal money stock. All the post-war data are quarterly and seasonally adjusted, if required, by X-11 method.[4] The nominal rate of interest is deleted from the post-war data set because of its conspicuous heteroskedasticity in Δx_t and possibility that the integration order may not be constant over time.

The following is a summary of results that are presented in Hatanaka and Koto (1994) in greater details. In all the tests we have adopted AR approximations to ARMA models, and the lag orders have been determined as described in Section 7.2.1 by the t-tests of highest-order coefficients.

[1] Kwiatkowski *et al*. (1992) perform a type of MA unit test as well as Dickey–Fuller test, though they do not refer to the encompassing analysis. Their MA unit-root test uses a non-parametric estimator of long-run variance.

[2] The real rate of interest is not in Nelson and Plosser (1982).

[3] See Section 2.5 on the logarithmic transformation.

[4] See Section 7.3.4 on the seasonal adjustment.

9.1 Deterministic Trends Amenable to the DS and the TS

I begin with the selection of models for deterministic trends, which is to be made separately within the DS models and within the TS models. A word of warning is appropriate in this regard. *When your eyes move along a rough contour of time-series charts such as Figure 9.1(a), you are tacitly assuming that the time series has a central line, i.e. it is trend stationary.*

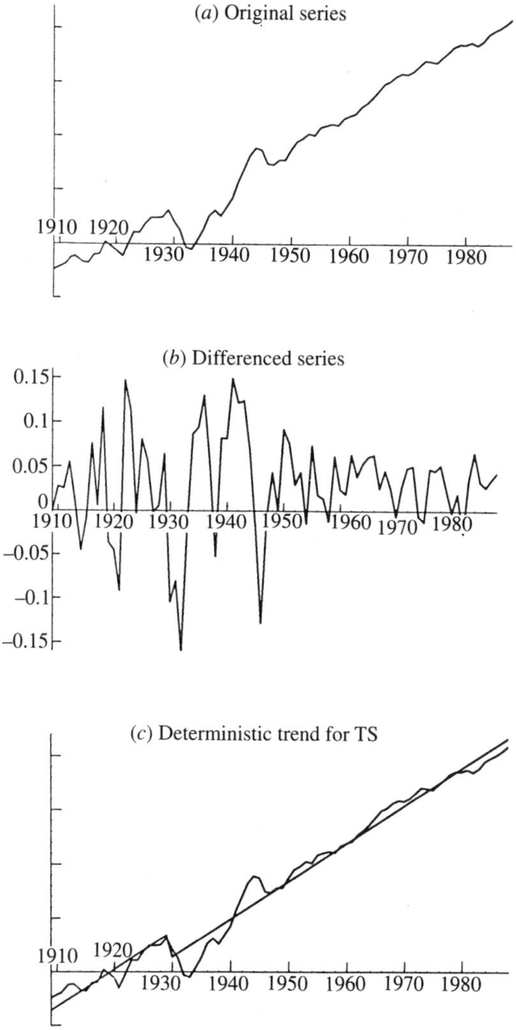

FIG. 9.1 *Historical data of real GNP, log: (a) Original series, (b) Differenced series, (c) Deterministic trend for TS*

Our model selection of deterministic trends is based on hypothesis testing, using equations such as (8.5) or (8.6). The results are that modes of the deterministic trends amenable to DS are often different from those amenable to TS, and that generally *deterministic trends for DS are simpler, often lacking structural changes, than those for TS.*[5] Determination of modes of deterministic trends is often difficult for TS.

These points may be illustrated by the historical data of real GNP. The chart is given in Figure 9.1(*a*). Virtually all the past studies concluded that a linear trend with an intercept shift, M^{1c}, fits the data with 1930 as the breakpoint (1930 is the beginning of the new regime.) Figure 9.1(*b*) shows the series of $\{\Delta x_t\}$, and we see no evidence of an outlier about the Great Crash or at any time. Moreover, tests with equations such as (8.6) reveal that neither the difference in means of Δx_t before and after 1929 nor the linear (or quadratic) trend in Δx_t is significant. Thus the best model of deterministic trend within the DS hypotheses is a simple, linear trend. On the other hand the test with equation (8.5) for TS models shows that the intercept shift is indeed significant but the slope change is not. Thus M_1^{1c} with breakpoint at 1930 is the best model of deterministic trend within the TS hypothesis (see Figure 9.1(*c*)).

As stated at the beginning of Chapter 8 structural changes in deterministic trends are exogenous to the stochastic parts of the variables. There may be doubts about the Great Crash being regarded as exogenous to the stochastic part of real GNP. Such interpretation is necessitated if the stochastic part is to be stationary, but it is not if the stochastic part is non-stationary with a unit root.

In general, different models tend to explain different aspects of observations, but the models that explain relatively a wider range of aspects (i.e. wider endogeneity) are thought superior to other models. Moreover, models with constant parameters are also superior to models with time-varying parameters. In terms of these criteria the DS models are superior to the TS models.

Concerning the historical data other than real GNP, the real and nominal rates of interest and stock price present some difficulties in determining modes of deterministic trends especially for the TS models. The difficulties are somewhat reduced in the post-war quarterly data.

9.2 Discrimination between TS and DS

The model selection by the encompassing principle compares different models in terms of their congruence with statistical observations. What seems to be the ideal procedure to discriminate DS and TS in the array, Figure 8.1(*a*), consists of the following steps: (i) assuming that the DGP is DS, choose the best model of deterministic trend in DS; (ii) assuming that the DGP is TS, choose the best model of deterministic trend in TS; (iii) investigate how well the DS model chosen in (i) encompasses the TS with the most general model of deterministic

[5] One exception is real rate of interest in the historical data.

trends; and (iv) see how well the TS model chosen in (ii) encompasses the DS with the most general model of deterministic trends. The ultimate discrimination between DS and TS is made by comparing the encompassing capability in (iii) and (iv) measured by the P-values.

This procedure cannot be adopted because I am unable to find a method that works well with $T = 100$ or so for step (iv), in which the model of deterministic trend in DS subsumes that in TS. I shall follow steps (i) and (ii) but then proceed to (iii′) in which we see how well the DS model chosen in (i) encompasses the TS model chosen in (ii), and finally (iv′) to see how well the TS model chosen in (ii) encompasses the DS model in (i). This procedure has a drawback in that selection of the best model of deterministic trends in (i) does not mean much when the DGP is TS. This selection is not used in (iv) but used in (iv′). Nevertheless step (iv′) is feasible because we have not encountered the best model of deterministic trends in DS properly subsuming that in TS as explained in Section 9.1 above. Incidentally, step (iii) is feasible, but the symmetrical treatment of DS and TS necessitates modification of (iii) into (iii′).

9.2.1 US historical data

In the historical data real GNP and real wage may be near the boundary between DS and TS; real rate of interest and unemployment rate are judged TS; CPI is $I(1)$ but not $I(2)$; and stock price, interest rate, and money stock are judged DS. These are the conclusions reached in Hatanaka and Koto (1994). Here I shall present the analysis on real GNP, 1909–88. It was found in the previous section that the best model of deterministic trend is a linear trend for DS while it is a linear trend with an intercept shift in 1930 for TS. Thus we shall perform our encompassing analysis between M_0^1 and M_1^{1c}.

Let us begin with $M_0^1 \overset{E}{\rightarrow} M_1^{1c}$. This is investigated using a type of the augmented Dickey-Fuller test. Consider

$$\Delta x_t = \mu_0 + \mu_1 I_{1930}(t) + \beta t + (\alpha_1 - 1)x_{t-1} + \alpha_2 \Delta x_{t-1} + \dots$$
$$+ \alpha_p \Delta x_{t-p+1} + \text{error}, \qquad (9.1)$$

with $I_{TB+1}(t)$ defined below (8.1). If $\alpha_1 < 1$ (9.1) defines a linear trend with an intercept shift at 1930, i.e. M_1^{1c}. If $(\mu_1, \beta, \alpha_1) = (0, 0, 1)$, (9.1) represents a DS model with a linear trend, i.e. M_0^1. The F-test is run for $(\mu_1, \beta, \alpha_1) = (0, 0, 1)$. In Koto and Hatanaka (1994) the limiting distribution of the test statistic under M_0^1 is tabulated by a simulation method described in Section 7.3.1. It is assumed that $(T - T_B)/T \equiv \lambda$ is kept fixed while T goes to infinity. Since (1988–1929)/(1988–1908) is close to 0.7, the table for $\lambda = 0.7$ is reproduced in Table 9.1, where p and x represent those in

$$p = \int_0^x f(z)dz,$$

with $f(\cdot)$ denoting the limiting p.d.f. of the statistic.

TABLE 9.1 *Limiting cumulative distribution of the statistic for* $M_0^1 \overset{E}{\rightarrow} M_1^{1c}$, $\lambda = 0.7$

p	0.1	0.2	0.3	0.4	0.5	0.6	0.7	0.8	0.9	0.95
x	1.45	1.79	2.08	2.26	2.66	2.98	3.35	3.83	4.56	5.23

To implement the F-test we first determine lag order $(p-1)$ in (9.1), which is the order of AR other than $(1-\rho L)$ as shown, for example, in (7.1) and (7.2). In the present data the highest lag order term, α_p, has t value equal to 2.04 with $(p-1)=7$. The F-test statistics for $(p-1)=7$ to 10 range between 7.0 and 9.0. Table 9.1 shows that their P-values are much less than 0.05.

As for $M_1^{1c} \overset{E}{\rightarrow} M_0^1$, we can use the $\hat{\mu}$ test. It was explained in (8.10) and (8.11) for $M_1^1 \overset{E}{\rightarrow} M_0^0$, and the method can easily be extended to $M_1^{1c} \overset{E}{\rightarrow} M_0^1$. The $\hat{\mu}$ is still the sample mean of Δx_t, which is a statistic of M_0^1. Since M_1^{1c} has deterministic trend, $\theta_0 + \theta_1 I_{1930}(t) + \theta_2 t$, it is seen that plim $\hat{\mu} = \theta_2$, which is estimated by regressing x_t upon $(1, I_{1930}(t),\ t)$. Analogously to (8.10) we have

$$(T-1)(\hat{\mu} - \hat{\theta}_2) = e_T - e_1,$$

where $(e_1, \ldots, e_T)$ are the residuals. It is again necessary that $\hat{\sigma}_v^2$ remains bounded under M_0^1. In the present case $n = 20$ is found adequate in estimating $\hat{\sigma}_v^2$ by the method described below (8.12). The limiting distribution of the $\hat{\mu}$-test statistic is $N(0, 1)$, and the P-value is about 0.2 in the present case.

The P-value in $M_1^{1c} \overset{E}{\rightarrow} M_0^1$ is larger than the P-value in $M_0^1 \overset{E}{\rightarrow} M_1^{1c}$, and we decide that M_1^{1c}, a member of TS models, fits the data better than M_0^1, a member of DS models. However, it is better to keep in mind that both of the two P-values are small, which may be indicative of a boundary case between DS and TS.[6]

As for the other real variables the real wage has the same deterministic trends that the real GNP has respectively in the DS and TS models. The P-value for DS is slightly larger than that for the TS, but both of the P-values are as low as 0.1 or 0.2. The real rate of interest has a constant trend in both the DS and TS models, and also an outlier in the differenced series. The encompassing analysis with the outlier included in the data shows P-value for TS overwhelmingly larger than that for DS, but the difference is reduced when the outlier is eliminated by a dummy variable introduced in both the DS and TS models. The unemployment rate has a constant trend in both the DS and TS models, and the P-value for TS is about 0.7 while that for TS is below 0.05. These results on the historical data may be summarized as follows. Unemployment rate and real rate of interest are definitely TS. Formal applications of our comparison criteria lead to real GNP being TS, but this variable as well as real wage appears to be near the boundary between DS and TS.

[6] Simulation results in Koto and Hatanaka (1994) lead us to think that the innovation variance in the pre-war period being four times as large as that in the post-war would not bring about any bias in either direction.

We conclude that *the data do not provide strong evidence to propose the unit roots to be incorporated in macrodynamics of real economic variables. The self-restoring force of the trend line can be neither assured nor refuted.*

9.2.2 US Post-war data

All variables, real variables, prices, and financial variables, are DS in the post-war period. This is the conclusion reached in Hatanaka and Koto (1994).

Below I shall show the analyses of real consumption, unemployment rate, and CPI. As for the CPI we shall be concerned with whether it is $I(2)$ or $I(1)$.

The data of real consumption for 1949 I–1992 IV are shown in Figure 9.2(*a*). To select the deterministic trend within DS models we initially look for outliers in Δx_t, which is shown in Figure 9.2(*b*). We have decided that there is none. Then (8.6) is used to see if the difference in means between the periods before and after the Oil Crisis is significant, and we have found it barely is. Thus we have chosen a linear trend with a slope change at 1973 I, M_0^{1s}. As for the deterministic trend within the TS models the analysis on the basis of (8.5) shows that a slope change at 1973 I is significant. Thus we shall compare M_0^{1s} and M_1^{1s} in the encompassing analysis.

As for $M_0^{1s} \overset{E}{\rightarrow} M_1^{1s}$ we use a type of Dickey–Fuller test based on (8.4), ignoring ξ_t therein. The F-test is run for $(\beta_0, \beta_1, \alpha_1) = (0, 0, 1)$. The limiting distribution of the test statistic under M_0^{1s} is tabulated in Koto and Hatanaka (1994). Noting that $\lambda = (T - T_B)/T$ is about 0.5, we cite the distribution for $\lambda = 0.5$ in Table 9.2.

The coefficient of the highest lag order term, α_p in (8.4), has t-values equal to -1.96 and -2.23 for $(p-1) = 23$ and 20 respectively. With $(p-1) = 23$ the F-statistic is about 2.5. Comparing this with Table 9.2 we see that the P-value is about 0.8.

$M_1^{1s} \overset{E}{\rightarrow} M_0^{1s}$ is investigated by the Saikkonen–Luukkonen test. The linear trend with slope change is initially subtracted from x_t. The asymptotic distribution of the Saikkonen–Luukkonen test statistic depends on what mode of deterministic trend is subtracted. Koto and Hatanaka (1994) show the distribution in the present case (linear trend with slope change, $\lambda = 0.5$) as in Table 9.3. The AR fitting is adopted as described in Section 3.4.2 to construct the Saikkonen–Luukkonen test statistic (3.14′), and $p = 24$ is chosen for the AR lag order. It turns out that the test statistic is 0.059 in the present data. The P-value is less than 0.2.

The P-value for $M_0^{1s} \overset{E}{\rightarrow} M_1^{1s}$ is much larger than the P-value for $M_1^{1s} \overset{E}{\rightarrow} M_0^{1s}$, and we conclude that the real consumption is DS in the post-war data.

I like to call readers' attention to very high lag orders that we may have to choose in analysing the seasonally adjusted quarterly data.

The data of unemployment rate for 1949 I–1991 IV is shown in Figure 9.3(*a*). The unemployment rate is the only variable that was judged TS in the analyses

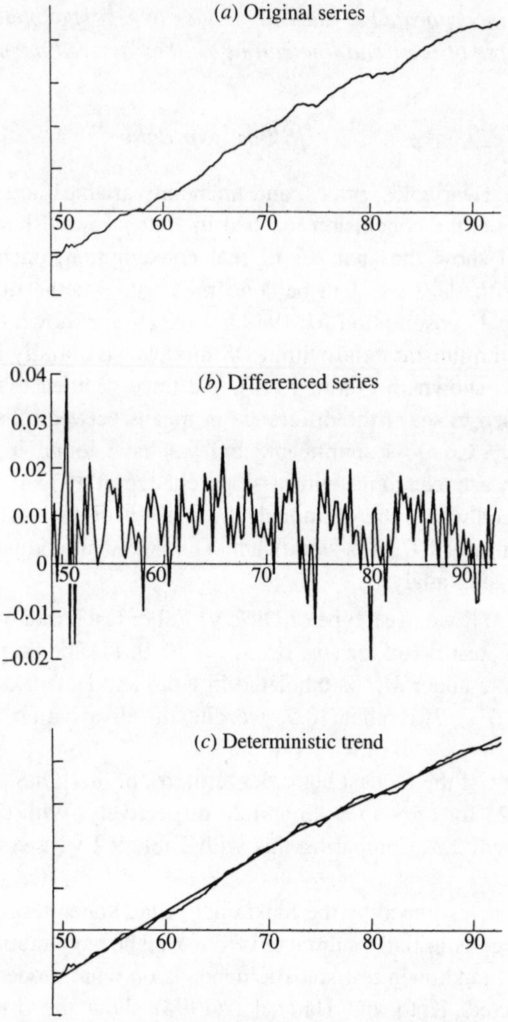

FIG. 9.2 *Post-war data of real consumption, log: (a) Original series, (b) Differenced series, (c) Deterministic trend*

TABLE 9.2 *Limiting cumulative distribution of the statistic for* $M_0^{1s} \xrightarrow{E} M_1^{1s}$, $\lambda = 0.5$

p	0.1	0.2	0.3	0.4	0.5	0.6	0.7	0.8	0.9	0.95
x	2.09	2.51	2.85	3.18	3.50	3.86	4.28	4.82	5.65	6.42

of historical data by Nelson and Plosser (1982). In Figure 9.3(*b*) the mean of Δx_t is not significantly different from zero in the analysis using an equation that

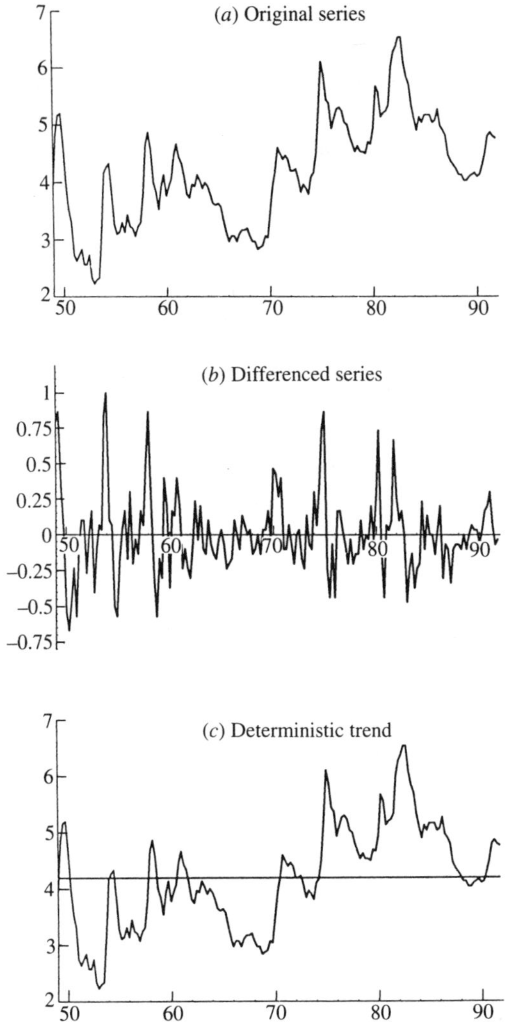

FIG. 9.3 *Post-war data of unemployment rate: (a) Original series, (b) Differenced series, (c) Deterministic trend*

TABLE 9.3 *Limiting cumulative distribution of the statistic for* $M_1^{1s} \overset{E}{\to} M_0^{1s}$, $\lambda = 0.5$

p	0.1	0.2	0.3	0.4	0.5	0.6	0.7	0.8	0.9	0.95
x	0.021	0.025	0.029	0.032	0.037	0.041	0.047	0.055	0.069	0.084

resembles (8.6) but lacks I_{TB+1}. In Figure 9.3(c) the coefficient of time variable is not significant in an equation that lacks I_{TB+1} and $\max(t - T_B, 0)$ in (8.5) but resembles it otherwise. Thus the deterministic trends are just a constant in both the DS and TS. As for $M_0^0 \xrightarrow{E} M_1^0$ we find t-value equal to -2.99 for the highest lag order term for $(p-1) = 12$. The F-statistics in the augmented Dickey–Fuller test range from 1.5 to 2.1 over $(p-1)$ between 13 and 16. The limiting distribution is given in Table 9.4. The P-values are roughly between 0.4 and 0.6. As for $M_1^0 \xrightarrow{E} M_0^0$ the limiting distribution of the Saikkonen–Luukkonen statistic, (3.14′), is given in Table 9.5 for the case where a constant trend is subtracted from x_t. In the present data the statistic is 0.50 with $p = 13$, and the P-value is less than 0.05. We thus conclude that the unemployment rate is DS in the post-war data.

As for some of the other variables the real GDP has P-value between 0.3 and 0.6 for DS, depending on what lag orders are chosen, and P-value between 0.05 and 0.10 for TS. There is some anxiety about the selection of deterministic trends in real wage, but between M_0^2 and M_1^2 the P-value for DS is about 0.5 while the P-value for TS is less than 0.05. The real rate of interest is difficult to analyse primarily in choosing the mode of deterministic trend for TS, another manifestation of the point emphasized in Section 9.1 above. We have abandoned the encompassing analysis of this variable. As for the nominal GNP, we found cubic trends significant in both the DS and TS. The P-values for DS are between 0.2 and 0.7, while the P-values for TS are much less than 0.05. As for the stock price we have compared M_0^3 and M_1^3. The P-value for DS is about 0.9, and that for TS is much less than 0.05. The conclusion is that real variables, price, and financial variables are all DS in the US post-war data except for some that we are unable to analyse.

It has also been found that none of the post-war data has both P_{01} and P_{10} small, which means that *none of them seems to be near the boundary* between DS and TS. In particular *none belongs to the Schwert ARMA*. This should be contrasted to the historical data, in which real GNP and real wage may be judged near the boundary between TS and DS.

Earlier on the historical data we were unable to decide if the real economic variables were DS except for unemployment rate and real rate of interest. Regarding the different results between the historical and post-war data there

TABLE 9.4 *Limiting cumulative distribution of the statistic for* $M_0^0 \xrightarrow{E} M_1^0$

p	0.1	0.2	0.3	0.4	0.5	0.6	0.7	0.8	0.9	0.95
x	0.68	0.95	1.19	1.45	1.73	2.04	2.42	2.93	3.79	4.58

TABLE 9.5 *Limiting cumulative distribution of the statistic for* $M_1^0 \xrightarrow{E} M_0^0$

p	0.1	0.2	0.3	0.4	0.5	0.6	0.7	0.8	0.9	0.95
x	0.046	0.062	0.079	0.097	0.118	0.146	0.184	0.240	0.344	0.459

cannot be an unequivocal explanation because the pre-war data alone are too short for a separate analysis. However, several conjectures are possible. First, economic regimes are different between the pre-war and post-war periods. Second, historical data are annual and cover longer time-spans, whereas post-war data are quarterly spanning shorter periods. If the DGP is TS, and if one quarter is short enough to assure $b(1) = 0$, then annual data covering longer time-spans would have higher discriminatory power to discern DS and TS (see Section 2.5)). It would lead to the interpretation that real variables are indeed TS but the post-war data cannot reveal it. The dominating characteristic root is about 0.95 on the quarterly basis, which is equivalent to 0.81 on the annual basis. The root, 0.95, cannot be distinguished from unity with $T = 150$, but 0.81 can be with $T = 100$.

At any rate it is the post-war data rather than the historical data that are used for most of econometric studies. There we must use statistical inference procedures that would be appropriate when unit roots may possibly be involved. Part II will show that the treatment of even a simple regression model should be different from the traditional econometrics when unit roots are involved. However, it is also important to bear in mind the uncertainty about the characteristic roots between 0.9 and 1.0 mentioned above.

9.2.3 Integration order of the post-war CPI

The integration order of log of CPI has been an issue in the unit-root field. No one has questioned that it is at least unity. The issue is whether it is 2 or not. As for the historical data Hatanaka and Koto (1994) find strong evidence to support that CPI is not $I(2)$.

Let us turn to the integration order of log of CPI in the post-war period. The same analysis as before is now applied to $\{\Delta x_t\}$ rather than $\{x_t\}$ in order to determine whether $\{x_t\}$ is $I(2)$ or $I(1)$. Initially the chart of $\{\Delta^2 x_t\}$ starting at 1949 I has been examined, and an outlier is found in 1951 I. Since interpretation of this outlier seems to pose a problem, and since 1951 I is so close to the beginning of the post-war era, we have chosen 1952 I–1992 IV as our sample period, for which charts are given in Figure 9.4.

As for the deterministic trend in DS a linear trend is not significant, but a constant term is significantly non-zero in (8.6). As for TS a quadratic trend is significant in (8.5). We have compared M_0^1 and M_1^2. The coefficient of highest lag order term for $(p-1) = 7$ is highly significant. The Dickey–Fuller statistics are not stable as lag orders are varied, and, when compared with Table 9.6, P-values range between 0.4 and 0.7 over $(p-1) = 9$ to 14. The $\hat{\mu}$ test has P-value, 0.4. As a supplement we have also compared M_0^2 and M_1^2. The P-values of Dickey–Fuller statistics are similar to the above, and the Saikkonen–Luukkonen statistic has P-value, 0.2. The inflation rate may well be DS, and CPI may be $I(2)$ in the post-war period.

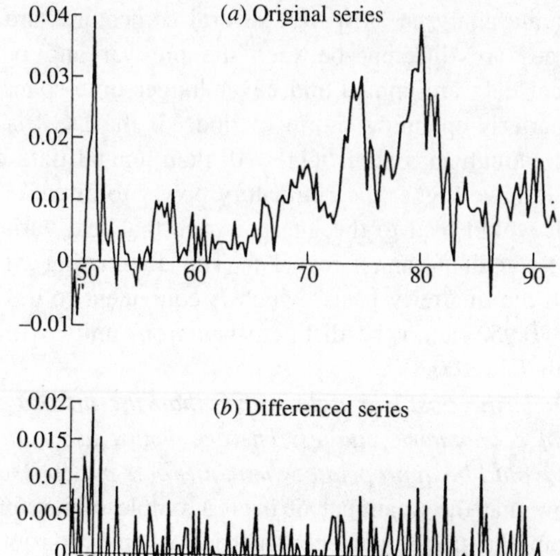

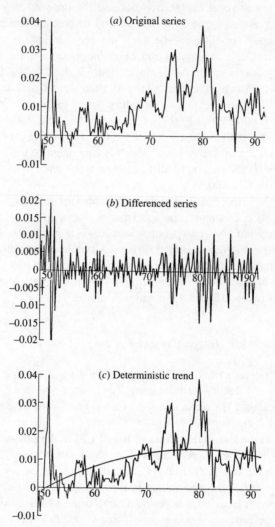

FIG. 9.4 *Post-war data of inflation rate: (a) Original series, (b) Differenced series, (c) Deterministic trend*

TABLE 9.6 *Limiting cumulative distribution of the statistic for* $M_0^1 \overset{E}{\to} M_1^2$

p	0.1	0.2	0.3	0.4	0.5	0.6	0.7	0.8	0.9	0.95
x	1.63	2.00	2.32	2.62	2.93	3.28	3.67	4.17	4.95	5.67

As for money stock, its historical data show that log M is $I(1)$ but not $I(2)$. As for the post-war data we find it difficult to decide whether it is $I(2)$ or $I(1)$.

Incidentally, Japanese real GNP and stock price in Figures 1.1 and 1.2 are both $I(1)$, if the breakpoint is set in 1974,[7] but there is some uncertainty about the choice of breakpoint (see Takeuchi, 1991).

[7] The highest-order coefficient in Dickey-Fuller equation is significant at $(p-1) = 11$, and the P-values of the Dickey-Fuller statistic are based upon lag orders $(p-1)$ larger than 11.

10
Bayesian Discrimination

The present Chapter surveys and assesses Bayesian studies of the unit root. Section 10.1 sets forth the notations. Section 10.2 presents three different categories of discrimination that have emerged in the Bayesian unit-root literature. Section 10.3 surveys the literature on the first category, in which stationarity is discriminated from non-stationarity. It is not directly related to the discrimination between DS and TS, but it is this category that both sides of the controversy between Sims (1988) and Phillips (1991*b*) refer to. It will be revealed that the prior should be model-dependent and hence a flat prior is ruled out, and that the Bayesian inference is standard in so far as the likelihood function is concerned, which should be contrasted to the classical inference equipped with a battery of non-standard limiting distributions. Section 10.4 explains problems that arise in the second and third categories of discrimination, in which a point-null hypothesis, $\rho = 1$, is compared with alternative hypotheses. It will be shown that the point-null hypothesis constrains our choice of prior distributions, virtually ruling out non-informative priors. The third category, which contains only Schotman and van Dijk (1991*a*, *b*, 1993), does deal with the discrimination between the DS and TS. The results are surveyed in Section 10.5. My survey does not include the recent literature on the Bayesian model selection such as Koop and Steel (1994), Phillips (1992*b*), Phillips and Ploberger (1992), Stock (1992), and Tsurumi and Wago (1993) due to lack of time.

10.1 Differences between the Bayesian and the Classical Theories

I assume some acquaintance with an elementary part of the Bayesian statistics on the reader's part, but some essential points will be mentioned here to compare them with the classical statistics. Differences between the two schools of statistics begin with the concept of probability. In the classical school the probability is the relative frequency of an event in a hypothetical sequence of experiments. In the Bayesian, the probability is the degree in which an event is thought likely to occur, or a proposition likely to hold, on the basis of someone's judgement. The Bayesian inference starts with a prior p.d.f., $f(\theta)$, of a parameter vector, θ, whereas the classical inference cannot incorporate such concept. The likelihood function may be written $f(x|\theta)$ in both schools, but here too is revealed an important difference. The x in the Bayesian likelihood is the actual observation.[1] The x in the classical likelihood is a random variable. Not only the actual observation of x but also all the x that might be observed are brought together to form a distribution of x in the sense of relative frequency. Therefore $f(x|\theta)$ is a stochastic function of θ, from which are derived probability distributions of the first- and the second-order derivatives of the likelihood function, which in turn form the basis of the classical inference. On the other hand the Bayesian inference is based on the posterior p.d.f.,

$$\alpha(\theta|x) \propto f(x|\theta)f(\theta).$$

Here again x is the actual observation.

The basic ingredients in the Bayesian inference are the prior distribution and the likelihood function. It will be seen later that it is the prior distribution that raises a number of difficult problems in the unit-root field.

Suppose that we wish to test H_i, $i = 0, 1$, where H_i states that $\theta \in \Theta_i$. Prior probabilities of H_i are

$$P(\Theta_0) = \pi_0, \qquad P(\Theta_1) = \pi_1, \qquad \pi_0 + \pi_1 = 1, \tag{10.1}$$

which may be further distributed each within the Θ_i as $\pi_i f^{(i)}(\theta)$, $i = 0, 1$, where

$$\int_{\Theta_i} f^{(i)}(\theta)d\theta = 1, \qquad i = 0, 1. \tag{10.2}$$

Posterior probabilities of the two hypotheses are

$$\begin{cases} \alpha(\Theta_0) = \pi_0 \displaystyle\int_{\Theta_0} f^{(0)}(\theta)f(x|\theta)d\theta/m(x) \\ \alpha(\Theta_1) = \pi_1 \displaystyle\int_{\Theta_1} f^{(1)}(\theta)f(x|\theta)d\theta/m(x), \end{cases} \tag{10.3}$$

where $$m(x) = \pi_0 \int_{\Theta_0} f^{(0)}(\theta)f(x|\theta)d\theta + \pi_1 \int_{\Theta_1} f^{(1)}(\theta)f(x|\theta)d\theta.$$

Both π_i and $\alpha(\Theta_i)$, $i = 0, 1$ are probabilities of H_i being true, and the transformation from π_i to $\alpha(\Theta_i)$ is brought about by assessing the observation, x, in light of the model and the observation.

The Bayesian inference often uses a p.d.f. such that its integral diverges to infinity as the domain of integration expands infinitely. Such a p.d.f. is said to be improper. When an improper p.d.f., $f(\theta)$, is adopted as a prior distribution for all θ in Θ_0 and Θ_1, the prior probabilities of H_0 and H_1 cannot be defined.

[1] This is a main point in the likelihood principle, which is often cited in the literature of Bayesian tests of difference stationarity. See e.g. Lindley (1965: 58–69), Berger (1985: 28–33), and Poirier (1988) for more about the likelihood principle.

But the ratio between the posterior probabilities, i.e. the posterior odds ratio,

$$\frac{\alpha(\Theta_0)}{\alpha(\Theta_1)} = \frac{\int_{\Theta_0} f(\theta) f(x|\theta) d\theta}{\int_{\Theta_1} f(\theta) f(x|\theta) d\theta} \tag{10.4}$$

can be defined in so far as the integrals in the nominator and the denominator are each bounded.

Finally, suppose that for $i = 0, 1$ the loss in accepting H_i is zero if H_i is true, and k_i if $H_j (j \neq i)$ is true. The expected loss involved in accepting H_1, i.e. rejecting H_0 is $k_1\alpha(\Theta_0)$, and the expected loss in accepting H_0, i.e. rejecting H_1 is $k_0\alpha(\Theta_1)$. Therefore H_1 is accepted when

$$\alpha(\Theta_0)/\alpha(\Theta_1) < k_0/k_1. \tag{10.5}$$

The two hypotheses are treated symmetrically here, whereas it is well known that the null and the alternative hypotheses in the classical inference are not.

Readers who wish to know more about the Bayesian inference are referred to Lindley (1965), Zellner (1971), Leamer (1978), and Berger (1985).

10.2 Different Versions of the Hypotheses

For the sake of simplicity let us consider the model (5.2), where $|\rho| < 1$ in the trend stationarity, and $\rho = 1$ in the difference stationarity. Earlier in Section 2.3 it was pointed out that explosive roots of the characteristic polynomial cannot be absorbed in the difference-stationary model. The explosive root has been a priori ruled out in all the classical inference on the unit root. Along with Sims (1988) and Phillips (1991*a*), however, explosive roots are brought into consideration in the Bayesian testing. Three versions of hypothesis-testing have emerged in the literature.

$$H_0^{(1)}: \quad \rho \geq 1 \quad \text{vs.} \quad H_1^{(1)}: \quad |\rho| < 1$$
$$H_0^{(2)}: \quad \rho = 1 \quad \text{vs.} \quad H_1^{(2)}: \quad \rho \neq 1$$
$$H_0^{(3)}: \quad \rho = 1 \quad \text{vs.} \quad H_1^{(3)}: \quad |\rho| < 1.$$

I have several comments: (i) In the first version the difference stationarity is merged with explosive roots in $H_0^{(1)}$. This version of tests does not answer questions regarding the difference stationarity. Rather it is directed to discriminating the stationarity and the non-stationarity. (ii) In the second version $H_0^{(2)}$ is precisely the difference stationarity, but $\rho > 1$ and $|\rho| < 1$ are grouped together in $H_1^{(2)}$. These two situations entail entirely diferent meanings and different methods to cope with. (iii) In the third version the prior probability for $\rho > 1$ is zero. Explosive roots are a priori ruled out. (iv) There can be an argument that explosive roots may very well be reality, in which case the third version is rendered meaningless; in fact the discrimination between DS and TS is meaningless. This argument would lead to the fourth version, in which three hypotheses,

$$H_0^{(4)}:\quad \rho = 1; \qquad H_1^{(4)}:\quad |\rho| < 1; \qquad H_2^{(4)}:\quad \rho > 1$$

are compared in terms of their posterior probabilities. It has not been investigated to the best of my knowledge.

There may be some scepticism about compounding a linear deterministic trend with an explosive ρ, though as $t \to \infty$ it is just an explosive trend. One might consider the following model of two regimes,

$$x_t = \mu + \beta t + \rho x_{t-1} + \varepsilon_t, \qquad |\rho| < 1 \tag{10.6a}$$

$$x_t = \mu + \rho x_{t-1} + \varepsilon_t, \qquad \rho \geq 1 \tag{10.6b}$$

The first regime is nothing but (5.4), but $\rho = 1$ is excluded from it because $\rho = 1$ forces β to zero, merging it to (10.6*b*). (10.6*a*) may be extended to include a deterministic trend more general than a linear.

10.3 Problems Associated with the First Version

In the classical test of a null hypothesis H_0 the P-value is the probability that a test statistic is farther away from Θ_0 beyond its observed value. In the first version of discrimination in Section 10.2 it is seen (i) that the whole parameter space is divided between Θ_0 and Θ_1, and (ii) that Θ_i lies on the 'other side' of $\Theta_j (i \neq j)$. In such cases the P-value in the classical inference is identical to the Bayesian posterior probability in so far as we are concerned with standard models in which data are generated independently and identically.

For example, consider a regression model with only one fixed regressor,

$$y_i = \beta x_i + \varepsilon_i, \qquad i = 1, \ldots, n \tag{10.7}$$

where $\{\varepsilon_i\}$ is i.i.d., ε_i is $N(0, \sigma_\varepsilon^2)$, and σ_ε^2 is known. The likelihood function is

$$(2\pi\sigma_\varepsilon^2)^{-n/2} \exp\left(-\frac{1}{2\sigma_\varepsilon^2}\sum\nolimits_1^n (y_i - \beta x_i)^2\right). \tag{10.8}$$

Writing

$$A = \sigma_\varepsilon^{-2}\sum x_i^2, \quad B = (2\pi\sigma_\varepsilon^2)^{-n/2} \exp\left(-\frac{1}{2\sigma_\varepsilon^2}\sum (y_i - \hat{\beta} x_i)^2\right), \tag{10.9}$$

where $\hat{\beta}$ is the OLS estimate of β, (10.8) is expressed as

$$B \exp\left(-\frac{A}{2}(\beta - \hat{\beta})^2\right). \tag{10.8$'$}$$

Note that β is not involved in either A or B. When (10.8′) is normalized so as to integrate to unity in the integration by β, (10.8′) is the density function of a normal variate with mean $\hat{\beta}$ and variance A^{-1}, which is sketched in Figure 10.1(*a*).

Suppose that H_0 states $\beta \geq 1$, which is Θ_0, and H_1 states $\beta < 1$, which is Θ_1. Assume that $\pi_0 = \pi_1$, the prior distribution is flat, and $k_0 = k_1$ in the notations given in Section 10.1 above. The Bayesian decision, (10.5), is then reduced to the comparison between two shaded areas over Θ_0 and Θ_1 in Figure 10.1(*a*). H_0 is rejected if the area over Θ_0 is smaller than that over Θ_1 as in Figure 10.1(*a*).

In the classical hypothesis test of H_0 using $\hat{\beta}$ as the test statistic we consider the sampling distribution of $\hat{\beta}$ under the assumption that the true value of β is unity. This sampling distribution is $N(1, A^{-1})$ and represented by a dotted curve in Figure 10.1(*b*). The *P*-value is the shaded area. Since the likelihood function in Figure 10.1(*a*) and the sampling distribution in Figure 10.1(*b*) share the common variance, A^{-1}, the posterior probability of Θ_0 in Figure 10.1(*a*) is equal to the *P*-value in Figure 10.1(*b*). The equality would hold even if we switch the null hypothesis from H_0 to H_1.

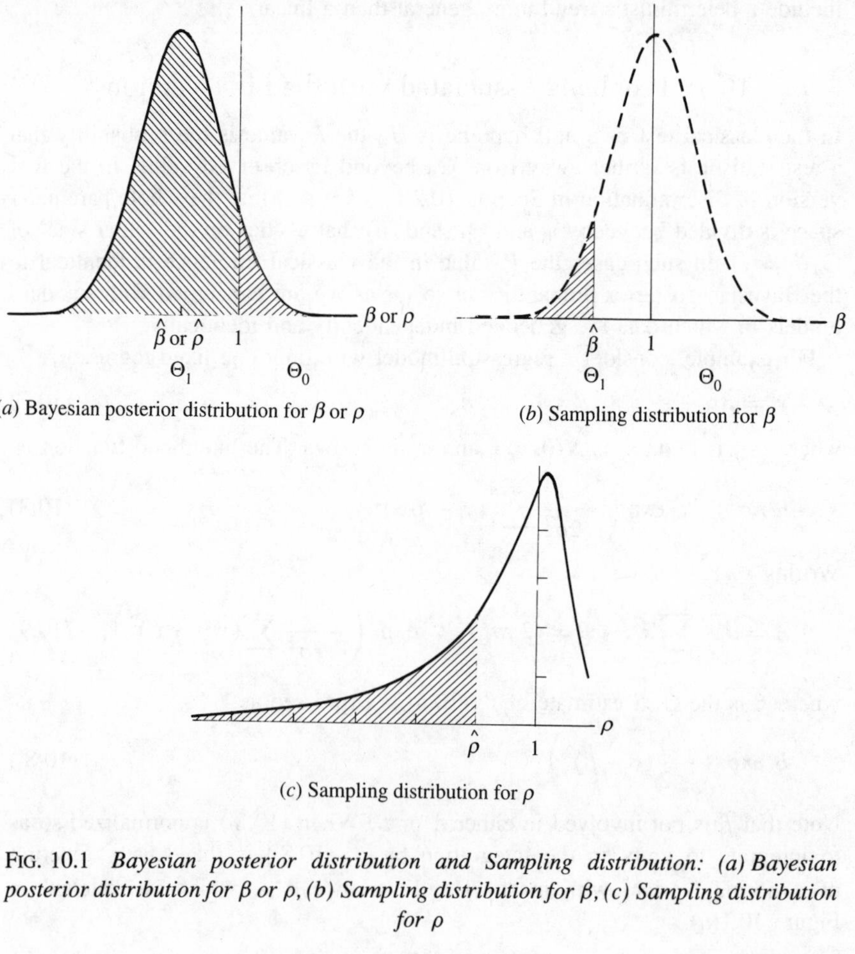

(*a*) Bayesian posterior distribution for β or ρ

(*b*) Sampling distribution for β

(*c*) Sampling distribution for ρ

FIG. 10.1 *Bayesian posterior distribution and Sampling distribution: (a) Bayesian posterior distribution for β or ρ, (b) Sampling distribution for β, (c) Sampling distribution for ρ*

The likelihood ratio test is another version of the classical inference based upon the likelihood function. In testing the null hypothesis H_0 it compares the maxima of likelihoods over Θ_0 and over Θ_1. The former maximum is attained at $\beta = 1$, and the latter at $\hat{\beta}$. Therefore $(-2) \times$ (the logarithm of the likelihood ratio) is $A(1 - \hat{\beta})^2$. This term is assessed by its sampling distribution under H_0, which is $\chi^2(1)$. The P-value should be identical to the one obtained in Figure 10.1(b) through $\hat{\beta} \sim N(1, A^{-1})$, and it is equal to the posterior probability of H_0.

This kind of relationship between the classical and the Bayesian inference holds in many models in so far as the data generation is standard.[2] Sims and Uhlig (1991) find that the relation does *not* hold in the first version of discrimination in Section 10.2.

To simplify our exposition let us consider an AR(1)

$$x_t = \rho x_{t-1} + \varepsilon_t, \qquad t = 1, \ldots, T \tag{10.10}$$

where ε_t is distributed in $N(0, \sigma_\varepsilon^2)$ and σ_ε^2 is known. Conditionally upon x_0 the p.d.f. of $(x_1, \ldots, x_T)$ is

$$(2\pi\sigma_\varepsilon^2)^{-T/2} \exp\left(-\frac{1}{2\sigma_\varepsilon^2}\sum\nolimits_1^T (x_t - \rho x_{t-1})^2\right), \tag{10.11}$$

no matter whether $\rho <$ or $=$ or > 1. If T is large the marginal p.d.f. of x_0 can be ignored even for $\rho > 1$.[3] (10.11) can be rewritten as

$$B \exp\left(-\frac{A}{2}(\rho - \hat{\rho})^2\right), \tag{10.11$'$}$$

where $\hat{\rho}$ is the OLS and

$$A = \sigma_\varepsilon^{-2}\sum x_{t-1}^2, \quad B = (2\pi\sigma_\varepsilon^2)^{-T/2} \exp\left(-\frac{1}{2\sigma_\varepsilon^2}\sum (x_t - \hat{\rho}x_{t-1})^2\right). \tag{10.12}$$

(10.12) is analogous to (10.9). The likelihood function of ρ is (10.11$'$) suitably normalized. (10.11$'$) is quite analogous to (10.8$'$). Continuing to assume the flat prior and $\pi_0 = \pi_1$ the Bayesian posterior distribution for ρ can be expressed by Figure 10.1(a). The posterior probability of $\rho \geq 1$ is the area shaded as ///. The Bayesian analysis of $H_0^{(1)}$ vs. $H_1^{(1)}$ does not differ much from the regression model.

[2] The equality was pointed out in Pratt (1965), and elaborated on in DeGroot (1973) and Casella and Berger (1987). In establishing the asymptotic equality in a general model the following theorem due to Lindley (1965: pp. 129–31) and Walker (1969) is useful. If T is sufficiently large and if the prior distribution is continuous, the posterior distribution is approximately a normal distribution with its mean vector equal to the maximum-likelihood estimator and its covariance matrix equal to the inverse of the second-order derivative of the log-likelihood function.

[3] This can be shown by comparing the log-likelihood conditional upon x_0 and the log-likelihood for the marginal distribution of $(x_1, \ldots, x_T)$ after x_0 is integrated out (see Fukushige, Hatanaka, and Koto (1994)).

Let us turn to the classical inference and consider the likelihood ratio test of $H_0(\rho \geq 1)$ against $H_1(0 < \rho < 1)$. Suppose that $\hat{\rho} < 1$ happens to hold in the data. The test statistic is $A(\hat{\rho} - 1)^2$, which is evaluated in terms of the sampling distribution of $\hat{\rho}$ assuming that the true value of ρ is unity. The asymptotic distribution is not $\chi^2(1)$, but

$$A(\hat{\rho} - 1)^2 \xrightarrow{D} \left(\int_0^1 w(r)^2 dr\right)^{-1} \left(\int_0^1 w(r) dw(r)\right)^2.$$

The asymptotic P-value of $\hat{\rho}$ can be obtained. Alternatively one could use simply $T(\hat{\rho} - 1)$ as the test statistic. The sampling distribution is sketched as the dotted curve in Figure 10.1(c). It is non-normal and skewed to the left of $\rho = 1$. The P-value is the shaded area, and it is not equal to the Bayesian posterior probability of $\rho \geq 1$ in Figure 10.1(a).

When a unit root is involved the likelihood function is standard but the sampling distribution is not, and as a result the P-value and the posterior probability diverge. Sims and Uhlig (1991) demonstrate this point visually through a simulation study with $T = 100$.

I have assumed a flat prior of ρ so that the posterior has been proportional to the likelihood function. Phillips (1991b) criticizes a flat prior as a non-informative prior. He stresses that the prior should incorporate the property of the model as it is not meant to be prior to the model (but only to observations). In the standard regression model, $y_i = \beta x_i + \varepsilon_i$, the Fisher information does not involve β, and the flat prior of β may be regarded as non-informative. In the autoregressive model (10.10) the Fisher information does involve ρ, and the flat prior of ρ is not non-informative. The Jeffreys non-informative prior is proportional to the square root of (the determinant of) the Fisher information (matrix). The best known example is σ^{-1} for σ. Its advantage is that the result of Bayesian inference is invariant through transformations of parameters if this prior is adopted (see Zellner (1971: 47–8)). The point is relevant if one wishes to keep the results comparable between annual and quarterly data. See Section 2.5.

As for the model (10.6a), in which $|\rho| < 1$, the Jeffreys prior density for $(\mu, \beta, \rho, \sigma)$ is approximately

$$\sigma^{-3}(1 - \rho^2)^{-1/2}, \qquad |\rho| < 1. \tag{10.13}$$

However, for $\rho > 1$ the density rises at the speed of ρ^{2T}, which would be contrary to many researchers' judgement. See Leamer (1991), Poirier (1991), Sims (1991), Wago and Tsurumi (1991), and Phillips (1991c). In my view the prior should be model-dependent, and hence its density should vary with ρ, but no economists would accept the Jeffreys prior.

DeJong and Whiteman (1991a, 1991b) perform a kind of the first version of testing, in which the discrimination is sought between $\tilde{H}_0^{(1)} : \rho \geq 0.975$ and $\tilde{H}_1^{(1)} : \rho < 0.975$. Their losses, k_0 and k_1, are such that $\tilde{H}_0^{(1)}$ is accepted if and only if $P[\rho \geq 0.975] \geq 0.05$. The model is (10.6$a$) extended to $\rho \geq 1$ as well as

$|\rho| < 1$, while leaving μ, β, and ρ variation free. Compare this with Section 5.2. In one prior $\tilde{H}_1^{(1)}$ is rejected only in CPI, bond yield, and velocity among the fourteen time series in Nelson and Plosser (1982). Some alternative priors add to this list nominal GNP, nominal stock price, and nominal wage. They observe a high negative correlation between β and ρ, but this may be explained by my theoretical observation given in Appendix 3.3.

I conclude the present Section as follows. The Bayesian discrimination between $H_0^{(1)}$ and $H_1^{(1)}$ is standard in so far as the likelihood function is concerned. In particular it does not require non-standard distributions such as those based on the Wiener process. However, the Bayesian discrimination between $H_0^{(1)}$ and $H_1^{(1)}$ is non-standard in requiring the prior distribution to be model-dependent and thus ruling out a flat prior for ρ. The latter point holds even when the domain of ρ is confined into $(-1, 1]$ as in the third type of discrimination.

10.4 Point Null Hypotheses

The hypotheses, $H_0^{(2)}$, $H_0^{(3)}$, and $H_0^{(4)}$, each restrict ρ to unity. The domains of parameters (ρ and all nuisance parameters) specified by these hypotheses have each zero measure in the whole space of parameters. Such hypotheses are called the point (or sharp) null hypothesis.

The Bayesians begin their argument with the remark that many point null hypotheses are not what researchers really wish to test. Concerning the difference stationarity the argument is that we really wish to test $\rho \in [1 - \delta, 1 + \delta]$ rather than $\rho = 1$. Then, turning to the case where researchers really wish to test a point-null hypothesis, the Bayesians such as Berger (1985: 156) admit that their inference does not work. In particular, no matter what π_0 and π_1 may be, $\alpha(\Theta_0)$ defined by (10.3) for a point null hypothesis $H_0 : \theta = \theta_0$ is approximately unity, when T is large and the distance between θ_0 and the mode of the likelihood function is in the order of $T^{-1/2}$. This is called Jeffreys paradox or Lindley paradox.[4] (Recall that the local alternative in the classical hypothesis testing deviates from θ_0 by the order of $T^{-1/2}$, and yet the test statistic rejects the null hypothesis when the P-value is small.) Readers may be relieved by the fact that long time-series data are not available to us. With small T, however, the Bayesian inference still faces two problems: (i) restrictions to our choice of prior distributions and (ii) an excessive favour on the point null hypothesis.

10.4.1 Restrictions to priors

I begin with the first problem, restrictions to prior distributions. Despite the emphasis upon the subjective probability many Bayesians in econometrics

[4] The statement follows from the reasoning in Berger (1985: pp. 148–56) and Zellner (1971: 302–6), assuming that data maintain the same P-value while $T \to \infty$.

and other disciplines perform an objective analysis by adopting some non-informative prior and/or by checking the sensitivity of posterior distributions to different prior distributions. The latter should be recommended in every study, but it is often the case that non-informative priors cannot be adopted in testing a point null hypothesis.

Suppose that a model contains only a scalar parameter, θ, and that H_0 states that θ is a point θ_0 while H_1 states that $\theta \neq \theta_0$. Let us consider the posterior odds ratio (10.4) with a continuous density function $f(\theta)$ as a prior. Then the prior probability of $\theta = \theta_0$ is zero, which forces the posterior probability to zero. No matter whether $f(\cdot)$ is proper or improper, a continuous p.d.f. cannot be adopted as a prior.

Consider then a narrow interval (null) hypothesis $\tilde{H}_\delta$ that specifies θ to be in $\Theta_\delta \equiv [\theta_0 - \delta, \theta_0 + \delta]$. In the framework of (10.1) and (10.2) the prior probability of $\tilde{H}_\delta$ is π_0, which is distributed within Θ_δ according to $f^{(0)}(\cdot)$. If $f^{(0)}(\cdot)$ is uniform in Θ_δ, the posterior probability of $\tilde{H}_\delta$ is

$$\alpha(\Theta_0) = \frac{\pi_0}{2\delta} \int_{\theta_0-\delta}^{\theta_0+\delta} f(x|\theta)d\theta/m(x).$$

As $\delta \to 0$ $\tilde{H}_\delta$ converges to the point null hypothesis H_0, and we have

$$\alpha(\theta_0) = \pi_0 f(x|\theta_0)/m(x) \tag{10.14}$$

by virtue of the mean value theorem. In testing H_0 we should place a discrete probability mass π_0 on the point θ_0 in the prior distribution. We would then get the posterior probability (10.14) by combining π_0 with the likelihood at $\theta = \theta_0$. It should also be clear that there is not much difference between a point ($\rho = 1$) and a narrow interval ($1 - \delta \leq \rho \leq 1 + \delta$) hypothesis in so far as the likelihood function is smooth about θ_0. This would be the case unless T is very large so that most of the likelihood is concentrated about θ_0.[5]

It is worth noting that the discrete mass in the prior induces a discrete mass on θ_0 in the posterior probability distribution.

Continuing the explanation on the scalar parameter, we place on H_1 the prior probability $\pi_1 \equiv 1 - \pi_0$, which is distributed through $f^{(1)}(\theta)$ over the whole straight line except the point θ_0. The function $f^{(1)}(\cdot)$ must integrate to unity as specified in (10.2) because otherwise the prior probability of H_1 cannot be made equal to π_1. Thus any improper p.d.f. is ruled out for $f^{(1)}(\cdot)$. Unfortunately most of known non-informative priors are improper.

Let us then consider a model which contains a vector parameter $\boldsymbol{\theta} = (\theta_1, \ldots, \theta_k)$. As a simple example of Θ_0 having zero measure, suppose that θ_1 is restricted to $\theta_1 = 1$ but $(\theta_2, \ldots, \theta_k)$ is free in Θ_0. The $\boldsymbol{\theta}$s not in Θ_0 form Θ_1. Suppose that θ_1 and $(\theta_2, \ldots, \theta_k)$ are independent in the prior distribution so that the p.d.f. is $\pi_1 f(\theta_1) f(\theta_2, \ldots, \theta_k)$ in Θ_1 and $P[\theta_1 = 1$ and $(\theta_2, \ldots, \theta_k) \epsilon$ an infinitesimal cube about $(\theta_2, \ldots, \theta_k)] = \pi_0 f(\theta_2, \ldots, \theta_k) d\theta_2 \ldots d\theta_k$. Then

[5] See Berger and Delampady (1987) for more about this point.

$f(\theta_2, \ldots, \theta_k)$ need not be proper because the posterior odds ratio (10.4) in the present case is

$$\frac{\pi_0 \int_{-\infty}^{\infty} \cdots \int f(\theta_2, \ldots, \theta_k) f(x|\theta_1 = 1, \theta_2, \ldots, \theta_k) d\theta_2 \ldots d\theta_k}{\pi_1 \int_{-\infty}^{\infty} f(\theta_1) \left[\int_{-\infty}^{\infty} \cdots \int f(\theta_2, \ldots, \theta_k) f(x|\theta_1, \theta_2, \ldots, \theta_k) d\theta_2 \ldots d\theta_k \right] d\theta_1} \tag{10.15}$$

The outer integral in the denominator of (10.15) is equal to that which excludes $\theta_1 = 1$ because all functions in the integrand are continuous.[6]

10.4.2 Favour on the point null

I now turn to the second problem, an excessive favour on the point null hypothesis. Consider a model that contains only a scalar parameter θ. H_0 is $\theta = \theta_0$ and H_1 is $\theta \neq \theta_0$. Suppose that we are given data such that the likelihood at θ_0 is low compared with the highest value of the likelihood function. The P-value would be small no matter what test statistic is used in the classical inference. But in the Bayesian approach a discrete mass of prior probability is placed on θ_0, and it would produce a large value of $\alpha(\theta_0)$, which may be regarded as undue favour on the point null hypothesis by the classical inference. If the hypothesis is not a point null, effects of the prior upon the posterior distributions eventually die down as $T \to \infty$ no matter whether the prior is informative or non-informative. When the hypothesis is a point null, effects of the discrete mass in the prior stay on while $T \to \infty$, as the Lindley paradox indicates.

Pure Bayesians reject outright the idea of comparing the $\alpha(\theta_0)$ to the P-value, but some Bayesians suggest how to protect researchers from an undue favour on a point null hypothesis.[7] In regard to the test of difference stationarity, which is a point null hypothesis, many researchers, Koop (1992) and Wago and Tsurumi (1991) among others, present the size and power of their Bayesian decision procedures (10.5) in terms of the relative frequency in hypothetical repetitions of data generation.

It is now clear that the second and the fourth versions of the testing in Section 10.2 involve both the first and the second problems due to point null hypotheses, whereas the third version has the second problem. The third version is free from the first problem because it deals with a bounded domain of parameters.

Concluding my explanations in Sections 10.3 and 10.4 I warn that *we should not expect the results of the classical and the Bayesian inference to be related in a simple manner*. In general, the parameter is a random variable in one, and a

[6] It is assumed that $f(\theta_1)$ integrates to unity over Θ_1 and that the integrals in the nominator and the denominator of (10.15) are both bounded.

[7] See Berger and Sellke (1987).

constant in the other. The inference is conditioned on just one set of available data in one, and based on a hypothetical sequence of data generations in the other. In particular, concerning the four versions of discrimination mentioned in Section 10.2, the Bayesian analysis of the likelihood function is standard, but the classical analysis is non-standard as demonstrated in Chapters 4–7. Bayesian prior distributions raise a number of problems. Use of non-informative priors is very much limited,[8] and this makes it difficult to compare the Bayesian and the classical results on the unit-root problems. However, the third version of discrimination, $H_0^{(3)}$ vs. $H_1^{(3)}$, which is the discrimination between DS and TS, is the least affected by the difficulties on prior distribution.

10.5 Results in the Second and the Third Versions

The test in Koop (1992) deals with the second version in spite of the announcement in its introduction that the TS will be tested against the DS. The model is

$$x_t = \beta_0 + \beta_1 x_{t-1} + \beta_2 x_{t-2} + \beta_3 x_{t-3} + \beta_4 t + \varepsilon_t, \tag{10.16}$$

where $\{\varepsilon_t\}$ is i.i.d. The DS is represented by $\beta_1 + \beta_2 + \beta_3 = 1$, upon which $\pi_0 = 0.5$ is placed. The priors are proper and symmetric about this line, using the Cauchy distribution and a family of distributions developed in Zellner (1986), which is called the *g*-priors. Koop (1992) analyses the Nelson–Plosser historical data and concludes that the DS is rejected in most of real variables but not rejected in nominal variables though this conclusion should not be taken as unequivocal.

Schotman and van Dijk (1991*a*) performs the third version of testing on the real exchange rate. The model is

$$(1 - \rho L)(x_t - \mu) = \varepsilon_t, \tag{10.17}$$

where $\{\varepsilon_t\}$ is Gaussian i.i.d. Unlike Dejong and Whiteman (1991*a*, *b*) they follow the modelling in the Dickey–Fuller test in Section 5.2 so that μ and ρ are not variation free. Since μ is not identified asymptotically at $\rho = 1$, any non-informative prior on μ leads to the posterior density diverging to ∞ at $\rho = 1$ as $T \to \infty$. They think of a prior of μ conditional upon ρ such that ranges of uniform distributions diverge to ∞ as ρ approaches unity from below. The idea may be useful to analyse the model of two regimes, (10.6*a*) (10.6*b*), but actually they choose some other prior on μ. They also choose the prior of ρ uniform over $[A, 1]$, where A is chosen so that most of the likelihoods are contained in this interval. Setting $\pi_0 = \pi_1 = 0.5$ the posterior probabilities of $\rho = 1$ in various real exchange rates range between 0.7 and 0.3.

[8] Occasionally a point null hypothesis is examined by the HPDI (highest posterior density interval) significance test. It checks if θ_0 is contained in a confidence interval based on the posterior distribution. See Lindley (1965: 58–61). If a continuous prior is used I would follow the criticism of the method by Berger and Delampady (1987) to the effect that it does not assess the distinguished point, θ_0. The point accepted by the decision rule (10.5) may very well be outside of the confidence interval.

Schotman and van Dijk (1991*b*) extend (10.17) to

$$(1 - \rho L)(x_t - \mu - \beta t) = \varepsilon_t, \qquad (10.17')$$

and apply it to the Nelson and Plosser historical data extended up to 1988. The results are that real variables are trend stationary, but nominal variables, prices, interest rates, velocity, and stock price are not. Schotman and van Dijk (1993) extends (1.17′) to

$$(1 - c_1 L - \ldots - c_p L^p)(x_t - \mu - \beta t) = \varepsilon_t,$$

and places a prior on $c(1) = 1 - c_1 - \ldots - c_p$. The prior on μ is normal conditionally upon $c(1)$ and σ_ε, and the conditional variance diverges as $c(1)$ approaches zero (i.e. unit root). They analysed the annual post-war data of real outputs in sixteen OECD countries with $p = 3$. Those of eight countries are judged DS.

Note that only Schotman and van Dijk (1991*a*, *b*, 1993) deal directly with the discrimination between DS and TS in Bayesian terms. It is interesting that the Bayesian discrimination gives results relatively more favourable to TS than the classical tests for DS against TS do.

I have not seen Bayesian analyses applied to the post-war data except for the exchange rate and annual data of real outputs in Schotman and van Dijk (1991*a*, 1993).

PART II
Co-integration Analysis in Econometrics

Overview

The co-integration research has made enormous progress since the seminal Granger representation theorem was proven in Engle and Granger (1987). A wide range of splendid ideas has emerged. Indeed, the development has been so rapid and divergent that the current state seems a little confusing. Part II presents the co-integration as I view it as an econometrician. My view has been influenced by my experiences with macroeconomic time-series data obtained in writing Part I. What I learned was that modes of deterministic trends are often difficult to determine, and that, partly because of this, integration orders are not easy to identify in some variables. The writing of Part II on the co-integration is thus orientated to giving more detailed consideration to deterministic trends, and to raising appreciation of the methods that are robust to the integration orders and different modes of deterministic trends. My view has also been influenced by results of simulation studies by my colleagues in Japan on the limited length of data. It leads me to mild scepticism about usefulness (for macroeconomics) of the widely applied analysis of co-integrated VAR (vector autogressive process) in Johansen (1991*a*), which otherwise excels all other inference methods. The methods which are developed by Phillips (1991*a*) on the econometric motivation assume rather than estimate some aspects of the co-integration. They might be of some use, however, unless the assumption is definitively rejected by the VAR method, which I do not imagine to happen frequently. These are the basic grounds on which Part II is written.

Chapter 11 compares two modelling strategies because this topic is related to the judgement just made in regard to the VAR and 'econometric' analyses of the co-integration. One of the two strategies is to start with the VAR modelling with as few economic theories as possible, and has been proposed most vigorously in Sims (1980*b*). The other is to incorporate fully the economic theories into the models, and has been the tradition of econometrics. The ideal procedure is undoubtedly to start with the minimum of economic theories and test rather than assume the validity of the theories. Its effective implementation is often hindered by limitations to the length of the time-series data available for macroeconomic studies. Chapter 11 also serves the purpose of introducing a number of basic concepts on the multiple economic time series such as Granger causality and weak exogeneity. Chapter 12 explains the co-integration and the Granger representation theorem. It also discusses in some length the relationship between the economic theories and the co-integration analysis especially about the meaning of long-run equilibrium. The methods that were called above 'econometric' are presented in Chapters 13 and 14. In Chapter 13 are explained the methods developed in Phillips (1991*a*) among others on the co-integrated (rather than spurious) regressions. As for the computations they involve nothing more than conventional t- and F-statistics, and, as for the distributions, nothing more than the standard normal and χ^2 distributions. Nevertheless we are freed from worrying about the correlation between the regressors and disturbance if the disturbance is stationary. In Chapter 14 these theories are applied to the inference problems on dynamic models such as the Hendry model and a class of general models that includes the linear, quadratic model in Kennan (1979), which is a basis for many empirical studies of rational expectations. The method in Johansen (1991*a*) is explained in Chapter 15, acknowledging the criticism by Phillips (1991*d*) but also clarifying what the method contributes to. This chapter also includes a brief summary of the simulation studies mentioned above. My opinion expressed in the first paragraph about the VAR and 'econometric' approaches are explained in Sections 13.4.2, and 13.4.3, and Sections 15.1.4, 15.1.5, 15.2.1, and 15.4.1.

A large number of topics are left out in my survey. (i) In Part I it has been discovered that CPI and money stock may well be $I(2)$, but I shall assume throughout Part II that the integration orders are at most unity.[1] Other topics that are not included in the book are (ii) the multi-co-integration, which may well be useful for studying stock–flow relationships,[2] (iii) the Bayesian studies,[3] (iv) heteroskedasticity in the co-integration,[4] (v) errors in variables,[5] (vi) time-varying parameters,[6] (vii) the asymmetric adjustment,[7] (viii) the non-linearity,[8] (ix) panel data,[9] (x) qualitative data,[10] (xi) ARCH models,[11] and (xii) forecasts.[12] I have transferred to Appendix 6 the explanation of methods that utilize a non-parametric estimation of the long-run covariance matrix on the ground explained in Section 7.3.3 of Part I. I have not included the potentially useful test on the restriction on VAR coefficients (such as Granger non-causality) in Toda and Yamamoto (1995). The test does not require any pretesting on the

[1] See Johansen (1992*a*, 1992*e*) and Juselius (1994) for $I(2)$ and Davidson (1991) and Engle and Yoo (1991) for a general treatment of integration orders. Park and Phillips (1989), Stock and Watson (1993), and Haldrup (1994) extend the analysis of co-integrated regression in Chapter 13 to higher integration orders. Engsted (1993), Johansen (1992*d*), Stock and Watson (1993), Juselius (1994), and Haldrup (1994) present empirical studies dealing with $I(2)$ variables. See also the literature on the multi-co-integration given in n. 2.

[2] The multi-co-integration is defined and analysed in Granger and Lee (1989, 1990), and also analysed in Johansen (1992*a*) and Park (1992). See Granger and Lee (1989) and Lee (1992) for the applications.

[3] DeJong (1992), Phillips (1992*a*), Kleibergen and van Dijk (1994), Chao and Phillips (1994), and Tsurumi and Wago (1994).

[4] Hansen (1992*b*).

[5] Nowak (1991).

[6] Canarella, Pollard, and Lai (1990), and Granger and Lee (1991).

[7] Granger and Lee (1989).

[8] Granger (1991, 1993) and Granger and Hallman (1991).

[9] Levin and Lin (1992) and Quah (1993) present a univariate unit root test on panel data. I do not know of any literature on the co-integration on panel data.

[10] McAleer, McKenzie, and Pesaran (1994).

[11] Bollerslev and Engle (1993).

[12] Engle, Granger, and Hallman (1989).

integration order or the co-integration rank, but it does not fit in the organization of Part II.[13]

A number of research topics clearly suggest themselves in the course of my survey, but there is no time to pursue them.

The expression of the characteristic polynomial used in mathematical economics is abandoned in Part II, and instead the convention in time-series analysis is adopted. See Section 2.3 (Part I) for the relation between characteristic polynomials in the time-series analysis and the mathematical economics.

The readers who are interested in the regression analysis rather than the multiple time series may start from Chapter 13. Major prerequisites for the understanding of Chapter 13 are Chapters 4–7 rather than Chapters 11 and 12. Readers will learn that the new econometrics differs from the traditional one even at the level of a simple regression model. However, an important portion of Chapter 13, that is Sections 13.4.2 and 13.4.3, cannot be understood without Chapters 11 and 12.

[13] Readers are referred to Hargreaves (1993) for a nice survey in a summary style, covering more methods than Part II does.

11
Different Modelling Strategies on Multiple Relationships

11.1 Economic Models and Statistical Models

11.1.1 Simultaneous equations model

The present book is primarily concerned with econometrics for macroeconomics, and the economic models here describe economic theories on the interrelations among macroeconomic variables. The variables are aggregate measures of quantities of transactions and of prices concerning goods and assets. The interrelations among these measures originate in the arbitraging and the optimizing behaviour of economic agents. The time units relevant to empirical investigations of these interrelations are those in which the data of the aggregate measures are available, usually a quarter. The interrelations suggest certain regularities upon the way in which past measures affect current measures. The interrelations may not completely determine the current measures, given the past, and the parts that are left indeterminate are accounted for by random variables with zero mean. In fact the shocks that play a fundamental role in many macroeconomic theories are the parts of current variables that are not determined by their past measures. Since one quarter is much longer than the time unit in which an economic agent decides on its transactions, the interrelations also suggest regularities on the way in which current measures of different variables are determined jointly with mutual interactions within the *same* quarter.

Functional forms of interrelations are not specified by economic theories. Econometrics has adopted, in fact too easily, a linear approximation to the interrelations among macroeconomic variables. We thus arrive at what is called the linear simultaneous equations model in econometrics,

$$\boldsymbol{A}_0\boldsymbol{x}_t = \boldsymbol{A}_1\boldsymbol{x}_{t-1} + \ldots + \boldsymbol{u}_t, \tag{11.1}$$

where $\{\boldsymbol{x}_t\}$ is a k-element vector stochastic process of macroeconomic variables, and $\{\boldsymbol{u}_t\}$ is a vector stochastic process with zero mean. $\{\boldsymbol{x}_t\}$ is observable, but $\{\boldsymbol{u}_t\}$ is not. In principle, all of the $k \times k$ coefficient matrices, $\boldsymbol{A}_0, \boldsymbol{A}_1, \ldots$ are to reflect economic theories on the interrelations among elements of $\{\boldsymbol{x}_t\}$. $\boldsymbol{A}_0$ is assumed to be non-singular. For simplicity we may assume that $\{\boldsymbol{u}_t\}$ is i.i.d. with $E(\boldsymbol{u}_t) = 0$ and $E(\boldsymbol{u}_t\boldsymbol{u}_t') = \boldsymbol{\Omega}$. Equating each of k elements of both sides of (11.1) yields k equations each called a *structural* equation emphasizing that it reflects economic theories on the agents and markets.

11.1.2 Identification

The identification of a (vector) parameter is defined as follows. Given a model, the entire space of parameter values is divided into observationally equivalent classes. Two points belong to the same class if and only if they produce the identical probability distribution of observations. If each class contains no more than a single point, the parameter is identified. In many models the parameters are identified from the outset. In some models the parameters are identified after some normalization rules are introduced. In (11.1) the normalization sets the diagonal elements of $\boldsymbol{A}_0$ to unities, which is innocuous for the purpose of the analysis. In Chapters 13 and 15 we shall find some normalization rule that is not innocuous. In (11.1) the remaining part of parameters, i.e. the off-diagonal elements of $\boldsymbol{A}_0$ and $\boldsymbol{A}_1, \ldots$, and distinct elements of $\boldsymbol{\Omega}$, are still left unidentified. In fact a model obtained by left multiplication of both sides of (11.1) by a non-singular matrix produces the same probability distribution of the stochastic process $\{x_t\}$ as the original model.

In general, any constraint upon parameters eliminates from each (observationally equivalent) class those points that violate the constraint. If a single point or none is left in each class, the parameter is identified by the constraint. When every class has one and only point, the parameter is said to be just-identified. When some classes are void and the other classes have only one point, the parameter is said to be overidentified. In regard to (11.1) proponents of the simultaneous equations model assumed that the economic theories provided constraints upon $\boldsymbol{A}_0, \boldsymbol{A}_1, \ldots$ and $\boldsymbol{\Omega}$ that are sufficiently strong to identify $\boldsymbol{A}_0, \boldsymbol{A}_1, \ldots$ and $\boldsymbol{\Omega}$ completely.

In what follows, when a (vector) parameter can be identified only with a normalization rule or a constraint provided by economic theories, I shall state the condition explicitly. When the parameter is identified (unidentified) without a normalization rule or a constraint, I shall simply write identified (unidentified).

11.1.3 VAR model

Sims (1980*b*) argued that applications of the simultaneous equations model to macroeconomics had in fact relied upon artificial constraints unjustified by economic theories in order to achieve the complete identification. In my judgement the criticism of Sims (1980*b*) is well acknowledged by econometricians.

As an alternative to the simultaneous equations model Sims (1980*b*) proposed the VAR model,

$$\boldsymbol{x}_t = \boldsymbol{B}_1\boldsymbol{x}_{t-1} + \boldsymbol{B}_2\boldsymbol{x}_{t-2} + \ldots + \boldsymbol{v}_t, \tag{11.2}$$

where $\{\boldsymbol{v}_t\}$ is i.i.d. with zero mean. (11.1) and (11.2) are alike and in fact (11.2) follows from (11.1) by multiplying $\boldsymbol{A}_0^{-1}$ on both sides. But an important difference between (11.1) and (11.2) is that the coefficient matrices, $\boldsymbol{B}_1, \boldsymbol{B}_2, \ldots$ in (11.2) are identified without any constraints derived from economic theories.

Moreover, the VAR model is a statistical model because $\boldsymbol{B}_1, \boldsymbol{B}_2, \ldots$ are determined solely on the basis of how well (11.2) fits the time-series data of $\{\boldsymbol{x}_t\}$.

As pointed out above, a VAR model is derived from the simultaneous equations model (11.1) by multiplying $\boldsymbol{A}_0^{-1}$ on both sides. Constraints on $\boldsymbol{A}_0, \boldsymbol{A}_1, \ldots$ due to economic theories may be transferred to $\boldsymbol{B}_1, \boldsymbol{B}_2, \ldots$. Thus some aspects of economic theories may place constraints upon the parameters of VAR models. Since $\boldsymbol{B}_1, \boldsymbol{B}_2, \ldots$ are identified without the aid of economic theories, the constraints provide overidentifying restrictions, which can be tested by observations. Moreover, in many such studies one does not have to deal with structural equations explicitly, thus motivating empirical studies of economic theories on the basis of the VAR rather than the simultaneous equation. There is a large amount of literature on this topic. I mention here tests of rational-expectations hypotheses on a co-integrated VAR in Shiller (1981*b*), Campbell and Shiller (1987, 1988), and Kunitomo and Yamamoto (1990).

11.1.4 Comparison

I shall now compare the simultaneous equations model (11.1) and VAR (11.2). In applications of (11.2) the lag orders are truncated at p so that the coefficient matrices are $\boldsymbol{B}_1, \ldots, \boldsymbol{B}_p$.[1] Altogether they involve pk^2 parameters when $\boldsymbol{x}_t$ has k elements. Since the sample size available for macroeconomic studies is 100 to 150, the VAR includes too many parameters in comparison with the sample size. On the other hand, the simultaneous equations model has many fewer (effective) parameters because of the constraints placed on the matrices $\boldsymbol{A}_0, \boldsymbol{A}_1, \ldots$. It must be admitted that economic theories do not constrain either lag orders or dynamic lag structures represented by $\boldsymbol{A}_1, \boldsymbol{A}_2, \ldots$ in (11.1), but in practice a large part of elements of $\boldsymbol{A}_1, \boldsymbol{A}_2, \ldots$ is suppressed to zero in the simultaneous equations model. The validity of such practices may be doubtful, but they contribute to reducing the number of unknown parameters to be estimated.

As stated above, constraints are placed upon $\boldsymbol{A}_0, \boldsymbol{A}_1, \ldots$ in the simultaneous equations model (11.1), while they need not be on $\boldsymbol{B}_1, \boldsymbol{B}_2, \ldots$ in the VAR model (11.2). This may lead us to think that the simultaneous equations models are logical specializations of the VAR models. However, if our consideration is confined to those models that can reasonbly be estimated with 100 or 150 observations of quarterly data, the simultaneous equations model can contain a larger number of variables (denoted by k above) than the VAR models do. This is because the effective number of parameters in $\boldsymbol{A}_0, \boldsymbol{A}_1, \ldots$ is much smaller than pk^2, even if it is assumed that the same lag order p is adopted between the simultaneous equations and VAR. The 'feasible' VAR models are not necessarily logical generalization of 'feasible' simultaneous equations models.

If feasible simultaneous equations models are logical specializations of a feasible VAR model, then the VAR model may be used as a benchmark to test the

[1] The determination of lag orders is an important problem. See Lütkepohl (1991: 118–50) for stationary multivariate models, and Morimune and Mantani (1993) for non-stationary models.

simultaneous equation models. In the VAR model $\boldsymbol{B}_1, \ldots, \boldsymbol{B}_p$ are just-identified. On the other hand, some of the constraints on $\boldsymbol{A}_0, \boldsymbol{A}_1, \ldots$ allegedly derived from economic theories may imply constraints upon $\boldsymbol{A}_0^{-1}\boldsymbol{A}_1 \equiv \boldsymbol{B}_1, \ldots \boldsymbol{A}_0^{-1}\boldsymbol{A}_p \equiv \boldsymbol{B}_p$, leading to overidentifying restrictions upon the VAR coefficient matrices, $\boldsymbol{B}_1, \ldots, \boldsymbol{B}_p$. This approach has been taken in Hendry and Mizon (1993). The basic logic here is identical to that mentioned in the last paragraph of 11.1.3 above.

11.1.5 Intermediate positions

Admitting that economic theories do not identify completely $\boldsymbol{A}_0, \boldsymbol{A}_1, \ldots$, and $\boldsymbol{\Omega}$, the theories do divide the entire space of parameter values into a number of observationally equivalent classes. Even though each class may comprise a number of parameter points, some aspects of economic theories can be tested empirically if each class is such that either *all* members of the class admit the aspects or *no* members of the class admit the aspects; in short, if the aspects are properties of the observationally equivalent classes.[2] This approach to save the simultaneous equations model from Sims's criticism has not long been explored in practice to the best of my knowledge, but it has been found in the co-integration analysis that some aspects of economic theories are properties of the observationally equivalent classes. See Section 15.2.1 below.

Recently a modelling strategy called the structural VAR has been proposed in Bernanke (1986), Blanchard and Quah (1989), Blanchard (1989), King *et al.* (1991). In my judgement the structural VAR is a variant of the simultaneous equations model rather than a VAR. It does not assume $\boldsymbol{A}_0 = \boldsymbol{I}$ in (11.1), and moreover employs some constraints on the parameters $\boldsymbol{A}_0, \boldsymbol{A}_1, \ldots$, and $\boldsymbol{\Omega}$ just sufficient to identify them completely. Common to all the structural VARs is the specification that $\boldsymbol{\Omega} = E(\boldsymbol{u}_t\boldsymbol{u}_t')$ is diagonal in (11.1) while assuming that $\{\boldsymbol{u}_t\}$ is i.i.d. In other words, shocks in different structural equations, for example, demand shocks and supply shocks, are uncorrelated at all leads and lags. It has been known in the simultaneous equations literature that this is not sufficient for complete identification of $\boldsymbol{A}_0, \boldsymbol{A}_1, \ldots$, and indeed additional constraints are introduced.

What deserves our particular attention is Blanchard and Quah (1989) and King *et al.* (1991). In Blanchard and Quah (1989) and also Gali (1992) constraints are placed upon the impact matrix of shocks in different structural equations, $\boldsymbol{u}_t$, upon long-run components of variables x_t. Conceptually this matrix is

$$\frac{\partial \boldsymbol{x}_{t+\infty}}{\partial \boldsymbol{u}_t'}$$

in (11.1), but it is easier to work along the methods given in Chapter 12. King *et al.* (1991) derive particular co-integration properties (rank and structure of

[2] Phillips (1989) expresses a similar suggestion by some reparametrization.

the co-integration space) from an economic theory. This implication upon the long-run impact of shocks is then used for the identification of parameters in the simultaneous equations. This will be further explained in Section 15.5. Models in Lee and Hamada (1991) and Ahmed *et al.* (1993) are simultaneous equations models on the relationships among long-run components of different variables.

In contrast to the standard VAR the structural VAR model achieves identification of its parameter through economic theories,[3] and thus may be subjected to criticisms such as Sims (1980*b*) about the validity of economic theories. However, the constraints due to long-run economic theories are less controversial than those due to the short-run dynamics. Moreover, the standard VAR is not without a drawback in other respects, as mentioned earlier. One way to test the economic theories is to just-identify the model by constraints derived from a portion of the theories and then test the validity of the rest against the observations. In my judgement there is no unequivocal choice between the standard VAR and the simultaneous equations model.[4]

It is the (standard rather than structural) VAR models that are adopted in most parts of Part II for the explanation of co-integration analysis. Economic theories are considered in implementing the co-integration analysis, but structural equations are not. This strategy is found adequate because many long-run economic relations do not directly deal with structural equations (for instance, demand function or supply function), but with some equations derived from them through the equilibrium conditions. However, we shall need some consideration analogous to the simultaneous equations in Section 15.2.1, where we discuss the unidentified co-integration matrix to be denoted by $\boldsymbol{B}'$. The simultaneous equations models are briefly touched on in Section 13.1.4, but by and large unexplored in the present book. The long-run version of structural VAR models may well be an important topic for future research.

11.2 Weak Exogeneity

Most of the models in econometrics are conditional upon exogenous variables, and the exogenous variables are not explicitly modelled. The concept of weak exogeneity provides conditions under which we can perform efficient inference on the conditional model without employing the entire model. The purpose of the present section is to give a brief explanation of weak exogeneity to the extent that is necessary for the reading of Part II. Readers are referred to Engle, Hendry, and Richard (1983) for more about weak exogeneity and to Ericsson (1992) for a good expository presentation.

[3] Sims (1980*b*) achieves identification of $A_0, A_1, \ldots$ in (11.1) by a particular causality ordering among different shocks, which ordering however is not founded on economic theories. This interpretation of Sims (1980*b*) has been provided in Bernanke (1986).

[4] I am indebted to suggestions from Yosuke Takeda on the writing of the present and previous paragraphs.

For illustration consider a bivariate normal distribution of $\boldsymbol{x}' = (x_1, x_2)$ with mean vector $\boldsymbol{\mu}' = (\mu_1, \mu_2)$ and covariance matrix

$$\boldsymbol{\Sigma} = \begin{bmatrix} \sigma_{11} & \sigma_{12} \\ \sigma_{21} & \sigma_{22} \end{bmatrix}.$$

The parameters are $(\mu_1, \mu_2, \sigma_{11}, \sigma_{12}, \sigma_{22})$. The p.d.f. of $\boldsymbol{x}$ is

$$f(\boldsymbol{x}) = (2\pi)^{-1} (\det\ [\boldsymbol{\Sigma}])^{-1/2} \exp\ \left(-\tfrac{1}{2}(\boldsymbol{x} - \boldsymbol{\mu})'\boldsymbol{\Sigma}^{-1}(\boldsymbol{x} - \boldsymbol{\mu})\right).$$

where $\det[\boldsymbol{\Sigma}]$ is the determinant of $\boldsymbol{\Sigma}$. This can be expressed as $f(x_2|x_1)f(x_1)$, where $f(x_2|x_1)$ is the conditional p.d.f. of x_2 upon x_1, i.e.

$$f(x_2|x_1) = (2\pi)^{-1/2}\sigma_{22.1}^{-1/2} \exp\ \left(-\tfrac{1}{2}\sigma_{22.1}^{-1}(x_2 - \beta x_1 - \mu_{2.1})^2\right), \tag{11.3}$$

$$\beta = \sigma_{12}\sigma_{11}^{-1}, \quad \sigma_{22.1} = \sigma_{22} - \sigma_{11}^{-1}\sigma_{12}^2,$$

$$\mu_{2.1} = \mu_2 - \beta\mu_1.$$

Moreover, $f(x_1)$ is the marginal p.d.f. of x_1, i.e.

$$f(x_1) = (2\pi)^{-1/2}\sigma_{11}^{-1/2} \exp\ \left(-\tfrac{1}{2}\sigma_{11}^{-1}(x_1 - \mu_1)^2\right). \tag{11.4}$$

The conditional p.d.f. contains three parameters, β, $\sigma_{22.1}$ and $\mu_{2.1}$, and the marginal p.d.f. contains two parameters, σ_{11} and μ_1. Suppose that $\boldsymbol{x}_t' = (x_{1t}, x_{2t})$ is distributed as $\boldsymbol{x}$ given above and $\{\boldsymbol{x}_t\}$ is i.i.d. Then over the sample period $t = 1, \ldots, T$ the log-likelihood is

$$\sum_{t=1}^{T} \log f(\boldsymbol{x}) = \sum_t \log f(x_{2t}|x_{1t}) + \sum_t \log f(x_{1t}). \tag{11.5}$$

The first term on the right-hand side of (11.5) contains parameters, $(\beta, \sigma_{22.1}, \mu_{2.1})$, and the second term has (σ_{11}, μ_1). The variations of $(\beta, \sigma_{22.1}, \mu_{2.1})$ are free from (σ_{11}, μ_1) so that the differentiation of (11.5) with respect to $(\beta, \sigma_{22.1}, \mu_{2.1})$ is in no way constrained by (σ_{11}, μ_1).

Suppose that we are concerned with the estimation of β only. Since β is not contained in the second term of the right-hand side of (11.5), the maximum-likelihood estimation of β is performed by maximizing the first term only, which comes from the conditional p.d.f., (11.3). The equation that is associated with (11.3) is

$$x_{2t} = \beta x_{1t} + \mu_{2.1} + u_t, \quad u_t \sim N(0, \sigma_{22.1}). \tag{11.6}$$

The marginal p.d.f. of x_1, (11.4), is irrelevant to the maximum-likelihood estimation of β. Then it is said that x_1 is *weakly exogenous* in (11.6) *with respect to* β. The β in this situation is called the *parameter of interest*. The equation (11.6) is called the *conditional model*, and

$$x_1 \sim N(\mu_1, \sigma_{11}) \tag{11.7}$$

is called the *marginal model*.

It is always important to specify the parameter of interest when one mentions weak exogeneity. In fact in the above example x_1 is weakly exogenous in (11.6) with respect to $(\beta, \mu_{2.1}, \sigma_{22.1})$ instead of β alone.

The formal definition of weak exogeneity is given in Engle, Hendry, and Richard (1983) as follows. Let $\{\boldsymbol{x}_t\}$ be a vector stochastic process, and that the joint p.d.f. of $(\boldsymbol{x}_T, \boldsymbol{x}_{T-1}, \ldots, \boldsymbol{x}_1, \boldsymbol{x}_0)$ is

$$f(\boldsymbol{x}_T, \boldsymbol{x}_{T-1}, \ldots, \boldsymbol{x}_1, \boldsymbol{x}_0) = \Pi_{t=1}^T f(\boldsymbol{x}_t|\boldsymbol{x}_{t-1}, \ldots, \boldsymbol{x}_1, \boldsymbol{x}_0). \tag{11.8}$$

This expression as a sequence of products of the conditional p.d.f.s is always possible, and in fact frequently used in time-series analysis. Throughout $t = T, \ldots, 1, 0$ $\boldsymbol{x}_t$ is partitioned identically as $\boldsymbol{x}'_t = (\boldsymbol{x}'_{1t}, \boldsymbol{x}'_{2t})$. Then (11.8) is written

$$\Pi_t f(\boldsymbol{x}_{2t}|\boldsymbol{x}_{1t}, \boldsymbol{x}_{t-1}, \ldots, \boldsymbol{x}_1, \boldsymbol{x}_0)\Pi_t f(\boldsymbol{x}_{1t}|\boldsymbol{x}_{t-1}, \ldots, \boldsymbol{x}_1, \boldsymbol{x}_0). \tag{11.9}$$

Moreover, assume that $f(\boldsymbol{x}_{2t}|\boldsymbol{x}_{1t}, \boldsymbol{x}_{t-1}, \ldots, \boldsymbol{x}_1, \boldsymbol{x}_0)$, $t = T, \ldots, 1, 0$, contains the vector parameter $\boldsymbol{\lambda}_1$; that $f(\boldsymbol{x}_{1t}|\boldsymbol{x}_{t-1}, \ldots, \boldsymbol{x}_1, \boldsymbol{x}_0)$, $t = T, \ldots, 1, 0$, contains the vector parameter $\boldsymbol{\lambda}_2$; and that $\boldsymbol{\lambda}_1$ and $\boldsymbol{\lambda}_2$ are *variation-free*, i.e. the variations of $\boldsymbol{\lambda}_1$ are in no way constrained either through equalities or inequalities by $\boldsymbol{\lambda}_2$ and vice versa.[5] (11.9) is expressed as

$$\Pi_t f(\boldsymbol{x}_{2t}|\boldsymbol{x}_{1t}, \boldsymbol{x}_{t-1}, \ldots, \boldsymbol{x}_1, \boldsymbol{x}_0; \boldsymbol{\lambda}_1)\Pi_t f(\boldsymbol{x}_{1t}|\boldsymbol{x}_{t-1}, \ldots, \boldsymbol{x}_1, \boldsymbol{x}_0; \boldsymbol{\lambda}_2). \tag{11.9'}$$

If $\boldsymbol{\lambda}_1$ is the parameter of interest, $\boldsymbol{x}_{1t}$ is weakly exogenous in the conditional model representing $f(\boldsymbol{x}_{2t}|\boldsymbol{x}_{1t}, \boldsymbol{x}_{t-1}, \ldots, \boldsymbol{x}_1, \boldsymbol{x}_0; \boldsymbol{\lambda}_1)$, $t = T, \ldots, 1, 0$. The maximum-likelihood estimation of $\boldsymbol{\lambda}_1$ can be based upon the conditional model alone. The marginal model is irrelevant to $\boldsymbol{\lambda}_1$.

When $\boldsymbol{\lambda}' = (\boldsymbol{\lambda}'_1, \boldsymbol{\lambda}'_2)$ is reparametrized into $\boldsymbol{\gamma}'$ as is often done in econometrics, $\boldsymbol{x}_{1t}$ remains weakly exogenous with respect to any elements of $\boldsymbol{\gamma}'$ that can be expressed by $\boldsymbol{\lambda}'_1$ alone.

Nowhere in the above explanation is assumed the stationarity of $\{\boldsymbol{x}_t\}$. In fact Banerjee *et al.* (1993: 245–52) demonstrate the importance of the weak exogeneity in the models in which $I(1)$ variables are involved.

Let us consider the weak exogeneity in the simultaneous equations model (11.1) with lag order p,

$$\boldsymbol{A}^{(0)}\boldsymbol{x}_t = \boldsymbol{A}^{(1)}\boldsymbol{x}_{t-1} + \ldots + \boldsymbol{A}^{(p)}\boldsymbol{x}_{t-p} + \boldsymbol{u}_t,$$

where $\{\boldsymbol{u}_t\}$ is Gaussian i.i.d. with $E(\boldsymbol{u}_t) = \boldsymbol{0}$ and $E(\boldsymbol{u}_t\boldsymbol{u}'_t) = \boldsymbol{\Omega}$ assumed to be positive definite. $\{\boldsymbol{x}_t\}$ may be non-stationary with unit roots. We partition $\boldsymbol{x}'_t$ as $(\boldsymbol{x}'_{1t}, \boldsymbol{x}'_{2t})$ with k_1 and k_2 elements in $\boldsymbol{x}_{1t}$ and $\boldsymbol{x}_{2t}$ respectively.

I shall proceed as though $k_1 = k_2 = 1$, but its extension to any k_1 and k_2 is straightforward. Let us write

$$\boldsymbol{x}'_t \equiv (x_{1t}, x_{2t}), \quad \boldsymbol{u}'_t \equiv (u_{1t}, u_{2t})$$

[5] Ericsson (1992) presents a nice explanation of variation-free parameters on the stable cobweb model.

$$\boldsymbol{A}^{(i)} \equiv \begin{bmatrix} a_{11}^{(i)}, & a_{12}^{(i)} \\ a_{21}^{(i)}, & a_{22}^{(i)} \end{bmatrix}, \quad i = 0, 1, \ldots, p$$

$$\boldsymbol{\Omega} \equiv \begin{bmatrix} \omega_{11}, & \omega_{12} \\ \omega_{21}, & \omega_{22} \end{bmatrix} \equiv E(\boldsymbol{u}_t \boldsymbol{u}_t').$$

Then the model is

$$\begin{bmatrix} a_{11}^{(0)}, & a_{12}^{(0)} \\ a_{21}^{(0)}, & a_{22}^{(0)} \end{bmatrix} \begin{bmatrix} x_{1t} \\ x_{2t} \end{bmatrix} = \sum_{i=1}^{p} \begin{bmatrix} a_{11}^{(i)}, & a_{12}^{(i)} \\ a_{21}^{(i)}, & a_{22}^{(i)} \end{bmatrix} \begin{bmatrix} x_{1t-i} \\ x_{2t-i} \end{bmatrix} + \begin{bmatrix} u_{1t} \\ u_{2t} \end{bmatrix}. \qquad (11.10)$$

I shall use notations

$$\boldsymbol{A}^{(0)-1} \equiv \begin{bmatrix} \boldsymbol{c}_1 \\ \boldsymbol{c}_2 \end{bmatrix},$$

$$\boldsymbol{a}_h^{(i)} \equiv \left(a_{h1}^{(i)}, a_{h2}^{(i)}\right); \quad h = 1, 2, i = 0, 1, \ldots, p.$$

Then

$$x_{1t} = \boldsymbol{c}_1 \left(\sum_{i=1}^{p} \boldsymbol{A}^{(i)} \boldsymbol{x}_{t-i} + \boldsymbol{u}_t\right) \qquad (11.11a)$$

$$x_{2t} = \boldsymbol{c}_2 \left(\sum_{i=1}^{p} \boldsymbol{A}^{(i)} \boldsymbol{x}_{t-i} + \boldsymbol{u}_t\right). \qquad (11.11b)$$

Consider then

$$E(x_{2t}|x_{1t}, \boldsymbol{x}_{t-1}, \boldsymbol{x}_{t-2}, \ldots, \boldsymbol{x}_0)$$
$$= \boldsymbol{c}_2 \left\{\sum_{i=1}^{p} \boldsymbol{A}^{(i)} \boldsymbol{x}_{t-i} + E(\boldsymbol{u}_t|x_{1t}, \boldsymbol{x}_{t-1}, \ldots, \boldsymbol{x}_0)\right\}.$$

Using (11.11a), and noting that $\boldsymbol{u}_t$ is uncorrelated with $\boldsymbol{x}_{t-1}, \boldsymbol{x}_{t-2}, \ldots, \boldsymbol{x}_0$, this is equal to

$$\boldsymbol{c}_2 \left\{\sum_{i=1}^{p} \boldsymbol{A}^{(i)} \boldsymbol{x}_{t-i} + E(\boldsymbol{u}_t|\boldsymbol{c}_1 \boldsymbol{u}_t)\right\},$$

but

$$E(\boldsymbol{u}_t|\boldsymbol{c}_1 \boldsymbol{u}_t) = \boldsymbol{\Omega} \boldsymbol{c}_1' (\boldsymbol{c}_1 \boldsymbol{\Omega} \boldsymbol{c}_1')^{-1} \boldsymbol{c}_1 \boldsymbol{u}_t. \qquad (11.12)$$

Therefore

$$E(x_{2t}|x_{1t}, \boldsymbol{x}_{t-1}, \boldsymbol{x}_{t-2}, \ldots, \boldsymbol{x}_0)$$
$$= \boldsymbol{c}_2 \left\{\sum_{i=1}^{p} \boldsymbol{A}^{(i)} \boldsymbol{x}_{t-i} + \boldsymbol{\Omega} \boldsymbol{c}_1' (\boldsymbol{c}_1 \boldsymbol{\Omega} \boldsymbol{c}_1')^{-1} \left(x_{1t} - \boldsymbol{c}_1 \sum_{i=1}^{p} \boldsymbol{A}^{(i)} \boldsymbol{x}_{t-i}\right)\right\} \qquad (11.13)$$
$$= \boldsymbol{c}_2 \boldsymbol{\Omega} \boldsymbol{c}_1' (\boldsymbol{c}_1 \boldsymbol{\Omega} \boldsymbol{c}_1')^{-1} x_{1t} + \left[\boldsymbol{c}_2 - \boldsymbol{c}_2 \boldsymbol{\Omega} \boldsymbol{c}_1' (\boldsymbol{c}_1 \boldsymbol{\Omega} \boldsymbol{c}_1')^{-1} \boldsymbol{c}_1\right] \sum_{i=1}^{p} \boldsymbol{A}^{(i)} \boldsymbol{x}_{t-i}.$$

The variance of x_{2t} conditional upon $x_{1t}, \boldsymbol{x}_{t-1}, \boldsymbol{x}_{t-2}, \ldots, \boldsymbol{x}_0$ is

$$\boldsymbol{c}_2 E\{(\boldsymbol{u}_t - E(\boldsymbol{u}_t|\boldsymbol{c}_1 \boldsymbol{u}_t))(\boldsymbol{u}_t - E(\boldsymbol{u}_t|\boldsymbol{c}_1 \boldsymbol{u}_t))'\}\boldsymbol{c}_2'. \qquad (11.14)$$

Since $\{\boldsymbol{x}_t\}$ is Gaussian, the conditional mean and conditional variance determine the conditional p.d.f. $f(x_{2t}|x_{1t}, \boldsymbol{x}_{t-1}, \ldots, \boldsymbol{x}_0)$.

So far no particular assumptions have been introduced, but let us now introduce two assumptions.

Assumption 1 $\omega_{12} = 0$

Assumption 2 $a_{12}^{(0)} = 0$.

Then $\boldsymbol{c}_1 = (a_{11}^{(0)-1}, 0)$, $\boldsymbol{c}_2 = (-a_{22}^{(0)-1} a_{21}^{(0)} a_{11}^{(0)-1}, a_{22}^{(0)-1})$. (11.12) is reduced to just $(u_{1t}, 0)'$. (11.13) is now,

$$E(x_{2t}|x_{1t}, \boldsymbol{x}_{t-1}, \boldsymbol{x}_{t-2}, \ldots, \boldsymbol{x}_0) \tag{11.13$'$}$$
$$= -a_{22}^{(0)-1} a_{21}^{(0)} x_{1t} + a_{22}^{(0)-1} \sum_{i=1}^{p} \boldsymbol{a}_2^{(i)} \boldsymbol{x}_{t-i},$$

and (11.14) is

$$a_{22}^{(0)-1} \omega_{22} a_{22}^{(0)-1}. \tag{11.14$'$}$$

The mean and variance of $\{x_{2t}\}$ conditional upon $(x_{1t}, \boldsymbol{x}_{t-1}, \boldsymbol{x}_{t-2}, \ldots)$, (11.13$'$) and (11.14$'$), contain $\boldsymbol{a}_{2.}^{(i)}$, $i = 0, 1, \ldots, p$ and ω_{22} only. On the other hand the mean and variance of $\{x_{1t}\}$ conditional upon $(\boldsymbol{x}_{t-1}, \boldsymbol{x}_{t-2}, \ldots)$ under Assumptions 1 and 2 contain $a_{11}^{(0)}$, $\boldsymbol{a}_1^{(i)}$, $i = 1, \ldots, p$ and ω_{11}, but do not contain $\boldsymbol{a}_2^{(i)}$, $i = 0, 1, \ldots, p$ and ω_{22}. The only additional assumption needed for the weak exogeneity is

Assumption 3 There exist no a priori constraints that relate $\boldsymbol{a}_1^{(i)}$, $i = 0, 1, \ldots, p$ and ω_{11} to $\boldsymbol{a}_2^{(i)}$, $i = 0, 1, \ldots, p$ and ω_{22}.

Under Assumptions 1, 2, and 3 x_{1t} is weakly exogenous in the conditional model,

$$a_{21}^{(0)} x_{1t} + a_{22}^{(0)} x_{2t} = \sum_{i=1}^{p} \boldsymbol{a}_2^{(i)} x_{t-1} + u_{2t}, \ \ u_{2t} \sim N(0, \omega_{22})$$

with respect to $\boldsymbol{a}_2^{(i)}$, $i = 0, 1, \ldots, p$ and ω_{22}. The result may be regarded as a special case of Theorem 4.3 of Engle, Hendry, and Richard (1983), which however deals with a rather complicated model.

Assumptions 1, 2, and 3 are only sufficient conditions, but I do not know of any weaker sufficient conditions.[6] In particular, x_{1t} *being predetermined is not sufficient* for an efficient estimation of $\boldsymbol{a}_2^{(i)}$ and ω_{22}, and therefore not sufficient for the weak exogeneity. Even though the predetermined x_{1t} yields a consistent estimation of $\boldsymbol{a}_2^{(i)}$ and ω_{22}, these parameters are contained in the marginal model as well. When Assumptions 1 and 2 hold, the simultaneous equations model is called recursive.

[6] For the stationary simultaneous equations model Hatanaka and Odaki (1983) shows that x_{1t} being predetermined in the second equation, i.e. $E(x_{1t}u_{2t}) = 0$, is equivalent to $\omega_{12} = a_{12}^{(0)} a_{22}^{(0)-1} \omega_{22}$, which in turn is equivalent to the conditions, (11.13$'$) and (11.14$'$), of the conditional model. However, this is not sufficient for the weak exogeneity, because the marginal model still contains $\boldsymbol{a}_2^{(i)}$ and ω_{22} unless either Assumption 1 or Assumption 2 is introduced. Needless to say that Assumption 3 is always needed for the weak exogeneity.

Neither Assumption 1 nor Assumption 2 can be verified by the data alone. Some a priori knowledge is needed to justify them because the parameters involved are not identified without such knowledge.

The VAR model (11.2) in the case of $k = 2$ is obtained by making $\boldsymbol{A}^{(0)} = \boldsymbol{I}_2$ in (11.10). Then $\boldsymbol{c}_1 = (1, 0)$ and $\boldsymbol{c}_2 = (0, 1)$. (11.12) becomes $E(\boldsymbol{u}_t|\boldsymbol{c}_1\boldsymbol{u}_t) = (1, \omega_{21}\omega_{11}^{-1})' u_{1t}$, and (11.13) becomes

$$E(x_{2t}|x_{1t}, \boldsymbol{x}_{t-1}, \ldots, \boldsymbol{x}_0) = \omega_{21}\omega_{11}^{-1}x_{1t} + \sum_{i=1}^{p}\left(\boldsymbol{a}_2^{(i)} - \omega_{21}\omega_{11}^{-1}\boldsymbol{a}_1^{(i)}\right)\boldsymbol{x}_{t-i}.$$

The conditional variance is $\omega_{22} - \omega_{21}\omega_{11}^{-1}\omega_{12}$. The conditional model may be written as

$$x_{2t} = \omega_{21}\omega_{11}^{-1}x_{1t} + \sum_{i}\left(\boldsymbol{a}_2^{(i)} - \omega_{21}\omega_{11}^{-1}\boldsymbol{a}_1^{(i)}\right)\boldsymbol{x}_{t-i} + v_t \tag{11.15}$$

$$v_t \sim N(0, \omega_{22} - \omega_{21}\omega_{11}^{-1}\omega_{12}),$$

and the marginal model for x_{1t} is

$$x_{1t} = \sum_{i}\boldsymbol{a}_1^{(i)}\boldsymbol{x}_{t-i} + u_{1t}, \quad u_{1t} \sim N(0, \omega_{11}) \tag{11.16}$$

The original parameters, $\boldsymbol{a}_1^{(i)}, \boldsymbol{a}_2^{(i)}, i = 1, \ldots, p, \omega_{11}, \omega_{12}, \omega_{22}$ may be reparametrized into $\boldsymbol{a}_1^{(i)}, \tilde{\boldsymbol{a}}_2^{(i)} \equiv \boldsymbol{a}_2^{(i)} - \omega_{21}\omega_{11}^{-1}\boldsymbol{a}_1^{(i)}, i = 1, \ldots, p, \omega_{11}, \beta_{2.1} \equiv \omega_{21}\omega_{11}^{-1}$, $\omega_{22.1} \equiv \omega_{22} - \omega_{21}\omega_{11}^{-1}\omega_{12}$. Then x_{1t} is weakly exogenous in (11.15) with respect to $\tilde{\boldsymbol{a}}_2^{(i)}, i = 1, \ldots, p, \beta_{2.1}, \omega_{22.1}$.

11.3 Granger Non-Causality

Granger (1969) considered the causality of y on x in regard to two optimal (minimum mean squared error) predictions of x_t, (i) using the information set of $x_{t-1}, x_{t-2}, \ldots$ and (ii) using the information set of $(x_{t-1}, y_{t-1}), (x_{t-2}, y_{t-2}), \ldots$. The second prediction never entails a mean squared error larger than the first prediction, but it is possible that two predictions have identical mean squared errors. When that occurs y fails to cause x as the information of $(y_{t-1}, y_{t-2}, \ldots)$ does not contribute to the prediction of x_t. This definition of (non-) causality may well be a misleading wording as the causality should refer to some intrinsic property of a system rather than a prediction. The concept, 'Granger- (non-) causality', was adopted in Sims (1972) to allow for this point, and has since been accepted by economic theorists and econometricians. It must be pointed out that prediction does reflect whatever one identifies as the intrinsic property.

Granger non-causality has since been found indispensable in economic theories to discern different channels in which expectation is formed by economic agents and markets. The concept has also played an important role in many empirical studies dealing with expectation. We shall need the concept of Granger non-causality to explain the framework of cointegration in Chapter 12 and the inference theory in Chapter 13. The present Section provides a brief explanation only to the extent that is necessary for the reading of Part II. Readers are referred to Granger (1969), Sims (1972), Geweke (1984), Granger and Newbold (1986, chs. 7 and 8), and Granger (1988*b*) for more about Granger non-causality, and Stock and Watson (1989) and Friedman and Kuttner (1993) for recent empirical studies in which Granger causality is examined.

If $\{(x_t, y_t)\}$ starts at $t = 0$, the optimal prediction of x_t from $(x_{t-1}, \ldots, x_0)$ is $E(x_t|x_{t-1}, \ldots, x_0)$, and the optimal prediction of x_t from $(x_{t-1}, y_{t-1}, \ldots, x_0, y_0)$ is $E(x_t|x_{t-1}, y_{t-1}, \ldots, x_0, y_0)$. The variances of errors in the two predictions are identical if and only if

$$E(x_t|x_{t-1}, \ldots, x_0) = E(x_t|x_{t-1}, y_{t-1}, \ldots, x_0, y_0) \tag{11.17}$$

holds for all realizations of $(x_{t-1}, y_{t-1}, \ldots, x_0, y_0)$. Thus y failing to cause x in Granger's sense is defined by (11.17) for all $t \geq 1$. If $\{(x_t, y_t)\}$ starts at $t = -\infty$, the conditioning variables in (11.17) must be replaced by $(x_{t-1}, \ldots, x_0, x_{-1}, \ldots)$ on the left-hand side and by $(x_{t-1}, y_{t-1}, \ldots, x_0, y_0, x_{-1}, y_{-1}, \ldots)$ on the right-hand side, and some specifications on $\{(x_t, y_t)\}$ would be required to perform our reasoning on the conditional expectations.

Suppose that

$$\boldsymbol{x}_t = \boldsymbol{B}^{(1)}\boldsymbol{x}_{t-1} + \ldots + \boldsymbol{B}^{(p)}\boldsymbol{x}_{t-p} + \boldsymbol{v}_t \tag{11.18}$$

is a bivariate, possibly non-stationary VAR. The reasoning made on (11.10) can be carried over here by setting $\boldsymbol{A}^{(0)}$ in (11.10) to $\boldsymbol{I}_2$ and equating $\boldsymbol{A}^{(i)}$ to $\boldsymbol{B}^{(i)}$ in (11.17). We write

$$\boldsymbol{B}^{(i)} = \begin{bmatrix} b_{11}^{(i)}, & b_{12}^{(i)} \\ b_{21}^{(i)}, & b_{22}^{(i)} \end{bmatrix}, \quad \boldsymbol{b}_1^{(i)} = [b_{11}^{(i)}, b_{12}^{(i)}], \quad i = 1, \ldots, p.$$

$E(\boldsymbol{v}_t\boldsymbol{v}_t') = \boldsymbol{\Sigma}$ is positive definite, but $\{\boldsymbol{v}_t\}$ need not be Gaussian. It will be shown that x_{2t} does not cause x_{1t} in Granger's sense if and only if $b_{12}^{(i)} = 0, i = 1, \ldots, p$. Proofs for the case where $\{\boldsymbol{x}_t\}$ is stationary and also for the case where $\{\boldsymbol{x}_t\}$ is non-stationary and not cointegrated will be shown below. The case where $\{\boldsymbol{x}_t\}$ is co-integrated will be discussed in Section 12.2.4.

Suppose that (11.18) is initiated by some random variables $(\boldsymbol{x}_{p-1}, \ldots, \boldsymbol{x}_0)$. From the first equation of (11.18)

$$E(x_{1t}|\boldsymbol{x}_{t-1}, \boldsymbol{x}_{t-2}, \ldots, \boldsymbol{x}_0) = \sum_{i=1}^{p} \boldsymbol{b}_1^{(i)}\boldsymbol{x}_{t-i} \ (t > p) \tag{11.19a}$$

$$E(x_{1t}|x_{1t-1}, x_{1t-2}, \ldots, x_{10}) = \sum_{i=1}^{p} b_{11}^{(i)}x_{1t-i} + \sum_{i=1}^{p} b_{12}^{(i)}E(x_{2t-i}|x_{1t-1}, x_{1t-2}, \ldots, x_{10}). \tag{11.19b}$$

As stated in (11.17) x_{2t} does not cause x_{1t} in Granger's sense if and only if (11.19*a*) and (11.19*b*) are identical with probability 1. The difference between the two is

$$\sum_{i=1}^{p} b_{12}^{(i)}(x_{2t-i} - E(x_{2t-i}|x_{1t-1}, x_{1t-2}, \ldots, x_{10})). \tag{11.20}$$

If (11.18) is a stationary VAR with stationary moments in the initials $(\boldsymbol{x}_{p-1}, \ldots, \boldsymbol{x}_0)$,[7] it is easy to prove that (11.20) vanishes with probability 1 if and only if $b_{12}^{(i)} = 0, i = 1, \ldots, p$. First of all, letting $\boldsymbol{\xi}'_{t-1} \equiv (\boldsymbol{x}'_{t-1}, \boldsymbol{x}'_{t-2}, \ldots, \boldsymbol{x}'_0)$, it is known that $E(\boldsymbol{\xi}_{t-1}\boldsymbol{\xi}'_{t-1})$ is positive definite. Since $\boldsymbol{\eta}'_{t-1} \equiv (x_{2t-1}, \ldots, x_{2t-p})$ and $\boldsymbol{\zeta}'_{t-1} \equiv (x_{1t-1}, x_{1t-2}, \ldots, x_{10})$ are both subvectors of $\boldsymbol{\xi}_{t-1}$, the covariance matrix of $\boldsymbol{\eta}_{t-1}$ conditional upon $\boldsymbol{\zeta}_{t-1}$ is positive definite. Therefore $(x_{2t-i} - E(x_{2t-i}|x_{1t-1}, x_{1t-2}, \ldots, x_{11}))$, $i = 1, \ldots, p$, is a p-dimensional, *non-degenerate* random vector. (11.20) vanishes if and only if $b_{12}^{(i)} = 0, i = 1, \ldots, p$. Thus $b_{12}^{(i)} = 0, i = 1, \ldots, p$, is necessary and sufficient for x_{2t} failing to cause x_{1t} in Granger's sense. This result can be obtained also when (11.18) starts at $t = -\infty$.

The above result is implicit in Granger (1969), and has been the most widely used version of Granger non-causality. Since $\boldsymbol{B}^{(1)}, \ldots, \boldsymbol{B}^{(p)}$ are identified Granger non-causality can be tested with the observation of $\{\boldsymbol{x}_t\}$.

Continuing with the stationary case of (11.18), it can be inverted into a VMA (vector moving-average process),

$$\boldsymbol{x}_t \equiv \boldsymbol{C}^{(0)}\boldsymbol{\varepsilon}_t + \boldsymbol{C}^{(1)}\boldsymbol{\varepsilon}_{t-1} + \ldots, \tag{11.21}$$

$$\boldsymbol{C}^{(i)} = \begin{bmatrix} c_{11}^{(i)}, & c_{12}^{(i)} \\ c_{21}^{(i)}, & c_{22}^{(i)} \end{bmatrix}, \quad i = 0, 1, \ldots .$$

If $b_{12}^{(i)} = 0, i = 1, \ldots, p$ in (11.18), then $c_{12}^{(i)} = 0, i = 0, 1, \ldots$, in (11.21).

Let us consider then a VMA (11.21), not necessarily one that is obtained through inversion of a VAR. $\{\boldsymbol{\varepsilon}_t\}$ is i.i.d. with $E(\boldsymbol{\varepsilon}_t) = \boldsymbol{0}$. We shall need later the following theorem.

Theorem 11.1 (Sims (1972)). Suppose that (11.21) starting at $t = -\infty$ is a stationary, linear, indeterministic process with $E(\boldsymbol{\varepsilon}_t\boldsymbol{\varepsilon}'_t) = \boldsymbol{I}_2$.[8] Then x_2 does not cause x_1 in Granger's sense if and only if *we can choose* either $c_{11}^{(i)} = 0, i = 0, 1, 2\ldots$ or $c_{12}^{(i)} = 0, i = 0, 1, 2, \ldots$.

The proof in Sims (1972) uses some advanced mathematics. Here I try to show plausibility of the theorem. First of all, the italicized words, *we can choose*, need explanation. In general two different stochastic processes may

[7] A word of explanation may be needed on stationary moments of initials. For illustration I use a stationary AR(1),

$$x_t = \mu + \alpha x_{t-1} + \varepsilon_t.$$

If the process starts from $t = -\infty$ and $(x_1, \ldots, x_T)$ are observed,

$$E(x_t) = (1-\alpha)^{-1}\mu, \ \text{var}\ (x_t) = \sigma_\varepsilon^2(1-\alpha^2)^{-1}, 1 \le t \le T.$$

Suppose that the process starts from $t = 0$ but

$$E(x_0) = (1-\alpha)^{-1}\mu, \ \text{var}\ (x_0) = \sigma_\varepsilon^2(1-\alpha^2)^{-1}.$$

Then we still have the moments on x_t given above. We say that x_0 has the stationary mean $(1-\alpha)^{-1}\mu$ and the stationary variance $\sigma_\varepsilon^2(1-\alpha^2)^{-1}$.

[8] A stationary process $\{\boldsymbol{x}_t\}$ is said to be indeterministic if there is no part of $\boldsymbol{x}_t$ that can be accurately predicted from $(\boldsymbol{x}_{t-1}, \boldsymbol{x}_{t-2}, \ldots)$.

be regarded identical if they share the same first- and second-order moments. (The second-order moments are the sequence of autocovariance matrices.) The same VMA process can then be represented in different ways even when we restrict $E(\boldsymbol{\varepsilon}_t\boldsymbol{\varepsilon}_t')$ to $\boldsymbol{I}_2$. Suppose that a bivariate process with $E(\boldsymbol{x}_t) = \boldsymbol{0}$ and a given autocovariance matrix sequence is derived for the process (11.21). Then a process with the same first- and second-order moments as (11.21) can be described by

$$\boldsymbol{x}_t = \tilde{\boldsymbol{C}}^{(0)}\boldsymbol{u}_t + \tilde{\boldsymbol{C}}^{(1)}\boldsymbol{u}_{t-1} + \ldots, \qquad E(\boldsymbol{u}_t\boldsymbol{u}_t') = \boldsymbol{I}_2.$$

if $\tilde{\boldsymbol{C}}^{(i)} = \boldsymbol{C}^{(i)}\boldsymbol{H}$, $\boldsymbol{u}_t = \boldsymbol{H}'\boldsymbol{\varepsilon}_t$, and $\boldsymbol{H}$ is an orthogonal matrix. (In short, the $\boldsymbol{C}$s in VMA (11.21) are not identified when differences among probability distributions are judged in terms of only the first- and second-order moments, which is justified if the process is Gaussian.) In the statement of Theorem 11.1 the conditions, $c_{11}^{(i)} = 0, i = 0, 1, 2, \ldots$, and/or $c_{12}^{(i)} = 0, i = 0, 1, 2, \ldots$ mean properties of one of many representations that all denote the process with the same first- and second-order moments.

Second, let us illustrate Theorem 11.1 with the first-order VMA,

$$\begin{bmatrix} x_{1t} \\ x_{2t} \end{bmatrix} = \begin{bmatrix} c_{11}^{(0)} & c_{12}^{(0)} \\ c_{21}^{(0)} & c_{22}^{(0)} \end{bmatrix} \begin{bmatrix} \varepsilon_{1t} \\ \varepsilon_{2t} \end{bmatrix} + \begin{bmatrix} c_{11}^{(1)} & c_{12}^{(1)} \\ c_{21}^{(1)} & c_{22}^{(1)} \end{bmatrix} \begin{bmatrix} \varepsilon_{1t-1} \\ \varepsilon_{2t-1} \end{bmatrix}, E(\boldsymbol{\varepsilon}_t\boldsymbol{\varepsilon}_t') = \boldsymbol{I}_2.$$

Denoting $(c_{11}^{(i)}, c_{12}^{(i)})$ by $\boldsymbol{c}_1^{(i)}$, it is seen that

$$E(x_{1t}|\boldsymbol{x}_{t-1}, \boldsymbol{x}_{t-2}, \ldots) = \boldsymbol{c}_1^{(1)}\boldsymbol{\varepsilon}_{t-1}$$

$$E(x_{1t}|x_{1t-1}, x_{1t-2}, \ldots) = \boldsymbol{c}_1^{(1)}\boldsymbol{c}_1^{(0)\prime}\left(\boldsymbol{c}_1^{(0)}\boldsymbol{c}_1^{(0)\prime}\right)^{-1}\boldsymbol{c}_1^{(0)}\boldsymbol{\varepsilon}_{t-1}.$$

Therefore x_2 does not cause x_1 in Granger's sense if and only if there exists a non-zero scalar d such that $\boldsymbol{c}_1^{(1)} = d\boldsymbol{c}_1^{(0)}$. (Of course, $\boldsymbol{c}_1^{(1)} = \boldsymbol{c}_1^{(0)} = \boldsymbol{0}$ is precluded from our consideration.) The condition $\boldsymbol{c}_1^{(1)} = d\boldsymbol{c}_1^{(0)}$ is equivalent to existence of a vector $\boldsymbol{f}$ such that $\|\boldsymbol{f}\| = 1$ and $\boldsymbol{c}_1^{(1)}\boldsymbol{f} = \boldsymbol{c}_1^{(0)}\boldsymbol{f} = 0$. Form an orthogonal matrix, either $[\boldsymbol{f}, \boldsymbol{g}]$ or $[\boldsymbol{g}, \boldsymbol{f}]$, with $\boldsymbol{g}$ such that $\boldsymbol{g}'\boldsymbol{f} = 0$ and $\|\boldsymbol{g}\| = 1$, and adopt it for $\boldsymbol{H}$ above. Then either $\tilde{c}_{11}^{(1)} = \tilde{c}_{11}^{(0)} = 0$ or $\tilde{c}_{12}^{(1)} = \tilde{c}_{12}^{(0)} = 0$.[9]

QED

In Chapter 13 I shall need another theorem on Granger non causality.

Theorem 11.2 (Sims (1972)). Suppose that (11.21) is a stationary, linear, indeterministic process with $E(\boldsymbol{\varepsilon}_t\boldsymbol{\varepsilon}_t') = \boldsymbol{\Sigma}$, which is positive definite. Then x_2 does not cause x_1 in Granger's sense if and only if the distributed lag relation

$$x_{2t} = \sum_{i=0}^{\infty} g_i x_{1t-i} + w_t, \tag{11.22}$$

holds with $E(w_t) = 0$ and $E(w_t x_{1t-s}) = 0$ for all positive, zero, negative values of s.

[9] A nice exercise is to extend the above reasoning to VMA in lag order 2. It seems that Granger non-causality implies a complicated condition in the vector ARMA.

The original proof of Sims (1972) relies on some advanced mathematics. I shall follow Yamamoto (1988: 170–1) to demonstrate a proof of 'only if', and a proof of 'if' will also be given later.

Let us start with the VAR, (11.18), assuming its stationarity and $b_{12}^{(i)} = 0$, $i = 1, \ldots, p$. It is known that such VAR models generate linear indeterministic processes. Appendix 5 gives a relevant determinantal equation for the stationary VAR, and when x_2 does not cause x_1 in Granger's sense it is simplified to

$$\det \begin{bmatrix} b_{11}(\lambda) & 0 \\ b_{21}(\lambda) & b_{22}(\lambda) \end{bmatrix} = 0, \tag{11.23}$$

where
$$b_{11}(\lambda) = 1 - b_{11}^{(1)}\lambda - \ldots - b_{11}^{(p)}\lambda^p$$
$$b_{21}(\lambda) = -b_{21}^{(1)}\lambda - \ldots - b_{21}^{(p)}\lambda^p$$
$$b_{22}(\lambda) = 1 - b_{22}^{(1)}\lambda - \ldots - b_{22}^{(p)}\lambda^p.$$

(11.23) is equivalent to

$$b_{11}(\lambda)b_{22}(\lambda) = 0, \tag{11.23$'$}$$

and because of the stationarity the roots of $b_{11}(\lambda) = 0$ and $b_{22}(\lambda) = 0$ must all be larger than unity in moduli. In particular both $b_{11}(L)$ and $b_{22}(L)$ are invertible.

Recalling $E(\boldsymbol{v}_t\boldsymbol{v}_t') = \boldsymbol{\Sigma}$ in (11.18), premultiply (11.18) by

$$\boldsymbol{S} \equiv \begin{bmatrix} 1, & 0 \\ -\sigma_{11}^{-1}\sigma_{12}, & 1 \end{bmatrix},$$

and let $\boldsymbol{\varepsilon}_t = \boldsymbol{S}\boldsymbol{v}_t$. Since $\{\boldsymbol{v}_t\}$ is i.i.d., so is $\{\boldsymbol{\varepsilon}_t\}$, and $E(\boldsymbol{\varepsilon}_t\boldsymbol{\varepsilon}_t') = \text{diag}[\sigma_{11}, \sigma_{22} - \sigma_{11}^{-1}\sigma_{12}^2]$. Therefore ε_{1t} and ε_{2s} are uncorrelated for all t and s. Since $x_{1t} = b_{11}(L)^{-1}\varepsilon_{1t}$, x_{1t} and ε_{2s} are also uncorrelated for all t and s.

After premultiplication by $\boldsymbol{S}$ the second equation of (11.18) is

$$x_{2t} - \sum_{i=1}^{p} b_{22}^{(i)} x_{2t-i} = \sigma_{11}^{-1}\sigma_{12}x_{1t} + \sum_{i=1}^{p} \left(b_{21}^{(i)} - \sigma_{11}^{-1}\sigma_{12}b_{11}^{(i)}\right) x_{1t-i} + \varepsilon_{2t},$$

from which we obtain

$$x_{2t} = b_{22}(L)^{-1}\left(\sigma_{11}^{-1}\sigma_{12}x_{1t} + \sum_{i=1}^{p} \left(b_{21}^{(i)} - \sigma_{11}^{-1}\sigma_{12}b_{11}^{(i)}\right) x_{1t-i}\right) + b_{22}(L)^{-1}\varepsilon_{2t}.$$

This is in the form of (11.22) with $w_t = b_{22}(L)^{-1}\varepsilon_{2t}$. The zero correlation between x_{1t} and w_s for all t and s follows from the zero correlation between x_{1t} and ε_{2s} for all t and s. It is important to remember that in general $\{w_t\}$ in (11.22) is not i.i.d.

Conversely suppose that the distributed lag relation (11.21) holds with the condition $E(w_t) = 0$ and $E(w_t x_{t-s}) = 0$ for all s. In general the conditional expectation in the linear process is given by the projection. Here (11.22) implies that the space spanned by $(x_{1t-1}, x_{2t-1}, x_{1t-2}, x_{2t-2}, \ldots)$ is also spanned by $(x_{1t-1}, w_{t-1}, x_{1t-1}, w_{t-2}, \ldots)$. Moreover, x_{1t} is uncorrelated with $w_{t-1}, w_{t-2}, \ldots$.

Therefore

$$E(x_{1t}|x_{1t-1}, x_{2t-1}, x_{1t-2}, x_{2t-2}, \ldots) = E(x_{1t}|x_{1t-1}, x_{1t-2}, \ldots),$$

i.e., x_2 does not cause x_1 in Granger's sense. QED

Let us turn to Granger non-causality in the non-stationary case. Suppose that in (11.18)

$$\begin{aligned} \boldsymbol{I}_2 - \boldsymbol{B}^{(1)}L - \ldots - \boldsymbol{B}^{(p)}L^p &= (1-L) \\ &\times \left(\boldsymbol{I}_2 - \tilde{\boldsymbol{B}}^{(1)}L - \ldots - \tilde{\boldsymbol{B}}^{(p-1)}L^{p-1}\right) \end{aligned} \tag{11.24}$$

so that

$$\begin{aligned} &\boldsymbol{B}^{(1)} = -\boldsymbol{I}_2 - \tilde{\boldsymbol{B}}^{(1)},\ \boldsymbol{B}^{(2)} = \tilde{\boldsymbol{B}}^{(1)} - \tilde{\boldsymbol{B}}^{(2)}, \ldots, \\ &\boldsymbol{B}^{(p-1)} = \tilde{\boldsymbol{B}}^{(p-2)} - \tilde{\boldsymbol{B}}^{(p-1)},\ \boldsymbol{B}^{(p)} = \tilde{\boldsymbol{B}}^{(p-1)}. \end{aligned} \tag{11.24$'$}$$

Let $b_{jh}^{(i)}$ and $\tilde{b}_{jh}^{(i)}$, $j, h, = 1, 2$, be (j, h) element of $\boldsymbol{B}^{(i)}$ and $\tilde{\boldsymbol{B}}^{(i)}$ respectively. It will be explained later in Chapter 12 that (11.24) means that x_{1t} and x_{2t} are not co-integrated. (11.24) enables us to rewrite (11.18) as

$$\Delta \boldsymbol{x}_t = \tilde{\boldsymbol{B}}^{(1)}\Delta \boldsymbol{x}_{t-1} + \ldots + \tilde{\boldsymbol{B}}^{(p-1)}\Delta \boldsymbol{x}_{t-p+1} + \boldsymbol{v}_t. \tag{11.25}$$

I assume that $\boldsymbol{x}_0 = 0$, and that $\{\Delta \boldsymbol{x}_t\}$ in (11.25) is stationary with stationary moments in initials. The information set may be represented either by $(\boldsymbol{x}_{t-1}, \ldots, \boldsymbol{x}_1)$ or by $(\Delta \boldsymbol{x}_{t-1}, \ldots, \Delta \boldsymbol{x}_1)$. Since $x_{1t-1} = \sum_{i=1}^{t-1} \Delta x_{1t-i}$, x_{1t-1} is in the information set $(\Delta x_{1t-1}, \ldots, \Delta x_{11})$. Therefore

$$\begin{aligned} E(\Delta x_{1t}|\Delta \boldsymbol{x}_{t-1}, \ldots, \Delta \boldsymbol{x}_1) &= E(x_{1t}|\Delta \boldsymbol{x}_{t-1}, \ldots, \Delta \boldsymbol{x}_1) - x_{1t-1}, \\ E(\Delta x_{1t}|\Delta x_{1t-1}, \ldots, \Delta x_{11}) &= E(x_{1t}|\Delta x_{1t-1}, \ldots, \Delta x_{11}) - x_{1t-1}. \end{aligned}$$

The Granger non-causality of x_{2t} upon x_{1t} holds if and only if

$$E(\Delta x_{1t}|\Delta \boldsymbol{x}_{t-1}, \ldots, \Delta \boldsymbol{x}_1) = E(\Delta x_{1t}|\Delta x_{1t-1}, \ldots, \Delta x_{11}). \tag{11.26}$$

Reintroducing the reasoning about (11.20) and redefining $\boldsymbol{\xi}'_{t-1}$, as $(\Delta \boldsymbol{x}_{t-1}, \ldots, \Delta \boldsymbol{x}_1)$, it is seen that (11.26) holds in (11.25) if and only if $\tilde{b}_{12}^{(i)} = 0$, $i = 1, \ldots, p-1$, which is equivalent to $b_{12}^{(i)} = 0$, $i = 1, \ldots, p$, by virtue of (11.24′).

Thus it is seen that Granger non-causality is the triangularity of $\boldsymbol{B}^{(1)}, \ldots, \boldsymbol{B}^{(p)}$ in the VAR (11.18).

12
Conceptual Framework of the Co-integration and its Relation to Economic Theories

The plan of the present chapter is as follows. In Section 12.1 we begin with the definition of co-integration in the MA representation as it is the easiest to understand. It will be followed in Section 12.2 by the seminal Granger representation theorem in Engle and Granger (1987). It transforms the definition into those in the VAR and the error-correction representation, and proves the equivalence among them. However, my explanation of the Granger representation theorem follows that in Engle and Yoo (1991) rather than the original. Since Engle and Yoo (1991) use mathematics of the polynomial matrix, an elementary exposition of the mathematics is provided in Appendix 5. The concept of common trends will be explained in both Sections 12.1 and 12.2. The theoretical structure of the Granger representation theorem is illustrated with economic interpretation by a bivariate process in Section 12.3. The error-correction form in the Granger representation is a *statistical* rather than an *economic* model. In Section 12.3, using the economic-error correction model as an example, I shall delineate the type of the long-run relationships that can be dealt with by the co-integration analysis. Also shown is how one can recover the parameter of the economic error-correction model from that of the statistical error-correction model. Highlights of Chapter 12 are given at the end to help readers to keep important results in their memory.

In the original definition in Granger (1981) an $I(1)$ vector time series has been said to be co-integrated when each element of the series is $I(1)$ individually but some linear combinations of the elements are $I(0)$. Many scholars find it more convenient for mathematical understanding to delete the above environmental condition that each element is $I(1)$ individually, thus allowing that some elements of the vector time series may be $I(0)$. This flexible definition will be adopted here. It still holds true that the co-integration relation must involve at least two $I(1)$ variables (with non-zero coefficients) if it involves any. The flexible definition also means that a co-integrating vector may have nothing to do with the long-run relationship, indicating only stationarity of some variables in the system. How to exclude such a co-integration from our consideration will be shown in Section 12.3.7.

The rank of a matrix $\boldsymbol{A}$ will be denoted by $\rho(\boldsymbol{A})$, and the determinant of a square matrix $\boldsymbol{A}$ by $\det[\boldsymbol{A}]$.

Identification problems will be brought up frequently, and as stated in Section 11.1.2 I shall write simply a (matrix) parameter unidentified (or identified) when the parameter is unidentified (or identified) without aid of normalization rules or constraints due to economic theories. The unidentified parameter could well be identified if such aid is available.

Throughout the present chapter I shall assume that $\{\Delta \boldsymbol{x}_t\}$ is stationary, i.e. the integration order is at most unity. This is an important assumption.

12.1 Co-integration in the MA Representation

The present section is a straightforward extension of Section 2.2 (Part I) to a multivariate model. Suppose that $\{\boldsymbol{x}_t\}$ is a vector stochastic process with k elements in the vector. We shall be concerned with the time series of $\Delta \boldsymbol{x}_t \equiv \boldsymbol{x}_t - \boldsymbol{x}_{t-1}$, which is assumed to be generated by a stationary vector MA with a possibly infinite order,

$$\Delta \boldsymbol{x}_t = \boldsymbol{C}_0 \boldsymbol{\varepsilon}_t + \boldsymbol{C}_1 \boldsymbol{\varepsilon}_{t-1} + \dots \quad = \boldsymbol{C}(L)\boldsymbol{\varepsilon}_t, \tag{12.1}$$

where $\{\boldsymbol{\varepsilon}_t\}$ is i.i.d. with $E(\boldsymbol{\varepsilon}_t) = \boldsymbol{0}$ and $E(\boldsymbol{\varepsilon}_t \boldsymbol{\varepsilon}_t') = \boldsymbol{\Sigma}_\varepsilon$ for all t. $\boldsymbol{\Sigma}_\varepsilon$ is positive definite. Each of the $\boldsymbol{C}$s is $k \times k$. $\boldsymbol{\Sigma}_\varepsilon$ can be made $\boldsymbol{I}_k$ by replacing $\boldsymbol{\varepsilon}_t$ by $\boldsymbol{\Sigma}^{-1/2}\boldsymbol{\varepsilon}_t$ and $\boldsymbol{C}_j$ by $\boldsymbol{C}_j \boldsymbol{\Sigma}^{1/2}$. However even with $\boldsymbol{\Sigma}_\varepsilon = \boldsymbol{I}_k$ the $\boldsymbol{C}$s are not uniquely determined by the second-order moments of $\{\Delta \boldsymbol{x}_t\}$ as pointed out in Section 11.3.

Denoting a norm of a matrix, say $\boldsymbol{A}$, by $\|\boldsymbol{A}\|$ (e.g., square root of the largest eigenvalue of $\boldsymbol{A}'\boldsymbol{A}$), the sequence of $\|\boldsymbol{C}_j\|$ must converge to zero as $j \to \infty$ sufficiently rapidly to ensure the mathematical validity of each statement that will be presented subsequently. But we shall not bother specifying the required speed of convergence because the MA representation of the stationary vector ARMA process always meets the required conditions.

12.1.1 Co-integration space

Just as in Section 2.2 the optimal prediction of $\boldsymbol{x}$ in the infinitely remote future on the basis of $(\boldsymbol{x}_t, \boldsymbol{x}_{t-1}, \dots)$ is

$$\hat{\boldsymbol{x}}_t = \boldsymbol{x}_t + \left(\sum\nolimits_1^\infty \boldsymbol{C}_j\right)\boldsymbol{\varepsilon}_t + \left(\sum\nolimits_2^\infty \boldsymbol{C}_j\right)\boldsymbol{\varepsilon}_{t-1} + \dots, \tag{12.2}$$

from which it is seen that

$$\hat{\boldsymbol{x}}_t - \hat{\boldsymbol{x}}_{t-1} = \left(\sum\nolimits_0^\infty \boldsymbol{C}_j\right)\boldsymbol{\varepsilon}_t. \tag{12.3}$$

The long-run component of $\Delta \boldsymbol{x}_t$ is $\left(\sum_0^\infty \boldsymbol{C}_j\right)\boldsymbol{\varepsilon}_t$. The identity, (2.7), in Part I is extended to the multivariate case as

$$\boldsymbol{C}(L) - \boldsymbol{C}(1) = (1 - L)\boldsymbol{C}^*(L), \tag{12.4}$$

where $\quad \boldsymbol{C}^*(L) \equiv \boldsymbol{C}_0^* + \boldsymbol{C}_1^* L + \boldsymbol{C}_2^* L^2 + \dots$

$$\boldsymbol{C}_0^* = -\sum\nolimits_1^\infty \boldsymbol{C}_j, \quad \boldsymbol{C}_1^* = -\sum\nolimits_2^\infty \boldsymbol{C}_j, \dots$$

From (12.1) and (12.4) it follows that

$$\begin{aligned} \boldsymbol{x}_t &= \boldsymbol{x}_0 + \sum\nolimits_1^t \Delta \boldsymbol{x}_s = \boldsymbol{x}_0 + \sum\nolimits_1^t \boldsymbol{C}(L)\boldsymbol{\varepsilon}_s \\ &= \boldsymbol{x}_0 + \boldsymbol{C}(1)\sum\nolimits_1^t \boldsymbol{\varepsilon}_s + \sum\nolimits_1^t \boldsymbol{C}^*(L)\Delta\boldsymbol{\varepsilon}_s \\ &= \boldsymbol{C}(1)\sum\nolimits_1^t \boldsymbol{\varepsilon}_s + \boldsymbol{C}^*(L)\boldsymbol{\varepsilon}_t + \boldsymbol{x}_0 - \boldsymbol{C}^*(L)\boldsymbol{\varepsilon}_0. \end{aligned} \tag{12.5}$$

All of the following analysis will be made conditional upon $\boldsymbol{x}_0 - \boldsymbol{C}^*(L)\boldsymbol{\varepsilon}_0$, which is assumed to be a well-defined random variable. Since $\boldsymbol{C}^*(L)\boldsymbol{\varepsilon}_t$ is stationary the stochastic trend in $\boldsymbol{x}_t$ can originate only in $\boldsymbol{C}(1)\sum_1^t \boldsymbol{\varepsilon}_s$. Apart from the initial effects, the $\boldsymbol{x}_t$ is decomposed into the long-run component $\boldsymbol{C}(1)\sum_1^t \boldsymbol{\varepsilon}_s$ and the short-run component $\boldsymbol{C}^*(L)\boldsymbol{\varepsilon}_t$. As in Section 2.2 we hereafter redefine $\hat{\boldsymbol{x}}_t$ as

$$\hat{\boldsymbol{x}}_t = \boldsymbol{C}(1)\sum\nolimits_1^t \boldsymbol{\varepsilon}_s. \tag{12.2$'$}$$

The co-integration as defined in Engle and Granger (1987) is concerned with the row null space of $\boldsymbol{C}(1)$. Let $\boldsymbol{b}$ be a $k \times 1$ non-stochastic, non-zero vector. If $\boldsymbol{C}(1)$ has full rank, i.e. $\rho(\boldsymbol{C}(1)) = k$, then $\boldsymbol{b}'\boldsymbol{C}(1) \neq \boldsymbol{0}'$ for any $\boldsymbol{b}$, so that $\boldsymbol{b}'\boldsymbol{x}_t$ is non-stationary having a stochastic trend. If $\rho(\boldsymbol{C}(1)) = k - 1$, there is $\boldsymbol{b}$ such that $\boldsymbol{b}'\boldsymbol{C}(1) = \boldsymbol{0}'$. In fact such $\boldsymbol{b}$ forms a one-dimensional vector subspace. For any $\boldsymbol{b}$ in the subspace $\boldsymbol{b}'\boldsymbol{x}_t$ is stationary and $\boldsymbol{b}'\hat{\boldsymbol{x}}_t = 0$, but for any $\boldsymbol{b}$ not in the subspace $\boldsymbol{b}'\boldsymbol{x}_t$ is non-stationary and $\boldsymbol{b}'\hat{\boldsymbol{x}}_t \neq 0$. If $\rho(\boldsymbol{C}(1)) = k - r (r > 0)$, there is an r-dimensional vector subspace of $\boldsymbol{b}$ such that $\boldsymbol{b}'\boldsymbol{C}(1) = \boldsymbol{0}'$. If and only if $\boldsymbol{b}$ belongs to the subspace, $\boldsymbol{b}'\boldsymbol{x}_t$ is stationary and $\boldsymbol{b}'\hat{\boldsymbol{x}}_t = \boldsymbol{0}'$. Finally, if $\boldsymbol{C}(1)$ is zero matrix, the identity (12.4) shows that $\boldsymbol{C}(L)$ has a factor, $(\boldsymbol{I} - \boldsymbol{I}L)$. In this case Δ in (12.1) is cancelled from both sides, and $\boldsymbol{x}_t$ is stationary so that $\boldsymbol{b}'\boldsymbol{x}_t$ is stationary for any $\boldsymbol{b}$. Moreover, $\hat{\boldsymbol{x}}_t \equiv \boldsymbol{0}$.

The $\boldsymbol{b}$ that makes $\boldsymbol{b}'\boldsymbol{x}_t$ stationary is called co-integrating vector, and the vector space of co-integrating vectors is the co-integration space. It is the left null space of $\boldsymbol{C}(1)$. If the space has r-dimensions one can select an $r \times k$ matrix, $\boldsymbol{B}'$, that consists of r linearly independent co-integrating vectors. The r is called the co-integration rank. $\boldsymbol{B}'$ may be called a co-integration matrix, but $\boldsymbol{B}'$ is not unique because $\boldsymbol{F}\boldsymbol{B}'$ is also a co-integration matrix in so far as $\boldsymbol{F}$ is non-singular.

If $\boldsymbol{B}'$ is a co-integration matrix we have a set of relations among long-run components,

$$\boldsymbol{B}'\hat{\boldsymbol{x}}_t = \boldsymbol{0},$$

so that $\boldsymbol{B}'$ may be thought of as representing the long-run relationship among elements of $\boldsymbol{x}_t$. This idea is further developed later in Section 12.2.2 in connection with the error-correction representation. It should be pointed out, however, that a unit vector like $(0, 1, 0, \ldots, 0)$ is not precluded from $\boldsymbol{b}$. If $\boldsymbol{b} = (0, 1, 0, \ldots, 0)$, then the second element of $\Delta\boldsymbol{x}_t$ has no long-run component, but this vector $\boldsymbol{b}$ cannot be called a relationship.

I shall often use the expression that the co-integration space 'annihilates' or 'nullifies' the stochastic trends of $\boldsymbol{x}_t$.

The covariance matrix of $\Delta\hat{\boldsymbol{x}}_t$, i.e. the long-run covariance matrix is $\boldsymbol{C}(1)\boldsymbol{\Sigma}_\varepsilon\boldsymbol{C}(1)'$, or $\boldsymbol{C}(1)\boldsymbol{C}(1)'$ if $\boldsymbol{\Sigma}_\varepsilon$ is normalized to $\boldsymbol{I}_k$. Since $\boldsymbol{\Sigma}_\varepsilon$ is positive definite the rank of $\boldsymbol{C}(1)\boldsymbol{\Sigma}_\varepsilon\boldsymbol{C}(1)'$ is equal to the rank of $\boldsymbol{C}(1)$, which in turn is equal to k minus the rank of the co-integration space. Unless the co-integration space is null the long-run covariance matrix is singular, indicating that the elements of the long-run component vector, $\Delta\hat{\boldsymbol{x}}_t$, are linearly dependent.

Let us consider identification of the co-integration space and rank. Admittedly the $\boldsymbol{C}$s are not uniquely determined by the second-order moments of $\{\Delta\boldsymbol{x}_t\}$ even with $\boldsymbol{\Sigma}_\varepsilon = \boldsymbol{I}_k$, but, as indicated in Section 11.3 above, different matrices of $\boldsymbol{C}(1)$ that produce the same second-order moments are related through $\boldsymbol{C}(1)\boldsymbol{H}$ with an arbitary orthogonal matrix $\boldsymbol{H}$. The left null space of $\boldsymbol{C}(1)\boldsymbol{H}$ is invariant through all $\boldsymbol{H}$s. Therefore the co-integration space is uniquely determined from the second-order moments of $\{\Delta\boldsymbol{x}_t\}$. The co-integration space is identified, and so is the rank.

12.1.2 *Common trends*

The above definition of co-integration leads us to the concept of common trends due to Stock and Watson (1988*b*). Suppose that the co-integration rank is r. Construct a $k \times k$ orthogonal matrix $\boldsymbol{H} \equiv (\boldsymbol{H}_1, \boldsymbol{H}_2)$ such that (i) $\boldsymbol{H}_1$ is $k \times r$ and $\boldsymbol{H}_2$ is $k \times (k-r)$ and (ii) $\boldsymbol{C}(1)\boldsymbol{H}_1 = \boldsymbol{0}$. Then $\boldsymbol{C}(1)\boldsymbol{\varepsilon}_s = \boldsymbol{C}(1)(\boldsymbol{H}_1\boldsymbol{H}_1' + \boldsymbol{H}_2\boldsymbol{H}_2')\boldsymbol{\varepsilon}_s = \boldsymbol{C}(1)\boldsymbol{H}_2\boldsymbol{H}_2'\boldsymbol{\varepsilon}_s$. Since $\{\boldsymbol{\varepsilon}_s\}$ is i.i.d. so is $\{\boldsymbol{H}_2'\boldsymbol{\varepsilon}_s\}$, but $\boldsymbol{H}_2'\boldsymbol{\varepsilon}_s$ has only $(k-r)$ elements. Let $\boldsymbol{\xi}_s \equiv \boldsymbol{H}_2'\boldsymbol{\varepsilon}_s$. From (12.5)

$$\boldsymbol{x}_t = \boldsymbol{C}(1)\boldsymbol{H}_2\boldsymbol{\Sigma}_1^t\boldsymbol{\xi}_s + \boldsymbol{C}^*(L)\boldsymbol{\varepsilon}_t + \boldsymbol{x}_0 - \boldsymbol{C}^*(L)\boldsymbol{\varepsilon}_0. \tag{12.6}$$

The stochastic trends $\boldsymbol{f}_t \equiv \boldsymbol{\Sigma}_1^t\boldsymbol{\xi}_s = \boldsymbol{H}'_2\boldsymbol{\Sigma}_1^t\boldsymbol{\varepsilon}_s$ have only $(k-r)$ dimensions, and they are allocated among k dimensions of $\boldsymbol{x}_t$ through $\boldsymbol{C}(1)\boldsymbol{H}_2$. In other words elements of $\boldsymbol{x}_t$ contain different linear combinations of the same $(k-r)$ elements of vector common trends $\boldsymbol{f}_t$. If $E(\boldsymbol{\varepsilon}_t\boldsymbol{\varepsilon}_t')$ is normalized to $\boldsymbol{I}_k$, $E(\boldsymbol{\xi}_t\boldsymbol{\xi}_t') = \boldsymbol{I}_{k-r}$, and the vector common stochastic trends $\boldsymbol{f}_t$ consist of $(k-r)$ mutually uncorrelated scalar common trends, which would perhaps facilitate the interpretation. Comparing (12.6) and (12.5), and noting (12.2′),

$$\hat{\boldsymbol{x}}_t = \boldsymbol{C}(1)\boldsymbol{H}_2\boldsymbol{f}_t,$$

which shows how the long-run component, $\hat{\boldsymbol{x}}_t$, and common trends, $\boldsymbol{f}_t$, are related. (If $\rho(\boldsymbol{C}(1)) = k$, i.e. $r = 0$, k variables share k stochastic trends so that the word, 'common', loses its real meaning. This is the situation where $\boldsymbol{x}_t$ is not co-integrated.) See also the representation of common trends given in expressions (12.25) and (12.25′) below, and a summary presentation of King *et al.* (1991) introduced in Section 15.5. In fact this aspect of co-integration has motivated a large number of empirical applications of the cointegration analysis as shown in Section 15.5.

12.1.3 *Deterministic linear trend*

So far we have considered the case where $E(\Delta \boldsymbol{x}_t) = \mathbf{0}$, and the non-stationarity has taken the form of stochastic trends. There are two different ways to introduce non-zero mean in $\Delta \boldsymbol{x}_t$. The first is

$$\Delta \boldsymbol{x}_t = \boldsymbol{\mu} + \boldsymbol{C}_0 \boldsymbol{\varepsilon}_t + \boldsymbol{C}_1 \boldsymbol{\varepsilon}_{t-1} + \ldots = \boldsymbol{\mu} + \boldsymbol{C}(L)\boldsymbol{\varepsilon}_t, \tag{12.7}$$

which leads to

$$\boldsymbol{x}_t = t\boldsymbol{\mu} + \boldsymbol{C}(1)\sum\nolimits_1^t \boldsymbol{\varepsilon}_s + \boldsymbol{C}^*(L)\boldsymbol{\varepsilon}_t + \boldsymbol{x}_0 - \boldsymbol{C}^*(L)\boldsymbol{\varepsilon}_0. \tag{12.8}$$

For $\boldsymbol{b}$ to be a co-integrating vector $\boldsymbol{b}'\boldsymbol{x}_t$ must be stationary, and in particular must not have a deterministic linear trend with a non-zero slope. We now investigate $k \times (k+1)$ matrix, $[\boldsymbol{\mu}, \boldsymbol{C}(1)]$. If $\rho([\boldsymbol{\mu}, \boldsymbol{C}(1)]) = k$, there is no $\boldsymbol{b}$ such that $\boldsymbol{b}'t\boldsymbol{\mu} = 0$ and $\boldsymbol{b}'\boldsymbol{C}(1) = \mathbf{0}$.[1] Thus $\boldsymbol{b}'\boldsymbol{x}_t$ cannot be stationary for any $\boldsymbol{b}$. If $\rho([\boldsymbol{\mu}, \boldsymbol{C}(1)]) = k-r$, there exists the r-dimensional co-integration space of $\boldsymbol{b}$ such that $\boldsymbol{b}'t\boldsymbol{\mu} = 0$ and $\boldsymbol{b}'\boldsymbol{C}(1) = \mathbf{0}$ so that $\boldsymbol{b}'\boldsymbol{x}_t$ is stationary. Note that $E(\boldsymbol{b}'\boldsymbol{x}_t) = E(\boldsymbol{b}'\boldsymbol{x}_0) =$ a constant for all t and so is the variance of $\boldsymbol{b}'\boldsymbol{x}_t$.

One might like to consider separately $\boldsymbol{b}'\boldsymbol{\mu} = 0$ and $\boldsymbol{b}'\boldsymbol{C}(1) = \mathbf{0}$. In the terminology of Ogaki and Park (1992) the existence of $\boldsymbol{b}$ such that $\boldsymbol{b}'\boldsymbol{C}(1) = \mathbf{0}$ is called 'stochastic co-integration', and the existence of $\boldsymbol{b}$ such that $\boldsymbol{b}'[\boldsymbol{\mu}, \boldsymbol{C}(1) = \mathbf{0}$ 'deterministic co-integration'. The $\boldsymbol{b}$ in the stochastic co-integration makes $\boldsymbol{b}'\boldsymbol{x}_t$ trend stationary but not necessarily stationary. The co-integration space in the deterministic co-integration annihilates the deterministic and the stochastic trends at once, while the co-integration space in the stochastic co-integration nullifies only the stochastic trends.

The second method to introduce a non-zero mean of $\Delta \boldsymbol{x}_t$ is to let the innovation have a non-zero mean, $\boldsymbol{\mu}$, i.e.

$$\Delta \boldsymbol{x}_t = \boldsymbol{C}_0(\boldsymbol{\varepsilon}_t + \boldsymbol{\mu}) + \boldsymbol{C}_1(\boldsymbol{\varepsilon}_{t-1} + \boldsymbol{\mu}) + \ldots = \boldsymbol{C}(L)(\boldsymbol{\varepsilon}_t + \boldsymbol{\mu}), \tag{12.9}$$

which gives

$$\begin{aligned} \boldsymbol{x}_t &= \boldsymbol{x}_0 + \boldsymbol{C}(1)\sum\nolimits_1^t (\boldsymbol{\varepsilon}_s + \boldsymbol{\mu}) + \boldsymbol{C}^*(L)\boldsymbol{\varepsilon}_t - \boldsymbol{C}^*(L)\boldsymbol{\varepsilon}_0 \qquad (12.10)\\ &= t\boldsymbol{C}(1)\boldsymbol{\mu} + \boldsymbol{C}(1)\sum\nolimits_1^t \boldsymbol{\varepsilon}_s + \boldsymbol{C}^*(L)\boldsymbol{\varepsilon}_t + \boldsymbol{x}_0 - \boldsymbol{C}^*(L)\boldsymbol{\varepsilon}_0. \end{aligned}$$

It is this form that we obtain when a VAR is inverted. Here we observe the MA counterpart of what Johansen (1991*a*) emphasized in relation to the VAR representation of co-integration. Note how (12.8) and (12.10) differ in their first terms of the right-hand sides. Suppose that the co-integration rank is r. Reintroducing the orthogonal matrix $\boldsymbol{H} = [\boldsymbol{H}_1, \boldsymbol{H}_2]$ such that $\boldsymbol{C}(1)\boldsymbol{H}_1 = \mathbf{0}$, we see that $\boldsymbol{C}(1)\boldsymbol{\mu} = \boldsymbol{C}(1)\boldsymbol{H}_2\boldsymbol{H}_2'\boldsymbol{\mu}$. Johansen (1991*a*) points out that if $\boldsymbol{H}_2'\boldsymbol{\mu} = \mathbf{0}$ the linear trend is absent in each element of $\boldsymbol{x}_t$ in spite of the presence of

[1] In connection with (12.7) Stock and Watson (1988*b*) seem to state that $\boldsymbol{b}'[\boldsymbol{\mu}, \boldsymbol{C}(1)] = \mathbf{0}$ implies that $\boldsymbol{\mu}$ belongs to the column space of $\boldsymbol{C}(1)$, but this is incorrect. A counter-example is that $k = 3$, the second and the third columns of $\boldsymbol{C}(1)$ are both some scalar multiples of the first column but $\boldsymbol{\mu}$ is not. The co-integrating space is one-dimensional.

$\boldsymbol{\mu}$ in (12.9). In fact $E(\boldsymbol{x}_t) = E(\boldsymbol{x}_0) =$ a constant vector. Another point worth mentioning regarding (12.9) is that the co-integration space can be represented by the condition $\boldsymbol{b}'\boldsymbol{C}(1) = \mathbf{0}$ alone rather than $\boldsymbol{b}'[\boldsymbol{\mu}, \boldsymbol{C}(1)] = \mathbf{0}$. If $\boldsymbol{H}_2'\boldsymbol{\mu} \neq \mathbf{0}$, k elements of $\boldsymbol{x}_t$ share $(k-r)$ dimensions of common trends $(t\boldsymbol{H}_2'\boldsymbol{\mu} + \boldsymbol{\Sigma}_1^t \boldsymbol{\xi}_s)$, which include the deterministic linear trend with a non-zero slope. The co-integration space is the left null space of $\boldsymbol{C}(1)$, and the co-integrating vectors annihilate the deterministic and stochastic trends at once. We can have only 'deterministic co-integration' in the terminology of Ogaki and Park (1992).

I shall adopt (12.9) rather than (12.7) in the rest of Part II.

Incidentally it makes no sense generally to investigate the relationship among deterministic linear trends of various variables. For example, if $\{x_{it}\}$, $i = 1, 2$, has a linear trend $a_i + b_i t$, the two linear trends are perfectly correlated unless one of the bs is zero.

12.2 Granger Representation Theorem

So far the co-integration has been defined in the framework of the VMA (vector moving average) representation of $\Delta \boldsymbol{x}_t$, assuming that the order of integration is at most unity. An important role that co-integration plays in econometrics, however, lies in its representation in the VAR and especially the error-correction form. The singularity involved in the co-integrated VMA makes its inversion into VAR non-trivial. It is the Granger representation theorem in Engle and Granger (1987) that shows the equivalence among the VMA, the VAR, and the error-correction representations of co-integration. Here I shall follow the demonstration of the theorem in Engle and Yoo (1991) (attributed to the Ph.D. dissertation of Byung Sam Yoo) rather than the original one in Engle and Granger (1987). Moreover, I shall concentrate on deriving the VAR and the error-correction representation from the VMA, thus omitting the reverse direction of derivation.[2] Initially $\boldsymbol{\mu}$ is suppressed to zero.

A factor that enhances the importance of the error-correction representation is that it is this representation in which Johansen (1991*a*) develops an asymptotically efficient inference procedure. This will be explained in Chapter 15. Because of this it is easier to perform the inference in the error-correction form initially, and, if necessary, to translate the results back to the VMA representation via (12.20′), (12.25), and (12.25′) below.

Mathematics of the polynomial matrix is explained in Appendix 5. Here I start where Appendix 5 ends. The $\boldsymbol{x}_t$ in Appendix 5 is replaced by $\Delta \boldsymbol{x}_t$. Thus the model of $\Delta \boldsymbol{x}_t$ is a k-elements VARMA (vector ARMA)

$$\boldsymbol{A}(L)\Delta \boldsymbol{x}_t = \boldsymbol{B}(L)\boldsymbol{\varepsilon}_t, \qquad (12.11)$$

which is slightly more restrictive than in Section (12.1) above. We wish to construct stationary ARMA models of $\Delta \boldsymbol{x}_t$ such that $\Delta \boldsymbol{x}_t$ is $I(0)$ but $\boldsymbol{B}'\Delta \boldsymbol{x}_t$ is

[2] See Johansen (1991*a*) and Banerjee *et al.* (1993: 146–50) for the reverse direction.

$I(-1)$ for $\boldsymbol{B}'$ with rank r. (For $I(-1)$ see the paragraph below (2.12) in Section 2.2 of Part I.) It is assumed that det $[\boldsymbol{A}(z)] = 0$ has all roots outside the unit circle, that det $[\boldsymbol{B}(z)] = 0$ has roots outside the unit circle and possibly real unit roots, but that det $[\boldsymbol{B}(z)] = 0$ has none of the complex unit roots nor roots inside the unit circle. Moreover, we normalize $\boldsymbol{\Sigma}_\varepsilon$ to $\boldsymbol{I}_k$. The presence of real unit roots in $\boldsymbol{B}(z)$ is a multivariate extension of (2.9) in Part I having an MA unit root. The m_is in (A5.12) of Appendix 5 are assumed to be unity. This assumption excludes the multi-co-integration developed in Granger and Lee (1990), in which m_i is at least 2 for $i = k, \dots, k-j$ for some $k-j$ that is $\geq k-r+1$.

12.2.1 VAR representation

Writing $\boldsymbol{C}(L) \equiv \boldsymbol{A}(L)^{-1}\boldsymbol{B}(L)$ in (12.11) it is seen that the co-integration was defined in the previous section by $\rho(\boldsymbol{C}(1)) = k-r$, where r is the co-integration rank. In transferring the result in Appendix 5 I drop ~ above $\boldsymbol{U}$ and $\boldsymbol{V}$.

$$\boldsymbol{C}(L) = \boldsymbol{U}(L)\boldsymbol{D}(L)\boldsymbol{V}(L), \tag{12.12a}$$

$$\boldsymbol{U}(L)^{-1}\Delta\boldsymbol{x}_t = \boldsymbol{D}(L)\boldsymbol{V}(L)\boldsymbol{\varepsilon}_t, \tag{12.12b}$$

$$\boldsymbol{D}(L) \equiv \text{diag}[\overbrace{1, \dots, 1}^{k-r}, \overbrace{(1-L), \dots, (1-L)}^{r}], \tag{12.12c}$$

where $\boldsymbol{U}(L)^{-1}$ and $\boldsymbol{V}(L)$ are both polynomial (rather than rational) matrices, $\boldsymbol{U}(L)$ is a rational matrix, and both det$[\boldsymbol{U}(z)^{-1}] = 0$ and det$[\boldsymbol{V}(z)] = 0$ have all roots outside the unit circle. Even though $\boldsymbol{U}(L)$ and $\boldsymbol{V}(L)$ are not uniquely determined by $\boldsymbol{C}(L)$, the above properties of $\boldsymbol{U}(L)$ and $\boldsymbol{V}(L)$ hold for all their representations.

For any $k \times k$ matrix, say $\boldsymbol{X}$, $(\boldsymbol{X})_{1.}$, $(\boldsymbol{X})_{2.}$, $(\boldsymbol{X})_{.1}$, $(\boldsymbol{X})_{.2}$ will denote the first $(k-r)$ rows, the last r rows, the first $(k-r)$ columns, and the last r columns of $\boldsymbol{X}$ respectively. Partitioning (12.12b) as

$$\begin{bmatrix} (\boldsymbol{U}(L)^{-1})_{1.} \\ (\boldsymbol{U}(L)^{-1})_{2.} \end{bmatrix} \Delta\boldsymbol{x}_t = \begin{bmatrix} \boldsymbol{I}_{k-r} & 0 \\ \boldsymbol{0} & (1-L)\boldsymbol{I}_r \end{bmatrix} [(\boldsymbol{V}(L))_{.1}, (\boldsymbol{V}(L))_{.2}]\boldsymbol{\varepsilon}_t,$$

and cancelling $(1-\boldsymbol{L})$ involved in the last r rows of both sides, we get

$$\boldsymbol{D}^*(L)\boldsymbol{U}(L)^{-1}\boldsymbol{x}_t = \boldsymbol{V}(L)\boldsymbol{\varepsilon}_t, \tag{12.13a}$$

$$\boldsymbol{D}^*(L) \equiv \text{diag}\,[\overbrace{(1-L), \dots, (1-L)}^{k-r}, \overbrace{1, \dots, 1}^{r}]. \tag{12.13b}$$

Since $\boldsymbol{V}(L)$ is invertible, let us write

$$\boldsymbol{\Pi}(L) = \boldsymbol{V}(L)^{-1}\boldsymbol{D}^*(L)\boldsymbol{U}(L)^{-1}. \tag{12.14}$$

Generally $\boldsymbol{V}(L)^{-1}$ is not a polynomial matrix but a converging power series of L with matrix coefficients, where the convergence is that of a decaying exponential.

Thus $\boldsymbol{\Pi}(L) = \boldsymbol{\Pi}_0 + \boldsymbol{\Pi}_1 L + \ldots$, and

$$\boldsymbol{\Pi}(L)\boldsymbol{x}_t = \boldsymbol{\varepsilon}_t \tag{12.15}$$

is a VAR possibly with infinite orders. The equation, $\det[\boldsymbol{\Pi}(z)] = 0$, has roots outside the unit circle and $(k - r)$ real unit roots. The rank of $\boldsymbol{\Pi}(1)$ is r. This is the VAR representation of the co-integration with rank r.[3]

12.2.2 *Error-correction representation*

Since the first $(k - r)$ diagonal elements of $\boldsymbol{D}^*(1)$ are zero,

$$\boldsymbol{\Pi}(1) = (\boldsymbol{V}(1)^{-1})_{.2}(\boldsymbol{U}(1)^{-1})_{2.} \tag{12.16}$$

Since both $\boldsymbol{U}(1)^{-1}$ and $\boldsymbol{V}(1)^{-1}$ are non-singular, ranks of $(\boldsymbol{V}(1)^{-1})_{.2}$ and $(\boldsymbol{U}(1)^{-1})_{2.}$ are each r. Let us write $-\boldsymbol{A} \equiv (\boldsymbol{V}(1)^{-1})_{.2}$ and $\boldsymbol{B}' \equiv (\boldsymbol{U}(1)^{-1})_{2.}$, and remember that $\boldsymbol{A}$ is $k \times r$ and $\boldsymbol{B}'$ is $r \times k$. Then

$$\boldsymbol{\Pi}(1) \equiv -\boldsymbol{A}\boldsymbol{B}'. \tag{12.16$'$}$$

Define $\boldsymbol{\Gamma}(L) = \boldsymbol{\Gamma}_0 + \boldsymbol{\Gamma}_1 L + \ldots$ by

$$\boldsymbol{\Pi}(L) \equiv \boldsymbol{\Pi}(1)L + (1 - L)\boldsymbol{\Gamma}(L). \tag{12.17}$$

Because of the identity

$$\boldsymbol{\Pi}(L) - \boldsymbol{\Pi}(1)L = (1 - L)(\boldsymbol{\Pi}_0 - \boldsymbol{\Pi}_2 L - \boldsymbol{\Pi}_3 L(1 + L) - \ldots),$$

the $\boldsymbol{\Gamma}$s are

$$\boldsymbol{\Gamma}_0 \equiv \boldsymbol{\Pi}_0, \quad \boldsymbol{\Gamma}_i \equiv -\sum_{s=i+1}^{\infty} \boldsymbol{\Pi}_s, \quad i = 1, 2, \ldots.$$

(12.15) is written as

$$\boldsymbol{\Gamma}(L)\Delta\boldsymbol{x}_t = \boldsymbol{A}\boldsymbol{B}'\boldsymbol{x}_{t-1} + \boldsymbol{\varepsilon}_t. \tag{12.18}$$

This is the error-correction representation of the co-integration. It is a variant of the VAR representation, but its role in econometrics is far more important than the original VAR representation.

It has been said that $\boldsymbol{B}'\boldsymbol{x}_{t-1} = \boldsymbol{0}$ is a set of equilibrium relations (except in the case where a row of $\boldsymbol{B}'$ is a unit vector), and that $\boldsymbol{B}'\boldsymbol{x}_{t-1}$ indicates deviations from the equilibrium when $\boldsymbol{x}_{t-1}$ is observed. The matrix $\boldsymbol{A}$ may be interpreted as the matrix of adjustment speeds. Its (i, j) element represents the speed at which the i-th element of $\boldsymbol{x}_t$ is adjusted from $\boldsymbol{x}_{t-1}$ in the light of the deviation in the j-th equilibrium relation. The matrix $\boldsymbol{A}$ is called the adjustment matrix or the loading matrix. In (12.18) the adjustment speed also depends upon $\Delta\boldsymbol{x}_{t-1}, \Delta\boldsymbol{x}_{t-2}, \ldots$. The equilibrium will be further explained in connection with economic theories in Section 12.3.

[3] Readers are recommended to study another derivation of the VAR from the VMA in the co-integrated system given in Banerjee *et al.* (1993: 257–60). It does not use the Smith–McMillan form, and follows closely the derivation of VMA from VAR given in Johansen (1991*a*).

The rank of $\mathbf{\Pi}(1)$ has an important role. Suppose that $\mathbf{\Pi}(1)$ has its full rank, k, i.e. $r = k$. Then both $\boldsymbol{A}$ and $\boldsymbol{B}'$ are $k \times k$ and non-singular, and $\boldsymbol{D}^*(L) = \boldsymbol{I}_k$ in (12.13b). The det$[\mathbf{\Pi}(z)]$ vanishes only outside of the unit circle. Therefore (12.15) is a stationary VAR for $\boldsymbol{x}_t$. In fact, since $\boldsymbol{A}$ and $\boldsymbol{B}$ may be replaced by $\boldsymbol{AF}$ and $\boldsymbol{BF}'^{-1}$ with any non-singular $\boldsymbol{F}$ (keeping $\boldsymbol{AB}'$ invariant), $\boldsymbol{B}'$ may be set to $\boldsymbol{I}_k$. Then $\boldsymbol{B}'\boldsymbol{x}_t$ being stationary means $\boldsymbol{x}_t$ being stationary.

Going to the other extreme on the rank of $\mathbf{\Pi}(1)$, suppose that $\mathbf{\Pi}(1) = \mathbf{0}$. Then both $\boldsymbol{A}$ and $\boldsymbol{B}$ are zero, and $\boldsymbol{D}^*(L) =$ diag $[(1-L), \ldots, (1-L)]$. (12.18) is reduced to a VAR for $\Delta\boldsymbol{x}_t$. Since $\mathbf{\Pi}(L) = (1-L)\mathbf{\Gamma}(L)$, $\mathbf{\Gamma}(L) = \boldsymbol{V}(L)^{-1}\boldsymbol{U}(L)^{-1}$. It is seen that $\mathbf{\Gamma}(L)$ is a converging power series of L with convergence as fast as a decaying exponential.

$$\mathbf{\Gamma}(L)\Delta\boldsymbol{x}_t = \boldsymbol{\varepsilon}_t$$

is a stationary VAR for $\Delta\boldsymbol{x}_t$. Its long-run covariance matrix is $\mathbf{\Gamma}(1)^{-1}\mathbf{\Sigma}_\varepsilon\mathbf{\Gamma}(1)^{-1'}$, which is non-singular. $\{\boldsymbol{x}_t\}$ is not co-integrated.

Let us consider the intermediate case between the above two extremes, $0 < \rho(\mathbf{\Pi}(1)) = r < k$. $\boldsymbol{A}$ has r columns, and $\boldsymbol{B}'$ has r rows. The last r rows of (12.13a) are

$$(\boldsymbol{U}(L)^{-1})_{2.}\boldsymbol{x}_t = (\boldsymbol{V}(L))_{2.}\boldsymbol{\varepsilon}_t. \tag{12.19}$$

Both $\boldsymbol{U}(L)^{-1}$ and $\boldsymbol{V}(L)$ are polynomial matrices. Writing $\boldsymbol{B}(L)' \equiv (\boldsymbol{U}(L)^{-1})_{2.}$ and $\boldsymbol{B}(L)' = \boldsymbol{B}(1)' + (1-L)\boldsymbol{B}^*(L)'$, it is seen that the left-hand side of (12.19) is $\boldsymbol{B}(1)'\boldsymbol{x}_t + \boldsymbol{B}^*(L)'\Delta\boldsymbol{x}_t$. Since the integration order of $\boldsymbol{x}_t$ is at most unity, $\boldsymbol{B}^*(L)'\Delta\boldsymbol{x}_t$ is stationary. So is the right-hand side of (12.19). Therefore $\boldsymbol{B}(1)'\boldsymbol{x}_t$ is stationary, and $\boldsymbol{B}(1)'$ is a co-integration matrix. $\boldsymbol{B}(1)'$ is what was written $\boldsymbol{B}'$ earlier. The co-integration rank is $\rho(\mathbf{\Pi}(1))$.

An expression that appeals to our intuition is that in the absence of co-integration the number of unit roots equal to that of variables ($\Delta\boldsymbol{x}_t$ being a stationary VAR) while in the co-integration the number of unit roots is reduced from that of variables by the co-integration rank.

Simulation studies often require small examples of finite order VARs that have specific co-integration properties. The following examples are presented also as exercises of the above mathematics.

Example 1. Suppose that we are requested to provide a VAR model of (x_{1t}, x_{2t}, x_{3t}) such that x_{1t}, x_{2t}, and x_{3t} are each $I(1)$, x_{1t} and x_{2t} not co-integrated, but x_{1t}, x_{2t}, x_{3t} co-integrated. The co-integration rank is 1 so that in (12.13b)

$$\boldsymbol{D}^*(L) = \text{ diag } [(1-L), (1-L), 1].$$

Triangular systems are convenient because determinants are products of diagonal elements. Set

$$\boldsymbol{U}(L)^{-1} = \begin{bmatrix} p_{11}(L) & 0 & 0 \\ p_{21}(L) & p_{22}(L) & 0 \\ p_{31}(L) & p_{32}(L) & p_{33}(L) \end{bmatrix},$$

where $p_{ij}(L)$ is a polynomial of L. (x_2 and x_3 do not cause x_1 in Granger's sense, and x_3 does not cause (x_1, x_2) in Granger's sense.) An important condition is that $p_{ii}(L)$, $i = 1, 2, 3$ have all roots outside the unit circle. Also set $\boldsymbol{V}(L) = \boldsymbol{I}_3$, and $E(\boldsymbol{\varepsilon}_t\boldsymbol{\varepsilon}_t') = \boldsymbol{I}_3$. In (12.14)

$$\boldsymbol{\Pi}(L) = \begin{bmatrix} (1-L)p_{11}(L) & 0 & 0 \\ (1-L)p_{21}(L) & (1-L)p_{22}(L) & 0 \\ p_{31}(L) & p_{32}(L) & p_{33}(L) \end{bmatrix},$$

and in (12.16) and (12.16′)

$$\boldsymbol{\Pi}(1) = \begin{bmatrix} 0 & 0 & 0 \\ 0 & 0 & 0 \\ p_{31}(1) & p_{32}(1) & p_{33}(1) \end{bmatrix}$$

$$-\boldsymbol{A} = \begin{bmatrix} 0 \\ 0 \\ 1 \end{bmatrix}, \boldsymbol{B}' = [p_{31}(1), p_{32}(1), p_{33}(1)].$$

In (12.17)

$$\boldsymbol{\Gamma}(L) = \begin{bmatrix} p_{11}(L) & 0 & 0 \\ p_{21}(L) & p_{22}(L) & 0 \\ \pi_{31}(L) & \pi_{32}(L) & \pi_{33}(L) \end{bmatrix},$$

where $p_{ij}(L) = p_{ij}(1)L + (1-L)\pi_{ij}(L)$, $i, j = 1, 2, 3$.

The VAR is

$$\boldsymbol{\Pi}(L)\boldsymbol{x}_t = \boldsymbol{\varepsilon}_t.$$

Its first equation is

$$(1-L)p_{11}(L)x_{1t} = \varepsilon_{1t},$$

and $\{x_{1t}\}$ is $I(1)$. The second equation is

$$(1-L)p_{22}(L)x_{2t} = -(1-L)p_{21}(L)x_{1t} + \varepsilon_{2t}.$$

The right-hand side is $I(0)$, and therefore $\{x_{2t}\}$ is $I(1)$. Assuming that $\boldsymbol{\varepsilon}_t = 0$ for $t \leq 0$,

$$x_{2t} = -p_{22}(L)^{-1}p_{21}(L)x_{1t} + p_{22}(L)^{-1}\sum_{s=1}^{t} \varepsilon_{2s}.$$

Since $E(x_{1t}\varepsilon_{2s}) = 0$ for all t and s, adding a non-stochastic multiple of x_{1t} to x_{2t} does not eliminate $p_{22}(L)^{-1}\sum_{s=1}^{t} \varepsilon_{2s}$, i.e. $\{x_{1t}\}$ and $\{x_{2t}\}$ are not co-integrated. The third equation is

$$p_{33}(L)x_{3t} = -p_{31}(L)x_{1t} - p_{32}(L)x_{2t} + \varepsilon_{3t}.$$

Unless $p_{31}(1) = p_{32}(1) = 0$, $\{x_{3t}\}$ is $I(1)$.

$$p_{31}(1)x_{1t} + p_{32}(1)x_{2t} + p_{33}(1)x_{3t}$$

is $I(0)$, and hence $\{(x_{1t}, x_{2t}, x_{3t})\}$ is co-integrated. Note that $p_{33}(1) \neq 0$ from the outset, but we must impose the condition that either $p_{31}(1) \neq 0$ or $p_{32}(1) \neq 0$.

Readers are advised to derive $C(1)$ through (12.12a) and confirm that the first and second rows are linearly independent (so that x_1 and x_2 are not co-integrated) and that $(p_{31}(1), p_{32}(1), p_{33}(1))$ is in the left null space of $C(1)$ as it should be.

The present example will play an important role in the co-integrated regression explained in Chapter 13, where regressors should not be co-integrated but a regressand and regressors are co-integrated.

Example 2. Suppose that we are asked to provide a VAR in which x_{1t} and x_{2t} are $I(1)$ but x_{3t} is $I(0)$, and x_{1t} and x_{2t} are co-integrated. The co-integration rank is 2.

$$D^*(L) = \text{diag}\,[(1-L), 1, 1].$$

Let us use the same $U(L)^{-1}$ as in Example 1. Here

$$\Pi(L) = \begin{bmatrix} (1-L)p_{11}(L) & 0 & 0 \\ p_{21}(L) & p_{22}(L) & 0 \\ p_{31}(L) & p_{32}(L) & p_{33}(L) \end{bmatrix},$$

$$\Pi(1) = \begin{bmatrix} 0 & 0 & 0 \\ p_{21}(1) & p_{22}(1) & 0 \\ p_{31}(1) & p_{32}(1) & p_{33}(1) \end{bmatrix}.$$

$$-A = \begin{bmatrix} 0 & 0 \\ 1 & 0 \\ 0 & 1 \end{bmatrix}, \quad B' = \begin{bmatrix} p_{21}(1) & p_{22}(1) & 0 \\ p_{31}(1) & p_{32}(1) & p_{33}(1) \end{bmatrix}.$$

$$\Gamma(L) = \begin{bmatrix} p_{11}(L) & 0 & 0 \\ \pi_{21}(L) & \pi_{22}(L) & 0 \\ \pi_{31}(L) & \pi_{32}(L) & \pi_{33}(L) \end{bmatrix}$$

$\{x_{1t}\}$ is $I(1)$. Since

$$p_{22}(L)x_{2t} = -p_{21}(L)x_{1t} + \varepsilon_{2t},$$

$\{x_{2t}\}$ is $I(1)$ unless $p_{21}(1) = 0$. $\{(x_{1t}, x_{2t}\}$ is co-integrated because $p_{21}(1)x_{1t} + p_{22}(1)x_{2t}$ is stationary. Note that $p_{22}(1) \neq 0$ from the outset, but we must impose the condition that $p_{21}(1) \neq 0$. From the third equation we have

$$p_{33}(L)x_{3t} = -p_{31}(L)x_{1t} - p_{32}(L)x_{2t} + \varepsilon_{3t}.$$

$\{x_{3t}\}$ being $I(0)$ requires $-p_{31}(L)x_{1t} - p_{32}(L)x_{2t}$ being $I(0)$, which in turn requires

$$p_{31}(1)/p_{32}(1) = p_{21}(1)/p_{22}(1).$$

Let $g \equiv p_{21}(1)/p_{31}(1)$ and

$$Q \equiv \begin{bmatrix} 1 & 0 \\ 1 & -g \end{bmatrix}.$$

The above $\boldsymbol{B}'$ may be replaced by

$$\boldsymbol{QB}' = \begin{bmatrix} p_{21}(1) & p_{22}(1) & 0 \\ 0 & 0 & -g p_{33}(1) \end{bmatrix}$$

provided that $-\boldsymbol{A}$ is replaced by

$$-\boldsymbol{AQ}^{-1} = \begin{bmatrix} 0 & 0 \\ 1 & 0 \\ 1 & g \end{bmatrix}.$$

It is seen that x_{3t} is $I(0)$.

12.2.3 *Properties of the error-correction representation*

From (12.12*a*) and (12.12*c*) it is seen that

$$\boldsymbol{C}(1) = (\boldsymbol{U}(1))_{.1}\boldsymbol{V}(1)_{1.}. \tag{12.20}$$

Since $\boldsymbol{U}(1)^{-1}\boldsymbol{U}(1) = \boldsymbol{I}_k$ and $\boldsymbol{V}(1)\boldsymbol{V}(1)^{-1} = \boldsymbol{I}_k$, (12.20) and (12.16) imply

$$(a)\, \boldsymbol{\Pi}(1)\boldsymbol{C}(1) = \boldsymbol{0}, \quad (b)\, \boldsymbol{C}(1)\boldsymbol{\Pi}(1) = \boldsymbol{0}. \tag{12.21}$$

(12.21) is a part of the Granger representation theorem, and called the *duality* between $\boldsymbol{\Pi}(1)$ for the VAR and $\boldsymbol{C}(1)$ for the VMA representations.

Since $(\boldsymbol{V}(1))_{1.}\boldsymbol{A} = \boldsymbol{0}$ and $\boldsymbol{B}'(\boldsymbol{U}(1))_{.1} = \boldsymbol{0}$, we may write $(\boldsymbol{V}(1))_{1.} \equiv \boldsymbol{A}'_{\perp}$ and $(\boldsymbol{U}(1))_{1.} \equiv \boldsymbol{B}_{\perp}$. Then $\boldsymbol{C}(1) = \boldsymbol{B}_{\perp}\boldsymbol{A}'_{\perp}$. In particular $\rho(\boldsymbol{C}(1)) = k - r$, which agrees with the explanation in the Section 12.1. Since $\boldsymbol{U}(L)$ and $\boldsymbol{V}(L)$ are not uniquely determined from (12.11), it may be appropriate to re-express $\boldsymbol{C}(1)$. Let $\boldsymbol{A}_{\perp}$ and $\boldsymbol{B}_{\perp}$ be *any* $k \times (k-r)$ column full-rank matrices such that $\boldsymbol{A}'_{\perp}\boldsymbol{A} = \boldsymbol{0}$ and $\boldsymbol{B}'_{\perp}\boldsymbol{B} = \boldsymbol{0}$ respectively. Different $\boldsymbol{A}_{\perp}$s are related through right multiplications by non-singular matrices, and so are different $\boldsymbol{B}_{\perp}$s. Construct $\boldsymbol{\Pi}^*(L)$ by

$$\boldsymbol{\Pi}(L) = \boldsymbol{\Pi}(1) + (1 - L)\boldsymbol{\Pi}^*(L). \tag{12.22}$$

Johansen (1991*a*) shows that

$$\boldsymbol{C}(1) = \boldsymbol{B}_{\perp}(\boldsymbol{A}'_{\perp}\boldsymbol{\Pi}^*(1)\boldsymbol{B}_{\perp})^{-1}\boldsymbol{A}'_{\perp}, \tag{12.20$'$}$$

which is apparently invariant through right multiplications of $\boldsymbol{A}_{\perp}$ and $\boldsymbol{B}_{\perp}$ by non-singular matrices. Johansen (1992*a*) also shows that the non-singularity of $\boldsymbol{A}'_{\perp}\boldsymbol{\Pi}^*(1)\boldsymbol{B}_{\perp}$ is necessary and sufficient for $\{x_t\}$ being $I(1)$ rather than $I(2)$.

Incidentally $\boldsymbol{\Pi}^*(L)$ in (12.22) is related to $\boldsymbol{\Gamma}(L)$ in (12.17) through

$$\boldsymbol{\Pi}^*(L) = \boldsymbol{\Gamma}(L) - \boldsymbol{\Pi}(1),$$

i.e.

$$\boldsymbol{\Pi}^*_0 = \boldsymbol{\Gamma}_0 - \boldsymbol{\Pi}(1),$$

$$\boldsymbol{\Pi}^*_i = \boldsymbol{\Gamma}_i, \quad i \geq 1.$$

Since $\boldsymbol{A}'_{\perp}\boldsymbol{\Pi}(1)\boldsymbol{B}_{\perp} = \boldsymbol{0}$ because of (12.16′), (12.20′) can also be written

$$\boldsymbol{C}(1) = \boldsymbol{B}_{\perp}(\boldsymbol{A}'_{\perp}\boldsymbol{\Gamma}(1)\boldsymbol{B}_{\perp})^{-1}\boldsymbol{A}'_{\perp}.^{4} \tag{12.20$''$}$$

[4] Hiro Toda has kindly suggested (12.20″) to me.

In most econometric applications an infinite power series $\mathbf{\Pi}(L)$ in (12.15) is approximated by a finite order, q. From now we free $\mathbf{\Sigma}_\varepsilon$ from the normalization, and instead normalize $\mathbf{\Pi}_0$ in $\mathbf{\Pi}(L)$ to $\boldsymbol{I}_k$ by adjusting $\mathbf{\Pi}_0, \mathbf{\Pi}_1, \ldots$, and $\mathbf{\Sigma}_\varepsilon$. Adopting a standard way to write a finite-order VAR, (12.15) is replaced by

$$(\boldsymbol{I} - \mathbf{\Pi}_1 L - \ldots - \mathbf{\Pi}_q L^q)\boldsymbol{x}_t = \boldsymbol{\varepsilon}_t, \qquad (12.23)$$

and (12.18) by

$$\Delta \boldsymbol{x}_t = \boldsymbol{A}\boldsymbol{B}'\boldsymbol{x}_{t-1} + (\mathbf{\Gamma}_1 L + \ldots + \mathbf{\Gamma}_{q-1} L^{q-1})\Delta \boldsymbol{x}_t + \boldsymbol{\varepsilon}_t. \qquad (12.24)$$

The truncation of the infinite power series of L in $\mathbf{\Pi}(L) \equiv \boldsymbol{V}(L)^{-1} \boldsymbol{D}^*(L)\boldsymbol{U}(L)^{-1}$ can be justified as follows. It has been assumed that $\boldsymbol{V}(z)$ is a polynomial matrix such that $\det[\boldsymbol{V}(z)] = 0$ has all roots outside the unit circle. Therefore in $\boldsymbol{V}(L)^{-1} \equiv \tilde{\boldsymbol{V}}_0 + \tilde{\boldsymbol{V}}_1 L + \tilde{\boldsymbol{V}}_2 L^2 + \ldots$, $\{\|\tilde{\boldsymbol{V}}(j)\|\}$ is bounded by a decaying exponential, by which I mean the existence of c such that $0 < c < 1$ and $\|\tilde{\boldsymbol{V}}(j)\| < c^j$, $j = 0, 1, \ldots$ $\boldsymbol{U}(L)^{-1}$ is a polynomial (rather than a rational) matrix, and $\boldsymbol{D}^*(L)$ is given in (12.13*b*). Then, in $\mathbf{\Pi}(L) \equiv \mathbf{\Pi}_0 + \mathbf{\Pi}_1 L + \mathbf{\Pi}_2 L^2 + \ldots$, it is easily seen that $\{\|\mathbf{\Pi}_j\|\}$ is also bounded by a decaying exponential, and $\mathbf{\Pi}(L)$ may be approximated by its truncated version. Once $\mathbf{\Pi}(L)$ is truncated as in (12.23). $\mathbf{\Gamma}(L)$ is also truncated as in (12.24).[5]

It has been noted that neither $\boldsymbol{A}$ nor $\boldsymbol{B}$ is unique. This is a nice opportunity to explain the identification problem. It is known that the $\mathbf{\Pi}$s in (12.23) are identified no matter whether unit roots are involved, in so far as the leading term $\mathbf{\Pi}_0$ is normalized to $\boldsymbol{I}$. Therefore $\boldsymbol{A}\boldsymbol{B}' \equiv -\mathbf{\Pi}(1)$ is identified though $\boldsymbol{A}$ and $\boldsymbol{B}'$ are not separately. In particular the rank of $\boldsymbol{A}\boldsymbol{B}'$, the co-integration rank, is identified, which is consistent with our previous result on the VMA representation. Moreover, all of $\mathbf{\Gamma}_1, \ldots, \mathbf{\Gamma}_{q-1}$ are identified.

12.2.4 Common trends once more

I briefly return to the MA representation in Section 12.1. Notice that $\boldsymbol{C}(L)$ in Section 12.2 is $\boldsymbol{A}(L)^{-1}\boldsymbol{B}(L)$ in (12.11). Once (12.11) is accepted, $\boldsymbol{C}(L)$ in Section 12.2 is identical to $\boldsymbol{C}(L)$ in (12.1) in Section 12.1. (In fact $\{\boldsymbol{\varepsilon}_t\}$ in Section 12.2 is also identical to $\{\boldsymbol{\varepsilon}_t\}$ in Section 12.1.) In Section (12.12) the common stochastic trends are $\sum_1^t \boldsymbol{\xi}_s = \boldsymbol{H}_2' \sum_1^t \boldsymbol{\varepsilon}_s$. Because of (12.20′) $\boldsymbol{H}_1$ may

[5] Engle and Yoo (1991) point out that Γ(L) may not be invertible. An easy way to appreciate the point is to investigate a single equation, $a(L)y_t + b(L)x_t = \varepsilon_t$, assuming that $a(L) = a_0 + a_1 L + \ldots + a_p L^p$ is invertible. Construct $a^*(L)$ and $b^*(L)$ by $a(L) = a(1)L + (1 - L)a^*(L)$, and $b(L) = b(1)L + (1 - L)b^*(L)$. We get $a^*(L)\Delta y_t + a(1)y_{t-1} + b(1)x_{t-1} + b^*(L)\Delta x_t = \varepsilon_t$, which is an error-correction form. But $a^*(L)$ may not be invertible as Engle and Yoo (1991) point out even if $a(L)$ is invertible. Construction of a counter-example is easy. One could also use $a(L) = a(1) + (1 - L)a^{**}(L)$ and $b(L) = b(1) + (1 - L)b^{**}(L)$. We then get a form analogous to the Bewley representation. See Bewley (1979), Hylleberg and Mizon (1989), and Banerjee *et al.* (1993: 54). It also has the same problem. Compare these expressions with (14.15). The present remark should not be taken as a criticism of the error-correction model and the Bewley model. It only warns readers about the treatment of $a^*(L)$ or $a^{**}(L)$.

be taken as $\boldsymbol{A}(\boldsymbol{A}'\boldsymbol{A})^{-1/2}$, and $\boldsymbol{H}_2$ as $\boldsymbol{A}_\perp(\boldsymbol{A}_\perp'\boldsymbol{A}_\perp)^{-1/2}$. The common stochastic trends, $\boldsymbol{f}_t \equiv \boldsymbol{H}_2'\sum_1^t \boldsymbol{\varepsilon}_s$, are also

$$(\boldsymbol{A}_\perp'\boldsymbol{A}_\perp)^{-1/2}\boldsymbol{A}_\perp' \sum_1^t \boldsymbol{\varepsilon}_s (\equiv \boldsymbol{f}_t). \tag{12.25}$$

From (12.20′) it is seen that they enter into $\boldsymbol{x}_t$ as

$$\boldsymbol{C}(1)\boldsymbol{H}_2 \sum_1^t \boldsymbol{\xi}_s = \boldsymbol{B}_\perp(\boldsymbol{A}_\perp'\boldsymbol{\Pi}^*(1)\boldsymbol{B}_\perp)^{-1}\boldsymbol{A}_\perp' \sum_1^t \boldsymbol{\varepsilon}_s \equiv (\hat{\boldsymbol{x}}_t).$$

While $\boldsymbol{B}'$ defines the long-run equilibrium, it is $\boldsymbol{B}_\perp$ and $\boldsymbol{A}_\perp$ that contribute to the formation of the common trends.

Gonzalo and Granger (1991) and Konishi and Granger (1992) note that the equilibrium error does not cause the common trend in Granger's sense. To be more concrete, consider the r-variates vector process of $\boldsymbol{\xi}_t \equiv \boldsymbol{B}'x_{t-1}$ and the $(k-r)$ variates vector process of $\Delta \boldsymbol{f}_t \equiv (\boldsymbol{A}_\perp'\boldsymbol{A}_\perp)^{-1/2}\boldsymbol{A}_\perp'\boldsymbol{\varepsilon}_t$. Then it can be shown that $\boldsymbol{\xi}_t$ does not cause $\Delta \boldsymbol{f}_t$ in Granger's sense. Suppose that $E(\boldsymbol{\varepsilon}_t\boldsymbol{\varepsilon}_t') = \boldsymbol{I}_k$ in (12.11), and that this normalization is carried through (12.15) and (12.18). Left multiplication of (12.18) by $(\boldsymbol{A}'\boldsymbol{A})^{-1}\boldsymbol{A}'$ leads to

$$\boldsymbol{B}'x_{t-1} = (\boldsymbol{A}'\boldsymbol{A})^{-1}\boldsymbol{A}'(\boldsymbol{\Gamma}(L)\Delta \boldsymbol{x}_t - \boldsymbol{\varepsilon}_t) = (\boldsymbol{A}'\boldsymbol{A})^{-1}\boldsymbol{A}'(\boldsymbol{\Gamma}(L)\boldsymbol{C}(L) - \boldsymbol{I})\boldsymbol{\varepsilon}_t.$$

Since

$$\boldsymbol{H} \equiv \begin{bmatrix} (\boldsymbol{A}_\perp'\boldsymbol{A}_\perp)^{-1/2}\boldsymbol{A}_\perp' \\ (\boldsymbol{A}'\boldsymbol{A})^{-1/2}\boldsymbol{A}' \end{bmatrix}$$

is an orthogonal matrix, let $\boldsymbol{u}_t \equiv \boldsymbol{H}\boldsymbol{\varepsilon}_t$, $\boldsymbol{u}_{1t} = (\boldsymbol{A}_\perp'\boldsymbol{A}_\perp)^{-1/2}\boldsymbol{A}_\perp'\boldsymbol{\varepsilon}_t$, and $\boldsymbol{u}_{2t} = (\boldsymbol{A}'\boldsymbol{A})^{-1/2}\boldsymbol{A}'\boldsymbol{\varepsilon}_t$. Then $E(\boldsymbol{u}_t\boldsymbol{u}_t') = \boldsymbol{I}_k$, and a VMA representation of $(\Delta \boldsymbol{f}_t', \boldsymbol{\xi}_t')'$ is

$$\begin{bmatrix} \Delta \boldsymbol{f}_t \\ \boldsymbol{\xi}_t \end{bmatrix} = \begin{bmatrix} \boldsymbol{I}_{k-r} & 0 \\ \boldsymbol{F}_{21}(L) & \boldsymbol{F}_{22}(L) \end{bmatrix} \begin{bmatrix} \boldsymbol{u}_{1t} \\ \boldsymbol{u}_{2t} \end{bmatrix},$$

where $\boldsymbol{F}_{21}(L) = (\boldsymbol{A}'\boldsymbol{A})^{-1}\boldsymbol{A}'(\boldsymbol{\Gamma}(L)\boldsymbol{C}(L) - \boldsymbol{I})\boldsymbol{A}_\perp(\boldsymbol{A}_\perp'\boldsymbol{A}_\perp)^{-1/2}$ and $\boldsymbol{F}_{22}(L) = (\boldsymbol{A}'\boldsymbol{A})^{-1}\boldsymbol{A}'(\boldsymbol{\Gamma}(L)\boldsymbol{C}(L) - \boldsymbol{I})\boldsymbol{A}(\boldsymbol{A}'\boldsymbol{A})^{-1/2}$. By a generalized version of Theorem 11.1 in Chapter 11 it is seen that $\boldsymbol{\xi}_t$ does not cause $\Delta \boldsymbol{f}_t$ in Granger's sense.

12.2.5 Non-zero $\boldsymbol{\mu}$

Replace $\{\boldsymbol{\varepsilon}_t\}$ by $\{(\boldsymbol{\mu} + \boldsymbol{\varepsilon}_t)\}$ in (12.11). Thus (12.24) is replaced by

$$\Delta \boldsymbol{x}_t = \boldsymbol{A}\boldsymbol{B}'\boldsymbol{x}_{t-1} + (\boldsymbol{\Gamma}_1 L + \ldots + \boldsymbol{\Gamma}_{q-1}\boldsymbol{L}^{q-1})\Delta \boldsymbol{x}_t + \boldsymbol{\mu} + \boldsymbol{\varepsilon}_t. \tag{12.26}$$

The only point worth noting is the one already mentioned at the end of the previous Section 12.1.3. In fact Johansen (1991*a*) derives the VMA representation (12.10) with (12.20′) from the error-correction representation (12.26) so that we may proceed with (12.10). As demonstrated in (12.10) $\boldsymbol{\mu}$ produces a linear trend in $\{\boldsymbol{x}_t\}$ only through $t\boldsymbol{C}(1)\boldsymbol{\mu}$. Recall that $\boldsymbol{C}(1)\boldsymbol{A} = \boldsymbol{0}$. If $\boldsymbol{\mu}$ is a linear combination of columns of $\boldsymbol{A}$, $\boldsymbol{C}(1)\boldsymbol{\mu} = \boldsymbol{0}$ and the linear trends are absent from every element of $\{\boldsymbol{x}_t\}$. Because of (12.20′)

$$t\boldsymbol{C}(1)\boldsymbol{\mu} = t\boldsymbol{B}_\perp(\boldsymbol{A}'_\perp\boldsymbol{\Pi}^*(1)\boldsymbol{B}_\perp)'\boldsymbol{A}'_\perp\boldsymbol{\mu},$$

and this shows how $\boldsymbol{\mu}$ enters into $\boldsymbol{x}_t$. This is parallel to the way in which the stochastic common trends are formed and entered into $\boldsymbol{x}_t$. Therefore it may be useful to define the common trends (as they enter into $\boldsymbol{x}_t$) as

$$t\boldsymbol{C}(1)\boldsymbol{\mu} + \boldsymbol{C}(1)\sum_{s=1}^{t}\boldsymbol{\varepsilon}_s = \boldsymbol{B}_\perp(\boldsymbol{A}'_\perp\boldsymbol{\Pi}^*(1)\boldsymbol{B}_\perp)^{-1}\boldsymbol{A}'_\perp\left(t\boldsymbol{\mu} + \sum_{s=1}^{t}\boldsymbol{\varepsilon}_s\right),$$

combining the deterministic linear trends and the stochastic trends. (Needless to say this does not mean that each element of $\boldsymbol{x}_t$ has the same slope of linear trend.) Note that $\boldsymbol{B}'$ annihilates both of these trends at once.

I now comment on constants in deterministic trends.

1. The model (12.10) admits a constant in the ith element of $\boldsymbol{x}_t$ only when the ith element of $E(\boldsymbol{x}_0)$ is non-zero and the ith element of $C(1)\boldsymbol{\mu}$ is zero. The model admits a non-zero constant term in the linear trend of the ith element of $\boldsymbol{x}_t$ only when the ith element of $E(\boldsymbol{x}_0)$ is non-zero.

2. It is also seen from (12.10) that $E(\boldsymbol{B}'\boldsymbol{x}_t) = \boldsymbol{B}'E(\boldsymbol{x}_0)$. If the equilibrium error has a non-zero mean at the initial stage, the non-zero mean stays on for ever. I shall comment on this problem in Section 12.3.2 below.

3. A constant term is identified if it is involved in a stationary process. In particular $E(\boldsymbol{B}'\boldsymbol{x}_t) = \boldsymbol{B}'E(\boldsymbol{x}_0)$ is identified once $\boldsymbol{B}'$ is identified. See Sections 11.1.2 and 15.2.1 on different ways to introduce identifiability into $\boldsymbol{B}'$.

Johansen (1992*d*) shows that a modification of (12.26) enables us to incorporate a co-integration space that annihilates only the stochastic trends. Introduce $\boldsymbol{\mu}_1 t$ into (12.26) to get

$$\Delta\boldsymbol{x}_t = \boldsymbol{A}\boldsymbol{B}'\boldsymbol{x}_{t-1} + (\boldsymbol{\Gamma}_1 L + \ldots + \boldsymbol{\Gamma}_{q-1}L^{q-1})\Delta\boldsymbol{x}_t + \boldsymbol{\mu}_0 + \boldsymbol{\mu}_1 t + \boldsymbol{\varepsilon}_t. \quad (12.27)$$

(12.10) is replaced by

$$\boldsymbol{x}_t = \frac{1}{2}t(t+1)\boldsymbol{C}(1)\boldsymbol{\mu}_1 + t\boldsymbol{C}(1)\boldsymbol{\mu}_0 + \boldsymbol{C}^*(L)\boldsymbol{\mu}_1 t \quad (12.28)$$

$$+\boldsymbol{C}(1)\sum_1^t\boldsymbol{\varepsilon}_s + \boldsymbol{C}^*(L)\boldsymbol{\varepsilon}_t + \boldsymbol{x}_0 - \boldsymbol{C}^*(L)\boldsymbol{\varepsilon}_0.$$

$\boldsymbol{B}'$ annhilates the stochastic trends $\boldsymbol{C}(1)\sum_1^t\boldsymbol{\varepsilon}_s$, but does not annihilate the linear trends because $\boldsymbol{B}'\boldsymbol{C}^*(L)\boldsymbol{\mu}_1 t \neq \boldsymbol{0}$. However, $\boldsymbol{B}'$ does annihilate the quadratic trends. If we wish $\{\boldsymbol{x}_t\}$ to lack quadratic trends in the first place before being annihilated by $\boldsymbol{B}'$, we must impose the condition, $\boldsymbol{A}'_\perp\boldsymbol{\mu}_1 = \boldsymbol{0}$.

12.2.6 Granger non-causality

Granger non-causality was explained in Section 11.3, but the case where x_{1t} and x_{2t} are co-integrated has been deferred. Suppose that $k = 2$ and $r = 1$ in (12.24):

$$\begin{bmatrix} \Delta x_{1t} \\ \Delta x_{2t} \end{bmatrix} = \begin{bmatrix} a_1 \\ a_2 \end{bmatrix} [b_1, b_2] \begin{bmatrix} x_{1t-1} \\ x_{2t-1} \end{bmatrix} + \sum_{i=1}^{q-1} \begin{bmatrix} \gamma_{11}^{(i)} & \gamma_{12}^{(i)} \\ \gamma_{21}^{(i)} & \gamma_{22}^{(i)} \end{bmatrix} \begin{bmatrix} \Delta x_{1t-i} \\ \Delta x_{2t-i} \end{bmatrix} + \begin{bmatrix} \varepsilon_{1t} \\ \varepsilon_{2t} \end{bmatrix}.$$

As explained in relation to (11.20) Granger non-causality of x_{2t} upon x_{1t} may be examined by comparing two predictions of Δx_{1t}. One is based upon $[\Delta x_{1t-1}, \ldots, \Delta x_{11}]$, and the other upon $[\Delta x_{t-1}, \ldots, \Delta x_1]$, assuming that $x_0 = 0$. Substituting $x_{ht-1} = \sum_{i=1}^{t-1} \Delta x_{ht-i}$, $h = 1, 2$, into the first equation, it is seen that

$$\begin{aligned} & E(\Delta x_{1t}|\Delta x_{t-1}, \ldots, \Delta x_1) - E(\Delta x_{1t}|\Delta x_{1t-1}, \ldots, \Delta x_{11}) \\ & = \sum_{i=1}^{q-1} \left(a_1 b_2 + \gamma_{12}^{(i)}\right) (\Delta x_{2t-i} - E(\Delta x_{2t-i}|\Delta x_{1t-1}, \ldots, \Delta x_{11})) \\ & + a_1 b_2 \sum_{i=q}^{t-1} (\Delta x_{2t-i} - E(\Delta x_{2t-i}|\Delta x_{1t-1}, \ldots, \Delta x_{11})). \end{aligned}$$

The reasoning set out in Section 12.1.3 is applicable even in the present case where $\boldsymbol{B}'\Delta \boldsymbol{x}_t$ is $I(-1)$, and x_{2t} does not cause x_{1t} in Granger's sense if and only if $a_1 b_2 + \gamma_{12}^{(i)} = 0, i = 1, \ldots, q-1$ and $a_1 b_2 = 0$. The condition can be rewritten as $a_1 b_2 = 0$ and $\gamma_{12}^{(i)} = 0, i = 1, \ldots, q-1$. Granger non-causality is the triangularity of $\boldsymbol{AB}', \boldsymbol{\Gamma}_1, \ldots, \boldsymbol{\Gamma}_{q-1}$ in the error-correction form of VAR (12.24).

12.3 Economic Theory and Co-integration

The co-integration in Sections (12.2) and (12.3) is a statistical rather than an economic model. This should be obvious from the explanation in Section 12.1. In Section 12.2 words such as the equilibrium and equilibrium error have been used, but the main conclusion such as (12.18) is simply rewriting the model in Section 12.1 in a different mathematical form. One may wonder why it has been written in the literature that $\boldsymbol{B}'\boldsymbol{x}_t$ is the equilibrium error which drives the system towards equilibrium. This association between economic theory and co-integration has been questioned in some literature. Here I justify the association.

Three introductory remarks are in order. First, economic theory requires a particular representation of the co-integrating vectors that are not unique otherwise. Let y, m, and i be the log income, log money stock, and interest rate, and suppose that y and m are $I(1)$ while i is $I(0)$. The variables are assembled in vector, (m,y,i). Since i is $I(0)$, (0,0,1) is a co-integrating vector. If demand function for money holds, $(1, -1, -b)$ is another co-integrating vector. Any non-singular transformations (rotations) of these two vectors are contained in the co-integration space. But the vector that is meaningful from the standpoint of the economic theory is only $(1, -1, -b)$. Others, for example $(1, -1, 0)$, have no economic meaning. Nor does (0,0,1). This point will be discussed further in Sections 12.3.7 and 15.2.1.

Second, it is said that the co-integration is related to the long-run equilibrium. However, what distinguishes the short-run and long-run equilibria in economic dynamics is the length of time that the system needs in order to restore the equilibria when the system is shocked once but left undisturbed afterwards. On the other hand, the long-run and short-run are distinguished by integration orders in the co-integration analysis. Therefore the short-run equilibrium in economics may well provide a co-integrating relation as the uncovered interest parity did in many studies.

Third, from the standpoint of equilibrium analysis of economic theory the co-integration space should nullify both the deterministic and the stochastic trends at once. The same opinion has been expressed in Han and Ogaki (1991). In this chapter I shall be concerned only with the deterministic co-integration in the terminology of Ogaki and Park (1992). We are naturally led to this restriction by introducing the drift term $\boldsymbol{\mu}$ as in (12.9) and/or (12.26). It is admitted however that some long-run economic relationships are thought to hold only in abstraction from the deterministic trends. For example, Stock and Watson (1989) investigate neutrality of money in terms of the stochastic trends only. Ogaki (1992) and Ogaki and Park (1992) note a case where only the stochastic co-integration is expected in connection with consumption of goods and the relative prices.

12.3.1 Long-run relations in economics and co-integration

Let us ask ourselves what economic sense one can make out of the co-integrating vectors assuming that the vectors may be rotated if necessary. To answer the question I consider a model sensible from the standpoint of economic theory, transform it in the error-correction form of the Granger representation, and examine the correspondence between the parameters of the economic model and the statistical error-correction form. This demonstration also provides a nice exercise of the mathematics in Sections 12.1 and 12.2.

Campbell (1987) and Campbell and Shiller (1988) prove that the present-value model given in Section 1.3 of Part I necessarily involves a co-integrating vector. The proof will be given in (12.29) and (12.40) of this Chapter.[6] Another example of the association between the co-integration and economic theories is the real business cycle theory. The business cycle is interpreted by the equilibrium analysis of processes in which effects of shocks are propagated. One kind of shock is that in the growth rate of productivity, and economic theory explains how stochastic trends are generated. This is not seen elsewhere. See King *et al.* (1991), of which a brief summary is given in Section 15.5.

Here I consider a model in the error-correction literature. In Alogoskoufis and Smith (1992) an economic agent wishes the target variable y_t^* to be equal to

[6] Campbell (1987) emphasizes the difference between the forward-looking nature of the present-value model and the disequilibrium adjustment of the error-correction model such as Davidson *et al.* (1978).

$k + x_t$, where x_t is exogenous, but actually adjusts the control variable y_t by

$$\Delta y_t = \beta(E(x_t|I_{t-1}) - x_{t-1}) + \gamma(y^*_{t-1} - y_{t-1}) + \varepsilon_{1t}, \tag{12.29}$$

$$y^*_t = k + x_t. \tag{12.30}$$

This is a type of the error-correction model which has been developed as an economic model in Sargan (1964), Davidson *et al.* (1978), and Hendry and von Ungern-Sternberg (1980) among others. The long-run equilibrium relation is (12.30), and (12.29) has the equilibrium error at $t-1$, $y^*_{t-1} - y_{t-1}$, on the right-hand side. It is assumed throughout the present explanation that $1 > \gamma > 0$. The β is not necessarily the discount factor,[7] and if $\beta = \gamma$, (12.29) is reduced to an expectation version of the partial-adjustment model,

$$\Delta y_t = \gamma(E(x_t|I_{t-1}) + k - y_{t-1}),$$

which was dominating in econometrics prior to the error-correction model.

Though embarassing it must be admitted that there are a number of different definitions of long-run equilibrium in the terminology of economic theory. In my judgement economic theory often considers a hypothetical situation where x_t is perfectly predictable and ε_{1t} is absent from (12.29). The long-run equilibrium relation is the one between y_t and x_t that would hold in this situation as $t \to \infty$. When x_t is perfectly forecastable and ε_{1t} is absent in the model that consists of (12.29) and (12.30), the relation at a finite t is

$$y_t = k + (1 - (1-\gamma)L)^{-1}(\beta\Delta x_t + \gamma x_{t-1}). \tag{12.31}$$

If $\beta = \gamma$ as in the partial adjustment, (12.31) is specialized to

$$y_t = k + \gamma \sum\nolimits_{j=0}^{\infty} (1-\gamma)^j x_{t-j}.$$

If $x_t = \mu + ct$, $c \neq 0$, we have as $t \to \infty$

$$y_t - (k + x_t - c(1-\gamma)/\gamma) \to 0.$$

To those economists who consider $y_t = k + x_t$ as the right long-run equilibrium this is a defect of the partial-adjustment model because the equilibrium is unattainable.[8] Let us turn to the more general error correction. If $\beta \neq \gamma$ and if $x_t = \mu + ct$, $c \neq 0$, we have as $t \to \infty$,

$$y_t - (k + x_t + (\beta - 1)c/\gamma) \to 0. \tag{12.32}$$

If $\beta = 1$ we attain the long-run relation, $y_t = k + x_t$, but otherwise the relation is again unattainable.

Finally, it is seen that, no matter what β and γ may be,

$$t^{-1}(x_t - y_t) \to 0 \tag{12.33}$$

[7] (12.29) and (12.30) should not be confused with the Euler equation in the linear quadratic model. A difference equation somewhat similar to (but different from) (12.29) appears in the planning horizon, but the equation has to be solved for the immediate decision variable to get the behaviour equation there. On the other hand (12.29) itself is the behaviour equation.

[8] See Salmon (1982) for more on this point.

as $t \to \infty$ if $x_t = \mu + ct$, $c \neq 0$. (12.23) is obtained as follows. In the spirit of the undetermined coefficient method set $x_t = \mu_1 + c_1 t$ and $y_t = \mu_2 + c_2 t$, and substitute them into (12.31). With $a(z) \equiv (1 - (1-\gamma)z)^{-1}$ the coefficient of t on the right-hand side is $a(1)\gamma c_1$, which is c_1. The coefficient of t on the left hand is simply c_2. Therefore, if and only if $c_1 = c_2$ the terms in $O(t)$ vanish from (12.31), and (12.33) holds. (Though μ_1 and μ_2 are determined so as to make (12.31) hold even in the terms in $O(1)$, they are irrelevant to the long-run equilibrium considered in (12.33).) We call (12.33) the *balanced-growth version* of long-run equilibrium.[9] Keep in mind the use of $a(1)$ to get the coefficient of t.

Now we must determine which one of the above relations is represented as the long-run equilibrium in the co-integration analysis. Suppose that

$$\Delta x_t = d(L)(\mu + \varepsilon_{2t}) = d(1)\mu + d(L)\varepsilon_{2t}, \tag{12.34}$$

where $d(L) = d_0 + d_1 L + \ldots + d_q L^q$, and $d(z) = 0$ has all roots outside the unit circle so that $d(L)$ is invertible. $\{\varepsilon_{1t}\}$ has appeared in (12.29), and we assume that $\{(\varepsilon_{1t}, \varepsilon_{2t})\}$ is i.i.d. with zero mean and covariance matrix I_2. By virtue of Theorem 11.1 in Section 11.3 it is seen that y_t does not cause x_t in Granger's sense, and that

$$E(x_t | I_{t-1}) - x_{t-1} = E(\Delta x_t | I_{t-1}) = d(1)\mu + (d(L) - d_0)\varepsilon_{2t}.$$

Substituting this into (12.29) and using (12.34) with the assumption that $x_t = 0$ for $t \leq 0$, we get

$$y_t = k + \gamma^{-1}\beta d(1)\mu + (1 - (1-\gamma)L)^{-1} \times [\beta(d(L) - d_0)\varepsilon_{2t} + \gamma x_{t-1} + \varepsilon_{1t}]. \tag{12.35}$$

Differencing and using (12.34) leads to

$$\Delta y_t = (1 - (1-\gamma)L)^{-1}[(\gamma d(1)L + \delta(L) \times (1 - L))(\mu + \varepsilon_{2t}) + (1 - L)\varepsilon_{1t}], \tag{12.35$'$}$$

where $\delta(L) \equiv \beta(d(L) - d_0) + \gamma d^*(L)L$ and $d(L) \equiv d(1) + (1 - L)d^*(L)$.

(12.34) and (12.35′) provide a nice exercise in order to understand the theoretical structure of co-integration. The two equations form a VARMA for $(\Delta x_t, \Delta y_t)'$,

$$\begin{pmatrix} 1 & 0 \\ 0 & 1 - (1-\gamma)L \end{pmatrix} \begin{pmatrix} \Delta x_t \\ \Delta y_t \end{pmatrix} = \begin{pmatrix} d(L) & 0 \\ \gamma d(1)L + \delta(L)(1 - L) & 1 - L \end{pmatrix} \times \begin{pmatrix} \mu + \varepsilon_{2t} \\ \varepsilon_{1t} \end{pmatrix}. \tag{12.36}$$

[9] When (12.30) is replaced by $y_t^* = k + cx_t$, (12.33) is $t^{-1}(cx_t - y_t)$. If $x_t = \log X_t$ and $y_t = \log Y_t$, the growth rates of X_t and Y_t are not equal unless $c = 1$. Perhaps we should look for a word other than balanced growth.

This is expressed as a VMA,

$$\begin{bmatrix} \Delta x_t \\ \Delta y_t \end{bmatrix} = \boldsymbol{C}(L) \begin{bmatrix} \mu + \varepsilon_{2t} \\ \varepsilon_{1t} \end{bmatrix},$$

where $c_{11}(L) = d(L)$, $c_{12}(L) = 0$, $c_{21}(L) = (1-(1-\gamma)L)^{-1}[\gamma d(1)L + \delta(L)(1-L)]$, $c_{22}(L) = (1-(1-\gamma)L)^{-1}(1-L)$. Therefore

$$\boldsymbol{C}(1) = \begin{bmatrix} d(1) & 0 \\ d(1) & 0 \end{bmatrix},$$

and a representation of the co-integrating vector is $(1, -1)$.

It follows that

$$\boldsymbol{C}(L) = \boldsymbol{U}(L)\boldsymbol{D}(L)\boldsymbol{V}(L), \tag{12.37}$$

where $\boldsymbol{U}(L) = \begin{bmatrix} 1 & 0 \\ 0 & (1-(1-\gamma)L)^{-1} \end{bmatrix} \begin{bmatrix} 1 & 0 \\ \gamma L & 1 \end{bmatrix}$

$$\boldsymbol{D}(L) = \begin{bmatrix} 1 & 0 \\ 0 & 1-L \end{bmatrix}$$

$$\boldsymbol{V}(L) = \begin{bmatrix} d(L) & 0 \\ \beta(d(L) - d_0) & 1 \end{bmatrix}.$$

$\boldsymbol{U}(L)^{-1}$ is a polynomial matrix, and so is $\boldsymbol{V}(L)$.[10]

$$(\boldsymbol{U}(L)^{-1})_{2.} = (-\gamma L, 1 - (1-\gamma)L)$$

$$\boldsymbol{D}^*(L) = \begin{bmatrix} 1-L & 0 \\ 0 & 1 \end{bmatrix}$$

$$(\boldsymbol{V}(L)^{-1})_{.2} = \begin{bmatrix} 0 \\ 1 \end{bmatrix}$$

[10] In the present case the desired result (12.37) follows directly from the construction of $\delta(L)$ without a Smith–McMillan form. The matrix of the MA part of (12.36) is

$$\begin{bmatrix} d(L) & 0 \\ \gamma d(1)L + \delta(L)(1-L) & 1-L \end{bmatrix},$$

and premultiplying this by

$$\begin{bmatrix} 1 & 0 \\ \gamma L & 1 \end{bmatrix},$$

produces

$$\begin{bmatrix} 1 & 0 \\ 0 & 1-L \end{bmatrix} \begin{bmatrix} d(L) & 0 \\ \beta(d(L) - d_0) & 1 \end{bmatrix}.$$

Therefore the matrix of the MA part of (12.36) is:

$$\begin{bmatrix} 1 & 0 \\ \gamma L & 1 \end{bmatrix} \begin{bmatrix} 1 & 0 \\ 0 & 1-L \end{bmatrix} \begin{bmatrix} d(L) & 0 \\ \beta(d(L) - d_0) & 1 \end{bmatrix}.$$

$$\boldsymbol{A} = -(\boldsymbol{V}(1)^{-1})_{.2} = \begin{bmatrix} 0 \\ -1 \end{bmatrix}$$

$$\boldsymbol{B}' = (\boldsymbol{U}(1)^{-1})_{.2} = (-\gamma, \gamma)$$

$$\boldsymbol{\Pi}(L) = \boldsymbol{V}(L)^{-1}\boldsymbol{D}^*(L)\boldsymbol{U}(L)^{-1}$$

$$= \begin{bmatrix} (1-L)d(L)^{-1} & 0 \\ -(1-L)d(L)^{-1}[\beta(d(L)-d_0)] - \gamma L, & 1-(1-\gamma)L \end{bmatrix}$$

$$\boldsymbol{\Pi}(1) = \begin{bmatrix} 0 & 0 \\ -\gamma & \gamma \end{bmatrix} = -\boldsymbol{A}\boldsymbol{B}'$$

$$\boldsymbol{\Gamma}(L) = \begin{bmatrix} d(L)^{-1} & 0 \\ -d(L)^{-1}[\beta(d(L)-d_0)], & 1 \end{bmatrix}.$$

The error-correction representation is

$$\begin{bmatrix} d(L)^{-1} & 0 \\ -d(L)^{-1}[\beta(d(L)-d_0], & 1 \end{bmatrix} \begin{bmatrix} \Delta x_t \\ \Delta y_t \end{bmatrix}$$

$$= \begin{bmatrix} 0 \\ -\gamma \end{bmatrix} [-1, 1] \begin{bmatrix} x_{t-1} \\ y_{t-1} \end{bmatrix} + \begin{bmatrix} \mu + \varepsilon_{2t} \\ \varepsilon_{1t} \end{bmatrix} \tag{12.38}$$

On the right-hand side of (12.38) the 2×2 coefficient matrix of $[x_{t-1}, y_{t-1}]'$ may be replaced by

$$\begin{bmatrix} 0 \\ \gamma \end{bmatrix} [1, -1], \quad \text{or} \quad \begin{bmatrix} 0 \\ -1 \end{bmatrix} [-\gamma, \gamma],$$

but the one in (12.38) makes sense from the standpoint of economic theory. The positive value of $y_{t-1} - x_{t-1}$ adjusts y_t downward. The co-integration nullifies the deterministic and the stochastic trends at once. The long-run relationship is $y_{t-1} = x_{t-1}$. It turns out that the first equation of (12.38) is a reproduction of (12.34), and the second equation is (12.29) rewritten with the aid of (12.34) except that k is missing from (12.38). In fact k has disappeared at (12.35′).

The economic model (12.29) that incorporates the *partial adjustment* as a special case ($\beta = \gamma$) has been expressed in the *error-correction* form in the terminology of co-integration analysis.

It was seen that economic theory had a number of versions of long-run equilibrium relations different from the co-integration vector $(1, -1)$. The one that comes closest to this is (12.33), the balanced-growth version of long-run equilibrium. It contains no information either about k or indicative of whether $\beta =$ or $\neq \gamma$.

If we had adopted the present-value model instead of (12.29), (12.30) in the above consideration, we would reach the same conclusion that it is the balanced-growth version of the long-run equilibrium that is dealt with in the co-integration analysis.

12.3.2 A short-cut alternative to 12.3.1

Suppose that $\{u_t\}$ is a stationary scalar process with zero mean, $v_t = \sum_{s=1}^{t} u_s$, $a(L)$ is a scalar infinite power series of L, and $a(L) = a(1) + (1 - L)a^*(L)$. Then note that $(a(L) - a(1))v_t$ is $I(0)$ because $(a(L) - a(1))v_t = a^*(L)u_t+$ initial terms.

Consider the economic-error correction model, (12.29) and (12.30). Earlier an undetermined coefficient method was applied to the deterministic version, (12.31). A method parallel to it is available for the stochastic model. Substituting (12.30) into (12.29) we get

$$(1 - (1 - \gamma)L)y_t = \beta(E(x_t|I_{t-1}) - x_{t-1}) + \gamma(k + x_{t-1}) + \varepsilon_{1t} \tag{12.39}$$

Let $a(L) = 1 - (1 - \gamma)L$. Then $a(1) = \gamma$. The part of $I(1)$ on the left-hand side of (12.39) is $\gamma\hat{y}_t$ because $(a(L) - a(1))y_t$ is $I(0)$. The $I(1)$ term on the right-hand side is $\gamma\hat{x}_t$, because $E(x_t|I_{t-1}) - x_{t-1}$ is generally $I(0)$. The $I(1)$ terms dominate the $I(0)$ terms. The long-run relation is $t^{-1/2}(x_t - y_t) \to 0$. This shows why it is the balanced-growth version of long-run relations that correspond to that in the co-integration analysis. In the present model the same relation holds on the deterministic and stochastic trends.

12.3.3 Parameters in the economic model and the co-integration model

As explained in Section 11.1.2 a (vector) parameter is identified in a model when a given probability distribution of observations uniquely determines the value of the parameter that produces the distribution in the model. In the model that consists of (12.29), (12.30), and (12.34) $(d_0, d_1, \ldots, d_q)$ is identified in (12.34), and (γ, β) in (12.29). However, k is not identified asymptotically as x_t and y_t are both $I(1)$. This is seen from the Fisher information of k failing to expand to infinity as T does. The Fisher information, which is (-1) times the expectation of second-order derivative of log-likelihood function, indicates a response of probability distribution to an infinitesimal difference in the parameter values.

Let us then consider how we can determine γ, β, and $(d_0, d_1, \ldots, d_q)$ from the probability distribution of observations $\{(x_t, y_t)\}$ in the statistical error correction model, (12.38), or, putting it equivalently, from the identified parameters of (12.38). This would also clarify how the parameter of the economic model can be recovered from that of the statistical error-correction model. The identification in the general error-correction form (12.24) has been considered at the end of Section 12.2.3. The co-integration rank is identified so that γ is determined as unity. Therefore $\boldsymbol{A}$ is $\boldsymbol{a} = (a_1, a_2)'$ and $\boldsymbol{B}'$ is $\boldsymbol{b}' = (b_1, b_2)$. $\boldsymbol{A}$ and $\boldsymbol{B}$ are not separately identified but $\boldsymbol{AB}'$ is. Therefore a_1b_1, a_2b_1, a_1b_2, and a_2b_2 are identified, and they can be uniquely determined from the probability distribution of observations. We also know from the distribution that y_t does not cause x_t in Granger's sense (see Section 11.3). Therefore as shown below in (12.43) we must have $a_1b_1 = a_1b_2 = 0$. The γ can be determined from a_2b_2 or $-a_2b_1$. $(d_0, d_1, \ldots, d_q)$ and β can be determined from $\boldsymbol{\Gamma}(L)$ as $\boldsymbol{\Gamma}(L)$ is identified.

12.3.4 *Stability condition*

In the economic theory it is important to ascertain whether a given equilibrium relation satisfies the stability condition. Let $\boldsymbol{B}'\boldsymbol{x}_t = \boldsymbol{0}$ be the equilibrium relations. In reality $\boldsymbol{B}'\boldsymbol{x}_t = \boldsymbol{u}_t$, where $\{\boldsymbol{u}_t\}$ is a stochastic process with zero mean, representing deviations from the equilibrium due to shocks. Suppose that if the shocks are absent after a time, t_0, $\boldsymbol{B}'\boldsymbol{x}_t$ converges to zero as $t \to \infty$. This means that the equilibrium is eventually restored when the extraneous shocks cease to disturb the system. The equilibrium is then said to be stable.

The equilibrium $\boldsymbol{B}'\boldsymbol{x}_t = \boldsymbol{0}$ does satisfy the stability condition in the error-correction representation (12.18) with $\boldsymbol{\mu} = \boldsymbol{0}$. To prove it we restart from (12.12*b*),

$$\Delta \boldsymbol{x}_t = \boldsymbol{U}(L)\boldsymbol{D}(L)\boldsymbol{V}(L)\boldsymbol{\varepsilon}_t.$$

If $\boldsymbol{\varepsilon}_t = \boldsymbol{0}$ after a time t_0, $\Delta \boldsymbol{x}_t \xrightarrow{P} \boldsymbol{0}$ as $t \to \infty$, where $\xrightarrow{P}$ means convergence in probability, because $\boldsymbol{V}(L)$ is a polynomial matrix and $\boldsymbol{U}(L)$ is expressed as a converging infinite power series of L. In (12.19) both $(\boldsymbol{V}(L))_{2.}$ and $(\boldsymbol{U}(L)^{-1})_{2.}$ are polynomials, and $(\boldsymbol{V}(L))_{2.}\boldsymbol{\varepsilon}_t$ is zero for $t > t_0 + q$, where q is the order of polynomial of $(\boldsymbol{V}(L))_{2.}$. Using $\boldsymbol{B}(L)' = \boldsymbol{B}(1)' + (1-L)\mathbf{B}^*(L)'$ and the reasoning presented below (12.19), it is seen that $\Delta \boldsymbol{x}_t \xrightarrow{P} \boldsymbol{0}$ implies $\boldsymbol{B}(1)'\boldsymbol{x}_t \xrightarrow{P} \boldsymbol{0}$ as $t \to \infty$.

In the model (12.26) with $\boldsymbol{\mu} \neq \boldsymbol{0}$ there is a possibility that $E(\boldsymbol{B}'\boldsymbol{x}_t) \neq \boldsymbol{0}$. When shocks cease to disturb the system at time t_0, $\boldsymbol{B}'\boldsymbol{x}_t$ may converge to a non-zero constant, which violates the stability of equilibrium (see Section 12.2.5 above). Therefore the examination of stability requires a test for $E(\boldsymbol{B}'\boldsymbol{x}_t) = \boldsymbol{0}$ after it is confirmed by the co-integration analysis that $\boldsymbol{B}'\boldsymbol{x}_t$ is stationary. For the investigation of $E(\boldsymbol{B}'\boldsymbol{x}_t)$ $\boldsymbol{B}$ must be identified by a normalization rule or by some constraints due to economic theories (see Section 15.2.1 below). Then the Johansen method described in Chapter 5 gives an estimate of $\boldsymbol{B}$, $\hat{\boldsymbol{B}}$. Since $\boldsymbol{B} - \hat{\boldsymbol{B}}$ is $O_p(T^{-1})$, we may regard it as though $\boldsymbol{B} = \hat{\boldsymbol{B}}$ in testing for the zero mean of $\boldsymbol{B}'\boldsymbol{x}_t$. Testing for zero mean in the stationary process is a standard problem. See, for example, Fuller (1976: 230–2).

Fukushige, Hatanaka, and Koto (1994) investigate the stability of a single equilibrium relation accounting for the possibility that the dominating root of the characteristic polynomial may be complex-valued.

12.3.5 *Adjustment towards the equilibrium*

In the model (12.29) it is the will of economic agents that restores the equilibrium. In the price model it is the arbitrage among market participants that drives the price system towards equilibrium. That the expectation of participants may also contribute to establishing the equilibrium is analysed in the literature of the theory of rational expectations (see, for example, Pesaran (1987, chs. 3, 4)) and also in the econometric literature such as Pagan (1985) and Nickell (1985). As explained in Section 11.3 Granger causality is an important concept in discriminating different channels of contributions to the prediction of multiple time series. Granger (1986) and Campbell and Shiller (1987, 1988) reveal an important Granger-causality relation that contributes to the movement toward equilibrium in the co-integrated VAR. The results in these studies are nearly identical, and I shall present here Campbell and Shiller (1987, 1988).

Campbell and Shiller (1988) begin by demonstrating that the general present-value relationship between x and y is a co-integrating relation. Let

$$y_t = \theta(1-\gamma)\sum_{i=0}^{\infty} \gamma^i E(x_{t+i}|I_t) + c, \tag{12.40}$$

where $1 > \gamma > 0$, and I_t is the information set at t, including (x_t, y_t), (x_{t-1}, y_{t-1}), ... Both x_t and y_t are $I(1)$. It is easy to show that $z_t \equiv y_t - \theta x_t$ is $I(0)$, because

$$\begin{aligned} z_t &= \theta(1-\gamma)\sum_{i=0}^{\infty} \gamma^i (E(x_{t+i}|I_t) - x_t) + c \\ &= \theta(1-\gamma)\sum_{i=0}^{\infty} \gamma^i \sum_{s=1}^{i} E(\Delta x_{t+s}|I_t) + c \\ &= \theta\sum_{i=0}^{\infty} \gamma^i E(\Delta x_{t+i}|I_t) + c. \end{aligned} \tag{12.41}$$

It should be obvious that the extreme right-hand side of (12.41) is a stationary stochastic process, but I will explain it in some detail. Note first that (12.40) is a stochastic process because the conditioning variables in I_t are random variables. A bivariate stochastic process, $\{(\Delta x_t, \Delta y_t)\}$ is generated by (12.1). $\{\varepsilon_t\}$ is a two elements i.i.d. process with zero mean and covariance matrix $\boldsymbol{I}_2$. The $\mathbf{C}_j$ s are each 2×2, and let $\mathbf{c}_{1j}$ be the first row of $\mathbf{C}_j$, $j = 0, 1, \ldots$. I assume c in (12.40) is zero for simplicity.

$$\Delta \boldsymbol{x}_t = \boldsymbol{c}_{10}\varepsilon_t + \boldsymbol{c}_{11}\varepsilon_{t-1} + \ldots.$$

Then $$\sum_1^{\infty} \gamma^i E(\Delta \boldsymbol{x}_{t+i}|I_t) = \left(\sum_1^{\infty} \gamma^i \boldsymbol{c}_{1i}\right)\varepsilon_t + \left(\sum_1^{\infty} \gamma^i \boldsymbol{c}_{1i+1}\right)\varepsilon_{t-1} + \ldots.$$

Therefore $$z_t = \left(\theta\sum_1^{\infty} \gamma^i \boldsymbol{c}_{1i}\right)\varepsilon_t + \left(\theta\sum_1^{\infty} \gamma^i \boldsymbol{c}_{1i+1}\right)\varepsilon_{t-1} + \ldots,$$

which is stationary.

Campbell and Shiller (1988) show that except for a pathological case z does cause Δx in Granger's sense, i.e. the equilibrium error has a net contribution beyond the past Δx to the prediction of future Δx. Since $\Delta y_t = \Delta z_t + \theta \Delta x_t$, the three-elements vector process $\{(\Delta x_t, \Delta y_t, z_t)\}$ is generated by the two-elements vector i.i.d. $\{\varepsilon_t\}$ as follows.

$$\begin{bmatrix} \Delta x_t \\ \Delta y_t \\ z_t \end{bmatrix} = \begin{bmatrix} c_{10} \\ \theta\sum_0^{\infty} \gamma^i c_{1i} \\ \theta\sum_1^{\infty} \gamma^i c_{1i} \end{bmatrix} \varepsilon_t + \begin{bmatrix} c_{11} \\ \theta(1-\gamma)\sum_0^{\infty} \gamma^i c_{1i+1} \\ \theta\sum_1^{\infty} \gamma^i c_{1i+1} \end{bmatrix} \varepsilon_{t-1} + \ldots$$

Suppose that z_t does not cause Δx_t in Granger's sense in the bivariate system $\{(\Delta x_t, z_t)\}$. Then by virtue of Theorem 11.1 in Section 11.3 either all of the first elements of $c_{10}, c_{11}, \ldots$ may be chosen to be zero, or all of the second elements of $c_{10}, c_{11}, \ldots$ may be chosen to be zero. Then $\{(\Delta x_t, \Delta y_t, z_t)\}$ is driven by a *scalar* i.i.d. process. The conclusion is that either z causes Δx in Granger's sense in the bivariate system or else z and Δx are essentially the same process.[11]

Ignoring the latter possibility we may say that the equilibrium error sets forth a movement toward the equilibrium through the expectation of future x. Earlier in Section 12.2.5 it was shown that the equilibrium error has no influence upon the common trends.

An interesting feature of the co-integration is its relation to the efficient market hypothesis, more precisely the martingale property (see Section 1.2.4). The result (12.18) states that if $\{x_t\}$ is $I(1)$ and at least one co-integrating vector exists,

$$\Delta \boldsymbol{x}_t = \boldsymbol{\Gamma}_1 \Delta \boldsymbol{x}_{t-1} + \ldots + \boldsymbol{A}\boldsymbol{B}' \boldsymbol{x}_{t-1} + \boldsymbol{\varepsilon}_t,$$

where $\boldsymbol{\Pi}(1) \equiv -\boldsymbol{A}\boldsymbol{B}'$ is not zero. Granger (1986) points out that this means $E(\Delta \boldsymbol{x}_t | \boldsymbol{x}_{t-1}, \boldsymbol{x}_{t-2}, \ldots) \neq \boldsymbol{0}$, which in turn means that $\{\boldsymbol{x}_t\}$ is not a martingale process. The price system in the efficient market cannot be co-integrated. My verbal explanation is that the efficient market completes the required adjustment within the same time unit so that there is no need to drive the system towards the equilibrium in the next period.[12] See Baillie and Bollerclev (1989), Hakkio and Ruch (1989), and Copeland (1991) for the applications to foreign-exchange markets and subsequent discussions in Diebold, Gardeazabal, and Yilmaz (1994) and Bailie and Bollerslev (1994). Doubts are cast on co-integrations among different daily spot nominal exchange rates.

Consider the adjustment towards the equilibrium when a sort of exogeneity is involved. Suppose (i) that $\Delta \boldsymbol{x}_t$ is partitioned as $\Delta \boldsymbol{x}'_t = (\Delta \boldsymbol{x}'_{1t}, \Delta \boldsymbol{x}'_{2t})$ with $(k-r)$ and r elements in $\Delta \boldsymbol{x}_{1t}$ and $\Delta \boldsymbol{x}_{2t}$ respectively, (ii) that both $\boldsymbol{A}(L)$ and $\boldsymbol{B}(L)$ in (12.11) have the same block lower triangularity,

$$\begin{array}{c c} & \begin{array}{ccc} k-r & & r \end{array} \\ \begin{array}{c} k-r \\ \\ r \end{array} & \left[\begin{array}{ccc} \times & \vdots & 0 \\ \cdots & \cdots & \cdots \\ \times & \vdots & \times \end{array}\right] \end{array}, \tag{12.42}$$

and (iii) that $\boldsymbol{\Sigma}_\varepsilon = \boldsymbol{I}_k$. (This means that $\boldsymbol{\Pi}_0$ is freed from the normalization.) Then $\boldsymbol{C}(L)$, $\boldsymbol{U}(L)$, and $\boldsymbol{V}(L)$ also have the same structure, and $\Delta \boldsymbol{x}_2$ does not cause $\Delta \boldsymbol{x}_1$ in Granger's sense. If this partitioning coincides with that in $\boldsymbol{D}(L)$ in (12.12*c*), $\boldsymbol{x}_{1t}$ and $\boldsymbol{x}_{2t}$ are co-integrated and $\boldsymbol{B}'\boldsymbol{x}_t$ is stationary. $\boldsymbol{A} \equiv -(\boldsymbol{V}(1)^{-1})_{.2}$

[11] An analysis in Johansen (1992*a*) can be used to show how this reasoning can be generalized. $\boldsymbol{B}'\boldsymbol{x}_t$ does cause at least one element of $\boldsymbol{x}_t$ in Granger's sense unless $\boldsymbol{A}'\boldsymbol{\Pi}^*(L)\boldsymbol{B}_\perp = \boldsymbol{0}$, where $\boldsymbol{\Pi}^*(L)$, $\boldsymbol{A}$, and $\boldsymbol{B}_\perp$ have been defined in Section 12.2.

[12] The theory of efficient market contains a number of aspects, some of which are not contradictory to the co-integration. See Dweyer and Wallace (1992) and Copeland (1991).

is now in the form

$$\begin{matrix} & r \\ k-r & \\ r & \end{matrix}\begin{bmatrix} 0 \\ \cdots \\ \times \end{bmatrix}, \tag{12.43}$$

The equilibrium errors $\boldsymbol{B}'\boldsymbol{x}_{t-1}$ do not subject $\Delta\boldsymbol{x}_1$ to the adjustment process towards equilibrium. The adjustment is made through $\Delta\boldsymbol{x}_2$ alone as it should be. Moreover, $\boldsymbol{\Pi}(L)$ and $\boldsymbol{\Gamma}(L)$ are block triangular in the form of (12.42). The point will be further discussed in Section 15.4 with a definitive concept of exogeneity.

12.3.6 Long-run parameters and short-run parameters

Classification between the long-run and the short-run parameters is vague. $\boldsymbol{B}'$ definitely belongs to the long-run parameters as it defines the long-run equilibrium relation. The adjustment matrix $\boldsymbol{A}$ is important in the movement towards equilibrium, and it contributes via $\boldsymbol{A}_\perp$ to the formation of common trends as seen from (12.25). On the other hand the $\boldsymbol{\Gamma}$ s in (12.24) definitely belong to the short-run parameters as they describe the short-run dynamics.

In the model that consists of (12.29) and (12.30), of which the error-correction form is (12.38), γ is an element of the adjustment matrix, but β is related to a short-run parameter. Thus what discriminates the partial adjustment and the economic error-correction models, i.e. $\beta =$ or $\neq \gamma$, is related to a short-run parameter.

In the example (12.38) the long-run and the short-run parameters are separated, but the separation may not be complete. In fact a simple model

$$\Delta x_t = \varepsilon_{1t}, \qquad y_t = bx_t + \varepsilon_{2t}$$

has the error-correction representation

$$\begin{bmatrix} 1 & 0 \\ -b & 1 \end{bmatrix}\begin{bmatrix} \Delta x_t \\ \Delta y_t \end{bmatrix} + \begin{bmatrix} 0 \\ 1 \end{bmatrix}[-b, 1]\begin{bmatrix} x_{t-1} \\ y_{t-1} \end{bmatrix} = \begin{bmatrix} \varepsilon_{1t} \\ \varepsilon_{2t} \end{bmatrix},$$

where b appears at once as the long-run and the short-run parameter. In such a case b is the long-run parameter, and there is no short-run parameter. More generally the two groups of parameters may be functionally related in part, and a reparametrization is advised in Sections 14.1 and 14.3 below.

12.3.7 Stationary elements and the long-run relationship

As was indicated in Section 12.1 above an element of $\{\boldsymbol{x}_t\}$ may be $I(0)$ even though $\{\boldsymbol{x}_t\}$ is $I(1)$ as a vector process. In such a case a unit vector is a co-integrating vector, but it cannot represent any relationship whatsoever, long run or not. We wish to discern long-run relationships from such co-integrating vectors when $I(0)$ variables are included in $\{\boldsymbol{x}_t\}$.[13] It is assumed below that integration orders of individual variables and the co-integration rank are known. For example, in $\{(x_{1t}, x_{2t}, x_{3t}, x_{4t})'\}$, $\{x_{1t}\}$ and $\{x_{2t}\}$ are $I(0)$ and $\{x_{3t}\}$ and $\{x_{4t}\}$ are $I(1)$. The co-integration ranks that are consistent with this set of integration orders are $r = 2$ or 3. The long-run relationship is in the form $c_3x_{3t} + c_4x_{4t} = 0$.

Let us begin with the case, $r = 2$. The co-integration space is generated by

$$\begin{pmatrix} q_{11}, & q_{12}, & q_{13} \\ q_{21}, & q_{22}, & q_{23} \end{pmatrix} \begin{pmatrix} 1, & 0, & 0, & 0 \\ 0, & 1, & 0, & 0 \\ 0, & 0, & c_3, & c_4 \end{pmatrix},$$

where the matrix of q_{ij} is arbitrary except that it has rank 2. When q_{13} and q_{23} are both restricted to zero, the co-integration space does not involve $\{x_{3t}\}$ or $\{x_{4t}\}$, and hence has nothing to do with a long-run relationship. The property that $q_{13} = q_{23} = 0$ is an identifiable property of the co-integration space, which is explained in section 15.2.1. The test (1) in section 15.2.2 with $\boldsymbol{H} = [\boldsymbol{I}_2, \boldsymbol{0}]'$ can be used to test for the property. If either one of q_{13} and q_{23} is non-zero, the co-integration space does contain the long-run relationship relating $\{x_{3t}\}$ and $\{x_{4t}\}$.

Then consider the case, $r = 3$. The co-integration space is generated by

$$\begin{pmatrix} q_{11}, & q_{12}, & q_{13} \\ q_{21}, & q_{22}, & q_{23} \\ q_{31}, & q_{32}, & q_{33} \end{pmatrix} \begin{pmatrix} 1, & 0, & 0, & 0 \\ 0, & 1, & 0, & 0 \\ 0, & 0, & c_3, & c_4 \end{pmatrix},$$

where the matrix of q_{ij} must have rank 3. The condition that $q_{13} = q_{23} = q_{33} = 0$ is excluded by this rank condition, and the long-run relationship relating $\{x_{3t}\}$ and $\{x_{4t}\}$ is necessarily included in the co-integration space.

The above statement on the case, $r = 2$, can be extended to general cases where the number of $I(0)$ variables is equal to the co-integration rank. There may be $I(1)$ variables more than 2, implying possibility of more than one long-run relationship. Exclusion of *all* long-run relationships from the co-integration space can be tested by (1) in Section 15.2.2. Needless to say that the above statement on the case, $r = 3$, can also be generalized.

The properties of long-run relationships thus admitted can be investigated by tests (3)–(8) in Section 15.2.2.

Highlights of Chapter 12

A k elements vector stochastic process is denoted by $\{\boldsymbol{x}_t\}$. $\{\Delta\boldsymbol{x}_t\}$ is assumed to be $I(0)$, i.e. $\{\boldsymbol{x}_t\}$ is at most $I(1)$. Initially it is assumed that $E(\Delta\boldsymbol{x}_t) = \boldsymbol{0}$.

1. In the VMA representation of $\Delta\boldsymbol{x}_t$,

$$\Delta\boldsymbol{x}_t = \boldsymbol{C}(L)\boldsymbol{\varepsilon}_t,$$

[13] Mototsugu Fukushige has suggested to me consideration of this problem.

the co-integration with rank r is defined by $\rho(\boldsymbol{C}(1)) = k - r$. Then there exists an $r \times k$ matrix $\boldsymbol{B}'$ such that $\rho(\boldsymbol{B}') = r$ and $\boldsymbol{B}'\boldsymbol{C}(1) = \mathbf{0}$. It can be shown that $\boldsymbol{B}'\boldsymbol{x}_t$ is $I(0)$. $\boldsymbol{B}'$ is a co-integration matrix, and the vector space spanned by the rows of $\boldsymbol{B}'$ is the co-integration space (Section 12.1.1). There also exists a $k \times r$ matrix $\boldsymbol{H}_1$ such that $\boldsymbol{C}(1)\boldsymbol{H}_1 = \mathbf{0}$ and $\boldsymbol{H}'_1\boldsymbol{H}_1 = I_r$. Let $\boldsymbol{H}_2$ be a $k \times (k - r)$ matrix such that $\boldsymbol{H}'_1\boldsymbol{H}_2 = \mathbf{0}$ and $\boldsymbol{H}'_2\boldsymbol{H}_2 = \boldsymbol{I}_{k-r}$. A representation of $(k - r)$ dimensional common stochastic trends is $\mathbf{f}_t \equiv \boldsymbol{H}'_2 \sum_1^t \boldsymbol{\varepsilon}_s$, and they enter into $\boldsymbol{x}_t$ as $\hat{\mathbf{x}}_t \equiv \boldsymbol{C}(1) \sum_1^t \boldsymbol{\varepsilon}_s = \boldsymbol{C}(1)\boldsymbol{H}_2\boldsymbol{H}'_2 \sum_1^t \boldsymbol{\varepsilon}_s$ (Section 12.1.2).

2. In the VAR representation for $\{\boldsymbol{x}_t\}$,

$$\boldsymbol{\Pi}(L)\mathbf{x}_t = \boldsymbol{\varepsilon}_t,$$

the co-integration with rank r is given by $\rho(\boldsymbol{\Pi}(1)) \equiv r$ (Section 12.2.1). The equation, $\det[\boldsymbol{\Pi}(z)] = 0$, has $(k - r)$ unit roots. In particular, $\boldsymbol{\Pi}(1) = \mathbf{0}$ if $\{\boldsymbol{x}_t\}$ is $I(1)$ and $r = 0$, having k unit roots, and $\boldsymbol{\Pi}(1)$ has its full rank, k, if $\{\boldsymbol{x}_t\}$ is $I(0)$ having no unit roots (Section 12.2.2). The definitions of co-integration in 1 and 2 are equivalent. (Section 12.2.1 proves only that the one in 1 implies the one in 2. The reverse implication is found in Engle and Granger (1987), Johansen (1991*a*), and Banerjee *et al.* (1993: 146–50).) There are duality relations between the VMA and VAR representations,

$$\boldsymbol{\Pi}(1)\boldsymbol{C}(1) = \mathbf{0}, \quad \boldsymbol{C}(1)\boldsymbol{\Pi}(1) = \mathbf{0}$$

(Section 12.2.3).

3. When $\rho(\boldsymbol{\Pi}(1)) = r$ there exist $\boldsymbol{A}$ and $\boldsymbol{B}$ such that both are $k \times r$, $\rho(\boldsymbol{A}) = \rho(\boldsymbol{B}) = r$ and $\boldsymbol{\Pi}(1) = -\boldsymbol{A}\boldsymbol{B}'$. Construct $\boldsymbol{\Gamma}(L)$ by

$$\boldsymbol{\Pi}(L) = \boldsymbol{\Pi}(1)L + (1 - L)\boldsymbol{\Gamma}(L).$$

Then we have the error-correction representation of co-integration with rank r,

$$\boldsymbol{\Gamma}(L)\Delta\boldsymbol{x}_t = \boldsymbol{A}\boldsymbol{B}'\boldsymbol{x}_{t-1} + \boldsymbol{\varepsilon}_t.$$

$\boldsymbol{B}'\boldsymbol{x}_{t-1}$ is $I(0)$, and $\boldsymbol{B}'$ annihilates the common stochastic trends (Section 12.2.2). The space of rows of $\mathbf{B}'$ is the co-integration space. $\mathbf{B}'\boldsymbol{x}_t = \mathbf{0}$ may be interpreted as the long-run equilibrium relation in the sense of balanced growth (Section 12.3.1). $\boldsymbol{B}'\boldsymbol{x}_{t-1}$ is then the error of equilibrium, and the equilibrium is stable in the sense in which the word is meant in mathematical economics (Section 12.3.4). $\boldsymbol{B}'\boldsymbol{x}_{t-1}$ causes $\boldsymbol{x}_t$ in Granger's sense, and this indicates a role that expectation may possibly play to help the covergence towards the equilibrium (Section 12.3.5). Co-integration is contradictory to some aspect of the efficient-market hypothesis (Section 12.3.5).

4. Construct $\boldsymbol{\Pi}^*(L)$ by

$$\boldsymbol{\Pi}(L) = \boldsymbol{\Pi}(1) + (1 - L)\boldsymbol{\Pi}^*(L).$$

Let $\boldsymbol{A}_\perp$ and $\boldsymbol{B}_\perp$ be each $k \times (k - r)$, $\rho(\boldsymbol{A}_\perp) = \rho(\boldsymbol{B}_\perp) = k - r$ and $\boldsymbol{A}'\boldsymbol{A}_\perp = \mathbf{0}$ and $\boldsymbol{B}'\boldsymbol{B}_\perp = \mathbf{0}$. Then the VMA and the error-correction representations of co-integration are related through

$$\boldsymbol{C}(1) = \boldsymbol{B}_\perp(\boldsymbol{A}'_\perp\boldsymbol{\Pi}^*(1)\boldsymbol{B}_\perp)^{-1}\boldsymbol{A}'_\perp = \boldsymbol{B}_\perp(\boldsymbol{A}'_\perp\boldsymbol{\Gamma}(1)\boldsymbol{B}_\perp)^{-1}\boldsymbol{A}'_\perp$$

(Section 12.2.3). Common stochastic trends $\boldsymbol{f}_t$ enter into $\boldsymbol{x}_t$ as $\boldsymbol{C}(1)\sum_1^t \boldsymbol{\varepsilon}_s$ in the VMA representation, and as

$$\boldsymbol{B}_\perp(\boldsymbol{A}'_\perp \boldsymbol{\Pi}^*(1)\boldsymbol{B}_\perp)^{-1}\boldsymbol{A}'_\perp \sum\nolimits_1^t \boldsymbol{\varepsilon}_s$$

in the error-correction representation (Section 12.2.4). Common trends are not caused by the equilibrium error $\boldsymbol{B}'\boldsymbol{x}_{t-1}$ in the Granger sense (Section 12.2.4).

5. The co-integration space is identified (Section 12.1.1). $\boldsymbol{AB}'$ is identified, but $\boldsymbol{A}$ and $\boldsymbol{B}$ are not separately (Section 12.2.3).

6. A co-integration space that annihilates only the stochastic common trends requires the VMA representation of $\Delta\boldsymbol{x}_t$ to be written as

$$\Delta\boldsymbol{x}_t - \boldsymbol{\mu} = \boldsymbol{C}(L)\boldsymbol{\varepsilon}_t$$

(Section 12.1.3). The VAR and error-correction representations are substantially complicated, but will be given later. On the other hand a co-integration space that annihilates both linear deterministic trends and stochastic common trends requires the VMA representation of $\Delta\boldsymbol{x}_t$,

$$\Delta\mathbf{x}_t = \mathbf{C}(L)(\boldsymbol{\mu} + \boldsymbol{\varepsilon}_t),$$

and the VAR representation of $\boldsymbol{x}_t$,

$$\boldsymbol{\Pi}(L)\boldsymbol{x}_t = \boldsymbol{\mu} + \boldsymbol{\varepsilon}_t$$

(Section 12.1.3 and 12.2.5). With $\boldsymbol{\Pi}(1) = -\boldsymbol{AB}'$ the error-correction representation is

$$\boldsymbol{\Gamma}(L)\Delta\boldsymbol{x}_t = \boldsymbol{AB}'\boldsymbol{x}_{t-1} + \boldsymbol{\mu} + \boldsymbol{\varepsilon}_t.$$

Linear deterministic trends are revealed in $\boldsymbol{x}_t$ only when $\boldsymbol{C}(1)\boldsymbol{\mu} \neq \boldsymbol{0}$ in the VMA representation, or equivalently $\boldsymbol{A}'_\perp\boldsymbol{\mu} \neq \boldsymbol{0}$ in the error-correction representation (Sections 12.1.3 and 12.2.5). $\boldsymbol{B}'\boldsymbol{x}_t$ is $I(0)$ having constant means. For a study of a long-run equilibrium relation it is necessary to confirm that $E(\boldsymbol{B}'\boldsymbol{x}_t) = E(\boldsymbol{B}'\mathbf{x}_0) = \boldsymbol{0}$ (Sections 12.2.5 and 12.3.4).

7. For a co-integration matrix to annihilate the stochastic common trends only we have to consider

$$\boldsymbol{\Gamma}(L)\Delta\boldsymbol{x}_t = \boldsymbol{AB}'\boldsymbol{x}_{t-1} + \boldsymbol{\mu}_0 + \boldsymbol{\mu}_1 t + \boldsymbol{\varepsilon}_t.$$

This opens a possibility of quadratic deterministic trends, and we must impose $\boldsymbol{A}'_\perp\boldsymbol{\mu}_1 = \boldsymbol{0}$ if we wish to trim the order of polynomial to unity (Section 12.2.5).

13
Asymptotic Inference Theories on Co-integrated Regressions*

Throughout the present chapter it will be assumed that integration orders of relevant individual variables have already been determined by the univariate method given in Part I. Even though a system (multivariate) method is also available for the determination, I recommend the univariate method on the ground that it is more flexible in modelling the deterministic trend and short-run dynamics, which are conceptually incidental to the integration order but nevertheless influence seriously the results on the integration order. Chapter 9 has revealed that most of macroeconomic variables are $I(1)$ and some may even be $I(2)$ over the period of twenty-five to forty years in the post-war quarterly US data. (The past studies in which the contrary conclusion was reached analysed the historical data.) The chapter also uncovered some difficulties that we face in determining integration orders. Two important ones are (i) possible changes in the orders during the sample period and (ii) effects of some arbitrariness that is inherent in the process of model selection for deterministic trends even when judicious judgement is exercised.

Co-integrating relations can be expressed as regression-like equations having $I(1)$ variables in the regressors and regressands. I have written regression-like because the errors may be correlated with the regressors, in which case the models are not really regression models. The traditional econometric theory must be re-examined for the co-integrating relations.

When integration orders of the variables are determined, they immediately have important implications on the regression model. Suppose that x_t, y_t, and u_t are respectively independent variable, dependent variable, and disturbance in

$$y_t = bx_t + u_t.$$

Assume for simplicity that no deterministic trends are involved. If x_t and y_t are $I(1)$ and $I(0)$ respectively, one can immediately see by matching the integration orders of both sides that u_t is $I(1)$ and x_t and u_t are co-integrated, which is perhaps not a useful model. Likewise in

$$y_t = b_1x_{1t} + b_2x_{2t} + u_t,$$

* I have benefited from comments by Kimio Morimune and Hiro Toda on earlier drafts of the present chapter. Especially Hiro Toda has saved me from an error in an earlier version of Section 13.3. Remaining errors are mine.

if x_{1t} and x_{2t} are both $I(1)$ and y_t is $I(0)$, x_{1t} and x_{2t} must be co-integrated in so far as u_t is $I(0)$. When the dependent variable and (a linear combination of) independent variables have identical integration orders, the equation is called *balanced* in Banerjee *et al.* (1993: 164). One could have an unbalanced regression, but one should be aware of the implications that it entails. It seems that most econometric models specify the disturbance to be stationary with zero mean.

The plan of Chapter 13 is as follows. Initially in Section 13.1.1 the spurious and the co-integrated regressions are distinguished. Then various cases of co-integrated regressions are explained in Sections 13.1.2–13.3. Most of the basic points can be demonstrated in Section 13.1, which deals with the case where Δx_t is i.i.d. without a drift. Section 13.2 treats the case where Δx_t is still i.i.d. but has a deterministic drift, and Section 13.3 explains the case where Δx_t is serially correlated. The remarkable result of Phillips (1991*a*) will be presented with emphasis placed slightly differently from his own. The conventional methods of estimation and testing based upon t- and F-statistics are robust to all different modes of deterministic trends. The robustness to the integration orders is confined to the case of strict exogeneity, but with the co-integration between $I(1)$ variables the applicability of the inference procedure is extended beyond that in $I(0)$ variables with a properly selected set of independent variables in the OLS. In particular *we are freed from worrying about the correlation between the regressors and disturbance in so far as the disturbance is stationary.* A summary of Section 13.1–3 is given for a general case at the end of the present chapter 13.

While co-integration is assumed in Sections 13.1.2–13.3, Sections 13.5–6 discuss testing for the co-integration. Actually Chapter 15 is devoted to this testing, and the method in Johansen (1991*a*) will be presented there. Sections 13.5–6 of this chapter consider two topics that do not fit well into Chapter 15—an a priori specified co-integrating vector and the reason why available methods other than Johansen (1991*a*) are not generally recommended for co-integration tests.

The above summary has skipped Section 13.4. What is presented there is that the co-integrated regression models assume not only the co-integration rank but also some basic aspect of the co-integration space that is called the location of non-singular submatrices in $\boldsymbol{B}'$. In fact, at least the co-integration rank can be estimated from the available data by the method developed in Johansen (1988, 1991*a*) as will be explained in Chapter 15. However, the method has limited capability when applied to economic time-series data of the length actually available (see Sections 15.1.4–5 below). The rank and the basic aspect of the space as specified by economic theories may well be accepted (unless they are definitively rejected by the Johansen method), thus concentrating verification to the remaining aspects of the co-integration space. The issue is just one example of the basic one discussed in Chapter 11, and the discussion will be continued in Chapter 15.

Readers will also find in Section 13.4.1 an application to the US post-war quarterly data of income and consumption. These variables have been found $I(1)$ in Part I, and most of the points that I like to emphasize can be brought up in connection with this application.

The present chapter also aids the understanding of inference theories on the co-integration space in Chapter 15 after the co-integration rank is determined. Section 13.1 also contains an important point on the ordinary regression model, say, for cross-section data, that seems little known among econometricians and even denied in many econometric textbooks.

An important topic that is left unexplored is to investigate how robust all inference methods are when the dominating characteristic root deviates from unity to 0.9, because the roots between 0.9 and 1.0 cannot be distinguished effectively from unity with $T = 100$ as demonstrated in Chapter 8.

13.1 Pure Random Walk

A scalar Wiener process has been used in Part I. It can be extended to the vector k-elements process. The standard vector Wiener process $\boldsymbol{w}(r)$ is distributed in $N(\mathbf{0}, rI_k)$, and $\boldsymbol{w}(s_2) - \boldsymbol{w}(s_1)$ and $\boldsymbol{w}(r) - \boldsymbol{w}(s_3)$ are independent if $0 \le s_1 \le s_2 \le s_3 \le r$. Suppose that $\boldsymbol{\Sigma}$ is a $k \times k$ positive definite matrix. Let $\boldsymbol{\Sigma}^{1/2}$ be either a symmetric, positive definite matrix such that $\boldsymbol{\Sigma}^{1/2}\boldsymbol{\Sigma}^{1/2} = \boldsymbol{\Sigma}$, or a lower triangular matrix such that $\boldsymbol{\Sigma}^{1/2}\boldsymbol{\Sigma}^{1/2'} = \boldsymbol{\Sigma}$. $\boldsymbol{\Sigma}^{1/2}\boldsymbol{w}(r)$ is called the vector Wiener process with the covariance matrix $\boldsymbol{\Sigma}$. Indeed, it is distributed in $N(\mathbf{0}, r\boldsymbol{\Sigma})$. I shall use the notation, $\boldsymbol{w}(r; \boldsymbol{\Sigma})$, with the lower-case letter $\boldsymbol{w}$ because it is a stochastic vector rather than a matrix. If $\boldsymbol{\Sigma}$ is diagonal, elements of $\boldsymbol{w}(r, \boldsymbol{\Sigma})$ are mutually independent because $\boldsymbol{w}(\ )$ is Gaussian. Partition a general positive definite $\boldsymbol{\Sigma}$ as

$$\boldsymbol{\Sigma} = \begin{bmatrix} \boldsymbol{\Sigma}_{11} & \boldsymbol{\Sigma}_{12} \\ \boldsymbol{\Sigma}_{21} & \boldsymbol{\Sigma}_{22} \end{bmatrix},$$

where $\boldsymbol{\Sigma}_{11}$ is $k_1 \times k_1$ and $k_2 = k - k_1$. Then the following two Wiener processes,

$$(\boldsymbol{I}_{k1}, 0)\boldsymbol{w}\ (r, \boldsymbol{\Sigma}) \equiv \boldsymbol{w}_1\ (r, \boldsymbol{\Sigma}), \tag{13.1a}$$

$$\left(-\boldsymbol{\Sigma}_{21}\boldsymbol{\Sigma}_{11}^{-1}, \boldsymbol{I}_{k2}\right)\boldsymbol{w}\ (r, \boldsymbol{\Sigma}) \equiv \boldsymbol{w}_{2.1}\left(r, \boldsymbol{\Sigma}_{22} - \boldsymbol{\Sigma}_{21}\boldsymbol{\Sigma}_{11}^{-1}\boldsymbol{\Sigma}_{12}\right) \tag{13.1b}$$

are mutually independent. In (13.1b) the part of the last k_2 elements of $\boldsymbol{w}\ (r, \boldsymbol{\Sigma})$ that is related to the first k_1 elements are subtracted from the last k_2 elements. The Wiener process (13.1b) has the covariance matrix, $\boldsymbol{\Sigma}_{22} - \boldsymbol{\Sigma}_{21}\boldsymbol{\Sigma}_{11}^{-1}\boldsymbol{\Sigma}_{12}$ (see Phillips 1989, lemma 3.1).

Suppose that a k-elements vector process $\{\boldsymbol{\varepsilon}_t\}$ is i.i.d. with $\boldsymbol{E}(\boldsymbol{\varepsilon}_t) = \mathbf{0}$ and $\boldsymbol{E}(\boldsymbol{\varepsilon}_t\boldsymbol{\varepsilon}_t') = \boldsymbol{\Sigma}$. Let $\boldsymbol{v}_t \equiv \sum_{s=1}^{t} \boldsymbol{\varepsilon}_s$. Then in the same way as in (4.2) of Part I we have as $T \to \infty$

$$T^{-3/2}\sum_{t=1}^{T} \boldsymbol{v}_t \xrightarrow{D} \int_0^1 \boldsymbol{w}\ (r, \boldsymbol{\Sigma})\, dr. \tag{13.2}$$

The k elements of $T^{-3/2}\boldsymbol{\Sigma v}_t$ are jointly distributed asymptotically the same as the k elements of $\int_0^1 \boldsymbol{w}(r, \boldsymbol{\Sigma})\,dr$. Also in the same way as in (4.3) of Part I we have as $T \to \infty$

$$T^{-2}\sum_{t=1}^{T} \boldsymbol{v}_t\boldsymbol{v}'_t \xrightarrow{D} \int_0^1 \boldsymbol{w}(r, \boldsymbol{\Sigma})\,\boldsymbol{w}(r, \boldsymbol{\Sigma})'\,dr. \tag{13.3}$$

The $k(k+1)/2$ distinct elements of $T^{-2}\sum \boldsymbol{v}_t\boldsymbol{v}'_t$ are jointly distributed asymptotically the same as the corresponding elements of $\int_0^1 \boldsymbol{w}(r, \boldsymbol{\Sigma})\,\boldsymbol{w}(r, \boldsymbol{\Sigma})'\,dr$. Finally, as in (4.7) of Part I

$$T^{-1}\sum_{t=1}^{T} \boldsymbol{v}_{t-1}\boldsymbol{\varepsilon}'_t \xrightarrow{D} \int_0^1 \boldsymbol{w}(r, \boldsymbol{\Sigma})\,d\boldsymbol{w}(r, \boldsymbol{\Sigma})' \tag{13.4}$$

as $T \to \infty$. The $\boldsymbol{\Sigma}$ within $\boldsymbol{w}(\ ,\ )$ will often be omitted in the following. See Phillips and Durlauf (1986) and Park and Phillips (1988) for the above asymptotic theory; also see Phillips and Ouliaris (1990) for other related formulae.

The following lemma is due to Park and Phillips (1988) and Park (1992).

LEMMA 13.1 (i) Partition $\boldsymbol{w}(r, \boldsymbol{\Sigma})$ into $\boldsymbol{w}_1$ and $\boldsymbol{w}_2$, where w_2 is a scalar and $\boldsymbol{w}_1$ has $(k-1)$ elements. Suppose $\boldsymbol{\Sigma}$ is $\text{diag}[\boldsymbol{\Sigma}_{11}, \sigma_{22}]$ where $\boldsymbol{\Sigma}_{11}$ is $(k-1)\times(k-1)$ positive definite. Then conditionally upon $\boldsymbol{G} \equiv \int \boldsymbol{w}_1(r)\boldsymbol{w}_1(r)'dr$, $\int \boldsymbol{w}_1(r)dw_2(r)$ is distributed in $\boldsymbol{N}(0, \sigma_{22}\boldsymbol{G})$. (ii) Partition $\boldsymbol{w}(r, \boldsymbol{\Sigma})$ into $\left(\boldsymbol{w}_1(r, \boldsymbol{\Sigma})', \boldsymbol{w}_2(r, \boldsymbol{\Sigma})'\right)'$, where $\boldsymbol{w}_1$ and $\boldsymbol{w}_2$ have k_1 and $k_2(= k - k_1)$ elements. Suppose that $\boldsymbol{\Sigma}$ is $\text{diag}[\boldsymbol{\Sigma}_{11}, \boldsymbol{\Sigma}_{22}]$ where $\boldsymbol{\Sigma}_{11}$ and $\boldsymbol{\Sigma}_{22}$ are respectively $k_1 \times k_1$ and $k_2 \times k_2$ positive definite. Then conditionally upon $\boldsymbol{G} \equiv \int \boldsymbol{w}_1(r)\boldsymbol{w}_1(r)'dr$, $\text{vec}\int \boldsymbol{w}_1(r)d\boldsymbol{w}_2(r)'$ is distributed in $\boldsymbol{N}(0, \boldsymbol{\Sigma}_{22} \otimes \boldsymbol{G})$, where $\text{vec}\,\boldsymbol{A}$ is the column vector constructed by stacking columns of $\boldsymbol{A}$.

I shall present a reasoning that may be useful to show the plausibility of this lemma. Suppose that two scalar processes $\{\varepsilon_{1t}\}$ and $\{\varepsilon_{2t}\}$ are mutually independent Gaussian, and each i.i.d with zero mean and variances σ_{11} and σ_{22} respectively. Let $v_{1t} \equiv \sum_{s=1}^{t} \varepsilon_{1s}$. For fixed values of $\varepsilon_{11}, \ldots, \varepsilon_{1T}$, $T^{-1}\sum v_{1t-1}\varepsilon_{2t}$ is Gaussian with zero mean and variance, $\sigma_{22}T^{-2}\sum v_{1t-1}^2$. This distribution depends not on the values of $\varepsilon_{11}, \ldots, \varepsilon_{1T-1}$ individually but on the value of $\sum v_{1t-1}^2$ only. Therefore the distribution of $T^{-1}\sum v_{1t-1}\varepsilon_{2t}$ conditional upon $T^{-2}\sum v_{1t-1}^2$ is $N\left(0, \sigma_{22}T^{-2}\sum v_{1t-1}^2\right)$. And $T^{-2}\sum v_{1t-1}^2 \xrightarrow{D} \int w_1(r)^2dr$ and $T^{-1}\sum v_{1t-1}\varepsilon_{2t} \xrightarrow{D} \int w_1(r)dw_2(r)$.

The exposition that follows uses the minimum number of variables necessary to demonstrate the basic point involved in each topic. The extension to higher dimensions is straightforward in every case.

13.1.1 Spurious regression and co-integrated regression

Suppose that a bivariate process $\{(\varepsilon_{1t}, \varepsilon_{2t})\}$ is i.i.d. with zero mean vector and the covariance matrix $\boldsymbol{\Sigma}$, which is positive definite. Let $v_{it} \equiv \sum_{s=1}^{t} \varepsilon_{is}$, $i = 1, 2$, and $x_t \equiv v_{1t}$. Consider two alternative models to generate y_t. One is

$$y_t = bx_t + \varepsilon_{2t}, \qquad b \neq 0, \tag{13.5}$$

and the other is

$$y_t = bx_t + v_{2t}, \tag{13.6}$$

In (13.5) x_t and y_t are co-integrated, but they are not in (13.6).

Having T observations of (x_t, y_t), compute the OLS, $\hat{b} = \left(\sum x_t y_t\right)\left(\sum x_t^2\right)^{-1}$. In (13.5)

$$\hat{b} - b = \left(\sum x_t \varepsilon_{2t}\right)\left(\sum x_t^2\right)^{-1}, \tag{13.7}$$

and in (13.6)

$$\hat{b} - b = \left(\sum x_t v_{2t}\right)\left(\sum x_t^2\right)^{-1}. \tag{13.8}$$

Let $\boldsymbol{w}(r) = (w_1(r), w_2(r))'$ be the two elements Wiener process with covariance matrix $\boldsymbol{\Sigma}$. As for (13.7)

$$T(\hat{b} - b) = \left(T^{-1}\sum \varepsilon_{1t}\varepsilon_{2t} + T^{-1}\sum v_{1t-1}\varepsilon_{2t}\right)\left(T^{-2}\sum v_{1t}^2\right)^{-1} \tag{13.7$'$}$$

$$\xrightarrow{D} \left(\sigma_{12} + \int w_1(r)dw_2(r)\right)\left(\int w_1(r)^2 dr\right)^{-1}.$$

As for (13.8)

$$\hat{b} - b = \left(T^{-2}\sum v_{1t}v_{2t}\right)\left(T^{-2}\sum v_{1t}^2\right)^{-1} \tag{13.8$'$}$$

$$\xrightarrow{D} \left(\int w_1(r)w_2(r)dr\right)\left(\int w_1(r)^2 dr\right)^{-1}.$$

Note that (13.7′) deals with $T(\hat{b}-b)$ while (13.8′) refers to $(\hat{b}-b)$. In (13.8′) the error of the OLS estimator does not converge in probability to zero, nor to any constant, but remains to be a random variable no matter how large T may be.[1] In (13.7′) $T(\hat{b}-b)$ converges to a random variable, and $(\hat{b}-b)$ is $O_p(T^{-1})$, i.e. $\hat{b}$ is nearly T-consistent. (It should not be called T-consistent because the right-hand side of (13.7′) generally has a non-zero mean, but I shall use the term, T-consistency, for brevity.)

The regression between non-co-integrated $I(1)$ variables such as (13.6) is called the *spurious regression*. The peculiar behaviour of the OLS $\hat{b}$ when the true b is zero was noted in Granger and Newbold (1974) by a simulation study, and explained mathematically as above in Phillips (1986). In fact the t-statistic

[1] See Phillips (1989) for a further analysis of the right-hand side of (13.8′).

to test for $b = 0$ diverges as $T \to \infty$ because if T is large the statistic is approximately

$$\left(T^{-1}\sum v_{2t}^2\right)^{-1/2} \cdot \hat{b} \cdot \left(\sum v_{1t}^2\right)^{1/2}$$
$$= T^{1/2}\left(T^{-2}\sum v_{2t}^2\right)^{-1/2} \cdot \hat{b} \cdot \left(T^{-2}\sum v_{1t}^2\right)^{1/2},$$

where $\left(T^{-2}\sum v_{2t}^2\right)^{-1/2}$, $\hat{b}$, and $\left(T^{-2}\sum v_{1t}^2\right)^{1/2}$ are each $O_p(1)$. When T is large, *the hypothesis* $b = 0$ *is surely rejected while* b *is zero in the data-generating process*. This motivates the word, 'spurious'. Banerjee *et al.* (1993: 70–81) re-examine the experiments in Granger and Newbold (1974), and describe how the spurious regressions are manifested in finite samples.

A situation in which we have a spurious regression in practice is that a regression is run between two $I(1)$ variables, while in fact three $I(1)$ variables including the two are co-integrated. Thus a spurious regression is closely related to the misspecification in regard to a list of variables to be included in a regression equation (see Section 15.5 below).

The regression equation on co-integrated variables such as (13.5) will be called the *co-integrated regression* below. It has a remarkable feature. The OLS is not just consistent but T-consistent. This holds true in spite of the fact that the regressor x_t and the error ε_{2t} are correlated. This result is conspicuously different from the traditional econometric theory dealing with $I(0)$ variables. There we have been troubled by the correlations between endogenous variables and disturbance in the simultaneous equations and/or between measurement errors in the regressors and the equation errors, which lead to inconsistency of the OLS. The T-consistency of OLS in the co-integrated regression was first noted in Stock (1987) and Phillips and Durlauf (1986).

How to discriminate the spurious and co-integrated regressions will be explained in Section 13.4.3 below.

Notwithstanding the T-consistency of OLS in the co-integrated regression, (13.7′) does not have zero expectation, and in fact the bias in (13.7′) may be substantial in finite samples such as $T = 100$, as has been shown in Stock (1987) and Banerjee *et al.* (1993: 215–23). Moreover, unless the relation between x_t and ε_{2t} is specialized, the limiting distribution of the t-statistic depends upon nuisance parameters, i.e. the parameters other than b. These defects of the simple OLS in (13.7) have motivated enormous progress in the theory of co-integrated regression, and this progress will be explained in the remainder of the present chapter. If the OLS is modified in a simple manner, we can have very simple inference procedures for estimation and testing that use only the standard normal distribution and χ^2 distributions. And problems due to correlations between regressors and disturbance in simultaneous equations or observation errors are all dissolved.

13.1.2 Co-integrated regression with an uncorrelated error

In the regression model, say $y_t = bx_t + u_t$, u_t is said to be a uncorrelated error if $E(x_t u_t) = 0$, and a correlated error if $E(x_t u_t) \neq 0$. In the standard regression model dealing with $I(0)$ variables the OLS of b is consistent if the error is uncorrelated, and inconsistent if the error is correlated.

Suppose that $\{(\varepsilon_{1t}, \varepsilon_{2t})'\}$ is i.i.d. with zero mean vector and covariance matrix $\mathbf{\Sigma}$, which is assumed to be diag$[\sigma_{11}, \sigma_{22}]$; in particular $\sigma_{12} = 0$. As before $x_t \equiv v_{1t} \equiv \sum_{s=1}^{t} \varepsilon_{1t}$, and

$$y_t = bx_t + \varepsilon_{2t}, \tag{13.9}$$

which is a co-integrated regression with the uncorrelated error. The bivariate process (x_t, y_t) has a co-integrating vector $(-b, 1)$, and we are interested in the inference about this vector.

Suppose that $\{(x_t, y_t)'\}$ is observable, and let $\hat{b}$ be the OLS of b. Let $(w_1(r), w_2(r))'$ have the covariance matrix, diag$[\sigma_{11}, \sigma_{22}]$. Setting $\sigma_{12} = 0$ in (13.7′), we have

$$T(\hat{b} - b) \xrightarrow{D} \int w_1(r)dw_2(r) \left(\int w_1(r)^2 dr \right)^{-1} \equiv \xi, \tag{13.10}$$

but $w_1(r)$ and $w_2(r)$ being independent introduces further important simplification. Let us write

$$g \equiv \left(\int w_1(r)^2 dr \right)^{-1}. \tag{13.11}$$

By virtue of Lemma 13.1. ξ in (13.10) is distributed in $N(0, \sigma_{22} g)$ conditionally upon g. The conditional p.d.f. is

$$(2\pi\sigma_{22} g)^{-1/2} \exp\left(-(2\sigma_{22} g)^{-1} \xi^2\right).$$

Therefore writing $f(g)$ for the marginal p.d.f. of g, the marginal p.d.f. of ξ is

$$\int_0^\infty (2\pi\sigma_{22} g)^{-1/2} \exp(-(2\sigma_{22} g)^{-1} \xi^2) f(g) dg. \tag{13.12}$$

This kind of distribution will be called the *mixed Gaussian* in the present book. It is a mixture of zero mean normal distributions with different variances. In particular $E(\xi) = 0$.

Consider the t-statistic to test for $b = b^0$,

$$\hat{t} = T(\hat{b} - b^0) \left(T^{-2} \mathbf{\Sigma} x_t^2 \right)^{1/2} s^{-1}, \quad s = \left(T^{-1} \mathbf{\Sigma} (y_t - \hat{b} x_t)^2 \right)^{1/2}. \tag{13.13}$$

If b^0 is the true value of b, plim $s = \sigma_{22}^{1/2}$ because plim $\hat{b} = b^0$. Thus

$$\hat{t} \xrightarrow{D} \sigma_{22}^{-1/2} \int w_1(r)dw_2(r) \left(\int w_1(r)^2 dr \right)^{-1/2} \equiv \eta. \tag{13.14}$$

Conditionally upon g in (13.11) η is found to be distributed in $N(0, 1)$ so that η is distributed, so to speak, in the mixed $N(0, 1)$ with the conditioning variable g. However the distribution of $N(0, 1)$ does not depend on g. In other words the conditional distribution of η is invariant throughout all values of the conditioning variable g. Therefore η and g are independent, and the marginal p.d.f. of η is also $N(0, 1)$. The t-statistic based on the mixed Gaussian estimator is asymptotically $N(0, 1)$ by virtue of the scale normalization involved in the construction of the t-statistic.

So far we have considered a hypothesis testing, but it goes without saying that the t-statistic can also be used to construct a confidence interval on b. See also Remark 6 in Section 13.4.2.

The above result is due to Krämer (1986) and Park and Phillips (1988). The result is easily extended to a regression with k regressors. Let $\{(\varepsilon_{1t}, \ldots, \varepsilon_{kt}, \varepsilon_{(k+1)t}\}$ be i.i.d. with zero mean vector and covariance matrix $\mathbf{\Sigma}$, and suppose that $\mathbf{\Sigma}$ is block-diagonal, diag $\left[\mathbf{\Sigma}_{11}, \sigma_{k+1}^2\right]$, where $\mathbf{\Sigma}_{11}$ is $k \times k$ and non-singular. The regressors, $x_t' \equiv (x_{1t}, \ldots, x_{kt})$, are constructed by $x_{it} \equiv \sum_{s=1}^{t} \varepsilon_{is}$, $i = 1, \ldots, k$. *They are not co-integrated.* This is because $\mathbf{\Sigma}_{11}$ is non-singular and what corresponds to $\boldsymbol{C}(1)$ in the MA representation (12.1) is $\boldsymbol{I}_k$ in the present case. The y_t is constructed by

$$y_t = \boldsymbol{b}'\boldsymbol{x}_t + \varepsilon_{(k+1)t}, \qquad \boldsymbol{b}'\boldsymbol{b} \neq 0. \tag{13.15}$$

Let $\hat{\boldsymbol{b}}$ be the OLS in (13.15). Let $\boldsymbol{w}^*(r)$ be the $(k+1)$ elements Wiener process with the covariance matrix $\mathbf{\Sigma} = \text{diag}\left[\mathbf{\Sigma}_{11}, \sigma_{k+1}^2\right]$, and partition $w^*(r)$ into $\boldsymbol{w}(r)$ and $w_{k+1}(r)$, where $\boldsymbol{w}(r)$ has k elements. Then

$$T(\hat{\boldsymbol{b}} - \boldsymbol{b}) \to \left(\int \boldsymbol{w}(r)\boldsymbol{w}(r)'dr\right)^{-1} \int \boldsymbol{w}(r)d\boldsymbol{w}_{k+1}(r) \equiv \boldsymbol{\zeta}.$$

Conditionally upon $\boldsymbol{G} \equiv \left(\int \boldsymbol{w}(r)\boldsymbol{w}(r)'dr\right)^{-1}$, $\boldsymbol{\zeta}$ is distributed in $\boldsymbol{N}(0, \sigma_{k+1}^2\boldsymbol{G})$. Consider a hypothesis, $\boldsymbol{H}\boldsymbol{b}^0 = \boldsymbol{h}$, where a known matrix $\boldsymbol{H}$ is $k_1 \times k$, $\rho(\boldsymbol{H}) = k_1$, and $\boldsymbol{h}$ is a known vector. The F-statistic multiplied by k_1 is

$$(\hat{\boldsymbol{b}} - \boldsymbol{b}^0)'\boldsymbol{H}'(\boldsymbol{H}(\boldsymbol{X}'\boldsymbol{X})^{-1}\boldsymbol{H}')^{-1}\boldsymbol{H}(\hat{\boldsymbol{b}} - \boldsymbol{b}^0)/s^2, \tag{13.16}$$

where $\boldsymbol{X}'\boldsymbol{X} = \sum \boldsymbol{x}_t\boldsymbol{x}'_t$, and s^2 is the square of the standard error of regression. Suppose that the hypothesis holds true. Then $T\boldsymbol{H}(\hat{\boldsymbol{b}} - \boldsymbol{b}^0)$ coverages to a mixed Gaussian distribution, which is $\boldsymbol{N}(0, \sigma_{k+1}^2\boldsymbol{HGH}')$ conditionally upon $\boldsymbol{G}$. Moreover, $T^2\boldsymbol{H}(\boldsymbol{X}'\boldsymbol{X})^{-1}\boldsymbol{H}'$ converges to $\boldsymbol{HGH}'$, and s^2 to σ_{k+1}^2. Therefore the limiting distribution of (13.16) is the mixed $\chi^2(k_1)$ with the conditioning variable $\boldsymbol{G}$. Since the distribution of $\chi^2(k_1)$ does not depend on $\boldsymbol{G}$, the marginal asymptotic distribution of (13.16) is also $\chi^2(k_1)$. This result can also be used to set a confidence interval on $\boldsymbol{Hb}$. When $k_1 = 1$ and $\boldsymbol{H}$ is a unit vector, one can use the standard normal distribution.

Since $\{(\varepsilon_{1t}, \ldots, \varepsilon_{kt}, \varepsilon_{(k+1)t})\}$ is assumed to be i.i.d. with $\mathbf{\Sigma} = \text{diag}\left[\mathbf{\Sigma}_{11}, \sigma_{k+1}^2\right]$, $\boldsymbol{x}_t$ in (13.15) is strictly exogenous. Later in Section (13.3) it will be shown that the strict exogeneity of $\boldsymbol{x}_t$ guarantees the mixed χ^2 property of an estimator of $\boldsymbol{b}$ even when the serial correlations are allowed.

Needless to say that if $\{\boldsymbol{x}_t\}$ in (13.9) or (13.15) is $I(0)$ and strictly exogenous the t- and F-statistics are asymptotically distributed in $N(0, 1)$ and χ^2 respectively. Therefore it can be said that *the conventional inference procedures based on the OLS are robust to integration orders in the case of strict exogeneity.*

One can further extend (13.15) to the case where y_t on its left-hand side is a vector rather than a scalar. However, $\{\boldsymbol{x}_t\}$ *should not be co-integrated.*

A remaining problem is how to test for the absence of co-integration in $\{(x_{1t}, \ldots, x_{kt})\}$ and presence of co-integration in $\{(x_{1t}, \ldots, x_{kt}, y_t)\}$. It will be given in Section 13.4.3 below.

The main result in the present section is analogous to an important point on the simple regression model, say, for cross-section data, which however seems little known among econometricians. (Indeed many textbooks state that the result does not hold.) In $\boldsymbol{y} = \boldsymbol{X}\boldsymbol{\beta}+\boldsymbol{u}$, $\boldsymbol{X}$ is $n \times k$ *random* matrix, $\boldsymbol{y}$ and $\boldsymbol{u}$ are each $n \times 1$ random vector, $\boldsymbol{\beta}$ is $k \times 1$ unknown parameter, and, conditionally upon $\boldsymbol{X}$, $\boldsymbol{u}$ is distributed in $N(0, \sigma^2 \boldsymbol{I}_n)$. Construct the F-statistic to test for $\boldsymbol{H}\boldsymbol{\beta} = \boldsymbol{h}$, where $\boldsymbol{H}$ is $k_1 \times k$. Then the *marginal* distribution of the F-statistic is distributed in $F(k_1, n-k)$. This is because, conditionally upon $\boldsymbol{X}$, the F-statistic is distributed in $F(k_1, n-k)$, but this distribution does not depend upon $\boldsymbol{X}$. *Both the confidence interval and significance test based upon the F-statistic are valid irrespective of the distribution of* $\boldsymbol{X}$. The conditional normality assumption can be removed in the asymptotic theory in which n is taken to infinity.

13.1.3 Co-integrated regression with a correlated error

Let us return to the case of a single regressor and a single regressand, and continue with $\{(\varepsilon_{1t}, \varepsilon_{2t})'\}$ being i.i.d. with zero mean vector and covariance matrix $\boldsymbol{\Sigma}$. But here I consider the case where $\boldsymbol{\Sigma}$ is not necessarily diagonal. The model is still (13.5) i.e. (13.9), which is reproduced here,

$$y_t = bx_t + \varepsilon_{2t}, \tag{13.9}$$

where $x_t \equiv v_{1t} \equiv \sum_{s=1}^{t} \varepsilon_{1s}$. The limiting distribution of the OLS is given in (13.7′).

The right-hand side of (13.7′) is not mixed Gaussian. The OLS is of little use, but Phillips (1991*a*) and Phillips and Loretan (1991) present an estimator which is asymptotically mixed Gaussian.[2]

Let σ_{11}, σ_{12}, and σ_{22} be the elements of $\boldsymbol{\Sigma}$. Even though ε_{2t} is correlated with $\Delta x_t = \varepsilon_{1t}$ in (13.9), we can eliminate that part of ε_{2t} which is linearly related to Δx_t by introducing Δx_t in the regressor set. In fact (13.9) can be rewritten as

$$y_t = bx_t + \sigma_{21}\sigma_{11}^{-1}\Delta x_t + \varepsilon_{2.1t} \tag{13.9′}$$

[2] I have benefited from a suggestion by Hiro Toda on the expository device in this subsection.

$$\varepsilon_{2.1t} = \varepsilon_{2t} - \sigma_{21}\sigma_{11}^{-1}\varepsilon_{1t}.$$

Writing $c \equiv \sigma_{21}\sigma_{11}^{-1}$, let $(\hat{b}, \hat{c})'$ be the OLS estimate of (b, c) along (13.9′) with y_t as the dependent variable and $(x_t, \Delta x_t)$ as the independent variable. Let $\boldsymbol{x}' = (x_2, \ldots, x_T)$, $\boldsymbol{y}' = (y_2, \ldots, y_T)$, $\Delta\boldsymbol{x}' = (\Delta x_2, \ldots, \Delta x_T)$, $\boldsymbol{X} = (\boldsymbol{x}, \Delta\boldsymbol{x})$, $\varepsilon_{2.1}' = (\varepsilon_{2.12}, \ldots, \varepsilon_{2.1T})$, and $\boldsymbol{D}_T = \text{diag}[T, T^{1/2}]$. Then

$$\begin{pmatrix} \hat{b} - b \\ \hat{c} - c \end{pmatrix} = \boldsymbol{D}_T^{-1}(\boldsymbol{D}_T^{-1}\boldsymbol{X}'\boldsymbol{X}\boldsymbol{D}_T^{-1})^{-1}\boldsymbol{D}_T^{-1}\boldsymbol{X}'\boldsymbol{\varepsilon}_{2.1}$$

$$= \begin{pmatrix} T^{-1} & 0 \\ 0 & T^{-1/2} \end{pmatrix} \begin{pmatrix} T^{-2}\boldsymbol{x}'\boldsymbol{x} & T^{-3/2}\boldsymbol{x}'\Delta\boldsymbol{x} \\ & T^{-1}\Delta\boldsymbol{x}'\Delta\boldsymbol{x} \end{pmatrix} \begin{pmatrix} T^{-1}\boldsymbol{x}'\boldsymbol{\varepsilon}_{2.1} \\ T^{-1/2}\Delta\boldsymbol{x}'\boldsymbol{\varepsilon}_{2.1} \end{pmatrix}. \tag{13.17}$$

Let $(w_1(r), w_2(r))'$ be the Wiener process with covariance matrix $\boldsymbol{\Sigma}$, and let $(w_1(r), w_{2.1}(r))'$ be the Wiener process that is derived from $(w_1(r), w_2(r))'$ as (13.1a) and (13.1b). Then the process, $(w_1(r), w_{2.1}(r))'$, has the covariance matrix, $\text{diag}[\sigma_{11}, \sigma_{22} - \sigma_{21}^2\sigma_{11}^{-1}]$. Concerning the elements in (13.17), it is seen that

$$T^{-2}\boldsymbol{x}'\boldsymbol{x} \xrightarrow{D} \int w_1(r)^2 dr$$

$$T^{-3/2}\boldsymbol{x}'\Delta\boldsymbol{x} = T^{-1/2}\left(T^{-1}\sum(\Delta x_t)^2 + T^{-1}\sum x_{t-1}\Delta x_t\right) \xrightarrow{P} 0$$

$$T^{-1}\Delta\boldsymbol{x}'\Delta\boldsymbol{x} \xrightarrow{P} \sigma_{11}$$

$$T^{-1}x'\varepsilon_{2.1} = T^{-1}\left(\sum x_{t-1}\varepsilon_{2.1,t} + \sum \varepsilon_{1t}\varepsilon_{2.1t}\right) \xrightarrow{D} \int w_1(r)dw_{2.1}(r) + 0.$$

Substituting these relations in (13.17) we see that

$$T(\hat{b} - b) \xrightarrow{D} \left(\int w_1(r)^2 dr\right)^{-1} \int w_1(r)dw_{2.1}(r). \tag{13.18}$$

Since the covariance matrix of $(w_1(r), w_{2.1}(r))'$ is diagonal, $T(\hat{b} - b)$ is asymptotically $N(0, (\sigma_{22} - \sigma_{21}^2\sigma_{11}^{-1})g)$ conditionally upon $g \equiv \left(\int w_1(r)^2 dr\right)^{-1}$. In particular the right-hand side of (13.18) has zero expectation, while (13.7′) based on the OLS (13.7) does not have zero expectation.

Thus the OLS to be run is

$$y_t = \hat{b}x_t + \hat{c}\Delta x_t + \text{error}. \tag{13.19}$$

The t-statistic to test for $b = b^0$ in (13.19) is

$$\hat{t} = s^{-1}(\hat{b} - b^0)(\boldsymbol{x}'\boldsymbol{Q}\boldsymbol{x})^{1/2}, \tag{13.20}$$

where $\boldsymbol{Q} = \boldsymbol{I}_{T-1} - \Delta\boldsymbol{x}(\Delta\boldsymbol{x}'\Delta\boldsymbol{x})^{-1}\Delta\boldsymbol{x}'$

$$s = \left(T^{-1}\boldsymbol{\Sigma}(y_t - \hat{b}x_t - \hat{c}\Delta x_t)^2\right)^{1/2}.$$

Let $\boldsymbol{x}'_{-1} = (x_1, \ldots, x_{T-1})$. Then

$$\begin{aligned} T^{-2}\boldsymbol{x}'\boldsymbol{Q}\boldsymbol{x} &= T^{-2}(\Delta\boldsymbol{x} + \boldsymbol{x}_{-1})'\boldsymbol{Q}(\Delta\boldsymbol{x} + \boldsymbol{x}_{-1}) = T^{-2}\boldsymbol{x}'_{-1}\boldsymbol{Q}\boldsymbol{x}_{-1} \\ &= T^{-2}\boldsymbol{x}'_{-1}\boldsymbol{x}_{-1} - T^{-2}\boldsymbol{x}'_{-1}\Delta\boldsymbol{x}(T^{-1}\Delta\boldsymbol{x}'\Delta\boldsymbol{x})^{-1}T^{-1}\Delta\boldsymbol{x}'\boldsymbol{x}_{-1} \\ &\xrightarrow{D} \int w_1(r)^2 dr - 0. \end{aligned}$$

It also follows from (13.9′) that $\text{plim}\, s^2 = \sigma_{22} - \sigma_{21}^2\sigma_{11}^{-1}$. Combining these with (13.18) it follows that (13.20) is asymptotically distributed in $N(0, 1)$.

Incidentally the limit distribution regarding $\hat{c}$ also follows from (13.17). Since $T^{-1/2}\sum \varepsilon_{1t}\varepsilon_{2.1t} \xrightarrow{D} N(0, \sigma_{11}\sigma_{22} - \sigma_{21}^2)$, it is seen that

$$T^{1/2}(\hat{c} - c) \xrightarrow{D} N(0, \sigma_{11}^{-1}(\sigma_{22} - \sigma_{21}^2\sigma_{11}^{-1})).$$

Phillips (1991*a*) derives the above result through the maximum-likelihood estimation of b in $y_t = bx_{t-1} + u_t$, $x_t = \sum_{s=1}^{t} \varepsilon_{1s}$, $u_t = b\varepsilon_{1t} + \varepsilon_{2t}$. He also shows that when the MLE is mixed Gaussian it is the optimal estimator. Its explanation however is beyond the scope of the present book.

Generally we have no a priori information about $\boldsymbol{\Sigma}$ in practice. Therefore the method in the present section rather than the one in Section 13.1.2 should be recommended.

If x_t and y_t in (13.9) are $I(0)$ and if x_t and ε_{2t} are correlated, any OLS estimators, including that on (13.19), do not yield consistent estimation of b. The OLS is not robust to integration orders when the error is correlated. It can be said that *the co-integration among I(1) variables extends the applicability of OLS beyond that in the I(0) variables by freeing us from worry about the correlation between the regressor and disturbance.* The instrumental variable estimator has been used for the regression model with a correlated error when the variables are $I(0)$. The instrumental variable estimator applied to the cointegrated regression with a correlated error is T-consistent, but some modifications are required to make it mixed Gaussian[3] (see Phillips and Hansen (1990)).

Extending (13.9) to $y_t = \boldsymbol{b}'\boldsymbol{x}_t + \varepsilon_{2t}$ with a k-element vector $\boldsymbol{x}_t$ is straightforward *if* $\{\boldsymbol{x}_t\}$ *is not co-integrated.* Moreover, y_t can be extended to a vector under the same condition.

13.1.4 An example of the simultaneous equations model[4]

The following example provides a number of interesting problems to consider. $\{(\varepsilon_{1t}, \varepsilon_{2t}, \varepsilon_{3t})\}$ is i.i.d. with zero mean vector and the covariance matrix $\boldsymbol{\Sigma}$. Let

[3] Phillips and Hansen (1990) modify the instrumental variable estimator just as they modify the OLS, which is explained in Appendix 6. Without the modification the instrumental variable estimator is not mixed Gaussian.

[4] I have benefited from discussions with Koichi Maekawa and Taku Yamamoto on the writing of this subsection.

$x_t = v_{1t} \equiv \sum_{s=1}^{t} \varepsilon_{1s}$, and

$$y_t = bx_t + \varepsilon_{2t}, \tag{13.21a}$$

$$z_t = c_1 x_t + c_2 y_t + \varepsilon_{3t}. \tag{13.21b}$$

I assume that $b \neq 0$, and $c_1 + bc_2 \neq 0$ so that x_t, y_t, and z_t are each $I(1)$. (13.21*a*) and (13.21*b*) contain two linearly independent co-integrating vectors, $(-b, 1, 0)$ and $(-c_1, -c_2, 1)$ in the three-elements vector process, $\{(x_t, y_t, z_t)\}$. The two variables on the right-hand side of (13.21*b*) are co-integrated.

(13.21*a*) and (13.21*b*) may be looked upon as a simultaneous equations model. The coefficient of z_t in (13.21*a*) is a priori specified zero. This a priori information identifies b in (13.21*a*) because mixing (13.21*a*) and (13.21*b*) to get a new (13.21*a*) necessarily introduces z_t into (13.21*a*). On the other hand (c_1, c_2) in (13.21*b*) are not identified unless we have a priori information about the correlation between ε_{2t} and ε_{3t}. If $\sigma_{23} = 0$ is known a priori, it precludes mixing of (13.21*a*) and (13.21*b*) to get a new (13.21*b*), and (c_1, c_2) is identified. In fact, if $\sigma_{23} = 0$, and if x is weakly exogenous with respect to b, c_1, and c_2, (13.21*a*) and (13.21*b*) are what is known as the recursive system in the field of simultaneous equations, in which the OLS is consistent in the case of $I(0)$ variables.

Rewrite (13.21*a*) and (13.21*b*) as

$$\begin{bmatrix} y_t \\ z_t \end{bmatrix} = \begin{bmatrix} b \\ c_1 + bc_2 \end{bmatrix} x_t + \begin{bmatrix} \varepsilon_{2t} \\ \varepsilon_{3t} + c_2\varepsilon_{2t} \end{bmatrix}. \tag{13.22}$$

This is analogous to a reduced form. Moreover, each of the two equations in (13.22) is in the form that has been analysed in Sections 13.1.2–3. If $\sigma_{12} = \sigma_{13} = 0$ is a priori known, the method in Section 13.1.2 can be used to estimate b and $c_1 + bc_2$. Otherwise the method in Section 13.1.3 should be used.

Whatever the model is, OLS calculations can be run with z_t as the dependent and (x_t, y_t) as the independent variables. In the present case it tries to estimate an unidentified parameter (c_1, c_2) in (13.21*b*). Following Park and Phillips (1989) let us ask ourselves how $(\hat{c}_1, \hat{c}_2)$ is related to (c_1, c_2). The data-generating model is (13.21*a*) and (13.21*b*). Let $\boldsymbol{x}$, $\boldsymbol{y}$, and $\boldsymbol{z}$ be each $T \times 1$ vectors of the data. Then (13.21*b*) is

$$\boldsymbol{z} = (\boldsymbol{x}, \boldsymbol{y})(c_1, c_2)' + \boldsymbol{\varepsilon}_3. \tag{13.23}$$

This is a nice place to introduce a transformation to canonical variables each having different orders in probability, which was initiated in Sims, Stock, and Watson (1990). Let

$$\boldsymbol{H} = (1 + b^2)^{-1/2} \begin{bmatrix} -b, & 1 \\ 1, & b \end{bmatrix}.$$

Then $\boldsymbol{H}\boldsymbol{H}' = \boldsymbol{I}_2$. Let

$$(\boldsymbol{x}, \boldsymbol{y})\boldsymbol{H} \equiv (\boldsymbol{\xi}, \boldsymbol{\eta}),\ \boldsymbol{H}'(c_1, c_2)' = (\gamma_1, \gamma_2)',$$

$$\boldsymbol{z} = (\boldsymbol{\xi}, \boldsymbol{\eta})(\gamma_1, \gamma_2)' + \boldsymbol{\varepsilon}_3. \tag{13.23'}$$

Then $\boldsymbol{\xi} = (1+b^2)^{-1/2}\boldsymbol{\varepsilon}_2$ and $\boldsymbol{\eta} = (1+b^2)^{-1/2}((1+b^2)\boldsymbol{x} + b\boldsymbol{\varepsilon}_2)$. The point is that we have transformed $(\boldsymbol{x}, \boldsymbol{y})$ into $(\boldsymbol{\xi}, \boldsymbol{\eta})$ by using the co-integrating relation (13.21a) so that $\boldsymbol{\xi}$ is $I(0)$ and $\boldsymbol{\eta}$ is $I(1)$.

We are concerned with the $(\hat{c}_1, \hat{c}_2) - (c_1, c_2)$. Regress $\boldsymbol{z}$ upon $(\boldsymbol{\xi}, \boldsymbol{\eta})$ to get $(\hat{\gamma}_1, \hat{\gamma}_2)$. Since b is unknown $(\hat{\gamma}_1, \hat{\gamma}_2)$ is not an estimator, but it is useful to analyse $(\hat{c}_1, \hat{c}_2)$. Since $(\hat{c}_1, \hat{c}_2)' = \boldsymbol{H}(\hat{\gamma}_1, \hat{\gamma}_2)'$, we have

$$\begin{aligned}\begin{bmatrix}\hat{c}_1\\ \hat{c}_2\end{bmatrix} - \begin{bmatrix}c_1\\ c_2\end{bmatrix} &= \boldsymbol{H}\left\{\begin{bmatrix}\hat{\gamma}_1\\ \hat{\gamma}_2\end{bmatrix} - \begin{bmatrix}\gamma_1\\ \gamma_2\end{bmatrix}\right\}\\ &= \boldsymbol{H}\begin{pmatrix}T^{-1/2} & 0\\ 0 & T^{-1}\end{pmatrix}\begin{pmatrix}T^{-1}\boldsymbol{\xi}'\boldsymbol{\xi} & T^{-3/2}\boldsymbol{\xi}'\boldsymbol{\eta}\\ T^{-3/2}\boldsymbol{\eta}'\boldsymbol{\xi} & T^{-2}\boldsymbol{\eta}'\boldsymbol{\eta}\end{pmatrix}^{-1}\\ &\quad\times\begin{pmatrix}T^{-1/2}\boldsymbol{\xi}'\boldsymbol{\varepsilon}_3\\ T^{-1}\boldsymbol{\eta}'\boldsymbol{\varepsilon}_3\end{pmatrix}.\end{aligned} \tag{13.24}$$

Note $\quad T^{-1}\boldsymbol{\xi}'\boldsymbol{\xi} \xrightarrow{P} (1+b^2)^{-1}\sigma_{22},\ T^{-3/2}\boldsymbol{\xi}'\boldsymbol{\eta} \xrightarrow{P} 0,$

$$T^{-2}\boldsymbol{\eta}'\boldsymbol{\eta} \xrightarrow{D} (1+b^2)\int w_1(r)^2 dr,\ T^{-1}\boldsymbol{\xi}'\boldsymbol{\varepsilon}_3 \xrightarrow{P} (1+b^2)^{-1/2}\sigma_{23},$$

$$T^{-2}\boldsymbol{\eta}'\boldsymbol{\varepsilon}_3 \xrightarrow{P} 0.$$

Investigating (3.24) it is seen that

$$\begin{pmatrix}T^{-1}\boldsymbol{\xi}'\boldsymbol{\xi} & T^{-3/2}\boldsymbol{\xi}'\boldsymbol{\eta}\\ T^{-3/2}\boldsymbol{\eta}'\boldsymbol{\xi} & T^{-2}\boldsymbol{\eta}'\boldsymbol{\eta}\end{pmatrix}$$

becomes diagonal asymptotically. Therefore $\text{plim}(\hat{\gamma}_1 - \gamma_1) = (\text{plim}\ T^{-1}\boldsymbol{\xi}'\boldsymbol{\xi})^{-1}$, $\text{plim}\ T^{-1}\boldsymbol{\xi}'\boldsymbol{\varepsilon}_3 = (1+b^2)^{1/2}\sigma_{22}^{-1}\sigma_{23}$, and $\text{plim}\ (\hat{\gamma}_2 - \gamma_2) = \text{plim}\ (T^{-2}\boldsymbol{\eta}'\boldsymbol{\eta})^{-1}T^{-2}\boldsymbol{\eta}'\boldsymbol{\varepsilon}_3 = 0$. The conclusion on $((\hat{c}_1 - c_1), (\hat{c}_2 - c_2))$ is $\text{plim}\ \hat{c}_1 = c_1 - b\sigma_{23}\sigma_{22}^{-1}$, $\text{plim}\hat{c}_2 = c_2 + \sigma_{23}\sigma_{22}^{-1}$. If $\sigma_{23} = 0$, the OLS $(\hat{c}_1, \hat{c}_2)$ is a consistent estimator. (However, it is $\sqrt{T}$ consistent because $\hat{\gamma}_1$ is.) Recall that $\sigma_{23} = 0$ enables us to identify (c_1, c_2). Notice also that $\gamma_2 = c_1 + bc_2$ is identified without any a priori information about $\boldsymbol{\Sigma}$.

It is seen that the inference theories involving $I(1)$ are parallel to the standard theories for the stationary processes in so far as the consistency condition is concerned. It is the stationary component, ξ_t, that brings this about.[5]

[5] Maekawa *et al.* (1993) consider

$$y_t = \alpha y_{t-1} + \beta z_t + u_t, \quad |\alpha| < 1 \tag{$*$}$$

$$u_t = \rho u_{t-1} + v_t, \quad |\rho| < 1$$

$$z_t = z_{t-1} + \varepsilon_t,$$

where $\{v_t\}$ and $\{\varepsilon_t\}$ are mutually independent and each i.i.d. with zero mean and finite variance. This is a standard econometric model except that $\{z_t\}$ is $I(1)$. While y_t and z_t are co-integrated, y_{t-1} and z_t are also co-integrated on the right-hand side of $(*)$. The situation is analogous to (13.23).

When the identifiability is achieved by $\sigma_{23} = 0$, the limit distribution of $(\hat{c}_1, \hat{c}_2)$ is different from that in the $I(0)$ case. Since

$$\sqrt{T}\begin{pmatrix}\hat{c}_1 - c_1 \\ \hat{c}_2 - c_2\end{pmatrix} = (1+b^2)^{-1/2}\begin{pmatrix}-b & T^{-1/2} \\ 1 & T^{-1/2}b\end{pmatrix}\begin{pmatrix}T^{-1}\xi'\xi & T^{-3/2}\xi'\eta \\ T^{-3/2}\eta'\xi & T^{-2}\eta'\eta\end{pmatrix}^{-1}$$

$$\times\begin{pmatrix}T^{-1/2}\xi'\varepsilon_3 \\ T^{-1}\eta'\varepsilon_3\end{pmatrix},$$

$$\sqrt{T}\begin{pmatrix}\hat{c}_1 - c_1 \\ \hat{c}_2 - c_2\end{pmatrix} \approx (1+b^2)^{1/2}\sigma_{22}^{-1}\begin{pmatrix}-b \\ 1\end{pmatrix}T^{-1/2}\varepsilon_2'\varepsilon_3,$$

which is asymptotically degenerate Gaussian. We have assumed $b \neq 0$ from the outset.

The above demonstration provides a hint regarding how one can eliminate the assumptions made in Sections 13.1.2–3 above that $\{\boldsymbol{x}_t\}$ should not be co-integrated when it is a vector stochastic process. Wooldridge (1991) and Hamilton (1994: 590–1) present a general proposition, which is specialized in the present example of (13.21*a*) and (13.21*b*) to the statement that even though $\{x_t\}$ and $\{y_t\}$ are co-integrated $\{(\hat{c}_1 x_t + \hat{c}_2 y_t)\}$ converges in probability to the image of projection of $\{z_t\}$ on to $\{(x_t, y_t)\}$. Saikkonen (1993) shows a method to estimate a general simultaneous equations model. Davidson (1994) reveals an interesting aspect of identifiability by exclusion of variables in simultaneous equations.

13.1.5 Mixing a stationary regressor in the regressor set

(13.23′) is

$$z_t = \gamma_1\xi_t + \gamma_2\eta_t + \varepsilon_{3t}. \qquad (13.23'')$$

Here ξ_t is stationary while η_t is non-stationary so that (13.23″) is a co-integrating relation with a vector $(\times, -\gamma_2, 1)$ in $(\xi_t, \eta_t, z_t,)$ where $\times$ means unspecified. As for the coefficient on the stationary ξ_t it is seen from (13.24) that if $E(\xi_t\varepsilon_{3t}) = 0$, $\hat{\gamma}_1$ is consistent, and that

$$\sqrt{T}(\hat{\gamma}_1 - \gamma_1) \approx (T^{-1}\xi'\xi)^{-1}T^{-1/2}\xi'\varepsilon_3,$$

In fact

$$y_{t-1} = \beta(1-\alpha)^{-1}z_t + w_t$$

$$(1-\alpha L)w_t = u_{t-1} - \beta(1-\alpha)^{-1}\varepsilon_t$$

if $y_0 = z_0 = 0$. What corresponds to the stationary component, ξ_t, in the text is here $(1+\tau^2)^{-1/2}w_t$, where $\tau = \beta(1-\alpha)^{-1}$. When $\rho \neq 0$, w_t and u_t are correlated. What corresponds to $\hat{\gamma}_1$ in the text is not consistent here, which makes the OLS $(\hat{\alpha}, \hat{\beta})$ in $(*)$ inconsistent. It has been known that the OLS is not consistent when $\rho \neq 0$ and $\{z_t\}$ is $I(0)$. Again it is the stationary component that produces the similarity between $I(0)$ and $I(1)$ cases.

is asymptotically normal. The test on γ_1 is standard. On the other hand, regarding the coefficient on the non-stationary $\boldsymbol{\eta}$ we have

$$T(\hat{\gamma}_2 - \gamma_2) \approx (T^{-2}\boldsymbol{\eta}'\boldsymbol{\eta})^{-1}T^{-1}\boldsymbol{\eta}'\boldsymbol{\varepsilon}_3,$$

which is like a number of expressions that have appeared previously in the non-stationary case.

In general, suppose that

$$z_t = c_1 x_t + c_2 y_t + \varepsilon_{3t},$$

where $\{x_t\}$ is stationary, but $y_t = \sum_{s=1}^{t} \varepsilon_{2s}.\{(\varepsilon_{2t}, \varepsilon_{3t})\}$ is i.i.d. with zero mean and covariance matrix $\boldsymbol{\Sigma}$, which is not necessarily diagonal. Let $(\hat{c}_1, \hat{c}_2)$ be the OLS of (c_1, c_2), and $\boldsymbol{D}_T = \text{diag}[T^{1/2}, T]$. Then

$$\boldsymbol{D}_T \begin{bmatrix} \hat{c}_1 - c_1 \\ \hat{c}_2 - c_2 \end{bmatrix} = \begin{bmatrix} T^{-1}\boldsymbol{x}'\boldsymbol{x} & T^{-3/2}\boldsymbol{x}'\boldsymbol{y} \\ & T^{-2}\boldsymbol{y}'\boldsymbol{y} \end{bmatrix}^{-1} \begin{bmatrix} T^{-1/2}\boldsymbol{x}'\boldsymbol{\varepsilon}_3 \\ T^{-1}\boldsymbol{y}'\boldsymbol{\varepsilon}_3 \end{bmatrix},$$

where $\boldsymbol{x}' = (x_1, \ldots, x_T)$, $\boldsymbol{y}' = (y_1, \ldots, y_T)$, $\boldsymbol{\varepsilon}_3' = (\varepsilon_{31}, \ldots, \varepsilon_{3T})$. Note that plim $T^{-3/2}\boldsymbol{x}'\boldsymbol{y} = 0$. Provided that $E(x_t\varepsilon_{3t}) = 0$, i.e. if the stationary regressor is uncorrelated with the error, then $\hat{c}_1$ is $\sqrt{T}$-consistent, and

$$\sqrt{T}(\hat{c}_1 - c_1) \to N(0, \sigma_{11}(\text{plim } T^{-1}\boldsymbol{x}'\boldsymbol{x})^{-1}),$$

which is just the same as in traditional econometrics. On the other hand, $\hat{c}_2$ is T-consistent even when $E(\varepsilon_{2t}\varepsilon_{3t}) \neq 0$. However, it is only when $E(\varepsilon_{2t}\varepsilon_{3t}) = 0$ that $T(\hat{c}_2 - c_2)$ is mixed Gaussian.

13.2 Deterministic Polynomial Trends

Concerning the vector processes $\{\boldsymbol{\varepsilon}_t\}$ and $\{\boldsymbol{v}_t\}$ constructed in connection with (13.2)–(13.4) we have

$$T^{-5/2}\sum_{t=1}^{T} t\boldsymbol{v}_t \overset{D}{\to} \int_0^1 r\boldsymbol{w}(r, \boldsymbol{\Sigma})dr \tag{13.25}$$

$$T^{-3/2}\sum_{t=1}^{T} t\boldsymbol{\varepsilon}_t \overset{D}{\to} \int_0^1 rd\boldsymbol{w}(r, \boldsymbol{\Sigma}). \tag{13.26}$$

They correspond to (6.14) and (6.15) in Part I.

13.2.1 A single regressor

Previous conclusions in Section 13.1 are substantially altered when x_t has a linear trend as well as a stochastic trend. Reconsider the models (13.5) and (13.6) in Section 13.1.1 replacing the data generation of x_t by

$$\Delta x_t = \mu + \varepsilon_{1t}, \quad \mu \neq 0. \tag{13.27}$$

As before $\{(\varepsilon_{1t}, \varepsilon_{2t})\}$ is i.i.d. with zero mean vector and covariance matrix $\mathbf{\Sigma}$. I use the same definition of $\{(v_{1t}, v_{2t})\}$ as before. As explained in Section 4.2 of Part I the deterministic part dominates the stochastic part in $\sum x_t^2$, and $T^{-3}\sum x_t^2 \xrightarrow{P} \mu^2/3$.

Let us begin with the spurious regression model (13.6) to generate y_t. Then

$$\sqrt{T}(\hat{b}-b) \xrightarrow{D} 3\mu^{-2}\int rw_2(r)dr,$$

where $w_2(r)$ is the Wiener process with variance $E(\varepsilon_{2t}^2) \equiv \sigma_{22}$. Thus the OLS is $\sqrt{T}$ consistent and asymptotically Gaussian in spite of the spurious regression. However, the t-statistic diverges because

$$\hat{t} \equiv s^{-1}(\hat{b}-b)\left(\sum x_t^2\right)^{1/2} \approx \left(T^{-1}\sum v_{2t}^2\right)^{-1/2}\left(\mu\sum tv_{2t}\right)\left(\mu^2\sum t^2\right)^{-1/2}$$

$$\approx T^{1/2}\left(T^{-2}\sum v_{2t}^2\right)^{-1/2}\left(T^{-5/2}\sum tv_{2t}\right)\left(T^{-3}\sum t^2\right)^{-1/2}.$$

The hypothesis, $b=0$, is surely rejected when b is indeed zero, and the word, 'spurious', maintains its proper meaning even when a linear trend is contained in x_t. Incidentally, the above also shows that it is only in the co-integrated regression that the (mixed) Gaussian property of $\hat{b}-b$ induces the asymptotic $N(0, 1)$ of t-statistic.

Let us then turn to the co-integrated regression, (13.5), to generate y_t from x_t, which is constructed in (13.27). $(-b, 1)$ is the co-integrating vector in the process $\{(x_t, y_t)\}$ such that the vector nullifies both the stochastic and deterministic trends. $\{(\varepsilon_{1t}, \varepsilon_{2t})\}$ is i.i.d. with zero mean vector and covariance matrix $\mathbf{\Sigma}$. Concerning the OLS,

$$y_t = \hat{b}x_t + \text{error}, \tag{13.28}$$

the deterministic trend dominates the stochastic trend in $\{x_t\}$, which makes the correlation between Δx_t and ε_{2t} irrelevant. It is seen that

$$T^{3/2}(\hat{b}-b) \xrightarrow{D} N(0, 3\mu^{-2}\sigma_{22}), \tag{13.29}$$

no matter whether x_t and ε_{2t} are correlated or uncorrelated. This limit distribution is unconditional Gaussian rather than mixed Gaussian. The asymptotic normality of OLS in the present context has been emphasized in West (1988). The t-statistic also converges to $N(0, 1)$ no matter whether the error is correlated or uncorrelated with the regressor.

The co-integrating regression that nullifies both the deterministic and stochastic trends allows a constant term. When we consider

$$y_t = a + bx_t + \varepsilon_{2t},$$

and the corresponding OLS

$$y_t = \hat{a} + \hat{b}x_t + \text{error}, \tag{13.28$'$}$$

all the above results remain unaltered except that $N(0, 3\mu^{-2}\sigma_{22})$ in (13.29) is replaced by $N(0, 12\mu^{-2}\sigma_{22})$. The t-statistic is asymptotically $N(0, 1)$.

The above reasoning can be extended to a wide class of modes of deterministic trends in x_t. Suppose (i) that $x_t = f_t + u_t$, where $\{f_t\}$ is deterministic and $T^{-\alpha}\sum f_t^2$ converges to $c(>0)$ as $T \to \infty$, (ii) that $\{u_t\}$ is stochastic and possibly non-stationary, but (iii) that f_t dominates u_t. If $\{u_t\}$ is $I(1)$ so that u_t is $O_p(t^{1/2})$, then the condition (iii) means that $\alpha > 1$. Let $y_t = a + bx_t + \varepsilon_{2t}$. Regarding $\hat{b}$ in (13.28′), $T^{\alpha/2}(\hat{b} - b)$ is asymptotically $N(0, \sigma_{22}c^{-1})$ unconditionally. The t-statistic, which is

$$s^{-1}(\hat{b} - b)\left(\sum x_t^2\right)^{1/2} = s^{-1}T^{\alpha/2}(\hat{b} - b)\left(T^{-\alpha}\sum x_t^2\right)^{1/2},$$

is asymptotically $N(0, 1)$.

I find some wisdom in the OLS

$$y_t = \hat{a} + \hat{b}x_t + \hat{c}\Delta x_t + \text{error}. \tag{13.28″}$$

In the OLS (13.28) and (13.28′) with a finite sample some size of μ^2/σ_{11} is required for the dominance of deterministic trend (of x) over the stochastic trend in order to make the correlation between $\Delta x_t = \varepsilon_{1t}$ and ε_{2t} irrelevant. In (13.28″) that correlation is eliminated by Δx_t and thereby the t-statistic on $\hat{b}$ converges to $N(0, 1)$ even when μ^2/σ_{11} is small or zero. When $\mu = 0$ the limit distribution of $\hat{b}$ is mixed Gaussian, while it is (simple) Gaussian when $\mu \neq 0$. In either case the t-statistic converges to $N(0, 1)$. More generally, for any f_t, it is advisable to have Δx_t in the regressor set because then the correlation between $\Delta x_t = \Delta f_t + \varepsilon_{1t}$ and ε_{2t} can be eliminated even when f_t does not dominate v_{1t}.

As for the co-integration vector that annihilates only the stochastic trend, we may consider the model

$$y_t = a + bt + cx_t + \varepsilon_{2t} \tag{13.5′}$$

in conjunction with (13.27). $\{(\varepsilon_{1t}, \varepsilon_{2t})\}$ continues to be i.i.d. with zero mean and covariance $\mathbf{\Sigma}$. If $b + c\mu \neq 0$, y_t also contains a linear deterministic trend. The vector $(-c, 1)$ for (x_t, y_t) is the co-integration vector that annihilates stochastic trends only. There remains a deterministic trend, $a + bt$, in $y_t - cx_t$.

If $\sigma_{12} = 0$ we may run OLS

$$y_t = \hat{a} + \hat{b}t + \hat{c}x_t + \text{error}. \tag{13.30}$$

It is well known that $\hat{c}$ is equivalent to the OLS estimate of c in $\tilde{y}_t = \hat{c}\tilde{x}_t +$ residual, where $\tilde{y}_t$ and $\tilde{x}_t$ are demeaned and detrended y_t and x_t respectively. $T(\hat{c} - c)$ is asymptotically mixed Gaussian. However, the conditioning variable is different from (13.11). Here we have

$$T(\hat{c} - c) \to \left(\int w^*(r)^2 dr\right)^{-1}\left(\int w^*(r)dw_2(r)\right), \tag{13.31}$$

TABLE 13.1 *Various OLS with regressors containing deterministic trends*

DGP of y	OLS	t-statistic converges to $N(0, 1)$
(a) $y_t = a + bx_t + \varepsilon_{2t}$ f_t dominating v_{1t}	$y_t = \hat{a} + \hat{b}x_t + \text{error}$	no matter whether $\sigma_{12} =$ or $\neq 0$
(b) $y_t = a + bx_t + \varepsilon_{2t}$	$y_t = \hat{a} + \hat{b}x_t + \hat{c}\Delta x_t$ + error	no matter whether $\sigma_{12} =$ or $\neq 0$
(c) $y_t = a + bt + cx_t + \varepsilon_{2t}$	$y_t = \hat{a} + \hat{b}t + \hat{c}x_t$ + error	only when $\sigma_{12} = 0$
(d) $y_t = a + bt + cx_t + \varepsilon_{2t}$	$y_t = \hat{a} + \hat{b}t + \hat{c}x_t + \hat{d}\Delta x_t$ + error	no matter whether $\sigma_{12} =$ or $\neq 0$

where $w^*(r) \equiv w_1(r) - \int w_1(r)dr - 12(r - \frac{1}{2}) \int (s - \frac{1}{2})w_1(s)ds$ (see Section 6.1 of Part I), and $(w_1(r), w_2(r))'$ is the Wiener process with $\mathbf{\Sigma} = \text{diag}[\sigma_{11}, \sigma_{22}]$. The conditioning variable here is $\left(\int w^*(r)^2 dr\right)^{-1}$. Nevertheless the t-statistic does converge to $N(0, 1)$.

If $\sigma_{12} \neq 0$ the OLS to be run is

$$y_t = \hat{a} + \hat{b}t + \hat{c}x_t + \hat{d}\Delta x_t + \text{error}. \tag{13.32}$$

The t-statistic for $\hat{c}$ converges to $N(0, 1)$. The results on (13.31) and (13.32) are invariant whether the true value of μ in (13.27) is zero or not.

The above results are summarized in Table 13.1. In (a) and (b) we are concerned with the co-integration that nullifies both the deterministic and the stochastic trends at once. The process of Δx_t is $\Delta f_t + \varepsilon_{1t}$ with some non-stochastic f_t. In (a) f_t dominates $v_{1t} = \sum_{s=1}^{t} \varepsilon_{1t}$, but in (b) f_t need not dominate v_{1t}. In (c) and (d) we are concerned with the co-integration that nullifies the stochastic trends only. The deterministic trends of x_t and y_t must be both linear in so far as the trend on the right-hand side of OLS equation is kept as $\hat{a} + \hat{b}t$. Any other forms of deterministic trends would entail a bias for the estimation of the co-integration vector. (A more complicated form of deterministic trend can be allowed for if the trend function on the right-hand of OLS equation subsumes the correct specifications of the models of deterministic trends in x and y.)

13.2.2 Two regressors

Next let us consider the case where two regressors x_{1t} and x_{2t} are involved. The result on the spurious regression is essentially identical to the case of a single regressor, but the result on the co-integrated regression is more complicated than in the case of a single regressor. Hansen (1992a) demonstrates the results in a mathematically unified form. I shall present a more elementary exposition of the results in Hansen (1992*a*).

Suppose that the regressors are generated by

$$\begin{bmatrix} \Delta x_{1t} \\ \Delta x_{2t} \end{bmatrix} = \begin{bmatrix} \mu_1 \\ \mu_2 \end{bmatrix} + \begin{bmatrix} \varepsilon_{1t} \\ \varepsilon_{2t} \end{bmatrix}, \qquad \mu_1^2 + \mu_2^2 \neq 0, \tag{13.33}$$

that the regression equation to generate y_t is

$$y_t = b_1 x_{1t} + b_2 x_{2t} + \varepsilon_{3t}, \tag{13.34}$$

and that $\{(\varepsilon_{1t}, \varepsilon_{2t}, \varepsilon_{3t})\}$ is i.i.d. with zero mean vector and covariance matrix $\sum = \text{diag}\,[\boldsymbol{\Sigma}^*, \sigma_{33}]$, where $\boldsymbol{\Sigma}^*$ is 2×2. Regressors x_1 and x_2 are uncorrelated with the disturbance. The submatrix of $\sum$ which consists of the first and second rows and columns is assumed to be non-singular so that x_{1t} and x_{2t} are not co-integrated. This is an important assumption maintained through the present section. In the three variables process (x_{1t}, x_{2t}, y_t) a vector $(-b_1, -b_2, 1)$ nullifies both the stochastic and deterministic trends. We are interested in the inference on (b_1, b_2) through the OLS,

$$y_t = \hat{b}_1 x_{1t} + \hat{b}_2 x_{2t} + \text{error}.$$

To analyse $(\hat{b}_1, \hat{b}_2)$, let us introduce a transformation to canonical variables by

$$\boldsymbol{H} = (\mu_1^2 + \mu_2^2)^{-1/2} \begin{bmatrix} \mu_1, & -\mu_2 \\ \mu_2, & \mu_1 \end{bmatrix}.$$

Then $\boldsymbol{HH}' = \boldsymbol{I}_2$. Writing (13.34) as

$$y_t = (x_{1t}, x_{2t})\boldsymbol{HH}' \begin{pmatrix} b_1 \\ b_2 \end{pmatrix} + \varepsilon_{3t}, \ \boldsymbol{H}' \begin{pmatrix} b_1 \\ b_2 \end{pmatrix} = \begin{pmatrix} c_1 \\ c_2 \end{pmatrix},$$

it is seen that

$$y_t = ((\mu t + \xi_{1t}), \xi_{2t}) \begin{pmatrix} c_1 \\ c_2 \end{pmatrix} + \varepsilon_{3t}, \tag{13.35}$$

where $\mu \equiv (\mu_1^2 + \mu_2^2)^{1/2}$, $\xi_{1t} \equiv \mu^{-1}(\mu_1 v_{1t} + \mu_2 v_{2t})$, $\xi_{2t} \equiv \mu^{-1}(-\mu_2 v_{1t} + \mu_1 v_{2t})$, and $v_{it} = \sum_{s=1}^{t} \varepsilon_{it}$. The time variable t appears only in the first of two regressors in (13.35).

$$\begin{aligned} \begin{pmatrix} \hat{c}_1 \\ \hat{c}_2 \end{pmatrix} - \begin{pmatrix} c_1 \\ c_2 \end{pmatrix} &= \begin{pmatrix} T^{-3/2} & 0 \\ 0 & T^{-1} \end{pmatrix} \\ &\times \begin{pmatrix} T^{-3} \sum (\mu t + \xi_{1t})^2, & T^{-5/2} \sum (\mu t + \xi_{1t})\xi_{2t} \\ T^{-5/2} \sum (\mu t + \xi_{1t})\xi_{2t}, & T^{-2} \sum \xi_{2t}^2 \end{pmatrix}^{-1} \\ &\times \begin{bmatrix} T^{-3/2} \sum \varepsilon_{3t}(\mu t + \xi_{1t}) \\ T^{-1} \sum \varepsilon_{3t}\xi_{2t} \end{bmatrix}. \end{aligned} \tag{13.36}$$

Let $(w_1(r), w_2(r), w_3(r))'$ be the Wiener process with covariance matrix $\mathbf{\Sigma} = \text{diag}\,[\mathbf{\Sigma}^*, \sigma_{33}]$. Also write $(w_1(r), w_2(r))\boldsymbol{H} \equiv (\tilde{w}_1(r), \tilde{w}_2(r))$. Then

$$T^{-3}\sum(\mu t + \xi_{1t})^2 \xrightarrow{P} \mu^2/3 \equiv \int_0^1 r^2 dr,$$

$$T^{-5/2}\sum(\mu t + \xi_{1t})\xi_{2t} \xrightarrow{D} \mu \int r\tilde{w}_2(r)dr,$$

$$T^{-2}\sum \xi_{2t}^2 \xrightarrow{D} \int \tilde{w}_2(r)^2 dr,$$

$$T^{-3/2}\sum \varepsilon_{3t}(\mu t + \xi_{1t}) \xrightarrow{D} \mu \int r dw_3(r),$$

$$T^{-1}\sum \varepsilon_{3t}\xi_{2t} \xrightarrow{D} \int \tilde{w}_2(r)dw_3(r).$$

Therefore

$$\begin{bmatrix} T^{3/2}(\hat{c}_1 - c_1) \\ T(\hat{c}_2 - c_2) \end{bmatrix} \xrightarrow{D} \left(\int \begin{bmatrix} \mu r \\ \tilde{w}_2 \end{bmatrix} \begin{bmatrix} \mu r \\ \tilde{w}_2 \end{bmatrix}' dr\right)^{-1} \times \left(\int \begin{bmatrix} \mu r \\ \tilde{w}_2 \end{bmatrix} dw_3(r)\right). \tag{13.37}$$

$(\tilde{w}_2(r), w_3(r))'$ is the Wiener process with the covariance matrix, $\text{diag}[\sigma_{22}^*, \sigma_{33}]$, where $\sigma_{22}^* = \mu^{-2}(-\mu_2, \mu_1)\mathbf{\Sigma}^*(-\mu_2, \mu_1)'$. Note that $\hat{c}_1 - c_1$ is $O_p(T^{3/2})$ while $\hat{c}_2 - c_2$ is $O_p(T^{-1})$. It is as though ξ_{1t} is dominated out and the regressors consist of μt and ξ_{2t}.

Conditionally upon

$$G \equiv \left(\int \begin{bmatrix} \mu r \\ \tilde{w}_2 \end{bmatrix} \begin{bmatrix} \mu r \\ \tilde{w}_2 \end{bmatrix}' dr\right)^{-1}. \tag{13.38}$$

$[T^{3/2}(\hat{c}_1 - c_1), T(\hat{c}_2 - c_2)]'$ is asymptotically distributed in $N(0, \sigma_{33}\boldsymbol{G})$. Keep in mind for a later reference that the asymptotic conditional distributions of $T^{3/2}(\hat{c}_1 - c_1)$ and $T(\hat{c}_2 - c_2)$ are respectively $N(0, \sigma_{33}G_{11})$ and $N(0, \sigma_{33}G_{22})$, where G_{ij} is the (i, j) element of $\boldsymbol{G}$.

However, we are interested in the original parameter (b_1, b_2) rather than (c_1, c_2). Consider a linear combination of $(\hat{b}_1 - b_1, \hat{b}_2 - b_2)$ with weights (d_1, d_2),

$$(d_1, d_2)\begin{pmatrix} \hat{b}_1 - b_1 \\ \hat{b}_2 - b_2 \end{pmatrix} = \mu^{-1}(d_1, d_2)\begin{pmatrix} \mu_1, & -\mu_2 \\ \mu_2, & \mu_1 \end{pmatrix}\begin{bmatrix} \hat{c}_1 - c_1 \\ \hat{c}_2 - c_2 \end{bmatrix}.$$

If $(d_1, d_2)(-\mu_2, \mu_1)' = 0$, the linear combination does not include $\hat{c}_2 - c_2$. The combination is $O_p(T^{-3/2})$. If $(d_1, d_2)(-\mu_2, \mu_1)' \neq 0$, the combination does include $\hat{c}_2 - c_2$, and it is $O_p(T^{-1})$. In this sense the asymptotic distribution of $(\hat{b}_1 - b_1, \hat{b}_2 - b_2)$ is degenerate, a point that was emphasized in Park and Phillips (1988).

Note that $(d_1, d_2)(-\mu_2, \mu_1)' = 0$ means that the relative weights in the linear combination are proportional to $\mu_1 : \mu_2$. Note also that $\mu_1 b_1 + \mu_2 b_2$ is the coefficient of time variable t on the right-hand side of (13.34). This coefficient can be estimated with error only in $O_p(T^{-3/2})$.[6]

At first sight one might think that the degeneracy might cause trouble in the inference. Hansen (1992*a*) shows it does not. Let us consider the null hypothesis, $d_1 b_1 + d_2 b_2 = d_3$, where (d_1, d_2, d_3) is a priori known. It can be shown that the t-statistic is asymptotically $N(0, 1)$ under the null hypothesis regardless of whether $(d_1, d_2)(-\mu_2, \mu_1)' =$ or $\neq 0$. Let $\boldsymbol{x}_1' = (x_{11}, \dots, x_{1T})$, $\boldsymbol{x}_2' = (x_{21}, \dots, x_{2T})$ and $\boldsymbol{X} = (\boldsymbol{x}_1, \boldsymbol{x}_2)$. The t-statistic is

$$s^{-1}(d_1\hat{b}_1 + d_2\hat{b}_2 - d_3)((d_1, d_2)(\boldsymbol{X}'\boldsymbol{X})^{-1}(d_1, d_2)')^{-1/2}, \tag{13.39}$$

where s is the standard error of regression in (13.34). Let $\boldsymbol{D}_T = \text{diag}[T^{3/2}, T]$, and consider

$$\begin{aligned}&(d_1, d_2)(\boldsymbol{X}'\boldsymbol{X})^{-1}(d_1, d_2)' \\ &\quad = (d_1, d_2)\boldsymbol{H}\boldsymbol{D}_T^{-1}(\boldsymbol{D}_T^{-1}\boldsymbol{H}'\boldsymbol{X}'\boldsymbol{X}\boldsymbol{H}\boldsymbol{D}_T^{-1})^{-1}\boldsymbol{D}_T^{-1}\boldsymbol{H}'(d_1, d_2)'.\end{aligned} \tag{13.40}$$

Write $\hat{\boldsymbol{G}} \equiv (\boldsymbol{D}_T^{-1}\boldsymbol{H}'\boldsymbol{X}'\boldsymbol{X}\boldsymbol{H}\boldsymbol{D}_T^{-1})^{-1}$ and denote its (i, j) element by $\hat{G}_{ij}$. In fact $\hat{G}$ appeared in the right-hand side of (13.36). If $(d_1, d_2)(-\mu_2, \mu_1)' \neq 0$, the second element of $(d_1, d_2)\boldsymbol{H}\boldsymbol{D}_T^{-1}$ dominates the first element, and $T^2 \times$ (13.40) is

$$\mu^{-2}(d_1, d_2)(-\mu_2, \mu_1)'\hat{\boldsymbol{G}}_{22}(-\mu_2, \mu_1)(d_1, d_2)' + O_p(T^{-1/2}).$$

If $(d_1, d_2)(-\mu_2, \mu_1) = 0$, the second element of $(d_1, d_2)\boldsymbol{H}\boldsymbol{D}_T^{-1}$ is zero, and $T^3 \times$ (13.40) is

$$\mu^{-2}(d_1, d_2)(\mu_1, \mu_2)'\hat{\boldsymbol{G}}_{11}(\mu_1, \mu_2)(d_1, d_2)'.$$

Then consider

$$(d_1, d_2)(\hat{b}_1 - b_1, \hat{b}_2 - b_2)' = (d_1, d_2)\boldsymbol{H}\boldsymbol{D}_T^{-1}\boldsymbol{D}_T(\hat{c}_1 - c_1, \hat{c}_2 - c_2)' \tag{13.41}$$

under the null hypothesis. If $(d_1, d_2)(-\mu_2, \mu_1)' \neq 0$, $T \times$ (13.41) is

$$\mu^{-1}(d_1, d_2)(-\mu_2, \mu_1)'T(\hat{c}_2 - c_2) + O_p(T^{-1/2}),$$

and if $(d_1, d_2)(-\mu_2, \mu_1)' = 0$, $T^{3/2} \times$ (13.41) is

$$\mu^{-1}(d_1, d_2)(\mu_1, \mu_2)'T^{3/2}(\hat{c}_1 - c_1).$$

[6] To test if the co-integration vector $(b_1^0, b_2^0, -1)$ for (x_1, x_2, y) annihilates the linear trend, we wish to test if $-\mu_1 b_1^0 - \mu_2 b_2^0 + \mu_3 = 0$, where μ_3 is the slope of the linear trend of y_t. The t-test considered in the text is not directly useful because

$$\begin{aligned}&-\hat{\mu}_1(\hat{b}_1 - b_1^0) - \hat{\mu}_2(\hat{b}_2 - b_2^0) + \hat{\mu}_3 = -\mu_1(\hat{b}_1 - b_1^0) - \mu_2(\hat{b}_2 - b_2^0) \\ &\quad + \mu_3 + (\hat{\mu}_3 - \mu_3) + O_p(T^{-6}),\end{aligned}$$

but $\hat{\mu}_3 - \mu_3$ cannot be $o_p(T^{-3/2})$.

If $(d_1, d_2)(-\mu_2, \mu_1)' \neq 0$, the t-statistic in (13.39) is looked upon as

$$s^{-1}(T \times (13.41))(T^2 \times (13.40))^{-1/2} = s^{-1}T(\hat{c}_2 - c_2)\hat{G}_{22}^{-1/2} + O_p(T^{-1/2}).$$

If $(d_1, d_2)(-\mu_2, \mu_1)' = 0$, it is looked upon as

$$s^{-1}(T^{3/2} \times (13.41))(T^3 \times (13.40))^{-1/2} = s^{-1}T^{3/2}(\hat{c}_1 - c_1)\hat{G}_{11}^{-1/2}.$$

Note that $\hat{G} \xrightarrow{D} G$ in (13.38). In either case the t-statistic converges asymptotically to $N(0, 1)$ by virtue of the asymptotic distributions of $(T^{3/2}(\hat{c}_1 - c_1), T(\hat{c}_2 - c_2))$ given in (13.37) under the null hypothesis. Conditionally upon any G the statistic is asymptotically $N(0, 1)$, and hence it is $N(0, 1)$ unconditionally as well.

Next consider twice the F-statistic to test for $(b_1, b_2) = (b_1^0, b_2^0)$,

$$s^{-2}(\hat{b}_1 - b_1^0, \hat{b}_2 - b_2^0)\boldsymbol{X}'\boldsymbol{X}(\hat{b}_1 - b_1^0, \hat{b}_2 - b_2^0)'. \tag{13.42}$$

Writing $(b_1^0, b_2^0)\boldsymbol{H} = (c_1^0, c_2^0)$, (13.42) is

$$s^{-2}(\hat{c}_1 - c_1^0, \hat{c}_2 - c_2^0)\boldsymbol{D}_T(\boldsymbol{D}_T^{-1}\boldsymbol{H}'\boldsymbol{X}'\boldsymbol{X}\boldsymbol{H}\boldsymbol{D}_T^{-1})\boldsymbol{D}_T(\hat{c}_1 - c_1^0, (\hat{c}_2 - c_2^0)'.$$

By virtue of (13.37) this is asymptotically $\chi^2(2)$, and the degeneracy is simply irrelevant.

If $\boldsymbol{\Sigma}$ is not block diagonal so that ε_{3t} is correlated with $(\varepsilon_{1t}, \varepsilon_{2t})$, we can use the method given in Section 13.1.3 above by running OLS

$$y_t = \hat{b}_1 x_{1t} + \hat{b}_2 x_{1t} + \hat{c}\Delta x_{1t} + \hat{d}\Delta x_{2t} + \text{error}.$$

If $\mu_2 = 0$ in (13.33) so that x_{2t} does not have a linear trend, the transformation matrix $\boldsymbol{H}$ is reduced to $\boldsymbol{I}_2$. The above reasoning is simplified when we are interested in the inference on b_1 only. Here $(d_1, d_2) = (1, 0)$ in the above analysis of t-statistic, and we have $(d_1, d_2)(-\mu_2, \mu_1)' \equiv 0$ so that $\hat{b}_1 - b_1$ does not include $\hat{c}_2 - c_2$. Nevertheless the situation here is different from (13.28) and (13.29), where a single regressor contains a deterministic as well as a stochastic trend. Here $\boldsymbol{G}$ is not block diagonal, and the limit distribution of $T^{3/2}(\hat{c}_1 - c_1)$ is not Gaussian unconditionally.

So far y_t has been generated by (13.34) so that the co-integrating vector nullifies both the deterministic and stochastic trends at once. Suppose now that we are concerned with a co-integration that nullifies the stochastic trend only. The model is

$$y_t = a + bt + c_1 x_{1t} + c_2 x_{2t} + \varepsilon_{3t},$$

in conjunction with (13.33) that generates (x_{1t}, x_{2t}). Run OLS

$$y_t = \hat{a} + \hat{b}t + \hat{c}_1 x_{1t} + \hat{c}_2 x_{2t} + \text{error}.$$

The t and $2F$ on (c_1, c_2) converge respectively to $N(0, 1)$ and $\chi^2(2)$ only when $\sigma_{13} = \sigma_{23} = 0$. However, the t and $2F$ on (c_1, c_2) in the OLS,

$$y_t = \hat{a} + \hat{b}t + \hat{c}x_{1t} + \hat{c}_2 x_{2t} + \hat{d}\Delta x_{1t} + \hat{e}\Delta x_{2t} + \text{error},$$

are respectively $N(0, 1)$ and $\chi^2(2)$ asymptotically even when $\sigma_{13} \neq 0$ or $\sigma_{23} \neq 0$.

Throughout the above the covariance matrix of $(\varepsilon_{1t}, \varepsilon_{2t})$ is non-singular so that x_1 and x_2 are not co-integrated.

13.2.3 West model

Yet another variant of models is

$$\begin{bmatrix} x_t \\ \Delta y_t \end{bmatrix} = \begin{bmatrix} \mu_1 \\ \mu_2 \end{bmatrix} + \begin{bmatrix} \varepsilon_{1t} \\ \varepsilon_{2t} \end{bmatrix}$$

$$z_t = b_1 x_t + b_2 y_t + \varepsilon_{3t}, \tag{13.43}$$

where $\boldsymbol{\varepsilon}_t \equiv (\varepsilon_{1t}, \varepsilon_{2t}, \varepsilon_{3t})'$, $\{\boldsymbol{\varepsilon}_t\}$ is i.i.d. with $E(\boldsymbol{\varepsilon}_t) = 0$, and $E(\boldsymbol{\varepsilon}_t\boldsymbol{\varepsilon}_t') \equiv \boldsymbol{\Sigma}$ is positive definite. The essential assumptions here are $\mu_2 \neq 0$ and $\sigma_{13} = 0$. However, μ_1 may possibly be zero, and σ_{23} may possibly be non-zero. (The present model is not subsumed in Section 13.2.2 because every variable is $I(1)$ in that section.) Note that x_t is $I(0)$, while y_t is $I(1)$ with a deterministic linear trend. Let $\boldsymbol{b}' = (b_1, b_2)$, and $\hat{\boldsymbol{b}}$ be the OLS of $\boldsymbol{b}$ in (13.43). Let $\boldsymbol{D}_T = \text{diag}[T^{1/2}, T^{3/2}]$, and $\boldsymbol{X}$ be the data matrix of (x_t, y_t). Then

$$\text{plim}\boldsymbol{D}_T^{-1}\boldsymbol{X}'\boldsymbol{X}\boldsymbol{D}_T^{-1} = \begin{bmatrix} \mu_1^2 + \sigma_{11}, & \frac{1}{2}\mu_1\mu_2 \\ & \frac{1}{3}\mu_2^2 \end{bmatrix} \equiv \boldsymbol{A}.$$

If $\mu_1 = 0$, $\boldsymbol{A}$ is diagonal. Neither σ_{12} nor σ_{22} appears in $\boldsymbol{A}$. Since $\mu_2 \neq 0$, the impact of the deterministic trend in y_t dominates that of ε_{1t} and ε_{2t} in regard to $T^{-2}\sum x_t y_t$ and $T^{-3}\sum y_t^2$. Moreover,

$$\begin{bmatrix} T^{-1/2}\sum x_t\varepsilon_{3t} \\ T^{-3/2}\sum y_t\varepsilon_{3t} \end{bmatrix} \xrightarrow{D} N(0, \sigma_{33}\boldsymbol{A}),$$

by virtue of $\mu_2 \neq 0$ and $\sigma_{13} = 0$. $\boldsymbol{D}_T(\hat{\boldsymbol{b}} - \boldsymbol{b})$ converges to a (simple) Gaussian, $N(0, \sigma_{33}\boldsymbol{A}^{-1})$. Standard testing procedures are applicable.

In my opinion we had better add Δy_t in the regressor set of the OLS because the deterministic trend does not completely dominate the stochastic trend in finite samples.

West (1988) extends the above analysis to the case where $\{\boldsymbol{\varepsilon}_t\}$ is generalized to a stationary process $\{\boldsymbol{u}_t\}$. It is necessary to assume that u_{3t}, the disturbance in (13.43), be uncorrelated with $u_{1t} \equiv x_t - \mu_1$ not only contemporaneously but also in all lags and forwards. However, Δy_t may be correlated with u_{3t}. If $\mu_2 \neq 0, \boldsymbol{D}_T(\hat{\boldsymbol{b}} - \boldsymbol{b})$ is asymptotically (simple) Gaussian. The regressor x_t can be easily extended to a vector. The extension of y_t to a vector necessitates consideration in Section 13.2.2, which deprives the model of the essence of West (1988). Stock and West (1988) apply the method to the consumption function as formulated in Hall (1978). See also Banerjee *et al.* (1993: 178).

I shall not give details on quadratic and cubic trends. A number of expressions in Hatanaka and Koto (1994) are useful to adapt the above reasoning to polynomial trends. I point out some basic points on the quadratic trend. Earlier it was found that the OLS was $\sqrt{T}$-consistent in the spurious regression with a linear trend. With a quadratic trend the OLS is $T^{3/2}$-consistent. Nevertheless the t-statistic to test $b = 0$ diverges when b is indeed zero in the DGP. As for the co-integrated regression the expression (13.29) should be altered to $T^{5/2}(\hat{b} - b)$ being asymptotically normal regardless of whether the error is correlated or uncorrelated with the regressor. In the case of two regressors, the regressors are transformed into vectors of two variables, one having t^2 and another having t but not t^2. The OLS is asymptotically Gaussian instead of mixed Gaussian. The t-statistic to test for $d_1 b_1 + d_2 b_2 = d_3$ converges to $N(0, 1)$, and twice the F-statistic to test for $(b_1, b_2) = (b_1^0, b_2^0)$ converges to $\chi^2(2)$ under the null hypothesis.

The conclusion of the present section is as follows. In so far as the co-integrated regression models are concerned, the applicability of conventional asymptotic inference procedures based on t- and F-statistics (using $N(0, 1)$ and χ^2) is maintained throughout all different modes of deterministic trends. The reasons vary among different modes. In some cases the estimators are mixed Gaussian, and in others the estimators are simple Gaussian. The t- and F-statistics are *robust to both the integration orders and the modes of deterministic trends* in so far as $\{x_t\}$ and $\{y_t\}$ are co-integrated and $\{x_t\}$ is strictly exogenous. Moreover, the device in Section 13.1.3 extends the applicability of t- and F-statistics to the case where $\{x_t\}$ is not strictly exogenous, but the device is not robust to integration orders.

13.3 Serially Correlated Case

We now abandon the assumption that $\Delta \boldsymbol{x}_t$ is i.i.d. Suppose that the k-elements stochastic process $\{\boldsymbol{u}_t\}$ is stationary with $E(\boldsymbol{u}_t) = \mathbf{0}$ and $E(\boldsymbol{u}_t \boldsymbol{u}'_{t+j}) \equiv \boldsymbol{\Gamma}_j$, $j = \ldots, -1, 0, 1, \ldots$. Note that $\boldsymbol{\Gamma}_{-j} = \boldsymbol{\Gamma}'_j$. Let $\boldsymbol{\Gamma} \equiv \sum_{j=-\infty}^{\infty} \boldsymbol{\Gamma}_j$, which is the long-run covariance matrix of $\Delta \boldsymbol{x} = \boldsymbol{u}$. Write $\boldsymbol{v}_t \equiv \sum_{s=1}^{t} \boldsymbol{u}_s$. Then instead of (13.2) we have

$$T^{-3/2} \sum_{t=1}^{T} \boldsymbol{v}_t \xrightarrow{D} \int_0^1 \boldsymbol{w}(r, \boldsymbol{\Gamma}) dr, \tag{13.44}$$

and instead of (13.3)

$$T^{-2} \sum_{t=1}^{T} \boldsymbol{v}_t \boldsymbol{v}'_t \xrightarrow{D} \int_0^1 \boldsymbol{w}(r, \boldsymbol{\Gamma}) \boldsymbol{w}(r, \boldsymbol{\Gamma})' dr. \tag{13.45}$$

(13.4) has to be replaced by the following more complicated formula,

$$T^{-1} \sum_{t=1}^{T} \boldsymbol{v}_{t-1} \boldsymbol{u}'_t \xrightarrow{D} \int_0^1 \boldsymbol{w}(r, \boldsymbol{\Gamma}) d\boldsymbol{w}(r, \boldsymbol{\Gamma})' + \boldsymbol{\Lambda},\ \boldsymbol{\Lambda} = \sum_{j=1}^{\infty} \boldsymbol{\Gamma}_j. \tag{13.46}$$

Compare (13.46) with (6.14) of Part I. The results in (13.44) and (13.46) are found in Phillips and Durlauf (1986), Park and Phillips (1988), and Phillips (1988*a*). Keep in mind that the covariance matrix of Wiener process is the long-run covariance matrix in all the above expressions.

Let $\{(u_{1t}, u_{2t})\}$ be a bivariate stationary process with mean zero and auto-covariance matrix sequence $\{\boldsymbol{\Gamma}_j\}$, and $v_{it} \equiv \sum_{s=1}^{t} u_{is}$, $i = 1, 2$, and $x_t \equiv v_{1t}$. Let $(w_1(r), w_2(r))'$ be a bivariate Wiener process with covariance matrix, $\boldsymbol{\Gamma} \equiv \sum_{-\infty}^{\infty} \boldsymbol{\Gamma}_j$. Also write $\boldsymbol{\Lambda} = \sum_{1}^{\infty} \boldsymbol{\Gamma}_j$. The $(i. j)$ element of 2×2 matrices $\boldsymbol{\Gamma}$, $\boldsymbol{\Gamma}_h$, and $\boldsymbol{\Lambda}$ are denoted by γ_{ij}, $\gamma_{ij}^{(h)}$, and λ_{ij} respectively. In the co-integrated regression,

$$y_t = bx_t + u_{2t}, \tag{13.47}$$

we have

$$\begin{aligned} T(\hat{b} - b) &= \left(T^{-1} \sum u_{1t}u_{2t} + T^{-1} \sum v_{1t-1}u_{2t}\right) \left(T^{-2} \sum v_{1t}^2\right)^{-1} \\ &\xrightarrow{D} \left(\gamma_{12}^{(0)} + \lambda_{12} + \int w_1(r)dw_2(r)\right) \left(\int w_1(r)^2 dr\right)^{-1}. \end{aligned} \tag{13.48}$$

In the spurious regression, $y_t = bx_t + v_{2t}$ we have

$$\begin{aligned} (\hat{b} - b) &= T^{-2} \sum v_{1t}v_{2t} \left(T^{-2} \sum v_{1t}^2\right)^{-1} \\ &\xrightarrow{D} \int w_1(r)w_2(r)dr \left(\int w_1(r)^2 dr\right)^{-1}. \end{aligned}$$

The OLS in the spurious regression does not converge in probability to any constant, while the OLS in the co-integrated regression is T-consistent.

13.3.1 Strict exogeneity

Suppose that u_{1t} and u_{2t} are uncorrelated not only contemporaneously but also in all lags and forwards. Then x_t in (13.47) is strictly exogenous. *First* $\gamma_{12}^{(0)} = \lambda_{12} = 0$, and (13.48) is simplified to

$$T(\hat{b} - b) \xrightarrow{D} \int w_1(r)dw_2(r) \left(\int w_1(r)^2 dr\right)^{-1}. \tag{13.49}$$

Second, since $\boldsymbol{\Gamma}$ is diagonal, $w_1(r)$ and $w_2(r)$ are independent, and the right-hand side of (13.49) is $N(0, \gamma_{22}g)$ conditionally upon $g \equiv \left(\int w_1(r)^2 dr\right)^{-1}$. With a consistent estimator of γ_{22} to be denoted by $\hat{\gamma}_{22}$

$$\hat{t} = (\hat{\gamma}_{22})^{-1/2}(\hat{b} - b) \left(\sum x_t^2\right)^{1/2} \tag{13.49'}$$

is asymptotically distributed in $N(0, 1)$, which is due to Krämer (1986) and Park and Phillips (1988).

What has necessitated estimation of long-run variance γ_{22} is that $\{u_{2t}\}$ is not i.i.d. This kind of problem has been dealt with in the traditional econometrics by the Cochrane–Orcutt transformation, assuming that $\{u_{2t}\}$ is an AR (p),

$$a(L)u_{2t} = \varepsilon_{2t} \tag{13.50}$$

$$a(L) \equiv 1 - a_1 L - \ldots - a_p L^P,$$

where $\{\varepsilon_{2t}\}$ is i.i.d. with $E(\varepsilon_{2t}) = 0$ and $E(\varepsilon_{2t}^2) = \sigma_{22}$. In fact, once this assumption is made, two methods are available to get statistics that are asymptotically $N(0, 1)$. One does not use the Cochrane–Orcutt transformation, but directly estimates γ_{22}. The other uses the transformation, but does not estimate γ_{22}.

Both methods begin with the OLS with y_t as the dependent variable and x_t as the independent variable. Estimates of $(a_1, \ldots, a_p)$ are obtained by fitting (13.50) to residuals $\{\hat{u}_{2t}\}$. Let $\hat{a}(L) \equiv 1 - \hat{a}_1 L - \ldots - \hat{a}_p L^p$. In the first of the two methods, we note that $\gamma_{22} = a(1)^{-2}\sigma_{22}$. The term $a(1)$ is estimated by $\hat{a}(1)$, and σ_{22} by the residuals in fitting (13.50) to $\{\hat{u}_{2t}\}$. The $\hat{\gamma}_{22}$ thus obtained is then substituted in (13.49′).

The second of the two methods is a two-step method. The first stage is again the OLS with y_t as the dependent variable and x_t as the independent variable: $\hat{a}(L)$ is obtained. The second stage is based on $y_t^* \equiv a(L)y_t$, and $x_t^* \equiv a(L)x_t$. From (13.47) and (13.50) it follows that

$$y_t^* = bx_t^* + \varepsilon_{2t}. \tag{13.51}$$

Write $\hat{y}_t^* \equiv \hat{a}(L)y_t$, and $\hat{x}_t^* \equiv \hat{a}(L)x_t$. In the second stage the dependent variable of OLS is $\hat{y}_t^*$ and the independent variable is $\hat{x}_t^*$. The $\hat{b}^*$ that results is our estimate of b.

Using (13.47) it is seen that

$$\hat{y}_t^* = b\hat{x}_t^* + \varepsilon_{2t} + (\hat{a}(L) - a(L))u_{2t}.$$

Therefore

$$T(\hat{b}^* - b) = T^{-2}\left(\sum \hat{x}_t^{*2}\right)^{-1}\left(T^{-1}\sum \hat{x}_t^*\varepsilon_{2t} + T^{-1}\sum \hat{x}_t^*(\hat{a}(L) - a(L))u_{2t}\right).$$

Note that $T^{-2}\sum \hat{x}_t^{*2} = T^{-2}\sum x_t^{*2} + o_p(1)$,

$$T^{-1}\sum \hat{x}_t^*\varepsilon_{2t} = T^{-1}\sum x_t^*\varepsilon_{2t} + o_p(1),$$

$$T^{-1}\sum \hat{x}_t^*(\hat{a}(L) - a(L))u_{2t} = o_p(1),$$

where the last equality is in part based on the strict exogeneity assumption. It is seen that

$$T(\hat{b}^* - b) \approx \left(T^{-2}\sum x_t^{*2}\right)^{-1}\left(T^{-1}\sum x_t^*\varepsilon_{2t}\right).$$

The long-run variance of x_t^* is $a(1)^2\gamma_{11}$. By the assumption in the present section, $\{x_t^*\}$ and $\{\varepsilon_{2t}\}$ are totally uncorrelated in all leads and lags. Let $(w_1^*(r), w_2^*(r))$ be the bivariate Wiener process with covariance matrix, $\mathrm{diag}[a(1)^2\gamma_{11}, \sigma_{22}]$. Then

$$T(\hat{b}^* - b) \xrightarrow{D} \left(\int w_1^*(r)^2 dr\right)^{-1} \int w_1^*(r) dw_2^*(r),$$

which is $N(0, \sigma_{22}\, g^*)$ conditionally upon $g^* \equiv \left(\int w_1^*(r)^2 dr\right)^{-1}$. The t-statistic on b in the second stage is

$$\hat{t} = s^{-1}(\hat{b}^* - b^0)\left(\sum \hat{x}_t^{*2}\right)^{1/2} = s^{-1}T(\hat{b}^* - b^0)\left(T^{-2}\sum \hat{x}_t^{*2}\right)^{1/2},$$

which converges to $N(0, 1)$ because $s^2 \xrightarrow{P} \sigma_{22}$.

That the single step OLS on (13.47), i.e. $T(\hat{b} - b)$ in (13.49), and the second step OLS on (13.51), i.e. $T(\hat{b}^* - b)$, are identically distributed asymptotically can be seen by comparing the expressions of two mixed Gaussian distributions. In fact this has been pointed out in Krämer (1986) and Phillips and Park (1988) in the context of comparison between GLS and OLS. Comparison in finite samples has not been made to the best of my knowledge. The first of the two methods proposed above bases its inference on $T(\hat{b} - b)$ as indicated in t-statistic (13.49′) in conjunction with an estimate of long-run variance, γ_{22}. On the other hand, the second method avoids direct-estimation of this long-run variance, which may be difficult with $T = 100$.

Extension to the case where $\{x_t\}$ is a vector process is straightforward in so far as $\{\boldsymbol{x}_t\}$ is not co-integrated. The extension to the case where $\{\boldsymbol{y}_t\}$ is a vector process will be explained at the end of the chapter.

13.3.2 Correlated error

Suppose that $\{(u_{1t}, u_{2t})\}$ is a bivariate stationary process with zero mean vector, that $x_t = \sum_{s=1}^{t} u_{1s} = v_{1t}$, and that y_t is generated by (13.47), in which u_{2t} and x_t are correlated. Earlier in the case where $\{(u_{1t}, u_{2t})\}$ is i.i.d. introduction of Δx_t in the regression (see (13.19)) enabled us to reach a mixed Gaussian estimator in spite of the correlated error. In the present case the process $\{u_{2t}\}$ can be projected on to $\{u_{1t}\}$ to get

$$u_{2t} = \sum_{j=-\infty}^{\infty} c_j u_{1t+j} + u_{2.1t} \tag{13.52}$$

where $\{u_{2.1t}\}$ is stationary with zero mean but not necessarily i.i.d., and $\{u_{2.1t}\}$ and $\{u_{1t}\}$ are uncorrelated not only contemporaneously but also in all lags and leads. In practice the leads and lags may be truncated while retaining the above condition approximately, so that

$$u_{2t} = \sum_{-q1}^{q2} c_j u_{1t+j} + u_{2.1t}. \tag{13.52′}$$

Substitution of (13.52′) into our data-generating process (13.47) yields

$$y_t = bx_t + \sum_{-q1}^{q2} c_j u_{1t+j} + u_{2.1t}.$$

Therefore we should run the OLS

$$y_t = \hat{b}x_t + \sum_{-q1}^{q2} \hat{c}_j \Delta x_{t+j} + \text{error}. \tag{13.53}$$

The relevant Wiener process is $(w_1(r), w_{2.1}(r))$ such that its covariance matrix is diag$[\gamma_{11}, \gamma_{22.1}]$, where γ_{11} is the long-run variance of $\Delta x_t = u_{1t}$, $\gamma_{22.1}$ is the long-run variance of $u_{2.1t}$, and the off-diagonal elements are zero because $\{u_{1t}\}$ and $\{u_{2.1t}\}$ are totally uncorrelated because of (13.52) or (13.52′). It follows that $T(\hat{b} - b)$ is asymptotically $N(0, \gamma_{22.1}g)$ conditionally upon $g = \left(\int w_1(r)^2 dr\right)^{-1}$. We may run here again two steps of OLS using the Cochrane–Orcutt transformation. The second step OLS is run along

$$\hat{a}(L)y_t = b\hat{a}(L)x_t + \sum_{-q1}^{q2} c_j \hat{a}(L)\Delta x_{t+j} + \text{error}.$$

The t-statistic on b is asymptotically $N(0, 1)$.

This is a revolution in econometric theory. Here regressor x_t and disturbance u_{2t} may be correlated in (13.47), but it does not pose any obstacle to estimation of b. This is made possible by x_t being $I(1)$. This result is due to Phillips (1991*a*), Phillips and Loretan (1991), Saikkonen (1991), and Stock and Watson (1993).

The x_t can be extended to a vector process in so far as $\boldsymbol{x}_t$ is not co-integrated within itself. The extension to the case where $\{\boldsymbol{y}_t\}$ is a vector process is explained at the end of the chapter.

Introduction of lagged and forwarded Δx_t frees us from worrying about the correlated regressors in so far as the disturbance is believed to be stationary.

If $\{u_{2t}\}$ does not cause $\{u_{1t}\}$ in Granger's sense, Theorem 11.2 in Section 11.3 suggests

$$u_{2t} = c_0 u_{1t} + c_1 u_{1t-1} + \ldots + u_{2.1t}, \tag{13.54}$$

where $\{u_{2.1t}\}$ satisfies all the conditions that are placed on $\{u_{2.1t}\}$ in (13.52). In other words the leads of Δx_t in (13.53) are not necessary. One would like to discriminate u_2 causing and not causing $u_1 (= \Delta x)$ on the basis of observations of (x_t, y_t). It is appropriate in practice to perform the discrimination by testing for y failing to cause x, but the precise relation is as follows.

LEMMA 13.2. Suppose that $\{(u_{1t}, u_{2t})\}$ is a stationary process starting at $t = -\infty$, and construct $\{(x_t, y_t)\}$ for $t \geq 1$ by $x_t = \sum_{s=1}^{t} u_{1s}$ and $y_{2t} = bx_t + u_{2t}$. (See Sections 2.2 and 11.3 for starting at $t = 1$ in construction of $I(1)$ variables.) Then

$$E(u_{1t}|u_{1t-1}, u_{2t-1}, \ldots, u_{11}, u_{21}) = E(u_{1t}|u_{1t-1}, \ldots, u_{11}) \tag{13.55}$$

is equivalent to

$$E(x_t|x_{t-1}, y_{t-1}, \ldots, x_1, y_1) = E(x_t|x_{t-1}, \ldots, x_1). \tag{13.56}$$

Remark 1. (13.56) is the definition of y failing to cause x, but (13.55) does not necessarily mean u_2 failing to cause u_1. The definition of u_2 failing to cause u_1 is

$$E(u_{1t}|u_{1t-1}, u_{2t-1}, \ldots, u_{11}, u_{21}, u_{10}, u_{20}, \ldots)$$
$$= E(u_{1t}|u_{1t-1}, \ldots, u_{11}, u_{10}, \ldots). \tag{13.57}$$

Proof of Lemma 13.2. The proof uses nothing more than the existence of relevant conditional expectations. $(x_{t-1}, y_{t-1}, \ldots, x_1, y_1)$ and $(u_{1t-1}, u_{2t-1}, \ldots, u_{11}, u_{21})$ are related by a non-singular transformation. (In fact the Jacobian is a constant, unity.) The probability density of u_{1t} conditional upon $(x_{t-1}, y_{t-1}, \ldots, x_1, y_1)$ is identical to that of u_{1t} conditional upon $(u_{1t-1}, u_{2t-1}, \ldots, u_{11}, u_{21})$, and

$$E(u_{1t}|x_{t-1}, y_{t-1}, \ldots, x_1, y_1) = E(u_{1t}|u_{1t-1}, u_{2t-1}, \ldots, u_{11}, u_{21}).$$

Likewise we get

$$E(u_{1t}|x_{t-1}, \ldots, x_1) = E(u_{1t}|u_{1t-1}, \ldots, u_{11}).$$

Therefore $E(x_t|x_{t-1}, y_{t-1}, \ldots, x_1, y_1)$

$$= x_{t-1} + E(u_{1t}|u_{1t-1}, u_{2t-1}, \ldots, u_{11}, u_{21})$$

and $E(x_t|x_{t-1}, \ldots, x_1) = x_{t-1} + E(u_{1t}|u_{1t-1}, \ldots, u_{11})$.

(13.55) and (13.56) are equivalent. QED

Remark 2. If $\{(u_{1t}, u_{2t})\}$ is a stationary, linear, indeterministic process,

$$|E(u_{1t}|u_{1t-1}, u_{2t-1}, \ldots, u_{11}, u_{21}) - E(u_{1t}|u_{1t-1}, u_{2t-1}, \ldots,$$
$$u_{11}, u_{21}, u_{10}, u_{20}, \ldots)|$$

becomes negligible as $t \to \infty$, and we have analogous relations on other conditional expectations. The difference between (13.55) and (13.57) becomes negligible. It thus holds true *asymptotically that u_2 fails to cause u_1 if and only if y fails to cause x.*

The Granger non-causality test in a possibly co-integrated VAR will be explained in Section 15.4.3.

There exist a number of methods to deal with the present case of correlated regression. The fully modified least squares due to Phillips and Hansen (1990) is given in Appendix 6. Phillips and Loretan (1991) consider methods that are analogous to the above (13.53) but include lags of $(y_t - bx_t)$ or Δy_t instead of leads of Δx_t. Banerjee *et al.* (1993: 242–52) summarize them with emphasis on the weak exogeneity, and subject them to experimental investigations.

13.3.3 Deterministic trend

It should be obvious how the reasoning in Section 13.2 is to be modified when $\{\boldsymbol{\varepsilon}_t\}$ there is replaced by $\{\boldsymbol{u}_t\}$. Some summary statements are found at the end of the present chapter.

13.4 Miscellaneous Remarks including Direction of Co-integration

13.4.1 Simulations and applications

A comprehensive simulation study of finite sample distributions of the OLS and the estimator $\hat{b}$ in (13.53) is found in Stock and Watson (1993) for the cases where $\{x_t\}$ is strictly exogenous and also where $\{x_t\}$ and $\{u_t\}$ are correlated. The results for $T = 100$ are close to what one derives from the above asymptotic analyses. The OLS has no bias in strict exogeneity, but has a substantial bias in correlated regression. The estimator $\hat{b}$ in (13.53) has no bias in strict exogeneity, and its bias in correlated regression is much less than that of the OLS. Increasing the orders of leads and lags of Δx_t in (13.53) reduces the bias, but increases the dispersion. The selection of these orders does pose a problem. It is worth noting that in the theoretical distributed lag relation (13.54) the lag order of u_1 terminates at q if $\{(u_{1t}, u_{2t}\}$ is a VMA with order q, but the order extends to infinity if $\{(u_{1t}, u_{2t}\}$ is a VAR.

An application of $\hat{b}$ in (13.53) is made on the demand for money in Stock and Watson (1993). They analyse the historical data, seeking for a stable long-run demand function.

The following application has been provided by Mototsugu Shintani and Yasuji Koto. It is concerned with a relation between the log of real income per capita, x, and the log of real consumption per capita, y, in the seasonally adjusted quarterly US data over the period, 1947 I–1993 I. $T = 185$. The time-series charts are presented in Figure 13.1. It is generally thought that income and consumption are mutually interdependent so that in

$$y_t = a + bx_t + u_t$$

x_t and u_t may well be correlated. In fact $\{x_t\}$ has a deterministic trend, and as it dominates the stochastic trend in $\{x_t\}$ asymptotically, the t-statistic on b in the

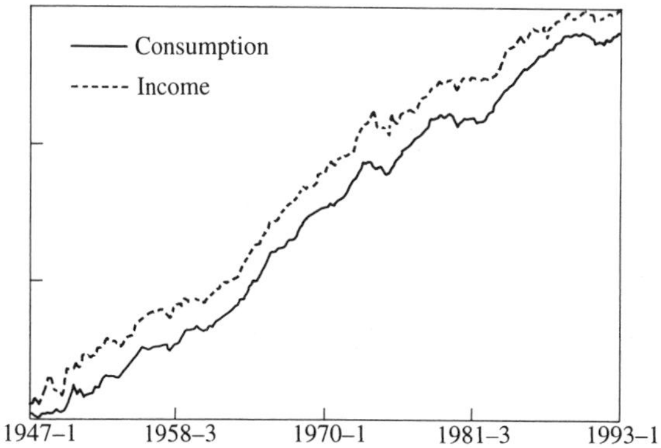

FIG. 13.1 *Consumption and income per capita*

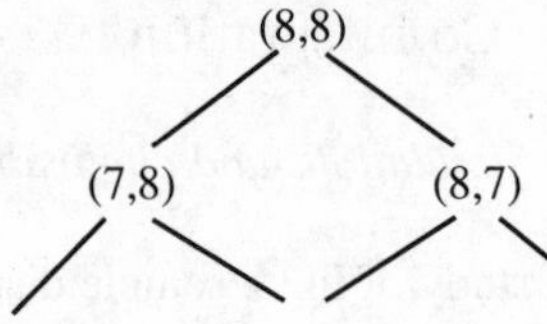

FIG. 13.2 *A tree of* (q_1, q_2)

OLS as simple as

$$y_t = \hat{a} + \hat{b}x_t + \text{error}$$

is asymptotically $N(0, 1)$. However, in finite samples the dominance is not complete, and we are thus led to the OLS,

$$y_t = \hat{a} + \hat{b}x_t + \sum\nolimits_{-q1}^{q2} \hat{c}_j \Delta x_{t+j} + \text{error}. \tag{13.58}$$

We are concerned with the co-integration in which the deterministic and stochastic trends are eliminated at once so that the time variable is not introduced in (13.58). It is not necessary to specify the model of deterministic trend.

The null hypothesis that y does not cause x in Granger's sense has been tested with a VAR containing a constant term, and the hypothesis has been rejected even at 1% significance level.[7] This means that leads of Δx are needed in (13.58). The general-to-specific principle in Mizon (1977) and Hendry (1979) has been used to select q_1 and q_2. Assuming that neither can exceed 8, the tree diagram such as Figure 13.2 is formed. Starting from the top, we step down when and only when the highest-order coefficient c_{-q1} or c_{q2} is not significant at 1% significance level. (If there is a serial correlation in residuals the significance should be judged in the equation with Cochrane–Orcutt transformed variables.) We have settled at $(q_1, q_2) = (5, 5)$. With this choice of (q_1, q_2) (13.58) has been estimated with Cochrane–Orcutt transformation. The t-statistic to test $b = 1$ is -3.72. The long-run elasticity of consumption to income is significantly less than unity.

13.4.2 *Co-integration space implied by a co-integrated regression*

In comparing (13.5) and (13.6) I have emphasized the importance of discriminating the spurious and the co-integrated regressions. Nevertheless my writing in the rest of Section 13.1 simply assumed that x and y are co-integrated. Noting that the co-integration rank is 1 in the co-integrated regression (with a scalar y) and zero in the spurious regression, I might rephrase the above assumption to

[7] Incidentally it has also been found that income does not cause consumption in Granger's sense, which reconfirms a point that Hall (1978) discovered in connection with the rational expectations hypothesis.

say that the co-integration rank has simply been assumed rather than estimated by the data.

In fact, what has been assumed is not just the co-integration rank. The following point is due to Johansen (1992*a*). Consider a regression equation in which both the dependent and independent variables are 2-elements vectors,

$$y_{1t} = c_{11}x_{1t} + c_{12}x_{2t} + u_{1t},$$
$$y_{2t} = c_{21}x_{1t} + c_{22}x_{2t} + u_{2t}, \tag{13.59}$$

where $\boldsymbol{u}'_t = (u_{1t}, u_{2t})$ is a stationary process with zero mean. One would naturally interpret (13.59) to mean that the co-integration rank is 2 in $\{(x_{1t}, x_{2t}, y_{1t}, y_{2t})\}$, and that, writing

$$\boldsymbol{C} = \begin{bmatrix} c_{11} & c_{12} \\ c_{21} & c_{22} \end{bmatrix},$$

$[-C, I_2]$ is a representation of $\boldsymbol{B}'$ in the error-correction representation, (12.18). The point to be emphasized is that the co-integration space is *not* just any one of the two-dimensional vector subspaces in the four-dimensional whole space. Denoting by $\boldsymbol{B}'_2$ the 2×2 submatrix of $\boldsymbol{B}'$ that consists of its third and fourth columns, left multiplications by any 2×2 non-singular matrices $\boldsymbol{F}$ never turns $\boldsymbol{B}'_2$ to a singular matrix. Therefore, a vector such as $(a, b, 0, 0)$ cannot be a co-integrating vector. Neither x_{1t} nor x_{2t} is $I(0)$, and no linear combinations of x_{1t} and x_{2t} are $I(0)$.

Let us consider this point in the general framework of Section 12.1. I reproduce the main points of the framework. $\{\Delta \boldsymbol{x}_t\}$ is a k-element vector linear process, $\Delta \boldsymbol{x}_t = \boldsymbol{C}(L)\boldsymbol{\varepsilon}_t$ ($\boldsymbol{\mu}$ is suppressed to zero). The co-integration rank is r so that $\rho(\boldsymbol{C}(1)) = k - r$. An $r \times k$ matrix $\boldsymbol{B}'$ is a co-integration matrix so that $\boldsymbol{B}'\boldsymbol{C}(1) = \boldsymbol{0}$. Since $\rho(\boldsymbol{B}') = r$, there must be at least one $r \times r$ submatrix of $\boldsymbol{B}'$ that is non-singular. Knowing which rows and columns of $\boldsymbol{B}'$ are included in such a non-singular submatrix will be called knowing the location of a non-singular submatrix. Then the following proposition characterizes the co-integrated regression model.

LEMMA 13.3. Knowing the co-integration rank r and location of a non-singular $r \times r$ submatrix of $\boldsymbol{B}'$ in Section 12.1 induces a co-integrated regression model with $(k - r)$ non-cointegrated regressors and r regressands.

Proof. For convenience of exposition let the non-singular submatrix be in the extreme right position of $\boldsymbol{B}'$. Non-singularity of this submatrix is invariant through left multiplications of $\boldsymbol{B}'$ by any non-singular matrices. It may then be convenient to normalize this submatrix to the unit matrix. $\boldsymbol{B}'$ is now $(-\boldsymbol{P}, \boldsymbol{I}_r)$, and $(-\boldsymbol{P}, \boldsymbol{I}_r)\boldsymbol{C}(1) = \boldsymbol{0}$. Let $\{\boldsymbol{x}_t\}$ be partitioned as $\{(\boldsymbol{x}'_{1t}, \boldsymbol{x}'_{2t})'\}$ with $(k - r)$ and r elements respectively for $\boldsymbol{x}_{1t}$ and $\boldsymbol{x}_{2t}$. Since

$$\begin{bmatrix} \boldsymbol{I}_{k-r} & \boldsymbol{0} \\ -\boldsymbol{P} & \boldsymbol{I}_r \end{bmatrix}$$

is non-singular, the rank of

$$\begin{bmatrix} \boldsymbol{I}_{k-r} & \boldsymbol{0} \\ -\boldsymbol{P} & \boldsymbol{I}_r \end{bmatrix} \boldsymbol{C}(1) = \begin{bmatrix} (\boldsymbol{I}_{k-r}, \boldsymbol{0})\boldsymbol{C}(1) \\ \boldsymbol{0} \end{bmatrix}$$

must be equal to $\rho(\boldsymbol{C}(1)) = k - r$, and $(\boldsymbol{I}_{k-r}, \boldsymbol{0})\boldsymbol{C}(1)$ has its full row rank. From the reasoning about (12.5) it is seen that $\{\boldsymbol{x}_{1t}\}$ is not co-integrated, and that $\{(-\boldsymbol{P}, \boldsymbol{I}_r)\boldsymbol{x}_t\}$ is stationary.

Remark 1. Location of a non-singular submatrix is an identified property of the co-integration space, because it is invariant through left multiplications of $\boldsymbol{B}'$ by any non-singular matrices.

Remark 2. It is important to bear in mind that the normalization used above is acceptable only when the extreme right $r \times r$ submatrix is non-singular. In general, a normalization of $\boldsymbol{B}'$ can be performed by imposing $\boldsymbol{B}'\boldsymbol{F} = \boldsymbol{I}_r$, where $\boldsymbol{F}$ is a known $k \times r$ matrix with rank r, and $\boldsymbol{B}'\boldsymbol{F} = \boldsymbol{I}_r$ is not generally associated with locations of non-singular submatrices. It is when $\boldsymbol{F}'$ takes special forms such as $(\boldsymbol{0}, \boldsymbol{I}_r)$ that $\boldsymbol{B}'\boldsymbol{F} = \boldsymbol{I}_r$ is related to location of a non-singular submatrix. It is the location of non-singular submatrices rather than normalizations that is basic in the co-integrated regression.[8]

Remark 3. The above reasoning justifies the expression that the co-integration is directed from $\boldsymbol{x}_1$ to $\boldsymbol{x}_2$. It implies some *asymmetry* between regressors and regressands, which resembles that between exogenous and endogenous variables in the analysis of economic theories dealing with non-stochastic variables. There the exogenous and endogenous variables have different roles as one is not concerned with relationships among exogenous variables but with relationships between endogenous and exogenous variables. (Incidentally the standard econometric definitions of exogenous and endogenous variables are not thought of in such analyses.) In empirical investigations of economic theories the location of a non-singular submatrix may be suggested by the economic theories.

Remark 4. It is possible for example that the extreme left and the extreme right submatrices are both non-singular. There can be a number of different co-integrated regressions with different sets of regressors, all of which are derived from the same model representation in Chapter 12.

Remark 5. As will be explained in Chapter 15 any normalization $\boldsymbol{B}'\boldsymbol{F} = \boldsymbol{I}_r$ identifies $\boldsymbol{B}'$. Thus $\boldsymbol{P}$ in $(-\boldsymbol{P}, \boldsymbol{I}_r)$ is identified.

Remark 6. $\{\boldsymbol{x}_{1t}\}$ must be non-co-integrated $I(1)$, but some or all elements of $\{\boldsymbol{x}_{2t}\}$ may well be $I(0)$. And, if the ith element of $\{\boldsymbol{x}_{2t}\}$ is $I(0)$, the ith row of $\boldsymbol{P}$ is a zero vector. The case has been excluded in Sections 13.1–3, as indicated by the condition, $b \neq 0$, in (13.5) for practical considerations on the balanced regression, but the condition is not really required for theoretical considerations.

[8] Phillips (1991*a*) develops his analysis of the co-integrated regression on the basis of a triangular representation of a co-integration matrix, and Hamilton (1994: 576–7) shows how this representation can be derived from the general representation of possibly co-integrated processes. The point emphasized here is that this derivation cannot be performed unless some property, indeed location of a non-singular $r \times r$ submatrix, is known.

The mathematical reasoning in (13.9)–(13.14) holds even when $b^0 = 0$ so that y_t is $I(0)$.

A reference related to the above remarks is Phillips (1994).

13.4.3 Relation to the co-integrated VAR analysis

The method developed in Johansen (1988, 1991*a*) on the co-integrated VAR estimates the co-integration rank, and tests the hypotheses about the structure of co-integration space. In particular, the spurious regression (13.6) and the co-integrated regression (13.5) can be discriminated as follows. Initially confirm that both x_t and y_t are $I(1)$ by the univariate analysis given in Part I. The confirmation rules out that $\{(x_t, y_t)\}$ has co-integration rank, r, equal to 2. Then test the hypothesis, $r = 0$. If it is rejected, accept the co-integrated regression. If it is not rejected, accept the spurious regression.

More generally, consider a $(k+1)$ elements process, $\{(\boldsymbol{x}'_t, y_t)\}$, where $\boldsymbol{x}_t$ has k elements, y_t is a scalar, and $\boldsymbol{x}'_t$ and y_t are each $I(1)$. It is assumed that $(\boldsymbol{x}'_t, y_t)$ contains all the relevant variables. A method such as (13.53) presupposes that $\{\boldsymbol{x}_t\}$ is not co-integrated and also that the co-integration is from $\boldsymbol{x}_t$ to y_t, i.e. the last element of the co-integrating vector is non-zero. It will be explained in a general framework in Section 15.2.1 that these conditions ($r = 1$ and the direction of co-integration) enable us to identify the normalized co-integrating vector, $(b_1, \ldots, b_k, 1)$. The conditions can be tested as follows. Initially test the hypothesis, $r = 0$, in $\{(\boldsymbol{x}'_t, y_t)\}$. If it is rejected, test the hypothesis, $r \leq 1$, against $r \leq 2$. If it is not rejected, judge that $r = 1$, and proceed to testing the hypothesis that the last element of the co-integrating vector is zero. See Section 15.2.2(5) and set $c' = (0, \ldots, 0, 1)$. The conditions required for (13.53) are accepted if the hypothesis is rejected. If $r = 0$ is not rejected, or if $r \leq 1$ is rejected, or if the last element of the vector being zero is not rejected, the required conditions are judged to fail.

When the above scalar y is extended to a vector with r elements, the co-integrating regression with y as regressands requires that the last $r \times r$ submatrix of $\boldsymbol{B}'$ for $\{(\boldsymbol{x}'_t, \boldsymbol{y}'_t)\}$ be non-singular. I do not find literature indicating a test useful to discriminate singularity and non-singularity of this submatrix.

It seems that all the materials presented above in the present chapter are subsumed into the method to be presented in Chapter 15. The reason why they have nevertheless been treated independently in the present chapter is that the method in Chapter 15 requires data covering a considerably longer period than available for macroeconomic studies to produce a reasonably accurate estimate of the co-integration rank.

To those readers who are engaged in empirical studies of economic theories my advice is to apply first the method in Chapter 15. If the results definitively deny the economic theories, accept the results. Otherwise assume the co-integration rank and the direction of co-integration as specified by the economic theories, and proceed to hypothesis testing along the co-integrated regression analysis given in the present chapter. Transition from the method in Chapter 15 to the regression method has been suggested in Johansen (1992*c*), and described in Section 15.4.1.

13.4.4 Long-run relation in the OLS in levels

I have so far explained the impact of co-integration upon the regression analysis. The co-integration relation is a relation among long-run components in $I(1)$ variables. If one starts the analysis from the standpoint of regression analysis, it is important to keep in mind that *the OLS in levels capture the relation among long-run components*, discarding short-run components.

Ignoring initial terms, x_t is decomposed into the long-run and short-run components as described in Section 2.2 of Part I.

$$x_t = b(1)\sum_{s=1}^{t} \varepsilon_s + b^*(L)\varepsilon_t,$$

and y_t is generated by

$$y_t = \beta b(1)\sum_{s=1}^{t} \varepsilon_s + \gamma b^*(L)\varepsilon_t + u_t, \tag{13.60}$$

where $\{u_t\}$ is a disturbance that may possibly be correlated with $\{\varepsilon_t\}$. It is supposed that long-run components of x and y are related as indicated by the first term on the right-hand side of (13.60), while short-run components are related as indicated by the second term. In particular $\gamma = 0$ in the permanent-income hypothesis.

Write $v_t = \sum_{s=1}^{t} \varepsilon_s$. The OLS in levels of x and y is

$$\begin{aligned}\left(\sum x_t^2\right)^{-1}\left(\sum x_t y_t\right) &= \left(T^{-2}\sum (b(1)v_t + b^*(L)\varepsilon_t)^2\right)^{-1}\left(T^{-2}\sum (b(1)v_t \right.\\ &\quad \left. + b^*(L)\varepsilon_t)\left(\beta b(1)v_t + \gamma b^*(L)\varepsilon_t + u_t\right)\right)\\ &= \left(T^{-2}b(1)^2\sum v_t^2 + O_p(T^{-1})\right)^{-1}\left(T^{-2}\beta b(1)^2\sum v_t^2 + O_p(T^{-1})\right) \xrightarrow{P} \beta\end{aligned}$$

13.5 A Priori Specified Co-integrating Vector

Frequently economic theories specify particular co-integrating vectors. For example, when the theory of present-value model, (12.40), is applied to the term structure of interest rates, the theory specifies $\theta = 1$ so that the co-integration is $x_t = y_t$; i.e. the short-term rate equals the long-term rate. This has been investigated in Campbell and Shiller (1987). The purchasing power parity on foreign-exchange rates is another example, and it is investigated in Mark (1990) and Ardeni and Lubian (1991) with a priori specified co-integrating vector $(1, -1, 1)$ for (p, p^*, f), where p, p^*, and f are each logarithms of domestic price, foreign price, and the exchange rate of domestic currency per foreign currency.

In terms of general notations, if we want to investigate whether or not $\boldsymbol{b}'$ is a co-integrating vector in a vector process $\{\boldsymbol{x}_t\}$ that annihilates deterministic and stochastic trends at once, and if $\boldsymbol{b}'$ is a priori specified, we only have to see whether $\{\boldsymbol{b}'\boldsymbol{x}_t\}$ is stationary or not. The discrimination to be sought is between the stationarity and the non-stationarity. Though the difference stationarity is a kind of non-stationarity, it is important to keep in mind that the trend stationarity is also a kind of non-stationarity unless the deterministic component is a constant. If one is concerned with the co-integration that nullifies stochastic trends only, one should examine whether $\{\boldsymbol{b}'\boldsymbol{x}_t\}$ is DS or TS.

It is useful to proceed along the classification adopted in Chapter 8. The stationarity is M_1^0, where the superscript 0 indicates a constant trend and the subscript 1 indicates absence of unit roots. In investigating the co-integration that nullifies both the deterministic and stochastic trends we must discriminate M_1^0 from all the rest as a model of $\boldsymbol{b}'\boldsymbol{x}_t$. The comparisons, $M_0^0 \overset{E}{\leftrightarrow} M_1^0$ and $M_1^0 \overset{E}{\leftrightarrow} M_1^1$, have been described in Chapter 8. The past studies seem to investigate only $M_0^1 \overset{E}{\rightarrow} M_1^1$ and $M_0^0 \overset{E}{\rightarrow} M_1^0$ by the Dickey–Fuller test, but this is evidently unsatisfactory.

When the stationarity of $\boldsymbol{b}'\boldsymbol{x}_t$ is confirmed it is necessary to test for the hypothesis $E(\boldsymbol{b}'\boldsymbol{x}_t) = 0$ from the standpoint of the equilibrium analyses of economic theories (see Section 12.3.4). There is a standard method for it (see, for example, Fuller (1976: 230–6)).

Part I was devoted to the discrimination between DS and TS that is needed for the investigation of $\boldsymbol{b}'\boldsymbol{x}_t$ that nullifies the stochastic trends only.

We may wish to perform a joint test of co-integration for r_0 multiple relationships with a priori specified coefficients. Extension of the above method to a vector time series has not been investigated. Hall, Anderson, and Granger (1992) use the maximum-likelihood method given in Chapter 15. Initially a sequence of tests for $r = 0, \leq 1, \leq 2, \ldots$ is performed. If $r = 0, \leq 1, \ldots, \leq r_0 - 1$ are all rejected but $r \leq r_0$ is not, we proceed to testing for the null hypothesis that the r_0 dimensional co-integration space includes the a priori specified vectors by the method given in Section 15.2.2. It should be noted that the presence of r_0 co-integrating relations is evaluated in terms of its absence as the null hypothesis (see Section 15.1.3).

13.6 Shortcomings in Many Past Empirical Studies

I continue on the testing of co-integration but now with a co-integrating vector that is unknown. As I stated earlier this study should be made by testing for the rank of co-integration along the analysis in Johansen (1988, 1991*a*). However, many past studies, especially those prior to Johansen (1988, 1991*a*), use the augmented Dickey–Fuller test applied to the residuals in the OLS regression along a co-integrating relation. In other words, the null hypothesis is a single equation, $y_t = \boldsymbol{b}'\boldsymbol{x}_t + v_t$, where $\{v_t\}$ is $I(1)$ so that $(y_t, \boldsymbol{x}'_t)$ is not co-integrated. In the first step the $\boldsymbol{b}$ is estimated by OLS, and the residuals, $\hat{v}_t$, are derived. In the second step the augmented Dickey–Fuller test statistic is computed to see if $\{\hat{v}_t\}$ is judged $I(1)$. Phillips and Ouliaris (1990) derive the limiting distribution of the augmented Dickey–Fuller test statistic and tabulate it, assuming that $E(\Delta\boldsymbol{x}_t) = \mathbf{0}$ in the data-generating process, while admitting demeaning and detrending of data along (13.30). Hansen (1992*a*) shows that, if the demeaning and detrending are not performed, the two-step test is not invariant to whether $E(\Delta\boldsymbol{x}_t) =$ or $\neq \mathbf{0}$ in the data-generating process, requiring some adjustment of dimensionality when $E(\Delta\boldsymbol{x}_t) \neq \mathbf{0}$ (see also Hamilton (1994: 591–601) for a lucid explanation of this point). What is more serious is the possible presence of co-integrating relations among elements of $\boldsymbol{x}_t$ (see Choi (1994) for the complicated limiting distribution of the test statistics). In my judgement the two-step test is applicable only when (i) the co-integration rank is a priori known to be at most 1 and (ii) the coefficient of y is known to be non-zero so that it can be normalized to 1. The test can hardly be useful to investigate the model specification of co-integrated regression regarding the points discussed in Section 13.4.3. [9]

Shintani (1994) emphasizes that the two-step method still retains some use because the case where x is a scalar variable arises often in applications. Let me give prescriptions for practitioners for this special case. $\{(u_{1t}, u_{2t})\}$ is a stationary bivariate AR process, $\Delta x_t = \mu + u_{1t}$, and

$$y_t = a + bx_t + \sum_{s=1}^{t} u_{2s}.$$

If $\mu \neq 0$, the limit distribution of the augmented Dickey–Fuller t-statistic on the residual, $y_t - \hat{a} - \hat{b}x_t$, is that given in Fuller (1976: 373, table 8.5.2, $\tau_\tau, n = \infty$), the table for the t-statistic in the case where detrending is performed. The finite sample distribution would depend upon the size of μ^2 in relation to the long-run variance of u_1. If $\mu = 0$, the limit distribution is provided in Phillips and Ouliaris (1990, table II*a*, $n = 1$). Suppose that

$$y_t = a + bt + cx_t + \sum_{s=1}^{t} u_{2s}.$$

The limit distribution of the augmented Dickey–Fuller t-statistic on the residual, $y_t - \hat{a} - \hat{b}t - \hat{c}x_t$, is given in Phillips and Ouliaris (1990, table II*c*, $n = 1$), no matter whether $\mu = 0$ or $\neq 0$.[10]

[9] Kremers, Ericsson, and Dolado (1992) investigate a two-step method applied to the Hendry model.

[10] $(1-R^2)$ is $O_p(1)$ in the spurious regression while it is $O_p(T^{-1})$ in the co-integrated regression. The Durbin–Watson statistic is $O_p(T^{-1})$ in the spurious regression while it is $O_p(1)$ in the co-integrated regression. Thus R^2 close to 1 is indicative of a co-integrated regression, while a very small value of the Durbin–Watson statistic is indicative of a spurious regression. However, these statistics are not useful in discriminating the spurious and co-integrated regressions because their limit distributions contain the long-run covariance matrix of $(\Delta x_t, \Delta y_t)$ as nuisance parameters.

Below follows a partial list of the literature on empirical studies of co-integration on the basis of the above two-step method; its purpose is to indicate the fields of economics in which co-integration analysis is useful rather than to demonstrate the results that past co-integration analyses have achieved. The literature on the application of the method of Johansen (1991*a*) is presented separately in Section 15.5.

Existence of co-integration between (real) stock price and (real) stock dividend is a piece of evidence against a version of rational bubbles. Diba and Grossman (1988) and Lim and Phoon (1991) test for absence of co-integration. The purchasing power parity with unknown coefficients has been investigated in Taylor (1988), McNown and Wallance (1989), Layton and Stark (1990), Kim (1990), and Patel (1990). Baillie and Selover (1987) study a monetary model of foreign exchange. Meese and Rogoff (1988) examine the co-integration between real exchange rates on the one hand and differentials between real interest rates of different countries on the other. Hall (1986) investigates the relation between wage, price, and productivity, and Drobny and Hall (1989) analyse the consumption function viewed as a co-integrating relation. In all of the above studies the null hypothesis is the absence of co-integration. Even if the Johansen (1991*a*) method were used, the null hypothesis would be the zero co-integration rank.

Highlights of Chapter 13

Here I present results in Sections 13.1–13.3 in a more general framework. Let $\{(\Delta \boldsymbol{x}_t', \boldsymbol{u}_t')\}$ be a jointly stationary, linear indeterministic process, and let $\boldsymbol{x}_t'$ and $\boldsymbol{u}_t'$ have respectively m and n elements. $\{\boldsymbol{y}_t\}$ is generated from $\{(\Delta \boldsymbol{x}_t', \boldsymbol{u}_t')\}$ by

$$\boldsymbol{y}_t' = \boldsymbol{a}' + \boldsymbol{x}_t'\boldsymbol{B} + \boldsymbol{u}_t', \tag{13.61}$$

where $\boldsymbol{a}'$ and $\boldsymbol{B}$ are respectively $1 \times n$ and $m \times n$ unknown parameters. (13.61) means that $\{\boldsymbol{x}_t\}$ and $\{\boldsymbol{y}_t\}$ are co-integrated. If $E(\Delta \boldsymbol{x}_t) \neq \boldsymbol{0}$ so that $\{\boldsymbol{x}_t\}$ has linear deterministic trends, $[-\boldsymbol{B}, \boldsymbol{I}]$ nullifies both the stochastic and deterministic trends in $(\boldsymbol{x}', \boldsymbol{y}')$. We may also consider

$$\boldsymbol{y}_t' = \boldsymbol{x}_t'\boldsymbol{B} + \boldsymbol{c}_0' + \boldsymbol{c}_1' t + \boldsymbol{u}_t'. \tag{13.62}$$

where $\boldsymbol{c}_0$ and $\boldsymbol{c}_1$ are each unknown n elements vector parameters. If deterministic trends in $\boldsymbol{y}_t$ and $\boldsymbol{x}_t$ are respectively $\boldsymbol{d}_{0y} + \boldsymbol{d}_{1y}t$ and $\boldsymbol{d}_{0x} + \boldsymbol{d}_{1x}t$, then (13.62) implies that $\boldsymbol{c}_0' = \boldsymbol{d}_{0y}' - \boldsymbol{d}_{0x}'\boldsymbol{B}$ and $\boldsymbol{c}_1' = \boldsymbol{d}_{1y}' - \boldsymbol{d}_{1x}'\boldsymbol{B}$. $[-\boldsymbol{B}, \boldsymbol{I}]$ is the co-integration matrix that nullifies only the stochastic trends in $(\boldsymbol{x}', \boldsymbol{y}')$. Deterministic trends are present in $\boldsymbol{y}_t' - \boldsymbol{x}_t'\boldsymbol{B}$ unless $\boldsymbol{c}_1' = 0$. The OLS on (13.62) is equivalent to the OLS on (13.61) in which $\boldsymbol{x}$ and $\boldsymbol{y}$ are demeaned and detrended.

The following results are based upon the assumption that $\{\boldsymbol{x}_t\}$ is not co-integrated.

1. If $\{\boldsymbol{u}_t\}$ and $\{\boldsymbol{x}_t\}$ are completely independent, (the degrees of freedom times) the F-statistics on (a portion of) $\boldsymbol{B}$ based upon the two-step least squares with

Cochrane–Orcutt transformation in either (13.61) or (13.62) are asymptotically χ^2 (see Section 13.3.1). When $\{\boldsymbol{x}_t\}$ contains one but only one element that is $I(1)$ and contains a linear or higher-order deterministic trend, the strict exogeneity condition can be eliminated on that element (see Section 13.2.1). Though very special logically, the case may be encountered frequently in econometric applications.

How to implement the Cochrane–Orcutt transformation in the case where $\boldsymbol{y}_t$ is a vector of n elements ($n > 1$) would require some explanation. Assume that

$$\boldsymbol{u}_t'\boldsymbol{A}(L) = \boldsymbol{\varepsilon}_t'$$
$$\boldsymbol{A}(L) = \boldsymbol{I} - \boldsymbol{A}_1 L - \ldots - \boldsymbol{A}_p L^p.$$

It is seen that

$$\boldsymbol{x}_t'\boldsymbol{B}\boldsymbol{A}(L) = (\text{vec}\,\boldsymbol{A}(L) \otimes \boldsymbol{x}_t)'(\boldsymbol{I}_n \otimes \text{vec}\,\boldsymbol{B}),$$

where vec is the column vector obtained by stacking columns. It follows from (13.61) that

$$\boldsymbol{y}_t'\boldsymbol{A}(L) = \boldsymbol{a}'\boldsymbol{A}(1) + (\text{vec}\,\boldsymbol{A}(L) \otimes \boldsymbol{x}_t)'(\boldsymbol{I}_n \otimes \text{vec}\,\boldsymbol{B}) + \boldsymbol{\varepsilon}_t'.$$

The second-step estimation must be based upon the SUR (seemingly unrelated regression) calculation with $\boldsymbol{y}_t'\hat{\boldsymbol{A}}(L)$ as the dependent variable and $(\text{vec}\,\hat{\boldsymbol{A}}(L) \otimes \boldsymbol{x}_t)'$ as the independent variables, where the coefficient vectors are identical among all equations. If $\boldsymbol{A}(L)$ is diagonal, $\text{diag}[a_{11}(L), \ldots, a_{nn}(L)]$,

$$\boldsymbol{x}_t'\boldsymbol{B}\boldsymbol{A}(L) = [a_{11}(L)\boldsymbol{x}_t'\boldsymbol{B}_1, \ldots, a_{nn}(L)\boldsymbol{x}_t'\boldsymbol{B}_n],$$

where $\boldsymbol{B} = [\boldsymbol{B}_1, \ldots, \boldsymbol{B}_n]$, and the ith equation has $y_{it}a_{ii}(L)$ as the dependent variable, and $a_{ii}(L)\boldsymbol{x}_t'$ as the independent variable.

2. If $\{\boldsymbol{u}_t\}$ does not cause $\{\Delta\boldsymbol{x}_t\}$ in Granger's sense, (the degrees of freedom times) the F-statistics on $\boldsymbol{B}$ based upon the two-step least squares with the Cochrane–Orcutt transformation on

$$\boldsymbol{y}_t' = \hat{\boldsymbol{a}}' + \boldsymbol{x}_t'\hat{\boldsymbol{B}} + \Delta\boldsymbol{x}_t'\hat{\boldsymbol{C}}_0 + \Delta\boldsymbol{x}_{t-1}'\hat{\boldsymbol{C}}_1 + \ldots + \text{error} \tag{13.63}$$

or

$$\boldsymbol{y}_t' = \boldsymbol{x}_t'\hat{\boldsymbol{B}} + \hat{\boldsymbol{c}}_0' + \hat{\boldsymbol{c}}_1' t + \Delta\boldsymbol{x}_t'\hat{\boldsymbol{C}}_0 + \Delta\boldsymbol{x}_{t-1}'\hat{\boldsymbol{C}}_1 + \ldots + \text{error} \tag{13.64}$$

are asymptotically χ^2. The condition that $\boldsymbol{u}$ does not cause $\Delta\boldsymbol{x}$ can be verified by testing for the non-causality of $\boldsymbol{y}$ on $\boldsymbol{x}$. It does not matter whether $\{\boldsymbol{x}_t\}$ has a linear deterministic trend, but no deterministic trend other than linear is permitted in (13.64).

3. More generally, even if $\{\boldsymbol{u}_t\}$ may cause $\{\Delta\boldsymbol{x}_t\}$ in Granger's sense, (the degrees of freedom times) the F-statistics on $\boldsymbol{B}$ based upon the two-step least squares with the Cochrane–Orcutt transformation on

$$\boldsymbol{y}_t' = \boldsymbol{x}_t'\hat{\boldsymbol{B}} + \Delta\boldsymbol{x}_t'\hat{\boldsymbol{C}}_0 + \Delta\boldsymbol{x}_{t-1}'\hat{\boldsymbol{C}}_1 + \ldots + \Delta\boldsymbol{x}_{t+1}'\hat{\boldsymbol{F}}_1 + \Delta\boldsymbol{x}_{t+2}'\hat{\boldsymbol{F}}_2 + \ldots + \text{error} \tag{13.65}$$

or

$$y_t' = x_t'\hat{B} + \hat{c}'_0 + \hat{c}'_1 t + \Delta x_t'\hat{C}_0 + \Delta x_{t-1}'\hat{C}_1 + \dots$$
$$+ \Delta x_{t+1}'\hat{F}_1 + \Delta x_{t+2}'\hat{F}_2 + \dots + \text{error} \qquad (13.66)$$

are asymptotically χ^2. It does not matter whether $\{x_t\}$ has a linear trend, but no deterministic trend other than linear is permitted in (13.66).

4. If $\{x_t\}$ is co-integrated, there appear stationary components, and the inference resembles the traditional econometric theories as far as the consistency condition is concerned (see Sections 13.1.4–5).

My practical advice consists of one major trunk line and a number of side lines. In the trunk line one determines initially the integration orders of $\{x_t\}$ and $\{y_t\}$, confirms that the regression is balanced, and, if both $\{x_t\}$ and $\{y_t\}$ are $I(1)$, proceeds to 3 above, assuming that $\{x_t\}$ and $\{y_t\}$ are co-integrated. This advice is applicable even to the special case where $\{x_t\}$ contains one but only one element that is $I(1)$ including a deterministic trend. If the co-integration is to annihilate both the deterministic and stochastic trends, adopt (13.65). Here models of deterministic trends need not be specified. If it is to annihilate the stochastic trends only, use (13.66). Here it is necessary to introduce the correct model specification of deterministic trends on the right-hand side of (13.66) if it is to be generalized beyond the linear form. Any misspecification would distort the results of inference. As for the side lines the co-integrated regression as opposed to spurious regression may be confirmed by the rank determined by the Johansen method in Chapter 15. We had better confirm that the co-integration is directed from x to y, but I do not know how to do this except in the case where y is a scalar (see Section 13.4.3). One can move from 3 above to the simpler 2 above if $\{y_t\}$ is found to fail to cause $\{x_t\}$ in Granger's sense.

14
Inference on Dynamic Econometric Models

Inference theories in the previous chapter will be applied to econometric models. An example of dynamic econometric models is the error-correction model that consists of (12.29), (12.30), and (12.34) in Chapter 12. Here it is modified slightly for the purpose of illustrating the inference method to be given in the present chapter. Earlier the target variable was constructed by (12.30), but here I generalize it to

$$y_t^* = k + \alpha x_t.$$

(12.34) is rewritten here with different notations,

$$\Delta x_t = c(L)(\mu + \varepsilon_{2t}), \qquad c_0 \equiv 1. \tag{14.1}$$

Using $c(L)\mu = c(1)\mu$ and $(c(L) - 1)\varepsilon_{2t} = (1 - c(L)^{-1})(\Delta x_t - c(1)\mu)$ it is seen that $E(x_t|I_{t-1}) - x_{t-1} = c(1)\mu + (1 - c(L)^{-1})(\Delta x_t - c(1)\mu) = \mu + (1 - c(L)^{-1})\Delta x_t$. The new model is

$$(1 - (1 - \gamma)L)y_t = \beta\mu + \gamma k + \gamma\alpha x_{t-1} + \beta(1 - c(L)^{-1})\Delta x_t + \varepsilon_{1t}; \tag{14.2}$$

which can also be written as

$$(1 - (1 - \gamma)L)y_t = \gamma k + \gamma\alpha x_{t-1} + \beta\Delta x_t - \beta\varepsilon_{2t} + \varepsilon_{1t}. \tag{14.2$'$}$$

(14.1) is added to them. It is assumed that $1 > 1 - \gamma > 0$ and that $\{(\varepsilon_{1t}, \varepsilon_{2t})\}$ is i.i.d. with zero mean. I shall discuss the condition on $E(\varepsilon_{1t}\varepsilon_{2t})$ as I proceed. The expression (14.2) involves $c(L)$ in (14.1) while the expression (14.2′) involves only the innovation in (14.1), and both expressions have been used in the literature of rational expectations.

Another example of econometric dynamic models is the linear quadratic model proposed in Kennan (1979). It has been used in many empirical studies of rational expectations, and analysed on stochastic trend and co-integration in Dolado, Galbraith, and Banerjee (1991) and Gregory, Pagan, and Smith (1993). Wickens (1993) also presents a related study. In Kennan (1979) an economic agent minimizes

$$E\left(\sum_{s=0}^{\infty} \beta^s[a(y_{t+s} - y_{t+s}^*)^2 + (y_{t+s} - y_{t+s-1})^2]|I_t\right),$$

where y_t^* is the target variable generated by

$$y_t^* = \alpha x_t + \varepsilon_{1t}. \tag{14.3}$$

$\{y_t\}$ is the decision variable, and $\{(x_t, \varepsilon_{1t})\}$ is exogenous to the agent. The β is the discount factor so that $1 > \beta > 0$, and $a(> 0)$ is the relative weight, w_1/w_2, between w_1 on the deviation from the target, $(y_{t+s} - y^*_{t+s})^2$, and w_2 on the adjustment cost, $(y_{t+s} - y_{t+s-1})^2$. $\{\varepsilon_{1t}\}$ is i.i.d. with zero mean. Kennan (1979) derives the behaviour equation as follows. The algebraic equation for z,

$$\beta z^2 - (1 + \beta + a)z + 1 = 0,$$

has two positive real roots, the smaller of which is less than unity. Let this root be λ, which of course depends on β and a. It then follows from the optimization of the agent that

$$(1 - \lambda L)y_t = (1 - \lambda)(1 - \beta\lambda) \sum_{j=0}^{\infty} (\beta\lambda)^j E(y^*_{t+j}|I_t), \tag{14.4}$$

which is equation (2.13) of Kennan (1979). Now suppose that x_t is generated by (14.1) and that $\{\varepsilon_{1t}\}$ in (14.3) is independent of $\{\varepsilon_{2t}\}$ in (14.1). Let

$$d(L) = \beta\lambda \frac{c(L) - c_0}{L} + (\beta\lambda)^2 \frac{c(L) - (c_0 + c_1 L)}{L^2} + \ldots, \; c_0 \equiv 1.$$

Then

$$\sum_{j=0}^{\infty} (\beta\lambda)^j E(y^*_{t+j}|I_t) = (1 - \beta\lambda)^{-1} \alpha[\mu \bar{d} + c(L)^{-1} d(L)\Delta x_t + x_t] + \varepsilon_{1t},$$

where $\bar{d} \equiv (1 - \beta\lambda)^{-1}(c_0\beta\lambda + c_1(\beta\lambda)^2 + \ldots)$. Substituting this into (14.4) we get the behaviour equation,

$$(1 - \lambda)^{-1}(1 - \lambda L)y_t = \alpha[\mu\bar{d} + x_t + c(L)^{-1} d(L)\Delta x_t] + (1 - \beta\lambda)\varepsilon_{1t}, \tag{14.5}$$

which can also be written as

$$(1 - \lambda)^{-1}(1 - \lambda L)y_t = \alpha\mu(\bar{d} + d(1)) + \alpha x_t + \alpha d(L)\varepsilon_{2t} + (1 - \beta\lambda)\varepsilon_{1t}. \tag{14.5'}$$

The model is (14.1) and (14.5), or (14.1) and (14.5′). (14.5) contains $c(L)$, but (14.5′) does not.

Both (14.2) and (14.5) can be regarded as special cases of

$$a(L)y_t = k + b(L)x_t + \varepsilon_{1t}. \tag{14.6}$$

where k and the as and bs in $a(L)$ and $b(L)$ are some known, possibly non-linear functions of an r dimensional vector parameter, $\boldsymbol{\theta}$. Writing $a(L) = a_0 + a_1 L + \ldots + a_p L^p$, a_0 should not be normalized to unity because the normalization would mean that a_0 is not a function of $\boldsymbol{\theta}$. The inference is to be made about $\boldsymbol{\theta}$ and not about k or the as and bs. It is assumed that all roots of $a(z) = 0$ lie outside of the unit circle so that $a(L)$ is invertible. If $\{\Delta x_t\}$ is stationary so is $\{\Delta y_t\}$, i.e. if $\{x_t\}$ is $I(1)$ so is $\{y_t\}$.[1] $b(L)$ may be an infinite power series of L,

[1] If $\{x_t\}$ is $I(1)$ and $\{a_j\}$ is bounded by a decaying exponential, then $y_t = \sum_{j=0}^{\infty} a_j x_{t-j}$ is $I(1)$. For example, if $x_t = \sum_{s=1}^{t} \varepsilon_s$ and $\{\varepsilon_t\}$ is i.i.d. with zero mean $\Delta y_t = a_0\varepsilon_t + a_1\varepsilon_{t-1} + \ldots$, which is $I(0)$. When the relation is expressed as $b(L)y_t = x_t$, where $b(L)$ is a polynomial of L, $b(L)$

but $\{b_j\}$ is bounded by a decaying exponential. The data-generating process of $\{x_t\}$ in (14.6) is (14.1), and in general $\boldsymbol{\theta}$ includes the cs in (14.1). The relation between $\{\varepsilon_{1t}\}$ in (14.6) and $\{\Delta x_t\}$ will be specified as we proceed. But $\{\varepsilon_{1t}\}$ and $\{\varepsilon_{2t}\}$ are i.i.d.,[2] and $\{c_j\}$ is bounded by a decaying exponential.

Another important class of dynamic relations is the one developed on the model specification methodology in Davidson *et al.* (1978), Hendry and Mizon (1978), Hendry and Richard (1982), Hendry, Pagan, and Sargan (1984), and Hendry (1987, 1993). It is

$$\Delta y_t = \delta(y_{t-1} - \alpha x_{t-1}) + a(L)\Delta y_{t-1} + b(L)\Delta x_t + \varepsilon_{1t}. \tag{14.7}$$

Two points worthy of emphasis are that an economic theory specifies $y_t = \alpha x_t$ as the long-run equilibrium and that $\{\varepsilon_{1t}\}$ should be none other than i.i.d. Both $a(L)$ and $b(L)$ are of finite orders, and the orders as well as the as and bs may be estimated by the standard time-series analysis with no reference to economic theories. The weak exogeneity of x_t with respect to δ, α, the as, and bs is also an important part of the specification. Writing $\phi(z) \equiv 1 - (1+\delta)z - a(z)z(1-z)$, it is assumed that the equation $\phi(z) = 0$ has all its roots outside of the unit circle so that if x_t is $I(1)$ so is y_t. An implication of this assumption is that $\phi(1) > 0$, as shown in Section 6.2.3 of Part I. In turn $\phi(1) > 0$ implies $\delta < 0$. It can be easily confirmed that if $\{x_t\}$ is $I(1)$, $y_t = \alpha x_t$ is the long-run equilibrium. I shall call (14.7) the Hendry model. (14.1) may be associated with (14.7). (14.7) does not logically follow from (12.18), but I accept (14.7) as an important strategy to model the reality.

In the present Chapter I shall describe inference methods on the general dynamic model (14.1) and (14.6) and the Hendry model, (14.1) and (14.7). Following Phillips (1991*a*) and Phillips and Loretan (1991) the methods are classified into two groups. In the first group the inference on the long-run parameter precedes that on the other parameters. It is called the two-step method. In the second group both the long-run and the short-run parameters are jointly subjected to the inference. It will be called the single-step method. My proposal on the general dynamic model (14.6) is based upon (14.15) below, which allows us to truncate the infinite power series, $b^*(L)$, but otherwise it closely follows Phillips and Loretan (1991). In my judgement the two-step method has wider applicability than the single-step method.

Throughout the present chapter we shall be concerned only with estimation and hypothesis testing on parameters, assuming that given models are validly specified. A part of the specification is the co-integration between x and y. This can be tested by the method in Chapter 15 within the framework of VAR, which is logically more general than the econometric models considered here. Kremers,

must represent a stable difference equation, and Boswijk (1994) presents a method to test for the instability.

[2] If ε_{1t} is replaced by a stationary AR, e.g., u_t such that $(1-\rho L)u_t = \varepsilon_{1t}$, then $a(L)$, k, and $b(L)$ are replaced by $a^*(L) = a(L)(1-\rho L)$, $k^* = k(1-\rho)$, and $b^*(L) = b(L)(1-\rho L)$; $\boldsymbol{\theta}$ is replaced by $\boldsymbol{\theta}^* = (\boldsymbol{\theta}', \rho)$; and the a^*s, k, and b^*s are new functions of $\boldsymbol{\theta}^*$.

Ericsson, and Dolado (1992) consider discrimination between co-integration and spurious regression specifically on the Hendry model assuming that α is known.

14.1 Hendry Model with the Two-Step Method

My explanation of the two-step method will begin with the Hendry model (14.7) in conjunction with the DGP for x_t, (14.1). To simplify the following exposition it is assumed that $a(L)$ and $b(L)$ in (14.7) are just a and b respectively so that the model is

$$\Delta y_t = \delta(y_{t-1} - \alpha x_{t-1}) + a\Delta y_{t-1} + b\Delta x_t + \varepsilon_{1t}. \qquad (14.7')$$

This can be rewritten as

$$(1 - (1 + \delta + a)L + aL^2)y_t = (b - (b + \alpha\delta)L)x_t + \varepsilon_{1t}. \qquad (14.8)$$

It is assumed that $1 - (1 + \delta + a)L + aL^2$ is invertible. With

$$b_0^* \equiv b - \alpha, \quad b_1^* \equiv a\alpha \qquad (14.9)$$

it is seen that

$$b - (b + \alpha\delta)L = (1 - (1 + \delta + a)L + aL^2)\alpha + (1 - L)(b_0^* + b_1^*L). \qquad (14.10)$$

This kind of reparametrization is found useful throughout the present chapter. It follows from (14.8) that

$$y_t = \alpha x_t + (1 - (1 + \delta + a)L + aL^2)^{-1}(b_0^* + b_1^*L)\Delta x_t$$
$$+ (1 - (1 + \delta + a)L + aL^2)^{-1}\varepsilon_{1t}, \qquad (14.11)$$

which implies that $y_t - \alpha x_t$ is stationary.

The first step of our two-step method is based on (14.11). Assume that an infinite power series of L, $(1-(1+\delta+a)L+aL^2)^{-1}(b_0^*+b_1^*L)$ can be truncated at, say, p. Let us run an OLS with y_t as the dependent variable and $(x_t, \Delta x_t, \ldots, \Delta x_{t-p})$ as the independent variable. Though (14.11) indicates constraints on the coefficients of independent variables, such constraints are ignored in the present OLS. Let the estimate of α be denoted by $\hat{\alpha}$. Suppose that the true value of μ in (14.1), μ^0, is zero. Then, if $(1 - (1 + \delta + a)L + aL^2)^{-1}\varepsilon_{1t}$ does not cause Δx_t in Granger's sense, the reasoning given in Section 13.3.2 shows that $T(\hat{\alpha} - \alpha)$ is asymptotically mixed Gaussian. Suppose next that $\mu^0 \neq 0$. Then whatever the relation between ε_{1t} and Δx_t may be, $T^{3/2}(\hat{\alpha} - \alpha)$ is asymptotically Gaussian. How to perform a statistical inference about α will be explained later.

In the second step of our two-step method we rewrite (14.7′) as

$$\Delta y_t = \delta(y_{t-1} - \hat{\alpha}x_{t-1}) + a\Delta y_{t-1} + b\Delta x_t + \varepsilon_{1t} + \delta(\hat{\alpha} - \alpha)x_{t-1}. \qquad (14.12)$$

If $\mu^0 = 0$, $\hat{\alpha} - \alpha$ is $O_p(T^{-1})$ and x_t is $O_p(T^{1/2})$ so that $(\hat{\alpha} - \alpha)x_{t-1}$ is $O_p(T^{-1/2})$. If $\mu^0 \neq 0$, $\hat{\alpha} - \alpha$ is $O_p(T^{-3/2})$ and x_t is $O_p(T)$ so that $(\hat{\alpha} - \alpha)x_{t-1}$ is again

$O_p(T^{-1/2})$. In either case the last term on the right-hand side of (14.12) may be ignored. We get

$$\Delta y_t \approx \delta(y_{t-1} - \hat{\alpha}x_{t-1}) + a\Delta y_{t-1} + b\Delta x_t + \varepsilon_{1t}. \tag{14.13}$$

If $\{\varepsilon_{1t}\}$ in (14.7′) and $\{\varepsilon_{2t}\}$ in (14.1) are mutually independent, Δx_t is weakly exogenous in (14.13) with respect to (δ, a, b). Noting that (14.13) is an equation on $I(0)$ variables, and also that ε_{1t} is uncorrelated asymptotically with other variables in (14.13), we run an OLS with Δy_t as the dependent variable and $((y_{t-1} - \hat{\alpha}x_{t-1}), \Delta y_{t-1}, \Delta x_t)$ as the independent variable to estimate (δ, a, b).

The feature of the two-step method is to take advantage of T- or $T^{3/2}$-consistency of the estimator of α, which can be achieved without bothering about the details of short-run relations. In fact the short-run relations are taken into consideration in the first step only in introducing $(\Delta x_t, \dots, \Delta x_{t-p})$ in the regressor set, while ignoring the constraints on the coefficients of these regressors. Moreover, the relation between $\{\varepsilon_{1t}\}$ and $\{\varepsilon_{2t}\}$ required in the first step is weaker than in the second step.

The inference on α is made in the first step. Since $(1-(1+\delta+a)L+aL^2)^{-1}\varepsilon_{1t}$ is not i.i.d. in (14.11), the t-statistic is not asymptotically $N(0, 1)$ as explained in Section 13.3.1. If a Cochrane–Orcutt transformation is performed on all the relevant variables, $y_t, x_t, \Delta x_t, \dots, \Delta x_{t-p}$, then the t-statistic on the coefficient of the transformed x is asymptotically $N(0, 1)$.

The inference on (δ, a, b) is made in the second step, treating $\hat{\alpha}$ as though it is the true value of α. This part of our inference is a standard one. $\sqrt{T}(\hat{\delta} - \delta, \hat{a} - a, \hat{b} - b)$ is asymptotically $N(0, \mathbf{V})$, where $\mathbf{V}$ is defined by

$$\sigma_{11}\left(\operatorname{plim} T^{-1}\begin{bmatrix} \sum \hat{\xi}_{t-1}^2, & \sum \hat{\xi}_{t-1}\Delta y_{t-1}, & \sum \hat{\xi}_{t-1}\Delta x_t \\ & \sum(\Delta y_{t-1})^2 & \sum \Delta y_{t-1}\Delta x_t \\ & & \sum(\Delta x_t)^2 \end{bmatrix}\right)^{-1}.$$

$\hat{\xi}_{t-1} \equiv y_{t-1} - \hat{\alpha}x_{t-1}$.

Frequently we encounter Hendry-models having multiple equations. It is easy to see that the above inference procedure for a single equation can be extended to multiple equations. The second step involves an SUR (seemingly unrelated regression) estimation. See Highlights of Chapter 13 for multiple equations.

The following will be found useful later in relation to the single-step method. Suppose that our inference on α is based upon the OLS on (14.11) without Cochrane–Orcutt transformation with y_t as the dependent variable and $(x_t, \Delta x_t, \dots, \Delta x_{t-p})$ as the independent variable. With $\phi(L) \equiv (1 - (1 + \delta + a)L + aL^2)^{-1}$, it is seen that the long-run variance of $\phi(L)\varepsilon_{1t}$ is $\delta^{-2}\sigma_{11}$. $T(\hat{\alpha} - \alpha)$ is asymptotically $N(0, \delta^{-2}\sigma_{11}g)$ conditionally upon $g \equiv (\int w(r)^2 dr)^{-1}$, where $w(r)$ is a scalar Wiener process with its variance equal to $c(1)^2\sigma_{22}$ i.e. the long-run variance of Δx_t. Therefore it is $\delta T(\hat{\alpha} - \alpha)$ instead of $T(\hat{\alpha} - \alpha)$ that is asymptotically mixed Gaussian with $N(0, \sigma_{11}g)$.

14.2 Dynamic Equation with the Two-Step Method

The model to be considered here is (14.1) and (14.6). Keep in mind that k, the as, and the bs are functions of $\boldsymbol{\theta}$. Define

$$\alpha \equiv \left(\sum_{j=0}^{\infty} b_j\right)\left(\sum_{j=0}^{p} a_j\right)^{-1}. \tag{14.14}$$

Then α is a function of $\boldsymbol{\theta}$, and $y_t = \alpha x_t$ is the long-run equilibrium. Construct $b^*(L) = b_0^* + b_1^* L + \ldots$ by

$$b(L) = \alpha a(L) + (1 - L)b^*(L). \tag{14.15}$$

It is seen that

$$\begin{aligned} b^*(L) &= (1 + L + \ldots)b(L) - \alpha(1 + L + \ldots)a(L) \\ &= \left(b(1) - \sum_1^{\infty} b_j\right) + \left(b(1) - \sum_2^{\infty} b_j\right) L + \ldots \\ &\quad - \alpha\left\{\left(a(1) - \sum_1^{\infty} a_j\right) + \left(a(1) - \sum_2^{\infty} a_j\right) L + \ldots\right\} \end{aligned}$$

so that $b_j^* = \alpha \sum_{h=j+1}^{\infty} a_h - \sum_{h=j+1}^{\infty} b_h$,
where $a_{p+1} = a_{p+2} = \ldots = 0$. Since $\{b_j\}$ is bounded by a decaying exponential, so is $\{b_j^*\}$.[3] Readers should recognize that a similar reparametrization was performed in (14.9) and (14.10). Using (14.15), (14.6) is rewritten as

$$y_t = \alpha x_t + a(1)^{-1}k + a(L)^{-1}b^*(L)\Delta x_t + a(L)^{-1}\varepsilon_{1t}. \tag{14.16}$$

The first step of the two-step method is concerned with estimation of α in (14.16). For this we regard y_t as the dependent variable and $(x_t, 1, \Delta x_t \ldots, \Delta x_{t-m})$ as the independent variable, assuming that $a(L)^{-1}b^*(L)$ can be truncated at m. The estimation consists of two stages. The $(a_1, \ldots, a_p)$ in $a(L)$ is estimated from residuals in the first OLS to get $\hat{a}(L)$. The second stage has $\hat{a}(L)y_t$ as the dependent variable, and $\hat{a}(L)(x_t, 1, \Delta x_t, \ldots, \Delta x_{t-m})$ as the independent variable. The t-statistic on $\hat{a}(L)x_t$ is asymptotically $N(0, 1)$. The asymptotic inference procedure is invariant to $\mu^0 =$ or $\neq 0$ in (14.1). It is sufficient for the reasoning to assume that $a(L)^{-1}\varepsilon_{1t}$ does not cause Δx_t in Granger's sense.

As for the second step of our two-step method consider

$$y_t - \hat{\alpha} x_t = a(1)^{-1}k + a(L)^{-1}b^*(L)\Delta x_t + a(L)^{-1}\varepsilon_{1t} - (\hat{\alpha} - \alpha)x_t. \tag{14.17}$$

We may ignore the last term on the right-hand side of (14.17) to obtain

$$a(L)(y_t - \hat{\alpha} x_t) - k - b^*(L)\Delta x_t \approx \varepsilon_{1t}. \tag{14.18}$$

This is a relation among $I(0)$ variables. If α is not an element of $\boldsymbol{\theta}$ but a function of $\boldsymbol{\theta}$, say, $\alpha = h(\theta_1, \ldots, \theta_r)$, it can be solved for θ_r to get $\theta_r = f(\theta_1, \ldots, \theta_{r-1}, \alpha)$. The new $\boldsymbol{\theta}$ is $(\theta_1, \ldots, \theta_{r-1}, \alpha)$, and the dependence of k, the as, and the bs upon the old $\boldsymbol{\theta}$ is re-expressed as the dependence upon the new

[3] Compare this with n. 5 of Chapter 12.

$\boldsymbol{\theta}$. Let $\boldsymbol{\theta}^* = (\theta_1, \ldots, \theta_{r-1})$. The entire parameters are classified into the long-run parameter $\alpha \equiv \theta_r$ and the short-run parameter $\boldsymbol{\theta}^*$.

We are concerned with the inference on $\boldsymbol{\theta}^*$ on the basis of (14.18). The *a*s, b^*s, and k may depend upon $\alpha \equiv \theta_r$, in which case α is replaced by $\hat{\alpha}$ in these parameters as well. $\boldsymbol{\theta}^*$ may be partitioned as $(\boldsymbol{\theta}_1^*, c_1, \ldots, c_q, \mu, \sigma_{22})$, where $c(L)$ in (14.1) is written $1 + c_1L + \ldots + c_qL^q$ and $\sigma_{22} = E(\varepsilon_{2t}^2)$. If $\{\Delta x_t\}$ is weakly exogenous in (14.18) with respect to $\boldsymbol{\theta}_1^*$, then the estimation of $\boldsymbol{\theta}_1^*$ may be based upon (14.18) alone. As for the MLE conditioned on $\{\Delta x_t\}$ one should recognize that the Gaussian likelihood contains the Jacobian determinant on the transformation from $(\varepsilon_{11}, \ldots, \varepsilon_{1T})$ to $(y_1, \ldots, y_T)$ because the determinant is not unity unless $a_0 \equiv 1$. Pursuing the non-linear least-squares approach, minimizing

$$\sum_t (a(L)(y_t - \hat{\alpha}x_t) - k - b^*(L)\Delta x_t)^2$$

does not even lead to a consistent estimate unless $\partial a_0/\partial\boldsymbol{\theta}_1^* \equiv 0$, but minimizing

$$\sum_t (a_0^{-1}a(L)(y_t - \hat{\alpha}x_t) - a_0^{-1}k - a_0^{-1}b^*(L)\Delta x_t)^2 \tag{14.19}$$

does provide a consistent estimator of $\boldsymbol{\theta}_1^*$. We may choose between the MLE and the non-linear least squares on (14.19). The latter is asymptotically less efficient but easier to compute.[4] (Although $a(L)$ was estimated previously in connection with (14.16), it is $\boldsymbol{\theta}_1^*$, not $a(L)$, that we like to estimate.)

If $\{\Delta x_t\}$ is not weakly exogenous in (14.18) with respect to $\boldsymbol{\theta}_1^*$, its efficient estimation requires joint estimation of $(\boldsymbol{\theta}_1^*, c_1, \ldots, c_q, \mu, \sigma_{22})$. If one is willing to sacrifice the efficiency for convenience in calculations, one may estimate $(c_1, \ldots, c_q, \mu, \sigma_{22})$ in (14.1), and substitute them in (14.18). It will be seen that $\{\Delta x_t\}$ is not generally weakly exogenous in the models that involve rational expectations.

The model (14.1) and (14.2) or (14.2′) may be used for illustration. The α there corresponds to α in (14.14), and it is an element of parameters to be estimated. The long-run relation is $y_t = \alpha x_t$. Assuming that $E(\varepsilon_{1t}\varepsilon_{2t}) = 0$, and that (14.2) instead of (14.2′) is used, Table 14.1 shows the correspondence between notations in the general model (14.1) and (14.6) and notations in the model (14.1) and (14.2). What is denoted by $b^*(L)$ in the general model is $\beta - \alpha - \beta c(L)^{-1}$ in the illustrated model. The estimation of α in the first step requires no explanation. The model to be considered at the second step is

$$(1 - (1 - \gamma)L)(y_t - \hat{\alpha}x_t) \approx \gamma k + \beta\mu + (\beta - \hat{\alpha} - \beta c(L)^{-1})\Delta x_t + \varepsilon_{1t}. \tag{14.20}$$

The a_0 is unity from the outset. However, $\{\Delta x_t\}$ is not weakly exogenous in (14.20). This is because $b^*(L) = \beta - \alpha - \beta c(L)^{-1}$ contains the parameters $(c_1, \ldots, c_q)$ in $c(L)$, which has been brought about by the behaviour

[4] An extremely general treatment of long-run and short-run parameters is found in appendix C of Johansen (1991*a*).

[5] Hiro Toda has kindly pointed out an error in the original draft.

TABLE 14.1

(14.1), (14.6)	(14.1), (14.2)
$a(L)$	$1-(1-\gamma)L$
$b(L)$	$\beta(1-c(L)^{-1})(1-L)+\gamma\alpha L$
$c(L)$	$c(L)$
α	α
k	$\beta\mu+\gamma k$
μ	μ
$\boldsymbol{\theta}$	$(\gamma, \beta, \alpha, k, c_1, \ldots, c_q, \mu, \sigma_{11}, \sigma_{22})$
$\boldsymbol{\theta}_1^*$	(γ, β, k)

equation (12.29) containing $E(x_t|I_{t-1})-x_{t-1}$. We might estimate $(c_1, \ldots, c_q)$ in (14.1), and substitute the estimates in (14.20) prior to the estimation of (γ, β, k).

The above has considered (14.2). We might instead consider (14.2′). It follows from (14.2′) that

$$y_t-\hat{\alpha}x_t \approx \gamma k+(1-\gamma)(y_{t-1}-\hat{\alpha}x_{t-1})+(\beta-\hat{\alpha})\Delta x_t-\beta\varepsilon_{2t}+\varepsilon_{1t}. \quad (14.20')$$

Note that Δx_t and ε_{2t} are correlated. However, since Δx_{t-1} is uncorrelated with ε_{2t} (but correlated with Δx_t unless $c(L)=c_0$), $(1, (y_{t-1}-\hat{\alpha}x_{t-1}), \Delta x_{t-1})$ is a valid instrument to estimate $(\gamma k, (1-\gamma), (\beta-\hat{\alpha}))$ by instrumental variable estimation. A consistent estimate of (γ, β, k) can be obtained from the estimate of $(\gamma k, (1-\gamma), (\beta-\hat{\alpha}))$.

In the model (14.5) the long-run relation is $y_t=\alpha x_t$, and α is again the long-run parameter. The second step here is more complicated than in the previous example. First of all $a_0 \neq 1$. It is easier to proceed along (14.5′) rather than (14.5), but it still leads us to a complicated equation

$$(1-\lambda L)(y_t-\hat{\alpha}x_t)=(1-\lambda)\hat{\alpha}\mu(1-\beta\lambda)^{-1}c(1)\beta\lambda-\lambda\hat{\alpha}\Delta x_t$$
$$+(1-\lambda)(\hat{\alpha}d(L)\varepsilon_{2t}+(1-\beta\lambda)\varepsilon_{1t}),$$

where I used $\overline{d}+d(1)=(1-\beta\lambda)^{-1}c(1)\beta\lambda$. The weak exogeneity of Δx_t does not hold, and Δx_t is correlated with ε_{2t}. We might estimate $(c_1, \ldots, c_q, \mu)$ from (14.1), and substitute them in $\mu c(1)$. Estimation of $(\lambda, \beta\lambda)$ is feasible with an instrumental variable method if we are willing to ignore the dependence of the disturbance variance upon $(\lambda, \beta\lambda)$.

14.3 Hendry Model with the Single-Step Method

In Sections 14.1–2 the inference on the long-run parameter has preceded that on the short-run parameters. It is also possible to perform inference on both the long-run and the short-run parameters at once.

Phillips and Loretan (1991) discuss a non-linear least-squares estimation of the Hendry model. I think that the non-linear least-squares method is useful for the estimation of the Hendry model. The model specification has been explained following (14.7). I assume again that $a(L)$ and $b(L)$ are just a and b respectively so that the model is (14.7′), which is reproduced below.

$$\Delta y_t = \delta(y_{t-1} - \alpha x_{t-1}) + a\Delta y_{t-1} + b\Delta x_t + \varepsilon_{1t}. \tag{14.7′}$$

Note that $y_t = \alpha x_t$ is the long-run equilibrium. The long-run parameter is α, and the short-run parameters comprise all the rest.

Initially I assume that $\{x_t\}$ is $I(1)$ without a deterministic trend. The minimum of

$$S \equiv \sum(\Delta y_t - \delta(y_{t-1} - \alpha x_{t-1}) - a\Delta y_{t-1} - b\Delta x_t)^2$$

is sought to estimate (δ, a, b, α). See Phillips and Loretan (1991) for their experiences with a number of algorithms for minimization of this particular type of functions. Let $(\hat{\delta}, \hat{a}, \hat{b}, \hat{\alpha})$ be the (δ, a, b, α) that minimizes S. For the theoretical analysis toward the asymptotic distribution derivatives of S with respect to (δ, a, b, α) are set to zero, and the non-linear expressions that result are linearly approximated about $(\delta^0, a^0, b^0, \alpha^0)$. This is a standard procedure in the non-linear regression. I show the approximation only on the differentiation with respect to α. From $\dfrac{\partial S}{\partial \alpha} = 0$

$$T^{-1}\sum(\Delta y_t - \delta(y_{t-1} - \alpha x_{t-1}) - a\Delta y_{t-1} - b\Delta x_t)x_{t-1} = 0. \tag{14.21a}$$

At the true values of the parameters

$$T^{-1}\sum(\Delta y_t - \delta^0(y_{t-1} - \alpha^0 x_{t-1}) - a^0\Delta y_{t-1} - b^0\Delta x_t)x_{t-1} = T^{-1}\sum \varepsilon_{1t}x_{t-1}. \tag{14.21b}$$

Therefore the linear approximation to (14.21b) minus (14.21a) yields

$$T^{-1}\left[(\delta - \delta^0)\sum \xi_{t-1}x_{t-1} + (a - a^0)\sum \Delta y_{t-1}x_{t-1} + (b - b^0)\sum \Delta x_t x_{t-1} - (\alpha - \alpha^0)\delta^0\sum x_{t-1}^2\right] \approx T^{-1}\sum \varepsilon_{1t}x_{t-1}, \tag{14.21c}$$

where $\xi_t \equiv y_t - \alpha^0 x_t$. Rewriting the left-hand side we get

$$\sqrt{T}(\delta - \delta^0)T^{-3/2}\sum \xi_{t-1}x_{t-1} + \sqrt{T}(a - a^0)T^{-3/2}\sum \Delta y_{t-1}x_{t-1} + \sqrt{T}(b - b^0)T^{-3/2}\sum \Delta x_t x_{t-1} - T(\alpha - \alpha^0)\delta^0 T^{-2}\sum x_{t-1}^2 \approx T^{-1}\sum \varepsilon_{1t}x_{t-1}. \tag{14.21d}$$

Turning to the derivatives with respect to δ, a, and b it is seen that they should be normalized by $T^{-1/2}$ rather than T^{-1} as in (14.21a) and (14.21b) on the derivative with respect to α.

Denote $\boldsymbol{\xi}'_{-1} \equiv (\xi_2, \dots, \xi_{T-1})$, $\Delta \mathbf{y}'_{-1} \equiv (\Delta y_2, \dots, \Delta y_{T-1})$, $\Delta \mathbf{x}' \equiv (\Delta x_3, \dots, \Delta x_T)$, $\boldsymbol{\varepsilon}' \equiv (\varepsilon_{13}, \dots, \varepsilon_{1T})$, and $\mathbf{x}'_{-1} \equiv (x_2, \dots, x_{T-1})$. Under the present assumption about $\{x_t\}$, i.e. absence of a deterministic trend, $T^{-3/2}\sum \xi_{t-1}\Delta x_t$,

$T^{-3/2}\sum \Delta y_{t-1}\Delta x_t$, $T^{-3/2}\sum \Delta x_t x_{t-1}$, $T^{-3/2}\sum x_{t-1}\xi_{t-1}$, $T^{-3/2}\sum x_{t-1}\Delta y_{t-1}$, $T^{-3/2}\sum x_{t-1}\Delta x_t$ are all $o_p(1)$. We obtain

$$\begin{bmatrix} T^{-1}(\boldsymbol{\xi}_{-1}, \Delta \boldsymbol{y}_{-1}, \Delta \boldsymbol{x})'(\boldsymbol{\xi}_{-1}, \Delta \boldsymbol{y}_{-1}, \Delta \boldsymbol{x}) & \mathbf{0} \\ \mathbf{0}' & \delta^0 T^{-2}\boldsymbol{x}_{-1}'\boldsymbol{x}_{-1} \end{bmatrix} \times$$

$$\begin{bmatrix} \sqrt{T}\begin{bmatrix} \delta - \delta^0 \\ a - a^0 \\ b - b^0 \end{bmatrix} \\ T(\alpha - \alpha^0) \end{bmatrix} \approx \begin{bmatrix} T^{-1/2}\boldsymbol{\varepsilon}'(\boldsymbol{\xi}_{-1}, \Delta \boldsymbol{y}_{-1}, \Delta \boldsymbol{x}) \\ T^{-1}\boldsymbol{\varepsilon}'\boldsymbol{x}_{-1} \end{bmatrix}. \tag{14.22}$$

Then $(\hat{\delta}, \hat{a}, \hat{b}, \hat{\alpha})$ satisfies (14.22) asymptotically.[6] Notice that the system of equations (14.22) is decomposed into two parts. One is just

$$\delta^0 T^{-2}\boldsymbol{x}_{-1}'\boldsymbol{x}_{-1} T(\alpha - \alpha^0) \approx T^{-1'}\boldsymbol{\varepsilon}'\boldsymbol{x}_{-1},$$

[6] Readers might wonder about the existence of solution and its consistency. The function to be minimized is $S(\boldsymbol{\theta})$ with $\boldsymbol{\theta}' = (\delta, a, b, \alpha)$. The Taylor expansion leads us to

$$S(\boldsymbol{\theta}) - S(\boldsymbol{\theta}^0) = \frac{\partial S}{\partial \boldsymbol{\theta}'}(\boldsymbol{\theta}^0)\boldsymbol{D}_T^{-1}\boldsymbol{D}_T(\boldsymbol{\theta} - \boldsymbol{\theta}^0)$$

$$+\tfrac{1}{2}(\boldsymbol{\theta} - \boldsymbol{\theta}^0)'\boldsymbol{D}_T\boldsymbol{D}_T^{-1}\frac{\partial^2 S}{\partial \boldsymbol{\theta}\partial \boldsymbol{\theta}'}(\boldsymbol{\theta}^0)\boldsymbol{D}_T^{-1}\boldsymbol{D}_T(\boldsymbol{\theta} - \boldsymbol{\theta}^0) \tag{$*$}$$

+ terms involving the third-, fourth-, ... order derivatives.

From our DGP it follows that

$$S(\boldsymbol{\theta}^0) = \boldsymbol{\varepsilon}'\boldsymbol{\varepsilon}$$

$$\frac{\partial S}{\partial \boldsymbol{\theta}'}(\boldsymbol{\theta}^0)\boldsymbol{D}_T^{-1} = -2[T^{-1/2}\boldsymbol{\varepsilon}'\boldsymbol{\xi}_{-1}, T^{-1/2}\boldsymbol{\varepsilon}'\Delta \boldsymbol{y}_{-1}, T^{-1/2}\boldsymbol{\varepsilon}'\Delta \boldsymbol{x}, -T^{-1}\delta^0\boldsymbol{\varepsilon}'\boldsymbol{x}_{-1}],$$

$$\boldsymbol{D}_T^{-1}\frac{\partial^2 S}{\partial \boldsymbol{\theta}\partial \boldsymbol{\theta}'}(\boldsymbol{\theta}^0)\boldsymbol{D}_T^{-1}$$

$$= 2\begin{bmatrix} T^{-1}(\boldsymbol{\xi}_{-1}, \Delta \boldsymbol{y}_{-1}, \Delta \boldsymbol{x})'(\boldsymbol{\xi}_{-1}\Delta \boldsymbol{y}_{-1}, \Delta \boldsymbol{x}) & \mathbf{0} \\ 0 & \delta^{02}T^{-2}\boldsymbol{x}_{-1}'\boldsymbol{x}_{-1} \end{bmatrix},$$

$$+o_p(1),$$

where the matrix in [ ] is positive definite in probability 1. (Earlier it was noted that $\delta^0 < 0$.) For the terms involving third-order derivatives e.g.

$$\frac{\partial^3 S}{\partial \alpha^2 \partial \delta} = 4\delta \boldsymbol{x}_{-1}'\boldsymbol{x}_{-1},$$

since it is $T^{-5/2}\dfrac{\partial^3 S}{\partial \alpha^2 \partial \boldsymbol{\delta}} \cdot T^{5/2}(\alpha - \alpha^0)^2(\delta - \delta^\circ)$ that enters into $(*)$ above, we note that

$$T^{-5/2}\frac{\partial^3 S}{\partial \alpha^2 \partial \delta} = o_p(1).$$

The conclusion is that when $S(\boldsymbol{\theta}) - S(\boldsymbol{\theta}^0)$ is looked upon as a function of $D_T(\boldsymbol{\theta} - \boldsymbol{\theta}^0)$, it is convex downward if T is sufficiently large. A unique minimum exists, in probability 1, i.e. the non-linear least-squares estimator exists, if T is sufficiently large. Plausibility of $\sqrt{T}$ consistency of (δ, a, b) and T-consistency of α has also been demonstrated because the argument is $D_T(\boldsymbol{\theta} - \boldsymbol{\theta}^0)$ rather than $(\boldsymbol{\theta} - \boldsymbol{\theta}^0)$.

which is analogous to the equations for the OLS estimator in the co-integrated regression in Chapter 13. The other is

$$T^{-1}(\boldsymbol{\xi}_{-1}, \Delta\boldsymbol{y}_{-1}, \Delta\boldsymbol{x})'(\boldsymbol{\xi}_{-1}, \Delta\boldsymbol{y}_{-1}, \Delta\boldsymbol{x}) \approx \sqrt{T}\begin{bmatrix} \delta - \delta^0 \\ a - a^0 \\ b - b^0 \end{bmatrix},$$

which is a standard result in the traditional econometrics dealing with $I(0)$ variables.

Let $E(\varepsilon_{1t}^2) = \sigma_{11}$, $E(\varepsilon_{1t}\varepsilon_{2t}) = 0$, and $E(\varepsilon_{2t}^2) = \sigma_{22}$ in (14.7′). Let $(w_1(r), w_2(r))$ be a Wiener process with covariance matrix, diag$[\sigma_{11}, c(1)^2\sigma_{22}]$. Then it is seen from (14.22) that

$$T(\hat{\alpha} - \alpha^0)\delta^0 \xrightarrow{D} \int w_2(r)dw_1(r)\left(\int w_2(r)^2 dr\right)^{-1}, \tag{14.23}$$

which is mixed Gaussian. Readers should recognize that this is identical to the limit distribution on $\hat{\alpha}$ in the first step of the two-step method that we would have if the Cochrane–Orcutt transformation were not performed there (see the last paragraph of Section 14.1 above). On the other hand the process, $\{(\boldsymbol{\xi}_{t-1}, \Delta\boldsymbol{y}_{t-1}, \Delta\boldsymbol{x}_t)\}$ is stationary, and the limiting distribution of $\sqrt{T}((\hat{\delta} - \delta^0), (\hat{a} - a^0), (\hat{b} - b^0))$ is standard, and represented as $N(0, \sigma_{11}\boldsymbol{A}^{-1})$, where $\boldsymbol{A} \equiv \text{plim}\, T^{-1}(\boldsymbol{\xi}_{-1}, \Delta\boldsymbol{y}_{-1}, \Delta\boldsymbol{x})'(\boldsymbol{\xi}_{-1}, \Delta\boldsymbol{y}_{-1}, \Delta\boldsymbol{x})$. It is interesting to observe that the present limit distribution on (δ, a, b) is identical to that in the two-step method given earlier in Section 14.1. Also note that the inference on (δ, a, b) and that on α are separated. See Phillips (1990) for the reasoning to establish the asymptotic independence between the estimators of long-run and short-run parameters.[7]

Since $(\hat{\delta} - \delta^0)$ is $O_p(T^{-1/2})$,

$$\begin{aligned} T(\hat{\alpha} - \alpha^0)\hat{\delta} &= T(\hat{\alpha} - \alpha^0)\delta^0 + O_p(T^{-1/2}) \\ &\xrightarrow{D} \int w_2(r)dw_1(r)\left(\int w_2(r)^2 dr\right)^{-1}, \end{aligned}$$

which is mixed Gaussian. Therefore on a sort of t-statistic

$$\frac{\hat{\delta}(\hat{\alpha} - \alpha^0)\left(\sum x_{t-1}^2\right)^{1/2}}{s} = \frac{\hat{\delta}T(\hat{\alpha} - \alpha^0)\left(T^{-2}\sum x_{t-1}^2\right)^{1/2}}{s} \xrightarrow{D} N(0, 1) \tag{14.24}$$

where s is the standard error of regression.

Let us turn to the case where $\{x_t\}$ is $I(1)$ with a linear deterministic trend so that $\Delta x_t = \mu +$ (a stationary process with zero mean). The long-run equilibrium is still $y_t = \alpha x_t$. The partial derivative of S with respect to α was previously normalized by T^{-1} in (14.21a)–(14.21d), but now the normalizer should be

[7] Koichi Maekawa has kindly pointed this out to me.

$T^{-3/2}$. (14.21d) is replaced by

$$\sqrt{T}(\delta-\delta^0)T^{-2}\sum\xi_{t-1}x_{t-1}+\sqrt{T}(a-a^0)T^{-2}\sum\Delta y_{t-1}x_{t-1}+\sqrt{T}(b-b^0)T^{-2}$$
$$\times\sum\Delta x_t x_{t-1} - T^{3/2}(\alpha-\alpha^0)\delta^0 T^{-3}\sum x_{t-1}^2 \approx T^{-3/2}\sum\varepsilon_{1t}x_{t-1}.$$

Since $T^{-2}\sum\xi_{t-1}x_{t-1}$, $T^{-2}\sum\Delta y_{t-1}x_{t-1}$, and $T^{-2}\sum\Delta x_t x_{t-1}$ are all $o_p(1)$,

$$T^{3/2}(\hat{\alpha}-\alpha^0) \xrightarrow{D} N(0, 3(\delta^0\mu^0)^{-2}\sigma_{11}).$$

A sort of t-statistic, (14.24), converges to $N(0, 1)$ because

$$\frac{\hat{\delta}(\hat{\alpha}-\alpha^0)\left(\sum x_{t-1}^2\right)^{1/2}}{s} = \frac{\hat{\delta}T^{3/2}(\hat{\alpha}-\alpha^0)\left(T^{-3}\sum x_{t-1}^2\right)^{1/2}}{s},$$

and $T^{-3}\sum x_{t-1}^2 \to 1/3\mu^{02}$. The conclusion is that our asymptotic inference procedure is invariant to $\mu^0 =$ and $\neq 0$.

14.4 Dynamic Equation with the Single-Step Method

Let us consider again the general dynamic model, (14.1) and (14.6), keeping in mind that k, the as, and the bs are functions of the r-dimensional vector parameter, $\boldsymbol{\theta} \equiv (\theta_1, \ldots, \theta_r)'$.

(14.15) enables us to rewrite (14.6) as

$$a_0^{-1}a(L)(y_t - \alpha x_t) = a_0^{-1}k + a_0^{-1}b^*(L)\Delta x_t + a_0^{-1}\varepsilon_{1t}, \tag{14.25}$$

where $a(L) \equiv a_0 + a_1 L + \ldots + a_p L^p$, $a(z) = 0$ has all roots outside of the unit circle, $b^*(L)$ may be an infinite power series, but $\{b_i^*\}$ is bounded by a decaying exponential. Moreover, I assume here that $\{\varepsilon_{1t}\}$ and $\{\varepsilon_{2t}\}$ in (14.1) are independent.

In general the as, bs, and k depend upon the parameters for (14.1), i.e. $c_1, \ldots, c_q, \mu, \sigma_{22}$, as indicated in Table 14.2 for the special case, (14.1) and (14.5). In practice we had better estimate them on the basis of (14.1) alone in order to save computation costs. The estimates are then substituted in the as, bs, and k. In the following description $\boldsymbol{\theta}$ does not include $c_1, \ldots, c_q, \mu, \sigma_{22}$.

Let us explore the least-squares method on (14.25). Writing $f(L) \equiv a_0^{-1}a(L) = 1 + f_1 L + \ldots + f_p L^p$, $d \equiv a_0^{-1}k$, and $g(L) \equiv a_0^{-1}b^*(L)$, and truncating $b^*(L)$ and hence $g(L)$ at a finite order,

$$S \equiv \sum_t (f(L)(y_t - \alpha x_t) - d - g(L)\Delta x_t)^2 \tag{14.26}$$

is minimized with respect to $\boldsymbol{\theta}$. The $\boldsymbol{\theta}$ affects S through α, d, the fs and gs, which may be assembled into a vector $\tilde{\boldsymbol{\theta}}$. The case where $\tilde{\boldsymbol{\theta}} = \boldsymbol{\theta}$ has been investigated in Phillips and Loretan (1991). In the present model $\tilde{\boldsymbol{\theta}}$ has a larger dimensionality than $\boldsymbol{\theta}$, and the linear approximation to $\partial S/\partial\boldsymbol{\theta}$ is developed through

TABLE 14.2

(14.1), (14.6)	(14.1), (14.5)
$a(L)$	$(1-\beta\lambda)^{-1}(1-\lambda)^{-1}(1-\lambda L)$
$f(L)$	$1-\lambda L$
k	$\alpha\mu(1-\beta\lambda)^{-1}\sum_{j=0}^{\infty}(\beta\lambda)^j c_j$
d	$(1-\lambda)\alpha\mu\sum(\beta\lambda)^j c_j$
$b(L)$	$(1-\beta\lambda)^{-1}\left\{\alpha+\alpha c(L)^{-1}\left[\beta\lambda\frac{c(L)-c_0}{L}+\dots\right](1-L)\right\}$
$b^*(L)$	$\alpha(1-\beta\lambda)^{-1}\left[-\lambda(1-\lambda)^{-1}+c(L)^{-1}\left(\beta\lambda\frac{c(L)-c_0}{L}+\dots\right)\right]$
$g(L)$	$-\alpha\lambda+\alpha(1-\lambda)c(L)^{-1}\left(\beta\lambda\frac{c(L)-c_0}{L}+\dots\right)$
α	α

$(\partial\tilde{\boldsymbol{\theta}}/\partial\boldsymbol{\theta}'(\boldsymbol{\theta}^0))(\boldsymbol{\theta}-\boldsymbol{\theta}^0)$ and $(\partial^2\tilde{\theta}_j/\partial\boldsymbol{\theta}\partial\boldsymbol{\theta}'(\boldsymbol{\theta}^0))(\boldsymbol{\theta}-\boldsymbol{\theta}^0)$. It is reasonable to assume that for each $i=1,\dots,r$, $\partial\tilde{\boldsymbol{\theta}}/\partial\theta_i$ is not a zero vector at the true value of $\boldsymbol{\theta}$.

I now suppose that $\alpha\equiv\theta_r$ because as indicated in Section 14.2 $\boldsymbol{\theta}$ can be reparametrized so that this holds. Let us assume that there are no functional relationships among elements of $\boldsymbol{\theta}$, because, if there are, the dimensionality of $\boldsymbol{\theta}$ can be reduced. Let us also assume that the true value of $\boldsymbol{\theta}$ is not on the boundary of the admissible domain of $\boldsymbol{\theta}$. Then each element of $\boldsymbol{\theta}$ is free to move in a small neighbourhood of the true value. It is such neighbourhood that we are concerned with in developing the asymptotic theory. Since α is an element of $\tilde{\boldsymbol{\theta}}$ as well as of $\boldsymbol{\theta}$, $\partial\alpha/\partial\boldsymbol{\theta}'$ is a portion of $\partial\tilde{\boldsymbol{\theta}}/\partial\boldsymbol{\theta}'$. And we have

$$\frac{\partial\alpha}{\partial\theta_r}\equiv 1,\quad \frac{\partial\alpha}{\partial\theta_i}\equiv 0,\ i=1,\dots,r-1. \tag{14.27}$$

However, partial derivatives of elements of $\tilde{\boldsymbol{\theta}}$ other than α may not be zero no matter whether they are with respect to θ_r or $\theta_i (i\neq r)$.

The sort of block-diagonality as observed in (14.22) is revealed without (14.27), but (14.27) certainly simplifies the asymptotic distribution of the non-linear least-squares estimator. The asymptotic theory requires that the truncation point of $g(L)$, m, should be increased with the sample size T at a speed slower than T, but I do not bother to consider such mathematical sophistication.

Let $\hat{\boldsymbol{\theta}}\equiv(\hat{\theta}_1,\dots,\hat{\theta}_r)$ be the $\boldsymbol{\theta}$ that minimizes S in (14.26). Construct for $i=1,\dots,r-1$

$$f(L)'_i\equiv\frac{\partial f_1}{\partial\theta_i}(\boldsymbol{\theta}^0)L+\frac{\partial f_2}{\partial\theta_i}(\boldsymbol{\theta}^0)L^2+\dots+\frac{\partial f_p}{\partial\theta_i}(\boldsymbol{\theta}^0)L^p$$

$$g(L)'_i\equiv\frac{\partial g_0}{\partial\theta_i}(\boldsymbol{\theta}^0)+\frac{\partial g_1}{\partial\theta_i}(\boldsymbol{\theta}^0)L+\dots+\frac{\partial g_m}{\partial\theta_i}(\boldsymbol{\theta}^0)L^m$$

$$d_i \equiv \frac{\partial d}{\partial \theta_i}(\boldsymbol{\theta}^0),$$

$$\xi_{it} \equiv f(L)_i'(y_t - \alpha^0 x_t) - d_i - g(L)_i' \Delta x_t$$

$$\boldsymbol{\xi}_i \equiv (\xi_{iq+1}, \ldots, \xi_{iT})', \qquad \boldsymbol{\varepsilon}_1' \equiv (\varepsilon_{1q+1}, \ldots, \varepsilon_{1T}) \tag{14.28}$$

where it is assumed that $p \leq m$. The process $\{(\boldsymbol{\xi}_1, \ldots, \boldsymbol{\xi}_{r-1})\}$ is stationary, and for $(\theta_1, \ldots, \theta_{r-1})$ we have

$$T^{-1}(\boldsymbol{\xi}_1, \ldots, \boldsymbol{\xi}_{r-1})'(\boldsymbol{\xi}_1, \ldots, \boldsymbol{\xi}_{r-1})\sqrt{T}\begin{bmatrix} \hat{\theta}_1 - \theta_1^0 \\ \vdots \\ \hat{\theta}_{r-1} - \theta_{r-1}^0 \end{bmatrix}.$$

$$\approx -a_0^{-1} T^{-1/2}(\boldsymbol{\xi}_1, \ldots, \boldsymbol{\xi}_{r-1})'\boldsymbol{\varepsilon}_1. \tag{14.29}$$

In deriving this $\partial f_0/\partial\theta_i \equiv 0$ plays an important role. The term a_0^{-1} comes from the last term in (14.25). Let

$$\boldsymbol{A} \equiv \operatorname{plim} T^{-1}(\boldsymbol{\xi}_1, \ldots, \boldsymbol{\xi}_{r-1})'(\boldsymbol{\xi}_1, \ldots, \boldsymbol{\xi}_{r-1}).$$

Then from (14.29) it follows that $\sqrt{T}(\hat{\theta}_1 - \theta_1^0, \ldots, \hat{\theta}_{r-1} - \theta_{r-1}^0)$ converges to $N(0, \sigma_{11} a_0^{-2} \boldsymbol{A}^{-1})$.

Concerning θ_r, if $\mu^0 = 0$ in (14.1), we obtain

$$T(\hat{\theta}_r - \theta_r^0) \approx a_0^{-1}\left(T^{-2}\sum (f(L)x_t)^2\right)^{-1}\left(T^{-1}\sum \varepsilon_{1t}(f(L)x_t)\right) \tag{14.30}$$

$$= \left(T^{-2}\sum (a(L)x_t)^2\right)^{-1}\left(T^{-1}\sum \varepsilon_{1t}(a(L)x_t)\right)$$

$$\rightarrow a(1)^{-1}\left(\int w_2(r)^2 dr\right)^{-1}\int w_2(r)dw_1(r),$$

where $(w_1(r), w_2(r))$ is a Wiener process with covariance matrix, diag$[\sigma_{11}, c(1)^2\sigma_{22}]$. For a sort of t-statistic it holds that

$$s^{-1}\hat{a}(1)(\hat{\theta}_r - \hat{\theta}_r^0)\left(\sum x_t^2\right)^{1/2} \xrightarrow{D} N(0, 1). \tag{14.31}$$

If $\mu^0 \neq 0$ in (14.1), $T^{3/2}(\hat{\theta}_r - \hat{\theta}_r^0) \xrightarrow{D} N(0, 3\mu^{-2}a(1)^{-2}\sigma_{11})$, and yet (14.31) holds true.

It is important to compare usefulness of the single-step and the two-step methods. First, concerning the long-run parameter, α, it is precisely the t-statistic (on the Cochrane–Orcutt transformed variable) that converges to $N(0, 1)$ in the two-step method, whereas it is the more complicated form, the left-hand side of (14.31) in the single-step method. The finite sample distributions of both statistics need to be investigated. Second, concerning the estimation of short-run parameters, the θs other than α, the single-step estimation and the minimization of (14.19) in the two-step method yield the identical limiting distribution. However, the finite sample distributions may well be different. Third, the requirement on the exogeneity is less severe in the two-step method than in the single-step method in so far as the estimation of the long-run parameter is concerned. When the OLS is run along (14.11) or (14.16) the coefficients of Δx_t, $\Delta x_{t-1}, \dots$ are unconstrained, and are determined automatically to eliminate the relation between x_t and ε_{1t}. The Granger non-causality condition is sufficient to ensure the mixed Gaussian property of $\hat{\alpha}$. Moreover, if the condition is in doubt, one could introduce the forwarded Δx_t as suggested in Section 13.3.2. In the single-step method the coefficients of Δx_t, $\Delta x_{t-1}, \dots$ are constrained as functions of the common parameter, $\boldsymbol{\theta}$. This is the reason why I assumed the strict exogeneity of x_t in the single-step method.

In my judgement the third point concerning the exogeneity would outweigh other points unless there is revealed an enormous difference in finite sample distributions between the two estimators.[8]

[8] Throughout the present chapter the disturbance terms are assumed to be i.i.d. Sugihara (1994) investigates the case where they are ARMA.

15
Maximum-Likelihood Inference Theory of Co-integrated VAR

Comprehensive inference procedures for the co-integration have been developed by Johansen (1988, 1991*a*, 1992*b*, 1992*c*, 1994) on the basis of the maximum-likelihood analysis of the VAR error-correction representation. The procedures include among others (i) data-based selection of the co-integration rank, and (ii) testing restrictions on the co-integration space with a given rank. Limiting distributions used for the selection of rank are completely free from all the nuisance parameters. Moreover, the test statistics on the co-integration space are distributed asymptotically in χ^2 like those in Chapter 13. Deterministic trends are properly taken into consideration, and the method can be easily adapted to structural changes in the deterministic trends.

Johansen (1988, 1991*a*) has been motivated in part by the literature in the field called the reduced-rank regression, which is closely related to the econometric model of simultaneous equations. Identifiability of coefficients in a structural equation is determined by the rank of a certain submatrix of the reduced-form parameters. In the reduced-form regression of p dependent variables, $\boldsymbol{y}$, upon $\boldsymbol{q}$ independent variables, $\boldsymbol{x}$, the independent variable is partitioned as $\boldsymbol{x}' = (\boldsymbol{x}_1', \boldsymbol{x}_2')$ where $\boldsymbol{x}_2$ consists of q_2 variables, The ith observation of $\boldsymbol{y}$ is generated by

$$\boldsymbol{y}_i = (\boldsymbol{B}_1, \boldsymbol{B}_2)\begin{pmatrix}\boldsymbol{x}_{1i}\\ \boldsymbol{x}_{2i}\end{pmatrix} + \boldsymbol{u}_i, \qquad i = 1, \ldots, n \tag{15.1}$$

where the matrix $\boldsymbol{B}_2$ is $p \times q_2$. Anderson (1951) considered how to test $\mathrm{H}_0 : \rho(\boldsymbol{B}_2) = r$ against $\mathrm{H}_1 : \rho(\boldsymbol{B}_2) \geq r$. The results are as follows: (i) The likelihood ratio is expressed by roots of a certain determinental equation, which roots are later found identical to the squares of the canonical correlation coefficients between $\boldsymbol{x}_2$ and $\boldsymbol{y}$ after eliminating linear effects of $\boldsymbol{x}_1$; (ii) $(-2)\times$ (the log-likelihood ratio) is asymptotically distributed under H_0 in the χ^2 distribution with $(p-r)(q_2-r)$ degrees of freedom, which is consistent with the general theory of the maximum-likelihood principle, because $\rho(\boldsymbol{B}_2) = r$ implies $(p-r)(q_2-r)$ constraints upon the elements of $\boldsymbol{B}_2$.[1] The likelihood ratio test is found useful to determine $\rho(\boldsymbol{B}_2)$.

[1] Given an $m \times n$ matrix $\boldsymbol{A}$, partition it as

$$\boldsymbol{A} = \begin{pmatrix}\boldsymbol{A}_{11} & \boldsymbol{A}_{12}\\ \boldsymbol{A}_{21} & \boldsymbol{A}_{22}\end{pmatrix},$$

where $\boldsymbol{A}_{11}$ is $r \times r$ and non-singular. Then $\rho(\boldsymbol{A}) = r$ implies $\boldsymbol{A}_{22} = \boldsymbol{A}_{21}\boldsymbol{A}_{11}^{-1}\boldsymbol{A}_{12}$, which is $(m-r)(n-r)$ constraints on the elements of $\boldsymbol{A}$.

The model such as (15.1) is called the reduced-rank regression. Its characteristic is that when the coefficient matrix is $p \times q$, the pq elements of the matrix are not free to move in the pq dimensional Euclidean space, but bound by some equality constraints. Anderson and Kunitomo (1992, 1994) extend Anderson (1951) to incorporate not only the likelihood ratio test but also the Wald and the Lagrange multiplier tests, and Kunitomo (1994) applies the results to the co-integration analysis in a general non-stationary process. However, I shall follow Johansen (1991*a*) in the following presentation.

The equation (15.1) resembles the VAR error-correction representation, (12.24). The variables, $\boldsymbol{y}$, $\boldsymbol{x}_1$, and $\boldsymbol{x}_2$ in (15.1) correspond respectively to $\Delta\boldsymbol{x}_t$, $(\Delta\boldsymbol{x}_{t-1}, \ldots, \Delta\boldsymbol{x}_{t-q+1})$, and $\boldsymbol{x}_{t-1}$ in (12.24). The canonical correlation in (15.1) between $\boldsymbol{x}_2$ and $\boldsymbol{y}$ after eliminating effects of $\boldsymbol{x}_1$ corresponds to the canonical correlation in (12.24) between $\Delta\boldsymbol{x}_t$ and $\boldsymbol{x}_{t-1}$ after eliminating effects of $(\Delta\boldsymbol{x}_{t-1}, \ldots, \Delta\boldsymbol{x}_{t-q+1})$. Needless to say that the distributions of the statistics are different between the two models because of the non-stationarity in (12.24).

Prior to the development of co-integration analysis the VAR models had been estimated either by the OLS on the levels of $\boldsymbol{x}_t$,

$$\boldsymbol{x}_t - \boldsymbol{\Pi}_1\boldsymbol{x}_{t-1} - \ldots - \boldsymbol{\Pi}_q\boldsymbol{x}_{t-q} = \boldsymbol{\varepsilon}_t,$$

or by OLS on the difference, $\Delta\boldsymbol{x}_t$,

$$\Delta\boldsymbol{x}_t - \boldsymbol{\Phi}_1\Delta\boldsymbol{x}_{t-1} - \ldots - \boldsymbol{\Phi}_q\Delta\boldsymbol{x}_{t-q} = \boldsymbol{\varepsilon}_t.$$

The former OLS is consistent under all conceivable conditions,[2] but not efficient if $\{\boldsymbol{x}_t\}$ has integration order $I(1)$ and co-integrated. The inefficiency is due to the reduced-rank condition being ignored, where the condition is that $\boldsymbol{\Pi}(1) \equiv \boldsymbol{I} - \boldsymbol{\Pi}_1 - \ldots - \boldsymbol{\Pi}_q$ has a rank less than the number of elements of $\boldsymbol{x}_t$ when $\{\boldsymbol{x}_t\}$ is co-integrated. The latter OLS on $\Delta\boldsymbol{x}_t$ is consistent only when $\{\boldsymbol{x}_t\}$ is $I(1)$ and not co-integrated. If $\{\boldsymbol{x}_t\}$ is co-integrated, the VAR in $\Delta\boldsymbol{x}_t$ is an invalid model as shown in Section 12.2.2.

Banerjee *et al.* (1993) present the Johansen method in detail. I shall omit the explanation of its mathematical aspect. Instead I shall give more consideration to those points that require clarification in light of the criticisms raised by Phillips (1991*d*) against its implementation.

The plan of the present chapter is as follows. Section 15.1 considers the determination of co-integration rank from the data. The derivation of the test statistic and the sequence of hypothesis testing for determination of rank are described in fair details following Johansen (1988, 1991*a*, *b*, 1992*b*) and incorporating a criticism made in Phillips (1991*d*). Results of simulation studies in Toda (1994, 1995) and Morimune and Mantani (1995) on the determination of rank and lag order are summarized. Structural changes are introduced in deterministic trends as they are found important in Part I. Section 15.2 is concerned

[2] Its limiting distribution is derived in Ahn and Reinsel (1988, 1990).

with the identification problem on $\boldsymbol{B}$ and the hypothesis testing on the co-integration space, following Johansen (1991*a*) and Johansen and Juselius (1990, 1992) and acknowledging a comment in Phillips (1991*d*). I shall do my best to explain differences between the co-integrated regression in Chapter 13 and the Johansen method in this chapter. Section 15.3 criticizes, following Phillips (1991*d*), a misleading practice of listing the estimates of co-integrating vectors. Section 15.4 deals with a system conditioned on exogenous variables. Following Johansen (1992*c*, 1992*d*) and Johansen and Juselius (1992) a condition for weak exogeneity is presented. Consideration of the weak exogeneity contributes again to clarifying the relationships between the VAR in this chapter and the co-integrated regression in Chapter 13. Granger non-causality in the long run is called co-integrating exogeneity in Hunter (1992). I shall point out a simple but useful case where the weak exogeneity, the non-causality in the long run, and the validity of co-integrated regressions are all united. I shall also introduce the results in Banerjee *et al.* (1993: 288–91) on the weak exogeneity and the results in Toda and Phillips (1993) on the Granger causality test. Section 15.5 surveys empirical applications of the maximum-likelihood analysis of VAR. It has influenced my entire writing of Part II.[3]

The notations such as det[ ] and $\rho(\ )$ are continued from Chapters 11 and 12. The Johansen method uses the flexible definition of co-integrations not requiring that each variable is $I(1)$ individually. As indicated in Section 12.1 and 12.3.7, when an $I(0)$ variable is included, a unit vector can be a co-integrating vector. How to distinguish such co-integrations from long-run relationships was indicated in Section 12.3.7.

15.1 Determination of Co-integration Rank

15.1.1 Introduction

Let us consider the model (12.26), which is reproduced here as

$$\Delta \boldsymbol{x}_t = \boldsymbol{A}\boldsymbol{B}' x_{t-1} + \boldsymbol{\Gamma}_1 \Delta \boldsymbol{x}_{t-1} + \ldots + \Gamma_{q-1} \Delta \boldsymbol{x}_{t-q+1} + \boldsymbol{\mu} + \boldsymbol{\varepsilon}_t$$

$$\rho(\boldsymbol{A}) = \rho(\boldsymbol{B}) = r, \quad 0 \le r \le k. \tag{15.2}$$

Johansen (1991*a*) has $\boldsymbol{x}_{t-q}$ instead of $\boldsymbol{x}_{t-1}$ on the right-hand side of (15.2), but the essence of the following reasoning does not depend on whether $\boldsymbol{x}_{t-1}$ or $\boldsymbol{x}_{t-q}$ is placed. Let $E(\boldsymbol{\varepsilon}_t \boldsymbol{\varepsilon}_t') \equiv \boldsymbol{\Omega}$. Unknown parameters are $\boldsymbol{A}$, $\boldsymbol{B}$, $\boldsymbol{\Gamma}_1, \ldots, \boldsymbol{\Gamma}_{q-1}$, $\boldsymbol{\mu}$, $\boldsymbol{\Omega}$, and r. It is assumed that the lag order, q, is known. The presence of $\boldsymbol{\mu}$ on the right-hand side generates a deterministic linear trend in $\boldsymbol{x}_t$ unless $\boldsymbol{A}_\perp' \boldsymbol{\mu} = \boldsymbol{0}$.

[3] Phillips (1993) applies the idea of fully modified least squares, given in Appendix 6, to the estimation of a possibly co-integrated VAR, and obtains results that are remarkable in terms of the asymptotic theory. It is not included in the present survey because it depends heavily upon the estimation of long-run covariance matrix.

The first problem is how to select r, the co-integration rank, in light of the available data. We are concerned with the hypotheses,

$$\mathrm{H}(r) : \rho(\boldsymbol{A}) = \rho(\boldsymbol{B}) \le r, \quad 0 \le r \le k. \tag{15.3}$$

It is important to bear in mind that the hypotheses here are inequalities $\le$ rather than equalities. (Different hypotheses will be introduced later.) Altogether $(k+1)$ hypotheses, $\mathrm{H}(k), \mathrm{H}(k-1), \ldots, \mathrm{H}(0)$ are available, and they form a nested sequence. What each hypothesis means can be considered on the basis of Section 12.2.2. $\mathrm{H}(k)$ places no restrictions upon the parameters. $\{\boldsymbol{x}_t\}$ may be stationary or non-stationary, and if it is non-stationary it may or may not be co-integrated. $\mathrm{H}(k-1)$ is equivalent to the singularity of $\boldsymbol{\Pi}(1)$. Recalling that the non-singularity of $\boldsymbol{\Pi}(1)$ is the stationarity of $\boldsymbol{x}_t$, we see that $\mathrm{H}(k-1)$ specifies $\{\boldsymbol{x}_t\}$ to be non-stationary, but it may or may not be co-integrated. Therefore testing for $\mathrm{H}(k-1)$ against $\mathrm{H}(k)$ is a test for non-stationarity with the non-stationarity as the null. $\mathrm{H}(k-2)$ specifies $\{\boldsymbol{x}_t\}$ to be non-stationary and moreover not to have $(k-1)$ linearly independent co-integrating vectors. Thus testing for $\mathrm{H}(k-2)$ against $\mathrm{H}(k-1)$ is a test for at most $(k-2)$ co-integrating vectors. Finally $\mathrm{H}(0)$ means absence of co-integration.

15.1.2 Derivation of likelihood ratio test statistics

The likelihood ratio test may be applied to the above sequence of hypotheses. For the determination of r all the parameters but r must be concentrated out of the log-likelihood function. It is seen that, given $\boldsymbol{B}$, (15.2) is a special case of the seemingly unrelated regression (SUR) model with $\boldsymbol{B}'\boldsymbol{x}_{t-1}, \Delta\boldsymbol{x}_{t-1}, \ldots, \Delta\boldsymbol{x}_{t-q+1}, 1$ as regressors. It is special in having the identical set of right-hand side variables in each equation, and it is well known for such a special SUR model that the maximum-likelihood estimators of all parameters are identical to the OLS estimators, in which the disturbance covariance structure is not exploited for the estimation. All the parameters other than r and $\boldsymbol{B}$ can be concentrated out by replacing them by their OLS estimators. But (15.2) is a reduced-rank SUR, and $\boldsymbol{B}$ will require special consideration.

Let $z_{0t} \equiv \Delta\boldsymbol{x}_t$, $z_{1t} \equiv \boldsymbol{x}_{t-1}$, $z_{2t} \equiv (\Delta\boldsymbol{x}'_{t-1}, \ldots, \Delta\boldsymbol{x}'_{t-q+1}, 1)'$, and $\boldsymbol{\Gamma} \equiv (\boldsymbol{\Gamma}_1, \ldots, \boldsymbol{\Gamma}_{q-1}, \boldsymbol{\mu})$. Then (15.2) is

$$z_{0t} = \boldsymbol{A}\boldsymbol{B}'z_{1t} + \boldsymbol{\Gamma}z_{2t} + \boldsymbol{\varepsilon}_t. \tag{15.4}$$

(15.4) is a reduced-rank regression model. Assume that $\{\boldsymbol{\varepsilon}_t\}$ is i.i.d. and $\boldsymbol{\varepsilon}_t$ is $N(\boldsymbol{0}, \boldsymbol{\Omega})$. The log-likelihood generated by (15.4) is asymptotically

$$\log L(\boldsymbol{A}, \boldsymbol{B}, \boldsymbol{\Omega}^{-1}, \boldsymbol{\Gamma}, r) = \frac{T}{2}\log\det[\boldsymbol{\Omega}^{-1}] - \tfrac{1}{2}\sum\nolimits_{t=q+1}^{T}(z_{0t} - \boldsymbol{A}\boldsymbol{B}'z_{1t} - \boldsymbol{\Gamma}z_{2t})'\boldsymbol{\Omega}^{-1}(z_{0t} - \boldsymbol{A}\boldsymbol{B}'z_{1t} - \boldsymbol{\Gamma}z_{2t}), \tag{15.5a}$$

ignoring the effect of initials.

The concentration will proceed in the order of $\boldsymbol{\Gamma}$, $\boldsymbol{\Omega}^{-1}$, $\boldsymbol{A}$, and $\boldsymbol{B}$. To concentrate $\boldsymbol{\Gamma}$ out let its OLS estimator be

$$\hat{\Gamma}(\boldsymbol{A}, \boldsymbol{B}, r) = \left(\sum\nolimits_t (z_{0t} - \boldsymbol{A}\boldsymbol{B}'z_{1t})z'_{2t}\right)\left(\sum\nolimits_t z_{2t}z'_{2t}\right)^{-1}. \tag{15.6}$$

Substituting (15.6) into $(z_{0t} - \boldsymbol{A}\boldsymbol{B}'z_{1t} - \boldsymbol{\Gamma}z_{2t})$ in (15.5a) we obtain residuals in the OLS, but the residuals are also obtained as follows. Regress z_{it}, $i = 0, 1$ upon z_{2t} to get

$$\zeta_{it} = z_{it} - \hat{\boldsymbol{\Gamma}}_i z_{2t}, \qquad i = 0, 1,$$

and form $\boldsymbol{\zeta}_{0t} - \boldsymbol{A}\boldsymbol{B}'\boldsymbol{\zeta}_{1t}$. The concentration with respect to $\boldsymbol{\Gamma}$ yields the log-likelihood

$$\log L(\boldsymbol{A}, \boldsymbol{B}, \boldsymbol{\Omega}^{-1}, r) = \frac{T}{2}\log\ \det[\boldsymbol{\Omega}^{-1}] - \tfrac{1}{2}\sum\nolimits_t (\boldsymbol{\zeta}_{0t} - \boldsymbol{A}\boldsymbol{B}'\boldsymbol{\zeta}_{1t})'\boldsymbol{\Omega}^{-1}$$

$$\times(\boldsymbol{\zeta}_{0t} - \boldsymbol{A}\boldsymbol{B}'\boldsymbol{\zeta}_{1t}). \tag{15.5b}$$

The maximum-likelihood estimator of $\boldsymbol{\Omega}$ based on (15.5b) is

$$\hat{\Omega}(\boldsymbol{A}, \boldsymbol{B}, r) \equiv T^{-1}\sum\nolimits_t (\boldsymbol{\zeta}_{0t} - \boldsymbol{A}\boldsymbol{B}'\boldsymbol{\zeta}_{1t})(\boldsymbol{\zeta}_{0t} - \boldsymbol{A}\boldsymbol{B}'\boldsymbol{\zeta}_{1t})'. \tag{15.7}$$

Substituting (15.7) in (15.5b), we obtain the further concentrated log-likelihood,

$$\log L(\boldsymbol{A}, \boldsymbol{B}, r) = -\frac{T}{2}\log\det[\hat{\boldsymbol{\Omega}}(\boldsymbol{A}, \boldsymbol{B}, r)], \tag{15.5c}$$

because the second term on the right-hand side of (15.5b) does not contain unknown parameters when $\hat{\boldsymbol{\Omega}}$ is substituted into $\boldsymbol{\Omega}$.

Define $\qquad \boldsymbol{S}_{ij} \equiv T^{-1}\sum\nolimits_t \zeta_{it}\zeta'_{jt} \qquad i, j = 0, 1.$

Let us consider first the case, $r = k$. Writing $\boldsymbol{\Pi} \equiv \boldsymbol{A}\boldsymbol{B}'$ and concentrating it out of (15.5c) through the OLS of $\boldsymbol{\Pi}$, $\hat{\boldsymbol{\Pi}} = \boldsymbol{S}_{01}\boldsymbol{S}_{11}^{-1}$, we have

$$\log L(\mathrm{H}(k)) = -\frac{T}{2}\log\ \det[\boldsymbol{S}_{00} - \boldsymbol{S}_{01}\boldsymbol{S}_{11}^{-1}\boldsymbol{S}_{10}], \tag{15.5d}$$

with

$$\hat{\boldsymbol{\Pi}} = \boldsymbol{S}_{01}\boldsymbol{S}_{11}^{-1} \tag{15.8}$$

Secondly, as for the other extreme case, $r = 0$ i.e. $\boldsymbol{A} = \boldsymbol{B} = \boldsymbol{0}$, (15.5$c$) is reduced to

$$\log L(\mathrm{H}(0)) = -\frac{T}{2}\log\ \det[\boldsymbol{S}_{00}]. \tag{15.5e}$$

Let us then consider an intermediate case, $0 < r < k$. To maximize (15.5c) we must minimize $\det[\hat{\Omega}(\boldsymbol{A}, \boldsymbol{B}, r)]$ in (15.5c). Given $\boldsymbol{B}$, $\det[\hat{\Omega}(\boldsymbol{A}, \boldsymbol{B}, r)]$ is minimized with respect to $\boldsymbol{A}$ by setting $\boldsymbol{A}$ to its OLS, $\hat{\boldsymbol{A}}(\boldsymbol{B}) = \boldsymbol{S}_{01}\boldsymbol{B}(\boldsymbol{B}'\boldsymbol{S}_{11}\boldsymbol{B})^{-1}$. Substituting it into (15.5c) we are led to minimizing

$$\det[\boldsymbol{S}_{00} - \boldsymbol{S}_{01}\boldsymbol{B}(\boldsymbol{B}'\boldsymbol{S}_{11}\boldsymbol{B})^{-1}\boldsymbol{B}'\boldsymbol{S}_{10}] \tag{15.9}$$

with respect to $\boldsymbol{B}$. This determinant is invariant when $\boldsymbol{B}$ is replaced by $\boldsymbol{BQ}$ with any non-singular $r \times r$ matrix $\boldsymbol{Q}$, which reflects the unidentifiability of $\boldsymbol{B}$. Let $\hat{\lambda}_1 > \ldots > \hat{\lambda}_k$ be the decreasingly ordered roots of

$$\det[\lambda \boldsymbol{S}_{11} - \boldsymbol{S}_{10}\boldsymbol{S}_{00}^{-1}\boldsymbol{S}_{01}] = 0. \tag{15.10}$$

The $\hat{\lambda}$s are real and non-negative as they are eigenvalues of $\boldsymbol{S}_{11}^{-1/2}\boldsymbol{S}_{10}\boldsymbol{S}_{00}^{-1}$ $\boldsymbol{S}_{01}\boldsymbol{S}_{11}^{-1/2}$. They are less than unity because $\boldsymbol{S}_{11} - \boldsymbol{S}_{10}\boldsymbol{S}_{00}^{-1}\boldsymbol{S}_{01}$ is positive definite. In fact the $\hat{\lambda}$s are squares of canonical correlation coefficients between $\boldsymbol{\zeta}_0$ and $\boldsymbol{\zeta}_1$. Let $\hat{\boldsymbol{v}}_i$ be a $k \times 1$ vector associated with $\hat{\lambda}_i$ such that

$$(\hat{\lambda}_i \boldsymbol{S}_{11} - \boldsymbol{S}_{10}\boldsymbol{S}_{00}^{-1}\boldsymbol{S}_{01})\hat{\boldsymbol{v}}_i = \boldsymbol{0}, \quad i = 1, \ldots, k. \tag{15.11}$$

The minimized value of (15.9) is $\det[\boldsymbol{S}_{00}]\Pi_{i=1}^{r}(1 - \hat{\lambda}_i)$,[4] and that *one way to attain the minimum* is to set

$$(a)\ \hat{\boldsymbol{B}} = [\hat{\boldsymbol{v}}_1, \ldots, \hat{\boldsymbol{v}}_r], \qquad (b)\ \hat{\boldsymbol{B}}'\boldsymbol{S}_{11}\hat{\boldsymbol{B}} = \boldsymbol{I}_r. \tag{15.12}$$

For $0 < r < k$ the concentrated log-likelihood is

$$\log L(\mathrm{H}(r)) = -\frac{T}{2}\log\ \det[\boldsymbol{S}_{00}] - \frac{T}{2}\sum_{i=1}^{r}\log(1 - \hat{\lambda}_i) \tag{15.5f}$$

We also have

$$\hat{\boldsymbol{A}} = \boldsymbol{S}_{01}\hat{\boldsymbol{B}}. \tag{15.13}$$

Note that only the largest r roots of (15.10) and the associated vectors enter into (15.12) and (15.5f) though (15.10) has altogether k roots. The above procedure is identical to calculations in the reduced-rank regression, and parallel to derivation of the limited information maximum-likelihood estimator in the simultaneous equations model as pointed out in Banerjee *et al.* (1993: 264–5).

[4] (15.9) is equal to $\det[\boldsymbol{S}_{00}]\det[\boldsymbol{B}'\boldsymbol{S}_{11}\boldsymbol{B} - \boldsymbol{B}'\boldsymbol{S}_{10}\boldsymbol{S}_{00}^{-1}\boldsymbol{S}_{01}\boldsymbol{B}]/\det[\boldsymbol{B}'\boldsymbol{S}_{11}\boldsymbol{B}]$ because

$$\det\left[\begin{pmatrix} \boldsymbol{S}_{00} & \boldsymbol{S}_{01}\boldsymbol{B} \\ \boldsymbol{B}'\boldsymbol{S}_{10} & \boldsymbol{B}'\boldsymbol{S}_{11}\boldsymbol{B} \end{pmatrix}\right] = \det[\boldsymbol{S}_{00}]\det[\boldsymbol{B}'\boldsymbol{S}_{11}\boldsymbol{B} - \boldsymbol{B}'\boldsymbol{S}_{10}\boldsymbol{S}_{00}^{-1}\boldsymbol{S}_{01}\boldsymbol{B}]$$

$$= \det[\boldsymbol{B}'\boldsymbol{S}_{11}\boldsymbol{B}]\det[\boldsymbol{S}_{00} - \boldsymbol{S}_{01}\boldsymbol{B}(\boldsymbol{B}'\boldsymbol{S}_{11}\boldsymbol{B})^{-1}\boldsymbol{B}'\boldsymbol{S}_{10}].$$

We must minimize

$$\det[\boldsymbol{B}'\boldsymbol{S}_{11}\boldsymbol{B} - \boldsymbol{B}'\boldsymbol{S}_{10}\boldsymbol{S}_{00}^{-1}\boldsymbol{S}_{01}\boldsymbol{B}]/\det[\boldsymbol{B}'\boldsymbol{S}_{11}\boldsymbol{B}] \tag{$*$}$$

with respect to $\boldsymbol{B}$. Let $\boldsymbol{\Lambda} = \mathrm{diag}[\hat{\lambda}_1, \ldots, \hat{\lambda}_k]$, where the $\hat{\lambda}$s are defined in relation to (15.10), and let $\mathbf{V}$ be the matrix that consists of $\hat{\boldsymbol{v}}_1, \ldots, \hat{\boldsymbol{v}}_k$ defined in (15.11). The matrix of orthonormalized eigenvectors of $\boldsymbol{S}_{11}^{-1/2}\boldsymbol{S}_{10}\boldsymbol{S}_{00}^{-1}\boldsymbol{S}_{01}\boldsymbol{S}_{11}^{-1/2}$ is $\boldsymbol{S}_{11}^{1/2}\boldsymbol{V}$, and the diagonal matrix of eigenvalues is $\boldsymbol{\Lambda}$. From these it follows that $\boldsymbol{V}'\boldsymbol{S}_{11}\boldsymbol{V} = \boldsymbol{I}_k$ and $\boldsymbol{V}'\boldsymbol{S}_{10}\boldsymbol{S}_{00}^{-1}\boldsymbol{S}_{01}\boldsymbol{V} = \boldsymbol{\Lambda}$. Transform $\boldsymbol{B}$ to $\boldsymbol{F}$ through $\boldsymbol{B} = \boldsymbol{VF}$, and then transform $\boldsymbol{F}$ to $\boldsymbol{Y}$ through $\boldsymbol{F}(\boldsymbol{F}'\boldsymbol{F})^{-1/2} = \boldsymbol{Y}$. Then ($*$) above is $\det[\boldsymbol{Y}'(\boldsymbol{I}_k - \boldsymbol{\Lambda})\boldsymbol{Y}]$, which is to be minimized subject to $\boldsymbol{Y}'\boldsymbol{Y} = \boldsymbol{I}_r$. The minimum is achieved by $\boldsymbol{Y} = [\boldsymbol{I}_r, \boldsymbol{0}]'$ because $1 > \hat{\lambda}_1 > \ldots > \hat{\lambda}_k > 0$. $\boldsymbol{F}$ is not unique, but we may take it as $\boldsymbol{Y}$. Then $\boldsymbol{B} = \boldsymbol{V}[\boldsymbol{I}_r, \boldsymbol{0}]'$.

The minimized value of ($*$) is $\Pi_{i=1}^{r}(1 - \hat{\lambda}_i)$, and the minimized value of $\det[\boldsymbol{S}_{00} - \boldsymbol{S}_{01}\boldsymbol{B}$ $(\boldsymbol{B}'\boldsymbol{S}_{11}\boldsymbol{B})^{-1}\boldsymbol{B}'\boldsymbol{S}_{10}]$ is $\det[\boldsymbol{S}_{00}]\Pi_{i=1}^{r}(1 - \hat{\lambda}_i)$.

We now find it more convenient to express (15.5d) also by the $\hat{\lambda}$s. In fact there is no obstacle to extending the above reasoning to $r = k$, and

$$\log L(\mathrm{H}(k)) = -\frac{T}{2}\log\ \det[\boldsymbol{S}_{00}] - \frac{T}{2}\sum_{i=1}^{k}\log(1-\hat{\lambda}_i). \qquad (15.5d')$$

The likelihood ratio test statistic for testing H(r) against H($r+1$), $r = 0, 1, \ldots, k-1$, is derived from (15.5e), (15.5f), and (15.5′) as

$$-2[\log L(\mathrm{H}(r)) - \log L(\mathrm{H}(r+1))] = -T\log(1-\hat{\lambda}_{r+1}). \qquad (15.14)$$

Also the likelihood ratio statistic for testing H(r) against H(k), $r = 0, 1, \ldots, k-1$, is

$$-2[\log L(\mathrm{H}(r)) - \log L(\mathrm{H}(k))] = -T\left[\sum_{i=1}^{k-r}\log(1-\hat{\lambda}_{r+i})\right]. \qquad (15.15)$$

15.1.3 Determination of co-integration rank

I now introduce

$$\overline{\mathrm{H}}(r) : \rho(\boldsymbol{A}) = \rho(\boldsymbol{B}) = r, \quad 0 \le r \le k.$$

Johansen (1991a) shows that under $\overline{\mathrm{H}}(r)$ $\hat{\lambda}_1, \ldots, \hat{\lambda}_r$, i.e. the r largest roots of (15.10) converge in probability to positive numbers (in fact, eigenvalues of a certain non-stochastic positive definite matrix), and $\hat{\lambda}_{r+1}, \ldots, \hat{\lambda}_k$ converge to zero in probability. Moreover, $(T\hat{\lambda}_{r+1}, \ldots, T\hat{\lambda}_k)$ do converge in distribution. To derive the limiting distributions under $\overline{\mathrm{H}}(r)$ let $\boldsymbol{w}(s)' = (w_1(s), \ldots, w_{k-r}(s)), 0 \le s \le 1$, be a vector standard Wiener process, and let $\boldsymbol{f}^{(1)}(s)$ be the first $(k-r-1)$ elements of $\boldsymbol{w}(s) - \int_0^1 \boldsymbol{w}(s)ds$, and $\boldsymbol{f}(s)' = (\boldsymbol{f}^{(1)}(s)', s - 1/2)$. Construct a $(k-r)\times(k-r)$ random matrix

$$\int_0^1 d\boldsymbol{w}(s)\boldsymbol{f}(s)'\left[\int_0^1 \boldsymbol{f}(s)\boldsymbol{f}(s)'ds\right]^{-1}\int_0^1 \boldsymbol{f}(s)d\boldsymbol{w}(s)'. \qquad (15.16)$$

Let $\boldsymbol{A}_\perp$ be a $k\times(k-r)$ matrix such that $\boldsymbol{A}_\perp'\boldsymbol{A} = \boldsymbol{0}$. If $\overline{\mathrm{H}}(r)$ holds true and if $\boldsymbol{A}_\perp'\boldsymbol{\mu} \neq \boldsymbol{0}$, $T\left(\sum_{i=1}^{k-r}\hat{\lambda}_{r+i}\right)$ is distributed asymptotically in the same distribution as that of the trace of (15.16), and $T\hat{\lambda}_{r+1}$ is distributed asymptotically in the same distribution as that of the maximum eigenvalue of (15.16). This is proved in appendices A and B of Johansen (1991a). Notice that (15.14) $\approx T\hat{\lambda}_{r+1}$ and (15.15) $\approx T\sum_1^{k-r}\hat{\lambda}_{r+i}$. Johansen and Juselius (1990) call (15.14) and (15.15) respectively the maximum eigenvalue and the trace test statistics, and tabulate the null asymptotic distributions. Osterwald-Lenum (1992) recalculates and extends the tables in Johansen and Juselius (1990). The condition $\boldsymbol{A}_\perp'\boldsymbol{\mu} \neq \boldsymbol{0}$ means presence of a linear trend in $\{\boldsymbol{x}_t\}$ as shown in Section 12.2.5. The distributions of the likelihood ratio test statistics for the case $\boldsymbol{A}_\perp'\boldsymbol{\mu} = \boldsymbol{0}$ are also given in Johansen (1991a). Of course it is different from that derived from (15.16). Reinsel and Ahn (1992) present an interesting aspect of the likelihood ratio, (15.15).

Even though the test statistics were derived from the assumption that ε_t is distributed in a normal distribution, the limiting distribution of the test statistic does not depend on this assumption as is often observed in many econometric models.

While H(0), H(1), ..., H(k) are nested (in fact the tree diagram has only one trunk and no branches), $\overline{\mathrm{H}}(0)$, $\overline{\mathrm{H}}(1)$, ..., $\overline{\mathrm{H}}(k)$ are not nested since $\overline{\mathrm{H}}(r) = \mathrm{H}(r) - \mathrm{H}(r-1)$. In the present problem Johansen (1992*b*) finds that the simple-to-general approach in H(0), H(1), ..., H(k) does lead to the correct selection of r with probability $(1-\alpha)$ if a significance level α is chosen. The reason is as follows.

Suppose that r^0 is the true value of co-integration rank. Let us use the maximum eigenvalue test statistic, (15.14), in the simple-to-general approach. The decision rule is (i) to start with $r = 0$, and (ii) to raise r whenever the test statistic $T\hat{\lambda}_{r+1}$ for testing H(r) against H($r+1$) is larger than the critical value determined by the distribution of the maximum eigenvalue of (15.16) with the significance level α. Throughout the trials the roots, $\hat{\lambda}_1, \ldots, \hat{\lambda}_k$ are the same roots of (15.10). But the numbers of rows and columns of (15.16) vary with r, and so does the critical value. If a tried value of r is smaller than r^0, $\hat{\lambda}_{r+1}$ converges in probability to a positive number, and $T\hat{\lambda}_{r+1}$ diverges to $+\infty$ as $T \to \infty$. Therefore we must reach r^0 with probability 1 (if T is sufficiently large). If the tried value of r is equal to r^0, $T\hat{\lambda}_{r+1}$ falls short of the critical value with probability $1-\alpha$. We stop at r^0 with probability $1-\alpha$, and go beyond r^0 with probability α. (If the tried value of r is larger than r^0, the limiting distribution of $T\hat{\lambda}_{r+1}$ is not that of the maximum eigenvalue of (15.16).) In the above sequence the maximum eigenvalue test may be replaced by the trace test.

The condition, $\boldsymbol{A}'_{\perp}\boldsymbol{\mu} \neq \boldsymbol{0}$, i.e. the existence of a linear trend in $\{x_t\}$, may be pre-tested for each element of $\{\boldsymbol{x}_t\}$ by the univariate method given in Chapter 8 on the testing for M_0^0 against M_0^1. If at least one element has a trend, it means $\boldsymbol{A}'_{\perp}\boldsymbol{\mu} \neq 0$. Johansen (1991*a*) shows a multivariate method to test the null hypothesis, $\rho(\boldsymbol{A}) = \rho(\boldsymbol{B}) = r$ and $\boldsymbol{A}'_{\perp}\boldsymbol{\mu} = \boldsymbol{0}$ against $\rho(\boldsymbol{A}) = \rho(\boldsymbol{B}) = r$, using a statistic distributed in χ^2 distribution with $(k-r)$ degrees of freedom under the null hypothesis. Moreover, Johansen (1992*b*) shows how to select r in conjunction with testing whether $\boldsymbol{A}'_{\perp}\boldsymbol{\mu} =$ or $\neq \boldsymbol{0}$ for each r.

Let $\hat{r}$ be the value of r thus selected. The maximum-likelihood estimates of $\boldsymbol{A}$ and $\boldsymbol{B}$, to be denoted by $\hat{\boldsymbol{A}}$ and $\hat{\boldsymbol{B}}$, are obtained through (15.13) and (15.12) with $r = \hat{r}$. The estimate of $\boldsymbol{\Omega}$ follows from (15.7), and $\boldsymbol{\Gamma}$ is estimated by (15.6). Johansen (1991*a*) proves that $\hat{\boldsymbol{\Gamma}}$, $\hat{\boldsymbol{\Omega}}$, and $\hat{\boldsymbol{A}}$ are all $\sqrt{T}$-consistent and the limiting distributions of their estimation errors are standard, and that, if B is somehow made identifiable (see Section 15.2.1), $\hat{\boldsymbol{B}}$ is T-consistent and the limiting distribution is represented by a mixed Gaussian. As indicated in Chapter 13 the t- and F-tests on $\boldsymbol{B}$ require only the standard normal and χ^2 distributions. Thus a non-standard test is confined to that on the co-integration rank.

[5] I am indebted to suggestions by Hiro Toda on the writing of the present paragraph.

15.1.4 Simulation studies on the co-integration rank

Toda (1994, 1995) performs a cleverly designed simulation experiment on the selection of co-integration rank. The lag order is 1 and a priori known, while the dimensionality of $\boldsymbol{x}$ is 2. The results are that $T = 100$ is inadequate to detect the true co-integration rank in a wide range of values of nuisance parameters. A part of the inadequacy is analogous to the weak power of the univariate unit root tests mentioned in Section 7.3.2, which means that $r = 0$ is not rejected often enough when the true state is $r \geq 1$. But here is an added aspect due to the multiple time series. This is the point that I referred to at the beginning of Part II and in Section 13.4.3. Specification errors on the mode of deterministic trends would further aggravate the difficulty.

I am not suggesting abandoning the determination of co-integration rank, but I am warning that it may be difficult in some cases of macroeconomic applications.

15.1.5 Determination of lag orders

So far I have assumed that the lag order, q, is known. In practice it is not, and it has to be determined from the available data before we begin the procedure described in Sections 15.1.2–3.

Consider a group of VAR models for a k elements vector stochastic process, $\{\boldsymbol{x}_t\}$,

$$\boldsymbol{x}_t = \boldsymbol{\Pi}_1 \boldsymbol{x}_{t-1} + \ldots + \boldsymbol{\Pi}_q \boldsymbol{x}_{t-q} + \boldsymbol{\mu} + \boldsymbol{\varepsilon}_t,$$

$$q = 0, 1, \ldots, q_{\max}.$$

Let q^0 be the true value of q, which means that $\boldsymbol{\Pi}_q = \boldsymbol{0}$ for $q = q^0 + 1, \ldots, q_{\max}$. The methods available for the estimation of q^0 can be classified into two classes.

One is to choose the q that minimizes some criterion function of q. Let $\boldsymbol{e}_{t(q)}$ be the k element residual vector at t in the OLS calculations with $(\boldsymbol{x}_{t-1}, \ldots, \boldsymbol{x}_{t-q})$ as regressors, and write $\boldsymbol{S}(q) = (T-q)^{-1} \sum_{t=q+1}^{T} \boldsymbol{e}_{t(q)} \boldsymbol{e}'_{t(q)}$. Akaike information criterion proposed in Akaike (1973) is

$$\tfrac{1}{2}(T-q) \log \det[\boldsymbol{S}(q)] + (k^2 q + k),$$

and Schwarz information criterion proposed in Schwarz (1978) is

$$\tfrac{1}{2}(T-q) \log \det[\boldsymbol{S}(q)] + \tfrac{1}{2}(k^2 q + k) \log(T-q).^6$$

The other class of methods is the general-to-specific model selection procedure similar to the order determination in the univariate model explained in Section 6.2.3. The hypotheses $\boldsymbol{\Pi}_q = \boldsymbol{0}$ are tested sequentially in the order of $q_{\max}, q_{\max} - 1, \ldots,$ and one chooses the first q for which $\boldsymbol{\Pi}_q = \boldsymbol{0}$ is rejected. A number of methods are available to test for $\boldsymbol{\Pi}_q = \boldsymbol{0}$. Sims, Stock, and Watson (1990) show that, no matter what the co-integration rank may be, the Wald

[6] Paulsen (1984) proves the consistency of the lag order selected by the Schwarz information criterion.

test statistic for $\mathbf{\Pi}_q = \mathbf{0}$ is distributed asymptotically in χ^2 distribution with k^2 degrees of freedom if $q \geq q^0 + 1$. Morimune and Mantani (1993) show that the likelihood ratio, $Tln(\det[\mathbf{S}(q-1)/\det[\mathbf{S}(q)])$, is distributed likewise, and also that the likelihood ratio is better than the Wald test statistic because the empirical size is closer to the nominal size for finite T. Another interesting result in Morimune and Mantani (1993) is that when OLS is run on

$$\Delta \boldsymbol{x}_t = \mathbf{\Pi}(1)\boldsymbol{x}_{t-1} + \mathbf{\Gamma}_1 \Delta \boldsymbol{x}_{t-1} + \ldots + \mathbf{\Gamma}_{q-1} \Delta \boldsymbol{x}_{t-q} + \boldsymbol{\mu} + \boldsymbol{\varepsilon}_t,$$

with $\Delta \boldsymbol{x}_t$ as the dependent variable and $(\boldsymbol{x}_{t-1}, \Delta \boldsymbol{x}_{t-1}, \ldots, \Delta \boldsymbol{x}_{t-q}, \boldsymbol{\iota})$ as the independent variables, the t-value for any element of $\mathbf{\Gamma}_1, \ldots, \mathbf{\Gamma}_{q-1}$ is asymptotically $N(0, 1)$ if its true value is zero. This can be used to search the highest lag order in which a given (i, j) position of $\mathbf{\Gamma}$s is non-zero. The levels of significance must be determined to implement the general-to-specific model selection procedures.

Finally, in both of the two classes of order-determination methods the selection of $q_{\max}$ affects the performance of the methods.

All the methods mentioned above are investigated in a simulation study in Morimune and Mantani (1993, 1995). They adopt respectively 1%, 1%, and $1/(k^2)$% for the significance levels of the Wald, likelihood ratio, and t-tests. Some highlights of the results are that both the likelihood ratio test and t-tests are useful to determine the lag order, and that especially the t-tests should be used to detect small values in $\mathbf{\Gamma}$ matrices. As for the information criterion the Akaike information criterion is better than the Schwarz in retaining the order with small values in elements of $\mathbf{\Gamma}$ matrices.

It is only when the true lag order is a priori known that the asymptotic theory for the determination of co-integration rank is valid. A theory is unavailable for the practical case where the lag order is determined from the data. In practice the method in Sections 15.1.2–3 has been used, treating the empirically determined lag order as though it were known a priori. A simulation study in Morimune and Mantani (1995) shows that different methods for the lag-order determination tends to produce an identical rank of co-integration (even though they may propose different lag orders), and that the rank shared by different methods is also identical to the co-integration rank determined in the hypothetical situation where the true lag order is known. However, this last determination of co-integration rank may err frequently with $T = 100$ as mentioned in Section 15.1.4.

Chao and Phillips (1994) adopt a Baysian model selection procedure to determine jointly the lag order and co-integration rank.

15.1.6 A research topic

If the MA unit root test in Section 3.4 is extended from a scalar MA process to a vector MA process for $\Delta \boldsymbol{x}_t$, it would meet a request from the testing of economic theories and also improve the selection of co-integration rank.

In the simple-to-general sequence of tests to determine the co-integration rank we test initially for the absence of co-integration against the presence of at most one co-integrating relation, next for at most one co-integrating relation against at most two relations, ... But in testing an economic theory we wish to have the null hypothesis indicate the existence of all the co-integrating relations derived from the economic theory. In terms of the notations used above we wish to test for $\overline{\mathrm{H}}(r)$ against $\mathrm{H}(r)$, which is a nested test, or test for $\overline{\mathrm{H}}(r)$ against $\mathrm{H}(r-1)$, which is a non-nested test.

In Chapter 8 the discrimination between M_0^1 and M_1^1 is made by combining two encompassing judgements, $M_0^1 \overset{E}{\rightarrow} M_1^1$ and $M_1^1 \overset{E}{\rightarrow} M_0^1$. In the present problem concerning two non-nested models, $\overline{\mathrm{H}}(r)$ and $\mathrm{H}(r-1)$, $H(r-1) \overset{E}{\rightarrow} \overline{\mathrm{H}}(r)$ can be analysed by comparing the observed value of $T\hat{\lambda}_r$ against its distribution that is applicable if the DGP is in $\mathrm{H}(r-1)$. In fact this comparison has been made in the simple-to-general sequence of tests. What is missing is $\overline{\mathrm{H}}(r) \overset{E}{\rightarrow} H(r-1)$, and it should be combined with $\mathrm{H}(r-1) \overset{E}{\rightarrow} \overline{\mathrm{H}}(r)$. It turns out that this is also what is requested in testing the economic theories.

$\overline{\mathrm{H}}(r)$ and $\mathrm{H}(r-1)$ are equivalent respectively to $\rho(\boldsymbol{C}(1)) = k-r$ and $\rho(\boldsymbol{C}(1)) \geq k-r+1$, where $\boldsymbol{C}(1)$ is associated with the long-run component of $\Delta \boldsymbol{x}_t$ in Section 12.1. Testing for $\overline{\mathrm{H}}(r)$ against $\mathrm{H}(r-1)$ is a non-standard problem in the maximum-likelihood theory, but it is not in the locally best invariant testing theory.[7]

15.1.7 Deterministic trends

The co-integration space that nullifies the stochastic trends only has been discussed in the last paragraph of Section 12.2.5. In relation to (12.27) the condition, $\boldsymbol{A}'_{\perp}\boldsymbol{\mu}_1 = \boldsymbol{0}$, can be tested, and if a quadratic trend is found missing from $\{\boldsymbol{x}_t\}$ we may proceed to the determination of co-integration rank, rewriting the model as

$$\Delta \boldsymbol{x}_t = \boldsymbol{A}\boldsymbol{B}^{*'}\boldsymbol{x}^*_{t-1} + (\boldsymbol{\Gamma}_1 L + \ldots + \boldsymbol{\Gamma}_{q-1}L^{q-1})\Delta \boldsymbol{x}_t + \boldsymbol{\mu}_0 + \boldsymbol{\varepsilon}_t, \tag{15.17}$$

where $\boldsymbol{B}^{*'} = [\boldsymbol{B}', \boldsymbol{b}_1]$, $\boldsymbol{b}_1 = (\boldsymbol{A}'\boldsymbol{A})^{-1}\boldsymbol{A}'\boldsymbol{\mu}_1$, and $\boldsymbol{x}_t^{*'} = (\boldsymbol{x}'_t, t)$. The reason is as follows. Using $\boldsymbol{I}_k = \boldsymbol{A}(\boldsymbol{A}'\boldsymbol{A})^{-1}\boldsymbol{A}' + \boldsymbol{A}_{\perp}(\boldsymbol{A}'_{\perp}\boldsymbol{A}_{\perp})^{-1}\boldsymbol{A}'_{\perp}$, i.e. $\boldsymbol{\mu}_1 = \boldsymbol{A}\boldsymbol{b}_1 + \boldsymbol{A}_{\perp}\boldsymbol{c}_1$ with $\boldsymbol{c}_1 = (\boldsymbol{A}'_{\perp}\boldsymbol{A}_{\perp})^{-1}\boldsymbol{A}'_{\perp}\boldsymbol{\mu}_1$, it is seen that $\boldsymbol{A}'_{\perp}\boldsymbol{\mu}_1 = \boldsymbol{0}$ implies $\boldsymbol{c}_1 = \boldsymbol{0}$ and hence $\boldsymbol{A}\boldsymbol{B}'\boldsymbol{x}_{t-1} + \boldsymbol{\mu}_1 t = \boldsymbol{A}\boldsymbol{B}^{*'}\boldsymbol{x}^*_{t-1} + \boldsymbol{\mu}_1$. (The $\boldsymbol{\mu}_0$ in (15.17) is $\boldsymbol{\mu}_0 + \boldsymbol{\mu}_1$ in (12.27).) The test and the limiting distribution are found in Johansen (1994), which also contains the test and the limiting distribution for the case where $\boldsymbol{A}'_{\perp}\boldsymbol{\mu}_1 \neq \boldsymbol{0}$. See also Osterwald-Lenum (1992) for the distribution.

From the result in Part I it is obvious that structural changes need to be introduced, which has already been revealed in Mizon (1991) and Mellander,

[7] Tanaka (1993), Harris and Inder (1992), and Leybourne and McCabe (1993) may be relevant to this problem.

Vredin, and Warne (1992). I illustrate the method by a one-time change in the slope of a linear trend. For each t let $\boldsymbol{\mu}_t$ be a $k \times 1$ deterministic vector such that

$$\mu_t = \begin{cases} \mu^0 \text{ if } 1 \leq t < T_0, \\ \mu^0 + \mu^1 \text{ if } T \geq t \geq T_0. \end{cases}$$

(15.2) is replaced by

$$\Delta \boldsymbol{x}_t = \boldsymbol{A}\boldsymbol{B}'\boldsymbol{x}_{t-1} + \boldsymbol{\Gamma}_1 \Delta \boldsymbol{x}_{t-1} + \ldots + \boldsymbol{\Gamma}_{q-1}\Delta \boldsymbol{x}_{t-q+1} + \boldsymbol{\mu}_t + \boldsymbol{\varepsilon}_t.$$

The derivation of the likelihood ratio test statistic is analogous to (15.5a–f), but the random matrix (15.16) has to be altered. Let $\lambda = (T - T_0)/T$, and consider the asymptotic theory with λ fixed while T goes to infinity. For $s \in [0, 1]$ construct

$$g(s) = \begin{cases} -\lambda & \text{if } 0 \leq s < 1 - \lambda \\ 1 - \lambda & \text{if } 1 \geq s \geq 1 - \lambda \end{cases}$$

$$h_1(s) = s - \tfrac{1}{2} - \tfrac{1}{2}g(s)$$

$$h_2(s) = \max(s - 1 + \lambda, 0) - \frac{\lambda^2}{2} - \frac{\lambda}{2}g(s) - \lambda^3(1 - 3\lambda + 3\lambda^2)^{-1}h_1(s).$$

Let $\boldsymbol{w}(s)$ be the $(k - r)$ dimensional standard Wiener process, and let $\boldsymbol{f}^{(1)}(s)$ be the first $(k - r - 2)$ elements of

$$\boldsymbol{w}(s) - \int \boldsymbol{w}(s)ds - \lambda^{-1}(1 - \lambda)^{-1}g(s) \int g(s)\boldsymbol{w}(s)ds.$$

Provided that $\boldsymbol{C}(1)\boldsymbol{\mu}^0 \neq \boldsymbol{0}$, $\boldsymbol{C}(1)\boldsymbol{\mu}^1 \neq \boldsymbol{0}$, and $\boldsymbol{C}(1)\boldsymbol{\mu}^0$ and $\boldsymbol{C}(1)\boldsymbol{\mu}^1$ are linearly independent, which implies that $r \leq k-2$, the $\boldsymbol{f}(s)$ in (15.16) should be replaced by $(\boldsymbol{f}^{(1)}(s)', h_1(s), h_2(s))$. The proof is analogous to appendices A and B of Johansen (1991a). Note that $g(s)$, $h_1(s)$, and $h_2(s)$ are mutually orthogonal over [0, 1] and also orthogonal each to a constant over [0, 1]. See Hatanaka and Koto (1994) for the other modes of structural changes and Kumitomo (1994) for a general treatment of deterministic trends.

15.2 Testing for Restrictions on the Co-integration Space

15.2.1 Identification problems and normalization rules

The co-integration matrix $\boldsymbol{B}'$ is not identified unless one introduces a normalization rule or a priori constraints derived from economic theories. If $\boldsymbol{B}'$ is a co-integration matrix, so is $\boldsymbol{Q}\boldsymbol{B}'$ with any non-singular $r \times r\,\boldsymbol{Q}$. (Remember, however, that $\boldsymbol{A}$ must also be transformed to $\boldsymbol{A}\boldsymbol{Q}^{-1}$ so that $\boldsymbol{A}\boldsymbol{B}'$ is invariant.) It is assumed that r is known below.

Different $\boldsymbol{B}$s can be grouped into observationally equivalent classes. Two $\boldsymbol{B}$s, $\boldsymbol{B}_1$ and $\boldsymbol{B}_2$, belong to the same class if and only if there exists a non-singular $r \times r\,\boldsymbol{Q}$ such that $\boldsymbol{B}_2' = \boldsymbol{Q}\boldsymbol{B}_1'$. Suppose that an economic theory postulates a set of long-run relations $B'x_t = 0$, and that we wish to test a property of B'. An example of the property is that b_1 is zero in $B' = (b_1, \ldots, b_k)$, i.e. the first element of x_t is not contained in any of the long-run relations though contained in some short-run relations. This property is invariant throughout all the left multiplications of B' by non-singular matrices. Thus all the observationally equivalent classes are classified into those in which all members have $b_1 = 0$ and those in which no members have $b_1 = 0$. The condition, $b_1 = 0$, is a property of (observationally equivalent) classes, and it can be tested by the data. For another example of the property of B' write $B' = (\tilde{b}_1, \ldots, \tilde{b}_r)'$ and denote a subvector of $\tilde{b}_1$ by $\tilde{b}_{11}$. Consider a property, $\tilde{b}_{11} = 0$. This means that a portion of the variables does not appear in the first long-run relation. This property is not invariant through left multiplications of B' by non-singular matrices. Each class contains those Bs such that $\tilde{b}_{11} = 0$ and those Bs such that $\tilde{b}_{11} \neq 0$. The condition, $\tilde{b}_{11} = 0$, is not a property of (observationally equivalent) classes, and cannot be tested by the data. Noting that all the members of the same class belong to the same column space of B (or the same row space of B'), Johansen (1988, 1991*a*) emphasized that one could test on the co-integration space but not on the co-integration vectors. Phillips (1991*d*) notes that many practitioners have not understood how the tests on the co-integrating space could be implemented.

A number of tests for the constraints on the co-integration space have been developed in Johansen (1988, 1991*a*) and Johansen and Juselius (1990, 1992), and they will be presented below. It is important to confirm that the constraints are properties of the observationally equivalent classes maintaining the invariance considered above. I emphasize two points involved in the basic methodology of Johansen (1988, 1991*a*).

1. Restrictions to the observationally equivalent classes may be interpreted as a result of compounding two restrictions. One is a just-identifying restriction represented by a normalization rule, and the other is an overidentifying restriction. Let F be a known $k \times r$ matrix such that $\rho(F) = r$. Then a normalization rule is provided by $F'B = I_r$ involving r^2 constraints.[8] Under the rule no $r \times r$ transformation matrices Q other than I_r are admitted for the transformation of B' into QB' to keep AB' invariant. (If $F'B_0 = I_r, F'B_0Q' = Q'$.) Therefore there is one and only one B' in a given (observationally equivalent) class that satisfies the normalization rule. In other words the rule just-identifies B'. Therefore any constraints that are introduced in addition to the normalization rule would lead to overidentification of B'. These constraints, which will be called effective in the following description of various tests, discriminate those classes which admit them and those which do not. One can test these effective constraints. The degrees of freedom are the numbers of these effective constraints. Illustrations will be provided in Section 15.2.2.

2. A given restriction may be represented by a combination of different rules of normalization and different over-identifying constraints, but, in so far as

[8] A seemingly more general form, $G'B = M$, can be put in the form $F'B = I_r$. M is a known $r \times r$ non-singular matrix, and G' is a known $r \times k$ matrix with full row rank.

the given restriction is a property of the observationally equivalent classes as defined above, the results of testing the restriction should be independent of the normalization rule adopted. Thus normalization rules are implicit in the Johansen method, but it is not important there which rules are adopted.

At this point it is appropriate to look back at the co-integrated regression in Chapter 13, considering the role that normalization rules might play there.

1. In Section 13.4.1 it was shown that it is the a priori knowledge about location of an $r \times r$ non-singular submatrix of $\boldsymbol{B}'$ that generates a co-integrated regression. In regard to this point it is important to bear in mind that if $\boldsymbol{F}'$ is not specialized beyond $r \times k$ and having a full row rank, the restriction $\boldsymbol{F}'\boldsymbol{B} = \boldsymbol{I}_r$ does not necessarily locate an $r \times r$ non-singular submatrix of $\boldsymbol{B}'$. It is a specific normalization such as $\boldsymbol{F}' = (\boldsymbol{0}, \boldsymbol{I}_r)$ that specifies location of an $r \times r$ non-singular submatrix, which in turn generates a co-integrated regression.

2. While a general normalization *selects* one representative from *each and every* observationally equivalent class, the specific normalization such as $\boldsymbol{F}' = (\boldsymbol{0}, \boldsymbol{I}_r)$ *rejects* those classes in which the last r rows of $\boldsymbol{B}$ form an $r \times r$ singular matrix. The specific normalization that generates a co-integrated regression excludes some observationally equivalent classes from our consideration from the outset. Such normalizations cannot be regarded as innocuous in our inference procedures.

3. Normalization rules in general free us from worry about the lack of identification in $\boldsymbol{B}$. The regression coefficients in the cointegrated regression models are identified.

Kleibergen and van Dijk (1994) present a methodology that is intermediate between the Johansen method and the co-integrated regression. They test for a co-integration rank, r, a priori specifying location of an $r \times r$ non-singular submatrix of $\boldsymbol{B}'$.

15.2.2 Various tests in light of the identification viewpoints

Based on a reasoning analogous to but more complicated than Chapter 13 concerning the mixed Gaussian estimator, Johansen (1991*a*) shows for a known value of r that $(-2) \times$ (the log-likelihood ratio) to test any p effective constraints upon $\boldsymbol{B}$ is asymptotically distributed in χ^2 distribution with p degrees of freedom. This general result may be specialized into several forms of linear hypotheses, for which the test statistics can be easily calculated. They are presented in the following subsections, 1–7, where r is known. In practice the rank selected in Section 15.1 is used without invalidating the asymptotic theory. A section below deals with a hypothesis on $\boldsymbol{A}$ as well.

I repeat two important points from Section 15.2.1. (*a*) Two $\boldsymbol{B}$s, $\boldsymbol{B}_1$ and $\boldsymbol{B}_2$, are observationally equivalent if and only if $\boldsymbol{B}_1 = \boldsymbol{B}_2\boldsymbol{P}$ with some non-singular $\boldsymbol{P}$; (*b*) a condition on $\boldsymbol{B}$ can be tested empirically only when it is a property of observationally equivalent classes, namely, the condition either holds in every member of an observationally equivalent class or fails in every member of an observationally equivalent class. An alternative statement is that a condition on $\boldsymbol{B}$ can be tested if and only if a $\boldsymbol{B}$ that meets the condition and another $\boldsymbol{B}$ that does not cannot be observationally equivalent. I shall show this testability on each one of the hypotheses that have been dealt with in the literature. *Users of these testing methods should keep in mind that what they investigate are not values of parameters, which are unidentified, but observationally equivalent classes of parameter values.*

The following results hold no matter what the modes of deterministic trends may be in so far as they are correctly specified and handled in Section 15.1.

1. $\boldsymbol{B} = \boldsymbol{HQ}$ with an a priori known $k \times r\,\boldsymbol{H}$.

Suppose that an economic theory specifies $\boldsymbol{H}'\boldsymbol{x}_t = \boldsymbol{0}$ as the long-run relations, where $\boldsymbol{H}$ is a priori specified and $\rho(\boldsymbol{H}) = r$. The $r \times r\,\boldsymbol{Q}$ is unspecified and arbitrary. This means that the base of the column space of $\boldsymbol{B}$ is completely specified. Take this for the null hypothesis, and consider testing it against $\overline{\boldsymbol{H}}(r)$, which is simply the statement that the co-integration rank is r but $\boldsymbol{B}'$ is completely unspecified otherwise.

Let $\boldsymbol{M}_H = \boldsymbol{I}_k - \boldsymbol{H}(\boldsymbol{H}'\boldsymbol{H})^{-1}\boldsymbol{H}'$. Then $\boldsymbol{M}_H\boldsymbol{H} = \boldsymbol{0}$. The condition of the hypothesis, $\boldsymbol{B} = \boldsymbol{HQ}$, is $\boldsymbol{M}_H\boldsymbol{B} = \boldsymbol{0}$. Concerning two $\boldsymbol{B}$s, $\boldsymbol{B}$ and $\boldsymbol{B}^*$, suppose that $\boldsymbol{M}_H\boldsymbol{B} = \boldsymbol{0}$ and $\boldsymbol{M}_H\boldsymbol{B}^* \neq \boldsymbol{0}$. Then it is not possible to have $\boldsymbol{B}^* = \boldsymbol{BP}$ with a non-singular $\boldsymbol{P}$. Therefore the condition of the hypothesis is a property of the observationally equivalent class.

The likelihood ratio test statistic is given in Johansen (1988) and Johansen and Jurelius (1992). The number of effective constraints is derived as follows. Partition $\boldsymbol{H}' = (\boldsymbol{H}_1', \boldsymbol{H}_2')$ and $\boldsymbol{B} = (\boldsymbol{B}_1', \boldsymbol{B}_2')'$, where $\boldsymbol{H}_1'$ and $\boldsymbol{B}_1'$ are both $r \times r$, and adopt the normalization rule $\boldsymbol{F}'\boldsymbol{B} = \boldsymbol{I}_r$ with $\boldsymbol{F}' = [\boldsymbol{I}_r, \boldsymbol{0}]$. Then $\boldsymbol{B}_1$ is set to $\boldsymbol{I}_r$ by the rule. Also $\boldsymbol{Q}$ is now restricted to $\boldsymbol{H}_1^{-1}$. The effective constraints bind $\boldsymbol{B}_2$ as $\boldsymbol{H}_2\boldsymbol{H}_1^{-1}$. The degrees of freedom are the number of effective constraints, i.e. the number of elements of $\boldsymbol{B}_2$, which is $r(k - r)$. The degrees of freedom do not depend on the particular $\boldsymbol{F}$ chosen above.

2. $\boldsymbol{B} = \boldsymbol{HQ}$ with a known $k \times r_1\,\boldsymbol{H}$, where $r_1 \geq r$.

The a priori specified matrix $\boldsymbol{H}$ is $k \times r_1$, $r \leq r_1 \leq k$, and $\rho(\boldsymbol{H}) = r_1$, and $\boldsymbol{Q}$ is $r_1 \times r$ but arbitrary otherwise. The null hypothesis, $\boldsymbol{B} = \boldsymbol{HQ}$, means that the base of the column space of $\boldsymbol{B}$ is contained in the vector space spanned by columns of $\boldsymbol{H}$, i.e. the column space of $\boldsymbol{B}$ is contained in the column space of $\boldsymbol{H}$. The constraint may be used to place a common restriction upon all columns of $\boldsymbol{B}$ as seen from the following example,

$$\boldsymbol{H} = \begin{pmatrix} 1 & 0 & 0 \\ -1 & 0 & 0 \\ 0 & 1 & 0 \\ 0 & 0 & 1 \end{pmatrix}, \qquad \boldsymbol{Q} \text{ is } 3 \times 2.$$

In $\boldsymbol{HQ}$ the first and the second elements of every column have identical absolute values with opposite signs. It can be shown in the same way as 1 above that $\boldsymbol{B} = \boldsymbol{HQ}$ is a property of observationally equivalent classes. See Johansen and Juselius (1992) for the derivation of the test statistic and its illustration.

The number of effective constraints is obtained as follows. Partition $\boldsymbol{B} = (\boldsymbol{B}_1', \boldsymbol{B}_2')'$, where $\boldsymbol{B}_1$ is $r \times r$, and $\boldsymbol{B}_2$ is $(k-r) \times r$, and also partition

$$\boldsymbol{H} = \begin{pmatrix} \boldsymbol{H}_{11} & \boldsymbol{H}_{12} \\ \boldsymbol{H}_{21} & \boldsymbol{H}_{22} \end{pmatrix}, \qquad \boldsymbol{Q} = \begin{pmatrix} \boldsymbol{Q}_1 \\ \boldsymbol{Q}_2 \end{pmatrix},$$

where $\boldsymbol{H}_{11}, \boldsymbol{H}_{12}, \boldsymbol{H}_{21}$, and $\boldsymbol{H}_{22}$ are respectively $r \times r$, $r \times (r_1 - r)$, $(k-r) \times r$, and $(k-r) \times (r_1 - r)$, and $\boldsymbol{Q}_1$ and $\boldsymbol{Q}_2$ are respectively $r \times r$, and $(r_1 - r) \times r$. Assume that $\boldsymbol{H}_{11}$ is non-singular. Then $\boldsymbol{B}_2 = \boldsymbol{H}_{21}\boldsymbol{H}_{11}^{-1}\boldsymbol{B}_1 + (\boldsymbol{H}_{22} - \boldsymbol{H}_{21}\boldsymbol{H}_{11}^{-1}\boldsymbol{H}_{12})\boldsymbol{Q}_2$. Set $\boldsymbol{B}_1 = \boldsymbol{I}_r$ by the normalization rule. Under the alternative hypothesis, which is $\overline{\mathrm{H}}(r)$, the number of free parameters is the number of elements of $\boldsymbol{B}_2$, i.e. $r(k-r)$. Under the null hypothesis, $\boldsymbol{B} = \boldsymbol{HQ}$, the number of free parameters is the number of elements of $\boldsymbol{Q}_2$, which is $r(r_1 - r)$. Therefore the number of effective constraints is the difference, i.e. $r(k - r_1)$. See Section 15.5 for applications.

3. $\boldsymbol{B} = (\boldsymbol{HQ}, \boldsymbol{R})$ with a known $k \times r_1\, \boldsymbol{H}$ and unspecified $r_1 \times r_1\, \boldsymbol{Q}$, where $r_1 < r$, if $\boldsymbol{B}$ is appropriately rotated.

The known matrix $\boldsymbol{H}$ is $k \times r_1$, $\boldsymbol{0} < r_1 < r$, and $\rho(\boldsymbol{H}) = r_1$. $\boldsymbol{Q}$ is $r_1 - r_1$ but arbitrary otherwise, and $\boldsymbol{R}$ is $k \times (r - r_1)$ but arbitrary otherwise. The null hypothesis means that the column space of $\boldsymbol{H}$ is a proper subspace of the co-integration space, in other words, the first r_1 columns of $\boldsymbol{B}$ can be made equal to $\boldsymbol{H}$ if it is properly rotated.

Let $\boldsymbol{H}_\perp$ be a $k \times (k - r_1)$ matrix such that $\boldsymbol{H}_\perp'\boldsymbol{H} = \boldsymbol{0}$ and $\rho(\boldsymbol{H}_\perp) = k - r_1$. Let $\boldsymbol{G} = \boldsymbol{H}(\boldsymbol{H}'\boldsymbol{H})^{-1/2}$, $\boldsymbol{G}_\perp = \boldsymbol{H}_\perp(\boldsymbol{H}_\perp'\boldsymbol{H}_\perp)^{-1/2}$. Then in general

$$\boldsymbol{B} = \boldsymbol{GG}'\boldsymbol{B} + \boldsymbol{G}_\perp\boldsymbol{G}_\perp'\boldsymbol{B} = \boldsymbol{H}(\boldsymbol{H}'\boldsymbol{H})^{-1}\boldsymbol{H}'\boldsymbol{B} + \boldsymbol{G}_\perp[\boldsymbol{0}, \boldsymbol{R}]\boldsymbol{P},$$

where $\boldsymbol{G}_\perp'\boldsymbol{B}$ and $[\boldsymbol{0}, \boldsymbol{R}]$ are each $(k - r_1) \times r$, $\boldsymbol{P}$ is $r \times r$ and non-singular, $\boldsymbol{R}$ is a $(k - r_1) \times \rho(\boldsymbol{G}_\perp'\boldsymbol{B})$ matrix, and $\boldsymbol{0}$ is $(k - r_1) \times (r - \rho(\boldsymbol{G}_\perp'\boldsymbol{B}))$ zero matrix. Multiplying $\boldsymbol{P}^{-1}$ from the right it is seen that the first $r - \rho(\boldsymbol{G}_\perp'\boldsymbol{B})$ columns of $\boldsymbol{BP}^{-1}$ are spanned by columns of $\boldsymbol{H}$. The condition of the hypothesis is that $\rho(\boldsymbol{G}_\perp'\boldsymbol{B}) \leq r - r_1$. This is a property of the observationally equivalent class, which can be shown as follows. Suppose that $\rho(\boldsymbol{G}_\perp'\boldsymbol{B}) \leq r - r_1$ and $\rho(\boldsymbol{G}_\perp'\boldsymbol{B}^*) > r - r_1$. It is impossible to have $\boldsymbol{B}^* = \boldsymbol{BP}^*$ with a non-singular $\boldsymbol{P}^*$.

See Johansen and Juselius (1992) for the derivation of the test statistic and its illustration. Partitioning $\boldsymbol{B} = (\boldsymbol{B}_1', \boldsymbol{B}_2')'$, where $\boldsymbol{B}_1$ is $r \times r$, it is seen that the constraints bind only the submatrix consisting of the last $(k - r)$ rows and the first r_1 columns.

4. $\boldsymbol{B} = (\boldsymbol{HQ}, \boldsymbol{R})$ with a known $k \times s\boldsymbol{H}$ and unspecified $s \times r_1\, \boldsymbol{Q}$, where $r_1 \leq s \leq k$, if $\boldsymbol{B}$ is appropriately rotated.

The present hypothesis is an extension of the earlier Subsection 3. In fact one obtains 3 above by making $s = r_1$ in 4. This is a property of the observationally equivalent class, which can be proven in the same way as in Subsection 3. An inference theory is found in theorem 3 of Johansen and Juselius (1992). The computation uses an iteration.

5. $\boldsymbol{c}'\boldsymbol{b} = 0$ where $r = 1, \boldsymbol{B}$ is denoted by $\boldsymbol{b}$, and $\boldsymbol{c}$ is a known non-stochastic vector.

This is clearly a property of the observationally equivalent class. A χ^2 test with 1 degree of freedom is available for this special case in corollary 5.3 of Johansen (1991*a*).

6. $\boldsymbol{A} = \boldsymbol{GP}$ and $\boldsymbol{B} = \boldsymbol{HQ}$ with known $\boldsymbol{G}$ and $\boldsymbol{H}$.

Let $\boldsymbol{G}$ and $\boldsymbol{H}$ be respectively $k \times r_a$ and $k \times r_b$ known matrices, and let $\boldsymbol{P}$ and $\boldsymbol{Q}$ be respectively $r_a \times r$ and $r_b \times r$ arbitrary matrices. It is assumed that $r \leq r_a \leq k$, $\rho(\boldsymbol{G}) = r_a$, $r \leq r_b \leq k$, and $\rho(\boldsymbol{H}) = r_b$. Notice that $\boldsymbol{B} = \boldsymbol{HQ}$ has been dealt with in 2 above. The null hypothesis is that $\boldsymbol{A} = \boldsymbol{GP}, \boldsymbol{B} = \boldsymbol{HQ}$, and $\rho(\boldsymbol{A}) = \rho(\boldsymbol{B}) = r$, which is tested against $\overline{H}(r)$. A test is given in Johansen (1991*a*).

7. Separation.

Block-diagonality of $\boldsymbol{B}'$ *after a proper rotation* is called the separability in Konishi and Granger (1992), which also presents a likelihood ratio test for the separability. Here I shall demonstrate that the separability is a property of the observationally equivalent class. Let $\boldsymbol{B}_1'$ and $\boldsymbol{B}_2'$ be respectively $r_1 \times k_1$ and $r_2 \times k_2$ where $r_1 + r_2 = r$, $k_1 + k_2 = k$. For a properly chosen $r \times r$ non-singular $\boldsymbol{P}$ we have $\boldsymbol{PB}' = \text{diag}\,[\boldsymbol{B}_1', \boldsymbol{B}_2']$. Suppose that $\boldsymbol{B}_*'$ is such that there is no $r \times r$ non-singular $\boldsymbol{P}_*$ that makes $\boldsymbol{P}_*\boldsymbol{B}_*' = \text{diag}\,[\boldsymbol{B}_{*1}', \boldsymbol{B}_{*2}']$, where $\boldsymbol{B}_{*1}'$ and $\boldsymbol{B}_{*2}'$ have the same numbers of rows and columns as $\boldsymbol{B}_1'$ and $\boldsymbol{B}_2'$ respectively. It can be shown that $\boldsymbol{B}_*' = \boldsymbol{QB}'$ with a non-singular $\boldsymbol{Q}$ does lead to contradiction, i.e. $\boldsymbol{B}_*$ and $\boldsymbol{B}$ cannot be observationally equivalent. If $\boldsymbol{B}_*' = \boldsymbol{QB}'$, $\boldsymbol{B}_*' = \boldsymbol{QP}^{-1}\,\text{diag}\,[\boldsymbol{B}_1', \boldsymbol{B}_2']$. The choice of $\boldsymbol{P}_* = \boldsymbol{PQ}^{-1}$ should make $\boldsymbol{P}_*\boldsymbol{B}_*' = \text{diag}\,[\boldsymbol{B}_1', \boldsymbol{B}_2']$.

8. Wald tests and likelihood ratio tests for general hypotheses.

Johansen (1991*a*) proposes the likelihood ratio tests for general hypotheses on the co-integration space, but Hoffman and Rasche (1991) point out that Wald tests are available for any linear constraints on the co-integration space. The constraints are interpreted as results of compounding appropriately chosen normalization rules and some effective constraints as explained in Section 15.2.1. The limit distribution of normalized $\hat{\boldsymbol{B}}$, which is mixed Gaussian, is given in Johansen (1991*a*, theorem C.1). The null distribution of the Wald test statistics are asymptotically χ^2 just as the likelihood ratio test statistics are. See Kunitomo (1994) for a full investigation of the Wald and Lagrange multiplier tests on the co-integrated VAR model.

My final remark on the testing is that procedures for testing constraints upon $(\boldsymbol{A}, \boldsymbol{\Gamma}_1, \ldots, \boldsymbol{\Gamma}_{q-1})$ in (15.2) are standard because $\sqrt{T} \times$ (the estimation errors) are asymptotically Gaussian. Even the constraints upon $(\boldsymbol{A}, \boldsymbol{B}, \boldsymbol{\Gamma}_1, \ldots, \boldsymbol{\Gamma}_{q-1})$ can be tested in a standard way with $\hat{\boldsymbol{B}}$ replacing $\boldsymbol{B}$ in the constraint because $\hat{\boldsymbol{B}} - \boldsymbol{B}$ is $\boldsymbol{O}_p(T^{-1})$.

15.3 A Common Practice on $\hat{\boldsymbol{B}}'$

A common practice in publishing applications of Johansen method is to present $\hat{\boldsymbol{B}}'$ in 15.12 (*a*), often normalizing one element of each row to unity. It has been noted above that $\boldsymbol{B}$ is not identified without some r^2 constraints. As emphasized in Phillips (1991*d*) $\hat{\boldsymbol{B}}'$ is an estimate of unidentified parameters, and hence devoid of any meaning.

Let us recall how $\hat{\boldsymbol{B}}'$ has been obtained. It was derived from minimizing the expression (15.9). But the minimization cannot determine $\boldsymbol{B}$ uniquely because (15.9) is invariant through transformations from $\boldsymbol{B}$ to $\boldsymbol{BQ}$ with non-singular $\boldsymbol{Q}$. Therefore (15.12) is only one of many ways to determine $\boldsymbol{B}$. Admittedly (15.12) (*b*) is a kind of normalization. But it has only $r(r+1)/2$ constraints not sufficient for the unique determination of $\boldsymbol{B}$. Moreover it means nothing from the standpoint of economic theory. Let $(\hat{\boldsymbol{w}}_1, \ldots, \hat{\boldsymbol{w}}_k)$ be the orthonormalized eigenvectors of $\boldsymbol{S}_{11}^{-1/2}\boldsymbol{S}_{12}\boldsymbol{S}_{00}^{-1}\boldsymbol{S}_{01}\boldsymbol{S}_{11}^{-1/2}$, and let $(\hat{\boldsymbol{v}}_1, \ldots, \hat{\boldsymbol{v}}_k) \equiv \boldsymbol{S}_{11}^{-1/2}(\hat{\boldsymbol{w}}_1, \ldots, \hat{\boldsymbol{w}}_k)$. Then $\hat{\boldsymbol{B}}$ is $(\hat{\boldsymbol{v}}_1, \ldots, \hat{\boldsymbol{v}}_r)$. This is an arbitrary way to determine $\boldsymbol{B}$.

One might argue that $\hat{\boldsymbol{B}}'$ is presented to let the readers perform any rotations of $\hat{\boldsymbol{B}}'$ that they desire. I do not deny its usefulness for informal judgement, but the final judgement should be based upon the hypothesis testing described in Section 15.2.2.

Admittedly the common practice criticized above does reflect some demand from econometricians. Johansen's method certainly enables us to *test* for constraints on the co-integration space, but if such constraints are not rejected we like to proceed to *estimating* the parameters using the constraints. For the estimation of $\boldsymbol{B}$ we need constraints strong enough to identify $\boldsymbol{B}$. The constraints that represent properties of observationally equivalent classes as given in Section 15.2.2 are not sufficient for the purpose. Not much has been investigated in the literature.

Incidentally, the impulse–response function does involve $\boldsymbol{AB}'$ but does not involve $\boldsymbol{A}$ or $\boldsymbol{B}$ separately. It is free from the identification problem. See Lütkepohl and Reimers (1992) and Mellander, Vredin, and Warne (1992) on the estimation of the impulse–response function using the error-correction form of co-integration.

15.4 Weak Exogeneity and Granger Non-causality

15.4.1 A relation among the weak exogeneity, Granger non-causality in the long-run, and the co-integrated regression

Conditional models are frequently used in econometric models, and the weak exogeneity condition enables us to perform efficient testing on such models (see Section 11.2). Suppose that the vector time series $\{\boldsymbol{x}_t\}$ in (15.2) with co-integration rank r is partitioned into $(\boldsymbol{x}_{1t}', \boldsymbol{x}_{2t}')'$, $\boldsymbol{x}_{1t}$, and $\boldsymbol{x}_{2t}$ having respectively k_1 and $k_2 = k - k_1$ elements. For simplicity of exposition $\boldsymbol{\mu}$ is suppressed to zero, q is assumed 2, and $\boldsymbol{\Gamma}_1$ is written $\boldsymbol{\Gamma}$. The first k_1 rows and the last k_2 rows of Γ and A are denoted respectively $\boldsymbol{\Gamma}_1$ and $\boldsymbol{A}_1$ and $\boldsymbol{\Gamma}_2$ and $\boldsymbol{A}_2 \cdot \boldsymbol{\Omega}$ is partitioned conformably as

$$\begin{bmatrix} \boldsymbol{\Omega}_{11} & \boldsymbol{\Omega}_{12} \\ \boldsymbol{\Omega}_{21} & \boldsymbol{\Omega}_{22} \end{bmatrix}.$$

Let us write the original model in the partitioned form,

$$\Delta \boldsymbol{x}_{1t} = \boldsymbol{A}_1 \boldsymbol{B}' \boldsymbol{x}_{t-1} + \boldsymbol{\Gamma}_1 \Delta \boldsymbol{x}_{t-1} + \boldsymbol{\varepsilon}_{1t}. \tag{15.18a}$$

$$\Delta \boldsymbol{x}_{2t} = \boldsymbol{A}_2 \boldsymbol{B}' \boldsymbol{x}_{t-1} + \boldsymbol{\Gamma}_2 \Delta \boldsymbol{x}_{t-1} + \boldsymbol{\varepsilon}_{2t}. \tag{15.18b}$$

The parameters are $\boldsymbol{A}_1, \boldsymbol{A}_2, \boldsymbol{B}', \boldsymbol{\Gamma}_1, \boldsymbol{\Gamma}_2$, vech($\boldsymbol{\Omega}_{11}$), $\boldsymbol{\Omega}_{12}$, vech($\boldsymbol{\Omega}_{22}$), where vech($\cdot$) is the vector of elements of the matrix in ( ) eliminating double-counting. Let us also partition $\boldsymbol{B}'$ as $[\boldsymbol{B}_1', \boldsymbol{B}_2']$.

The conditional and the marginal models were derived in (11.15) and (11.16). Though $k_1 = k_2 = 1$ there, its extention to general cases is straightforward. The marginal log-likelihood function is seen equal to

$$-\frac{T}{2} \log \det[\boldsymbol{\Omega}_{11}] - \tfrac{1}{2} \sum\nolimits_t (\Delta \boldsymbol{x}_{1t} - \boldsymbol{A}_1 \boldsymbol{B}' \boldsymbol{x}_{t-1} - \boldsymbol{\Gamma}_1 \Delta \boldsymbol{x}_{t-1})' \boldsymbol{\Omega}_{11}^{-1}$$
$$\times (\Delta \boldsymbol{x}_{1t} - \boldsymbol{A}_1 \boldsymbol{B}' \boldsymbol{x}_{t-1} - \boldsymbol{\Gamma}_1 \Delta \boldsymbol{x}_{t-1}), \tag{15.19a}$$

and the conditional log-likelihood function is

$$-\tfrac{T}{2} \log \det[\boldsymbol{\Omega}_{22.1}] - \tfrac{1}{2} \sum\nolimits_t (\Delta \boldsymbol{x}_{2t} - \boldsymbol{F}_2 \boldsymbol{B}' \boldsymbol{x}_{t-1}$$
$$- \boldsymbol{G}_2 \Delta \boldsymbol{x}_{t-1} - \boldsymbol{H}_{21} \Delta \boldsymbol{x}_{1t})'$$
$$\times \boldsymbol{\Omega}_{22.1}^{-1} (\Delta \boldsymbol{x}_{2t} - \boldsymbol{F}_2 \boldsymbol{B}' \boldsymbol{x}_{t-1} - \boldsymbol{G}_2 \Delta \boldsymbol{x}_{t-1} - \boldsymbol{H}_{21} \Delta \boldsymbol{x}_{1t}), \tag{15.19b}$$

where $\boldsymbol{F}_2 \equiv \boldsymbol{A}_2 - \boldsymbol{H}_{21} \boldsymbol{A}_1, \quad \boldsymbol{G}_2 \equiv (\boldsymbol{\Gamma}_2 - \boldsymbol{H}_{21} \boldsymbol{\Gamma}_1)$

$$\boldsymbol{H}_{21} \equiv \boldsymbol{\Omega}_{21} \boldsymbol{\Omega}_{11}^{-1}, \quad \boldsymbol{\Omega}_{22.1} \equiv \boldsymbol{\Omega}_{22} - \boldsymbol{\Omega}_{21} \boldsymbol{\Omega}_{11}^{-1} \boldsymbol{\Omega}_{12}.$$

The model of $\boldsymbol{x}_{2t}$ conditioned on $\boldsymbol{x}_{1t}$ is

$$\Delta \boldsymbol{x}_{2t} = \boldsymbol{F}_2 \boldsymbol{B}' \boldsymbol{x}_{t-1} + \boldsymbol{G}_2 \Delta \boldsymbol{x}_{t-1} + \boldsymbol{H}_{21} \Delta \boldsymbol{x}_{1t} + \boldsymbol{u}_t, \tag{15.20}$$

where $\boldsymbol{u}_t = \boldsymbol{\varepsilon}_{2t} - \boldsymbol{H}_{21} \boldsymbol{\varepsilon}_{1t}$ is i.i.d. with $N(\boldsymbol{0}, \boldsymbol{\Omega}_{22.1})$. The marginal model of $\boldsymbol{x}_{1t}$ is (15.18a).

It is difficult to envisage the weak exogeneity unless the relevant parameters are at least just-identified. Since $\rho(\boldsymbol{B}) = r$ there must be at least one $r \times r$ submatrix of $\boldsymbol{B}'$ that is non-singular. Denote it by $\boldsymbol{B}_F'$. We shall assume that a priori information is available to determine which columns of $\boldsymbol{B}'$ compose a $\boldsymbol{B}_F'$. It was shown in Section 13.4 that this information enables us to identify the entire $\boldsymbol{B}'$ uniquely by normalizing $\boldsymbol{B}_F'$ to a unit matrix.

What is important from the practical point of view is the case where $\boldsymbol{B}_2'$, which is $r \times k_2$, contains a $\boldsymbol{B}_F'$. (This is possible only when $k_2 \geq r$.) It will be shown for this case that $\boldsymbol{A}_1 = \boldsymbol{0}$ is equivalent to both the Granger non-causality in the long run and the weak exogeneity. I shall begin with the Granger non-causality. As shown in Section 12.2.6 $\boldsymbol{A}_1\boldsymbol{B}_2' = \boldsymbol{0}$ is an important part of the condition for $\boldsymbol{x}_2$ failing to cause $\boldsymbol{x}_1$ in Granger's sense, and may be regarded non-causality *in the long run*. Hunter (1992) calls it the co-integrating exogeneity, but I shall adopt the term, Granger non-causality in the long run. As explained in Hunter (1992), it means that $\boldsymbol{x}_{2t}$ does not contribute to the long-run forecasts of $\boldsymbol{x}_{1t}$. If $\boldsymbol{B}_2'$ contains a $\boldsymbol{B}_F'$ then $\boldsymbol{A}_1\boldsymbol{B}_2' = \boldsymbol{0}$ is equivalent to $\boldsymbol{A}_1 = \boldsymbol{0}$. This is because $\boldsymbol{A}_1\boldsymbol{B}_2' = \boldsymbol{0} \Rightarrow \boldsymbol{A}_1\boldsymbol{B}_F' = \boldsymbol{0} \Rightarrow \boldsymbol{A}_1 = \boldsymbol{0}$ and obviously $\boldsymbol{A}_1 = \boldsymbol{0} \Rightarrow \boldsymbol{A}_1\boldsymbol{B}_2' = \boldsymbol{0}$.

Johansen (1992*c*, 1992*d*) state that $\boldsymbol{A}_1 = \boldsymbol{0}$ is necessary and sufficient for the weak exogeneity of $\boldsymbol{x}_{1t}$, Indeed if $\boldsymbol{A}_1 = \boldsymbol{0}$, the marginal log-likelihood function, (15.19*a*), has the parameters, $\boldsymbol{\Gamma}_1$ and vech$(\boldsymbol{\Omega}_{11})$ only, while the conditional log-likelihood function, (15.20), has $\boldsymbol{A}_2, \boldsymbol{B}', \boldsymbol{G}_2, \boldsymbol{H}_{21}$, vech$(\boldsymbol{\Omega}_{22.1})$, where a submatrix of $\boldsymbol{B}', \boldsymbol{B}'_F$, is normalized. Johansen (1992*c*) demonstrates that the two groups of parameters are variation-free when $\boldsymbol{A}_1 = \boldsymbol{0}$. (15.18*a*) and (15.20) are now respectively

$$\Delta\boldsymbol{x}_{1t} = \boldsymbol{\Gamma}_1\Delta\boldsymbol{x}_{t-1} + \boldsymbol{\varepsilon}_{1t}, \tag{15.18$'$}$$

$$\Delta\boldsymbol{x}_{2t} = \boldsymbol{A}_2\boldsymbol{B}'\boldsymbol{x}_{t-1} + \boldsymbol{G}_2\Delta\boldsymbol{x}_{t-1} + \boldsymbol{H}_{21}\Delta\boldsymbol{x}_{1t} + \boldsymbol{u}_t. \tag{15.20$'$}$$

Even though $\Delta\boldsymbol{x}_{2t-1}$ is involved in the marginal model, it is irrelevant to the problem as shown in the explanation associated with (11.9). The $\boldsymbol{x}_{1t-1}, \Delta\boldsymbol{x}_{1t-1}$, and $\Delta\boldsymbol{x}_{1t}$ are weakly exogenous in (15.20′) with respect to not only $\boldsymbol{B}'$ but also $\boldsymbol{A}_2, \boldsymbol{G}_2, \boldsymbol{H}_{21}$, and vech$(\boldsymbol{\Omega}_{22.1})$. The necessity of $\boldsymbol{A}_1 = \boldsymbol{0}$ for the weak exogeneity is stated in Johansen (1992*d*).

When $\boldsymbol{A}_1 = \boldsymbol{0}$ the maximum-likelihood estimation of the parameters in (15.20′) can be based upon (15.20′) only. In reference to (15.4) we now set $z_{0t} = \Delta\boldsymbol{x}_{2t}, z_{1t} = \boldsymbol{x}_{t-1}(\text{not } \boldsymbol{x}_{2t-1}), z_{2t} = (\Delta\boldsymbol{x}_{1t}', \Delta\boldsymbol{x}_{t-1}')', \boldsymbol{A} = \boldsymbol{A}_2, \boldsymbol{\Gamma} = (\boldsymbol{H}_{21}, \boldsymbol{G}_2), \boldsymbol{\Omega} = \boldsymbol{\Omega}_{22.1}$. The rank r is determined from the conditional model, and a testing on the co-integration space is also performed on the conditional model.

Let us consider what is meant by the condition $\boldsymbol{A}_1 = \boldsymbol{0}$. When $\boldsymbol{A}_1 = \boldsymbol{0}$, (15.18*a*) involves differenced variables only, and hence it cannot represent a co-integrated regression. (Summing over time on each side of (15.18*a*) generates a random walk for the disturbance.) The co-integration is confined to the conditional model, (15.20), between $\boldsymbol{x}_1$ and $\boldsymbol{x}_2$. We have had a similar situation in Section 13.4.2. Moreover, when $\boldsymbol{A}_1 = \boldsymbol{0}$, the upper half of $\boldsymbol{AB}'$ is zero, and $\boldsymbol{B}'\boldsymbol{x}_{t-1}$ does not subject $\Delta\boldsymbol{x}_{1t}$ to the adjustment toward equilibrium (see Section 12.3.3).

In the present context of $\boldsymbol{B}_2'$ containing a $\boldsymbol{B}_F'$ it is impossible to have $k_1 > k-r$, i.e. more than $(k-r)$ variables cannot be weakly exogenous. Therefore pragmatic advice on the inference procedure is to begin with the determination of co-integration rank in the entire system. If it is determined as r_0, then at most $(k - r_0)$ variables are candidates for the weakly exogenous variables. The next step of our inference is to test for $\boldsymbol{A}_1 = \boldsymbol{0}$. Johansen and Juselius (1990, 1992) show that a standard χ^2 test is available.

Continuing with the assumption, $A_1 = 0$, an important special case is $k_1 = k - r$, i.e. $r = k_2$. Regarding $B' = (B_1', B_2')$ B_1' and B_2' have $k - r$ and r columns respectively. Co-integrating relations provide r equations to be solved for r elements of x_2 because B_2' is now B_F' and hence non-singular. Thus x_1 and x_2 are respectively exogenous and endogenous variables.

Johansen (1992*c*) notes that, if $r = k_2$, (15.20) or (15.20′) is no longer a reduced-rank regression, because all rk elements of $A_2 B'$ are free to move in the rk dimensional Euclidean space.[9] The process of concentrating the log-likelihood is much simplified when applied to this special case of the conditional model. Setting $B_2' = I_r$, (15.20′) can be rewritten as

$$x_{2t} = Cx_{1t} + D_1 \Delta x_{2t} + D_2 \Delta x_{2t-1} + D_3 \Delta x_{1t} + D_4 \Delta x_{1t-1} + v_t, \qquad (15.21)$$

where $C \equiv -B_1', D_1 \equiv I + A_2^{-1}, D_2 \equiv -A_2^{-1} G_{22}, D_3 \equiv B_1' - A_2^{-1} H_{21}, D_4 \equiv A_2^{-1} G_{21}$, and $v_t \equiv -A_2^{-1} u_t$. (15.21) is analogous to the co-integrated regression considered in Chapter 13. From (15.21) we see that $\Delta x_{2t} = C \Delta x_{1t} +$ terms in $I(-1)$, and on substituting it in (15.18′) we get

$$(I - (\Gamma_{11} + \Gamma_{12} C) L) \Delta x_{1t} = \varepsilon_{1t} + \text{terms in } I(-1),$$

which indicates that the long-run component of $\{x_{1t}\}$ can be expressed by $\{\varepsilon_{1t}\}$ only. Since $v_t = -A_2(\varepsilon_{2t} - H_{21} \varepsilon_{1t})$, it is possible to show that the OLS estimator of C in (15.21) is mixed Gaussian. In fact this also follows from the theory of the present chapter, because the inference on the basis of the conditional model (15.21) must be identical to the inference on the basis of the entire system (15.2) under the weak exogeneity. Thus it can be said that the co-integrated regression is essentially a special case where $(k - r)$ variables are weakly exogenous. This is what I meant in Section 13.4.3, where the materials in Chapter 13 are said to be subsumed in Chapter 15.

Nevertheless I gave a certain role to the co-integrated regression in Section 13.4.3 in view of the limited capability that the maximum-likelihood method of VAR has with the length of time-series data available for macroeconomic studies. This was shown in Section 15.1.4.

It is seen from the above development that $A_1 = 0$ continues to be necessary and sufficient for the weak exogeneity even if B_2' does not contain a B_F', in which case, however, $A_1 = 0$ is not related either to Granger non-causality in the long run or to the co-integrated regression with x_2 as the dependent variable. I do not think that this is an interesting case to consider in practice.

15.4.2 Partitioning the co-integrating space

It makes sense to partition B as

$$B = [B_a, B_b]$$

[9] There exist $r(k - r)$ free parameters in B' after the normalization, and the entire r^2 elements of A_2 are free.

provided that just-identifying constraints are introduced in the co-integration space. In some applications we are interested in the co-integrating relations, $\boldsymbol{B}_b'\boldsymbol{x}_t = \boldsymbol{0}$ only under the supposition that neither the just-identifying constraints nor any other constraints relate $\boldsymbol{B}_b'$ to $\boldsymbol{B}_a'$. The just-identifying constraints in no way bind $\boldsymbol{A}$, which is however identified.

Banerjee *et al.* (1993: 288–91) investigate the above partitioning in conjunction with the partitioning of $\boldsymbol{x}_t' = (\boldsymbol{x}_{1t}', \boldsymbol{x}_{2t}')$ and the conditioning of $\boldsymbol{x}_{2t}$ upon $\boldsymbol{x}_{1t}$. Thus $\boldsymbol{A}$ and $\boldsymbol{B}$ are further partitioned as

$$\boldsymbol{A} = \begin{bmatrix} \boldsymbol{A}_{1a}, & \boldsymbol{A}_{1b} \\ \boldsymbol{A}_{2a}, & \boldsymbol{A}_{2b} \end{bmatrix}, \qquad \boldsymbol{B} = \begin{bmatrix} \boldsymbol{B}_{1a}, & \boldsymbol{B}_{1b} \\ \boldsymbol{B}_{2a}, & \boldsymbol{B}_{2b} \end{bmatrix},$$

and (15.18*a*) and (15.18*b*) are rewritten as

$$\Delta \boldsymbol{x}_{1t} = (\boldsymbol{A}_{1a}, \boldsymbol{A}_{1b}) \begin{bmatrix} \boldsymbol{B}_{1a}', & \boldsymbol{B}_{2a}' \\ \boldsymbol{B}_{1b}', & \boldsymbol{B}_{2b}' \end{bmatrix} \begin{bmatrix} \boldsymbol{x}_{1t-1} \\ \boldsymbol{x}_{2t-1} \end{bmatrix} + \boldsymbol{\Gamma}_1 \Delta \boldsymbol{x}_{t-1} + \boldsymbol{\varepsilon}_{1t} \tag{15.22a}$$

$$\Delta \boldsymbol{x}_{2t} = (\boldsymbol{A}_{2a}, \boldsymbol{A}_{2b}) \begin{bmatrix} \boldsymbol{B}_{1a}', & \boldsymbol{B}_{2a}' \\ \boldsymbol{B}_{1b}', & \boldsymbol{B}_{2b}' \end{bmatrix} \begin{bmatrix} \boldsymbol{x}_{1t-1} \\ \boldsymbol{x}_{2t-1} \end{bmatrix} + \boldsymbol{\Gamma}_2 \Delta \boldsymbol{x}_{t-1} + \boldsymbol{\varepsilon}_{2t}. \tag{15.22b}$$

The marginal model is (15.22*a*), and the conditional model is

$$\Delta \boldsymbol{x}_{2t} = (\boldsymbol{A}_{2a} - \boldsymbol{H}_{21}\boldsymbol{A}_{1a}, \boldsymbol{A}_{2b} - \boldsymbol{H}_{21}\boldsymbol{A}_{1b}) \begin{bmatrix} \boldsymbol{B}_{1a}', & \boldsymbol{B}_{2a}' \\ \boldsymbol{B}_{1b}', & \boldsymbol{B}_{2b}' \end{bmatrix} \begin{bmatrix} \boldsymbol{x}_{1t-1} \\ \boldsymbol{x}_{2t-1} \end{bmatrix}$$
$$+ \boldsymbol{G}_2 \Delta \boldsymbol{x}_{t-1} + \boldsymbol{H}_{21} \Delta \boldsymbol{x}_{1t} + \boldsymbol{u}_t, \quad \boldsymbol{u}_t \sim N(\boldsymbol{0}, \boldsymbol{\Omega}_{22.1}). \tag{15.23}$$

Suppose that the parameters of interest are $(\boldsymbol{A}_{2b}, \boldsymbol{B}_{1b}', \boldsymbol{B}_{2b}')$. A sufficient condition to make $\Delta \boldsymbol{x}_{1t}$ and $\Delta \boldsymbol{x}_{1t-1}$ weakly exogenous in the conditional model is that $\boldsymbol{A}_{1b} = \boldsymbol{0}$ and $\boldsymbol{A}_{2a} - \boldsymbol{H}_{21}\boldsymbol{A}_{1a} = \boldsymbol{0}$. The parameters in the marginal model are $\boldsymbol{A}_{1a}, \boldsymbol{B}_{1a}', \boldsymbol{B}_{2a}', \boldsymbol{\Gamma}_1$, vech$(\boldsymbol{\Omega}_{11})$, and the parameters in the conditional model are $\boldsymbol{A}_{2b}, \boldsymbol{B}_{1b}', \boldsymbol{B}_{2b}', \boldsymbol{H}_{21}, \boldsymbol{G}_2$, vech$(\boldsymbol{\Omega}_{22.1})$. The two sets of parameters are variation-free. The co-integrating relation $\boldsymbol{B}_a'\boldsymbol{x}_t = \boldsymbol{0}$ appears in the marginal model but not in the conditional model, and $\boldsymbol{B}_b'\boldsymbol{x}_t = \boldsymbol{0}$ appears in the conditional model but not in the marginal model. How to test for $\boldsymbol{A}_{1b} = \boldsymbol{0}$ and $\boldsymbol{A}_{2a} - \boldsymbol{H}_{21}\boldsymbol{A}_{1a} = \boldsymbol{0}$ is described briefly also in Banerjee *et al.* (1993: 290).

15.4.3 Granger non-causality

Let us turn to Granger non-causality. The concept was explained in Section 11.3 on two types of VAR models, the stationary one and the one that is non-stationary and not co-integrated, and also in Section 12.2.6 on the VAR that is non-stationary and co-integrated. The explanation dealt with the case, $k_1 = k_2 = 1$, but its extension is straightforward. In all cases Granger non-causality is the block triangularity of the VAR system. Here we are concerned with testing. Mosconi and Giannini (1992) implement the likelihood ratio test by an iteration procedure, and Toda and Phillips (1993, 1994) analyse the limiting distributions of the Wald test statistics. I shall present the results of Toda and Phillips (1993, 1994).

Suppose that $x_t' = (x_{1t}', x_{2t}', x_{3t}')$, where x_{1t}, x_{2t}, and x_{3t} have respectively, k_1, k_2, k_3 elements, and that we are concerned with Granger causality of x_3 upon x_1. The null hypothesis is the absence of causality. Toda and Phillips (1993, 1994) consider two types of Wald test. One is the F-test based on the OLS of the ordinary VAR form,

$$x_t = \Pi_1 x_{t-1} + \ldots + \Pi_q x_{t-q} + \varepsilon_t. \tag{15.24}$$

Partitioning

$$\Pi_i = \begin{bmatrix} \Pi_{i11}, & \Pi_{i12}, & \Pi_{i13} \\ \Pi_{i21}, & \Pi_{i22}, & \Pi_{i23} \\ \Pi_{i31}, & \Pi_{i32}, & \Pi_{i33} \end{bmatrix}, i = 1, \ldots, q,$$

conformably with the partitioning of x_t, the null hypothesis is $\Pi_{i13} = 0, i = 1, \ldots, q$. (However, the limiting distribution of the F-statistics is derived on the assumption that the data-generating process is a possibly co-integrated VAR.) The other Wald test is based on the reduced-rank estimator of the error-correction form, (15.2). The null hypothesis is $\Gamma_{i13} = \mathbf{0}, i = 1, \ldots, q-1$ and $A_1 B_3' = 0$, where Γ_{i13} is analogous to Π_{i13} above, and $A = (A_1', A_2', A_3')', B' = (B_1', B_2', B_3')$. Derivation of the second Wald test is not as straightforward as many other problems in econometrics (see Toda and Phillips (1993)).

We have $\rho(B_3') = k_3$ if columns of B_3' are contained in a non-singular $r \times r\, B_F'$. Toda and Phillips (1991) show that provided that $\rho(B_3') = k_3$, the F-statistic based on (15.24) is distributed asymptotically in χ^2 with degrees of freedom equal to the number of constraints under the null hypothesis. Otherwise the limiting distributions are complicated. For example, if $k = 3, k_1 = k_2 = k_3 = 1, r = 1$, and $b_3 \neq 0$, then the F-statistic is χ^2.[10] But it is not if $k = 3, k_1 = 1, k_2 = 0, k_3 = 2$, and $r = 1$. As for the test based upon the reduced-rank statistics two alternative sufficient conditions for the null limiting distributions being χ^2 are $\rho(A_1) = k_1$ and $\rho(B_3') = k_3$.

It may be useful to test for $A_1 B_3' = \mathbf{0}$, which is a case of Granger non-causality in the long run.[11]

15.5 Applications

There are a large number of empirical studies using the method in Johansen (1991*a*). The following survey describes (i) difficulties that have been recognized in the course of implementing the method and (ii) contributions toward the empirical testing of economic theories.

King *et al.* (1991) investigate a particular version of the real business cycle theory, in which a series of shocks to the productivity growth generates the business cycle while driving the logarithms of output (y), consumption (c),

[10] This is the case which Sims, Stock, and Watson (1990) analysed.

[11] Granger and Lin (1995) propose a measure of causality in the long run.

and investment (i) in a balanced growth. In applying the Johansen method $\boldsymbol{x}_t'$ is (y_t, c_t, i_t), and the data are seasonally adjusted for post-war USA.[12] It is confirmed that $r = 2$, and that one way to represent the co-integration space is

$$\boldsymbol{B}' = \begin{pmatrix} -1 & 1 & 0 \\ -1 & 0 & 1 \end{pmatrix}.$$

Therefore $k - r = 1$, $\boldsymbol{B}_\perp'$ may be taken as $(1, 1, 1)$, and since $\rho(\boldsymbol{C}(1)) = 1$, $\boldsymbol{H}_2' = \boldsymbol{A}_\perp'$ may be taken as $(1, 0, 0)$. $\boldsymbol{C}(1)$ is $(1, 1, 1)'(1, 0, 0)$ (see Section 12.2.3). Let ε_{1t} be the first element of ε_t. The ε_{1t} can be interpreted as the shock to the productivity growth rate. The contribution of the common trend to $\boldsymbol{x}_t$ is $\boldsymbol{C}(1)\boldsymbol{H}_2 \sum_{s=1}^{t} \boldsymbol{\xi}_s$ in (12.6), which is $(1, 1, 1)' \sum_{s=1}^{t} \varepsilon_{1s}$ in the present case.

For readers interested in the structural VAR model and also the identification problem I mention that King *et al.* (1991) in fact start with a simultaneous equations model. They impose a priori the balanced growth in $\boldsymbol{x}_t$. Since $\boldsymbol{x}_t$ is $I(1)$, it implies the co-integration space given above. They further impose an a priori condition that among three shock variables the shock to productivity growth is uncorrelated with the other two. Then it is proven that these two a priori conditions together identify all the parameters in the simultaneous equations. The Johansen method was used afterwards to confirm the co-integration property a priori imposed earlier. Note that a particular structure of the co-integration space contributes to the identification.

King *et al.* (1991) ask themselves what percentage of the observed variations in y, c, and i are accounted for by the single common stochastic trend just found. The variations are represented by the error of prediction in different horizons. For the horizon τ the error is

$$\sum_{h=0}^{\tau-1} \boldsymbol{C}_h \boldsymbol{\varepsilon}_{t+\tau-h} \tag{15.25}$$

in the MA representation (12.1). Diagonal elements of the convariance matrix of (15.25) are each compared with the variance of $(1, 1, 1)' \sum_{h=0}^{\tau-1} \varepsilon_{1,t+\tau-h}$ for $\tau = 1, 2, \ldots$. The results on US post-war quarterly data are that relative contributions of the common trends are large in y and c but not in i. The above measure of variability is often used in econometrics, and the similar analysis is expected to be useful in many econometric analyses.

King *et al.* (1991) then consider a six-variables system in which the inflation rate, nominal interest rate, and real money stock are added to (y, c, i). Macroeconomic theories suggest two additional co-integrating relations, the money demand equation, and the Fisher effect. That $r = 3$ in the six-variables system is confirmed by the statistical analysis, but relative contributions of the common stochastic trend produced by the shock to productivity growth are much reduced from the three-variables system.

[12] The invariance of the co-integration matrix before and after the seasonal adjustment is shown nicely in Banerjee *et al.* (1993: 301–2). It assumes that the adjustment is a linear filter, while the method in practical use, such as $\boldsymbol{X} - 11$, is not. I imagine that the non-linear effect is negligible.

Mellander, Vredin, and Warne (1992) also investigate the real business cycle theory, but differ from King *et al.* (1991) in adding the terms of trade to (y, c, i) and in using the annual, historical data of Sweden. Moreover their deterministic trends include structural changes. Kunst and Neusser (1990) and Neusser (1991) extend King *et al.* (1991) to many countries, not only within each country but also across the countries with the real interest rate added to (y, c, i).

The long-run and short-run *market equilibrium* conditions have been investigated by the co-integration analysis. Juselius (1991) and Johansen and Juselius (1992) analyse the macroeconomic aspects of the exchange rate incorporating the PPP and UIP (uncovered interest parity). Johansen and Juselius (1992) study the UK quarterly data from 1972 I to 1987 II so that T is as small as 62. The system has five variables: UK price (x_1), the world price (x_2), UK exchange rate *vis-à-vis* all other currencies (x_3), UK interest rate (x_4), and Eurodollar interest rate (x_5). To these is added the oil price as the exogenous variable, because it eliminates non-stationarity in the variances of disturbances. As for the co-integration rank the trace test and the maximum eigenvalue test give $r = 2$ and $= 0$ respectively. They chose $r = 2$. A test for weak exogeneity suggests that the world price is, but Eurodollar interest rate is not, weakly exogenous. Method 2 in Section 15.2.2 is employed to test for the null hypothesis that the two-dimensional co-integration space has the particular structure $(1, -1, 1, \times, \times)$, where $\times$ means unspecified. The hypothesis is accepted. Then method 3 in the same section is employed to test for the hypothesis that $(1, -1, 1, 0, 0)$ is included in the co-integration space. The hypothesis is rejected. This means that the PPP relation appears in both of the two co-integrating relations, but the relation is accompanied in both by the interest-rate variables, i.e. the PPP cannot stand by itself. I think this is a new, interesting evaluation of the PPP. It is found that the UIP can stand by itself.[13] Hunter (1992) re-examines Johansen and Juselius (1992) especially in regard to the role of oil price.

The co-integration analysis of behaviour equations is feasible only when the equations are identified. But some co-integrating relationships are implications of the specifications of behaviour equations (for example, on the selection of variables), and the equations may be tested by way of testing for the relationships.

Hoffman and Rasche (1991) examine the long-run relationship between real money, real income, and either short-term or long-term interest rates, acknowledging in a footnote that the relationship is the demand for money only if the latter is identified. (It is possible that the demand function is identified in the long run but not in the short run.) The data are the post-war monthly data for the USA. The long-run relationship involving a short-term interest rate is confirmed, but that involving a long-term interest rate is not. McNown and Wallace (1992) are concerned with what is called the McKinnon hypothesis on the demand for money, i.e. the stability of the demand function requires

[13] Kugler and Lenz (1993) analyse the monthly data for PPP. Diebold, Gareazabal, and Yilmaz (1994) find that different daily nominal exchange rates are co-integrated without μ in (15.2), but not co-integrated with μ.

exchange rate as an explanatory variable (see McKinnon *et al.* (1984) for this hypothesis). On the US quarterly data from 1973 II to 1988 IV the P-values of the statistics to test for $r = 0$ are compared between the systems with and without the exchange rate. The hypothesis is supported. I think this is an interesting application of the co-integration analysis that it is hoped may be useful in many branches of applied econometrics. However, the inference procedure in McNown and Wallace (1992) should be modified. Consider a four-variables system, (m, y, i, f), where f is the exchange rate. If r is found equal to zero, there is no money demand function. If r is found ≤ 1, apply 5 of Section 15.2.2 with $\boldsymbol{c}' = (0, 0, 0, 1)$. If r is found $\leq r_0$ and $r_0 \geq 2$, apply 4 of the same section with $\boldsymbol{H} = [I_3, 0]'$ and a 3×1 matrix $\boldsymbol{Q}$. The four-variables system is used throughout the study. The results on the three variables (m, y, i) are hard to interpret as the effect of f is not made explicit.[14] The Fisher effect specifically upon long-term interest rates has been examined in Wallace and Warner (1993), using post-war US quarterly data. Co-integration between the inflation rate and long-term rates is confirmed by the maximum eigenvalue test.

It has been pointed out in Section 11.1 that if feasible simultaneous equations models are a logical specialization of feasible (standard) VAR models the over-identifying constraints in the former models can be tested against time-series data. This kind of approach has been pursued in Mizon (1991), Clements and Mizon (1991), and Hendry and Mizon (1993) in the framework of the model selection methodology of the British School, including the encompassing, which is described most fully in Hendry and Mizon (1993). Since the VAR may possibly be co-integrated they estimate the VAR by the Johansen method. After the rank is determined, the constraints on the simultaneous equations models can be expressed as those on $(\boldsymbol{A}, \boldsymbol{B}, \boldsymbol{\Gamma}_1, \ldots, \boldsymbol{\Gamma}_{q-1})$ in (15.2), and the constraints can be tested by traditional likelihood ratios dealing with the estimation errors in the standard $O_p(T^{-1/2})$. Placing the error-correction term at $(t - q)$ rather than at $(t - 1)$ as in (15.2), they consider an autoregressive form, with order 1, of $\boldsymbol{\xi}_t' \equiv (\Delta \boldsymbol{x}_t, \ldots, \Delta \boldsymbol{x}_{t-q+1}, \boldsymbol{B}'\boldsymbol{x}_{t-q})$. It plays a role of a bridge between the VAR and the simultaneous equations model. This autoregressive form is also useful to perform diagnostic investigations of the estimated VAR, because $\{\boldsymbol{\xi}_t\}$ is $I(0)$, the autoregressive form is stable, and $\boldsymbol{B}$ may be replaced by $\hat{\boldsymbol{B}}$ (see equation (5) of Hendry and Mizon (1993)).

Hendry and Mizon (1993) analyse four variables $(m - p, \Delta p, y, r)$, where r is the logarithm of interest rate. The data are seasonally adjusted quarterly UK data. A preliminary univariate analysis shows that $m - p$, y, and r are TS around linear trends and Δp is $I(1)$, i.e. p is $I(2)$. They formulate an error-correction form of VAR on $(m - p, \Delta p, y, r)$. The Johansen method shows that $r = 2$. The estimated model successfully passes all the diagnostic tests including the constancy of parameters. However, some dummy variables are introduced to deal with regime changes. The VAR can be a basis on which simultaneous

[14] See also Hafer and Jansen (1991) for the demand for money.

equations models are to be judged. One such model is not rejected.

In similar fashion Mizon (1991) analyses the relation between aggregate price change and relative price variability in conjunction with real earnings, logarithms of average hours of work, productivity and unemployment. Moreover Clements and Mizon (1991) investigate $(e - r, \Delta r, p - a, a, u)$ where e, r, p, a, and u are respectively earnings per hour worked, CPI, productivity, average hours worked, and unemployment all in logarithms. A large number of dummy variables is introduced.[15]

Johansen (1992*d*) shows that the income (y) and the rate of interest (r) are weakly exogenous in the study of money demand in Hendry and Mizon (1993) discussed above. Brodin and Nymoen (1992) apply the weak exogeneity test in the system of the logs of consumption (x_1), income (x_2), and wealth (x_3). The co-integration rank is found equal to 1, not 2 as one might suspect. The adjustment vector, $a = (a_1, a_2, a_3)'$, is such that it is only a_1 that is significantly different from zero. Thus income and wealth are weakly exogenous.

Friedman and Kuttner (1992) find that the relationship among money, real or nominal income, interest rate, and price observed prior to 1980 in the USA ceased to hold after 1980. The structural changes seem to be important in many fields of time series for economic studies.

I now turn to the financial markets. Baillie and Bollerslev (1989), McDermott (1990), and Copeland (1991) analyse daily data of spot rates in foreign-exchange markets. As indicated in Section 12.3.3 existence of a co-integrating relation contradicts the efficient-market hypothesis, and a day should be an appropriate time unit for this consideration. Absence of co-integration is supported in Copeland (1991) but not in the other studies mentioned above. Cross-re-examinations are needed. Baillie and Bollerslev (1989) and Copeland (1991) analyse also the forward rates and their relations to the spot rates in foreign-exchange markets.

Kasa (1992) finds stock price in different countries driven by a single common trend. Quarterly data are found more efficient than monthly data in determining the co-integration rank. It might be interesting to analyse the point in terms of the framework that Toda (1995) adopts for his simulation. Selection of lag order is found important in Kasa (1992). Hall, Anderson, and Granger (1992) investigate spreads among the yields of assets with different maturities in the US monthly data. All the spreads are driven by a single common trend as they should be if the present-value model holds true. However, the study is somewhat handicapped by the regime change in September 1979 and October 1982 and the drastic changes in the volatility, much greater volatility in 1980–3 than in the remaining periods.

The following conclusions emerge. The major difficulties that one faces in applying the Johansen method are due to structural changes, not just in the

[15] A review, Kirchgässner (1991), conjectures that a simultaneous equations model with a larger set of economic variables might be better than the feasible VAR in reducing the number of dummy variables. Needless to say that it requires substantiation.

deterministic trends but more seriously in the variance. Since T is small, especially in the studies of foreign-exchange markets, there is uncertainty about the determination of co-integration rank. All researchers use the relevant economic theories as a guide for the interpretation of the results. Partly because of this practice it is seldom that the economic theories are rejected outright. The most likely contribution of the co-integration analysis to economics seems to be modifications of economic theories in regard to the *selection of explanatory variables* as shown in Johansen and Juselius (1992) and McNown and Wallace (1992). A systematic inference procedure is desired for the selection. My earlier comment on McNown and Wallace (1992) is just a hint.

Appendix 1
Spectral Analysis

This appendix supplies proofs for several well-known statements on the spectral analysis that appear in the text of Chapters 3 and 7. Mathematical rigour is sacrificed for emphasis on the basic ideas. The readers who want more about the spectral analysis are advised to study Fuller (1976, ch. 7), Granger and Newbold (1986, ch. 2), and Hamilton (1994, ch. 6). More advanced readings are Anderson (1971, chs. 7, 8, 9, and 10) and Brillinger (1981).

(*a*) In a sequence of real numbers that extends in both directions, $\ldots, \gamma_{-1}, \gamma_0, \gamma_1, \ldots$ suppose that $\gamma_j = \gamma_{-j}$, $j = 1, 2, \ldots$.

$$f(\lambda) \equiv \frac{1}{2\pi} \sum_{j=-\infty}^{\infty} \gamma_j \exp(-i\lambda j), \qquad \pi \geq \lambda \geq -\pi \tag{A1.1}$$

is the Fourier transform of the sequence. In (A1.1) $i = \sqrt{-1}$. Noting that $\exp(-i\lambda j) = \cos \lambda j - i \sin \lambda j$, $\cos \lambda j = \cos \lambda(-j)$, $\sin \lambda j = -\sin \lambda(-j)$, (A1.1) is written as

$$\frac{1}{2\pi}\left(\gamma_0 + 2\sum_{j=1}^{\infty} \gamma_j \cos \lambda j\right) \tag{A1.1$'$}$$

and also as

$$\frac{1}{2\pi}\sum_{j=-\infty}^{\infty} \gamma_j \exp(i\lambda j) \tag{A1.1$''$}$$

When $f(\lambda)$ is defined by (A1.1) we have for $j = \ldots, -1, 0, 1, \ldots$

$$\int_{-\pi}^{\pi} f(\lambda) \exp(i\lambda j) d\lambda, \tag{A1.2}$$

$$= \int_{-\pi}^{\pi} \frac{1}{2\pi} \sum_{h=-\infty}^{\infty} \gamma_h \exp(-i\lambda h) \exp(i\lambda j) d\lambda$$

$$= \int_{-\pi}^{\pi} \frac{1}{2\pi} \gamma_j d\lambda = \gamma_j,$$

where the second equality follows from

$$\int_{-\pi}^{\pi} \exp(i\lambda(j-h))d\lambda = 0 \qquad \text{if } j \neq h.$$

The expression (A1.2) is called the Fourier inverse transform of $f(\lambda)$.

Given a stationary stochastic process, $\{x_t\}$, such that $E(x_t) = 0$, the auto-covariance for lag j is $E(x_t x_{t-j}) = E(x_{t+j} x_t)$, and thus $\gamma_j = \gamma_{-j}$. The Fourier transform of the sequence, $\ldots, \gamma_{-1}, \gamma_0, \gamma_1, \ldots$ is the (power) spectral density function, $f(\lambda)$, where the argument λ is called the frequency. The Fourier inverse transform of $f(\lambda)$ is the autocovariance sequence.

(*b*) Given two sequences, $\ldots, \alpha_{-1}, \alpha_0, \alpha_1, \ldots$ and $\ldots, \gamma_{-1}, \gamma_0, \gamma_1, \ldots$ we are interested in the sequence, $\ldots, \alpha_{-1}\gamma_{-1}, \alpha_0\gamma_0, \alpha_1\gamma_1, \ldots$.
Define

$$f_\alpha(\lambda) = \frac{1}{2\pi}\sum_j \alpha_j \exp(-i\lambda j)$$

$$f_\gamma(\lambda) = \frac{1}{2\pi}\sum_j \gamma_j \exp(-i\lambda j)$$

$$f_{\alpha\gamma}(\lambda) = \frac{1}{2\pi}\sum_j \alpha_j\gamma_j \exp(-i\lambda j).$$

Then

$$\int_{-\pi}^{\pi} f_\alpha(\zeta) f_\gamma(\lambda - \zeta) d\zeta \tag{A1.3}$$

$$= \int_{-\pi}^{\pi} \frac{1}{2\pi}\sum_j \alpha_j \exp(-i\zeta j)\frac{1}{2\pi}\sum_h \gamma_h \exp(-i(\lambda - \zeta)h) d\zeta$$

$$= \int_{-\pi}^{\pi} \left(\frac{1}{2\pi}\right)^2 \sum_j\sum_h \alpha_j\gamma_h \exp(-i\lambda h)\exp(-i\zeta(j-h))d\zeta$$

$$= \frac{1}{2\pi}\sum_h \alpha_h\gamma_h \exp(-i\lambda h) = f_{\alpha\gamma}(\lambda),$$

where we have used that $\int_{-\pi}^{\pi} \exp(-i\zeta(j-h))d\zeta = 0$ if $j \neq h$, and $=$ 2π if $j = h$.

(*c*) If $\{x_t\}$ is a scalar stationary process with $E(x_t) = 0$ and the spectral density function $f(\lambda)$, there is the Cramer representation

$$x_t = \int_{-\pi}^{\pi} \exp(it\lambda) dZ(\lambda),$$

where $Z(\cdot)$ is a complex valued, random function such that

$$E(dZ(\lambda)\overline{dZ(\zeta)}) = \begin{cases} 0 & \text{if } \lambda \neq \zeta \\ f(\lambda)d\lambda & \text{if } \lambda = \zeta. \end{cases}$$

Consider $y_t \equiv \sum_{j=-\infty}^{\infty} a_j x_{t-j}$. Then

$$y_t = \sum_j a_j \int_{-\pi}^{\pi} \exp(i(t-j)\lambda) dZ(\lambda)$$

$$= \int_{-\pi}^{\pi} \exp(it\lambda)\left(\sum_j a_j \exp(-ij\lambda)\right) dZ(\lambda).$$

The spectral density function of $\{y_t\}$ is

$$\left|\sum_j a_j \exp(-ij\lambda)\right|^2 f(\lambda).$$

Setting $a_0 = 1, a_1 = -1$, all other as to zero, the spectral density function of Δx_t is

$$|1 - \exp(-i\lambda)|^2 f(\lambda) = 2(1 - \cos\lambda) f(\lambda).$$

Appendix 2 Wiener (Brownian Motion) Process

Suppose that the pointer on your computer display is initially at the origin of X-axis, and begins to move either left or right by a non-stochastic amount, Δx, every Δt second. Probabilities of moving left and right are each 1/2, and directions in successive movements are mutually independent. Let x_i be a random variable defined by

$$x_i = \begin{cases} +1 & \text{if the } i\text{th movement is to the right} \\ -1 & \text{if the } i\text{th movement is to the left,} \end{cases}$$

and let $[a]$ be the largest integer that does not exceed a. The position of the pointer t seconds after the initial movement is

$$X(t) = (\Delta x)(x_1 + \ldots + x_{[t/\Delta t]}).$$

Since $E(x_i) = 0$ and $\text{var}(x_i) = 1$, $E(X(t)) = 0$ and $\text{var}(X(t)) = (\Delta x)^2[t/\Delta t]$. Let c be a positive real number, and let $\Delta x \to 0$ and $\Delta t \to 0$ while keeping $\Delta x = c\sqrt{\Delta t}$. In the limit we have a continuous time, and

$$E(X(t)) = 0, \qquad \text{var}(X(t)) = c^2 t.$$

Moreover, as $\Delta x \to 0$, $[t/\Delta t] \to \infty$, and $X(t)$ is a sum of mutually independent, infinitely many $(\Delta x)x_i$. By virtue of the central-limit theorem $X(t)$ is distributed in the normal distribution with the first- and the second-order moments given above. Finally, since the x_i s over two non-overlapping time periods are independent, we have the same independence property in the continuous time obtained by $\Delta x \to 0$.

This is the motivation behind the Wiener process, or the Brownian motion process, defined on a continuous time $t \geq 0$ by the following conditions,

(i) $w(0) = 0$

(ii) $w(t)$ is $N(0, c^2 t)$ for all $t > 0$

(iii) $w(s_2) - w(s_1)$ and $w(t) - w(s_3)$ are independent if $0 \leq s_1 < s_2 < s_3 \leq t$.

When $c = 1$, $w(t)$ is called the standard Wiener process. In the present book $w(\cdot)$ is the standard Wiener process, and the one with $c \neq 1$ will be written $cw(t)$. Thus $w(1)$ is $N(0, 1)$. Note that if $s \leq t$

$$\begin{aligned}\operatorname{cov}(w(s), w(t)) &= \operatorname{cov}(w(s), w(s) + w(t) - w(s)) \\ &= \operatorname{cov}(w(s), w(s)) + 0 = s.\end{aligned}$$

In general $\operatorname{cov}(w(s), w(t)) = \min(s, t)$. A good, elementary explanation of the Wiener process is found in Ross (1983) and Karlin (1975), the former being more elementary than the latter.

Suppose that a scalar process $\{\varepsilon_t\}$ is i.i.d. and $E(\varepsilon_t) = 0$ and $E(\varepsilon_t^2) = \sigma^2$, and let $S_T \equiv \varepsilon_1 + \ldots + \varepsilon_T$. Whatever the distribution of ε_t may be, $T^{-1/2}\sigma^{-1}S_T$ is distributed asymptotically as $T \to \infty$ in $N(0, 1) \equiv w(1)$. For a real number r such that $1 \geq r \geq 0$ let $[Tr]$ be the largest integer not exceeding Tr, and denote

$$X_T(r) = T^{-1/2}\sigma^{-1}S_{[Tr]}, \qquad 1 \geq r \geq 0.$$

$S_{[Tr]}$ is $\varepsilon_1 + \ldots + \varepsilon_t$ for some t and called a partial sum of $(\varepsilon_1, \varepsilon_2, \ldots)$. Given $T, X_T(r)$ may be regarded a stochastic process defined on a continuous time, r, such that $1 \geq r \geq 0$. As $T \to \infty$ we have the following theorems.

(i) $X_T(r) \xrightarrow{D} w(r), \qquad 1 \geq r \geq 0$

(ii) when $r_1, \ldots, r_m$ are arbitrary numbers between 0 and 1

$$X_T(r_1), \ldots, X_T(r_m)) \xrightarrow{D} (w(r_1), \ldots, w(r_m))$$

(iii) (ii) holds true even when $m \to \infty$.

These theorems are called Donsker's theorem, and may be regarded as an extension of the central-limit theorem. It is an extension because (i), (ii), and (iii) are concerned with a random function of r instead of a single random variable.

Recall a well-known theorem to the effect that (i) if for a stochastic process $\{x_T\}$ $x_T \xrightarrow{D} x$ as $T \to \infty$ and (ii) if $f(\cdot)$ is a continuous mapping, then $f(x_T) \xrightarrow{D} f(x)$. An analogous theorem holds on a functional of the stochastic process $X_T(r)$. As $T \to \infty$

(iv) $f(X_T(r)) \xrightarrow{D} f(w(r))$.

For example, $X_T(r)^2 \xrightarrow{D} w(r)^2$. Proofs of the above theorems (i)–(iv) require an advanced level of mathematics. A relatively elementary one is in Chung (1974: 217–22). More standard but also more advanced references are Billingsley (1968), Hall and Heyde (1980), Pollard (1984), and Tanaka (1995*b*).

The above (i), (ii), (iii), and (iv) are called the functional central-limit theorem and also the invariance principle. The Wiener process here is defined over [0, 1]. The convergence in distribution, $\xrightarrow{D}$, should in fact be the weak convergence, but I shall write $\xrightarrow{D}$ throughout the present book because the convergence in distribution and the weak convergence are identical in so far as they are applied in econometrics. Descriptions of $X_T(r)$ more detailed than the above are found in Banerjee *et al.* (1993: 21–5) and Hamilton (1994: 477–86), and they are useful to understand visually the convergence involved in (i) above.

On the $\{\varepsilon_t\}$ introduced above let $v_t \equiv \sum_{s=1}^{t} \varepsilon_s$. Then

$$\sigma^{-1}T^{-3/2}\sum_{t=1}^{T} v_t = T^{-1}\sum_{t=1}^{T} T^{-\frac{1}{2}}\sigma^{-1}\sum_{s=1}^{t} \varepsilon_s$$

$$= T^{-1}\sum_{t=1}^{T} X_T\left(\frac{t}{T}\right). \tag{A2.1}$$

Extending (ii) and (iii) it can be shown that

$$\sigma^{-1}T^{-3/2}\sum v_t \xrightarrow{D} \int_0^1 w(r)dr. \tag{A2.2}$$

Appendix 3 Asymptotic Theories involving a Linear Deterministic Trend

The present appendix explains the asymptotic theories that are used in Chapters 4 and 5 to deal with deterministic trends.

A3.1 Asymptotic Normality Involving a Linear Trend

Suppose that

$$x_t = \mu + \beta t + \varepsilon_t,$$

where $\{\varepsilon_t\}$ is i.i.d. with $E(\varepsilon_t) = 0$ and $E(\varepsilon_t^2) = \sigma_\varepsilon^2$. Let $\boldsymbol{\iota}' = (1, \ldots, 1), \boldsymbol{t}' = (1, \ldots, T), \boldsymbol{\varepsilon}' = (\varepsilon_1 \ldots, \varepsilon_T), \boldsymbol{x}' = (x_1, \ldots, x_T), \boldsymbol{X} = [\boldsymbol{\iota}, \boldsymbol{t}], \boldsymbol{D}_T = \text{diag}[T^{1/2}, T^{3/2}]$. Also let $\hat{\boldsymbol{\theta}}' \equiv (\hat{\mu}, \hat{\beta})$ be the OLS estimator of $\boldsymbol{\theta}' \equiv (\mu, \beta)$. We analyse $\boldsymbol{D}_T(\hat{\boldsymbol{\theta}} - \boldsymbol{\theta}) = (\boldsymbol{D}_T^{-1}\boldsymbol{X}'\boldsymbol{X}\boldsymbol{D}_T^{-1})^{-1}\boldsymbol{D}_T^{-1}\boldsymbol{X}'\varepsilon$. It is easy to see that as $T \to \infty$

$$(\boldsymbol{D}_T^{-1}\boldsymbol{X}'\boldsymbol{X}\boldsymbol{D}_T^{-1})^{-1} \to \begin{bmatrix} 1 & 1/2 \\ 1/2 & 1/3 \end{bmatrix}^{-1} \equiv \boldsymbol{\Omega}^{-1}.$$

The main task here is to investigate

$$\boldsymbol{D}_T^{-1}\boldsymbol{X}'\boldsymbol{\varepsilon} = \begin{bmatrix} T^{-1/2}\sum \varepsilon_t \\ T^{-3/2}\sum t\varepsilon_t \end{bmatrix}. \tag{A3.1}$$

It is well known that $T^{-1/2}\sum \varepsilon_t \xrightarrow{D} N(0, \sigma_\varepsilon^2)$. Readers might wonder about $T^{-3/2}\sum t\varepsilon_t$ since the weights on ε_ts increase with t. It can be shown that the vector random variable in (A3.1) jointly converges to a multivariate normal distribution.

To prove this we must show for any non-stochastic (α_1, α_2) that $\alpha_1 T^{-1/2}\sum \varepsilon_t + \alpha_2 T^{-3/2}\sum t\varepsilon_t$ converges to a scalar normal variate. This term may be written $\sum c_{tT}\varepsilon_t$, where

$$c_{tT} \equiv \alpha_1 T^{-1/2} + \alpha_2 T^{-3/2} t.$$

As $T \to \infty$, $\sum c_{tT}^2$ is $O(1)$, and the maximum of c_{tT}^2 over $t = 1, \ldots, T$ goes to zero. Therefore as $T \to \infty$

$$\max_{1,\ldots,T} c_{tT}^2 \Big/ \sum c_{tT}^2 \to 0. \tag{A3.2}$$

This condition establishes the Lindeberg–Feller condition, which is that for any $\delta(> 0)$

$$\sum_{t=1}^{T} S_T^{-2} \int_{|c_{tT}x| > \delta S_T} c_{tT}^2 x^2 f(x)dx \to 0. \tag{A3.3}$$

Here $f(\cdot)$ is the p.d.f., not necessarily normal, of ε_t common to all t and $S_T^2 = \sum c_{tT}^2$. The reason why (A3.3) follows from (A3.2) is as follows.

$$\text{(A3.3)} = \sum \left(\sum c_{tT}^2\right)^{-1} c_{tT}^2 \int_{x^2 > \delta^2 \left(\sum c_{tT}^2\right) c_{tT}^{-2}} x^2 f(x)dx$$

$$\leq \int_{x^2 > \delta^2 \left(\sum c_{tT}^2\right)(\max c_{tT}^2)^{-1}} x^2 f(x)dx,$$

and the last term goes to zero as $T \to \infty$ due to (A3.2) and existence of the second-order moment, $E(\varepsilon_t^2)$. I have followed Anderson (1971: 24).

The normal variate to which (A3.1) converges has the covariance matrix, $\sigma_\varepsilon^2 \lim \boldsymbol{D}_T^{-1}\boldsymbol{X}'\boldsymbol{X}\boldsymbol{D}_T^{-1} \equiv \sigma_\varepsilon^2 \boldsymbol{\Omega}$, and the conclusion is that

$$\begin{bmatrix} T^{1/2}(\hat{\mu} - \mu) \\ T^{3/2}(\hat{\beta} - \beta) \end{bmatrix} \xrightarrow{D} N(0, \sigma_\varepsilon^2 \boldsymbol{\Omega}^{-1}). \tag{A3.4}$$

Notice that $\hat{\beta}$ is $T^{3/2}$-consistent.

The essential point in the above derivation is that $\sum_1^T t^2 = O(T^3)$ while t^2 is at most T^2, from which it follows that a weight of one observation in the whole set is made as small as we wish by taking T sufficiently large. An exponential growth violates this condition.

A3.2 Proofs of (4.17)–(4.19)

Regarding the model

$$x_t = \mu + \rho x_{t-1} + \varepsilon_t,$$

the OLS estimator of $\boldsymbol{\theta}' = (\mu, \rho)$ is $\hat{\boldsymbol{\theta}} \equiv (\boldsymbol{X}'\boldsymbol{X})^{-1}\boldsymbol{X}'\boldsymbol{x}$, where $\iota' = (1, \ldots, 1)$, $\boldsymbol{x}'_{-1} = (x_1, \ldots, x_{T-1})$, $\boldsymbol{x}' = (x_2, \ldots, x_T)$, $\boldsymbol{X} = (\iota, \boldsymbol{x}_{-1}) \cdot \{\varepsilon_t\}$ is i.i.d. with zero mean. We derive the limiting distribution of $\hat{\boldsymbol{\theta}}$ when the true value of $\boldsymbol{\theta}$ is $\boldsymbol{\theta}^{0'} = (\mu^0, 1)$, where $\mu^0 \neq 0$. $\{x_t\}$ is generated by

$$x_t = \mu^0 t + \sum_{s=0}^{t-1} \varepsilon_{t-s} + x_0,$$

where x_0 is assumed to be independent of ε_t, $t > 0$. Let $\boldsymbol{D}_T =$ diag $[T^{1/2}, T^{3/2}]$. It is seen that

$$\begin{aligned}
\text{plim } T^{-2}\sum_2^T x_{t-1} &= \mu^0 \lim T^{-2}\sum_1^{T-1} t + \text{plim } T^{-2}\sum_1^{T-1}\sum_0^{t-1} \varepsilon_{t-s} \\
&= (\mu^0/2) + 0 \\
\text{plim } T^{-3}\sum_2^T x_{t-1}^2 &= \mu^{02} \lim T^{-3}\sum_1^{T-1} t^2 + 2\mu^0 \text{ plim } T^{-3}\sum_1^{T-1} t \\
&\quad \times \sum_{s=0}^{t-1} \varepsilon_{t-s} + \text{ plim } T^{-3}\sum_1^{T-1}\left(\sum_{s=0}^{t-1} \varepsilon_{t-s}\right)^2 \\
&= (\mu^{0^2}/3) + 0 + 0.
\end{aligned}$$

Let

$$\boldsymbol{\Sigma} \equiv \begin{bmatrix} 1 & \mu^0/2 \\ \mu^0/2 & \mu^{0^2}/3 \end{bmatrix}$$

Then it follows from the above calculations that $\lim_{T\to\infty} \boldsymbol{D}_T^{-1}\boldsymbol{X}'\boldsymbol{X}\boldsymbol{D}_T^{-1} \equiv \boldsymbol{\Sigma}$.

I now turn to $\boldsymbol{D}_T^{-1}\boldsymbol{X}'\boldsymbol{\varepsilon}$, where $\boldsymbol{\varepsilon}' = (\boldsymbol{\varepsilon}_2, \ldots, \boldsymbol{\varepsilon}_T)$. Noting that

$$T^{-3/2}\left(\sum_2^T x_{t-1}\varepsilon_t - \mu^0 \sum_2^T t\varepsilon_t\right) = T^{-3/2}\left(-\mu^0 \sum \varepsilon_t + \sum \varepsilon_t \sum_s \varepsilon_{t-1-s}\right)$$

converges in probability to zero, it is seen that

$$\boldsymbol{D}_T^{-1}\boldsymbol{X}'\boldsymbol{\varepsilon} - \begin{bmatrix} T^{-1/2}\sum \varepsilon_t \\ \mu^0 T^{-3/2}\sum t\varepsilon_t \end{bmatrix} \xrightarrow{P} \boldsymbol{0}.$$

As just shown in Section A3.1

$$\begin{bmatrix} T^{-1/2}\sum \varepsilon_t \\ \mu^0 T^{-3/2}\sum t\varepsilon_t \end{bmatrix} \xrightarrow{D} N\left(\boldsymbol{0}, \sigma_\varepsilon^2 \boldsymbol{\Sigma}\right).$$

Therefore

$$\boldsymbol{D}_T(\hat{\boldsymbol{\theta}} - \boldsymbol{\theta}^0) \xrightarrow{D} N\left(\mathbf{0}, \sigma_\varepsilon^2 \boldsymbol{\Sigma}^{-1}\right).$$

In particular, $T^{3/2}(\hat{\rho} - 1) \xrightarrow{D} N(0, 12\sigma_\varepsilon^2 \mu^{02})$.

A3.3 OLS along Equation (5.3)[1]

The least-squares estimator in (5.3) plays an important role in testing for DS against TS. The OLS is to be run along

$$x_t = \mu + \beta t + \rho x_{t-1} + \text{ residual}, \quad t = 2, \ldots, T. \tag{A3.5}$$

The data matrix of regressors in (A3.5) is $\boldsymbol{X} \equiv [\boldsymbol{\iota}, \boldsymbol{t}, \boldsymbol{x}_{-1}]$, where $\boldsymbol{x}_{-1} = (x_1, \ldots, x_{T-1})'$, and the data vector of the regressand is $\boldsymbol{x} \equiv (x_2, \ldots, x_T)'$. Let

$$\hat{\boldsymbol{\gamma}} \equiv (\hat{\mu}, \hat{\beta}, \hat{\rho})' \equiv (\boldsymbol{X}'\boldsymbol{X})^{-1}\boldsymbol{X}'\boldsymbol{x}. \tag{A3.6}$$

A3.3.1 Difference stationary DGP

Initially the data-generating process is

$$x_t = \theta_0 + \theta_1 t + v_t, \tag{A3.7}$$

where $v_t = \sum_{s=1}^t \varepsilon_s$ and $\{\varepsilon_t\}$ is i.i.d. with $E(\varepsilon_t) = 0$ and $E(\varepsilon_t^2) = \sigma_\varepsilon^2$. It is assumed that $x_0 = 0$, but note that θ_0 and x_0 cannot be distinguished. It will be seen later that neither is involved in $\hat{\beta}$, $\hat{\rho}$, and the t- and F-statistics.

Let $\boldsymbol{v} = (v_2, \ldots, v_T)'$, $\boldsymbol{v}_{-1} = (v_1, \ldots, v_{T-1})'$, $\boldsymbol{\varepsilon} = (\varepsilon_2, \ldots, \varepsilon_T)'$, $\boldsymbol{\varepsilon}_{-1} = (\varepsilon_1, \ldots, \varepsilon_{T-1})'$. From (A3.7) it follows that

$$\boldsymbol{x} = \boldsymbol{X}[\theta_1, 0, 1]' + \boldsymbol{\varepsilon}, \tag{A3.7$'$}$$

and from (A3.6) we get

$$\hat{\boldsymbol{\gamma}} - [\theta_1, 0, 1]' = (\boldsymbol{X}'\boldsymbol{X})^{-1}\boldsymbol{X}'\boldsymbol{\varepsilon}. \tag{A3.8}$$

Let

$$\boldsymbol{A} \equiv \begin{bmatrix} 1 & 0 & -(\theta_0 - \theta_1) \\ 0 & 1 & -\theta_1 \\ 0 & 0 & 1 \end{bmatrix}.$$

Then $\boldsymbol{XA} = [\boldsymbol{\iota}, \boldsymbol{t}, \boldsymbol{v}_{-1}]$. Let

$$\boldsymbol{B}_T \equiv \begin{bmatrix} 1 & -\dfrac{T+2}{2} & 0 \\ 0 & 1 & 0 \\ 0 & 0 & 1 \end{bmatrix}.$$

[1] I have benefited from a comment by Hiro Toda on an earlier draft of the present section.

Then $[\iota, t, v_{-1}]B_T \equiv [\iota, \tilde{t}, v_{-1}]$ and $\iota'\tilde{t} = 0$. Writing $AB_T \equiv A_T$, we have $XA_T = [\iota, \tilde{t}, v_{-1}]$. Let $D_T \equiv$ diag $[T'^{1/2}, \left(\frac{T'^3}{12}\right)^{1/2}, T']$ where $T' \equiv T - 1$.

$$(X'X)^{-1}X'\varepsilon = A_T D_T^{-1}[(XA_T D_T^{-1})'(XA_T D_T^{-1})]^{-1}(XA_T D_T^{-1})'\varepsilon, \tag{A3.9}$$

and

$$(XA_T D_T^{-1})'(XA_T D_T^{-1}) = \begin{bmatrix} 1 & 0 & T'^{-3/2}\sum v_{t-1} \\ 0 & 1 + 0(T^{-2}) & T'^{-5/2}\sqrt{12}\sum \tilde{t}v_{t-1} \\ T'^{-3/2}\sum v_{t-1} & T'^{-5/2}\sqrt{12}\sum \tilde{t}v_{t-1} & T'^{-2}\sum v_{t-1}^2 \end{bmatrix},$$

where $\tilde{t} = t - (T+2)/2$. Note that (A3.9) is nothing but (A3.8).

Introduce a lemma,

$$\begin{bmatrix} 1 & 0 & a_1 \\ 0 & 1 & a_2 \\ a_1 & a_2 & b \end{bmatrix}^{-1} = \begin{bmatrix} 1 & 0 & 0 \\ 0 & 1 & 0 \\ 0 & 0 & 0 \end{bmatrix} + \Delta^{-1}\begin{bmatrix} a_1 \\ a_2 \\ -1 \end{bmatrix}[a_1, a_2, -1],$$

where $\Delta = b - a_1^2 - a_2^2$, which incidentally can be extended to a higher dimensionality. (A3.9) is equal to

$$\begin{bmatrix} T'^{-1}\sum \varepsilon_t - 6T'^{-2}\sum \tilde{t}\varepsilon_t \\ 12T'^{-3}\sum \tilde{t}\varepsilon_t \\ 0 \end{bmatrix} - \frac{\Delta_1}{\Delta} \times \begin{bmatrix} T'^{-2}\sum v_{t-1} - 6T'^{-3}\sum \tilde{t}v_{t-1} + (\theta_0 - \theta_1)T'^{-1} \\ 12T'^{-4}\sum \tilde{t}v_{t-1} + \theta_1 T'^{-1} \\ -T'^{-1} \end{bmatrix} + \begin{bmatrix} O_p(T^{-5/2}) \\ O_p(T^{-7/2}) \\ O_p(T^{-3}) \end{bmatrix},$$

where

$$\Delta = T'^{-2}\sum v_{t-1}^2 - T'^{-3}\left(\sum v_{t-1}\right)^2 - 12T'^{-5} \times \left(\sum \tilde{t}v_{t-1}\right)^2 = O_p(1) \tag{A3.10a}$$

$$\Delta_1 = T'^{-1}\sum \varepsilon_t v_{t-1} - T'^{-2}\left(\sum \varepsilon_t\right)\left(\sum v_{t-1}\right) - 12T'^{-4}\left(\sum \tilde{t}\varepsilon_t\right) \times \left(\sum \tilde{t}v_{t-1}\right) = O_p(1). \tag{A3.10b}$$

Thus from (A3.8) and (A3.9)

$$\begin{cases} \hat{\mu} \approx \theta_1 + O_p(T^{-1/2}), \\ \hat{\beta} \approx -T'^{-1}\theta_1 \dfrac{\Delta_1}{\Delta} + 12T'^{-3}\sum \tilde{t}\varepsilon_t - 12T'^{-4}\dfrac{\Delta_1}{\Delta}\sum \tilde{t}v_{t-1}, \\ (\hat{\rho}-1) \approx T'^{-1}\dfrac{\Delta_1}{\Delta}, \end{cases} \tag{A3.11}$$

which proves that $\text{plim}\hat{\rho} = 1$, $\text{plim}\hat{\beta} = 0$, $\text{plim}\hat{\mu} = \theta_1$.

The last equation of (A3.11) by itself can be derived as follows. Let $\boldsymbol{Z} = [\iota, \hat{t}]$, and $\boldsymbol{Q}_z = \boldsymbol{I} - \boldsymbol{Z}(\boldsymbol{Z}'\boldsymbol{Z})^{-1}\boldsymbol{Z}'$. Then $T'(\hat{\rho}-1) = (T'^{-2}\boldsymbol{x}'_{-1}\boldsymbol{Q}_z\boldsymbol{x}_{-1})^{-1}T'^{-1}\boldsymbol{x}'_{-1}\boldsymbol{Q}_z(\boldsymbol{x}-\boldsymbol{x}_{-1}) = (T'^{-2}\boldsymbol{v}'_{-1}\boldsymbol{Q}_z\boldsymbol{v}_{-1})^{-1}T'^{-1}\boldsymbol{v}'_{-1}\boldsymbol{Q}_z\boldsymbol{\varepsilon}$.

The limiting distribution of $\sigma_\varepsilon^{-2}\Delta$ is given in (6.3) in the text, and the limiting distribution of $T(\hat{\rho}-1)$ is given in (6.8*a*). From (A3.11) it is obvious that $T(\hat{\rho}-1)$ is invariant to whether $\theta_1 =$ or $\neq 0$ in the data-generating process. However, $\hat{\beta}$ does depend upon $\theta_1 =$ or $\neq 0$. It is $O_p(T^{-1})$ if $\theta_1 \neq 0$, but $O_p(T^{-3/2})$ if $\theta_1 = 0$.

(*i*) *Multicolinearity between* $\hat{\beta}$ *and* $\hat{\rho}$.

Since $T'^{-3}\sum \tilde{t}\varepsilon_t$ and $T'^{-4}\sum \tilde{t}v_{t-1}$ are both $O_p(T^{-3/2})$, (A3.11) also shows that, if $\theta_1 \neq 0$, $\theta_1(\hat{\rho}-1)+\hat{\beta} = o_p(T^{-1})$, which means that $\hat{\beta}$ and $\hat{\rho}$ are perfectly correlated in $O_p(T^{-1})$. The correlation is negative (positive) if $\theta_1 > (<)\ 0$. The perfect correlation is caused by the following relation between two regressors, t and x_{t-1}: (*a*) $x_{t-1} = (\theta_0 - \theta_1) + \theta_1 t + v_{t-1}$, and as $T \to \infty$ $\theta_1 t$ dominates v_{t-1} in so far as $\theta_1 \neq 0$; (*b*) according to (A3.5) the dominating part of x_t is thus $(\theta_1\rho + \beta)t$. Subtracting x_{t-1} from both sides of (A3.5) it is seen that $\theta_1(\hat{\rho}-1)+\hat{\beta}$ is the coefficient in the effect of t upon Δx_t, which is expected to be zero.

(*ii*) *F-test statistic.*

Let $\boldsymbol{e} \equiv \boldsymbol{x} - \boldsymbol{X}\hat{\boldsymbol{\gamma}}$. Then $\boldsymbol{e}'\boldsymbol{e} = \boldsymbol{x}'[\boldsymbol{I} - \boldsymbol{X}(\boldsymbol{X}'\boldsymbol{X})^{-1}\boldsymbol{X}']\boldsymbol{x}$. From (*A*3.7′) it follows that

$$\boldsymbol{e}'\boldsymbol{e} = \boldsymbol{\varepsilon}'\boldsymbol{\varepsilon} - \boldsymbol{\varepsilon}'\boldsymbol{X}(\boldsymbol{X}'\boldsymbol{X})^{-1}\boldsymbol{X}'\boldsymbol{\varepsilon}.$$

We have

$$\begin{aligned} &\boldsymbol{\varepsilon}'\boldsymbol{X}(\boldsymbol{X}'\boldsymbol{X})^{-1}\boldsymbol{X}'\boldsymbol{\varepsilon} \\ &= \boldsymbol{\varepsilon}'\boldsymbol{X}\boldsymbol{A}_T\boldsymbol{D}_T^{-1}(\boldsymbol{D}_T^{-1}\boldsymbol{A}'_T\boldsymbol{X}'\boldsymbol{X}\boldsymbol{A}_T\boldsymbol{D}_T^{-1})^{-1}\boldsymbol{D}_T^{-1}\boldsymbol{A}'_T\boldsymbol{X}'\boldsymbol{\varepsilon} \\ &= T'^{-1}\left(\sum \varepsilon_t\right)^2 + 12T'^{-3}\left(\sum \tilde{t}\varepsilon_t\right)^2 + \frac{\Delta_1^2}{\Delta} + O_p(T^{-2}). \end{aligned}$$

Thus

$$\boldsymbol{e}'\boldsymbol{e} \approx \sum \varepsilon_t^2 - T'^{-1}\left(\sum \varepsilon_t\right)^2 - 12T'^{-3}\left(\sum \tilde{t}\varepsilon_t\right)^2 - \frac{\Delta_1^2}{\Delta}.$$

Then let $\tilde{\boldsymbol{e}}$ be the residual vector in the constrained least squares with the constraint, $(\beta, \rho) = (0, 1)$, in (A3.5). Then $\tilde{e}'\tilde{e} \approx \sum \varepsilon_t^2 - T'^{-1}\left(\sum \varepsilon_t\right)^2$, and

$$\tilde{e}'\tilde{e} - e'e \approx \frac{\Delta_1^2}{\Delta} + 12T'^{-3}\left(\sum \tilde{t}\varepsilon_t\right)^2. \tag{A3.12}$$

We can also prove that $\text{plim}(T-4)^{-1}e'e = \sigma_\varepsilon^2$. The limiting distribution of the F-statistic is given in (6.8c) of the text.

A3.3.2 The trend stationary DGP

Let us turn to the case where the data-generating process is

$$x_t = \theta_0 + \theta_1 t + u_t,$$

where $\{u_t\}$ is a stationary process with zero mean and the sequence of the serial correlation coefficients, $r_0 \equiv 1, r_1, \ldots,$ and the variance, σ_u^2. Let $u' = (u_2, \ldots, u_T)$. Then

$$x = \theta_0 \iota + \theta_1 t + u.$$

Concerning $\hat{\gamma}$ in (A3.6),

$$\begin{aligned}\hat{\gamma} &= [\theta_0, \theta_1, 0]' + (X'X)^{-1}X'u \\ &= [\theta_0, \theta_1, 0]' + A_T D_T^{-1}(D_T^{-1}A_T'X'XA_TD_T^{-1})^{-1}D_T^{-1}A_T'X'u,\end{aligned}$$

where A, B_T, and hence A_T are defined in the same way as above, but here D_T is diag $[T'^{1/2}, (T'^3/12)^{1/2}, T'^{1/2}]$. Therefore

$$\text{plim} D_T^{-1}A_T'X'XA_TD_T^{-1} = \text{diag}[1, 1, \sigma_u^2].$$

Thus

$$\hat{\gamma} \approx \begin{bmatrix}\theta_0\\ \theta_1\\ 0\end{bmatrix} + \begin{bmatrix} T'^{-1}\sum u_t - \frac{1}{2}\sqrt{(12)}T'^{-2}\sum \tilde{t}u_t - T'^{-1}(\theta_0 - \theta_1)\sigma_u^{-2} \times \sum u_{t-1}u_t \\ 12T'^{-3}\sum \tilde{t}u_t - T^{-1}\theta_1\sigma_u^{-2}\sum u_{t-1}u_t \\ T'^{-1}\sigma_u^{-2}\sum u_{t-1}u_t \end{bmatrix}.$$

Therefore $\text{plim}\hat{\rho} = r_1$, $\text{plim}\hat{\beta} = \theta_1(1 - r_1)$, and $\text{plim}\hat{\mu} = \theta_0(1 - r_1) + \theta_1 r_1$. If $\theta_1 \neq 0$, $\theta_1(\hat{\rho} - 1) + \hat{\beta} = o_p(T^{-1})$, i.e. *$\hat{\rho}$ and $\hat{\beta}$ are perfectly correlated* just in the same way as in the difference-stationary case. This is relevant to some findings in the Bayesian discrimination between the trend and the difference stationarity as noted in Chapter 10 of the text.

Appendix 4 OLS Estimator of Difference-Stationary Autoregressive Process

A4.1 Proof of (6.27)

The limiting result, (6.27), is due to Fuller (1976: 373–7). Here I shall show a proof based on the Wiener process rather than his original. The DGP is (6.23′) with $\alpha_1^0 = 1$, i.e. (6.19). Let $(\hat{\alpha}_1, \ldots, \hat{\alpha}_p)$ be the OLS of $(\alpha_1, \ldots, \alpha_p)$ along (6.23′). Let $\boldsymbol{X}$ be the data matrix of regressors, $(x_{t-1}, \Delta x_{t-1}, \ldots, \Delta x_{t-p+1})$; $\boldsymbol{\varepsilon}$ be the vector of ε_t; and $\boldsymbol{D}_T \equiv \text{diag}[T, T^{1/2}, \ldots, T^{1/2}]$, which is $p \times p$. We are concerned with $T(\hat{\alpha}_1 - 1)$, which is the first element of

$$\boldsymbol{D}_T(\boldsymbol{X}'\boldsymbol{X})^{-1}\boldsymbol{X}'\boldsymbol{\varepsilon} = (\boldsymbol{D}_T^{-1}\boldsymbol{X}'\boldsymbol{X}\boldsymbol{D}_T^{-1})^{-1}\boldsymbol{D}_T^{-1}\boldsymbol{X}'\varepsilon. \tag{A4.1}$$

Regarding the (1,1) element of $\boldsymbol{D}_T^{-1}\boldsymbol{X}'\boldsymbol{X}\boldsymbol{D}_T^{-1}$ we see from (6.13) that

$$T^{-2}\sum x_{t-1}^2 \xrightarrow{D} \sigma^2 \int_0^1 w(r)^2 dr \tag{A4.2}$$

where σ^2 is the long-run variance of u_t, i.e. (6.26). For $(1, j+1)$ elements, $j = 1, \ldots, p-1$, we have from (6.14)

$$T^{-3/2}\sum x_{t-1}\Delta x_{t-j} \xrightarrow{P} 0. \tag{A4.3}$$

Remaining elements converge in probability to the autocovariances of $\{u_t\}$. Because of (A4.3) $\boldsymbol{D}_T^{-1}\boldsymbol{X}'\boldsymbol{X}\boldsymbol{D}_T^{-1}$ is asymptotically block diagonal, and the (1,1) element is a block by itself.

In the DGP $\Delta x_t = u_t$, and $\{u_t\}$ is constructed by $AR(p-1)$, (6.20′). Let us invert this $AR(p-1)$ into an MA, and write

$$u_t = b(L)\varepsilon_t$$

with the same $\{\varepsilon_t\}$ as in (6.20′). Then an expression of σ^2 alternative to (6.26) is

$$\sigma^2 = b(1)^2\sigma_\varepsilon^2. \tag{A4.4}$$

We have been concerned with the first element of (A4.1). In view of the asymptotic block diagonality of $(\boldsymbol{D}_T^{-1}\boldsymbol{X}'\boldsymbol{X}\boldsymbol{D}_T^{-1})^{-1}$ we are now interested in the first element of $\boldsymbol{D}_T^{-1}\boldsymbol{X}'\varepsilon$, which is $T^{-1}\sum x_{t-1}\varepsilon_t$. Applying (2.8) to $\Delta x_t = u_t$ we see that

$$T^{-1}\sum x_{t-1}\varepsilon_t = b(1)T^{-1}\sum_t\left(\sum_{s=1}^{t-1}\varepsilon_s\right)\varepsilon_t + T^{-1}\sum \varepsilon_t b^*(L)\varepsilon_{t-1} + o_p(1).$$

The second term on the right-hand side converges to zero in probability, and by virtue of (4.7)

$$T^{-1}\sum x_{t-1}\varepsilon_t \xrightarrow{D} b(1)\sigma_\varepsilon^2\int_0^1 w(r)dw(r). \tag{A4.5}$$

Combining (A4.2) and (A4.5), and noting (A4.4), it is seen that

$$T(\hat{\alpha}_1 - 1) \xrightarrow{D} b(1)^{-1}\left(\int_0^1 w(r)^2 dr\right)^{-1}\int_0^1 w(r)dw(r). \tag{A4.6}$$

Note that $b(1) = (1 - a_1 - \ldots - a_{p-1})^{-1} > 0$. The distribution of $\hat{\alpha}_1$ involves nuisance parameters $(a_1, \ldots, a_{p-1})$.

As regards the t-statistic,

$$\hat{t} = s^{-1}T(\hat{\alpha}_1 - 1)\left(T^{-2}\sum x_{t-1}^2\right)^{1/2} \xrightarrow{D} \left(\int_0^1 w(r)^2 dr\right)^{-1/2}\int_0^1 w(r)dw(r),$$

since $\sigma = \sigma_\varepsilon b(1)$ and $\operatorname{plim} s = \sigma_\varepsilon$. Notice that $b(1)$ has disappeared from $\hat{t}$, and the limiting distribution of $\hat{t}$ is free from the nuisance parameters.

It has been seen that $\boldsymbol{D}_T^{-1}\boldsymbol{X}'\boldsymbol{X}\boldsymbol{D}_T^{-1}$ is asymptotically block-diagonal. This kind of block diagonality will be observed frequently in the unit-root field between the non-stationary and the stationary variables.

A4.2 Other Statistics

If $\alpha_1 = 1$, $\hat{\alpha}' = (\hat{\alpha}_2, \ldots, \hat{\alpha}_p)$ is asymptotically identical to the OLS estimator of $(a_1, \ldots, a_{p-1})$ in (6.20′). Using the well-known limiting distribution of the latter (see, e.g. Anderson (1971: 164–200)) the limiting distribution of $\hat{\alpha}$ is given by

$$\sqrt{T}(\hat{\boldsymbol{\alpha}} - \boldsymbol{\alpha}) \xrightarrow{D} N(\boldsymbol{0}, \sigma_\varepsilon^2\boldsymbol{\Gamma}^{-1}),$$

where $\boldsymbol{\alpha} \equiv (\alpha_2, \ldots, \alpha_p)$,

$$\boldsymbol{\Gamma} \equiv \begin{bmatrix} \gamma_0 & \gamma_1 & \cdots & \gamma_{p-2} \\ \gamma_1 & \ddots & \ddots & \vdots \\ \vdots & \ddots & \ddots & \gamma_1 \\ \gamma_{p-2} & \cdots & \gamma_1 & \gamma_0 \end{bmatrix} \qquad (p-1)\times(p-1),$$

and $\gamma_j \equiv E(u_t u_{t-j})$.

Appendix 5 Mathematics for the VAR, VMA, and VARMA

A bivariate AR may be written, for example, as either

$$\left\{\begin{bmatrix} a_{11}^0 & a_{12}^0 \\ a_{21}^0 & a_{22}^0 \end{bmatrix} + \begin{bmatrix} a_{11}^1 & 0 \\ a_{21}^1 & a_{22}^1 \end{bmatrix} L + \begin{bmatrix} 0 & 0 \\ 0 & a_{22}^2 \end{bmatrix} L^2 \right\} \begin{bmatrix} x_{1t} \\ x_{2t} \end{bmatrix} = \begin{bmatrix} \varepsilon_{1t} \\ \varepsilon_{2t} \end{bmatrix} \tag{A5.1}$$

or

$$\begin{bmatrix} a_{11}^0 + a_{11}^1 L, & a_{12}^0 \\ a_{21}^0 + a_{21}^1 L, & a_{22}^0 + a_{22}^1 L + a_{22}^2 L^2 \end{bmatrix} \begin{bmatrix} x_{1t} \\ x_{2t} \end{bmatrix} = \begin{bmatrix} \varepsilon_{1t} \\ \varepsilon_{2t} \end{bmatrix}. \tag{A5.2}$$

Econometricans are more familiar with (A5.1), but the system theory adopts (A5.2). I shall give an elementary, non rigorous explanation of the system theory used in Section 12.2.

I distinguish the words, polynomials, and infinite power series, by restricting the former to finite orders. The matrix on the left-hand side of (A5.2) has a polynomial of lag operator L in each element. More generally we consider a matrix of which each element is a polynomial function of a scalar argument z. It will be denoted by $\boldsymbol{A}(z)$. The coefficients of polynomials are assumed to be real numbers. Such a matrix is called the polynomial matrix. When a polynomial matrix is factored below, the factor polynomial matrix must also have coefficients in real numbers.

The determinant of a square polynomial matrix, $\boldsymbol{A}(z)$, is defined in the same way as in the ordinary matrix. The determinant will be denoted by $\det[\boldsymbol{A}(z)]$. $\boldsymbol{A}(z)$ is said to be non-singular if $\det[\boldsymbol{A}(z)] = 0$ holds only at a finite number of real or complex values of z, i.e. $\det[\boldsymbol{A}(z)]$ is not identically zero. $\boldsymbol{A}(z)$ is singular if and only if there exists a polynomial vector $\boldsymbol{b}(z)'$ such that $\boldsymbol{b}(z)'\boldsymbol{A}(z) \equiv \boldsymbol{0}$.

The k-variate VAR (vector autoregressive process) is represented by

$$\boldsymbol{A}(L)\boldsymbol{x}_t = \boldsymbol{\varepsilon}_t. \tag{A5.3}$$

$\boldsymbol{A}(z)$ is assumed to be non-singular. We are concerned with the stationarity of $\{\boldsymbol{x}_t\}$ generated by (A5.3) with an i.i.d. $\{\boldsymbol{\varepsilon}_t\}$. (A5.3) is a linear difference equation for $\{\boldsymbol{x}_t\}$ with $\{\boldsymbol{\varepsilon}_t\}$ as a forcing function. The stationarity of $\{\boldsymbol{x}_t\}$ is equivalent to the stability of the difference equation just in the same way as in the univariate AR. And the stability of (A5.3) is that the roots of the equation for z

$$\det[\boldsymbol{A}(z)] = 0 \tag{A5.4}$$

are all larger than unity in moduli, i.e. all lie outside the unit circle of the complex plane. If the characteristic polynomial of the difference equation is written as in mathematical economics, the stability would be represented by the characteristic roots being less than unity in moduli as we learn in economic dynamics (see Section 2.3).

In the present appendix and Section 12.2 we frequently refer to the roots of a determinental equation such as (A5.4) lying all outside of the unit circle of the complex plane. In every such statement I simply write that $\det[\boldsymbol{A}(z)] = 0$ has all roots outside the unit circle, omitting the words such as the equation and the complex plane.

Let $\boldsymbol{B}(z)$ be a $k \times k$ polynomial matrix. Then the k-variate VMA (vector moving average process) is represented by

$$\boldsymbol{x}_t = \boldsymbol{B}(L)\boldsymbol{\varepsilon}_t. \tag{A5.5}$$

We are concerned with the invertibility of VMA. To explain the invertibility I revert to an expression such as (A5.1). $\boldsymbol{B}(z)$ may be written $\boldsymbol{B}_0+\boldsymbol{B}_1 z+\ldots+\boldsymbol{B}_q z^q$, where the $\boldsymbol{B}$s are each $k \times k$ matrices. $\boldsymbol{B}(z)$ is said to be invertible if one can find a unique sequence of matrices, $\boldsymbol{A}_0, \boldsymbol{A}_1, \ldots$, such that

$$(\boldsymbol{A}_0 + \boldsymbol{A}_1 z + \boldsymbol{A}_2 z^2 + \ldots)(\boldsymbol{B}_0 + \boldsymbol{B}_1 z_1 + \ldots + \boldsymbol{B}_q z^q) = \boldsymbol{I}_k$$

holds identically and $\sum_{j=0}^{\infty} \|\boldsymbol{A}_j\|$ converges in terms of some measure of the norm $\|\ \|$ of $\boldsymbol{A}$s. A necessary and sufficient condition for the invertibility of $\boldsymbol{B}(z)$ is that roots of

$$\det[\boldsymbol{B}(z)] = 0 \tag{A5.6}$$

all lie outside the unit circle. This generalizes the well-known invertibility condition for a univariate MA.

VARMA is written as

$$\boldsymbol{A}(L)x_t = \boldsymbol{B}(L)\varepsilon_t. \tag{A5.7}$$

Just as a (scalar) polynomial may be factored into two or more (scalar) polynomials, $\boldsymbol{A}(z)$ may be factored into two or more polynomial matrices, and so is $\boldsymbol{B}(z)$. If $\boldsymbol{A}(z)$ and $\boldsymbol{B}(z)$ have a factor polynomial matrix common between them, it should be cancelled in (A5.7). When all the common factors are cancelled between $\boldsymbol{A}(z)$ and $\boldsymbol{B}(z)$, $\boldsymbol{A}(z)^{-1}\boldsymbol{B}(z)$ is called the irreducible MFD (matrix fraction description). The irreducibility is assumed throughout the following description.

A matrix with a rational function of z in each element is called the rational matrix. When $\boldsymbol{A}(z)$ is non-singular $\boldsymbol{C}(z) \equiv \boldsymbol{A}(z)^{-1}\boldsymbol{B}(z)$ is a rational matrix. The determinant of a rational matrix is also defined in the same way as in the ordinary matrix, and the concept of non-singularity follows from it in the same way as in the polynomial matrix. In fact,

$$\boldsymbol{C}(z) = (\det[\boldsymbol{A}(z)])^{-1}\tilde{\boldsymbol{A}}(z)\boldsymbol{B}(z),$$

where $\tilde{\boldsymbol{A}}(z)$ is the adjoint (adjunct) of $\boldsymbol{A}(z)$ and hence is a polynomial matrix. $\tilde{\boldsymbol{C}}(z) \equiv \tilde{\boldsymbol{A}}(z)\boldsymbol{B}(z)$ is also a polynomial matrix. Since $\det[\boldsymbol{C}(z)] =$

[1] See Kailath (1980: 367) for a more accurate description of the irreducibility.

$(\det[\boldsymbol{A}(z)])^{-k}\det[\tilde{\boldsymbol{C}}(z)]$, the non-singularity of $\boldsymbol{C}(z)$ is equivalent to the non-singularity of $\tilde{\boldsymbol{C}}(z)$.[2]

I assume that the $k \times k$ $\boldsymbol{C}(z) \equiv \boldsymbol{A}(z)^{-1}\boldsymbol{B}(z)$ is non-singular in (A5.7), which implies that $\boldsymbol{B}(z)$ is non-singular. The assumption precludes linear dependency among elements of $\{\boldsymbol{x}_t\}$ in (A5.7). When $\boldsymbol{C}(z)$ is non-singular, it can be represented in the Smith–McMillan form with the following properties.

$$\boldsymbol{C}(z) = \boldsymbol{U}(z)\boldsymbol{\Lambda}(z)\boldsymbol{V}(z), \tag{A5.8}$$

where
(i) three matrices on the right-hand side are each $k \times k$;
(ii) $\boldsymbol{U}(z)$ and $\boldsymbol{V}(z)$ are polynomial matrices, and $\det[\boldsymbol{U}(z)]$ and $\det[\boldsymbol{V}(z)]$ are both non-zero *constants* not involving z;
(iii) $\boldsymbol{\Lambda}(z) = \text{diag}[\lambda_1(z), \ldots, \lambda_k(z)]$ and $\lambda_i(z) = f_i(z)/g_i(z)$, $i = 1, \ldots, k$ such that
(iii*a*) $f_i(z)$ and $g_i(z)$ are polynomials not sharing a common factor;
(iii*b*) $f_i(z)|f_{i+1}(z), \quad i = 1, \ldots, k-1$;
(iii*c*) $g_{i+1}(z)|g_i(z), \quad i = 1, \ldots, k-1$;
(iv) $\boldsymbol{\Lambda}(z)$ is uniquely determined by $\boldsymbol{C}(z)$, but $\boldsymbol{U}(z)$ and $\boldsymbol{V}(z)$ are not.

Concerning (iii*b*) and (iii*c*) above, $a(z)|b(z)$ means that $a(z)$ divides $b(z)$, i.e. $a(z)$ is a factor of $b(z)$. See Kailath (1980: 443–4) for the Smith–McMillan form.

The polynomial matrix of which the determinant is a non-zero constant (i.e. a polynomial in zero degree) is called unimodular. Any products of unimodular matrices are unimodular, and the inverse of a unimodular matrix is unimodular. The reason why unimodular matrices appear in (A5.8) is that elementary row operations and column operations are unimodular. The elementary row operations consist of (i) an interchange of two rows, (ii) addition to a row of a polynomial multiple of another row, and (iii) scaling all elements of a row by a non-zero constant. The elementary column operations are likewise defined.

For example, consider

$$\boldsymbol{A}(z) = \begin{bmatrix} 1 & z \\ 0 & 1+az \end{bmatrix}, \boldsymbol{B}(z) = \begin{bmatrix} 1+bz & 0 \\ cz & 1 \end{bmatrix}, c \neq 0.$$

Then

$$\boldsymbol{C}(z) = \boldsymbol{A}(z)^{-1}\boldsymbol{B}(z) = (1+az)^{-1}\begin{bmatrix} (1+az)(1+bz) - cz^2 & -z \\ cz & 1 \end{bmatrix}. \tag{A5.9}$$

To express $\boldsymbol{C}(z)$ in a Smith–McMillan form it is convenient to rewrite

$$\begin{bmatrix} (1+az)(1+bz) - cz^2 & -z \\ cz & 1 \end{bmatrix} \tag{A5.10}$$

[2] The roots are not necessarily identical. If the highest power of z in $\det[\boldsymbol{A}(z)]$ exceeds that of every element of $\hat{\boldsymbol{C}}(z)$, $\det[\boldsymbol{C}(\pm\infty)] = 0$, while $\det[\hat{\boldsymbol{C}}(\pm\infty)] \neq 0$.

in what is called the Smith form. A polynomial matrix with rank 2 can be represented in a Smith form,

$$U_1(z)\Lambda_1(z)V_1(z). \tag{A5.11}$$

Here both $U_1(z)$ and $V_1(z)$ are 2×2 and unimodular and $\Lambda_1(z) = \text{diag}[\lambda_1(z), \lambda_2(z)]$ where $\lambda_1(z)|\lambda_2(z)$. How to obtain a Smith form is explained in Kailath (1980: 375–6, 391). It consists of elementary row and column operations. (A5.10) is equal to (A5.11) with

$$U_1(z) = \begin{bmatrix} 0 & 1 \\ 1 & 0 \end{bmatrix} \begin{bmatrix} 1 & 0 \\ c^{-1}(a+b) + c^{-1}(ab-c)z & 1 \end{bmatrix} \begin{bmatrix} 0 & 1 \\ 1 & 0 \end{bmatrix} \begin{bmatrix} 1 & 0 \\ cz & 1 \end{bmatrix}.$$

$$\Lambda_1(z) = \begin{bmatrix} 1 & 0 \\ 0 & (1+az)(1+bz) \end{bmatrix}.$$

$$V_1(z) = \begin{bmatrix} 1 & -c^{-1}(a+b) - c^{-1}abz \\ 0 & 1 \end{bmatrix}.$$

Then the Smith–McMillan form of (A5.9) is (A5.8) with $U(z) = U_1(z)$, $V(z) = V_1(z)$, and

$$\Lambda(z) = \begin{bmatrix} 1/(1+az) & 0 \\ 0 & (1+bz) \end{bmatrix}.$$

$$f_1(z) = 1,\ f_2(z) = 1 + bz,\ g_1(z) = 1 + az,\ g_2(z) = 1.$$

$V(z)^{-1}$ represents an elementary column operation, and the four matrices that form $U(z)$ are each obtained by inverting some matrices that represent elementary row operations.

The above result has a number of implications. First, for any finite values of z in general and for a root of $f_i(z) = 0$, z_0, in particular $U(z_0)$ and $V(z_0)$ are non-singular so that the rank of $C(z_0)$ is equal to the rank of $\Lambda(z_0)$. (There should be no contradiction between $C(z)$ being non-singular and $C(z_0)$ being singular.) Second, if z_0 is not a root of $f_{k-r}(z) = 0$ nor of $g_1(z) = 0$ but is a root of $f_{k-r+1}(z) = 0$, then z_0 is a root of $f_{k-r+2}(z) = 0, \ldots, f_k(z) = 0$, and $\Lambda(z_0)$ has rank, $k - r$, which is also the rank of $C(z_0)$. As a third implication I quote a lemma from Hannan and Deistler (1988: 54). Roots of $f_1(z) = 0, \ldots, f_k(z) = 0$ are roots of $\det[B(z)] = 0$, and roots of $g_1(z) = 0, \ldots, g_k(z) = 0$ are roots of $\det[A(z)] = 0$.

For any matrix A its rank will be denoted by $\rho(A)$ below.

In Section 12.2 we consider (A5.7), especially the case where $\det[A(z)] = 0$ has all roots lying outside the unit circle and $\det[B(z)] = 0$ has *real unit roots* as well as other roots lying outside the unit circle. It follows from the third implication mentioned above that, for some $(k - r)$ such that $0 \le k - r \le k - 1$, $f_{k-r+1}(1) = f_{k-r+2}(1) = \ldots = f_k(1) = 0$ while $f_1(1), \ldots, f_{k-r}(1)$ are not zero. (The latter is void if $k - r = 0$.) From the assumption about $A(z)$ we have $g_1(1) \neq 0, \ldots, g_k(1) \neq 0$, and it follows that $\rho(\Lambda(1)) = k - r$, which is also equal to $\rho(\boldsymbol{C}(1))$ as stated in the first implication. Since $\boldsymbol{C}(1) = \boldsymbol{A}(1)^{-1}\boldsymbol{B}(1)$ and $\boldsymbol{A}(1)$ is non-singular by the assumption about $\boldsymbol{A}(z)$, $\rho(\boldsymbol{B}(1))$ is also $k - r$.

The conclusions are that $\boldsymbol{C}(1)$ and $\boldsymbol{B}(1)$ have the identical rank, which is equal to the number of non-zero terms among $f_1(1), \ldots, f_k(1)$.

Incidentally, if $\det[\boldsymbol{B}(z)] = 0$ has all roots outside the unit circle and none of the real unit root, than $\rho(\boldsymbol{B}(1)) = k$.

Reverting to the case where $\det[\boldsymbol{B}(z)] = 0$ has real unit roots, Engle and Yoo (1991) suggest the following rearrangement of (A5.8). Write

$$f_i(z) \equiv \tilde{f}_i(z), \quad i \leq k - r$$
$$f_i(z) \equiv (1 - z)^{m_i}\tilde{f}_i(z), \quad i \geq k - r + 1, \tag{A5.12}$$

where $\tilde{f}_i(z) = 0$ has all roots lying outside the unit circle. This is possible by virtue of the third implication and the assumption about $\boldsymbol{B}(z)$. Moreover, let us suppose for the exposition in Section 12.2 that all the m_is in (A5.12) are unity. Let

$$\boldsymbol{\Lambda}(z) \equiv \boldsymbol{D}_g(z)^{-1}\boldsymbol{D}(z)\boldsymbol{D}_{\tilde{f}}(z) \tag{A5.13}$$
$$\boldsymbol{D}_g(z) \equiv \operatorname{diag}[g_1(z), \ldots, g_k(z)]$$
$$\boldsymbol{D}_{\tilde{f}}(z) \equiv \operatorname{diag}[\tilde{f}_1(z), \ldots, \tilde{f}_k(z)]$$
$$\boldsymbol{D}(z) \equiv \operatorname{diag}[\overbrace{1, \ldots, 1}^{k-r}, \overbrace{(1 - z), \ldots, (1 - z)}^{r}].$$

Then

$$\boldsymbol{C}(z) = (\boldsymbol{U}(z)\boldsymbol{D}_g(z)^{-1})\boldsymbol{D}(z)(\boldsymbol{D}_{\tilde{f}}(z)\boldsymbol{V}(z)). \tag{A5.14}$$

Setting $\tilde{\boldsymbol{U}}(z) \equiv \boldsymbol{U}(z)\boldsymbol{D}_g(z)^{-1}$ and $\tilde{\boldsymbol{V}}(Z) \equiv \boldsymbol{D}_{\tilde{f}}(z)\boldsymbol{V}(z)$, (A5.7) can be rewritten as

$$\tilde{\boldsymbol{U}}(L)^{-1}\boldsymbol{x}_t = \boldsymbol{D}(L)\tilde{\boldsymbol{V}}(L)\boldsymbol{\varepsilon}_t. \tag{A5.15}$$

In regard to $\tilde{\boldsymbol{U}}(z)^{-1} = \boldsymbol{D}_g(z)\boldsymbol{U}(z)^{-1}$, since $\det[\boldsymbol{U}(z)^{-1}] = 0$ has no (finite) roots,[3] and since $\det[\boldsymbol{A}(z)] = 0$ and hence $\det[\boldsymbol{D}_g(z)] = 0$ have all roots outside the unit circle, $\det[\tilde{\boldsymbol{U}}(z)]^{-1} = 0$ has all roots outside the unit circle. Moreover, since $\det[\boldsymbol{U}(z)]$ is a constant not involving z, $\tilde{\boldsymbol{U}}(z)^{-1}$ is a polynomial (rather than rational) matrix. $\tilde{\boldsymbol{V}}(z)$ is a polynomial matrix, and $\det[\tilde{\boldsymbol{V}}(z)] = 0$ has all roots outside the unit circle. $\tilde{\boldsymbol{V}}(L)$ is invertible, but $\boldsymbol{D}(L)$ is non-invertible. Therefore (A5.15) is VARMA with non-invertible MA, which (A5.7) is. The difference between (A5.7) and (A5.15) is that the presence of unit root is made more visible in (A5.15).

[3] In general, if $\boldsymbol{A}(z)$ is a non-singular $k \times k$ polynomial matrix and $\boldsymbol{B}(z)$ is its adjoint matrix, then $\det[\boldsymbol{B}(z)] = (\det[\boldsymbol{A}(z)])^{k-1}$. The roots of $\det[\boldsymbol{B}(z)] = 0$ must also be roots of $\det[\boldsymbol{A}(z)] = 0$. Concerning the text, $\det[\boldsymbol{U}(z)] = 0$ has no roots because $\boldsymbol{U}(z)$ is unimodular. Let $\boldsymbol{U}^*(z)$ be the adjoint of $\boldsymbol{U}(z)$. Then $\det[\boldsymbol{U}^*(z)] = 0$ has no finite roots. Though $\det[\boldsymbol{U}(z)^{-1}] = 0$ may have $z = \pm\infty$ as a root, it is outside the unit circle.

Appendix 6 Fully Modified Least-Squares Estimator

In Section 13.3 we have introduced a mixed Gaussian estimator proposed in Phillips (1991*a*) on the co-integrated regression, in which $\{(\Delta x_t, \Delta y_t)\}$ are serially correlated. On the same model Phillips and Hansen (1990) proposed another mixed Gaussian estimator called the fully modified least squares.

Initially the notations in Section 13.3 will be reproduced. $\{\boldsymbol{u}_t\}$ is a stationary process with zero mean vector, $\boldsymbol{u}_t' = (u_{1t}, u_{2t})$, and $E(\boldsymbol{u}_t\boldsymbol{u}_{t+j}') \equiv \boldsymbol{\Gamma}_j, \boldsymbol{\Gamma} \equiv \sum_{j=-\infty}^{\infty} \boldsymbol{\Gamma}_j$, and $\boldsymbol{\Lambda} \equiv \sum_{j=1}^{\infty} \boldsymbol{\Gamma}_j$. The (i, j) element of $\boldsymbol{\Gamma}, \boldsymbol{\Gamma}_h$, and $\boldsymbol{\Lambda}$ are respectively $\gamma_{ij}, \gamma_{ij}^{(h)}$, and λ_{ij}. The additional notation is $\boldsymbol{\Delta} = \boldsymbol{\Gamma}_0 + \boldsymbol{\Lambda}$, of which the (i, j) element is Δ_{ij}. Note that neither $\boldsymbol{\Lambda}$ nor $\boldsymbol{\Delta}$ is symmetric in general but $\boldsymbol{\Gamma}$ is. The model is $x_t = \sum_{s=1}^{t} u_{1s}$, and $y_t = bx_t + u_{2t}$. We estimate b from $\{(x_t, y_t)\}$.

The fully modified least-squares estimator of b begins with a consistent estimation of $(\gamma_{11}, \gamma_{21})$ and $(\Delta_{11}, \Delta_{12})$, but I like to delay description of the estimation method. The estimators are denoted by $(\hat{\gamma}_{11}, \hat{\gamma}_{21})$ and $(\hat{\Delta}_{11}, \hat{\Delta}_{12})$ respectively. Construct

$$\hat{y}_t^+ \equiv y_t - \hat{\gamma}_{21}\hat{\gamma}_{11}^{-1}\Delta x_t. \tag{A6.1}$$

Then the fully modified least-squares estimator of b is

$$\hat{b}^+ = \left[\sum \hat{y}_t^+ x_t - T(-\hat{\gamma}_{21}\hat{\gamma}_{11}^{-1}, 1)(\hat{\Delta}_{11}, \hat{\Delta}_{12})'\right]\left[\sum x_t^2\right]^{-1}. \tag{A6.2}$$

It is easy to derive the limiting distribution of $T(\hat{b}^+ - b)$. Since

$$\hat{b}^+ - b = \left[\sum(-\hat{\gamma}_{21}\hat{\gamma}_{11}^{-1}, 1)(u_{1t}, u_{2t})'x_t - T(-\hat{\gamma}_{21}\hat{\gamma}_{11}^{-1}, 1)(\hat{\Delta}_{11}, \hat{\Delta}_{12})'\right]$$
$$\times \left[\sum x_t^2\right]^{-1}, \tag{A6.3}$$

let us investigate $T^{-1} \times$ (the nominator of the right-hand side of (A6.3)). Let $\boldsymbol{w}(r) = (w_1(r), w_2(r))'$ be the Wiener process with covariance matrix $\boldsymbol{\Gamma}$. Then using (13.46) in the text it is seen that

$$T^{-1}\sum(-\hat{\gamma}_{21}\hat{\gamma}_{11}^{-1}, 1)(u_{1t}, u_{2t})'x_t = T^{-1}\sum(-\hat{\gamma}_{21}\hat{\gamma}_{11}^{-1}, 1)(u_{1t}, u_{2t})'$$
$$\times(x_{t-1} + u_{1t})] \xrightarrow{D} (-\gamma_{21}\gamma_{11}^{-1}, 1)\left[\int d\boldsymbol{w}(r)w_1(r) + (\Delta_{11}, \Delta_{12})'\right]. \tag{A6.4}$$

Therefore in (A6.3)

$$T^{-1}\sum\{(-\hat{\gamma}_{21}\hat{\gamma}_{11}^{-1},1)(u_{1t},u_{2t})'x_t-(-\hat{\gamma}_{21}\hat{\gamma}_{11}^{-1},1)(\Delta_{11},\Delta_{12})'\}$$
$$\xrightarrow{D}(-\gamma_{21}\gamma_{11}^{-1},1)\int d\boldsymbol{w}(r)w_1(r)=\int dw_{2.1}(r)w_1(r), \tag{A6.5}$$

where $w_{2.1}(r)$ is obtained from $\boldsymbol{w}(r)$ as in (13.1*a*) and (13.1*b*). See also Section 13.1.3. Finally we obtain

$$T(\hat{b}^+-b)\xrightarrow{D}\int dw_{2.1}(r)w_1(r)\left(\int w_1(r)^2dr\right)^{-1} \tag{A6.6}$$

just as in (13.18) of the text. This is mixed Gaussian because $(w_1(r), w_{2.1}(r))$ has a diagonal covariance matrix, $\text{diag}[\gamma_{11}, \gamma_{22}-\gamma_{21}^2\gamma_{11}^{-1}]$.

Modifications of the OLS have been made in two points to obtain $\hat{b}^+$. The first is introduction of $(\hat{\Delta}_{11}, \hat{\Delta}_{12})'$ in the nominator of (A6.2). It contributes to cancelling $(\Delta_{11}, \Delta_{12})'$ that appears in (A6.4). The second is the modification of y_t to get $\hat{y}_t^+$ in (A6.1). It contributes to eliminating the linear effect of $w_1(r)$ from $w_2(r)$ as seen from (A6.3) and (A6.5).

Both x_t and y_t may be extended to vector processes.

Now I return to the estimation of $(\gamma_{11}, \gamma_{21})$ and $(\Delta_{11}, \Delta_{12})$. Phillips and Hansen (1990) propose to estimate these parameters from OLS residuals non-parametrically in the same way as the spectral density function is estimated. The $\boldsymbol{\Gamma}$ is the matrix spectral density function of $\boldsymbol{u}_t = (u_{1t}, u_{2t})'$ at zero frequency. The case where a norm of the matrix spectral density function is lowest at zero frequency in its neighbourhood is a multivariate extension of the Schwert ARMA discussed in Sections 7.2.2–3. The non-parametric estimation of $\boldsymbol{\Gamma}$ would be extremely difficult in such cases. Phillips and Hansen (1990) estimate $\boldsymbol{\Lambda}$ in the same way as $\boldsymbol{\Gamma}$. Thus if the Bartlett window is used, $\sum\hat{u}_t\hat{u}_{t+k}'$, $k=0,1,\ldots$ are weighted with weights given in (3.4). To the best of my knowledge, not much is known about its finite sample properties.

The fully modified least-squares estimator is asymptotically equivalent to the estimator in (13.53) of Section 13.3. Users have to choose between the two estimators. A difficulty with the latter is how to choose the lag and forward orders in (13.53). On the other hand the fully modified least-squares method faces a problem regarding how to choose the truncation point in the non-parametric estimation of $\boldsymbol{\Gamma}$ and $\boldsymbol{\Lambda}$. In the simulation study conducted by Hargreaves (1993) the fully modified least-squares method fares better than the one in Section 13.3. As I see it, however, the study does not include the multivariate extension of the Schwert ARMA explained in Section 7.2.2. I expect that the method in Section 13.3 is more robust to the Schwert ARMA than the fully modified least squares. This is based on the ground that the augmented Dickey–Fuller test is more robust to the Schwert MA in the univariate analysis. An experimental study is required. Inder (1993) is partly relevant to the present problem.

In the univariate analysis of US macroeconomic data presented in Chapter 9 I have found none indicative of the univariate Schwert ARMA in the post-war quarterly data.

Phillips (1993) applies the idea of fully modified least squares to the estimation of a possibly co-integrated VAR, and obtains results that are remarkable in terms of the asymptotic theory.

References

Agiakloglou, C., and Newbold, P. (1992), 'Empirical Evidence on Dickey–Fuller-Type Tests,' *Journal of Time Series Analysis*, 13: 471–83.

Ahmed, Shagheil, Ickes, Barry W., Wang, Ping, and Yoo, Byung Sam (1993), 'International Business Cycles', *American Economic Review*, 83: 335–59.

Ahn, Sung K. (1993), 'Some Tests for Unit Roots in Autoregressive-Integrated-Moving Average Models with Deterministic Trends', *Biometrica*, 80: 855–68.

—— and Reinsel, Gregory C. (1988), 'Nested Reduced-Rank Auto Regressive Models for Multiple Time Series', *Journal of the American Statistical Association*, 83: 849–56.

—— —— (1990), 'Estimation of Partially Non-stationary Multivariate Autoregressive Model,' *Journal of the American Statistical Association*, 85: 813–23.

Akaike, Hirotsugu (1973), 'Information Theory and an Extension of the Likelihood Principle', in B. N. Petrov and F. Csaki (eds.), *Proceedings of the Second International Symposium of Information Theory, Akademia Kiado*, 267–81.

Alogoskoufis, George, and Smith, Ron (1991), 'On Error Correction Models: Specification, Interpretation, Estimation', *Journal of Economic Surveys*, 5: 97–128.

Anderson, T. W. (1951), 'Estimating Linear Restrictions on Regression Coefficients for Multivariate Normal Distributions', *Annals of Mathematical Statistics*, 22: 327–51.

—— (1971), *The Statistical Analysis of Time Series*, Wiley, New York.

—— and Kunitomo, Naoto (1992), 'Tests of Overidentification and Predeterminedness in Simultaneous Equation Models,' *Journal of Econometrics*, 54: 49–78.

—— —— (1994), 'Asymptotic Robustness of Tests of Overidentification and Predeterminedness', *Journal of Econometrics*, 62: 383–414.

Ansley, Craig F. (1979), 'An Algorithm for the Exact Likelihood of a Mixed Autoregressive-Moving Average Process', *Biometrika*, 66: 59–65.

Aoki, Masanao (1968), 'Control of Large Scale Dynamic Systems by Aggregation,' *IEEE Transactions on Automatic Control*, AC-13: 246–53.

—— (1990), *State Space Modeling of Time Series*, 2nd rev. edn., Springer-Verlag, Berlin.

Ardeni, Pier Giorgio, and Lubian, Diego (1991), 'Is There Trend Reversion in Purchasing Power Parity', *European Economic Review*, 35: 1035–55.

Baillie, Richard T., and Bollerslev, Tim (1989), 'Common Stochastic Trends in a System of Exchange Rates', *Journal of Finance*, 44: 167–81.

—— —— (1994), 'Cointegration, Fractional Cointegration, and Exchange Rate Dynamics,' *Journal of Finance*, 69: 737–45.

—— and Selover, David (1987), 'Cointegration and Models of Exchange Rate Determination', *International Journal of Forecasting*, 3: 43–51.

Balke, Nathan S., and Fomby, Thomas B. (1991), 'Shifting Trends, Segmented Trends, and Infrequent Permanent Shocks', *Journal of Monetary Economics*, 28: 61–85.

Banerjee, Anindya, Dolado, Juan, Galbraith, John W., and Hendry, David F. (1993), *Co-integration, Error-Correction, and the Econometric Analysis of Non-stationary Data*, Oxford University Press.

Banerjee, Anindya, Lumsdaine, Robin L., and Stock, James H. (1992), 'Recursive and Sequential Tests of the Unit-Root and Trend-Break Hypotheses: Theory and International Evidence', *Journal of Business and Economic Statistics*, 10: 271–87.

Basawa, I. V., Mallik, A. K., Mccormick, W. P., Reeves, J. H., and Taylor R. L. (1991*a*), 'Bootstrapping Unstable First Order Autoregressive Processes', *Annals of Statistics*, 19: 1098–111.

—— —— —— —— —— (1991*b*), 'Bootstrap Test of Significance and Sequential Bootstrap Estimation for Unstable First Order Autoregressive Processes', *Communications in Statistics, Theory and Methods*, 20: 1015–26.

Beaudry, Paul, and Koop, Gary (1993), 'Do Recessions Permanently Change Output?', *Journal of Monetary Economics*, 31: 149–63.

Beaulieu, J. Joseph, and Miron, Jeffrey A. (1993), 'Seasonal Unit Roots in Aggregate US Data', *Journal of Econometrics*, 55: 305–28.

Berger, James O. (1985), *Statistical Decision Theory and Bayesian Analysis*, 2nd edn., Springer-Verlag, Berlin.

—— and Delampady, Mohan (1987), 'Testing Precise Hypotheses', *Statistical Science*, 2: 317–52.

—— and Sellke, Thomas (1987), 'Testing a Point Null Hypothesis: The Irreconcilability of P Values and Evidence', *Journal of the American Statistical Association*, 82: 112–22.

Bernanke, Ben S. (1986), 'Alternative Explanations of the Money-Income Correlation', *Carnegie Rochester Conference Series on Public Policy*, 25: 49–100.

Beveridge, Stephen, and Nelson, Charles R. (1981), 'A New Approach to Decomposition of Economic Time Series into Permanent and Transitory Components with Particular Attention to Measurement of the "Business Cycle" ', *Journal of Monetary Economics*, 7: 151–74.

Bewley, R. A. (1979), 'The Direct Estimation of the Equilibrium Response in a Linear Dynamic Model', *Economics Letters*, 3: 357–61.

Billingsley, Patrick (1968), *Convergence of Probability Measures*, John Wiley, New York.

Blanchard, Oliver Jean (1989), 'A Traditional Interpretation of Macroeconomic Fluctuations', *American Economic Review*, 79: 1146–64.

—— and Quah, Danny (1989), 'The Dynamic Effects of Aggregate Demand and Supply Disturbances', *American Economic Review*, 79: 655–73.

Bollerslev, Tim, and Engle, Robert F. (1993), 'Common Persistence in Conditional Variances', *Econometrica*, 61: 167–86.

Boswijk, H. Peter (1994), 'Testing for an Unstable Root in Conditional and Structural Error Correction Models', *Journal of Econometrics*, 63: 37–60.

Box, G. E. P., and Jenkins, G. M. (1976), *Time Series Analysis: Forecasting and Control*, 2nd edn., Holden-Day, San Francisco.

—— and Tiao, G. C. (1977), 'A Canonical Analysis of Multiple Time Series', *Biometrika*, 64: 355–65.

Brillinger, David R. (1981), *Time Series: Data Analysis and Theory*, 2nd edn., Holden-Day, San Francisco.

Brodin, P. A., and Nymoen, R. (1992), 'Wealth Effects and Exogeneity: The Norwegian Consumption Function 1966(1)–1989(4)', *Oxford Bulletin of Economics and Statistics*, 54: 431–54.

Campbell, John Y. (1987), 'Does Saving Anticipate Declining Labor Income? An Alternative Test of the Permanent Income Hypothesis', *Econometrica*, 55: 1249–273.

Campbell, John J., and Deaton, Angus (1989), 'Why is Consumption so Smooth?', *Review of Economic Studies*, 56: 357–74.

—— and Mankiw, N. Gregory (1987), 'Are Output Fluctuations Transitory?', *Quarterly Journal of Economics*, 102: 857–80.

—— —— (1989), 'International Evidence on the Persistence of Economic Fluctuations', *Journal of Monetary Economics*, 23: 319–33.

—— and Perron, Pierre (1991), 'Pitfalls and Opportunities: What Macroeconomists should know about Unit Roots', *Macroeconomics Annual, 1991*, NBER, 141–201.

—— and Shiller, Robert J. (1987), 'Cointegration and Tests of Present Value Models', *Journal of Political Economy*, 95: 1062–88, repr. in R. F. Engle and C. W. J. Granger (eds.), *Long-Run Economic Relationships, Reading in Cointegration*, Oxford University Press.

—— —— (1988), 'Interpreting Cointegrated Models', *Journal of Economic Dynamics and Control*, 12: 505–22.

Canarella, Giorgio, Pollard, Stephen K., and Lai, Kon S. (1990), 'Cointegration between Exchange Rates and Relative Prices: Another View', *European Economic Review*, 14: 1303–22.

Casellea, George, and Berger, Roger L. (1987), 'Reconciling Bayesian and Frequentist Evidence in the One-Sided Testing Problem', *Journal of the American Statistical Association*, 82: 106–11.

Chan, N. H., and Wei, C. Z. (1988), 'Limiting Distributions of Least Squares Estimates of Unstable Autoregressive Processes', *Annals of Statistics*, 16: 367–401.

Chao, John C., and Phillips, Peter C. B. (1994), 'Bayesian Model Selection in Partially Nonstationary Vector Autoregressive Processes with Reduced Rank Structure', mimeo.

Cheung, Yin-Wong (1993), 'Long Memory in Foreign Exchange Rates', *Journal of Business and Economics Statistics*, 11: 93–101.

Choi, In (1992), 'Durbin–Hausman Tests for a Unit Root', *Oxford Bulletin of Economics and Statistics*, 54: 289–304.

—— (1993), 'Asymptotic Normality of the Least-Squares Estimates for Higher Order Autoregressive Integrated Processes with some Applications', *Econometric Theory*, 9: 263–82.

—— (1994), 'Spurious Regressions and Residual-Based Tests for Cointegration when Regressors are Cointegrated', *Journal of Econometrics*, 60: 313–20.

Christiano, Lawrence J., and Eichenbaum, Martin (1990), 'Unit Roots in Real GNP: Do We know, and Do We Care?', *Carnegie-Rochester Conference Series on Public Policy*, 32: 7–62.

Chung, Kai Lai (1974), *A Course in Probability Theory*, Academic Press, New York.

Clark, Peter K. (1987), 'The Cyclical Component of US Economic Activity', *Quarterly Journal of Economics*, 102: 797–814.

—— (1988), 'Nearly Redundant Parameters and Measure of Persistence in Economic Time Series', *Journal of Economic Dynamics and Control*, 12: 447–61.

—— (1989), 'Trend Reversion in Real Output and Unemployment', *Journal of Econometrics*, 40: 15–32.

Clements, Michael P., and Mizon, Graham E. (1991), 'Empirical Analysis of Macroeconomic Time Series', *European Economic Review*, 35: 887–932.

Cochrance, John H. (1988), 'How Big is the Random Walk in GNP?', *Journal of Political Economy*, 96: 893–920.

Cogley, Timothy (1990), 'International Evidence on the Size of the Random Walk in Output', *Journal of Political Economy*, 98: 501–18.

Copeland, Laurence S. (1991), 'Cointegration Tests with Daily Exchange Rate Data', *Oxford Bulletin of Economics and Statistics*, 53: 185–98.

Cox, D. R. (1961), 'Tests of Separate Families of Hypotheses', *Proceedings of the Fourth Berkeley Symposium on Mathematical Statistics and Probability*, I, University of California Press, 105–23.

—— and Hinkley, D. V. (1974), *Theoretical Statistics*, Chapman & Hall, London.

Davidson, James (1991), 'The Cointegration Properties of Vector Autoregression Models', *Journal of Time Series Analysis*, 12: 41–62.

—— (1994), 'Identifying Cointegrating Regressions by the Rank Condition', *Oxford Bulletin of Economics and Statistics*, 56: 105–9.

—— Hendry, David F., Srba, Frank, and Yeo, Stephen (1978), 'Econometric Modelling of the Aggregate Time Series Relationship between the Consumers' Expenditure and Income in the United Kingdom', *Economic Journal*, 88: 661–92.

Deaton, Angus (1987), 'Life-Cycle Models of Consumption: Is the Evidence Consistent with the Theory', in T. F. Bewley (ed.), *Advances in Econometrics, the 5th World Congress*, II, Cambridge University Press, 121–48.

DeGroot, Morris H. (1973), 'Doing What Comes Naturally: Interpreting a Tail Area as a Posterior Probability or as a Likelihood Ratio', *Journal of the American Statistical Association*, 68: 966–9.

DeJong, David N. (1992), 'Co-integration and Trend-Stationarity in Macroeconomic Time Series', *Journal of Econometrics*, 52: 347–70.

—— Nankervis, John C., Savin, N. E., and Whiteman, Charles H. (1992*a*), 'The Power Problems of Unit Root Tests in Time Series with Autoregressive Errors', *Journal of Econometrics*, 53: 323–43.

—— (1992*b*), 'Integration versus Trend-Stationarity in Time Series', *Econometrica*, 60: 423–33.

—— and Whiteman, Charles H. (1991*a*), 'The Temporal Stability of Dividends and Stock Prices: Evidence from the Likelihood Function', *American Economic Review*, 81: 600–17.

—— —— (1991*b*), 'Reconsidering "Trends and Random Walks in Macroeconomic Time Series"', *Journal of Monetary Economics*, 28: 221–54.

Delong, J. Bradford, and Summers, Lawrence H. (1988), 'How does Macroeconomic Policy affect Output?', *Brookings Papers on Economic Activity*, 1988, No. 2: 433–80.

Demery, D., and Duck, N. W. (1992), 'Are Economic Fluctuations really Persistent? A Reinterpretation of Some International Evidence', *Economic Journal*, 102: 1094–101.

Diba, Behzad T., and Grossman, Herschel I. (1988), 'Explosive Rational Bubbles in Stock Prices?', *American Economic Review*, 78: 520–30.

Dickey, David A., and Fuller, Wayne A. (1979), 'Distribution of the Estimators for Autoregressive Time Series with a Unit Root', *Journal of the American Statistical Association*, 74: 427–31.

—— —— (1981), 'Likelihood Ratio Statistics for Autoregressive Time Series with a Unit Root', *Econometrica*, 49: 1057–72.

Diebold, Francis X. (1988), *Empirical Modelling of Exchange Rate Dynamics*, Lecture Notes in Economics and Mathematical Systems, No. 303, Springer-Verlag, Berlin.

—— (1993), 'Discussion, the Effect of Seasonal Adjustment Filters on Tests for a Unit Root', *Journal of Econometrics*, 55: 99–103.

Diebold, Francis X., Gardeazabel, Javier, and Yilmaz, Kamil (1994), 'On Cointegration and Exchange Rate Dynamics', *Journal of Finance*, 69: 727-35.

—— Husted, Steven, and Rush, Mark (1991), 'Real Exchange Rates under the Gold Standard', *Journal of Political Economy*, 99: 1252-71.

Dolado, Juan, Galbraith, John W., and Banerjee, Anindya (1991), 'Estimating Intertemporal Quadratic Adjustment Cost Models with Integrated Series', *International Economic Review*, 32: 919-36.

Drobny, A., and Hall, S. G. (1989), 'An Investigation of the Long-Run Properties of Aggregate Non-Durable Consumers' Expenditure in the United Kingdom', *Economic Journal*, 99: 454-60.

Durbin, J., and Watson, G. S. (1971), 'Testing for Serial Correlation in Least Squares Regression, III', *Biometrika*, 58: 1-19.

Durlauf, Steven N. (1989), 'Output Persistence, Economic Structure, and the Choice of Stabilization Policy', *Brookings Papers on Economic Activity*, 1989/2: 69-116.

—— and Phillips, Peter C. B. (1988), 'Trends versus Random Walks in Time Series Analysis', *Econometrica*, 56: 1333-54.

Dweyer, Gerald P. Jr., and Wallace, Myles S. (1992), 'Cointegration and Market Efficiency', *Journal of International Money and Finance*, 11: 318-27.

Elliott, Graham, Rothenberg, Thomas J., and Stock, James H. (1992), 'Efficient Tests for an Autoregressive Unit Root', National Bureau of Economic Research, Technical Working Paper No. 130.

Engle, Robert F., and Granger, C. W. J. (1987), 'Co-integration and Error Correction: Representation, Estimation, and Testing', *Econometrica*, 55: 251-76, repr. in R. F. Engle and C. W. J. Granger (eds.), *Long-Run Economic Relationships, Readings in Cointegration*, Oxford University Press.

—— —— and Hallman, J. J. (1989), 'Merging Short- and Long-Run Forecasts: An Application of Seasonal Cointegration to Monthly Electricity Sales Forecasting', *Journal of Econometrics*, 40: 45-62, repr. in R. F. Engle and C. W. J. Granger (eds.), *Long-Run Economic Relationships, Readings in Cointegration*, Oxford University Press.

—— Hendry, David F., and Richard, Jean-François (1983), 'Exogeneity', *Econometrica*, 51: 277-304.

—— and Yoo, Byung Sam (1987), 'Forecasting and Testing in Co-integrated Systems', *Journal of Econometrics*, 35: 143-59, repr. in R. F. Engle and C. W. J. Granger (eds.), *Long-Run Economic Relationships, Readings in Cointegration*, Oxford University Press.

—— —— (1991), 'Cointegrated Economic Time Series: An Overview with New Results', in R. F. Engle and C. W. J. Granger (eds.), *Long-Run Economic Relationships, Readings in Cointegration*, Oxford University Press, 237-66.

Engsted, Tom (1993), 'Cointegration and Cagan's Model of Hyperinflation under Rational Expectations', *Journal of Money, Credit, and Banking*, 25: 350-60.

Ericsson, Neil R. (1992), 'Cointegration, Exogeneity, and Policy Analysis: An Overview', *Journal of Policy Modeling*, 14: 251-80.

Fama, Eugene F., and French, Kenneth R. (1988), 'Permanent and Temporary Components of Stock Prices', *Journal of Political Economy*, 96: 246-73.

Ferguson, Thomas S. (1967), *Mathematical Statistics: A Decision Theoretic Approach*, Academic Press, New York.

Flavin, Marjorie A. (1981), 'The Adjustment of Consumption to Changing Expectations about Future Income', *Journal of Political Economy*, 89: 974-1009.

Friedman, Benjamin M., and Kuttner, Kenneth N. (1992), 'Money, Income, Prices, and Interest Rates', *American Economic Review*, 82: 472–92.

—— —— (1993), 'Another Look at the Evidence on Money-Income Causality', *Journal of Econometrics*, 57: 189–203.

Froot, Kenneth A., and Obstfeld, Maurice (1991), 'Intrinsic Bubbles: The Case of Stock Prices', *American Economic Review*, 81: 1189–214.

Fukushige, M., Hatanaka, M., and Koto, Y. (1994), 'Testing for the Stationarity and the Stability of Equilibrium', in C. A. Sims (ed.), *Advances in Econometrics, Sixth World Congress*, i, Cambridge University Press, 3–45.

Fuller, Wayne A. (1976), *Introduction to Statistical Time Series*, John Wiley, New York.

Gali, Jordi (1992), 'How well does the IS-LM Model fit Postwar U.S. Data', *Quarterly Journal of Economics*, 107: 709–38.

Geweke, John (1984), 'Inference and Causality in Economic Time Series Models', in Z. Griliches and M. D. Intriligator (eds.), *Handbook of Econometrics*, II, North-Holland, Amsterdam.

Ghysels, Eric (1994), 'On the Economics and Econometrics of Seasonality', in C. A. Sims (ed.), *Advances in Econometrics, Sixth World Congress*, Cambridge University Press, 257–316.

—— and Perron, Pierre (1993), 'The Effect of Seasonal Adjustment Filters on Tests for a Unit Root', *Journal of Econometrics*, 55: 57–98.

Gonzalo, Jesus, and Granger, Clive W. J. (1991), 'Estimation of Common Long-Memory Components in Cointegrated Systems', mimeo.

Granger, C. W. J. (1969), 'Investigating Causal Relations by Econometric Models and Cross-Spectral Methods', *Econometrica*, 37: 424–38.

—— (1981), 'Some Properties of Time Series Data and Their Use in Econometric Model Specification', *Journal of Econometrics*, 16: 121–30.

—— (1986), 'Developments in the Study of Cointegrated Economic Variables', *Oxford Bulletin of Economics and Statistics*, 48: 213–28, repr. in R. F. Engle and C. W. J. Granger (eds.), *Long-Run Economic Relationships, Readings in Cointegration*, Oxford University Press.

—— (1988*a*), 'Models that Generate Trends', *Journal of Time Series Analysis*, 9: 329–43.

—— (1988*b*), 'Some Recent Developments in a Concept of Causality', *Journal of Econometrics*, 39: 199–211.

—— (1991), 'Some Recent Generalizations of Cointegration and the Analysis of Long-run Relationships', in R. F. Engle and C. W. J. Granger (eds.), *Long-Run Economic Relationships, Readings in Cointegration*, Oxford University Press, 277–87.

—— (1993), 'What are we learning about the Long-Run?' *Economic Journal*, 103: 307–17.

—— and Hallman, Jeff (1991), 'Long Memory Series with Attractors', *Oxford Bulletin of Economics and Statistics*, 53: 11–26.

—— and Joyeux, Roselyne (1980), 'An Introduction to Long-Memory Time Series Models and Fractional Differencing', *Journal of Time Series Analysis*, 1: 15–29.

Granger, C. W. J., and Lee, Hahn S. (1991), 'An Introduction to Time-Varying Parameter Cointegration', in P. Hackl and A. H. Westlund (eds.), *Econometric Structural Change*, Springer-Verlag, 139–57.

—— and Lee, T.-H. (1989), 'Investigation of Production, Sales and Inventory Relationships Using Multicointegration and Non-Symmetric Error Correction Models, *Journal of Applied Econometrics*, 4: 145–59.

—— —— (1990), 'Multicointegration', in G. F. Rhodes and T. B. Fomby (eds.), *Advances in Econometrics*, 8: 71–84, repr. in R. F. Engle and C. W. F. Granger (eds.), *Long-Run Economic Relationships, Readings in Cointegration*, Oxford University Press.

—— and Lin, Jin-Lung (1993), 'Causality in the Long Run', *Econometric Theory*, forthcoming.

—— and Newbold, P. (1974), 'Spurious Regressions in Econometrics', *Journal of Econometrics*, 2: 111–20.

—— —— (1986), *Forecasting Economic Time Series*, 2nd edn., Academic Press, New York.

—— and Teräsvirta, T. (1993), *Modelling Nonlinear Economic Relationships*, Oxford University Press.

—— and Weiss, A. A. (1983), 'Time Series Analysis of Error-Correction Models', in S. Karlin, T. Amemiya, and L. Goodman (eds.), *Studies in Econometrics, Time Series, and Multivariate Statistics*, Academic Press, New York.

Gregory, Allan W., Pagan, Adrian R., and Smith, Gregor W. (1993), 'Estimating Linear Quadratic Models with Integrated Processes', in P. C. B. Phillips (ed.), *Models, Methods, and Applications of Econometrics: Essays in Honour of A. R. Bergstrom*, Blackwell, Oxford, 220–39.

Grenander, Ulf, and Rosenflat, Murray (1957), *Statistical Analysis of Stationary Time Series*, Wiley, New York.

Hafer, R. W., and Jansen, Dennis W. (1991), 'The Demand for Money in the United States: Evidence from Cointegration Tests', *Journal of Money, Credit, and Banking*, 23: 155–68.

Hakkio, Craig S. (1986), 'Does the Exchange Rate follow a Random Walk', *Journal of International Money and Finance*, 5: 221–9.

—— and Rush, Mark (1989), 'Market Efficiency and Cointegration and Application to the Sterling and Deutschmark Exchange Markets', *Journal of International Money and Finance*, 8: 75–88.

Haldrup, Niels (1994), 'The Asymptotics of Single-Equation Cointegration Regressions with $I(1)$ and $I(2)$ Variables', *Journal of Econometrics*, 63, 153–81.

Hall, Alastair (1989), 'Testing for a Unit Root in the Presence of Moving Average Errors', *Biometrika*, 76: 49–56.

—— (1992*a*), 'Joint Hypothesis Tests for a Random Walk based on Instrumental Variable Estimators', *Journal of Time Series Analysis*, 13: 29–45.

—— (1992*b*), 'Testing for a Unit Root in Time Series using Instrumental Variable Estimators with Pretest Data Based Model Selection', *Journal of Econometrics*, 54: 223–50.

Hall, Anthony D., Anderson, Heather M., and Granger, Clive W. J. (1992), 'A Cointegration Analysis of Treasury Bill Rates', *Review of Economics and Statistics*, 75: 116–26.

Hall, P., and Heyde, C. C. (1980), *Martingale Limit Theory and its Applications*, Academic Press, New York.

Hall, Robert E. (1978), 'Stochastic Implications of the Life Cycle Permanent Income Hypothesis: Theory and Evidence', *Journal of Political Economy*, 86: 971–87.

Hall, S. G. (1986), 'An Application of the Granger and Engle Two-Step Estimation Procedure to United Kingdom Aggregate Wage Data', *Oxford Bulletin of Economics and Statistics*, 48: 229–39.

Hamilton, James D. (1994), *Time Series Analysis*, Princeton University Press.

Han, Hsiang-Ling, and Ogaki, Masao (1991), 'Consumption, Income, and Cointegration, Further Analysis', mimeo.

Hannan, E. J., and Deistler, Manfred (1988), *The Statistical Theory of Linear Systems*, John Wiley, New York.

Hansen, Bruce E. (1992*a*), 'Efficient Estimation and Testing of Cointegrating Vectors in the Presence of Deterministic Trends', *Journal of Econometrics*, 53: 87–121.

—— (1992*b*), 'Heteroskedastic Cointegration', *Journal of Econometrics*, 54: 139–58.

Hargreaves, Colin (1993), 'A Review of Methods of Estimating Cointegrating Relationships', mimeo.

Harris, David, and Inder, Brett (1992), 'A Test of the Null Hypothesis of Cointegration', mimeo.

Harrison, J. Michael, and Kreps, David M. (1979), 'Martingales and Arbitrage in Multiperiod Securities Market', *Journal of Economic Theory*, 20: 381–408.

Harvey, A. C. (1985), 'Trends and Cycles in Macroeconomic Time Series', *Journal of Business and Economic Statistics*, 3: 216–27.

—— (1989), *Forecasting Structural Time Series Models and the Kalman Filter*, Cambridge University Press.

—— (1990), *The Econometric Analysis of Time Series*, 2nd edn., MIT Press, Cambridge, Mass.

Hatanaka, Michio, and Koto, Yasuji (1994), 'Are There Unit Roots in Real Economic Variables? (An Encompassing Analysis of Difference and Trend Stationarity)', mimeo.

—— and Odaki, Mitsuhiro (1983), 'Policy Analyses with and without A Priori Conditions', *Economic Studies Quarterly*, 34: 193–210.

Hayashi, Fumio (1982), 'The Permanent Income Hypothesis: Estimation and Testing by Instrumental Variables', *Journal of Political Economy*, 90: 895–916.

Hendry, D. F. (1979), 'Predictive Failure and Econometric Modelling in Macroeconomics: The Transactions Demand for Money', in P. Ormerod (ed.), *Modelling the Economy*, Heinemann, London, 217–42.

—— (1987), 'Econometric Methodology: A Personal Perspective', in T. F. Bewley (ed.), *Advances in Econometrics Fifth World Congress*, II, Cambridge University Press, 29–48.

—— (1993), *Econometrics, Alchemy or Science?*, Blackwell, Oxford.

Hendry, D. F., and Mizon, Grayham E. (1978), 'Serial Correlation as a Convenient Simplification, Not a Nuisance: A Comment on a Study of the Demand for Money by the Bank of England', *Economic Journal*, 88: 549-63.

—— —— (1993), 'Evaluating Dynamic Econometric Models by Encompassing the VAR', in P. C. B. Phillips (ed.), *Models, Methods, and Applications of Econometrics: Essays in Honour of A. R. Bergstrom*, Blackwell, Oxford, 272-300.

—— and Neale, Adrian J. (1991), 'A Monte Carlo Study of the Effects of Structural Breaks on Tests for Unit Roots', in P. Hackl and A. H. Westlund (eds.), *Economic Structural Change*, Springer-Verlag, Berlin, 95-119.

—— Pagan, Adrian R., and Sargan, J. Dennis (1984), 'Dynamic Specification', in Z. Griliches and M. D. Intriligator (eds.), *Handbook of Econometrics*, II, North-Holland, Amsterdam.

—— and Richard, Jean-François (1982), 'On the Formulation of Empirical Model in Dynamic Econometrics', *Journal of Econometrics*, 20: 3-33.

—— and von Ungern-Sternberg, Thomas (1980), 'Liquidity and Inflation Effects on Consumers' Expenditure', in A. Deaton (ed.), *Essays in the Theory and Measurement of Consumers' Behaviour*, Cambridge University Press, 237-60.

Hoffman, Dennis L., and Rasche, Robert H. (1991), 'Long-Run Income and Interest Elasticities of Money Demand in the United States', *Review of Economics and Statistics*, 74: 665-74.

Hosking, J. R. M. (1981), 'Fraction Differencing', *Biometrika*, 68: 165-76.

Huizinga, John (1987), 'An Empirical Investigation of the Long-Run Behavior of Real Exchange Rates', *Carnegie-Rochester Conference Series on Public Policy*, 27: 149-214.

Hunter, John (1992), 'Tests of Cointegrating Exogeneity for PPP and Uncovered Interest Rate Parity in the United Kingdom', *Journal of Policy Modeling*, 14: 453-63.

Hylleberg, Svend (1994), 'The Economics of Seasonal Cycles: A Comment', in C. A. Sims (ed.), *Advances in Econometrics, Sixth World Congress*, i, Cambridge University Press, 252-5.

—— Engle, R. F., Granger, C. W. J., and Yoo, B. S. (1990), 'Seasonal Integration and Cointegration', *Journal of Econometrics*, 44: 215-38.

—— and Mizon, Grayham E. (1989), 'Cointegration and Error Correction Mechanisms', *Economic Journal*, 99 (Suppl.), 113-25.

Inder, Brett (1993), 'Estimating Long-Run Relationships in Economics', *Journal of Econometrics*, 57: 53-68.

Johansen, Søren (1988), 'Statistical Analysis of Cointegration Vectors', *Journal of Economic Dynamics and Control*, 12: 231-54.

—— (1991*a*), 'Estimation and Hypothesis Testing of Cointegration Vectors in Gaussian Vector Autoregressive Model', *Econometrica*, 59: 1551-80.

—— (1991*b*), 'Statistical Analysis of Cointegration Vectors', in R. F. Engle and C. W. J. Granger (eds.), *Long-run Economic Relationships, Readings in Cointegration*, Oxford University Press, 131-52.

—— (1992*a*), 'A Representation of Vector Autoregressive Processes Integrated of Order 2', *Econometric Theory*, 8: 188-202.

—— (1992*b*), 'Determination of Cointegration Rank in the Presence of a Linear Trend', *Oxford Bulletin of Economics and Statistics*, 54: 383-97.

—— (1992*c*), 'Cointegration in Partial Systems and the Efficiency of Single-Equation Analysis', *Journal of Econometrics*, 52: 389-402.

Johansen, Søren (1992*d*), 'Testing Weak Exogeneity and the Order of Cointegration in UK Money Demand Data', *Journal of Policy Modeling*, 14: 313–34.

—— (1992*e*), 'A Statistical Analysis of Cointegration for I(2) Variables', mimeo.

—— (1994), 'The Role of the Constant Term in Cointegration Analysis of Nonstationary Variables', *Econometric Reviews*, 13: 205–19.

—— and Juselius, Katarina (1990), 'Maximum Likelihood Estimation and Inference on Cointegration-with Applications to the Demand for Money', *Oxford Bulletin of Economics and Statistics*, 52: 109–210.

—— —— (1992), 'Some Structural Hypotheses in a Multivariate Cointegration Analysis of the Purchasing Power Parity and the Uncovered Interest Parity for U.K.', *Journal of Econometrics*, 53: 211–44.

Judge, George G., Griffiths, W. E., Hill, R. Carter, Lütkepohl, Helmut, and Lee, Tsoung-Chao (1985), *The Theory and Practice of Econometrics*, 2nd edn., John Wiley, New York.

Juselius, Katarina (1991), 'Long Run Relations in a Well Defined Statistical Model for the Data Generating Process, Cointegration Analysis of the PPP and the UIP Relation', in J. Gruber (ed.), *Econometric Decision Models: New Methods of Modelling and Applications*, Springer-Verlag, Berlin, 336–57.

—— (1994), 'On the Duality between Long-Run Relations and Common Trends in $I(1)$ versus $I(2)$ Model: An Application to Aggregate Money Holding', *Econometric Reviews*, 13: 151–78.

Kailath, Thomas (1980), *Linear Systems*, Prentice-Hall, New York.

Kariya, Takeaki (1980), 'Locally Robust Tests for Serial Correlation in Least Squares Regression', *Annals of Statistics*, 8: 1065–70.

Karlin, Samuel (1975), *A First Course in Stochastic Processes*, 2nd edn. Academic Press, New York.

Kasa, Kenneth (1992), 'Common Stochastic Trends in International Stock Markets', *Journal of Monetary Economics*, 29: 95–124.

Kennan, John (1979), 'The Estimation of Partial Adjustment Models with Rational Expectations', *Econometrica*, 47: 1441–55.

Kim, Yoonbai (1990), 'Purchasing Power Parity in the Long Run: A Cointegration Approach', *Journal of Money, Credit, and Banking*, 22: 491–503.

Kim, Myung Jig, Nelson, Charles R., and Startz, Richard (1991), 'Mean Reversion in Stock Prices? A Reappraisal of the Empirical Evidence', *Review of Economic Studies*, 58: 515–28.

King, M. L. (1980), 'Robust Tests for Spherical Symmetry and Their Application to Least Squares Regression', *Annals of Statistics*, 8: 1265–71.

—— and Hillier, Grant H. (1985), 'Locally Best Invariant Tests of the Error Covariance Matrix of the Linear Regression Model', *Journal of the Royal Statistical Society*, series B, 47: 98–102.

King, Robert G., Plosser, Charles I, Stock, James H., and Watson, Mark W. (1991), 'Stochastic Trends and Economic Fluctuations', *American Economic Review*, 81: 819–40.

Kirchgässner, Gebhard (1991), 'Comment on G. E. Mizon, "Modelling Relative Price Variability and Aggregate Inflation in the United Kingdom", *Scandinavian Journal of Economics*, 93: 189–211.

Kleibergen, Frank, and Van Dijk, Herman K. (1992), 'On the Shape of the Likelihood/Posterior in Cointegration Models', *Econometric Theory*, 10: 514–51.

Kleibergen, Frank, and Van Dijk, Herman K. (1994), 'Direct Cointegrating Testing in Error Correction Models', *Journal of Econometrics*, 63: 61-103.

Kleidon, Allan W. (1986), 'Variance Bounds Tests and Stock Price Valuation Models', *Journal of Political Economy*, 94: 953-1001.

Konishi, Toru, and Granger, Clive W. J. (1992), 'Separation in Cointegrated Systems', mimeo.

—— Ramsey, Valerie A., and Granger, Clive W. J. (1993), 'Stochastic Trends and Short-Run Relationships between Financial Variables and Real Activity', NBER Working Paper No. 4275.

Koop, G. (1992), "Objective" Bayesian Unit Root Tests', *Journal of Applied Econometrics*, 7: 65-82.

—— and Steel, Mark F. (1994), 'A Decision-Theoretic Analysis of the Unit-Root Hypothesis Using Mixtures of Elliptical Models', *Journal of Business and Economic Statistics*, 12: 95-107.

Kormendi, Roger, and Meguire, Philip (1990), 'A Multicountry Characterization of the Nonstationarity of Aggregate Output', *Journal of Money, Credit, and Banking*, 22: 77-93.

Koto, Yasuji, and Hatanaka, Michio (1994), 'A Simulation Study of the P-values Discrimination between the Difference and Trend Stationarity', mimeo.

Krämer, Walter (1986), 'Least Squares Regression when the Independent Variable follows an ARIMA Process', *Journal of the American Statistical Association*, 81: 150-4.

Kremers, Jeroen J. M., Ericsson, Neil R., and Dolado, Juan J. (1992), 'The Power of Cointegration Tests', *Oxford Bulletin of Economics and Statistics*, 54: 325-48.

Kugler, Peter, and Lenz, Carlos (1993), 'Multivariate Cointegration Analysis and the Long-Run Validity of PPP', *Review of Economics and Statistics*, 75: 180-4.

Kunitomo, Naoto (1994), 'Tests of Unit Roots and Cointegration Hypotheses in Econometric Models', mimeo.

—— and Yamamoto, Taku (1990), 'Conditions on Consistency by Vector Autoregressive Models and Cointegration', *Economic Studies Quarterly*, 41: 15-33.

Kunst, Robert, and Neusser, Klaus (1990), 'Cointegration in a Macroeconomic System', *Journal of Applied Econometrics*, 5: 351-65.

Kwiatkowski, Denis, Phillips, Peter C. B., Schmidt, Peter, and Shin, Yongcheol (1992), 'Testing the Null Hypothesis of Stationarity against the Alternative of a Unit Root: How Sure are We that Economic Time Series Have a Unit Root?', *Journal of Econometrics*, 54: 159-78.

Lamotte, Lynn Roy, and Mcwhorter Jr., Archer (1978), 'An Exact Test for the Presence of Random Walk Coefficients in a Linear Regression Model', *Journal of the American Statistical Association*, 73: 816-20.

Layton, Allan P., and Stark, Jonathan P. (1990), 'Cointegration as an Empirical Test of Purchasing Power Parity', *Journal of Macroeconomics*, 12: 125-36.

Leamer, Edward E. (1978), *Specification Searches*, John Wiley, New York.

—— (1991), 'Comment on "To Criticize the Critics"', *Journal of Applied Econometrics*, 6: 371-3.

Lee, Inpyo, and Hamada, Koichi (1991), 'International Monetary Regimes and Times Series Properties of Macroeconomic Behavior: A Cointegration Approach', mimeo.

Lee, Tae-Hwy (1992), 'Stock-Flow Relationships in US Housing Construction', *Oxford Bulletin of Economics and Statistics*, 54: 419-30.

Leroy, Stephen F. (1973), 'Risk Aversion and the Martingale Property of Stock Prices', *International Economic Review*, 14: 436–46.

Levin, Andrew, and Lin, Chien-Fu (1992), 'Unit Root Tests in Panel Data: Asymptotic and Finite-Sample Properties', mimeo.

Leybourne, S. J., and Mccabe, B. P. M. (1993), 'A Simple Test for Cointegration', *Oxford Bulletin of Economics and Statistics*, 55: 97–103.

—— (1994), 'A Consistent Test for a Unit Root', *Journal of Business and Economic Statistics*, 12: 157–66.

Lim, Kian-Guan, and Phoon, Kok-Fai (1991), 'Tests of Rational Bubbles using Cointegration Theory', *Applied Financial Economics*, 1: 85–7.

Lindley, D. V. (1965), *Introduction to Probability and Statistics*, Pt. 2, *Inference*, Cambridge University Press.

Lippi, Marco, and Reichlin, Lucrezia (1992), 'On Persistence of Shocks to Economic Variables', *Journal of Monetary Economics*, 29: 87–93.

Lo, Andrew W. (1991), 'Long-Term Memory in Stock Market Prices', *Econometrica*, 59: 1279–313.

—— and MacKinlay, A. Craig (1989), 'The Size and Power of the Variance Ratio Test in Finite Samples, A Monte Carlo Investigation', *Journal of Econometrics*, 40: 203–38.

Lucas, Robert F. Jr. (1978), 'Asset Prices in an Exchange Economy', *Econometrica*, 46: 1429–45.

Lütkepohl, Helmut (1991), *Introduction to Multiple Time Series Analysis*, Springer-Verlag, Berlin.

—— and Reimers, Hans-Eggert (1992), 'Impulse Response Analysis of Cointegrated Systems', *Journal of Economic Dynamics and Control*, 16: 53–78.

McAleer, Michael, McKenzie, C. R., and Pesaran, M. Hashem (1994), 'Cointegration and Direct Tests of the Rational Expectations Hypothesis', *Econometric Reviews*, 13: 231–58.

Mcdermott, C. J. (1990), 'Cointegration: Origins and Significance for Economists', *New Zealand Economic Papers*, 24: 1–23.

Mckinnon, Donald I., Radcliffe, Christopher, Tan, Kong-Yam, Warga, Arthur D., and Willet, Thomas D. (1984), 'International Influences on the US Economy: Summary of an Exchange', *American Economic Review*, 74: 1132–4.

MacNeill, Ian B. (1978), 'Properties of Sequences of Partial Sums of Polynomial Regression Residuals with Applications to Tests for Change of Regression at Unknown Times', *Annals of Statistics*, 6: 422–33.

McNown, Robert, and Wallace, Myles S. (1989), 'National Price Levels, Purchasing Power Parity, and Cointegration', *Journal of International Money and Finance*, 8: 533–45.

—— —— (1992), 'Cointegration Tests of a Long-Run Relation between Money Demand and the Effective Exchange Rate', *Journal of International Money and Finance*, 11: 107–14.

Maekawa, K., Yamamoto, T., Takeuchi, Y., and Hatanaka, M. (1993), 'Estimation in Dynamic Regression with an Integrated Process', mimeo.

Mankiw, N. Gregory, and Shapiro, Matthew (1985), 'Trends, Random Walks and Tests of the Permanent Income Hypothesis', *Journal of Monetary Economics*, 16: 163–74.

Mark, Nelson C. (1990), 'Real and Nominal Exchange Rates in the Long Run: An Empirical Investigation', *Journal of International Economics*, 28: 115–36.

Meese, R. A., and Rogoff, K. (1988), 'Was It Real? The Exchange Rate–Interest Differential Relation over the Modern Floating Rate Period', *Journal of Finance*, 43: 933–48.

Mellander, E., Vredin, A., and Warne, A. (1992), 'Stochastic Trends and Economic Fluctuations in a Small Open Economy', *Journal of Applied Econometrics*, 7: 369–94.
Mills, Terence C. (1992), 'How Robust is the Finding that Innovations to UK Output are Persistent?', *Scottish Journal of Political Economy*, 39: 154–66.
Mizon, Grayham E. (1977), 'Model Selection Procedures', in M. J. Artis and A. R. Nobay (eds.), *Studies in Modern Economic Analysis*, Blackwell, Oxford, 97–120.
—— (1984), 'The Encompassing Approach in Econometrics', in D. F. Hendry and K. F. Walles (eds.), *Econometrics and Quantitative Economics*, Blackwell, Oxford, 135–72.
—— (1991), 'Modelling Relative Price Variability and Aggregate Inflation in the United Kingdom', *Scandinavian Journal of Economics*, 93: 189–211.
—— and Richard, Jean-François (1986), 'The Encompassing Principle and its Application to Testing Non-nested Hypotheses', *Econometrica*, 54: 657–78.
Morimune, Kimio, and Mantini, Akihisa (1993), 'The Order of the Vector Autoregressive Process with Unit Roots', mimeo.
—— —— (1995), 'Estimating the Rank of Co-integration after Estimating the Order of a Vector Autoregression', *Japanese Economic Review*, forthcoming.
Mosconi, Rocco, and Giannini, Carlo (1992), 'Non-Causality in Cointegrated Systems: Representation, Estimation and Testing', *Oxford Bulletin of Economics and Statistics*, 54: 399–417.
Nabeya, Seiji, and Tanaka, Katsuto (1988), 'Asymptotic Theory of a Test for the Constancy of Regression Coefficients against the Random Walk Alternative', *Annals of Statistics*, 16: 218–35.
—— —— (1990), 'A General Approach to the Limiting Distribution for Estimators in Time Series Regression with Nonstable Autoregressive Errors', *Econometrica*, 58: 145–63.
Neave, Henry R. (1972), 'Observations on "Spectral Analysis of Short Series: A Simulation Study" by Granger and Hughes', *Journal of the Royal Statistical Society*, Series A, 135: 393–405.
Nelson, Charles R., and Plosser, Charles I. (1982), 'Trends and Random Walks in Macroeconomic Time Series', *Journal of Monetary Economics*, 10: 139–62.
Neusser, Klaus (1991), 'Testing the Long-Run Implications of the Neoclassical Growth Models', *Journal of Monetary Economics*, 27: 3–27.
Nickell, Stephen (1985), 'Error Correction, Partial Adjustment and all That: An Expository Note', *Oxford Bulletin of Economics and Statistics*, 47: 119–29.
Nowak, Eugen (1991), 'Discovering Hidden Cointegration', mimeo.
Nyblom, Jukka (1986), 'Testing for Deterministic Linear Trend in Time Series,' *Journal of the American Statistical Association*, 81: 545–9.
—— and Mäkeläinen, Timo (1983), 'Comparisons of Tests for the Presence of Random Walk Coefficients in a Simple Linear Model', *Journal of the American Statistical Association*, 78: 856–64.
Ogaki, Masao (1992), 'Engel's Law and Cointegration', *Journal of Political Economy*, 100: 1027–46.
—— and Park, Joon Y., 'A Cointegration Approach to Estimating Preference Parameters', mimeo.
Osborn, Denise R. (1990), 'A Survey of Seasonality in U.K. Macroeconomic Variables', *International Journal of Forecasting*, 6: 327–36.
Osterwald-Lenum, Michael (1992), 'A Note on Quantiles of the Asymptotic Distribution of the Maximum Likelihood Cointegration Rank Test Statistic', *Oxford Bulletin of Economics and Statistics*, 54: 461–72.

Ouliaris, Sam, Park, Joon Y., and Phillips, Peter C. B. (1989), 'Testing for a Unit Root in the Presence of a Maintained Trend', in B. Raj (ed.), *Advances in Econometrics and Modeling*, Kluwer, Kingston-upon-Thames, 7-28.

Pagan, Adrian (1985), 'Time Series Behaviour and Dynamic Specification', *Oxford Bulletin of Economics and Statistics*, 47: 199-211.

—— and Wickens, M. R. (1989), 'A Survey of Some Recent Econometric Methods', *Economics Journal*, 99: 962-1025.

Pantula, Sastry G., and Hall, Alastair (1991), 'Testing for Unit Roots in Autoregressive Moving Average Models', *Journal of Econometrics*, 48: 325-53.

Park, Joon Y. (1992), 'Canonical Cointegrating Regressions', *Econometrica*, 60: 119-43.

—— and Phillips, Peter C. B. (1988), 'Statistical Inference in Regressions with Integrated Processes': 1, *Econometric Theory*, 4: 468-97.

—— —— (1989), 'Statistical Inference in Regressions with Integrated Processes': 2, *Econometric Theory*, 5: 95-131.

Paulsen, Jostein (1984), 'Order Determination of Multivariate Autoregressive Time Series with Unit Roots', *Journal of Time Series Analysis*, 5: 115-27.

Patel, Jayendu (1990), 'Purchasing Power Parity as a Long-Run Relation', *Journal of Applied Econometrics*, 5: 367-79.

Perron, Pierre (1988), 'Trends and Random Walks in Macroeconomic Time Series: Further Evidence from a New Approach', *Journal of Economic Dynamics and Control*, 12: 297-332.

—— (1989*a*), 'The Great Crash, the Oil Price Shock, and the Unit Root Hypothesis', *Econometrica*, 57: 1361-401.

—— (1989*b*), 'Testing for a Random Walk: A Simulation Experiment of Power when the Sampling Interval is Varied', in B. Raj (ed.), *Advances in Econometrics and Modelling*, Kluwer, Kingston-upon-Thames, 47-68.

—— (1990), 'Testing for a Unit Root in a Time Series with a Changing Mean', *Journal of Business and Economic Statistics*, 8: 153-62.

—— (1991*a*), 'Test Consistency with Varying Sampling Frequency', *Econometric Theory*, 7: 341-68.

—— (1991*b*), 'A Test for Changes in a Polynomial Trend Function for a Dynamic Time Series', mimeo.

—— and Vogelsang, Timothy J. (1992*a*), 'Nonstationarity and Level Shifts with an Application to Purchasing Power Parity', *Journal of Business and Economic Statistics*, 10: 301-20.

—— —— (1992*b*), 'Testing for a Unit Root in a Time Series with a Changing Mean: Corrections and Extensions', *Journal of Business and Economic Statistics*, 10: 467-70.

Pesaran, M. Harshem (1987), *The Limits to Rational Expectations*, Blackwell, Oxford.

Phillips, P. C. B. (1986), 'Understanding Spurious Regressions in Econometrics', *Journal of Econometrics*, 33: 311-40.

—— (1987), 'Time Series Regression with a Unit Root', *Econometrica*, 55: 277-301.

—— (1988*a*), 'Weak Convergence of Sample Covariance Matrices to Stochastic Integrals via Martingale Approximations', *Econometric Theory*, 4: 528-3.

—— (1988*b*), 'Multiple Regression with Integrated Time Series', *Contemporary Mathematics*, 80: 79-105.

—— (1989), 'Partially Identified Econometric Models', *Econometric Theory*, 5: 181-240.

—— (1990), 'Solution', *Econometric Review*, 6: 431-3.

—— (1991*a*), 'Optimal Inference in Cointegrated Systems', *Econometrica*, 59: 283-306.

Phillips, P. C. B. (1991*b*), 'To Criticize the Critics: An Objective Bayesian Analysis of Stochastic Trends', *Journal of Applied Econometrics*, 6: 333-64.

—— (1991*c*), 'Bayesian Routes and Unit Roots: De Rebus Prioribus Semper Est Disputandum', *Journal of Applied Econometrics*, 6: 435-73.

—— (1991*d*), 'Unidentified Components in Reduced Rank Regression Estimation of ECM's', mimeo.

—— (1992*a*), 'The Long-Run Australian Consumption Function Reexamined: An Empirical Experience in Baysian Inference', in C. Hargreaves (ed) *Macroeconomic Modelling of the Long Run*, Edward Elgar, Cheltenham, 287-322.

—— (1992*b*), 'Bayesian Model Selection and Prediction with Empirical Applications', mimeo.

—— (1993), 'Fully Modified Least Squares and Vector Autoregression', mimeo.

—— and Durlauf, S. N. (1986), 'Multiple Time Series Regression with Integrated Processes', *Review of Economic Studies*, 53: 473-95.

—— (1994), 'Some Exact Distribution Theory for Maximum Likelihood Estimators of Cointegrating Coefficients in Error Correction Models', *Econometrica*, 62: 73-93.

—— and Hansen, Bruce E. (1990), 'Statistical Inference in Instrumental Variables Regression with I(1) Processes', *Review of Economic Studies*, 57: 99-125.

—— and Loretan, Mico (1991), 'Estimating Long-Run Economic Equilibria', *Review of Economic Studies*, 58: 407-36.

—— and Ouliaris, S. (1990), 'Asymptotic Properties of Residual Based Tests for Cointegration,' *Econometrica*, 58: 165-93.

—— and Park, Joon Y. (1988), 'Asymptotic Equivalence of Ordinary Least Squares and Generalized Least Squares in Regressions with Integrated Regressors,' *Journal of the American Statistical Association*, 83: 111-15.

—— and Perron, Pierre (1988), 'Testing for a Unit Root in Time Series Regression', *Biometrika*, 75: 335-46.

—— and Ploberger, W. (1992), 'Posterior Odds Testing for a Unit Root with Data-Based Model Selection', mimeo.

Poirier, Dale J. (1988), 'Frequentist and Subjectivist Perspectives on the Problem of Model Building in Economics', *Journal of Economic Perspective*, 2/1: 121-44.

—— (1991), 'A Comment on "To Criticize the Critics: An Objective Bayesian Analysis of Stochastic Trends", *Journal of Applied Econometrics*, 6: 381-6.

Pollard, David (1984), *Convergence of Stochastic Processes*, Springer-Verlag, Berlin.

Poterba, James M., and Summers, Lawrence H. (1988), 'Mean Reversion in Stock Prices, Evidence and Implications', *Journal of Financial Economics*, 22: 27-59.

Pratt, John W. (1965), 'Bayesian Interpretation of Standard Inference Statements', *Journal of the Royal Statistical Society*, Series B, 27: 169-92.

Quah, Danny (1990), 'Permanent and Transitory Movements in Labor Income: An Explanation for "Excess Smoothness" in Consumption', *Journal of Political Economy*, 98: 449-75.

—— (1993), 'Exploiting Cross Section Variation for Unit Root Inference in Dynamic Data', mimeo.

Raj, Baldev (1992), 'International Evidence in Persistence in Output in the Presence of an Episodic Change', *Journal of Applied Econometrics*, 7: 281-93.

Rappoport, Peter, and Reichlin, Lucrezia (1989), 'Segmented Trends and Non-Stationary Time Series', *Economic Journal*, 99 (Conference): 168-77.

Reinsel, Gregory C., and Ahn, Sung K. (1992), 'Vector Autoregressive Models with Unit Roots and Reduced Rank Structure: Estimation, Likelihood Ratio Test, and Forecasting', *Journal of Time Series Analysis*, 13: 353–75.

Romer, Christina D. (1986*a*), 'Spurious Volatility in Historical Unemployment Data', *Journal of Political Economy*, 94: 1–37.

—— (1986*b*), 'Is the Stabilization of the Postwar Economy a Figment of the Data?', *American Economic Review*, 76: 314–34.

—— (1989), 'The Prewar Business Cycle Reconsidered: New Estimates of Gross National Product, 1869–1908', *Journal of Political Economy*, 97: 1–37.

Rose, Andrew K. (1988), 'Is the Real Interest Rate Stable?', *Journal of Finance*, 43: 1095–112.

Ross, Sheldon M. (1983), *Stochastic Processes*, John Wiley, New York.

Rudebusch, Glenn D. (1992), 'Trends and Random Walks in Macroeconomic Time Series: A Re-Examination', *International Economic Review*, 33: 661–80.

Said, Said E., and Dickey, David A. (1984), 'Testing for Unit Roots in Autoregressive-Moving Average Models of Unknown Order', *Biometrika*, 71, 599–607.

Saikkonen, Pentti (1991), 'Asymptotically Efficient Estimation of Cointegration Regression', *Econometric Theory*, 7: 1–21.

—— (1993), 'Estimation of Cointegration Vectors with Linear Restrictions', *Econometric Theory*, 9: 19–35.

—— and Luukkonen, Ritva (1993*a*), 'Testing for a Moving Average Unit Root in Autoregressive Integrated Moving Average Models,' *Journal of the American Statistical Association*, 88: 596–601.

—— —— (1993*b*), 'Point Optimal Tests for Testing the Order of Differencing in ARIMA Models', *Econometric Theory*, 9: 343–62.

Salmon, Mark (1982), 'Error Correction Mechanisms', *Economic Journal*, 92: 615–29.

Sargan, J. D. (1964), 'Wages and Prices in the United Kingdom: A Study in Econometric Methodology', repr. in D. F. Hendry and K. F. Wallis (eds.), *Econometrics and Quantitative Economics*, Blackwell, Oxford, 275–314.

Sargent, Thomas (1979), *Macroeconomic Theory*, Academic Press, New York.

Schmidt, Peter, and Phillips, Peter C. B. (1992), 'LM Tests for a Unit Root in the Presence of Deterministic Trends', *Oxford Bulletin of Economics and Statistics*, 54: 257–87.

Schotman, Peter C., and Van Dijk, Herman K. (1991*a*), 'A Bayesian Analysis of the Unit Root in Real Exchange Rates', *Journal of Econometrics*, 49: 195–238.

—— —— (1991*b*), 'On Bayesian Routes to Unit Roots', *Journal of Applied Econometrics*, 6: 387–401.

—— —— (1993), 'Posterior Analysis of Possibly Integrated Time Series with an Application to Real GNP', in D. Brillinger, P. Caines, J. Geweke, E. Parzen, M. Rosenblatt, and M. Taqqu (eds.), *New Directions in Time Series Analysis*, Springer-Verlag, 341–63.

Schwarz, Gideon (1978), 'Estimating the Dimension of a Model', *Annals of Statistics*, 6: 461–4.

Schwert, G. William (1987), 'Effects of Model Specification on Tests for Unit Roots in Macroeconomic Data', *Journal of Monetary Economics*, 20: 73–103.

—— (1989), 'Tests for Unit Roots: A Monte Carlo Investigation', *Journal of Business and Economic Statistics*, 7: 147–59.

Shapiro, Matthew D., and Watson, Mark W. (1988), 'Sources of Business Cycle Fluctuations', NBER *Macroeconomics Annual*, 3: 111–48.

Shiller, Robert J. (1981*a*), 'Do Stock Prices Move Too Much to Be Justified by Subsequent Changes in Dividends?', *American Economic Review*, 71: 421-36.

—— (1981*b*), 'Alternative Tests of Rational Expectation Models: The Case of Term Structures', *Journal of Econometrics*, 16: 71-87.

Shintani, Mototsugu (1994), 'Cointegration and Tests of the Permanent Income Hypothesis: Japanese Evidence with International Comparisons', *Journal of the Japanese and International Economies*, 8: 144-72.

Sims, Christopher A. (1972), 'Money, Income, and Causality', *American Economic Review*, 62: 540-52.

—— (1980*a*), 'Martingale-Like Behavior of Prices', Working Paper No. 489, NBER.

—— (1980*b*), 'Macroeconomics and Reality', *Econometrica*, 48: 1-48.

—— (1988), 'Bayesian Skepticism on Unit Root Econometrics', *Journal of Economic Dynamics and Control*, 12: 463-74.

—— (1991), 'Comment by Christopher A. Sims on "To Criticize the Critics", by Peter C. B. Phillips', *Journal of Applied Econometrics*, 6: 423-34.

—— Stock, James H., and Watson, Mark W. (1990), 'Inference in Linear Time Series Models with Some Unit Roots', *Econometrica*, 58: 113-44.

—— and Uhlig, Harald (1991), 'Understanding Unit Rooters: A Helicopter Tour', *Econometrica*, 59: 1591-9.

Solo, Victor (1984), 'The Order of Differencing in ARIMA Models', *Journal of the American Statistical Association*, 79: 916-21.

Spanos, Aris (1986), *Statistical Foundations of Economic Modelling*, Cambridge University Press.

Stock, James H. (1987), 'Asymptotic Properties of Least Squares Estimators Cointegrating Vectors', *Econometrica*, 55: 1035-56.

—— (1992), 'Deciding between I(1) and I(0)', NBER, Technical Working Paper No. 121.

—— and Watson, Mark W. (1988*a*), 'Variable Trends in Economic Time Series', *Journal of Economic Perspectives*, 2/3, 147-74, repr. in R. F. Engle and C. W. J. Granger (eds.), *Long-Run Economic Relationships, Readings in Cointegration*, Oxford University Press.

—— —— (1988*b*), 'Testing for Common Trends', *Journal of the American Statistical Association*, 83: 1097-107, repr. in R. F. Engle and C. W. J. Granger (eds.), *Long-Run Economic Relationships, Readings in Cointegration*, Oxford University Press.

—— —— (1989), 'Interpreting the Evidence on Money-Income Causality', *Journal of Econometrics*, 40: 161-81.

—— —— (1993), 'A Simple Estimator of Cointegrating Vectors in Higher Order Integrated Systems', *Econometrica*, 61: 783-820.

Stock, James H. and West, Kenneth D. (1988), 'Integrated Regressors and Tests of the Permanent-Income Hypothesis', *Journal of Monetary Economics*, 21: 85-95.

Stultz, René M., and Wasserfallen, Walter (1985), 'Macroeconomic Time Series, Business Cycles and Macroeconomic Policies', *Carnegie-Rochester Conference Series on Public Policy*, 22: 9-54.

Sugihara, Soichi (1994), 'Error Correction Representation of a Dynamic Equation Model and its Estimation', mimeo. in Japanese.

Takeuchi, Yoshiyuki (1991), 'Trends and Structural Changes in Macroeconomic Time Series', *Journal of the Japan Statistical Society*, 21: 13-25.

Tanaka, Katsuto (1990), 'Testing for a Moving Average Unit Root', *Econometric Theory*, 6: 433-44.

Tanaka, Katsuto (1993), 'An Alternative Approach to the Asymptotic Theory of Spurious Regression, Cointegration, and Near Cointegration', *Econometric Theory*, 9: 36–61.

—— (1995*a*), 'The Optimality of Extended Score Tests with Applications to Testing for a Moving Average Unit Root', in S. Maddala, P. C. B. Phillips, and T. N. Srinivasan (eds.), *Advances in Econometrics*, Blackwell, Oxford.

—— (1995*b*), *Nonstationary and Noninvertible Time Series Analysis: A Distribution Theory*, Wiley, New York, forthcoming.

Taylor, Mark P. (1988), 'An Empirical Examination of Long-Run Purchasing Power Parity using Cointegration Techniques', *Applied Economics*, 20: 1369–81.

Toda, Hiro Y. (1994), 'Finite Sample Properties of Likelihood Ratio Tests for Cointegrating Ranks when Linear Trends are Present', *Review of Economics and Statistics*, 76: 66–79.

—— (1995), 'Finite Sample Performance of Likelihood Ratio Tests for Cointegrating Ranks in Vector Autoregressions', *Econometric Theory*, forthcoming.

—— and Mckenzie, C. R. (1994), 'LM Tests for Unit Roots in the Presence of Missing Observations', mimeo.

—— and Phillips, P. C. B. (1993), 'Vector Autoregression and Causality', *Econometrica*, 61: 1367–93.

—— —— (1994), 'Vector Autoregression and Causality: A Theoretical Overview and Simulation Study', *Econometric Reviews*, 13: 259–85.

—— and Yamamoto, Taku (1995), 'Statistical Inference in Vector Autoregressions with Possibly Integrated Processes', *Journal of Econometrics*, forthcoming.

Tsay, Ruey S. (1988), 'Outliers, Level Shifts, and Variance Changes in Time Series', *Journal of Forecasting*, 7: 1–20.

Tsurumi Hiroki, and Wago, Hajime (1993), 'A Bayesian Analysis of Unit Root under Unknown Order of an ARMA(p.q) Error', mimeo.

—— —— (1994), 'A Bayesian Analysis of Unit Root and Cointegration with an Application to a Yen–Dollar Exchange Rate Model', mimeo.

Wago, Hajime, and Tsurumi Hiroki (1991), 'A Bayesian Analysis of Unit Root and Stationarity Hypotheses with an Application to the Exchange Rate for Yen', mimeo.

Walker, A. M. (1969), 'On the Asymptotic Behaviour of Posterior Distributions', *Journal of the Royal Statistical Society*, Series B, 31: 80–8.

Wallace, Myles S., and Warner, John T. (1993), 'The Fisher Effect and the Structure of Interest Rates: Tests of Cointegration', *Review of Economics and Statistics*, 75: 320–4.

Wasserfallen, Walter (1986), 'Non-stationarities in Macro-economic Time Series: Further Evidence and Implications', *Canadian Journal of Economics*, 19: 498–510.

Watson, Mark W. (1986), 'Univariate Detrending Methods with Stochastic Trends', *Journal of Monetary Economics*, 18: 49–75.

West, Kenneth D. (1988), 'Asymptotic Normality When Regressors Have a Unit Root', *Econometrica*, 56: 1397–417.

White, John S. (1958), 'The Limiting Distribution of the Serial Correlation Coefficient in the Explosive Case', *Annals of Mathematical Statistics*, 29: 1188–97.

Wickens, Michael R. (1993), 'Rational Expectations and Integrated Variables', in P. C. B. Phillips (ed.), *Models, Methods, and Applications of Econometrics: Essays in Honour of A. R. Bergstrom*, Blackwell, Oxford, 317–36.

Wooldridge, Jeffrey M. (1991), 'Notes on Regression with Difference-Stationary Data', mimeo.

Yamamoto, Taku (1988), *Time Series Analysis in Economics*, Sobunsha, Tokyo (in Japanese).

Zellner, Arnold (1971), *An Introduction to Bayesian Inference in Econometrics*, John Wiley, New York.

—— (1986), 'On Assessing Prior Distributions and Bayesian Regression Analysis with g-Prior Distributions', in P. Goel and A. Zellner (eds.), *Bayesian Inference and Decision Techniques*, 233–43.

Zivot, Eric, and Andrews, Donald W. (1992), 'Further Evidence on the Great Crash, the Oil-Price Shock, and Unit-Root Hypothesis', *Journal of Business and Economic Statistics*, 10: 251–70.

Subject Index

Author Index